DATE DUE

DEMCO 128-5046

Children's
Literature
Review

Guide to Gale Literary Criticism Series

When you need to review criticism of literary works, these are the Gale series to use:

If the author's death date is:

You should turn to:

After Dec. 31, 1959
(or author is still living)

CONTEMPORARY LITERARY CRITICISM

for example: Jorge Luis Borges, Anthony Burgess,
William Faulkner, Mary Gordon,
Ernest Hemingway, Iris Murdoch

1900 through 1959

TWENTIETH-CENTURY LITERARY CRITICISM

for example: Willa Cather, F. Scott Fitzgerald,
Henry James, Mark Twain, Virginia Woolf

1800 through 1899

NINETEENTH-CENTURY LITERATURE CRITICISM

for example: Fyodor Dostoevsky, Nathaniel Hawthorne,
George Sand, William Wordsworth

1400 through 1799

LITERATURE CRITICISM FROM 1400 TO 1800
(excluding Shakespeare)

for example: Anne Bradstreet, Daniel Defoe,
Alexander Pope, François Rabelais,
Jonathan Swift, Phillis Wheatley

SHAKESPEAREAN CRITICISM

Shakespeare's plays and poetry

Antiquity through 1399

CLASSICAL AND MEDIEVAL LITERATURE CRITICISM

for example: Dante, Homer, Plato, Sophocles, Vergil,
the Beowulf Poet

Gale also publishes related criticism series:

CHILDREN'S LITERATURE REVIEW

This series covers authors of all eras who have written for the preschool through high school audience.

SHORT STORY CRITICISM

This series covers the major short fiction writers of all nationalities and periods of literary history.

POETRY CRITICISM

This series covers poets of all nationalities and periods of literary history.

ISSN 0362-4145

volume 25

Children's Literature Review

Excerpts from Reviews,
Criticism, and Commentary
on Books for Children
and Young People

Gerard J. Senick
Editor

Sharon R. Gunton
Associate Editor

 **Gale Research Inc.** • *DETROIT* • *LONDON*

STAFF

Gerard J. Senick, *Editor*

Sharon R. Gunton, *Associate Editor*

Jeanne A. Gough, *Permissions & Production Manager*
Linda M. Pugliese, *Production Supervisor*
Lorna Mabunda, Maureen A. Puhl, Jennifer VanSickle, *Editorial Associates*
Donna Craft, Paul Lewon, Camille Robinson, Sheila Walencewicz, *Editorial Assistants*

Maureen Richards, *Research Supervisor*
Mary Beth McElmeel, *Editorial Associate*
Kathleen Jowiak, Amy Kaechele, Julie Karmazin, Tamara C. Nott, Julie Synkonis, *Editorial Assistants*

Sandra C. Davis, *Permissions Supervisor (Text)*
Josephine M. Keene, Denise M. Singleton, Kimberly F. Smilay, *Permissions Associates*
Maria Franklin, Rebecca A. Hartford, Michele M. Lonoconus, Shelly Rakcozy, Shalice Shah, Nancy Sheridan, *Permissions Assistants*

Margaret A. Chamberlain, *Permissions Supervisor (Pictures)*
Pamela A. Hayes, *Permissions Associate*
Karla Kulkis, Nancy Rattenbury, Keith Reed, *Permissions Assistants*

Mary Beth Trimper, *Production Manager*
Mary Winterhalter, *Production Assistant*

Arthur Chartow, *Art Director*
C. J. Jonik, *Keyliner*

Contents

Preface   vii

Acknowledgments   xi

Cumulative Index to Authors   225

Cumulative Index to Nationalities   233

Cumulative Index to Titles   237

Preface

Children's literature has evolved into both a respected branch of creative writing and a successful industry. Currently, books for young readers are considered the most popular segment of publishing, while criticism of juvenile literature is instrumental in recording the literary or artistic development of the creators of children's books as well as the trends and controversies that result from changing values or attitudes about young people and their literature. Designed to provide a permanent, accessible record of this ongoing scholarship, *Children's Literature Review* (*CLR*) presents parents, teachers, and librarians—those responsible for bringing children and books together—with the opportunity to make informed choices when selecting reading materials for the young. This audience will find balanced overviews of the careers of the authors and illustrators of the books that they and their children are reading; these entries, which contain excerpts from published criticism in books and periodicals, assist users by sparking ideas for papers and assignments and suggesting supplementary and classroom reading. Ann L. Kalkhoff, president and editor of *Children's Book Review Service Inc.,* writes that "*CLR* has filled a gap in the field of children's books, and it is one series that will never lose its validity or importance."

Scope of the Series

Each volume of *CLR* profiles the careers of authors and illustrators of books for children from preschool through high school. Author lists in each volume reflect these elements:

- author lists are international in scope.

- approximately fifteen authors of all eras are represented.

- author lists represent the variety of genres covered by children's literature: picture books, fiction, nonfiction, poetry, folklore, and drama.

Although earlier volumes of *CLR* emphasized critical material published after 1960, successive volumes have expanded their coverage to encompass important criticism written before 1960. Since many of the authors included in *CLR* are living and continue to write, it is necessary to update their entries periodically. Thus, future volumes will supplement the entries of selected authors covered in earlier volumes as well as include criticism on the works of authors new to the series.

Organization of This Book

An author section consists of the following elements: author heading, author portrait, author introduction, excerpts of criticism (each followed by a bibliographical citation), and illustrations, when available.

- The **author heading** consists of the author's name followed by birth and death dates. The portion of the name outside the parentheses denotes the form under which the author is most frequently published. If the majority of the author's works for children were written under a pseudonym, the pseudonym will be listed in the author heading and the real name given on the first line of the author introduction. Also located at the beginning of the introduction are any other pseudonyms used by the author in writing for children and any name variations, including transliterated forms for authors whose languages use nonroman alphabets. Uncertainty as to a birth or death date is indicated by question marks.

- An **author portrait** is included when available.

- The **author introduction** contains information designed to introduce an author to *CLR* users by presenting an overview of the author's themes and styles, occasional biographical facts that relate to the author's literary career or critical responses to the author's works, and information about major awards and prizes the author has received. Introductions also list a group of representative titles for which the author or illustrator being profiled is best known; this section, which begins with the words "major works include," follows the genre line of the introduction. Where applicable, introductions conclude with references to additional entries in biographical and critical reference series published by Gale Research Inc. These sources include past volumes of *CLR* as well as *Authors & Artists for Young Adults, Contemporary Authors, Contemporary Literary Criticism, Dictionary of Literary Biography, Nineteenth-Century Literature Criticism, Short Story Criti-*

cism, Something about the Author, Something about the Author Autobiography Series, Twentieth-Century Literary Criticism, and *Yesterday's Authors of Books for Children.*

- **Criticism** is located in three sections: **author's commentary** (when available), **general commentary** (when available), and **title commentary** (in which commentary on specific titles appears). Centered headings introduce each section, in which criticism is arranged chronologically. Titles by authors being profiled are highlighted in boldface type within the text for easier access by readers.

The **author's commentary** presents background material written by the author or by an interviewer. This commentary may cover a specific work or several works. Author's commentary on more than one work appears after the author introduction, while commentary on an individual book follows the title entry heading.

The **general commentary** consists of critical excerpts that consider more than one work by the author or illustrator being profiled. General commentary is preceded by the critic's name in boldface type or, in the case of unsigned criticism, by the title of the journal. Occasionally, *CLR* features entries that emphasize general criticism on the overall career of an author or illustrator. When appropriate, a selection of reviews is included to supplement the general commentary.

The **title commentary** begins with title entry headings, which precede the criticism on a title and cite publication information on the work being reviewed. Title headings list the title of the work as it appeared in its first English-language edition. The first English-language publication date of each work is listed in parentheses following the title. Differing U.S. and British titles follow the publication date within the parentheses.

Entries in each title commentary section consist of critical excerpts on the author's individual works, arranged chronologically by publication date. The entries generally contain two to six reviews per title, depending on the stature of the book and the amount of criticism it has generated. The editors select titles that reflect the entire scope of the author's literary contribution, covering each genre and subject. An effort is made to reprint criticism that represents the full range of each title's reception—from the year of its initial publication to current assessments. Thus, the reader is provided with a record of the author's critical history. Publication information (such as publisher names and book prices) and parenthetical numerical references (such as footnotes or page and line references to specific editions of works) have been deleted at the editor's discretion to provide smoother reading of the text.

- Selected excerpts are preceded by **explanatory notes,** which provide information on the critic or work of criticism to enhance the reader's understanding of the excerpt.

- A complete **bibliographical citation** designed to facilitate the location of the original book or article follows each piece of criticism.

- Numerous **illustrations** are featured in *CLR.* For entries on illustrators, an effort has been made to include illustrations that reflect the characteristics discussed in the criticism. Entries on major authors who do not illustrate their own works may also include photographs and other illustrative material pertinent to the authors' careers.

Special Features

Entries on authors who are also illustrators will occasionally feature commentary on selected works illustrated but not written by the author being profiled. These works are strongly associated with the illustrator and have received critical acclaim for their art. By including critical comment on works of this type, the editors wish to provide a more complete representation of the author's total career. Criticism on these works has been chosen to stress artistic, rather than literary, contributions. Title entry headings for works illustrated by the author being profiled are arranged chronologically within the entry by date of publication and include notes identifying the author of the illustrated work. In order to provide easier access for users, all titles illustrated by the subject of the entry will be boldfaced.

CLR also includes entries on prominent illustrators who have contributed to the field of children's literature. These entries are designed to represent the development of the illustrator as an artist rather than as a literary stylist. The illustrator's section is organized like that of an author, with two exceptions: the introduction presents an overview of the illustrator's styles and techniques rather than outlining his or her literary background, and the commentary written by the illustrator on his or her works is called illustrator's commentary rather than author's commentary. Title entry headings are followed by explanatory notes identifying the author of the illustrated work. All titles of books containing illustrations by the artist being profiled as well as individual illustrations from these books are highlighted in boldface type.

Other Features

- An **acknowledgments,** which immediately follows the preface, lists the sources from which material has been reprinted in the volume. It does not, however, list every book or periodical consulted for the volume.

- The **cumulative index to authors** lists authors who have appeared in *CLR* and includes cross-references to *Authors & Artists for Young Adults, Contemporary Authors, Contemporary Literary Criticism, Dictionary of Literary Biography, Nineteenth-Century Literature Criticism, Short Story Criticism, Something about the Author, Something about the Author Autobiography Series, Twentieth-Century Literary Criticism,* and *Yesterday's Authors of Books for Children.*

- The **cumulative nationality index** lists authors alphabetically under their respective nationalities. Author names are followed by the volume number(s) in which they appear. Authors who have changed citizenship or whose current citizenship is not reflected in biographical sources appear under both their original nationality and that of their current residence.

- The **cumulative title index** lists titles covered in *CLR* followed by the volume and page number where criticism begins.

A Note to the Reader

When writing papers, students who quote directly from any volume in the Literature Criticism Series may use the following general forms to footnote reprinted criticism. The first example pertains to material drawn from periodicals, the second to material reprinted from books.

[1] T. S. Eliot, "John Donne," *The Nation and the Athenaeum,* 33 (9 June 1923), 321-32; excerpted and reprinted in *Literature Criticism from 1400 to 1800,* Vol. 10, ed. James E. Person, Jr. (Detroit: Gale Research, 1989), pp. 28-9.

[1] Henry Brooke, *Leslie Brooke and Johnny Crow* (Frederick Warne, 1982); excerpted and reprinted in *Children's Literature Review,* Vol. 20, ed. Gerard J. Senick (Detroit: Gale Research, 1990), p. 47.

Suggestions Are Welcome

In response to various suggestions, several features have been added to *CLR* since the series began, including author entries on retellers of traditional literature as well as those who have been the first to record oral tales and other folklore; entries on prominent illustrators featuring commentary on their styles and techniques; entries on authors whose works are considered controversial or have been challenged; occasional entries devoted to criticism on a single work by a major author; sections in author introductions that list major works by the author or illustrator being profiled; explanatory notes that provide information on the critic or work of criticism to enhance the usefulness of the excerpt; more extensive illustrative material, such as holographs of manuscript pages and photographs of people and places pertinent to the authors' careers; a cumulative nationality index for easy access to authors by nationality; and occasional guest essays written specifically for *CLR* by prominent critics on subjects of their choice.

Readers who wish to suggest authors to appear in future volumes, or who have other suggestions, are cordially invited to write the editor.

Acknowledgments

The editors wish to thank the copyright holders of the excerpted criticism included in this volume, the permissions managers of many book and magazine publishing companies for assisting us in securing reprint rights, and Anthony Bogucki for assistance with copyright research. We are also grateful to the staffs of the Detroit Public Library, the Library of Congress, the University of Detroit Library, Wayne State University Purdy/Kresge Library Complex, and the University of Michigan Libraries for making their resources available to us. Following is a list of the copyright holders who have granted us permission to reprint material in this volume of *CLR*. Every effort has been made to trace copyright, but if omissions have been made, please let us know.

THE EXCERPTS IN *CLR,* VOLUME 25, WERE REPRINTED FROM THE FOLLOWING PERIODICALS:

The ALAN Review, v. 11, Spring, 1984. Reprinted by permission of the publisher.—*American Book Collector,* n.s. v. 4, March-April, 1983. Copyright 1983 by The American Book Collector, Inc. Reprinted by permission of the publisher.—*The American Society Legion of Honor Magazine,* v. 38, 1967. © copyright by The American Society of the French Legion of Honor Magazine 1967. Reprinted by permission of the publisher.—*Appraisal: Children's Science Books,* v. 2, Fall, 1969; v. 3, Spring, 1970; v. 4, Fall, 1971; v. 5, Spring, 1972; v. 5, Fall, 1972; v. 6, Winter, 1973; v. 6, Spring, 1973; v. 6, Fall, 1973; v. 8, Fall, 1975. Copyright © 1969, 1970, 1971, 1972, 1973, 1975 by the Children's Science Book Review Committee. All reprinted by permission of the publisher.—*Appraisal: Science Books for Young People,* v. 5, Fall, 1972; v. 14, Winter, 1981; v. 14, Spring, 1981; v. 16, Fall, 1983; v. 18, Winter, 1985; v. 18, Spring, 1985; v. 20, Winter, 1987; v. 20, Spring. 1987; v. 21, Summer, 1988; v. 22, Winter & Spring, 1989. Copyright © 1972, 1981, 1983, 1985, 1987, 1988, 1989 by the Children's Science Book Review Committee. All reprinted by permission of the publisher.—*The Atlantic Monthly,* v. 202, December, 1958 for a review of "Science Can Be Fun" by Charlotte Jackson. Copyright 1958, renewed 1986 by The Atlantic Monthly Company, Boston, MA. Reprinted by permission of the author.—*Best Sellers,* v. 37, June 1977; v. 40, September, 1980; v. 44, September, 1984. Copyright © 1977, 1980, 1984 by the Helen Dwight Reid Educational Foundation. All reprinted by permission of the publisher.—*Book Week—The Washington Post,* May 7, 1967. © 1967, *The Washington Post.* Reprinted by permission of the publisher.—*Book Window,* v. 7, Winter, 1979 for a review of "Come Follow Me" by M. W. © 1979 S. C. B. A. and contributors. Reprinted by permission of the publisher.—*Book World—The Washington Post,* November 3, 1968 for a review of "The Ferlie" by Polly Goodwin; November 8, 1970 for a review of "The Walking Stones" by Jane Yolen. © 1968, 1970 by Postrib Corp. Both reprinted with permission of *The Washington Post* and the respective authors./ November 9, 1986. © 1986, *The Washington Post.* Reprinted with permission of the publisher.—*The Booklist,* v. 67, December 1, 1970; v. 70, February 1, 1974; v. 73, December 15, 1976; v. 74, April 1, 1978; v. 75, February 15, 1979; v. 76, September 1, 1979; v. 78, July, 1982; v. 80, May 15, 1984; v. 80, August, 1984; v. 81, January 1, 1985; v. 81, February 1, 1985; v. 82, March 15, 1985; v. 82, December 1, 1985; v. 82, May 1, 1986; v. 83, September 1, 1986; v. 83, September 15, 1986; v. 83, October 1, 1986; v. 83, April 1, 1987; v. 84, December 1, 1987; v. 84, February 1, 1988; v. 84, June 15, 1988; v. 85, September 15, 1988; v. 85, April 15, 1989; v. 86, September 15, 1989; v. 86, November 1, 1989; v. 86, February 15, 1990; v. 86, March 1, 1990; v. 86, April 15, 1990; v. 87, October 15, 1990. Copyright © 1970, 1974, 1976, 1978, 1979, 1982, 1984, 1985, 1986, 1987, 1988, 1989, 1990, by the American Library Association. All reprinted by permission of the publisher.—*Books for Keeps,* n. 41, November, 1986; n. 56, May, 1989. © School Bookshop Association 1986, 1989. Both reprinted by permission of the publisher.—*Books for Young People,* v. 2, December, 1988 for "Bruno, Boots & Margaret Worth Another Look" by Callie Israel. All rights reserved. Reprinted by permission of the publisher and the author.—*Books for Your Children,* v. 23, Summer, 1988; v. 25, Autumn-Winter, 1990. © *Books for Your Children* 1988, 1990. Both reprinted by permission of the publisher.—*British Book News Children's Books,* Summer, 1988. © The British Council, 1988. Reprinted by permission of the publisher.—*Bulletin of the Center for Children's Books,* v. 15, October, 1961; v. 22, February, 1969; v. 23, March, 1970; v. 25, October, 1971; v. 26, September, 1972; v. 26, March, 1973; v. 26, April, 1973; v. 27, December, 1973; v. 27, April, 1974; v. 29, January, 1976; v. 30, September, 1976; v. 30, October, 1976; v. 30, March, 1977; v. 30, April, 1977; v. 30, May, 1977; v. 31, June, 1978; v. 32, December, 1978; v. 33, March, 1980; v. 33, April, 1980; v. 33, June, 1980; v. 34, December, 1980; v. 34, January, 1981; v. 35, April, 1982; v. 36, September, 1982; v. 37, October, 1983; v. 37, November, 1983; v. 37, June, 1984; v. 39, November, 1985; v. 39, December, 1985; v. 39, June, 1986; v. 40, November, 1986; v. 40, January, 1987; v. 40, February, 1987; v. 40, June, 1987; v. 40, July, 1987; v. 41, April, 1988; v. 42, April, 1989; v. 42, May, 1989; v. 43, March, 1990. Copyright © 1961, 1969, 1970, 1971, 1972, 1973, 1974, 1976, 1977, 1978, 1980, 1981, 1982, 1983, 1984, 1985, 1986, 1987, 1988, 1989, 1990 by The University of Chicago. All reprinted by permission of The University of Chicago Press.—*Canadian Children's Literature,* n. 14, 1979; n. 15 & 16, 1980; n. 20, 1980; n. 38, 1985; n. 43, 1986; n. 52, 1988. Copyright © 1979, 1980, 1985, 1986, 1988 Canadian Children's Press. All reprinted by permission of the publisher.—*Chicago Tribune,* Part 4, November 13, 1955. © copyrighted 1955, renewed 1983, Chicago Tribune Company. All rights reserved.—*Children's Book News,* Toronto, v. 6, Sep-

COPYRIGHTED EXCERPTS IN *CLR,* VOLUME 25, WERE REPRINTED FROM THE FOLLOWING BOOKS:

Children's
Literature
Review

Marcel Aymé

1902-1967

French author of short stories.

Major works include *The Wonderful Farm* (1951) and *The Magic Pictures: More about the Wonderful Farm* (1954).

The following entry emphasizes general criticism of Aymé's literature for children. It also includes a selection of reviews to supplement the general criticism.

One of France's most celebrated modern writers, Aymé is well known for his adult short stories, novels, and plays, in which he satirizes French life and attitudes in a humorous and often acerbic voice. Considered an exceptional storyteller and philosopher, he is compared to such writers as Voltaire and Molière for his insightful observations of both human and animal nature. Aymé's works, which are often set in rural France, include such characteristics as the use of child or animal narrators, sensitive delineation of simple creatures, and inclusion of supernatural elements in a realistic fashion, attributes with which he also invests his books for primary graders. Several tales from the French editions of *Les Contes du Chat Perché* (1934) and *Autres Contes du Chat Perché* (1950) were collected and translated as *The Wonderful Farm* and *The Magic Pictures: More about the Wonderful Farm;* two additional "Wonderful Farm" books, *Derniers Conte du Chat Perché* (1958) and *Contes Bleus du Chat Perché* (1975) are as yet untranslated. Written for his granddaughter Françoise in Aymé's characteristically spare style and reflecting his provincial background, these collections of whimsical yet solid short stories blend fantasy and realism to present young readers with an original, distinctively French world that draws on the tradition of such fabulists as La Fontaine and Lewis Carroll. Called by critic Graham Lord "a milestone of French children's literature," the stories are considered international classics that possess both earthiness and charm.

In *The Wonderful Farm,* Aymé introduces Marinette and Delphine, lively and imaginative sisters who live on a French farm with their stolid, thrifty parents and a variety of barnyard and woodland animals that are both anthropomorphic and capable of magical feats. Both *The Wonderful Farm* and *The Magic Pictures,* in which the animals take on qualities attributed to the portraits that the sisters have painted of them, revolve around the attempts of the girls to promote the rights of the animals, to try and protect them from being eaten or overworked, or to try and alter the laws of nature or the family's usual farm procedures. The events of most of the stories occur when mischievous Marinette and Delphine disobey their parents by doing the opposite of what they have been asked; the resulting predicaments are often solved by the magical solutions of the animals, who speak in eloquent language only the girls can understand. At the end of each story, the farm returns to normal; both girls and animals learn lessons that center on the rewarding of good deeds and the

punishing of negative attitudes. Although Aymé underscores his books with realistic situations, such as the deaths of a few of the animals that attempt to deviate from the laws of nature, he is often praised for evoking pastoral innocence in a kindly and charming fashion. *Les Contes du Chat Perché* was awarded the Prix Chanteclair and had several of its tales adapted as a play by the Parisian troupe Compagnie de la Licorne in 1979; in their U.S. editions, the "Wonderful Farm" books are illustrated by the well-known American artist Maurice Sendak. Aymé has also received honors for his adult works.

(See also *Contemporary Literary Criticism,* Vol. 11; *Contemporary Authors,* Vols. 89-92; and *Dictionary of Literary Biography,* Vol. 72.)

Virginia Kirkus' Bookshop Service

[*The Wonderful Farm* is] a gently meandering little group of animal stories, with an incisive caricature edging into fable. On the wonderful farm where Marinette and Delphine live with their parents, the animals not only talk but seem particularly anxious to assert themselves, in oddly human ways. There is the pig who decides to reduce for

1

beauty's sake; the irascible gander who wishes to be treated with respect; the silly cock who is incited to rebellion against the stew-pot of the henyard by a wily-tongued and empty-stomached fox, and a lovely wild deer who discovers that one born to the danger of a free life cannot exchange freedom for safe barnyard security. The adventures of the little girls and the farmyard animals are deftly shaped, neatly packaged, but the air of carefree innocence and summer pastoral, a tone engagingly captured by many of the European moralists-on-holiday in juvenile literature, relieves the somewhat austere undertones for young children.

> *A review of "The Wonderful Farm," in* Virginia Kirkus' Bookshop Service, *Vol. XIX, No. 1, November 1, 1951, p. 633.*

New York Herald Tribune Book Review

Come to a farm in France where all the animals talk, but talk and act not at all like those talking creatures of whom, in America, we are a bit weary. An adult reading [*The Wonderful Farm*] aloud will be as much amused as the children from about five to eight, who will love naughty Delphine and Marinette, and will laugh heartily at the sly old fox, and the Bantam's discussion of how he would rather be eaten. Then there is the enchanting captive deer, who hated to work like an ox; you will weep at his death. Most magical of all is the seventh tale of the swans; at its end, the French parents and the children, who all along have differed about animals, now understand them together.

This French novelist has given us a very well written, most truly imaginative book, ably translated by Norman Denny. It is full of sharp wit, and has the usual French overtones from La Fontaine; the sharply etched glimpses of French farm life are very telling.

> *A review of "The Wonderful Farm," in* New York Herald Tribune Book Review, *November 11, 1951, p. 5.*

Alice S. Morris

Writers of adult literature who venture to address themselves to children are prone to wind up with that sometimes charming anomaly, a child's story for grown-ups. Marcel Aymé is among the rare ones. In **The Wonderful Farm** he demonstrates that the wit and feeling and intelligence that make him one of the distinguished modern writers of France can perform with delightful and apropos results on a juvenile level.

The wonderful farm of Aymé's title is severely down-to-earth in every respect except one: its animals can talk and are capable, at unexpected and isolated moments, of magic. Moreover, these pleasing attributes, so matter-of-fact is Mr. Aymé's managing of them, succeed in making the farm rather more real, if anything.

The stories themselves—about the cock who ran afoul of an alligator and the pig with delusions of grandeur and the donkey who gave the lie to the epithets usually attached to donkeys—have another magic. In every tale a moral view, an almost William Blakian view not restricted to the

province of the child but related to the whole human world, emerges delicately and without emphasis.

Maurice Sendak's drawings are close to the writings in their just balance of solidity and grace, of gravity and humor.

> *Alice S. Morris, "The Pig Had Delusions," in* The New York Times Book Review, *November 11, 1951, p. 26.*

The Junior Bookshelf

[In **The Wonderful Farm** the] incidents are a happy blend of the fantastic and commonplace while the animals talk in a convincing and matter of fact tone. Expectations of writing of quality were not at first realised and the early stories tended to be somewhat prosaic and devoid of depth of thought and feeling. The book gains momentum however, as it proceeds, and a naivety and charm peculiar to itself are gradually revealed. The rippling surface becomes a mirror of unexpected and deepening reflections while the last few stories reach heights of true imaginative power and insight. **"The Pig and the Peacock"** and **"The Little Black Cock"** are sensitive and delicate pieces of writing while **"The Swans"** is an idyllic and poetic sketch which stands out as an etching in clear and vivid relief.

> *A review of "The Wonderful Farm," in* The Junior Bookshelf, *Vol. 16, No. 3, October, 1952, p. 158.*

Virginia Kirkus' Bookshop Service

[The stories of **The Magic Pictures: More about the Wonderful Farm** tell more] about Marinette and Delphine, those two beguiling heroines of the French playwright's **The Wonderful Farm,** [and] . . . the pastoral innocence of their fable-like adventures on the farm. Now they start off with a morning painting session—and the animals they draw take on the qualities attributed to them in the little girls' pictures. Then there is the evil wolf who turned good—the panther who came all the way from Africa only to suffer with the cold and die—the pig who got the buzzard's wings and was happy he could fly. Gently told, these have their charm and mystery, their play of words, colors, sounds and very human characteristics that bring a certain earthiness into the magic, and will enchant with their timeless quality of fairy tale and fable.

> *A review of "The Magic Pictures," in* Virginia Kirkus' Bookshop Service, *Vol. XXII, No. 4, February 15, 1954, p. 109.*

Alice S. Morris

When a talented novelist addresses himself to children, they may expect enjoyment of a special caliber; so may the elders who read aloud to them. Marcel Aymé's **The Wonderful Farm,** one of the most refreshing and distinctive children's books of recent years, proved a case in point when it appeared in this country in 1951.

In **The Magic Pictures** the two little girls and the collection of eloquent beasts who peopled M. Aymé's farm continue their uncommon adventures. If these are a shade less brisk and economical and the moral implications a whit less sly than in the earlier book, they are still comic and winning. Here, as before, Mother and Father are abysmally addicted to common sense and the mercenary view; Delphine and Marinette are disarmingly naughty and nice, and the animals comfortably gifted with human speech—a gift which they honor in their flawless use of it. M. Aymé, meanwhile—whether he is revealing an unexpected instance of nature undertaking to emulate art, or telling about a wolf who tries to give up eating little girls (and comes very near to succeeding)—maintains that easy balance between the magical and the matter-of-fact which is the essence of his enchantment.

> *Alice S. Morris, "Eloquent Beasts," in* The New York Times Book Review, *May 2, 1954, p. 26.*

Maria Cimino

[In *The Magic Pictures: More about the Wonderful Farm*] Delphine and Marinette see the world through their own eyes and very spirited and imaginative eyes they are, for all their innocence. That they live on a farm in France where the animals can talk and do other amazing feats—while still remaining animals—is their great good fortune. That the life of a French farm is often hard creates the tensions which set off the absurd situations that arise between the children, their parents, and their animals. Only a writer with a vein of poetry in him could have created this touching children's world.

> *Maria Cimino, in a review of "The Magic Pictures: More About the Wonderful Farm," in* The Saturday Review, *New York, Vol. XXXVII, No. 20, May 15, 1954, p. 60.*

New York Herald Tribune Book Review

Adults who work on a farm are used to the idea that animals are meant to work hard for them, and in some cases, to be eaten at a suitable time, or, in the case of an old horse, to be sent off to the glue-maker. To children, these moments of tragedy are overwhelming, and for little Delphine and Marinette, who lived on a farm where the animals could talk, there simply had to be ways of evading the normal farm procedures. [In *The Magic Pictures: More about the Wonderful Farm* Aymé] gives us one delightful story after another, each proving the stern parents in the wrong, the clever animals right, and the little girls the anxious, busy agents between the two.

It all happens in France, and the scene offers the essence of French farm life. But the little girls could happen anywhere: they are painting the animals, and their crudely defective pictures come true; they know the story of Red Riding Hood, yet they let the wolf in to play at their fire, with almost disastrous results; they are studying geography—and the threatened drake goes off around the world, to bring home a panther from India; they long to be a horse and a donkey, and lo, they are, to their sorrow. Meanwhile, the stern natures of Father and Mother are somewhat softened by each strange experience.

If your young listeners from six up liked *The Wonderful Farm,* they will like its sequel even better. . . . The combination of stern realism and most original make-believe is wonderfully well done.

A review of "The Magic Pictures," in New York Herald Tribune Book Review, *May 16, 1954, p. 10.*

Mark J. Temmer

[*In the following excerpt, Temmer refers to an incident in "Le Loup" in which the wolf eats Marinette and Delphine. In the English-language translation of Aymé's tale by Norman Denny the wolf swallows a flat iron instead.*]

Fables should have a moral that pleases the reader's mind as well as his heart, and there is no doubt that Aymé's tales meet this first condition. He appeals to the intellect, and, as for matters of conscience, he follows the tradition of French fabulists who are not intent upon improving the world but prefer to analyze it in a manner that is both lucid and humerous. His **Contes du Chat Perché** is a lively commentary on French life, and his wit spares neither beast nor man. The viewpoint is more fantastic than poetic, the language more natural than formal, and it is precisely this smooth juxtaposition of the fantastic and the natural which characterizes not only his fables but also his many short stories. Aymé's works exhibit *le bon sens français* that shuns poetic exaggeration and seeks what he has defined as *le confort intellectuel,* namely "ce qui assure la santé de l'esprit, son bien-être, ses joies et ses aises dans la sécurité." Fortunately, Aymé is a better writer than philosopher, and the interest of his stories, resides less in their moral than in their dramatic action, which differs in every tale.

These fables, however, do share common traits in terms of their setting, style, formal development and characters. The human protagonists, as opposed to their animal counterparts, are few: a nameless Father and Mother and their children, Delphine and Marinette. Occasionally sentimental, rarely loving and never poetic, the parents are forever badgering their little girls with threats and admonitions. Typical French farmers, they tend to be thrifty and unimaginative—the black rooster is to them but a *coq-au-vin.* Furthermore, they seem cruel—are they not willing to sell their children after they have assumed the shape of a donkey and a horse? In contrast to *les parents,* who reflect the author's disenchantment, Delphine and Marinette are delightful heroines. Invested with a goodness and mischievousness abstracted from real life, these little girls have no personal history and yet they live, representative of girlhood in particular and mankind in general. Knowingly, the fabulist appeals to adult nostalgia for lost innocence and purifies this yearning of sadness. There is a breath of fresh air in these stories which relate the girl's adventures with fox and hens in the timeless setting of a French farm. Our fantasy is freed, and our belief and trust in the pleasures of childhood are once more justified.

It is likewise possible to isolate certain constants in the structure of the intrigues. Hostile intrusions or misdeeds with unforeseeable consequences disrupt the daily life of play and study. The girls consult their animal friends who offer advice and intervene to prevent disaster. The gods, however, are neither called upon nor even mentioned. The *dénouement* contains elements of surprise that are often imaginative or fantastic in nature. Frequently the logical order of life breaks down. Causes are no longer efficient: effects no longer predictable. Yet, despite this seeming reversal of the actual order, the essential facts of life are never disregarded, for Aymé's fantasy does not invoke supernatural powers. As in *Alice in Wonderland,* the result of fancy is truth, and madness but disguise. (pp.453-54)

Although the implications of Aymé's stories are sometimes sad, the *genre* and forms of the apologue are, by their very nature, gay and sprightly and thus mitigate any satire the apologue may contain. Aymé stops short of exaggeration and eschews the now fashionable gloom of expressionistic allegorists such as Kafka and Beckett. Quite circumspect in his use of the principle of the *reductio ad absurdum,* he criticizes what is, without, however, questioning ideals of loyalty, camaraderie and compassion. (pp.454-55)

Aymé's fables demonstrate a basic truth, that life triumphs over those who are victims of preconceived ideas about their destiny and instincts. Fate and instinct, however, are not always in accord. Such is the moral of **"Le Cerf et le chien."** A stag arrives in the courtyard pursued by hounds. The girls hide him and the lead dog, Pataud, taking pity on him, leads the pack astray: "Après tout le cerf ne m'a rien fait. D'un autre côté, bien sûr, le gibier est le gibier et je devrais faire mon-métier. Mais, pour une autre fois. . . . " The noble stag remains on the farm to assume an oxen's yoke. But after being beaten and brutalized by the parents, he returns to the life of the forest. Pataud, unable to prevent his death, and sickened by his trade, becomes a watch-dog: "Je ne veux plus entendre parler de la chasse. C'est fini." His remorse, so simple and evident, is far more telling than wordy self-accusations and confessions. Although one's guilt be only circumstantial, it should be redeemed by self-awareness if not by change. Passions must be curbed, for, as the pig declares: ". . . s'il ne fallait écouter que son appétit, on aurait bientôt dévoré ses meilleurs amis." (pp. 455-56)

It is of paramount importance that everyone, men and beasts, act according to the prescribed rules of society. To transgress openly their limits is to court disaster: witness *le petit coq noir* who lives on the assumption that to be eaten by one's master is a "règle sans exception." Seduced by Reynard's call to live freely and encouraged by the children to become the leader of his race, he is soon killed by the fox and eaten by the parents. Worst of all, the girls are scolded for meddling, and they now realize that "le mensonge et la désobéissance sont d'affreux péchés." Thus, Aymé derides empty precepts by contrasting them with a reality that operates under its own laws. There is a lag between the logic of life and the logic of justice. Indeed, the punishment does not always fit the crime, and sometimes one is chastized regardless of what one has done. Cognizant of this fact, the girls soon learn to defend themselves by assuming a rôle, and the resulting contrast between pretense and reality creates comic effects. As the wolf stares at them through the window, Marinette laughs at his pointed ears. But Delphine knows better. Clasping her sister's hand she declares: "C'est le loup. Le loup? dit Marinette, alors on a peur? Bien sûr, on a peur."

Despite these oscillations between sincerity and irony,

Aymé takes great care to inform the reader of the true feelings of any given character at any given time. Even the wolf enjoys feelings of tenderness and contrition until the confession of his evil deeds turns into torment when he is overcome by "le souvenir d'une gamine potelée et fondant sous la dent". The insertion of colloquial expressions in the dialogue furthers the dramatic development of his character. Thus, the girls propose to *jouer au loup* and as he participates in the game of being himself he quite *naturally* becomes himself and devours them. However, in contrast to Thurber, whose fables and morals are often derived from a commonplace (e.g. "Early to rise and early to bed makes a male healthy and wealthy and dead.") Aymé rarely subordinates his intrigue to the dramatic possibilities offered by a reinterpretation of a proverbial saying. Puns and jests have their place, but action is prior to style.

In order to be fabulistic, this action must be both human and animal, that is to say, the successful fabulist should understand man and beast, capture the essences of each and then invest the animal with those human qualities that best stress its respective folkloristic character. At the same time, he should grant the human protagonists a clear insight into animal psychology. Aymé is a master at treating a natural interplay between the children and the denizens of the barnyard and surrounding fields. Their conversations are spontaneous, their dialogues dramatic. Narration alternates pleasingly with direct discourse which enlivens the intrigue and serves as a convenient vehicle for parodying braggarts and pedants. In this respect, he belongs to a distinguished tradition of French writers that begins with the anonymous authors of *Le Roman de Renart* and has as its most illustrious member the immortal La Fontaine. Surely his *Fables* must have been Aymé's *livre de chevet,* for **Les Contes du chat perché** are pervaded by a similar spirit of classical restraint and mediaeval realism. And above all, Aymé, like La Fontaine, is an acute observer of the human and animal kingdoms. (pp. 456-58)

It would be unjust to Aymé as well as to poetry, to classify him as a poetic prose-writer. His **Confort intellectuel** is a traditional bourgeois attack against Baudelaire in particular, and, in general against all forms of symbolist prose and poetry, "celle qui consiste à dire des choses fausses ou à ne rien dire." Whether or not this refusal or incomprehension is the negative side of his talent is debatable. Yet poetic he is, at times, not in terms of metaphor, concept or rhythm, but in terms of his dramatic situations. They should not be simply subsumed under the heading of "realistic fantasy" and any difficulty we may encounter in defining this poetic feeling should not deny its residual presence. His poetry is an integral part of his composition: perhaps it is the fabular spirit itself. Despite his prejudices against those who do not write "clearly," Aymé may well be more closely allied to the surrealists than is good for his own *confort.* His revolt against, and transcendance of, the sociological norms of perception and behavior, suggest surrealistic influences.Above all, Aymé the fabulist rejects utilitarianism and in this respect. Jules Monnerot's definition of poetry is à propos: "Il y a poésie quand l'affectivité charge une manifestation humaine d'un sens qui ne se laisse pas ramener sans résidu à la notion vulgaire de

Aymé at his desk.

l'utile. L'efficace poétique est autre que l'efficience d'une modification du monde préméditée et exécutée selon le principe de réalité, les normes de l'entendement." (pp.458-59)

It is regrettable that Aymé's style does not always match the excellence of his fantasy and imagination. His prose, dry and functional, is not marred by any specific flaw or "little rift within the flute," but rather by a dull absence of ornament, design and metaphor. Admittedly, Aymé's ideal is simplicity, and he has bitterly attacked misuse of language: "Quand les mots se mettent à enfler, quand leur sens devient ambigu, incertain, et que le vocabulaire se charge de flou, d'obscurité et néant péremptoire, il n'y a plus de recours pour l'esprit." Yet this refusal of pretentiousness may well mask his weakness. Wanting to be natural, he tends to be *artless,* and his discourse lacks the diction, tension and luster of great prose. In art, nature is fashioned of art. Had he been as exacting towards himself as towards others, his fables might already be a part of France's literary patrimony. To be sure, Aymé, the fabulist, holds a very respectable position among the representatives of the *genre mineur,* of the fabular spirit which refuses to die, but the question of whether or not he has suc-

ceeded in immortalizing Delphine and Marinette remains the subject of much doubt. (pp. 461-62)

> *Mark J. Temmer, "Marcel Aymé, Fabulist and Moralist," in* The French Review, *Vol. XXXV, No. 5, April, 1962, pp. 453-62.*

Dorothy Brodin

Some critics have described Marcel Aymé as essentially a fabulist. He has, in fact, like La Fontaine and Charles Perrault, often used allegory and fable to speak of the world and its inhabitants. His *Contes du Chat perché* are ironical tales of children and animals on a typical French farm. From these tales morals can often be derived. Aymé, through the device of a non-realistic purely imaginative story, pokes fun at prejudices and conventions, and indirectly, almost carelessly, points up a lesson.

Although Aymé's world is not the "comédie aux cent actes divers" which we find in La Fontaine, we nevertheless can discover in his animal kingdom the image of a human world with the stratification, preconceived ideas, clichés, bromides, and pomposity of men engaged in the choreography of social relationships. To that world and society children bring the freshness of doubt. They are not convinced by the teachings of adults. They do not believe that the donkey is stupid, the wolf necessarily bad, or the panther something other than an overgrown but playful cat. The adults are wrong when they attach labels to God's creatures, but, at the same time, they are not entirely wrong since even the worst prejudices and platitudes have some basis in truth.

Some of Aymé's fables and apologues suggest strongly that people should not aim beyond their talents. This is one of the several meanings of **"Les Boeufs"** in which the good little girls, Delphine and Marinette, impressed with a traditional speech on the benefits of education, want the oxen to reap those benefits. They are children and can be excused for not understanding that what may be appropriate in some cases is not necessarily appropriate in others. As for the white ox who takes seriously to the idea of learning, he is like those Bouvards and Pécuchets who accumulate knowledge without making any headway in the direction of wisdom or culture. Although somewhat proud and ambitious, he had been a good hard-working ox. With his introduction to the world of books and arithmetic, however, his inherent faults began to develop and might have ruined him entirely. It is dangerous to be too proud and too ambitious, or to acquire an education unsuited to one's real capacities. The children are flexible enough to realize their mistake and, after the white ox has found refuge in a circus, they carefully refrain from teaching the other animals to read, because they have learned that oxen do not benefit from education. But are their elders equally wise? It would seem that there are many who still do not understand that what might be helpful for a future engineer can perhaps prove useless or even harmful for an ox. Nor do the officials in a petrified system of education, or the ambitious parents who believe blindly in its "benefits" (usually envisaged in strictly material terms) often distinguish any more intelligently than Aymé's little heroines; and countless bovine students continue to solve problems of the "if two faucets fill a hundred-gallon container . . ." type in countless classrooms all over the world.

"Le Petit Coq noir" is a fable which tells of the revolt of the poultry against its masters. The well-meaning, but naïve and conceited, little black cock leads the other barnyard denizens to accept as true the fox's promise that they will acquire teeth if they live in the forest far away from their masters. The conclusion of the story, of course, is the triumph of the truism that hen's teeth are indeed rare. We behold the return of the prodigal poultry, or at least of those animals which have not been eaten by the fox, and witness the fate of the leader of the insurrection who ends his life as a "coq au vin." The apologue points to the moral that there is no safer—or surer—happiness than to be eaten by one's masters. But the real lesson of the fable, insofar as there is a lesson, is perhaps that a leader should not lightly expose his troops to complete annihilation. The girls, of course, are scolded severely and made to realize that telling lies and being disobedient are horrid sins, a basic tenet of well-ordered family life.

In **"Le Loup"**, Marinette and Delphine, who disobey their parents again, are eaten by the wolf. Fortunately the grown-ups come home in time, open the wolf, and find both little girls unharmed although, says the author, that was not strictly according to Hoyle. The wolf, solidly sewed up once more with two meters of string, makes this amusing and unexpected resolution: "I swear that in the future you won't catch me being so greedy. And besides, when I see children, my first impulse will be to run away." He has learned that greediness is a sin, but also that it is safer to avoid temptation than to try to resist it. (pp. 42-5)

Men as individuals, or men in society, sometimes through ignorance or stupidity, sometimes with malice and selfishness, deform or flout certain "natural laws" and their doing so engenders suffering. Most of Aymé's fables contain this truth.

The natural laws which should govern human relationships, and which must enter into account if man and societies are to be saved, are exposed by Marcel Aymé in a cosmos which more often than not is quite different from the one of our daily lives. Indeed the supernatural and the mechanisms of science fiction and of surrealism are frequently the chief ingredients of his universe. His characters move in a world where reality extends beyond the limits we usually assign to it. For an American reader, there are striking and inescapable similarities between that world and the looking-glass kingdom where Alice discourses with objects, animals, and people according to some new dimension of logic where words mean what one wants them to mean. When he was asked about this, Marcel Aymé replied that he had read Lewis Carroll's work many years before, in translation, and had not particularly liked it. This seems to be true whenever a French person is questioned about *Alice in Wonderland.* The very essence of the English book and its particular outlook on life, as well as its way of dealing with language and literature, appear to be completely lost in the course of translation and exportation. Aymé, in spite of his afinities with Carroll, has made his "fantastic-ironical world" quite Gallic and very much his own. In it animals and human beings undergo varied and striking metamorphoses. A little white hen is asked by Delphine and Marinette to play the part of an elephant, since there is no elephant available on the French farm which is their home; the hen does it with such vigorous sincerity that in some essential way she really becomes an elephant, thus creating definite problems as she moves about the house. The little girls, as well as their animals, travel freely in the realm of imagination. If they wish sincerely to become a donkey or a horse, they wake up to find the transformation accomplished. Their thoughts and concepts give shape to the world in which they move. If they paint a four-legged animal and grant him only two legs, the live animal becomes a biped also. Oxen one day stop existing except for two pairs of horns, because the girls painted only their horns. Creatures repeatedly change size with respect to each other because the young artists have represented "a horse not quite half as big as a rooster" or a dog of absolutely monstrous size. (pp. 48-50)

The miracles which happen so frequently in Marcel Aymés' world are not all of the same kind or of the same duration . . .

At [some] times the miracle is in a sense a real one, but stems from the poetic vision and deep compassion of the author. Such is the lovely occurrence which is described in **"Le Paon"**, when the ridiculous young pig who has been starving itself to death in an effort to be as beautiful as the peacock, is assured by the children that he needs not diet any longer since he has already reached his goal; he makes a tremendous effort and, as he looks over his shoulder, "the rainbow suddenly came down and rested on him in colors so tender, but also so vivid, that the peacock's feathers would have seemed grayish in comparison." (p.51)

The miracles are not all of the same duration and need not be permanent, for Aymé often abandons the supernatural as soon as he has made his point. Delphine and Marinette, in spite of their many adventures, always return to being real little girls on a real farm. (pp.51-2)

The laws of reality cannot be permanently set aside, but Aymé's writings show that imagination and poetic vision can create a new and wonderful world which allows a momentary escape from the one we know, but also permits us to come back to it refreshed, and perhaps to see it in a new light and therefore appreciate it better. (p.52)

> *Dorothy Brodin, "A Fabulist for Our Times: Marcel Aymé," in* The American Society Legion of Honor Magazine, *Vol. 38, No. 1, 1967, pp. 41-52.*

Bettina Hürlimann

Marcel Aymé is a writer for adults and a man of typically French *esprit*, but he has written a series of children's books in which the subject of children and animals is wittily and warm-heartedly set out. It is not surprising that a poet from the country of La Fontaine has adapted the fable formula to suit his own purpose. His heroines are two little girls through whom the animals and their ways are reflected. As in *Peter Pan* the children and the animals speak the same language, and cats and wolves, dogs and birds, cows and donkeys all unite together. Although the stories which go to make up the volumes of *Les contes du chat perché* move along with the speed and excitement of a fairy tale, they contain an astonishing amount of dialogue, which belongs with the cleverest and the most enjoyable that can be found in modern children's literature.

The two little girls in the story, Marinette and Delphine, are left alone in their parents' farmhouse during a cloudburst and they decide to play at 'Noah's Ark'. They fetch one of each of the farmyard animals into the kitchen:

> The cow was very interested in the things she could see through the glass doors of the dresser. In particular she could scarcely take her eyes off a cheese and a bowl of milk and she murmured several times: "I see! . . . *Now* I understand!"

It is necessary for a white hen to play the part of an elephant in this imaginative game, where the Great Flood recurs once more in a no-man's-land between play and fantasy and reality, for the rain and the animals and the kitchen are all quite real. The hen which has indeed become an imaginary elephant is so big that it cannot get out before the children's parents return and they hide it in the bedroom. But when their parents finally go to the bedroom and open the door the veil of childish magic dissolves and out flutters a terrified white hen.

Then there is the wise story of the wolf whom the children allow into the house, in spite of all their parents' prohibitions. Mind you, he promises always to be a well-behaved wolf and he plays with the children and talks to them like a little brother, although he does admit that in a weak moment he had gobbled up Little Red Riding Hood. They all play the wildest games together and all goes well until his return visit, when Delphine, who has grown too confident, calls out, 'Wolf, would you like to play "Wolf-where-are-you"?' (A game that the two girls had invented.) Then, alas, this reformed character of a wolf momentarily forgets himself and swallows his two little friends whole. But they are, of course, saved and even the wolf with his sewn-up tummy renews his promise never more to eat up little girls.

This story and many another is told in a beautifully delicate but piquant manner. It brings the French child, with his thorough grounding in technical and intellectual matters, into a remarkable dialogue with nature—and indeed is conducted in such a plain, unadorned language that it has an appeal for all ages, delighting even grown-ups.

Les contes du chat perché are a mixture of fable, fairy tale, and straight story and they have a popularity in France similar to that of King Babar among younger children. Since the appearance of the first story in 1934 they have become some of the most-read books of France. (pp. 87-8)

> *Bettina Hürlimann, "Fantasy and Reality," in her* Three Centuries of Children's Books in Europe, *second edition, edited and translated by Brian W. Alderson, Oxford University Press, London, 1967, pp. 76-92.*

Graham Lord

Commentators trying to analyse Aymé's extremely varied use of the physically unreal have had recourse to a multitude of terms to qualify it: *fantaisie, merveilleux, surréel, fantastique, fabuleux, absurde, non-sens, miraculeux, féerique, science-fiction*. This list makes the analysis of Aymé's unreal stories seem a particularly daunting project, but in fact many of these terms are wrongly or too vaguely applied. Aymé's unreal has little connection with the vogue of Surrealism, the 'literature of the Absurd' or the rather anglophone trend towards verbal nonsense, and the theoreticians of the unreal tend to condemn the terms *merveilleux* and *fantaisie* as being too general, along with the once precise but now vague use of *miraculeux* and *fabuleux*.

Part of Aymé's originality is that he dabbles in several different currents of fantasy. Apart from a thin vein of science fiction, Aymé's imagination can be divided between the two widely accepted currents of *féerique* and *fantastique*. It is important to make a clear distinction between these two because Aymé tends to disregard literary convention by mingling them and adapting them to his own purposes. The *féerique* implies a world apart, like C. S. Lewis's Narnia or J. R. R. Tolkien's Middle Earth, a world inhabited by fairies, unicorns and sorcerers. Its normal phenomena are spells, magic lamps and moonlight. Describing the faerie world of Perrault, Marcel Schneider writes of 'un monde où tout vit, où tout parle, où tout agit. Ce monde a un sens.' It is also a moral world where man's causality is absent even though his attributes may be reflected in humanized animals; Isabelle Jan underlines the tradition of 'L'Ours-valeureux', 'le Cochon-tyran', 'le Renard-fripon' and 'le Chat-brigand'. Man's presence is not obligatory but Aymé obviously finds that faerie is much more relevant and interesting if man participates. Yet this participation will usually be temporary; man will return to the security of his own world at the end.

The literature of the fantastic tends to be taken more seriously than faerie because it talks of our world, our own time and space coordinates. Humans provide most of its protagonists even if they have some frightening new power, and where there are monsters—vampires and werewolves—they often reflect man in their creation. Several common themes recur: metamorphoses, time manipulation, invisibility, voyages to a 'beyond', statues that come to life, pacts with occult powers, monstrous psychological reflections of human feelings or experiences. The essence of the fantastic is the intrusion of something strange and frightening into our secure world. The fear is stressed because our security is threatened; man himself is closely involved and usually helpless before the fantastic. He could kill a fire-breathing dragon but the spectres that he encounters now are often part of himself, the *fantastique intérieur* that is so important in the work of Hoffmann and Poe.

There are elements of both faerie and the fantastic in the stories of Marcel Aymé. He admits appreciation of the work of Andersen and Perrault and has written prefaces to the stories of both. In his comments on his own childhood Aymé refers to the influence of fairy stories as well as to his penchant for Jules Verne and the comtesse de Ségur. All of these influences are to be seen in borrowings of material, but what is more interesting is the way Aymé adapts, distorts and often parodies that material. (pp.20-1)

Aymé's rather liberal attitude towards literary convention is visible . . . in the special case of *Les Contes du chat perché.* This collection is one of Aymé's best-known works. It won him the Prix Chanteclair and has been consistently re-edited ever since its first publication. In 1979 several of the tales were even adapted for the theatre by a young Parisian troupe, the Compagnie de la Licorne. Outwardly, these stories seem to have been written for children. Aymé intimated quite early that they were part of 'l'art d'être grand-père' and that they were written for his granddaughter Françoise, but he later confessed: 'Mes contes pour enfants, je les ai écrits pour moi-même. Je ne crois pas à la littérature enfantine.' His second *prière d'insérer* to these tales was probably more honest: like so many so-called children's books, *Les Contes du chat perché* were 'écrits pour les enfants âgés de quatre à soixante-quinze ans'. For Marcel Aymé there was certainly an element of personal nostalgia in them too: they harked back to his games of 'chat' in the Cours St Maurice at Dôle and

to the happy days of his early childhood in Villers-Robert and his adventures with his cousins in his uncle's mill.

These tales are special in two ways: firstly, because Aymé makes a faerie world apart out of a very real setting, and, secondly, because some of the unreal within that world is distinctly fantastic in character. The seventeen stories are set in a special farmyard and centered on the farmer's two young daughters, Delphine ('l'aînée') and Marinette ('la plus blonde') and their animal friends. This is an ideal frame for faerie. Aymé encourages the feeling of this being a world apart not only be setting the action in the farmyard and its surrounds but also because the stories feature an esoteric child's point of view. The farm is a children's world like so many that have been exploited in literature, an

> univers enfantin séparé, replié sur lui-même
> et où peuvent faire irruption l'improbable,
> l'étrange et même l'impossible.

We are much closer here to the Wonderland of Peter Pan or Alice than to a Fairyland of giants and magic spells. Alice and Wendy are surely related to Delphine and Marinette and a long line of young girls whose imagination and sensitivity have been exploited to link fantasy and reality.

The magic of the farm mainly surrounds the animals. It is not the simple magic proposition of Aymé's earlier novel *La Jument verte,* where he proposed a storytelling horse with a highly refined sensuality; here it is much more episodic. The animals can talk and play humanized roles and to a certain extent they can use their reason. Aymé is clearly conscious of the tradition which produced the 'Cochon-tyran' and the 'Renard-fripon' but he varies his characterization. His fox is the traditional wily creature but his pig is usually stupid, vain and rather nasty, his duck very clever and helpful, his cat rather passive and his rooster proud, arrogant and even treacherous. Yet any stability from story to story depends on Aymé's whim and on the girls' imagination. The pig turns out smart enough to play the detective in **'Les Vaches'** and the ass, normally stupid and obstinate of course, appears as sensitive and intelligent in **'Le mauvais jars'.**

Most of the action depends on contact between the girls and their animal friends. There is complicity and understanding only between them. The girls try to educate an ox; the animals help the girls with their homework and troop into the classroom to see the results. As well as occasionally adopting human roles, the beasts change roles among themselves: a deer swaps with an ox, a panther comes to live on the farm, a wolf wants to play 'chat perché' with the girls and a duck turns world-traveller. Animals talking and thinking is not an end to the magic. Aymé waves his wand once more and we see blindness transferred by telepathy, a hen that changes into an elephant, two white cows that disappear and a horse that shrinks to the size of a rooster. The fantastic even touches Delphine and Marinette to change them into an ass and a horse. This potentially frightening situation is eased somewhat by the fact that it occurs within a frame where such events seem almost acceptable.

The magic often starts with mischief; one of the girls'

pranks backfires on them or one of the animals does something unnatural. A frequent story pattern starts with the parents going to town for the day and warning their daughters against doing one particular thing in their absence. Of course Delphine and Marinette disobey and promptly get into a fix. Their situation worsens as they try to repair the damage and the ominous moment when their parents will return approaches. This tension is usually eased by a convenient last-minute solution. It is the girls' curious predicaments and the inventive solutions that provide much of the charm of these tales.

Delphine and Marinette's pranks are caused by their very innocence. Aymé is presenting the world through unconditioned eyes. He has created a frame where the girls can question the constraints, the conventions and the routines of the adult world and find them lacking. There is fantasy not only in the metamorphoses but also in the girls' minds: perhaps the wolf would make a nice playmate after all; perhaps the donkey is really quite clever despite what people say; and why should a panther not live on the farm? It is their fecund and strangely logical imagination that often provokes the magic. In **'Les Boîtes de peinture'** Delphine and Marinette try to draw the two white cows, but it is not possible to draw them on white paper, say the girls, or at least they would not be visible: 'C'est comme si vous n'existiez pas.' So the offended animals promptly disappear. The animals apply the same innocent process to the girls' homework. The problem is to calculate how many trees there are in a hypothetical forest, so the animals simply set out to count the trees in their own real forest. And when the girls want it to rain so they will not have to go and visit their nasty old aunt, what more natural solution than to ask Alphonse the cat, transposed from the Aymé apartment on the rue Paul-Féval, to wash his whiskers?

Naturally the parents cannot participate in this innocence. They are depersonalized, being referred to and even addressed as 'les parents'. In fact the other adults suffer the same fate, becoming 'la maîtresse', 'l'inspecteur' and 'l'aveugle'. Even aunt Mélina and uncle Alfred tend to be stereotyped figures. When they are active, the parents are always enemy figures. They seem hard-hearted, suspicious and miserly. What little dialogue they are accorded is unsympathetic: they spend their time scolding the girls or else rather optimistically warning them to 'soyez sages . . .', and they whisper ominously to each other as they watch the pig or the chicken growing plumper each day. There is a communication barrier represented by different attitudes to the animals. For the practical parents they are beasts of burden and work and candidates for the cooking pot, while for the girls they are playmates. The parents' main function in this faerie is obviously to represent the parallel, real world, the world of farm chores, homework and the threatened 'pain sec', a world to which the girls usually return after each episodic tale.

Strange things may occur and the girls will get into all sorts of scrapes, but in the end all will be put right. The animals will be restored to their proper forms and proportions, Delphine and Marinette will cease to be a horse and an ass and the blind man will retrieve his blindness. The kidnapped hens are brought back, the lost cows are found and the little black rooster can employ all the guile he can muster but will end up *au vin* in the pot all the same.

Often a return to reality includes a moral ending. Good deeds are rewarded and pride, hard-heartedness, arrogance and treachery are suitably punished whether in the pig, the rooster, the drunken soldier or the parents. Yet these moral punishments almost never involve Delphine and Marinette. Grandfather Aymé is clearly trying to teach the girls a lesson without actually punishing them. The threatened punishments for disobedience are miraculously waived (an exception: their 'affreux péchés' of falsehood and disobedience in 'Le petit coq noir'). Sometimes this is simply because Aymé finds the parents too malicious: the girls fool their parents and allow Alphonse the cat to escape his drowning in **'La Patte du chat'** because the parents were being quite unjust. Sometimes it is because the girls have had a fright and already learned their lesson: they are temporarily eaten by the wolf in **'Le Loup'**, harshly whipped as animals in **'L'Ane et le cheval'** and made to feel thoroughly ashamed in **'Les Boîtes de peinture'**. But more often it is simply that the girls have got into a fix through their own innocence or generosity: they are let into mischief in **'Le Loup'** and **'Le petit coq noir'**. Good intentions and the saviour figure of uncle Alfred retrieve the situation in **'Le Mouton'**. The girls seem to deserve punishment in **'Les Cygnes'** because they have again disobeyed their parents, but their pure hearts and good intentions save them once more.

Delphine and Marinette are not wilfully disobedient; it is just that girls will be girls. . . . This same reasoning is even applied to the animals. The pig's raving vanity should perhaps be punished in **'La Buse et le cochon'** but he is let off because Nature made him the ugliest of all; and when the wolf eats the girls he is only being his natural self. So when he is painfully cut open to free them he is sewn up again instead of being left to die. And in any case, he seems to have learned a lesson so why punish him? It is he, rather than the scolding parents or a moralizing Aymé who rounds off the tale: 'Je vous jure qu'à l'avenir on ne me prendra plus à être aussi gourmand. Et d'abord, quand je verrai des enfants je commencerai par me sauver'.

The reprieve in **'Les Cygnes'** gives the entertainer in Aymé a chance to show off his talents in a superb ending. The girls have crossed the road in spite of their parents' admonitions and are being held prisoner by some swans who turn out to be harsh disciplinarians. They are finally liberated by a wise old swan and returned to the farmhouse just in time to welcome their parents. But the effort costs their liberator his life: it is his swansong that will enchant the parents just long enough to let the girls scurry home. The final irony lies in the parents' comment: 'Quel dommage que vous n'ayez pas traversé la route tout à l'heure. Un cygne a chanté sur les prés'.

Les Contes du chat perché are the work of a storyteller much more than of a moralist. This is clear above all in his endings. When the animals cause an uproar in the classroom trying to help the girls with their arithmetic homework, the teacher gives them 'zéro de conduite'. But the inspector, fortuitously present that day, saves the story by giving them the 'croix d'honneur' for their originality! This is the Aymé who, having allowed an ass a certain measure of cunning to teach the nasty gander a lesson, rounds off his tale with:

> Aussi n'est-il plus question, depuis ce jour-là, de la bêtise de l'âne; et l'on dit, au contraire, d'un homme à qui l'on veut faire compliment de son intelligence qu'il est fin comme un âne.

Aymé has often been called a fabulist more than a moralist. Indeed there is something of the simple world of La Fontaine or the medieval *fabliaux* in stories like **'Le petit coq noir'**, **'Le Paon'** or **'Le mauvais jars'**, where the animals interact among themselves. The moral character of this world cannot be denied. It has been stressed by almost all those who have written on Aymé. Yet for him the purity lies not so much in the moral character as in the lack of artificial adult preoccupations. In his first *prière d'insérer* Aymé wrote:

> Je les écrivais pour reposer mes lecteurs éventuels de leurs tristes aventures où l'amour et l'argent sont si bien entremêlés qu'on les prend à chaque instant l'un pour l'autre, ce qui est forcément fatigant. Mes histoires sont donc des histoires simples, sans amour et sans argent.

The fact that we are adventuring in a moral world should not necessarily provoke a search for an individual lesson at the end of each story. This has been a common failing among commentators, who have felt obliged to label as many stories as possible. The formulae 'A chacun sa fonction dans la vie', 'la sottise des gens qui vont à l'encontre de leurs talents naturels' or the more complicated 'la dangereuse séduction dont jouissent les révolutionnaires dans les milieux intellectuels' may not be actually wrong, but to sum up Aymé's tales like this is absolutely to miss the essence of his talent. This kind of formulation (and thus limitation) quite destroys the *conteur's* nostalgic, whimsical, grandfatherly charm. Such activity is as futile as the criticism of André Rousseaux, who missed the point entirely when he accused Aymé of 'lèse-réalisme', asserting that 'Si les bêtes parlaient, elles tiendraient un tout autre langage.' Aymé's ironic reply is contained in his second *prière d'insérer*:

> Il avait bien raison. Rien n'interdit de croire en effet que si les bêtes parlaient, elles parleraient de politique ou de l'avenir de la science dans les îles Aléoutiennes. Peut-être même qu'elles feraient de la critique littéraire avec distinction.

(pp. 30-6)

Graham Lord, in his The Short Stories of Marcel Aymé, *University of Western Australia Press, 1980, 181 p.*

Gunnel Beckman

1910-

Swedish author of fiction.

Major works include *Admission to the Feast* (1971; also published as *Nineteen Is Too Young to Die*), *Mia* (1974; U. S. edition as *Mia Alone*), *A Room of His Own* (1973), *The Loneliness of Mia* (1975; U. S. edition as *That Early Spring*).

One of Sweden's most popular authors of contemporary realistic fiction for young adults and middle graders, Beckman is recognized as being among the first writers to address problems related to sexuality and other topical issues in her works. Often praised for her sensitivity to the emotions of her characters, her nonjudgmental approach, her frankness, and her clarity as a literary stylist, Beckman describes young people, both female and male, who grow stronger in their identities by facing personal dilemmas. Her novels also feature such subjects as death, divorce, loneliness, and the physical and emotional consequences of being sexually active as well as endings that are not neatly resolved. In *Tillträde till festen* (*Admission to the Feast*), the first of Beckman's books to be translated into English and one of her most respected titles, nineteen-year-old Annika, who learns that she is dying of leukemia, writes a stream-of-consciousness letter to a friend about her new appreciation for life, her reconcilation with her late alcoholic father, her relationship with her mother, and her acceptance of her own imminent death. Beckman is perhaps best known for her novel *Tre veckor över tiden* (*Mia;* also translated as *Three Weeks Overdue*); in this story, sixteen-year-old Mia, who discovers that she may be pregnant, agonizes over whether to continue the pregnancy or to have an abortion as she waits for the results of her pregnancy test. Often considered the first book of its kind, the success of the novel caused Beckman to be in demand as a school lecturer on sexuality and the problems of the young; *Mia* was also published in several editions, one of which includes an appendix with abortion statistics and information about pregnancy outside of marriage. Beckman is also the creator of a sequel, *Våren då allting hände* (*The Loneliness of Mia*), in which Mia must decide how she feels about women's liberation as she deals with the death of her beloved grandmother and has an affair with a sexist music student.

Formerly a probation officer and a lay assessor for the Swedish courts, experiences which prompted the ideas for several of her books, Beckman began her writing career as a newspaper journalist and reviewer of children's books; in addition, she has written detective novels and short stories for adults and has been a translator. Beckman's first books for children were directed to early graders and had traditional family life as their theme; her third novel *Visst gör det ont* (*It Certainly Hurts*) (1963), which draws on her childhood, was the first to include both her

unflinching view of reality and the use of her own life as subject matter. Beckman's next novel, *Misstänkt* (*Suspected*) (1965), is about thirteen-year-old Anders, who suspects that his friend has injured a woman when driving while intoxicated; Anders is also the protagonist of several of Beckman's other novels, including *Försök att förstå* (*A Room of His Own*), in which the character, now seventeen, leaves his country home for Stockholm and becomes involved with a troubled girl. In her fifth story, *Flickan utan namn* (*The Girl without a Name*) (1967), Beckman describes how nine-year-old Sara, a character based on one of her daughters, befriends a secretive Iranian orphan who has lost her family in an earthquake. Among her other works, Beckman is the author of two young adult novels about Fanny, a teenage girl from a divorced family, and her understanding grandmother, and *Oskuld* (*Innocence*) (1978), an autobiographical novel about her student years. *Tillträde till festen* was awarded the Bonnier's Prize for best book for young people in 1969, while *Att trösta Fanny* (*To Comfort Fanny*) (1981) was named one of the best young adult books of the 1980s by the Swedish Institute for Children's Books. Beckman also received the Nils Holgersson Plaque from the Swedish Library Association for her body of work in 1975.

(See also *Contemporary Literary Criticism,* Vol. 26; *Something about the Author,* Vol. 6; *Something about the Author Autobiography Series,* Vol. 9; *Contemporary Authors New Revision Series,* Vol. 15; and *Contemporary Authors,* Vols. 33-36, revised edition.)

GENERAL COMMENTARY

Bob Dixon

For young people of about thirteen and over, [*Mia* and *The Loneliness of Mia*] deal in an outspoken way with sexual questions teenagers have to come to terms with. However, this is all within a context of relationships. Mia, her parents and her grandmother—and even another generation has to be taken into account while Mia is possibly pregnant—all these are linked by questions of love and responsibility, one generation to another. In the first book, especially, powerful emotions are handled with understanding and realism as when, towards the turning point of the novel, Mia's father tells her that he and her mother are going to try living apart:

> Now it had been said. Now it was irretrievable. Not only that Mother and Dad weren't fond of each other and wanted to live apart . . . [sic] but they'd behaved and thought like this for ages, almost all of Mia's childhood, all the years she'd lived with them and laughed and talked and eaten and done her homework and celebrated Christmas and birthdays and gone on outings

Beckman in 1925.

and kissed and hugged, all that time was like one great betrayal; a pretending game that she'd never seen through, a security which was totally hollow.

It seems to me that Beckman tries to deal with too many very serious problems at once and therefore the overall structure of her work suffers. Her clear-sightedness and honesty, however, compel attention. Here is a writer dealing with the world of today. (p. 39)

> *Bob Dixon, "Sexism: Birds in Gilded Cages," in his* Catching Them Young: Sex, Race and Class in Children's Fiction, Vol. 1, *Pluto Press, 1977, pp. 1-41.*

TITLE COMMENTARY

The Girl without a Name (1970)

The pleasant story of a Swedish girl, Sara, and of her friendship with a young Persian girl who comes to live next door to her in Stockholm. Having lost her family a few years ago in an earthquake, the Persian girl has been adopted from a missionary orphanage by a Swedish couple in Iran on business. Burdened with some terrible secret connected with the earthquake, the girl cannot talk about the tragedy, and either cannot or will not tell anyone her Persian name. How she and Sara spend the summer, and how her secret comes out into the open form the plot. Characterizations are adequate; the text, though a translation, is smoothly written; and details of Swedish life are well-integrated into the story.

> *Sister Rita Angerman, in a review of "The Girl without a Name," in* School Library Journal, *Vol. 17, No. 1, September, 1970, p. 112.*

Nine-year-old Sara of Stockholm has happy times with the Iranian girl next door but sometimes she tires of always having to be kind and to remember not to question Gunilla about her life in Iran. Gunilla lost her entire family in an earthquake and since then has terrible nightmares and cannot or will not remember anything of the past, not even her name. One day Sara becomes impatient with Gunilla and lashes out at her, a shocking action which opens the way to Gunilla's recovery. Girls will enjoy the warm friendship between the two, the mystery surrounding Gunilla's past, and the psychological problem which, though complex for this age level, is satisfactorily explained.

> *A review of "The Girl without a Name," in* The Booklist, *Vol. 67, No. 7, December 1, 1970, p. 305.*

Admission to the Feast (1971)

Annika Hallin, alone in an isolated Swedish cottage, spills out her thoughts in a last letter to a friend; last, because Annika has leukaemia and knows death is not far away. She is a modern miss: at seventeen she lived with her boyfriend, Jacob, and Mother, a doctor, "had helped with contraceptives". She finds Betty Friedan's *The Feminine*

Mystique "terrifically interesting" and is concerned about the generation gap, Vietnam and racial discrimination.

Her father and mother have failed in their marriage: mother is working for Oxfam in Pakistan and father, a neurotic failure, is dead. Annika thinks back to a vital few days before he died when he laid his soul bare and father and daughter began to understand each other a little.

Annika's rambling discourse is basically a search for identity, for a still point in the turning world into which her shattering discovery has flung her. Her love for Jacob, her work in an old people's home, her unsatisfactory relationships with her parents, her bewilderment in the face of imminent death . . . Annika's turmoil gushes like a waterfall, a poignant and convincing apologia likely to arouse a warm response in middle and older teenagers. (pp. 407-08)

> *G. Bott, in a review of "Admission to the Feast," in* The Junior Bookshelf, *Vol. 35, No. 6, December, 1971, pp. 407-08.*

Stream of consciousness meditations on her 19 year life and imminent death typed out in anguish by Annika Hallin after learning—accidentally—that she has leukemia. What begins as random expressions of disbelieving grief, opinions on the state of the world (Betty Friedan's *Feminine Mystique* influences her tremendously), and remembered lines of poetry, soon coalesces into a memoir of her recently deceased alcoholic father. Rejecting the available bottle of sleeping pills, Annika soon begins to long in spite of herself for comfort from her boyfriend Jacob—whose intellectual dominance she'd only begun to resist. The final suggestion that Jacob may need her help (did he try to cross the thin ice of the lake on his way to her isolated cabin?) is somehow a less than satisfactory way of demonstrating her commitment to the days of life still ahead. Still, what other conclusion could there be? Annika is not profound enough to come to a real accommodation with death, but her gropings toward understanding and acceptance have a universal validity. Her reactions could be anyone's given the circumstances—there lie the story's limitations, and also its undeniable fascination.

> *A review of "Admission to the Feast," in* Kirkus Reviews, *Vol. XL, No. 18, September 15, 1972, p. 1106.*

Through a letter written to a friend, 19-year-old Annika Hallin tells most effectively of her discovery of and reaction to having leukemia. . . . The ending is stunning in its ambiguity: the possibility that Jacob may have been killed accidentally in his hurry to reach the cottage; that Annika might commit suicide; that everything might turn out happily. The avoidance of a neat wrap up is the capstone to a well-controlled story with fresh, balanced characterizations. Teenage girls will find it easy to identify with Annika's conflicting feelings about Jacob and her own identity and appreciate the well-handled treatment of an admittedly melodramatic situation. The author has resisted the many obvious opportunities to preach on subjects ranging from individual happiness to social justice, allowing the fully-developed character of Annika to speak for herself. (pp. 63-4)

> *Margaret A. Dorsey, in a review of "Admission to the Feast," in* School Library Journal, *Vol. 19, No. 4, December, 1972, pp. 63-4.*

She cannot write to the people who love her most, her fiance and her mother, because what Annika has to say would shock them too much. She writes to an old friend, and her story is grim and pathetic, yet not morbid. . . . In her long letter, she describes a meeting with her father, whom she had met the year before after not seeing him (divorce) since she was a very small child, she tells her friend Helen about her love affair, she describes the agony she feels and her adjustment to the fact that she is going to die. Translated from the Swedish title *Tillträde Till Festen,* the story may be found depressing by some readers, but it is strong and candid, remarkably varied and well-paced for a monologue, and certainly unusual in its theme.

> *Zena Sutherland, in a review of "Admission to the Feast," in* Bulletin of the Center for Children's Books, *Vol. 26, No. 8, April, 1973, p. 118.*

A Room of His Own (1973)

One begins to wish that publishers would cease to import the troubles of young Sweden when young Britain seems to have problems enough and to spare. I did not like Doris Dahlin's *The Sit-in Game* and I do not enjoy *A Room of His Own* for similar reasons. Both enforce too gloomy a picture of student/adolescent types, and one survey after another encourages the belief that comparatively few young people between school and a career go off the rails to any serious extent. One can't help feeling that Mrs. Beckman's story of a homesick country boy subjected to the desperation of a girl in a neighbouring apartment has the appearance of being "dated". There are some good things in it: the changing pattern of relationship between Anders and his family in the country, and the portrait of the factory-owner's widow, "kindly, deaf, and with a phobia about bacteria", who runs the apartment house and responds to every crisis without panic but without real involvement. Otherwise there seems to be little justification for the labour of translation and importation.

> *A. R. Williams, in a review of "A Room of His Own," in* The Junior Bookshelf, *Vol. 37, No. 5, October, 1973, p. 326.*

Very little is coherent about this story of a boy on his own for the first time in a big city. His feelings about himself are muddled, his feelings about the family he left behind are muddled, his relationship to the girl who lives in his building is muddled. There is no plot to speak of, no story to tell, no discovery, no resolution. The outpouring of adolescent ruminations is depressingly unrevealing . . .

Possibly part of the problem with the book is the translation from Swedish. But I don't think so. As the prose is insufficient, so is the plot, the characterization, the conception. It's just a muddled, dull story about another teenager struggling through his adolescence, with little insight, insignificant relationships and little meaning.

> *Dale Carlson, in a review of "A Room of His*

Own," in The New York Times Book Review, *June 23, 1974, p. 8.*

Several plot strands are inexpertly threaded through this story of a Swedish boy's second year at school in Stockholm. Anders' parents' health and economic problems, the conflict between a rebellious girl and her mother who live upstairs, and Anders' growing need for identity and sexual maturity are superficially treated. Needless profanity and stylistic awkwardness further detract from the novel. Though there are a couple of interesting characters and entertaining incidents (e.g., flashbacks of Anders' relationships with his grandfather and an elderly neighbor in Stockholm) they do not compensate for the book's weaknesses.

Peggy Sullivan, in a review of "A Room of His Own," in School Library Journal, *Vol. 21, No. 1, September, 1974, p. 97.*

Mia (1974; U.S. edition as *Mia Alone*)

Mia is a seventeen-year-old schoolgirl who becomes convinced that she is pregnant. This worry is deepened and aggravated, by an unhappy family background in which her mother and father are planning separation, and against this scene she tries to make decisions about her own future actions. The whole book centres around her thoughts regarding contraceptives, abortion, her career and of course her boy friend whom she tells of the predicament. The writing is good, giving a true picture of the circling, tangled thoughts of a girl in such a position, and is healthy in that it gives the right sense of overall depression and fear which inevitably darkens a situation of this kind—even those of a less complicated pattern. Mia's deliberations continue throughout the book until she finally finds that she is not pregnant, but the reader is still left with a thought-provoking work which will perhaps lead a teenager to a clearer realisation of the complications and values of human relationships and behaviour—thinking which is too often pushed summarily aside in these days. It is a pity perhaps that there is a need for such a book— the subject is paramount in much literature today—but unfortunately there is and the author handles it in the way in which it is needful. (pp. 288-89)

E. A. Astbury, in a review of "Mia," in The Junior Bookshelf, *Vol. 38, No. 5, October, 1974, pp. 288-89.*

Mia is a savagely ironical indictment of the clinical approach to sex and relationships arising out of materialism and urban rootlessness. At no point does any character show the slightest understanding of the wholeness of sex, love and marriage. Adult wisdom is represented by Gran: 'It's independence and responsibility that count . . . The only thing to do is to get a qualification and money of your own', and by Dad: 'You can only do what you think is right and true at that moment, don't you think?'. But they have no principles from which to derive their ideas of right and wrong. People may be kind, have a notion of doing right, but the foundation of life is expediency: get a job, qualifications and a safe contraceptive or you'll be in a mess.

Beckman at the time she received the Nils Holgersson Plaque in 1975.

The book is in every way, construction, characterisation, dialogue, imagery, depiction of surroundings, inept, cliche-ridden and lifeless. It can be hilarious: 'Jan had said it would be perfectly safe. He must have had plenty of experience, she'd thought. He was twenty and soon would be a qualified engineer'. The satire is, of course, unintentional. Mrs. Beckman is preaching the gospel of expediency. I hope that any young people who have the bad luck to read the book will see it for what it is. I commend to them, and to Mrs. Beckman, Stevie Smith's poem 'Girls, You are Valuable'. The title alone contains more wisdom than a million *Mia*s ever could.

M. H. Miller, in a review of "Mia," in Children's Book Review, *Vol. IV, No. 4, Winter, 1974-75, p. 149.*

Suspense is meant to mount as Mia Järeberg marks time awaiting results of her pregnancy test, but there's no need for nail biting since the scare is just that. Mia gets "the curse" (a surprising Victorianism for a modern-day story set in sexually free Sweden) and Beckman gets an easy way out of the not-so-simple issues raised: Mother had to get married before abortion on demand and where would Mia be if . . . ; boyfriend Jan opposes the operation (" 'That's against everything I've ever been taught at home' "); Mia's option to choose abortion means accepting responsibility for her own body; etc. Lacking any concrete action, the story becomes a bloodless marathon talk fest. Still, Beckman keeps a lid on moralizing and melodrama, and the absence of some of the genre's creakier conventions—one-shot pregnancies (here it's five times); Neanderthal parents (though in the throes of divorce, Mr. Järeberg is a model supportive father); bad-guy boyfriends (well-meaning Jan offers marriage)—makes this a mild improvement over run-of-the-abortion-mill tracts like Eyerly's *Bonnie Jo, Go Home* (Lippincott, 1972) and Madison's *Growing Up in a Hurry* (Little, 1973).

> *Pamela D. Pollack, in a review of "Mia Alone," in* School Library Journal, *Vol. 21, No. 5, January, 1975, p. 52.*

The Loneliness of Mia   (1975; U.S. edition as *That Early Spring*)

[**The Loneliness of Mia** broadens] the terms of reference which, in the earlier **Mia,** seemed painfully narrow. Mia's concern is not now exclusively with her own body and she shows herself capable of responding with some emotional strength to the troubles that now beset her—her parents' separation and the loss of her boy friend Jan. As an outlet for her feelings she turns to Martin, a music student who has no intention of treating her as anything but a pastime and a pleasant companion. Far more rewarding, in fact, is the confidence the girl places in her grandmother, who is able to help her to some sense of proportion, especially in regard to the Women's Liberation movement which Mia and her school friends endlessly discuss. Here the stylistic rigidity of the book is most in evidence. Conversations, especially in a group of young people, are neither naturally consistent nor orderly and it takes a writer of the calibre of William Mayne to give point and order to dialogue without seeming to do so. In **The Loneliness of Mia** we hear the sound of a debating society, not of an informal group talking naturally about what truly concerns them. The result is not—could never be—good fiction.

> *Margery Fisher, in a review of "The Loneliness of Mia," in* Growing Point, *Vol. 14, No. 1, May, 1975, p. 2644.*

Mia's equation of personal and societal ills and the schoolgirl seriousness with which she attacks both simultaneously may be peculiarly Scandinavian, yet the characters of Gram (a major presence here and never merely a colorful oldster) and of Martin, the likably ingenuous sexist, have dimensions that go beyond the issues they represent. Their existence is an affirmation—and proof that the "problem novel" can transcend its good intentions.

> *A review of "That Early Spring," in* Kirkus Reviews, *Vol. XLV, No. 3, February 1, 1977, p. 97.*

The mission of the author is to the portray today's dilemmas; the method is involvement in *every* social problem that's come down the pike. There's no preaching per se, but warm fireside talks on the importance of proper contraceptives and the importance of doing one's own thing make a cold, almost clinical story. From a lot of sensational mishmash, one or two chapters stand out as particularly well done. (A diamond among heaps of detritus are a pattern for Beckman.) Mia is the only one who realizes that death is a topic that many old people can and, indeed, *want* to discuss, an important event in their lives. Then, in trying to understand the callousnous of her party partner, Mia puzzles over his explanation of equal rights; "one standard" commits *her* to the pleasure but not any romantic involvement with her companion in one-night stands, an emotional arrangement few females are really ready for!

> *Hildagarde Gray, in a review of "That Early Spring," in* Best Sellers, *Vol. 37, No. 3, June, 1977, p. 95.*

Bruce Brooks

1950-

American author of fiction and nonfiction.

Major works include *The Moves Make the Man* (1984), *Midnight Hour Encores* (1986), *No Kidding* (1989), *Everywhere* (1990).

One of the most acclaimed creators of literature for young adults and middle graders to have emerged in the 1980s, Brooks is regarded as an original and daring writer whose works reflect his exceptional understanding of human nature as well as his skill as a literary stylist. He is also celebrated for bringing a fresh perspective to the teenage coming-of-age novel and for providing his books with distinctive protagonists, independent boys and girls who come from divorced families or from those affected by mental or physical illness. Setting his novels in past and future times as well as in the present and primarily using the American South as locale, Brooks presents situations often told in flashback in which his characters gain deeper insight into themselves and their values; in addition, Brooks addresses such issues as friendship, control, commitment, the nature of deceit, and the power of love. Frequently praised for his expository writing on subjects such as sports and music as well as for his imaginative use of metaphor, Brooks writes his books in fast-paced prose which ranges from lyrical and graceful to irreverent and satiric.

Born in Washington, D. C., the setting for his second novel *Midnight Hour Encores*, Brooks spent much of his childhood in North Carolina, where he moved after the divorce of his parents. His first novel, *The Moves Make the Man,* is considered an especially original first effort. Set during the time of the Supreme Court's decision on desegregation of public schools, it introduces thirteen-year-old Jerome Foxworthy, an outstanding scholar and basketball player who is the first black student to be admitted to a white junior high in Wilmington, North Carolina. Narrated irreverently by Jerome, the story focuses on his perceptions of the white world, his fascination with the deceptive "moves" of basketball, which he equates with survival skills in life, and his friendship with Bix, a talented but troubled white baseball player obsessed with telling the truth; attempting to retain Bix's sanity by teaching him the game of basketball, Jerome begins to better understand his own motives and behavior. Brooks also portrays the friendship between southern black and whites in *Everywhere,* the first of his offerings for younger children. In this sensitive story set in Richmond, Virginia, the love of ten-year-old Turley for his grandfather, who has had a series of heart attacks, helps to prevent him from giving in to death; Turley is aided by eleven-year-old Dooley, who attempts to switch the soul of Turley's grandfather with that of a turtle in emulation of an Indian ritual. As he did in *The Moves Make the Man,* Brooks introduces another talented and witty narrator in the contemporary novel

Midnight Hour Encores; at sixteen, Sib is an internationally famous cellist who is the child of divorced parents. She asks her father Taxi, a sixties idealist, to take her on a cross-country journey to meet her mother, a career woman who abandoned her at birth. Caustic and manipulative at the beginning of her story, Sib reveals her love for her father when she must choose to live with one of her parents at the end of the novel. Brooks draws upon his experience as the child of an alcoholic mother in *No Kidding,* a novel set in the next century in which alcoholics make up the majority of the population of the United States and children are forced to take responsibility for their families. Deserted by his father, fourteen-year-old Sam has placed his mother in an alcohol treatment center and his younger brother with a foster family; the story describes how Sam, who is awaiting his mother's imminent release, realizes that he cannot successfully control his family and their destinies. Brooks is also the author of *On the Wing: The Life of Birds from Feathers to Flight* (1989), a survey of bird physiology and behavior that is a companion volume to a segment of the public television series "Nature." *The Moves Make the Man* won the *Boston Globe-Horn Book* Award and was named a Newbery Award honor book in 1985.

(See also *Something about the Author,* Vol. 53.)

GENERAL COMMENTARY

Christine McDonnell

Talented, confident, independent, disciplined, excited by challenge: these characteristics describe Jerome Fox-worthy, the smart, steady basketball player who narrates *The Moves Make the Man,* and Sib Spooner, the world-class cellist, daughter of former hippies, who describes a journey in *Midnight Hour Encores.* The description also fits Bruce Brooks, creator of both characters, who admits, "I have an affinity for independence, for loners, for smart people who are watchers."

Armed with talent and technique, Bruce Brooks strode into the world of children's and young adult fiction as if on stilts. His first book, *The Moves Make the Man,* received the Boston Globe-Horn Book Award and a New-bery Honor Book citation. His second novel, *Midnight Hour Encores,* displays a similar power in its strong voice, unusual characters, and powerful emotional ties.

Several characteristics make his writing noteworthy: the confident, intense first-person voice; the insightful probing into characters' complicated inner lives; the imaginative metaphors, often funny, always fresh. Like Jerome and Sib, Brooks's tough, cocky narrators, the author insists on independence, values honesty, and goes his own way. He does not accept any limits in the structure, style, or content of his books.

Bruce Brooks never set out to write for children. The story that interested him happened to involve adolescents, and, as was the case with Robert Cormier, the book led him to discover, by accident, children's and young adult litera-ture. Thirty years ago, a teenage protagonist would not have pushed Brooks off the adult list—as evidenced by *The Catcher in the Rye* (Little) or *A Separate Peace* (Mac-millan)—but in this era of age-specific marketing, his ado-lescent characters directed the manuscript to the chil-dren's department of Harper and Row. Although the chil-dren's book department is his editorial home now, it does not define or limit him. "I don't know what *young adult* means. I don't want to know the field. Nothing exists for me except the shape my books have. I need that freedom, that cockiness, to write my own books."

After years of writing practice, using the twenty hours a week he had in the evenings and early morning before and after work, Brooks felt ready to write a book. Attending the prestigious Iowa Writer's Workshop gave him two years to write. "I went there very aggressive intellectually and came out very ambitious and increasingly confident. I used the workshop to boost my feeling that anything is possible. The only things I want to do are books that are unique and different."

When Bruce Brooks mentions authors he admires, the range is wide: Charles Dickens and Henry James; P. G. Wodehouse for the first-person voice; Raymond Chandler for his outrageous images—"He looked about as incon-spicuous as a tarantula on a slice of angel food cake" and

"Dead men are heavier than broken hearts." Mentioning Pynchon's *Gravity's Rainbow* (Bantam) and the work of Nabokov and Percy, Brooks likes books that are unlike anything anybody's ever done before. "That's the only kind of book I want to write."

The Moves Make the Man is a daring book in voice and plot. Brooks tells the story in the voice of Jerome Fox-worthy, a thirteen-year-old black basketball player. The choice of the voice was, to an extent, naive. Unfamiliar with the field of children's literature, Brooks was not ham-pered by the controversy about the depiction of black characters and black perspectives by white authors and the arguments that have surrounded books such as *Sound-er* (Harper), *The Slave Dancer* (Bradbury), and *The Snowy Day* (Viking). Brooks chose Jerome's voice because it in-terested him.

"I don't pretend to know what all thirteen-year-old black kids sound like, but I know what Jerome sounds like. The verisimilitude that depends on duplicating a type never comes into it. The accuracy of the voice arises from identi-ty; the character is not a type but an individual. It does not reflect an age group or a race. I can speak as this kid speaks. I know this guy and how he speaks. The voice arises entirely from who Jerome is."

Brooks defends fiction, the author's right to create, to lis-ten to his ear and trust his ability to invent. Jerome is not a universal symbol; he is a specific character created by Bruce Brooks. So is Bix, Jerome's white friend. In defend-ing the freedom of fiction, Brooks states, "I have no delu-sions about Jerome and Bix–they are words on paper, en-tirely fabricated, derived from ideas. But as we all know, words have effects, and fabrications are no less powerful for being invented rather than being born."

Both of Bruce Brooks's novels are told in the first-person voice. In *The Moves Make the Man* Jerome is reflecting over the events, writing the story down during the summer after it happened. In *Midnight Hour Encores* Sib relates her cross-country journey with her father as it happens. In both cases the voice allows for a double layer of infor-mation: we know what the character understands, and we can see beyond it to a deeper truth. As Brooks states, "I enjoy the fullness of character that you have to have to speak in a first-person voice. I enjoy the limitations. You are restricted to what a character sees and knows. I am not an omniscient human being. I see the world from one standpoint. In my books my characters see the world from one standpoint." The first-person voice is an extension of a long interest. "I am a mimic; I notice the way people speak. Voice has always been an interest of mine." His childhood creations, characters in a comic strip, were soon eclipsed by the size of the word-filled balloons in each square. Voice is primary to his characters.

The use of the first-person voice influences not only a novel's language but also its plot. Brooks explains, "I enjoy the cunning needed in the first person, thinking about what your character doesn't know and has to learn. It allows for the invisible solution of a mystery that the character is not facing. The reader sees; the character doesn't. That built-in irony adds to the fullness of the story."

This irony is at the heart of *Midnight Hour Encores.* In her trip across country with Taxi, her father, Sib seems unaware of the special quality of their relationship. The reader appreciates Taxi long before Sib does. Through the first-person voice, the reader witnesses the gradual growth of Sib's understanding. Although Sib is the source of information, the reader draws independent conclusions. In order to understand the end of the book, the reader must unravel a trick of voice: who is speaking? Where is Sib in the last pages? Bruce Brooks trusts the reader to decipher the ending.

Brooks loves the difficult and the subtle because it requires more from a reader. "Subtlety draws me out as a reader. I am not interested in spelling things out. I do it deliberately so that people who want to work hard will have a marvelous experience." Subtlety and ambiguity characterize the central argument in *The Moves Make the Man.* Bix, fiercely opposed to deceit in any form, refuses to use fakes in basketball. "Whatever my problem is, it ain't lying. I do not spend all my time teaching my body to trick people like you do. Part of the game, you tell me. Well, if that's so, this game is not a game at all but pure bullshit. Not for me. If this game is worth playing it is worth playing straight, clean."

Are moves equivalent to lies? Or are the moves necessary ammunition for any clever player in the complex game of life? Is it preferable, or even possible, to be crystal clear, using no devices, no deceptions? This question applies to fiction as well as to basketball. Bruce Brooks deliberately crafts books that avoid simple answers and obvious resolutions. Is he withholding information or presenting a deeper truth, acknowledging that, like life, fiction is deceptive and opaque? Rather than being a lie, perhaps a move is a greater truth.

At the end of *The Moves Make the Man,* Jerome muses, "One thing I have picked up from this whole story of Bix and me and seeing how things you start and stop so neatly by yourself do not always end up on the spot. The fact is–if you are faking, somebody is taking. . . . If nobody else is there to take the fake, then for good or bad a part of your own self will follow it. There are no moves you truly make alone."

Writers need readers, and readers need writers. A willing collaborator, I look forward to the moves of Bruce Brooks in future books. (pp. 188-91)

> *Christine McDonnell, "New Voices, New Visions: Bruce Books," in* The Horn Book Magazine, *Vol. LXIII, No. 2, March–April, 1987, pp. 188-91.*

Leonard S. Marcus

The new book that Bruce Brooks brings out to show [*Publishers Weekly*], on a recent visit to the writer's Silver Spring, Md., home, is not the one we were expecting. Brooks is the author of three highly acclaimed young adult novels. . . . This fall, HarperCollins will publish *Everywhere,* a gem-like, smaller-scale story, Brooks's first work of middle-grade fiction.

But the tallish illustrated volume Brooks plunks down on the dining room table of the airy suburban townhouse he shares with his wife and small son is neither a book for young readers nor a novel. *On the Wing: The Life of Birds from Feathers to Flight* . . . is instead the author's companion guide to a segment of the PBS television series *Nature.*

One reason he wanted to write a book about birds, Brooks says, is that "they're so different" from humans. "It's hard at first to feel much empathy for birds because their beaks, their feathers, their hearts which beat 600 times a minute, will seem so peculiar to us. So my premise"—and here Brooks might almost be describing his approach to fiction-writing—"is that by explaining why they have the equipment they do, and how they use it to satisfy elements of their nature that are not so very different from our own, we can begin to understand their behavior while still enjoying that wonderful sense of difference."

Brooks's impassioned, often psychologically complex novels are similarly clearsighted exercises in imaginative empathy. The author, who is white, cast *The Moves Make the Man* in the voice of a black teenager, Jerome Foxworthy. His second novel, *Midnight Hours Encores,* is narrated by a musically gifted teenage girl. Crossing gender and race are, however, only two of the more apparent means by which Brooks has drawn his young readers into his absorbing game.

Brooks describes his own childhood dispassionately as "broken-up, improvised, not the classic family set-up." He was born in 1950 in Washington, D.C., and spent much of his childhood in North Carolina, where he and his mother moved after his parents' divorce when Brooks was six. An intensely investigative child—"only children usually are," he suggests—he was also a strong reader. Enjoyment of reading soon fostered an active wish to write. "I started by doing comic books," he recalls. Before long, the young author was packing "about six sentences into each speech balloon," leaving barely enough room for a little talking head in the bottom corner of the frame.

A realist by temperament, Brooks was not, he thinks, a "great fantasizer" in the sense that he would lose himself in speculations about realities that were not his own—"the planet Znarg, say." His curiosity tended instead to gravitate toward near-at-hand anomalies: the precise nature, for instance, of a certain activity observed in the street from a passing bus. Impulsively but deliberately, the boy would get off the bus and return to the scene. Brooks's novels are similarly grounded in realistic particulars and in a fascination with process—the way things work—whether in music-making or competitive sports or seventh-grade home economics class.

Life in North Carolina during the '50s was to affect him forcibly. In Washington, Brooks recalls, he had had little experience to prepare him for the segregationist practices openly accepted in places like the downtown Durham restaurant into which he innocently wandered on his own one day in search of lunch. While sitting at the counter, he was aware only of an inexplicable tension building in the room. By the time he left, however, he realized that the section he'd entered had been for black customers only, that the partition dividing the restaurant was a racial barrier. "I saw with horror," he recalls, "how insulting it might have seemed for me to go in," and how, had he been a black child venturing into the all-white side, his presence would not even have been tolerated. "It made me think a lot," he says. "That awareness of racial conflict has been a part of my life all my life."

Both *The Moves Make the Man* and *Everywhere* examine a relationship between two youngsters, one black, the other white. In certain scenes of the earlier book, especially, the day-to-day consequences of living in a prejudiced society are brought searingly to the fore. Nonetheless, Brooks notes, the racial differences in *The Moves Make the Man* "turn out not to be nearly as strong as other differences, and certain similarities of circumstance and internal makeup" that ultimately define the complex relationship between Jerome and the elusive Bix Rivers.

Brooks's mother was an alcoholic. Following one of a series of nervous breakdowns she experienced, he "sort of ran away" at age 12, returning to Washington to live with his grandmother. In this new home, he was provided with the basic necessities and given considerably more freedom than middle class parents typically grant their teenagers. He remembers himself then as "an earnest, credulous white boy always going downtown to sneak into black clubs. I had to make up a lot about my childhood as I went along," he says. "Because of that, I really identify with the people who, to take care of themselves, have to come up with a way of silently manipulating events—rather than with the people who simply give orders."

The young protagonists of each of Brooks's first three novels also enjoy and, at times, suffer from varying degrees of immunity from conventional adult supervision. While the reader is made to admire their street smarts and extraordinary competence and passions, Brooks also casts a knowing eye on the emotional costs to young people of being forced to grow up early. The title of his third novel, *No Kidding,* refers in part to the fact that Sam, the story's 14-year-old central figure, is too busy looking after his younger brother and alcoholic mother to have much occasion for kidding around, let alone for *being* a kid.

Brooks, though, is also wary of reducing any young person's experience, however difficult, to the story of an "unhappy" childhood. "If you're a kid," he says, "you take as the definition of life whatever your own life happens to consist of." While his books explore much of what has come to be regarded as the standard territory of the adolescent "problem novel"—the consequences of living with parents who are divorced, alcoholic or mentally ill, and so on—they do so with refreshingly few traces of the humorless self-absorption typical of the genre.

Brooks can, for one thing, be a hilarious mimic. His caricatures in *The Moves Make the Man* of a junior high school communications teacher and a guidance counselor, neither of whom has much to communicate, are scathingly on target.

Equally important, his characters are bright, articulate, adventurous young people whose accomplishments are every bit as central to their self-definition—and to the reader's sense of who they are—as are any deficits they've suffered in their family arrangements. Sib Spooner, the protagonist/narrator of *Midnight Hours Encores,* is a world-class cellist. Both Bix and Jerome are fine ball players who draw strength, as countless youngsters do, from their solitary efforts to perfect their games.

When Brooks visits schools around the country, he talks to his young audiences about writing in strikingly similar terms. Literary activity, he tells them, is not so much about "the piling up of Christ images" (as some English teachers make it out to be), as it is about the mastering of certain "small skills"—for example, the artful use of the passive voice to imply powerlessness, as in Kafka—that gradually extend the "equipment" of the writer's "heart and mind."

Brooks, who attended the Iowa Writers' Workshop from 1978 to 1980, never intended to become a "young adult" novelist. He submitted *The Moves Make the Man* to several general trade houses before sending the manuscript to Harper Junior Books, where he was pleasantly surprised to find an editor, Laura Geringer, who, he recalls, admired the book in all its "strangeness and difficulty" and wanted to publish it, as is, for young readers.

That his career should have taken that particular turn strikes the author as a happy coincidence. "I've never written *for* kids," he suggests, but for "intelligent people. I write *about* kids because my own childhood is still something I am very much wondering about."

In the half-dozen years since his first novel was published, Brooks has enjoyed the respect of the children's book world and been honored with some of its highest accolades. He has also experienced his share of the condescension with which the larger literary community—including fellow novelists, university hiring committees and the like—will sometimes dismiss as sub-literary any work published under a children's imprint.

Such dispiriting episodes, however pale for Brooks beside the widespread, thoughtful attention his books have received from his "first readership," the nation's librarians and teachers. "They don't just read a book," he has found, "they *use* it. And reading matters so much to the kids themselves that it's enthralling to have them respond to my books." (pp. 214-15)

Among Brooks's current projects is a series of nature books for children to be published by Farrar, Straus & Giroux. The first two titles are about animal predation and animal architecture. Something of a literary chameleon himself, he doubtless has more fiction ahead of him as well, though whether his "next 10 books" will concern "relationships between parents and kids or between septuagenarians and octogenarians" is not yet clear to him. Writing is satisfying, Brooks finds, for much the same reasons that sports were rewarding for him as a teenager: "Because what happens can't be predicted. And yet you have certain abilities and certain tricks you're going to play if the opportunity arises. It's a perfect combination of structure, improvisation—and adventure." (p. 215)

Leonard S. Marcus, "Bruce Brooks," in Publishers Weekly, *Vol. 237, No. 30, July 27, 1990, pp. 214-15.*

TITLE COMMENTARY

The Moves Make the Man   (1984)

AUTHOR'S COMMENTARY

[*The following excerpt is from Brooks's acceptance speech for the* Boston Globe-Horn Book *Award in 1985.*]

One of the best things about awards is the feeling of companionship they almost always inspire. An artist or athlete receiving an award doesn't say, "Hey, sure, I'll take it all alone," but rather, "Thanks to everyone who helped," after which he gushes a catalogue of names and shares. I'll hold off on the catalogue for the moment, but I want to elaborate on the particular feelings of companionship and collaboration I've enjoyed in the year since *The Moves Make the Man* was published.

This feeling of collaboration is something I've hung on to without too much close study, probably because I was afraid it would vanish if I plucked at it. I've sometimes disliked the necessary solitude of producing fiction, envying the member of a string quartet or hockey team or any other unit that demands *interaction* to produce. So the sense that I was working with someone made me happy, even without pinning down exactly who that someone was. I suppose I vaguely assumed my feeling included my wife, my son, my editor Laura Geringer, Harper's promotion director Bill Morris—the people who obviously helped me make my *Moves.*

But today I realized I was wrong. Today, as I listened to Stephanie Loer quoting back at me my description of how much I enjoyed writing in the momentum of Jerome's voice, I realized who the collaborators I've felt behind me were: they were my characters.

This is not an original revelation in the world of fiction. Writers have admitted for centuries that they get a lot of help from the wills and identities of figures they create. Perhaps the most eloquent—and awe-struck—description of this comes from Henry James, in one of the critical prefaces to the 1909 New York edition of his works. Essentially, James said, "I get all of this fabulous credit for making and then weaving together the lives of complex, natural characters, especially when they have important conversations. But I really 'do' much less than it seems—I really only invent their initial shape and conditions, and then cut them loose, asking humbly if I may tag along and watch what they do to progress in their lives."

I am paraphrasing, of course—the Master would have rather run a mile in tight shoes than use such a locution as "cut them loose." But the insights is his: we really have a wonderfully easy job when we create a true character who naturally follows the life we've envisioned for him or her. We feel as if he or she is doing a good share of the work. We're collaborating.

This is not to construct a romantic picture of the writer as some kind of plasma-wizard, whipping beings into life and then communing with them. I have no delusions about Jerome and Bix—they are words on paper, entirely fabricated, derived from ideas. But as we all know, words have effects, and fabrications are no less powerful for being invented rather than being born. Jerome and Bix—and everyone else in the book I was writing, right down to the kids with the upside-down numbers on their Beefy's Lunch jerseys—simply developed a momentum that kept me more easily abreast of my story's ins and outs and details.

They also kept me from getting lonely and imperial. They made me feel the novel was a democratic act instead of a manipulative one. Maybe one day I had the idea Jerome should wear a red shirt, but something in Jerome's nature practically reared up and said, "No, man—no way the Jayfox wears some jive thing the color of a kiddie-school valentine card!" And instead of forcing his arms through the shirt holes, I shrugged, asked what color he'd prefer, and heard him say, "Light blue, man—color of tap water in a tall glass," and listened. Maybe all of this took place in less than a half-second; probably so, because that's how fast the decisions have to be in writing fiction: every word chosen or not chosen is a decision.

Let me mention one last bit of evidence that I owe my characters a great deal for their collaborative influence. I first wrote the story of Bix and Jerome as fourteen pages of summary background in a mammoth, towering novel about certain other characters later on in their lives. I had grandiose designs for this sprawling castle of a story, and the tale of "Jarome and Bix" served only as a fillip of crenelation in my architecture.

But the boys wouldn't shut up, once I had let them show their faces. They kept nagging me as I forged pedantically ahead with my bigger plans. "If you're going to tell my story, tell it right," Bix insisted. "Hey, man," yelled Jerome, "don't just go sticking me on the end of the bench. You got to give me the ball and watch me commence to move." They were right—their story was far better than my huge one, and their voices deserved the play I was denying them. So, after a few months of trying to ignore them, I took those fourteen pages and started from the top, using them as a kind of densely concentrated outline. The story was all in there; the trick was simply lettting Jerome tell it the way he should.

I am, of course, delighted that I had the sense to accept this collaboration. I had a lot of fun writing this book, and I have been thrilled with the way it has been received. To be frank, I didn't write it as a novel for young readers—the decision to publish it that way was Harper & Row's. This has turned out to be a wonderful break for me; it has brought me into a world I did not know existed, the world of the most devoted, vigilant, aggressive, critical, progressive, and preservational species in the literary environment—by which I mean the librarians, teachers, and critics whose province is children's literature. (pp. 38-40)

Bruce Brooks, "In Collaboration with My Characters," in The Horn Book Magazine, *Vol. LXII, No. 1, January-February, 1986, pp. 38-40.*

"Just listen to me and you'll get the story," says Jerome Foxworthy, the cheeky, irreverent, adolescent hero of *The Moves Make the Man.* And not only do we get the story, we get one of the most charming, witty protagonists you're likely to encounter. The moves referred to in the title are primarily the feints and jukes that basketball players use to fake out their opponents on the basketball court but, as Jerome discovers, "moves" may have a much deeper meaning in life.

Bruce Brooks's first novel is set in Wilmington, N.C., at about the time of the Supreme Court decision on desegregation of public schools in the 1950's. It is told from the viewpoint of Jerome, a black junior high school student who is outstanding academically and athletically—"the Jayfox can fly, the Jayfox can sneak . . . here come the Jayfox and havoc he wreak," his friends intone when he approaches the basketball court. He has been chosen as the only black student to be admitted to Chestnut, one of the town's white junior high schools.

At the outset the novel is focused on Jerome's initiation into the white world. There is the inevitable encounter with the school bully, Turk, who is, of course, not enthralled with Jerome's presence at Chestnut. But Jerome's reaction after he has demonstrated that he "can throw the hands," quickly establishes that the book's theme is not racial.

Instead, Mr. Brooks concentrates on Jerome's insightful and humorous perception of this new world—on being "the only coon in the forest." "The first day," Jerome says, "the lady in counseling asked if wanted Spanish, French, or German. Hey, I thought she was talking about what kind of salad dressing for lunch." Later he says, "These white kids learned like they didn't pay attention but picked it up like eating breakfast. . . . they didn't even try. . . . Listen, when blacks learned they KNEW they were learning."

Although a racist coach prevents Jerome from trying out for the school basketball team, he remains obsessed with "hoops," and that obsession becomes the novel's central theme and symbol. Early on Jerome observes Bix, a white athlete who is a superb baseball player. Jerome disdains baseball because it is too simple a game, "no tricks"—"Bunch of dudes in kneepants standing straight and watching each other do very little. Here, Sir, I am throwing this sphere at you. Thank you, Sir, I believe I shall bop it with this stick." On the other hand, "hoops is for the tricksters"; and it is the deceptive aspect of the game—the wizardry of feinting, faking and fooling an opponent with your moves—that makes the game fascinating. Still, Jerome is impressed with Bix's athletic ability and makes him his imaginary "mystery enemy." When he is transferred to the white school, he and Bix, who is a loner and something of an outsider at Chestnut, become friends.

Bix, it turns out, knows nothing about basketball. More-over, he is obsessed with the idea of never lying. He loves baseball precisely because it is a straight game. When Jerome begins teaching him the fundamentals of basketball (dribbling, shooting, passing and rebounding), he picks them up quickly. But he refuses to learn the subtle moves that Jerome tries to teach him. He insists on using only the "pure and honest" elements of the game. To Jerome, Bix's attitude is startling and strange, but no more so than Bix's sullen, standoffish behavior off the basketball court or his silence about his mentally ill mother.

Mr. Brooks uses the conflict of values between Jerome and Bix to speed the tale to a touching, bittersweet conclusion. In addition to Jerome's humorous asides, there is a marvelous scene in which Bix challenges his father, a former college basketball player, to a game that is reminiscent of the encounter between father and son in the film "The Great Santini." Both Jerome and Bix learn serious lessons about life from the other's attitudes, and readers may learn something about the nature of moves and what they do to the people who are deceived by them.

The Moves Make the Man is an excellent novel about values and the way people relate to one another. It is entertaining and accessible; the chapters in which Jerome teaches Bix how to play basketball could serve as a primer for any young athlete. Because Jerome is such an intelligent, street-wise narrator, it is a novel that adults will relish as well.

Mel Watkins, "A Trickster and His Upright Friend," in The New York Times Book Review, *November 11, 1984, p. 54.*

Brooks' fine first novel has a basketball theme and plenty of action but is no more about basketball than say, Mark Harris' *Bang the Drum Slowly* (Buccaneer, 1981) is about baseball. The sport is merely the vehicle for delivering a serious story of friendship and madness. The main character, Jerome Foxworthy, is a black junior high student in Wilmington, North Carolina, in the early 1960s. He is also brilliant, and an athlete of great talent who is extraordinarily cocksure of his abilities (perhaps too much so, on all accounts, but readers will accept it because the story depends on it). Jerome is the first black to attend his junior high, and the first chapters give readers an interesting account of middle class black life in a Southern city as a new era dawns. The real story develops further along when Jerome comes into contact with Bix Rivers, a white athlete, to whom Jerome is unaccountably attracted. Bix is mentally ill. He can tolerate no lies or deceit in life or in sports, and his definitions of these are disturbingly narrow. Bix's mother is in a mental institution, and much of the latter part of the novel deals with Jerome's attempts to keep Bix sane through basketball and to resolve the conflict between Bix and his stepfather. The story is not perfect: Jerome is wise well beyond his years; and body language, which plays a humorous part in Jerome's description of his school classes, was barely heard of in the '60s, never mind being taught in classes. This is a difficult story to read, but better readers will enjoy its humor, electric tension and great characters, and their efforts will be well rewarded. The description of the basketball action is simply excellent, but all the writing is top rank. Brooks is, indeed, a major new talent in the YA field.

Robert E. Unsworth, in a review of "The Moves Make the Man," in School Library Journal, *Vol. 31, No. 4, December, 1984, p. 103.*

Told in a fast hilarious prose this first novel begs to be read aloud. Brooks captures his characters' complexities, their language and style and delights the reader with vivid settings that evoke sights, sounds and aromas. Shattering in its execution, Brooks shakes the reader to respond with chuckling affirmation. Jerome Foxworthy is a tour de force black character—his thoughts and experiences, especially a first day episode in home economics cooking class making hamburgers out of newspaper, are fodder for many booktalks . . . Fascinated with Bix's erratic behavior and compulsion for truth, Jerome seeks the inner Bix in a complex friendship to be savored.

Although Foxworthy moves fast, many of the basketball scenes are belabored and pace lessens. The ending sputters and flattens although Jerome's final message "if nobody else is there to take the fake, then for good or bad a part of your own self will follow it. There are no moves you truly make alone" is finely tuned.

Allan A. Cuseo, in a review of "The Moves Make the Man," in Voice of Youth Advocates, *Vol. 7, No. 6, February, 1985, p. 322.*

In a savvy monologue, Jerome Foxworthy gradually discloses the bitter story of how his friend, a white boy named Bix, came to run away from home after the mental breakdown of his mother. Central to the story is the game of basketball, which Jerome plays like an ace and which he teaches Bix—and which becomes a metaphor for life's choices: is truth enough, or must we dissemble to survive in a harsh game? Is Bix innocent or bad, or both? Jerome's singular voice is intent and often funny. Although the writer has made him 13, he seems much older in perception and experience, and high school age readers will be drawn to his story by the brilliant sportswriting and by the trenchant examination of a friendship with a boy in trouble. The novel is memorable for its successful experimentation with language and for the shrewd exposition that grows out of complex characterization. Some readers may be disturbed by scenes of racial bigotry. (pp. 782-83)

Denise M. Wilms, in a review of "The Moves Make the Man," in Booklist, *Vol. 81, No. 11, February 1, 1985, pp. 782-83.*

The breezy, irreverent first-person narration may offend some readers with its talk of "niggers," "crackers," and "coons." Except for Jerome's mother, a paragon, the adults are nasty or incompetent; the taunts of Bix and his stepfather crackle with an animosity similar to that of Edward Albee's characters. But the distinctive voice, while not always convincing, is fresh, funny, and engaging. Furthermore, the basketball scenes encapsulate enough action and lingo to arouse even nonbasketball enthusiasts to the ball's "bammata bammata bammata bam" resonating through the bottoms of their feet.

Nancy C. Hammond, in a review of "The

Moves Make the Man," in The Horn Book Magazine, *Vol. LXI, No. 2, March-April, 1985, p. 185.*

Midnight Hour Encores   (1986)

Raised by Taxi, a devoted single-parent father, Sib is a world-famous cellist prodigy at 16. She's convinced she's done it all herself: Taxi "stands behind me so quietly I don't even know he's there." On their cross-country journey to meet her mother, Connie, who gave Sib up at birth, Taxi tries to explain the sixties so that Sib will understand her mother's desertion in the context of those times. Sib responds harshly with sarcastic gibes at Connie's superficial hippie pursuits, until slowly Sib comes to see that it is Taxi who loves the sixties and remains committed to its ideals. Perhaps predictably, Connie turns out to be a cool, sophisticated real-estate whiz, contemptuous of her self-indulgent hippie past and of Taxi's lack of "ego." Yet, to her own surprise, Sib likes her mother, even understanding Connie's inability to nurture a baby (Sib herself couldn't even care for a puppy). The rich, clever novel has some problems. The plot is unconvincing at times, straining for neat parallels, particularly in Sib's concert-world experiences. Wise, gentle Taxi is idealized: too often his wry, humane comments seem to be in the author's voice. But Sib's first-person narrative is rendered with wonderful control: arrogant, unselfconscious, sharp, and funny, she is also cunning and mean; so fiercely disciplined, she is almost obsessive; so sure of her identity, she is also able to "spread out everywhere like light and water" when great music moves her. As he did with basketball in *Moves Make the Man,* Brooks steeps this novel in the world of music—jazz and rock as well as classical cello and improvisation. He mocks the sixties stereotypes mercilessly and then revitalizes them, giving fresh meaning to love and innocence, commitment and self-realization. And the novel's stunning ending—when Sib chooses among mother, mentor, lover, and father—subverts the typical coming-of-age conventions.

Hazel Rochman, in a review of "Midnight Hour Encores," in Booklist, *Vol. 83, No. 2, September 15, 1986, p. 120.*

With his first book *The Moves Make the Man,* Bruce Brooks established himself as a master of the extended metaphor. In that multiple award winning novel, basketball was the dazzling language of life; now, before readers have really caught their breath from that achievement, Brooks has turned his considerable storytelling powers to the world of music and the coming of age of a prodigy.

Sibilance T. Spooner plays both life and the cello with "cunning and arrogance," two words which keep cropping up in the reviews of her concerts. Sib (who also renamed herself at the age of 8) has, from her own account, pretty much raised herself. She lives in the District of Columbia with Taxi her father, an exile from the '60s who edits an environmental newsletter. In a wonderful introductory first chapter, Sib tells how at 9, when all the other girls in her class were in love with horses, she asks Taxi to show her a horse.

He puts her in the car, drives her to a camping area six hours from home, then gets her up at dawn and walks her to the top of an enormous sand dune.

> I suddenly notice that the pounding of the surf is getting louder from a specific direction, the way a secondary theme sneaks into melody from the violas in an orchestra. And when I look in that direction, off to my left, instead of surf I see a sudden wild spray of beautiful monsters from Mars swirl out from behind a dune, gracefully rolling toward me, not snorting or shivering but just *running*, running on the flat beach beneath me, splashing in the edges of the tide and emptying those little pools with a single stroke of a hoof.

The remainder of the book unravels the mesh of feelings and history, personal and public, tangled in Sib's request at age 16 that Taxi show her her mother.

Early on in the book, Sib compares books to music and books lose because " . . . books are so damn locked up. To me, the little black words on a page are stiffer than steel forks, more closed than the stones in the Great Wall of China . . . Music is different. Music is written down, but it's not stony and stiff—in fact, the guy who wrote it wants me to fool around with it a bit, to poke into the special places I discover, to set my own pace, to tell the story with my own accents."

The other 200-odd pages of the book give a lie to that distinction. This is a book the reader will have to fool around with, poke into, and tell in his own accents. Brooks keeps you going on at least three lines of suspense, not including the question of whether, through all this, Sib will become a more likeable human being. And in the end, as you applaud the gesture which reveals her humanity, you are appalled by the cost of it. Then you remember the missing cello case and begin rewriting the ending to satisfy the accents of your own life.

I was reminded again of Holden Caulfied's definition of a good book as one that "when you're all done reading it, you wish the author that wrote it was a terrific friend of yours and you could call him up on the phone whenever you felt like it."

I want to call up Bruce Brooks and say that the trouble with a book so far ahead of the pack is that by page 15 I'm demanding it be perfect. So I notice Sib's abuse of "like" and "into" and Taxi's lapses into didacticism, and I want to quarrel about the ending, or at least make the author explain exactly what he was about which he probably won't. But anyhow, while I have him on the line, I can tell him thanks for another terrific book.

> *Katherine Paterson, "Heart Strings and Other Attachments," in* Book World—The Washington Post, *November 9, 1986, p. 17.*

Bruce Brooks just gets better and better with his writing. Although Sibilance is a very strong character from the first page, Taxi is brought alive from his beginnings as a rather flat, though idiosyncratic, cardboard father to one who is full-fleshed and filled with non-smothering love. The reader is slowly made aware that this trip to meet

Mom, turned by Taxi into a memory lane of the 60s, is of equal importance to Taxi and Sibilance. Where the reader had originally centered on Sibilance's reaction to her mother, Brooks urges you to consider Taxi and his feelings at the possibility of losing Sibilance.

The relationships explored by Brooks and the characters he has developed are just wonderful. Brooks also brings you into the world of music—composing, practicing, performing—in a way that is technical and accurate yet still easily understandable to the layperson. Just as good music flows and has rhythm, so does *Midnight Hour Encores.*

> *Pam Spencer, in a review of "Midnight Hour Encores," in* Voice of Youth Advocates, *Vol. 9, No. 5, December, 1986, p. 213.*

Midnight Hour Encores is a narrative in Sibilance's voice; naturally she gives herself all the good lines.

She is an arrogant, accomplished child of extraordinary and narrow intelligence; she is a whiz at music, sarcasm and manipulating people, yet does poorly in school, doesn't read books, has no friends and, as it turns out, has deluded herself about her feelings for her nurturing father. Bruce Brooks keeps his heroine's scintillatingly cynical voice consistent throughout, but the tone of this monologue is bound to create difficulties for its intended audience, the MTV generation, one of the objects of his heroine's scorn.

It will be difficult for a young reader to cultivate sympathy for a character so flashily contemptuous of pop culture. Most teenagers don't know the Debussy Quartet from the Ravel; most probably don't care, either. But as Sibilance rattles along snottily, using musical jargon miles beyond the comprehension of the average young adult, she sounds tauntingly superior. This is bound to be off-putting and frequently bewildering. Early in the story, for example, she makes a casual, derogatory comment about "Ma doing the Bach suites." True, that is precisely how a real child-cellist would have articulated the phrase, but most American teen-agers won't have heard of Yo-Yo Ma and will probably deduce that Sibilance is talking about her missing mother—who has been mentioned already on the dust jacket and in the story.

Van Halen fans aside, there does exist a substantial pool of classically trained students who would relish a novel that reflects their rarefied milieu so unapologetically, but unfortunately *Midnight Hour Encores* suffers from inconsistencies sure to alienate the musical child, too. Sibilance blithely states, "the circle of international music critics puts me about third or fourth in the world right now," then proceeds to specify today's most renowned cellists (to whom she considers herself superior). This is an outrageous assertion, even for the most egomaniacal of Juilliard freshmen. Sibilance claims to be a self-made woman, but musically that's impossible. If she has won so many competitions, where is her mentor? Who is her coach? She refers to her beloved first teacher, long dead—but who has helped her get to Brussels, Prague and Rome? No matter how talented, no 16-year-old blossoms into an artistically consummate world-class instrumentalist on her own. To pretend otherwise is an insult to the discipline, and those who study music know this.

Conspicuously absent from Sibilance's monologue is any consciousness of the business side of her career. Who has booked all the concerts with the major symphonies? Who has negotiated those recording contracts? In an atmosphere where teen-age virtuosos jockey for positions on pretigious rosters and agents cluster like flies around young talent it is inconceivable that Sibilance could produce such a long monologue with no references to this aspect of her life.

Also problematic are the discussions about music which sound researched and tend to flatten the natural drama of the story. When Sibilance and Taxi improvise a tone poem, as an homage to the "Age of Aquarius," it does not seem spontaneous. This is a lengthy, pivotal scene, but dull. In his award-winning first novel, *The Moves Make the Man,* Mr. Brooks used similar expository techniques with great success—but he was describing basketball, not musical passages. It might be that sports are intrinsically more exciting on paper than classical music—or, more likely, that the author is more excited by sports. In any case, *Midnight Hour Encores* lacks the zip of his earlier work and such listlessness obscures what would have been an engaging story about selfishness, self-exploration and self-discovery. One hopes that Mr. Brooks, who has a keen ear for the adolescent voice, will focus his next attempts on a protagonist less pretentious.

> *Karen Rile, in a review of "Midnight Hour Encores," in* The New York Times Book Review, *January 4, 1987, p. 33.*

No Kidding (1989)

After peeking back at the '60s in *Midnight Hour Encores,* Brooks takes readers into the next century, to a world that has some very specific extremes, but, in other ways, has changed very little. Sam, 14, has placed his younger brother Ollie with a foster family for a year, after committing his mother to Soberlife, a treatment center for alcoholics—who make up 60% of the population. Sam and Ollie's father, a member of a fire-and-brimstone religious group, the Steamers, left years before. Now Sam is ready to let his mother out, to find out if she is ready to have Ollie back or if the younger boy should be signed over to the foster parents permanently. Sam's control over everyone is a running treme of the book; but in a denouement that is as debilitating as it is surprising, Sam finds that if he has grown up too soon, he still needs some nurturing—and discovers it from a most unexpected source. The first chapters of the book seem to deliberately throw readers off, forcing them to examine each word and phrase for clues as to the time and place of the story. But as the intricacies of each character's personality come into play, the setting matters less. Brooks reveals his canny understanding of the complexities of human nature, and brings off an emotional tour de force that is as harrowing as it is real.

> *A review of "No Kidding," in* Publishers Weekly, *Vol. 235, No. 6, February 10, 1989, p. 73.*

Brooks' placement of an almost textbook alcoholic family into a bleak future time is a daring and believable flourish, and it is used to great effect in Sam's mimicking of the society he hates, making believe "you're going to be able to handle something you can't." The novel is written screenplay-style, in the present tense; definite, controlled, and observing rather than analytical or interpretive. The technique, while thematically wedded to the material, does become self-conscious, particularly in the dialogue, which often comes off as directed rather than motivated. The characterization of Ollie, especially, shows the limitations of the point-of-view: private and secret, he doesn't say much, and because readers don't know what he's thinking, his eventual explosion of rage, while credible, is vented in what seems to be an arbitrary rather than inevitable outlet. Mother has the great part here; shrewd and dangerous, she loves Sam with a passion that threatens to destroy the armor that she put around him to begin with. While the conclusion is over-explained, surrounding Sam's heartrending request to his mother (and himself) "Can I just be your boy?" with too much else, the question still has a sad urgency. We hope things can work out for the two of them.

> *Roger Sutton, in a review of "No Kidding," in* Bulletin of the Center for Children's Books, *Vol. 42, No. 8, April, 1989, p. 189.*

When experience is too painful to confront directly, novelists often find it necessary to transform it. Dealing with the love and anxiety, hope and humiliation that tug at children of alcoholic parents, Bruce Brooks removes his new novel, *No Kidding* to the 21st century.

No Kidding is about a lonely, willful boy who has been given the power to do what he thinks is right for his family. Never mind what they want; Sam makes the decisions. But no plan is foolproof, and Sam discovers that his family has a mind of its own, and that control is an illusion.

The 14-year-old has missed out on childhood in a bleak setting in the near future in which 69 percent of the adult population is alcoholic. A well-meaning Government funds drying-out centers and decrees universal education for AO's (Alcoholic Offspring).

The same Government has given Sam custody of his little brother Ollie and his alcoholic mother, who is about to be released from a treatment program. How will she handle her freedom? Will she drink?

Apparently unaware of his mother's alcoholism, 10-year-old Ollie dodges the foster parents Sam has placed him with to make secret adventures in the deserted city. Weaving like broken-field runners, the boys navigate a weirdly complex society, defined by regulations and peopled by recovering alcoholics and religious fanatics called Steemers.

Mr. Brooks's ambitious scheme pushes him into the narrative traps that await a writer trying out the future. A complicated past demands description, distancing the reader. Everything—AO, custody rules, splinter groups, Steemers—has to be explained. Mr. Brooks overloads his dialogue with expository lumps.

For example, one character asks a Roman Catholic cardinal: "Are you above worrying about the decline of your membership here—about eight percent last year, I recall . . . as the overall population grows more and more aligned with what the statisticians refer to as 'the church'? Almost ninety percent of the sober people in this city go to church four or more times a week. But they come *here* less and less."

Elsewhere, Ollie's foster father says: "We obviously know the probation period ends tomorrow. . . . Now, of course, there is a ten-day period for the decision of, you know, whether to grant custody or to extend into a new probationary term, or to retain."

The engaging character of Foxy Jerome pulled the reader into Mr. Brooks's first novel, **The Moves Make the Man,** . . . . It took as its themes both adolescence and basketball. The voice of young Sib, a teen-age cellist, engaged the reader and sharpened the focus in his second novel, **Midnight Hour Encores.**

Forsaking the intimacy and control of first-person narration, here Mr. Brooks is in riskier territory. Still he offers a strong, if fragmented, cautionary tale to young readers tempted by alcohol. To the gallant, desperate children of alcoholics, he sends word that they are not alone, and they will survive. If the narrative voice is uneven, it is also passionate. When Sam's mother's decision about her sobriety and the family's future comes, it seems almost arbitrary—a bittersweet expression of wish fulfillment—and a powerful expression of pain caught in mid-transformation.

> *Kit Reed, in a review of "No Kidding," in* The New York Times Book Review, *June 25, 1989, p. 30.*

Set in a future time when alcoholism has become an epidemic in the United States, this novel offers a chilling prediction of a society in which children have become the responsible family leaders and alcoholic parents are the dependents. . . . Sam's character is well drawn and believable, no matter how regrettable. Other characters are not so easily believed or understood. Ollie's motivation and actions are obscure, and Sam's mother's attempt to explain her rejection of Ollie is oblique and inconsistent with Sam's description of her alcoholism. While the experienced adult reader can fill in the gaps, supply the motivation, and in so doing create some of the missing plot detail, it will be harder for the young person to grasp the full import of the story and its subtle messages: we put too many burdens on children, pushing them into adulthood too fast; alcoholism is an insidious disease promising fun and power but producing sorrow and impotence. Brooks is a fine writer: the structure is taut; the rhythm pulsing; narrative and dialogue are crisp. The point of view changes constantly, which makes for a fast pace but is confusing at first. Although this powerful, accessible novel has some problems, Brooks has created a wonderful vehicle for discussion in advanced middle school and high school classes.

> *Elizabeth S. Watson, in a review of "No Kidding," in* The Horn Book Magazine, *Vol. LXV, No. 4, July-August, 1989, p. 486.*

On the Wing: The Life of Birds from Feathers to Flight (1989)

Brooks launches another survey of avian physiology and behavior, this one keyed to the PBS TV series "Nature," with a consideration of the feather, which naturalists agree separates birds from other animals. He emphasizes how birds' physical characteristics influence their flight, song, and population. For instance, flying is aided by feathers, hinged ribs, large quantities of red corpuscles, and hollow bones. Although he cites particular species as examples, Brooks' total effort is a generalized discussion of all avians and, additionally and with uncanny insight, of the relationships, both mutually beneficial and clashing, of birds with man.

> *George Hampton, in a review of "On the Wing," in* Booklist, *Vol. 86, No. 2, September 15, 1989, p. 126.*

This [is an] attractive, enticing book. . . . Through lively text, skillful overview, and anecdote, Brooks examines the structure and behavior of birds. Interspersed throughout the text are 150 excellent color photos reinforcing points made by Brooks. In only six chapters he describes the world of birds. . . . This is a thoughtful look at birds, fully worthy of association with this excellent TV series. Recommended for lay readers and experts alike.

> *Henry T. Armistead, in a review of "On the Wing," in* Library Journal, *Vol. 114, No. 18, November 1, 1989, p. 109.*

Everywhere (1990)

After ten-year-old Turley's grandfather has a heart attack, comfortable old Lucy Pettibone, self-styled nurse, comes to care for him—bringing her 11-year old grandson Dooley to keep the younger boy company. Certain that the grandfather will die, Dooley proposes saving him by a unique combination of voodoo and something he read in a comic book: they must find the animal most like Grandfather and kill it at the moment of his death so that the animal's soul can perpetuate his life. Turley is skeptical, but Dooley is imaginative as well as persuasive; the ritual is culminated when Grandfather really does turn the corner just as Dooley seems to behead a hapless turtle (which later turns up, healthy, in Grandfather's workshop; the bloody "head" was a bit of chicken neck).

With uncommon insight, Brooks reveals the feelings and concerns of a boy dealing with a loss of special magnitude: his grandfather has been his best friend, a rare spirit who nurtures the spirit of play that can mature into creative productivity. The two boys' brief, intense relationship is subtly drawn; realistically, the younger boy considers the fact that Dooley is black and he is not, but this in no way deters their sudden close friendship, while Dooley's quiet compassion warms the story. A beautifully written, notably perceptive brief novel.

> *A review of "Everywhere," in* Kirkus Reviews, *Vol. LVIII, No. 15, August 1, 1990, p. 1082.*

[*Everywhere* is] a lyrical, mystical excursion into the realm of the spirit and a testament to the power of hope and love. . . . Brooks's achievement lies in the degree to which readers, along with the narrator, will suspend disbelief and begin to trust in Dooley's mysterious and clearly improvised ministrations. His active insistence that the grandfather can and will be saved proves totally compelling. And the precise prose throughout paints a memorable portrait of a sensitive, reflective child, while highlighting the large and small moments from which the closest human ties are forged.

> *A review of "Everywhere," in* Publishers Weekly, *Vol. 237, No. 32, August 10, 1990, p. 445.*

Rarely has a first novel generated so much critical acclaim and heartfelt love as Bruce Brooks' extraordinary *The Moves Make the Man*. . . . While the two novels that followed—*Midnight Hour Encores* and *No Kidding*—were admired as well, many of his readers felt more distanced from the characters in those stories. Now comes a new book as original as each of its predecessors. *Everywhere* fulfills Brooks' promise as a writer capable of creating the kind of emotional resonance that strikes the heart as well as the mind.

By some quirk of criticism, novelists from the South are inevitably seen as regional writers, perhaps because their sense of place is often profound. Brooks' setting is unmistakably Southern, but his use of place expands beyond any concept of region. As reflected in the title, the idea of "everywhere" becomes the book's central metaphor.

Set in Richmond, Virginia, *Everywhere* begins with the matter-of-fact observations of [a] 10-year-old white boy as he worries about his grandfather, who has suffered a heart attack and seems likely to die. When a black nurse comes to help the grandmother, she brings her 11-year-old nephew, Dooley, to keep the boy company. Dooley becomes the spark to the boy's emotional kindling, and, once Dooley appears, the narrative blazes into a story whose un-

compromised humanity will draw and hold readers regardless of age.

In a flashback, the boy describes sharing with his grandfather an epiphany in which he is at one with all creation. No longer contained in his body, his soul is everywhere. Despite that intensely moving experience, the boy is understandably reluctant for his grandfather to die and go, irreversibly, everywhere.

Matter-of-fact about death and intuitively wise about the boy's needs, Dooley claims to have learned the art of "soul switching" from a comic book about Indians. He dares the boy to help find and sacrifice a turtle in order to save his grandfather's life. Emotionally and structurally, the book climaxes when, simultaneously, Dooley seems to sacrifice the turtle, the grandfather suffers another heart attack, and the boy pulls him back from death, calling out and reaching him with his love, his need, and his will.

Brooks involves readers by saying some things directly, others indirectly, and leaving some things unsaid. The limited first-person of the narrator is a confiding voice, not a stream of consciousness. At times, he keeps his own counsel, allowing readers the opportunity to observe and to draw their own conclusions. Some may wonder if Dooley believed in the ritual. Brooks never spells it out, but an early reference to catfish gives the first clue: "You can't trick them. They smarter than most white people."

Too often the denouement is the weakest part of a novel, the wrap-up of a story that has outlasted its author's interest. That isn't the case with *Everywhere.* The magnetic force that underlies Brooks' graceful prose seems to increase right to the end, drawing readers further into the hearts of his characters and into the mystery of the human heart.

> *Carolyn Phelan, " 'Everywhere,' by Bruce Brooks," in* Booklist, *Vol. 87, No. 4, October 15, 1990, p. 441.*

Anne Fine

1947-

English author of fiction and playwright.

Major works include *The Summer–House Loon* (1978), *The Stone Menagerie* (1980), *The Granny Project* (1983), *Madame Doubtfire* (1987; U. S. edition as *Alias Madame Doubtfire*), *Goggle-Eyes* (1989; U. S. edition as *My War with Goggle-Eyes*).

Acclaimed as a writer for primary graders, middle graders, and young adults, Fine blends realism and humor to address serious themes in works considered both funny and thought-provoking. Often praised for her insightful depiction of contemporary family life and for creating distinctive, often eccentric characters and universal situations with unusual twists, Fine is also acknowledged for her vigorous prose style and lively, accurate dialogue as well as for her humor, which ranges from gentle irony to caustic wit. Fine is perhaps best known for her young adult novels and stories for middle graders; in these works, she treats the problems of children and young people with their parents, their siblings, and each other at home or in school, documenting the growth of her male and female protagonists while considering such issues as the effects of divorce and aging and the importance of tolerance and respect in relationships. Several of her books also include philosophical discussions and subplots centering on such topics as nuclear disarmament, famine relief, stereotyping, and the nature of truth. Although some observers have stated that Fine's books may be too sophisticated or bizarre for the general reader, most agree that her works are valuable both for the messages they provide and for the manner in which they are delivered.

Coming from a large family and marrying into one, Fine has noted that her interest in family relationships provides the basis for many of her books. Before beginning her writing career, Fine taught English at a secondary school for girls, in an Edinburgh jail, and as a second language; she is also an adult novelist and scriptwriter of radio plays. Fine served as an information officer for OXFAM (Oxford Committee for Famine Relief) for two years, an experience that she reflects in *The Other, Darker Ned* (1979), a stylish comic novel for young adults which, along with her first book *The Summer–House Loon,* describes how Ione Muffet, the mischievous daughter of a blind history professor, brings together her father's beautiful secretary Caroline with Ned, an unconventional graduate student, and then tries to raise money for him through OXFAM. Among Fine's most popular works is *Madame Doubtfire,* the story of how Daniel, an actor whose ex-wife continually alters his plans to see his children, disguises himself as the nanny Madame Doubtfire, is hired by the family, and, once his identity is revealed, is allowed to see his children on a more regular basis; Fine is praised for treating her subject amusingly without negating the pain of divorce for

both her adult and child characters. With *Goggle-Eyes,* she recently created another notable comedy, a story told in flashback about how teenager Kitty learns to accept her divorced mother's boyfriend, Gerald, whom she dubs Goggle-Eyes for the way he stares at her mother's legs; Kitty has been asked to try and console her classmate Helen, whose mother has become involved with a man whom Helen has named Toad Shoes. In addition to her stories for middle graders and high school students, Fine is the creator of humorous, realistic short fiction for early readers noted for its substance, a play based on her story *The Granny Project* in which the four Harris children are given their wish to take care of their elderly grandmother rather than to have her placed in a nursing home, and two comic fantasies in a projected trilogy which describe the events that occur when the young protagonists encounter a genie. *The Summer-House Loon* was a runner-up for the *Guardian/Kestrel* Award in 1978, while *Madame Doubtfire* was nominated both for this award and for *The Observer* Prize for Teenage Fiction in 1987. Currently a Scottish resident, Fine received the Scottish Arts Council Award in 1986. She was also awarded the Carnegie Medal for *Goggle-Eyes* in 1990.

(See also *Something about the Author,* Vol. 29 and *Contemporary Authors,* Vol. 105.)

GENERAL COMMENTARY

Chris Powling

Last year Anne Fine's **Madame Doubtful** was a hot contender for both *The Guardian* Award and *The Observer*'s Prize for Teenage Fiction. It didn't win either and I'm not a bit surprised. After all, what self-respecting panel of judges could overlook the fact that this beady-eyed account of post-divorce wrangling is also sublimely, creasingly, *funny?* Reward that sort of thing and you risk giving the impression that comedy—a preferred mode for most youngsters—is just as potent as tragedy and just as difficult to write well. What implications might this have for the serious business of bookishness?

Anne Fine, though, appears to be incorrigible. [**Crummy Mummy and Me** and **A Pack of Liars**] are two more books whose prime intent is to make young people laugh. Both exploit the standard comic techniques of taking a familiar situation, turning it on its head, and shaking it vigorously to see what giggles and insights fall into the reader's lap. In the case of **Crummy Mummy and Me** the joke is role-reversal: "At last, she comes downstairs. And even then she's never dressed right. You'd think, honestly you would, that we didn't have any windows upstairs, the way she chooses what to wear. She certainly can't bother to look through them at the weather."

No, not a parent complaining about a child but the reverse. Minna is the looker-after in this household since her mother, a punk with all the trimmings, isn't up to the job. Minna becomes Minder Extraordinary as she copes with baby brother, boyfriend (Mum's) bed-time (hers) and much else besides. The authorial sharpness flags a bit here and there, but never the warm goodwill towards all Minnas and their dependants.

Goodwill warms **A Pack of Liars,** too, which explores the proposition that "Truth isn't the only virtue . . . there's always charity as well." Well, there is if you're like Laura whose attempt to enliven her own image as a penpal exposes a nifty approach to burglary and precipitates her into another Fine mess. Once again the narrative shamelessly favours ingenuity over plausibility on the pretty safe assumption that a reader can't complain effectively while grinning broadly.

Without matching the sheer panache of **Madame Doubtfire,** both these books offer welcome confirmation that humour is closer to humanity than apostles of high seriousness care to admit. Much more of this Ayckbournian flair and, who knows, Anne Fine may yet win a prize. But perhaps she'd better not hold her breath.

> *Chris Powling, "Relative Values," in* The Times Educational Supplement, *No. 3753, June 3, 1988, p. 49.*

Margery Fisher

The journey into adolescence is beset with pitfalls. Things might be easier if the young were allowed to develop unhindered but their collisions with other people's vagaries help in the process of growing up, painfully at times but usefully as well. Anne Fine's lively sense of the ridiculous and her talent for composing dialogue with the real sound of individual voices are seen at their best in [**The Summer House Loon** and **The Other Darker Ned**], two exhilarating and pointed domestic comedies . . . about the meeting of seemingly irreconcilable personalities. Ione has reached her middle teens in a comfortable but hardly conventional family. Her widowed father, a blind Professor of History, relies on her rather less, perhaps, than he does on Mandy, his much-tried guide-dog, but she is possibly more useful to him than Caroline Hope, engaged as reader and typist but mainly engrossed in the beautification of her glamorous self. Certainly Ione is going to have to face for herself that absorbing question of who she is and what she may become. Musing on the question in the summer house in the garden, she is interrupted by Ned Hamp, a pupil of her father's currently at odds with him over Early Sardinian Trade Routes, a dispute which could lose him his graduate degree. The temptation to compromise for the sake of his thesis provides one theme for the first story while in the second a village jumble-sale got up by Ione for Indian victims of drought is the focal point towards which the girl's feelings for Ned and her exasperated sympathy for wayward Caroline are somehow directed. Through her puzzled observations of other people we see that ups and downs of the love affair and marriage, hilariously and painfully real, of Ned and Caroline; we glimpse the Professor's control of his lonely but fruitful life and we have that delighted sense of recognition which comes in reading novels whose characters burst noisily and eccentrically out of the pages. (pp. 5343-44)

> *Margery Fisher, in a review of "The Summer House Loon" and "The Other Darker Ned," in* Growing Point, *Vol. 29, No. 1, May, 1990, pp. 5343-44.*

TITLE COMMENTARY

The Summer-House Loon   (1978)

[*The Summer-House Loon*] is vigorous and authentic. It covers the space between one summer evening and the next in the life of her teenage heroine, Ione, the daughter of a blind university professor. It is a wild, anarchic, hilarious day and night, as Ione interferes successfully in the turbulent love affair between her father's secretary and one of his students, a gifted buffoon called Ned Hump. In strict moral terms Ione is not a model heroine: she tells lies, she schemes, she meddles. She also gets drunk, as indeed do student, secretary and father: this unseemly and memorable episode is the understandable climax of some fierce romantic and academic quarrels. Meddling and lying to good effect, Ione copes with the foibles of her elders, plotting their happiness with wit, unselfishness and affection, and clearly maturing as she does so.

The Summer-House Loon is an original and engaging book, mischievous, inventive and very funny. It also has a fine emotional delicacy which sensitively captures, among all the comic upheaval, the passionate solitude of adolescence.

Peter Hollindale, "Teenage Tensions," in The Times Literary Supplement, *No. 3979, July 7, 1978, p. 767.*

Here is a winner, if ever I saw one. Anne Fine is one of the genuine discoveries of the decade.

Funny books for children, rare enough anyway, are nearly always fantasies. The humour springs from the incongruities of improbable juxtapositions. In *The Summer-House Loon* the abundant fun comes out of a recognisable, if more than a little unusual, human situation.

Ione Muffet—she does not like being called Miss Muffet—lives with her blind History Professor father in a chaotic house, to which Mrs. Phipps, a 'treasure', brings an occasional and superficial tidiness, while Miss Hope, from the Agency, transcribes Professor Muffet's braille notes and injects a transient order into his researches. Into this curious Eden comes Ned Hump, history undergraduate, very tall, very thin, to Ione's eyes entirely delightful. Ned loves the efficient Miss Hope, but even for her he cannot compromise his historical conscience. (He holds disastrously unconventional views on the Early Sardinian Trade Routes, and, unless he can change them or dissemble, his hopes of a good degree and a better job, and the means to keep the delectable Miss Hope in an appropriate manner, are vain.)

In the space of twenty-four hours—the compass of this compact and finely wrought novel—Ned makes his journey to Damascus and emerges, happy and with conscience more or less intact. No more of the story. Enough to say that it is told with fine skill and economy. The narrative is brisk, the dialogue beautifully characterised. The hero is not Ned, the loon, but the little girl who is working out her own personal destiny all the time she is helping Ned towards his lovely Caroline Hope. Ione has everything to look forward to. "Soon, not long from now, how super for *her*".

Not just a funny book, although it is certainly that. Here is a book with deep understanding, wisdom and compassion. It tosses the reader between laughter and tears with expert dexterity. (pp. 202-03)

M. Crouch, in a review of "The Summer-House Loon," in The Junior Bookshelf, *Vol. 42, No. 4, August, 1978, pp. 202-03.*

An elegant, bubbly British comedy, which gets much farcical mileage from an old convention: the assumption that people in love behave in a charmingly idiotic and highly stereotyped manner. Today's young people might be charmed or exasperated by the exaggerated looniness of both young Ned Hump—a graduate student of Ione Muffet's history-professor father—and of Ned's security-minded ladylove Caroline Hope, who is employed as blind Professor Muffet's Braille transcriber. But those moved to read on will be at least intermittently amused by the dithery doings that begin with Ione meeting the lovelorn young man in the Muffet summer house and end with his impromptu engagement party. . . . Ione, displaying more

cool than she knew she had, plays a role in resolving Ned's moral dilemma; but even though the action is seen through her eyes, the teenager's is decidedly a supporting part. One might wonder, in fact, if she isn't there mainly to make a children's book of a piece of fluff too passé for another audience. Nevertheless Ione is an alert and sympathetic observer, and the delightful evening when the professor and Ned get drunk in the study while Ione and Caroline get drunk on cooking-sherry in the kitchen would be less hilarious without her youthful perception of the goings-on.

A review of "The Summer-House Loon," in Kirkus Reviews, *Vol. XLVII, No. 7, April 1, 1979, p. 392.*

A buoyant, often humorous, and occasionally insightful tale which lacks plot (there *isn't* one to hang a real description on) and has that far-too-common problem of not being for any particular age group. Including a lovely drunken bash in the moonlight, the amorous habits of the student and his girlfriend, and a strong inclination toward having babies ("cots and cots of them," in thoroughly British idiom) it isn't quite young enough for young readers, and, being light and short and juvenile in approach, it isn't quite old enough for older ones. A writer to keep in mind for the future, since she has a way with words, but her first novel lacks substance and focus.

Sara Miller, in a review of "The Summer-House Loon," in School Library Journal, *Vol. 25, No. 9, May, 1979, p. 60.*

The Other, Darker Ned (1979)

In a sequel to the author's first book *The Summer-House Loon,* . . . the same group of original characters appears—the blind Professor, the odd but sensitive Ned Hump, his lovely, vain wife who is the Professor's secretary, and Ione the Professor's daughter who has a habit of eavesdropping and enjoys being solitary.

Ione 'sees' Ned as he might have been had he been born in a country suffering from poverty and drought. So she plans to raise money to buy two bullocks for that 'other darker Ned' through the medium of Oxfam. Her Jumble Sale is a riotous and funny operation, held in the churchyard and involving all the village.

Ione's connection of Ned with the deprived and suffering people on the other side of the world seems a little contrived. The strength of the book lies in its highly original characters and their reaction to each other.

E. Colwell, in a review of "The Other Darker Ned," in The Junior Bookshelf, *Vol. 43, No. 5, October, 1979, p. 277.*

The Stone Menagerie (1980)

Since he was a small boy Ally has endured a weekly visit, with his parents, to the mental hospital where Aunt Chloe sits silent and withdrawn. He has accepted that his nagging mother represents normality and his aunt a departure from the normal. One day, standing in boredom by the ward window, he sees a distant figure digging among the brambled thickets of the estate, and tracks down Flora and Riley, living outside society in the empty cages that once housed wild animals, in a way that astonishes and captivates the sheltered boy. This sensitive, sparkling tragi-comedy of convention and individuality is conducted in what seems at first to be a drifting series of scenes and dialogue but which looks at a second glance like an intricate dance, devised with a strict economy of words, an acute sense of personality and a shrewd, ironic humour that once more shows Anne Fine to be one of the sharpest and humorous observers of the human condition writing today for the young.

> *Margery Fisher, in a review of "The Stone Menagerie," in* Growing Point, *Vol. 19, No. 3, September, 1980, p. 3756.*

Writers nowadays seem to be pre-occupied with illness and the seamy side of life, and feel it their duty to present them to young readers. In this book the background is a mental hospital where Ally's Aunt Charlotte is a silent and withdrawn patient. Ally, a teenage boy, discovers a strange pair of squatters in the hospital grounds, Flora and Riley, who have made their home in the cages of what was once the menagerie of the big house. . . . Ally takes his Aunt to see his friends, and something in their odd surroundings rouses response in her clouded mind. The ending is unconvincingly fortuitous, but does leave a hope of possible happiness in the dim future.

This is certainly an original story, but a bizarre one. At times it excites repulsion in the reader—the sordid ant-infested cages, the unspeakable soup Flora concocts, the dirt and decay everywhere provide only a grim kind of humour. Behind the story is Ally's frustrated unhappiness released in his adolescent love for Flora, and the glimpses of the patients in the hospital, lost in a mysterious world of their own. (pp. 245-46)

> *E. Colwell, in a review of "The Stone Menagerie," in* The Junior Bookshelf, *Vol. 44, No. 5, October, 1980, pp. 245-46.*

A boy with his parents, visiting his aunt in a mental hospital, discovers an unconventional couple living on the far side of a lake in the hospital grounds. There is much irony about sanity and insanity and the unconventional couple end up happily, helping the boy to endure his mother's anxious nagging. The reality of mental hospitals makes me reject this fantasy in which a pregnant woman sets up house inside the stone cages of a small menagerie, once part of an estate, and there are vegetarian jokes all round. The story intends to make points about mental hospitals and menageries, but this uneasy mixture of realism and whimsy won't meet the situation.

> *D. Atkinson, in a review of "The Stone Menagerie," in* The School Librarian, *Vol. 28, No. 4, December, 1980, p. 393.*

Round behind the Ice-House (1981)

[*Round Behind the Icehouse*] is set deep in the country-side, and describes the relationship between a pair of adolescent twins. But . . . there is no sense of false romance; the farm is seen as an impersonal, sometimes cruel place, with the twins themselves caught up with each other in a destructive confusion of affection and resentment. All this is outlined well and convincingly; disquiet sets in, though, when the use of the first person singular is taken to such an extent that the "I" of the narrator begins to appear on each page with the monotony of telegraph poles seen from a train window. Certainly, adolescents frequently do think and write like this, but self-absorption does not always attract interest from others, and there are moments when Tom—the omnipresent ego—goes on too much for his, or our, own good. Yet there are passages of genuine power and feeling in this novel, and it is nice to see the twin relationship stripped, for a change, of its immediate glamour and shown as something altogether more complex and sometimes even damaging. There are distinct rewards here for readers who persevere with this occasionally disjointed and highly emotional narrative, and Anne Fine too is clearly a good novelist who should go on to write even better books.

> *Nicholas Tucker, "Confrontations," in* The Times Literary Supplement, *No. 4103, November 20, 1981, p. 1355.*

A boy and his sister are accomplices in childish mischief and later in campaigns against Jamieson, the farm's handyman, whose uncouth and secretive behaviour is as distasteful as his effective way with vermin. But as Tom grows older he realises that Cass is seeing Jamieson in a different light, while he himself, resenting her drawing away from him, is troubled also by a change in his view of Jamieson's daughter Lisa. Anne Fine writes with such controlled energy and such precision that she seems to have created a new, unique vocabulary for herself; accumulating minute details of behaviour, of landscape, of event, she builds up a narrative which compels attention for every word and phrase.

> *Margery Fisher, in a review of "Round behind the Ice-House," in* Growing Point, *Vol. 20, No. 5, January, 1982, p. 4010.*

During childhood the twins have been close, the bond between them being The List, a collection of the apparently harsh things their parents have called them. Now they are growing up: Cass, who has come to like pretty things and sneaking out to be with Halloran, faster than Tom. The boy's resultant loneliness is intensified when his growing feelings for Lisa lead him into a careless unkindness and he loses her company also.

Despite the final impression that Tom has reached maturity the prevailing mood in this book is misery, made worse rather than better by the high quality writing. May Anne Fine realise that young readers, like the rest of us on this sad old earth, have troubles enough of their own and accordingly make her next book jollier. (pp. 71-2)

> *R. Baines, in a review of "Round Behind the Ice-House," in* The Junior Bookshelf, *Vol. 46, No. 2, April, 1982, pp. 71-2.*

Fine with a group of schoolchildren.

The Granny Project   (1983)

[The] four Harris children are horrified when they realize that their parents are planning to put Granny in a home. They devise a master plan that works up to a point—but when that point is reached, the irate parents rebel, announcing that if the children are that concerned, they can take over caring for the old woman. Gran is incontinent, at times irrational, demanding, capricious, and querulous. The power struggle that revolves around her is almost in balance, with a compromise plan for care worked out, when Granny dies. This has some witty dialogue; it is based on a situation many children encounter and about which many of them have strong convictions. The weakness of the book is not in the writing style, but in the concept of the family situation and of the characterization and attitudes of individual family members; especially weak is the depiction of the mother and father: the mother, Natasha, plays the role of Tragic Queen, is given to muttering Russian proverbs (printed in Russian) and reviling her progeny; the father, Henry, is the archetypical wimp, and both are extremely casual about their parental responsibilities.

> *Zena Sutherland, in a review of "The Granny Project," in* Bulletin of the Center for Chil-

dren's Books, *Vol. 37, No. 2, October, 1983, p. 25.*

Although essentially dealing with aging and death, the novel crackles with life. Mordantly funny, ruthlessly honest, yet compassionate in its concern, the narrative contains rich, philosophical arguments embedded in the intense action and dialogue. The superbly drawn characters are reminders of how rarely writers create characters who not only act and react, but think.

> *Nancy C. Hammond, in a review of "The Granny Project," in* The Horn Book Magazine, *Vol. LIX, No. 5, October, 1983, p. 573.*

The cast of characters here consists of Henry Harris (overwhelmed father); Natasha Dolgorova (beautiful, intelligent, aloof mother); Ivan, Sophie, Tanya, and Nicholas (precocious, undisciplined children) and Mrs. Harris (slightly senile and physically deteriorating grandmother). The conflict begins when Henry and Natasha take steps to put Granny in a home, causing the children to hatch a plot to keep her with the family. . . . Henry and Natasha retaliate by leaving Granny's care totally up to the children and resuming an active social life. This action precipitates a counter-plot by the children, who convince their parents that Ivan's schoolwork is suffering because of his burdensome home duties. A compromise under which everyone makes a few sacrifices proves unnecessary when the starchy old woman contracts pneumonia and dies. Although Fine does succeed in giving all characters equal time, her caustic humor pervades even the more tender episodes, robbing them of the warmth they might have had. Her characters (particularly the shrewd Natasha, who falls for the most obvious of ploys) lack depth and come across as mere two-dimensional bundles of idiosyncrasies.

> *C. Nordhielm Wooldridge, in a review of "The Granny Project," in* School Library Journal, *Vol. 30, No. 2, October, 1983, p. 157.*

Scaredy-Cat (1985)

Poppy is not wholly a **Scaredy-Cat** but though she is used to Primary School she is nervous about the Senior School's Horror Show to which the juniors have been invited, so when Miss Patel says that nobody will go if there is any trouble in the classroom Poppy wonders whether this could be a solution. In fact it is entirely by accident that she does something reprehensible but the caretaker, finding her preparing to run away, advises her to tell the head about her troubles; to her surprise the sympathetic woman entirely understands the problem. A good deal is said in a short space in this domestic episode; the author evokes schoolroom atmosphere and one or two school personalities, abetted by [Vanessa Julian-Ottie], whose drawings are lively and briskly expressive.

> *Margery Fisher, in a review of "Scaredy-Cat," in* Growing Point, *Vol. 24, No. 4, November, 1985, p. 4520.*

Anneli the Art Hater (1986)

The idea of messing about with paints, crayons, pastels and collages is anathema to Anneli, especially when admiring parents display the results around the house. Anneli's hate turns to love when the discovery of a painting owned by an elderly neighbour provides not only funds to save the local children's home from closure, but a sensitive link with the past. This is an enjoyable story for juniors with several facets of substance. All the characters from elderly Mrs. Pears to three-year-old Josh, son of Jodie, Anneli's mum's lodger, are very real. The dialogue is particularly good: it comes in short staccato bursts and is as we speak. Medium-length stories for eight- to ten-year-olds are beginning to proliferate. This one is a little out of the ordinary and is well worth a place in the class library. (pp. 42, 44)

> *Julia Marriage, in a review of "Anneli the Art Hater," in* The School Librarian, *Vol. 35, No. 1, February, 1987, pp. 42, 44.*

Madame Doubtfire (1987; U.S. edition as Alias Madame Doubtfire)

When Miranda and Daniel were divorced, their three chil-

dren were supposed to visit their father at regular intervals but Miranda ruthlessly altered arrangements to suit herself, arguing that Daniel, an actor out of work, could rearrange his life at short notice; missing Lydia, Christopher and spoilt, babyish Natalie, and learning that Miranda's domestic arrangements had broken down, Daniel decided on bold measures. Disguised as the somewhat startling *Madame Doubtfire*, he applied for the job of working housekeeper and childminder and was engaged by Miranda, who found him a treasure in the household; moreover, the children took to the bedizened woman at once and their self-absorbed mother never suspected that they had soon recognised their father. It was certainly not her intuition which put an end to the arrangement but the lifeclass for which Daniel was currently posing; when he had to arrange for the students to attend at Miranda's house, and she returned unexpectedly early from work, the shocked adults were dragooned by their more sensible children into a radical experiment in living. The comedy of disguise allows the author to skate over the sexual hates and impulses inherent in the situation without lessening the candour of her insights into the irreconcileable feelings of both adults and children; readers of the teenage novel, weary of perfunctory blue-prints of reality, should be thankful to Anne Fine for giving them such nourishing food for thought within an entertaining piece of fiction.

> *Margery Fisher, in a review of "Madame Doubtfire," in* Growing Point, *Vol. 26, No. 3, September, 1987, p. 4858.*

Novels about divorce for children are rarely funny; here's one that will have readers laughing from the first page. Lydia, Christopher, and little Natalie have arrived, for their regular Tuesday tea with Dad, carrying yet another letter from Mom (" 'Aha!' he cried. 'Another missive from the Poisoned Pen. How *is* your mother, anyway?' ") which, as usual, says she'll have to cut the children's next visit short, and which, also as usual, the children have already opened and read. "It came under their general heading of self-defense." . . . While Daniel gets most of the good lines (" 'Fractions are useful,' Daniel told his son. 'Nobody ever gets all they want out of life.' ") it gradually becomes apparent that this wit is also his weakness, a carelessness that can hurt his children. Miranda, at first seeming a cold career woman, is equally revealed as a mother who works terribly hard at her job and family. This novel is a special combination of high humor and genuine pain (the first often expressing the second), showing, ironically and perfectly, in this "broken home" the bonds of shared history and love that keep a family together.

> *Roger Sutton, in a review of "Alias Madame Doubtfire," in* Bulletin of the Center for Children's Books, *Vol. 41, No. 8, April, 1988, p. 155.*

Beneath the farce, the story deals with a serious subject: the pain children experience when their parents divorce and then keep on battling. Some of that pain—the way one child hums to himself when his parents argue and another holds her ears—is poignantly portrayed.

But the novel . . . isn't told solely from the point of view of one of the youngsters. The narration shifts almost from paragraph to paragraph. The reader is sometimes told what different characters are thinking—but much more comes from Daniel's point of view than anyone else's. It might have been a better book for children if it had been told entirely from a child's point of view.

In the end, after Miranda has discovered Daniel's deception and there has been one more terrible fight, the parents, chastised by the children, share a tender moment in which both admit mistakes and arrangements are made for Daniel to see the children more. *Alias Madame Doubtfire* is sweet and amusing. I can't imagine anyone not enjoying it.

> *Mark Geller, in a review of "Alias Madame Doubtfire," in* The New York Times Book Review, *May 1, 1988, p 34.*

A Pack of Liars   (1988)

A funny-risible book depending on words and ideas rather than slapstick is to be cherished. Such a one is Anne Fine's *A Pack of Liars.* The high point is the beginning. What is a lie? Such arguments arise between 'sensitive' Laura and clever, rational Oliver who puts truth before tact when the class has been given a pack of pen-pal letters and told to write replies. What letters too—the utterly banal; the occasionally mad. Laura and Oliver look at each other's answers; disputations start, the wrong one is posted and the plot takes over. Fair enough, but the best of the book has gone.

> *Naomi Lewis, "Strange Encounters," in* The Observer, *April 3, 1988, p. 43.*

From a normal and innocuous start, a class exercise in letter-writing, *A Pack of Liars* develops into an unusual contest of deception. Laura, with the rest of her class, embarks on the first exploratory letter to the penfriend their teacher has allotted to her, only to find a strange similarity in the replies to her friends. To make the answering of the plodding letter she receives a little more interesting, Laura pretends to be a certain Lady Melody of eccentric habit, while Oliver, her best friend, reproves his pen-friend for his persistent anxieties. It turns out that this particular correspondent, Simon Huggett, is the only genuine one of the batch. When Laura goes to Sticklebury to investigate she finds that all the other letters come from the same address in the close, where a new-style Robin Hood has stored computers, televisions and other large items from his burglarious raids before handing them over to needy individuals and retirement homes. With Simon's help Laura and Oliver run the trickster to ground but they begin to wonder uneasily whether this strange thief may in fact be more nearly morally jusitifed than they are with their deliberately deceitful letters. This unusual problem in which school children have to cope with a totally unexpected situation, is partly resolved in what is a crackling, bizarre piece of reporting, conducted in the main in lively dialogue cheerfully pointing to traits of character as motive for some ingenious and inventive social prevarications.

> *Margery Fisher, in a review of "A Pack of Liars," in* Growing Point, *Vol. 27, No. 3, September, 1988, p. 5037.*

A book mildly mad from the very beginning, and the solution is the most outrageous part of this delightfully witty romp. An entertainment, lacking the 'layers' of the highly acclaimed *Madame Doubtfire* perhaps, but with a solid school background against which the reader has the satisfaction of watching Oliver and Laura 'rub off against each other.' Highly recommended.

> *L. M. K. Whitwell, in a review of "A Pack of Liars," in* The School Librarian, *Vol. 36, No. 4, November, 1988, p. 144.*

Crummy Mummy and Me   (1988)

[The] reversal of roles, and the edge and vigour of Minna's voice, make her account of her life with her family sharp and funny. Under her exasperation we sense her affection for these credible characters, and an awareness of how very different people can manage to live together. For boys as well as girls.

> *G. L., in a review of "Crummy Mummy and Me," in* Books for Your Children, *Vol. 23, No. 2, Summer, 1988, p. 13.*

Anne Fine is good at portraying the ups and downs of family life and in this novel, aimed at eight-to-elevens, she employs comical role-reversal to great effect. Minna's attractive and flamboyant mother stays up late, cannot get ready to take Minna to school on time, wears outrageous clothes and prefers junk food and watching telly to fresh air and exercise. The household includes Mum's punk boyfriend, Crusher Maggot, whose awe-inspiring exterior conceals a kind nature, and baby sister Miranda aka Crummy Dummy. Minna feels it is up to her to be the responsible member of the family and the book consists of a series of episodes related by the sensible Minna with plenty of funny asides and amusing dialogue. The characterization is excellent throughout. . . .

> *Ingrid Broomfield, in a review of "Crummy Mummy and Me," in* British Book News Children's Books, *Summer, 1988, p. 15.*

The jaunty narrator of these humorous family stories is Minna, a dutiful, sensible little girl with a feckless, happy-go-lucky, essentially child-like mum. This role reversal provides a running joke throughout the book: Minna's mother is never ready when it's time to go to school, has to be reminded about mealtimes, and always insists on their finishing any board game before she will let Minna go to bed. . . .

Further comic interest is supplied by the baby ('Crummy Dummy') and mum's punk boyfriend, Crusher Maggot, who sports a blue Mohican spiked haircut and a 'Made in Birmingham' tattoo on the shaven part of his head. Blue-rinsed gran is thoroughly disapproving, but several of the stories serve to reveal that Crusher's fierce appearance belies a very kindly, gentle nature. . . . My junior testers fell straight in with the humour of the book and its underlying message of tolerance. The questions that it raises make it less lightweight than it looks.

> *Chris Stephenson, in a review of "Crummy Mummy and Me," in* The School Librarian, *Vol. 36, No. 3, August, 1988, p. 99.*

Stranger Danger? (1989)

Stranger Danger? is . . . aimed at the child who is beginning to tackle something longer than a picture book. The theme of the story is how a small boy, Joe, copes in his everyday life with interpreting the 'safety rules' about dealing with strangers.

However, the plot lacks real excitement and the characters are portrayed indifferently, so that while the initial idea is a good one, the book seems rather 'thin'. . . .

It will probably be an acceptable purchase for a junior school or public library, as additional reading matter for the keener young readers, but by no means essential.

> *S. M. Ashburner, in a review of "Stranger Danger?" in* The Junior Bookshelf, *Vol. 53, No. 2, April, 1989, p. 69.*

Bill's New Frock (1989)

Bill wakes up (or dreams he does) to find himself a girl, a fate which his mother at once confirms by sending him to school in a pretty pink dress. Poor Bill: despite the anatomical and sartorial disasters which befall him, his mind and character stay incorrigibly male, a fact borne out by the gradual ruin of his frock. Before normality is restored at teatime, Bill has undergone a high speed training in what life is like for girls.

The story is excellent but quite subtle. Left to themselves, junior school children are likely to bring to it the strong sexual preconceptions they already have. A boy turned into a girl! A boy wearing a frock! The ribald merriment of most primary classes can be readily imagined. Not for a moment does the author question the importance of firm sexual identity, and only in passing does she challenge the male sex-stereotype; the effect is to reinforce both. So the surface of the story is fully occupied with Bill's hilarious predicament, and left to themselves most children (boys and girls alike) will enjoy this and see nothing more. Just as important, but much less conspicuous, is the book's critique of the female sex-stereotype, which is inappropriate not just for Bill but for the girls themselves. Trailing home in his devastated frock at teatime, Bill is whistled at by one Mean Malcolm, and all the revelations of his trying day are collected in his furious retort: "I am a *person!*" To understand the author's mischievous and telling observations on Bill's ordeal, children need the tactful intervention of a teacher who can mediate the book as ideology.

> *Peter Hollindale, "The Mediator and the Message," in* The Times Educational Supplement, *No. 3797, April 7, 1989, p. B9.*

Anne Fine has found a very entertaining way to make eight-to eleven-year-olds think about sexist attitudes. This novel may lead its readers to question the validity of some prevalent attitudes and it will at least bring them to their attention. However this is no heavy treatise but a simple light-hearted story. . . .

This book is well written and the easy style will appeal to most children. There is enough meat for fluent readers and the clear print, the jolly black and white illustrations [by Philippe Dupasquier], and the pace of the story will encourage the less able to keep going. *Bill's new frock* is particularly recommended for reading aloud to junior classes.

> *Valerie Caless, in a review of "Bill's New Frock," in* The School Librarian, *Vol. 37, No. 2, May, 1989, p. 59.*

Goggle-Eyes (1989; U.S. edition as *My War with Goggle-Eyes*)

When Helen runs out of the classroom, crying, the teacher sends Kitty Killin after her. Miss Lupey knows that like Helen, Kitty has had problems dealing with her mother's boyfriend. So while Helen hides in the cloakroom, Kitty sits outside the door and relates how Gerald Faulkner, nicknamed Goggle-eyes for the way he ogles Mrs. Killin, came into her life—and how she tried to get him out. Kitty dislikes Gerald from the moment he comes to pick up her mother for a date and can't understand what liberal Mrs. Killin sees in stuffy Goggle-eyes. He doesn't understand the family's passion about nuclear disarmament, and he seems more concerned with making sure the lights are shut off than letting them express their individuality. Kitty wants him out of their lives, and she fights the battle long after she's lost her passion for it. When it seems as if Gerald might really go, Kitty finally realizes just what he has brought to their family. Writing about the results of divorce is Fine's forte, and as she did in *Alias Madame Doubtfire* the author provides a comic yet perceptive look at life after marriage. Sophisticated in tone, and dripping with icy British wit, this may not be for every reader. But for those up to its challenge, the book offers wonderful, unique characterizations, thought-provoking ideas, and a fine depiction of the way people change, even when they don't want to.

> *Ilene Cooper, in a review of "My War with Goggle-Eyes," in* Booklist, *Vol. 85, No. 16, April 15, 1989, p. 1465.*

Anne Fine writes some of the funniest—and truest—family fight scenes to be found. Kitty's room is a bit, well, disorganized. Or, as mother's boyfriend Gerald (nicknamed Goggle-eyes by Kitty for the way he looks at mother's legs) prefers, the room is *disgusting*. "He put his foot in it right there. It was quite clear from the expression on Mum's face that, for the moment, she had heard enough from Gerald Faulkner about his views on natty housekeeping." But Gerald is tenacious, pointing out to Mum that her defence of Kitty is "utter baloney," and soon Mum is completely taken in. " 'Take care, Gerald,' she giggled. 'Mind what you say! You'll end up in terrible trouble with Kitty.' " That's just one skirmish in an ongoing war; perhaps even more pointed is the scene where staunch conservative Gerald accompanies Kitty, little sister Judith, and Mum to an anti-nuclear demonstration witnessed only by the police ("It's not as easy as you might think to get arrested") and some sheep. Contemptuous of their politics as he is, Gerald nevertheless takes Kitty and Jude home when Mum is arrested, and Kitty finds herself beginning to love him. In a benignly barbed family comedy peppered with Hepburn-and-Tracy repartee, readers will empathize with Kitty's step-by-step acceptance of Gerald while at the same time finding this self-described "boring" man magnetically charming from the start.

> *Roger Sutton, in a review of "My War with Goggle-Eyes," in* Bulletin of the Center for Children's Books, *Vol. 42, No. 9, May, 1989, p. 222.*

From the attention-grabbing first chapter to the happy-ever-after-maybe ending, Fine conveys a story about relationships filled with a humor that does not ridicule and sensitivity that is not cloying. . . . Fine's gentle antinuclear subplot never overshadows the main theme of acceptance and tolerance in relationships. Her characters are neither fanatics nor buffoons, but people with a wide range of feelings and reactions; the dialogue is especially expressive and full of feeling. A book that is thoroughly delightful to read.

> *Susan Schuller, in a review of "My War with Goggle-Eyes," in* School Library Journal, *Vol. 35, No. 9, May, 1989, p. 104.*

Fine has embarked on another exemplary study of the contemporary family, characterized in original style by piercing insights laced with delicious humor. Kitty, the narrator, is horrified when she finds that her divorced mother has taken up with a staid, rather fastidious man. . . . Gerald—or Goggle-eyes as Kitty prefers to think of him—takes a dim view of her mother's antinuclear stance, believing that the marches and rallies that she and the girls attend are hopelessly ill-planned and ineffective. Indeed, some of the funniest moments in the book describe in hilarious detail the peculiarly British form of civilized anarchy engaged in by these polite nuclear-weapons foes who are escorted by an even more polite police force to isolated, rural nuclear facilities for their demonstrations. It take a man of Gerald's organizational abilities to straighten the lot of them out. ' 'Why go to out-of-the-way holes where only the sheep can see you? It's crazy,' " he scolds. "I didn't answer that one. I've often thought myself that the sheep in the west of Scotland must be the most politically informed sheep in the world." The story is told in one long flashback, which seems unnecessary, but the characterizations are humorously to the point. As in this book's excellent predecessor, *Alias Madame Doubtfire,* Fine aims deadly accurate darts at modern relationships.

> *Nancy Vasilakis, in a review of "My War with Goggle-Eyes," in* The Horn Book Magazine, *Vol. LXV, No. 4, July-August, 1989, p. 482.*

[It] is by telling her own story that Kitty helps Helly to come to terms with the enormous changes in her world. A rattling good story it is too, consisting of many memorable anecdotes which range from the excruciatingly painful to the downright hilarious. In telling it from Kitty's point

of view, Anne Fine gives a complete and honest picture of the traumas and insecurities suffered by children whose mothers are embarking upon new and potentially permanent relationships.

Many readers will identify closely with Kitty and Helly and the details described by them. Although some very difficult emotions such as fear and jealously are explored, all the characters are likeable for their vulnerability. This is an excellent novel, told with sensitivity and humor, which also manages to make a strong case for nuclear disarmament.

> *Julie Blaisdale, in a review of "Goggle-Eyes," in* The School Librarian, *Vol. 37, No. 3, August, 1989, p. 113.*

A Sudden Puff of Glittering Smoke (1989)

In this lighthearted tale, a young girl 'summons up' a little genie from a ring which she finds. Far from bringing her prosperity he causes havoc at her school.

The interest of the book lies in the gentle humour of the descriptions rather than in a complex or fast-paced plot or in character development.

Most appropriate for the junior school age-group, it is likely to appeal mostly to girls, and would be an acceptable addition to a school or public library.

> *S. M. Ashburner, in a review of "A Sudden Puff of Glittering Smoke," in* The Junior Bookshelf, *Vol. 53, No. 5, October, 1989, p. 226.*

The Country Pancake (1990)

Lance and the other children in Miss Mirabelle's class choose an unusual method of raising money at the school fair; with a raffle involving guessing where on the school field Flossie the cow will deposit her 'pancake'. This is a storyline which is likely to appeal to children, who are usually amused by the unmentionable and the unconventional, the 'lavatory joke' which shocks their parents and teachers.

The plot develops slowly at first, which might deter some less quick readers. The characterisation of the central people in the book—Lance, Miss Mirabelle and Mrs. Spicer, the Head—is reasonably good for a book at this level, and the language is easy and undemanding. . . .

> *S. M. Ashburner, in a review of "The Country Pancake," in* The Junior Bookshelf, *Vol, 54, No. 1, February, 1990, p. 26.*

"A Country Pancake? said one of the same young friends. That's a dollop of cowmuck!" And so, of course, it is, and it is a dollop of cowmuck which is, in a way, the central, er, feature of this entirely charming tale of an unconventional teacher, a suspicious head, an imaginative class and a co-operative cow. The very best compliment I can pay to this story is to say that throughout my reading of it I longed to see before me on the carpet a group of eight-year olds braiding each other's hair and hugging themselves with anticipation and delight.

> *Gerald Haigh, in a review of "The Country Pancake," in* The Times Educational Supplement, *No. 3855, May 18, 1990, p. B10.*

A Sudden Swirl of Icy Wind   (1990)

When William is banished to his granny's store room, he doesn't know what he's done to upset her. And then a genie appears. It seemed the genie had helped out William's grandfather. A gentle story with a subtle secondary theme of respect for other people's beliefs, and a satisfying ending.

> *G. Kipling, in a review of "A Sudden Swirl of Icy Wind," in* Books for Your Children, *Vol. 25, No. 3, Autumn-Winter, 1990, p. 23.*

Gyo Fujikawa

1908-

Japanese American author and illustrator of picture books and fiction and editor.

Major works include *Babies* (1963), *Mother Goose* (1968), *A Child's Book of Poems* (1969), *Gyo Fujikawa's A to Z Picture Book* (1974), *Gyo Fujikawa's Oh, What a Busy Day!* (1976).

Considered among the first illustrators to include multi-ethnic children in her pictures, Fujikawa is an internationally popular creator of works for preschoolers and primary graders which show cherubic boys and girls involved in everyday activities and reacting with natural feelings. Well known for her drawings and paintings of round-faced children with lightly blushed cheeks and dots for eyes, she is acknowledged for depicting realistic and fantastic situations as well as a variety of emotions, both positive and negative, in works praised both as charming and true to child experience. Fujikawa is the creator of concept books; board books, both textual and wordless; an alphabet book; and stories featuring young children and their pets; she is also the compiler of several collections of poems and stories. Writing in a casual style, she includes combinations of prose, poetry, and sentence fragments in several of her works, and addresses such themes as friendship, cooperation, and loneliness as she describes the activities and moods of her young protagonists. As an illustrator, Fujikawa is noted for her success in two distinct styles: sharply defined black and white line drawings which often incorporate crosshatching and double-page spreads in soft watercolor that are filled with detail.

Named for a Chinese emperor, Fujikawa is often thought to be male. Before entering the field of children's literature, she was an art teacher, designer, and art director, working in the latter two capacities for Walt Disney Studios, an experience that she says made her aware of the importance of the details in her pictures. Fujikawa was also an artist and designer for advertising and magazine illustrations and for greeting cards and is the designer of several United States postage stamps. While working as a freelance artist, she illustrated Robert Louis Stevenson's *A Child's Garden of Verses* (1957), an assignment which led her to provide the pictures for Clement Clarke Moore's *The Night Before Christmas* (1961) as well as for collections of nursery rhymes and stories. Her first book, *Babies,* is often recognized as the first children's book to feature children of all races and nations in its illustrations. Fujikawa's subsequent works continue her exploration of the world of childhood; for example, in *Gyo Fujikawa's Oh, What a Busy Day!* she depicts the varying moods of a child's day through familiar activities such as playing in a treehouse. In addition to realistic subjects, Fujikawa includes supernatural creatures in her books, as in *Come Follow Me . . . to the Secret World of Elves and Fairies and Gnomes and Trolls* (1979), a collection of internation-

al poems and stories which also includes several original tales. Fujikawa is also the author and illustrator of the "Checkerboard Books" series, adventures of a group of friends—Jenny, Sam, Nicholas, Mei Su, and their dog Shags—who learn about the meaning of friendship.

(See also *Something about the Author,* Vols. 30, 39 and *Contemporary Authors,* Vol. 113.)

GENERAL COMMENTARY

Publishers Weekly

The illustrations by Miss Fujikawa mirror [a concern for small details]. "I like to include lots of details, small objects and variety that make children give a lot of attention to the illustrations. Children want facts. While they can understand visual abstractions they enjoy realistic renderings more. In illustrating children's stories and rhymes, for example, when many things are mentioned, I include them all in the art because I know children sit and look for them when the stories are read to them." (p. 46)

In her books, two styles of illustration are evident. The colored illustrations are watercolor paintings with hazy washes of color that set the mood for richly detailed pictures of children, adults, animals, the out-of-doors, objects, which are a pleasant balance between realistic renderings and stylized fancy. Her individuality of style is evident also in her use of colors. While she employs a wide range of colors, often together, they have a certain softness, even the bright colors. The entire effect of the illustration is soft.

In her other style, seen in the black-and-white line drawings, sharp details predominate. She uses many strokes to build forms and shades, and textures, often using the crosshatch technique. Finally, probably her trademark: many of her children and adults have round faces, round noses, black dots for eyes, and a delicate blush of cheek coloring that is delightful rather than coy. (pp. 46, 48)

Arthur Rackham, N. C. Wyeth, Edmund Dulac and Howard Pyle are a few of the great children's illustrators of the past that Gyo singles out for their timeless and firm personal approach. She feels that too few of today's illustrators are concerned with that warm personal involvement, and their brilliant inventive techniques alone fail to hold children's attention for very long.

Gyo Fujikawa has fulfilled her goals for becoming a children's illustrator. Aside from the large popularity and sales of her books, she knows by her mail that she has reached the children. (p. 48)

> *M. R. K., "Gyo Fujikawa: An Illustrator Children Love," in* Publishers Weekly, *Vol. 199, No. 1, January 4, 1971, pp. 45-6, 48.*

TITLE COMMENTARY

A Child's Book of Poems   (1969)

A carefully compiled and delightful collection of poems for young children with many charming illustrations by the talented Japanese artist Gyo Fujikawa—some in black and white, but every other double-page spread a coloured drawing in soft, appealing shades.

There are many well-known poems, and many attractive lesser-known ones, but the whole collection of over 120 poems includes mostly the classic poets, fifteen being from the pen of Christina Rossetti. Altogether an admirable collection.

> *B. Clark, in a review of "A Child's Book of Poems," in* The Junior Bookshelf, *Vol. 35, No. 1, February, 1971, p. 33.*

Gyo Fujikawa's A to Z Picture Book   (1974)

You could travel far and never find as thoroughly satisfying an alphabet book as Ms. Fujikawa's. Her pictures (some in color and some in black-and-white) are utterly captivating whether they feature her endearing children, animals or things. The drawings are precise and delicate and for each letter she presents not a measly one or two examples but a flock of them: "E" features edelweiss, Emma cleaning her ears, elephant, Eskimo, Edward is eat-

ing, eggs, eye, elf—all with appropriate action. A bonus follows some letters, verses which the artist has created to express a child's reactions to various experiences.

> *A review of "Gyo Fujikawa's A to Z Picture Book," in* Publishers Weekly, *Vol. 206, No. 6, August 5, 1974, p. 59.*

At last, a really good alphabet book for children—one they will enjoy and return to over the years. The book is richly illustrated with black-and-white and color drawings that show children of different races scampering through the alphabet world. The book includes an abundance of items for children to identify for each letter; this variety will enable children to continue to enjoy the book much longer than those showing only one thing for each letter so that the child is ready to put away the book once the single object is identified.

The very young child will enjoy the pages of busy babies for the letter B, and the pages of children and animals jumping for the letter J. Dangerous, delicious, dreadful, delightful and disgusting dreams will capture the older child, as will the mean, marvelous monster. Birds, plants and animals are plentiful to provide something for everyone to enjoy, including the adults who purchase this book.

> *Mary Shepard, in a review of "Gyo Fujikawa's A to Z Picture Book," in* Interracial Books for Children Bulletin, *Vol. 5, No. 6, 1974, p. 4.*

Once one has recovered from a first impression of overcrowding, one starts to unearth from the pages of Gyo Fujikawa's **A to Z Picture Book** many quite beautiful drawings. Full colour double spreads are interspersed with closely packed black pen illustrations. Whilst the rosy-cheeked cherubs populating these pages seem to owe something to Mabel Lucie Attwell, much of the sugariness has been happily avoided. The book should be a source of delight for many children. (p. 30)

> *Tony Dyson, in a review of "Gyo Fujikawa's A to Z Picture Book," in* The School Librarian, *Vol. 24, No. 1, March, 1976, pp. 29-30.*

Let's Play!   (1975)

Very short, very slight, with illustrations that show round-faced children who are a bit on the cute, or greeting card side, this should nevertheless be welcomed by the preschool child because it depicts familiar activities and because the pages are easy-to-turn heavy board. The text is casual and rambling: "Would you like to play 'grown-up' . . . or would you rather hide in boxes? That's such fun! Let's run . . . and chase around . . . and climb a tree." All of these, and other, activities are shown in uncluttered, spacious format.

> *Zena Sutherland, in a review of "Let's Play!" in* Bulletin of the Center for Children's Books, *Vol. 29, No. 5, January, 1976, p. 76.*

Gyo Fujikawa's Oh, What a Busy Day!   (1976)

[A] gentle and old-fashioned view of the frenetic life comes

From Gyo Fujikawa's Oh, What a Busy Day!, *written and illustrated by Gyo Fujikawa.*

across in Gyo Fujikawa's **Oh What a Busy Day.** This busy day shows children playing together in various shades of busyness—in the leafy deeps of a treehouse, in scratchy black pen-and-ink romps, in Grandma Moses winter scenes, in misty Japanese vistas. Every other page presents a different mood and style, which sometimes creates a bit of disjointedness. But there's room in this book—spanning a day from breakfast to dusk—for fantasy, jingles and rhymes, visits with old ladies, motley weather and a little of that sense of sadness and doubt which tells children that rage, melancholy and tenderness are feelings worth cultivating.

> *Mopsy Strange Kennedy, in a review of "Oh, What a Busy Day!" in* The New York Times Book Review, *November 14, 1976, p. 44.*

Beginning with a rooster waking everybody up, the overly **. . . Busy Day** consists of groups of children eating breakfast; playing outside; walking through sunshine, rain, and snowstorms; deciding what to be when they grow up; and realizing the value of friendship (among too many other lessons) through a medley of nursery rhymes, songs, sayings, and poetry. There's also too much going on in the pages of pen-and-ink drawings, full of detail and action, which alternate with soft watercolor spreads. The concept itself is misleading—the four seasons cannot all occur in one 12-hour period—and the book would be a lot

less hectic if Fujikawa had everything happen in one year, not one day.

> *Mary Sue Valovich, in a review of "Oh, What a Busy Day!" in* School Library Journal, *Vol. 23, No. 5, January, 1977, p. 82.*

While many of the activities are familiar, the settings are seldom those with which a child can identify; for example, the breakfast scene is a long table, out of doors, where a dozen small children of various ethnic origins eat together. The pictures are lively and deft, saved from greeting-card sweetness by their humor; the text is a jumble of captions, jingles, and rhymes; the pictures show both winter and summer scenes. There's a lot to look at but no discernible arrangement, the layout is often confusing, and the morning-to-night progression is completely forgotten at times.

> *Zena Sutherland, in a review of "Gyo Fujikawa's Oh, What a Busy Day!" in* Bulletin of the Center for Children's Books, *Vol. 30, No. 7, March, 1977, p. 106.*

Let's Grow a Garden   (1978)

Fujikawa's books never fail to ring up sales, for good reasons. She paints the most winning little children and shows them always engaged in zesty adventures. Here, wee boys and girls from various racial backgrounds keep busy planting seeds and caring for a burgeoning crop of vegetables until the gladsome harvest. The colors are lovely, the artist's touch is delicate and the overall effect is, in a word, irresistible.

> *A review of "Let's Grow a Garden," in* Publishers Weekly, *Vol. 213, No. 21, May 22, 1978, p. 232.*

Millie's Secret; My Favorite Thing   (1978)

Gyo Fujikawa might well take a cue from Mercer Mayer, John Goodall, and other authors of wordless books. Her latest offerings for the very young have sturdy, washable pages but little else of appeal to those cutting their teeth on books. The plots are pablum: **Millie's Secret,** disclosed after days of anticipation, turns out to be a dog having puppies—a nice surprise but not exciting enough to compensate for the tedious wait. **My Favorite Things** is a laundry list of pleasant occupations, ending with the predictable warm snuggle in a cozy bed. Decidedly dull.

> *Kathy Coffey, in a review of "Millie's Secret" and "My Favorite Things," in* School Library Journal, *Vol. 25, No. 5, January, 1979, p. 42.*

Gyo Fujikawa's Come Follow Me . . . to the Secret World of Elves and Fairies and Gnomes and Trolls (1979)

Any child who accepts Gyo Fujikawa's invitation will discover a world of magic and delight in this marvellous book of stories and verse. It is as the cover says a "secret world of elves and fairies and gnomes and trolls" brought alive in the most vivid manner by the superb illustrations. Did you know there was a space elf? Have you heard about the first Japanese fairy? Read this book and find out all about these and other attractive creatures. The illustrations create an atmosphere of magic and wonder and this book will delight everyone. It is absolutely beautiful.

> *M. W., in a review of "Come Follow Me," in* Book Window, *Vol. 7, No. 1, Winter, 1979, p. 12.*

This big book represents hours of enchantment for little ones. Fujikawa has chosen fail-safe stories and poems, a generous collection about magical creatures—gnomes, elves, fairies and trolls. Endowing the paintings and drawings with the dainty and pixieish touches that have made her books about wee children extremely popular, the artist beguiles the eye on every page. The entries are from several countries and range from **"The Fairy Queen,"** a ballad penned by an unknown poet in the 17th century, all the way to a modern tale about **"Jupie the Space Elf."** When his saucer sails off without him, he meets kind Earth elves and, thanks to their help, finds his way home. And Fujikawa's new book is sure to find its way under many a Christmas tree this year.

> *A review of "Come Follow Me . . . ," in* Publishers Weekly, *Vol. 216, No. 8, August 20, 1979, p. 81.*

Meet Jupie the Space Elf, Old Nosey Gnome and Chi-chan, a Japanese fairy, among other trolls, goblins and leprechauns in this large, colorful book of poems and stories about the creatures of fantasy and the imagination.

Gyo Fujikawa illustrates her little people with bright eyes and smiles, round heads and active bodies amid scenes rich in pastel colors. Particularly well done are the double-page spreads of elves, fairies and children playing together in twilight gardens.

The text is another matter. In style and language, the poems by little-remembered children's poets of the 1920's and 30's (Rose Fyleman, Margaret Tod Ritter, Elizabeth Godley, etc.) are remote from today's children. The stories, written by Gyo Fujikawa, have plots of only slight interest. Her artistic talents could have been used more effectively with the work of better writers and poets.

To appreciate this kind of book, of course, one must be willing to accept unabashed sentimentality. Small children will find the book appealing and ultimately satisfying because of the illustrations. They will have no trouble enjoying the gentle, happy pictures or imagining themselves frolicking with the little folk who inhabit the book's pages in large, happy numbers.

> *Joel Fram, in a review of "Come Follow Me . . . ," in* The New York Times Book Review, *August 26, 1979, p. 34.*

Welcome Is a Wonderful Word   (1980)

A simple little story is quietly told and illustrated by Fujikawa's fetching pictures, in color and black-and-white. Four of the artist's familiar, cute toddlers are featured on a special day. Jenny goes from house to house in her town, collecting castoffs from fond neighbors. These treasures she shares with pals Nicholas and Sam, and she has news as well to parcel out with fancy costumes for dress-up (even a derby for Shags, their dog). A family has moved into the vacant house near Jenny's. She tells the boys she hopes a girl her age now lives there, so the friends will be even, two boys and two girls. Mei Su, a Chinese child, is the newcomer but she won't come out to play when Jenny calls, a problem that Nicholas and Sam help solve.

> *A review of "Welcome Is a Wonderful Word," in* Publishers Weekly, *Vol. 218, No. 22, November 28, 1980, p. 50.*

Jenny and Jupie to the Rescue   (1982)

[A] lightweight story but graced by the piquant drawings and extraordinarily pretty scenes in color that make the artist's works bestsellers. Jenny is settled in bed when the space children, Jupie and twins Orrie and Zorrie, fly in with an SOS. The Space Teasers have stolen Jupie's dog Sunspot, and Jenny joins her friends, going to the rescue in their spaceship. The high-flying chase ends with Sunspot back in Jupie's craft, but the Teasers move his rescuers to pity the abductors since they are sorry to lose the little pet. A compromise is agreeable to all, for Jupie and the twins promise to bring Sunspot back for visits, and so antagonists become friends.

> *A review of "Jenny and Jupie to the Rescue," in* Publishers Weekly, *Vol. 222, No. 13, September 24, 1982, p. 73.*

Sam's All-Wrong Day (1982)

A group of multi-ethnic sweet-faced children jump and run through alternating two-page spreads of color and black and white. The text is slow and sluggish as Sam has one mishap after another. Everyone ends up in trouble when a bear finds their berries, but Sam saves the day by scaring the bear away. Then his luck takes a turn for the better. It's improbable Sam could have as bad a day as described here, but more improbable is that he could scare a bear or even that a bear would live in the pleasant suburbia pictured. For a funny and very possible all-wrong day, read Judith Viorst's *Alexander and the Terrible, Horrible, No Good, Very Bad Day* (Atheneum, 1976).

> *Pamela Warren Stebbins, in a review of "Sam's All-Wrong Day," in* School Library Journal, *Vol. 29, No. 6, February, 1983, p. 66.*

Shags Finds a Kitten; That's Not Fair! (1983)

[These two books] deal with loneliness and being a good winner. In **Shags Finds a Kitten,** Sam and his dog Shags save a kitten during a rainstorm. The next day Sam and his friends fuss over the kitten, ignoring Shags. The kitten almost chokes when the bonnet they dress her in becomes tangled in a bush, but Shags saves her and becomes a hero.

In **That's Not Fair!** the four friends become angry at each other following a sled race and a snowball fight; in the end they make up and agree it's no fun to play in the snow alone. Both stories deal with very common events in children's lives: being left out and losing. The concepts are handled well and convincingly; the detailed illustrations alternate between black and white and snappy colors.

> *Julie Tomlianovich, in a review of "Shags Finds a Kitten" and "That's Not Fair!" in* School Library Journal, *Vol. 30, No. 3, November, 1983, p. 62.*

Are You My Friend Today? (1988)

This disjointed effort offers a hodgepodge of cuddly animals and cherubic children vaguely celebrating the joys of friendship. While Fujikawa's illustrations have a brightly colored child appeal, the composition is so jumbled that on one page readers find a child in a snowsuit skiing over a blazing summer sun, and on another, a child on a swing appears to be suspended over water and just about to strike an unsuspecting swimmer. The less-cluttered pages fare better, but unfortunately, the text offers nothing but sentence fragments and pseudo-poetry. Preschoolers may enjoy the cheerful pictures, but for a book with child appeal and substance, stick with Aliki's *We Are Best Friends* (Greenwillow, 1982).

> *Lori A. Janick, in a review of "Are You My Friend Today?" in* School Library Journal, *Vol. 35, No. 8, April, 1989, p. 82.*

John S(trickland) Goodall

1908-

English author and illustrator of picture books.

Major works include *The Adventures of Paddy Pork* (1968), *Naughty Nancy, the Bad Bridesmaid* (1975; U. S. edition as *Naughty Nancy*), *An Edwardian Summer* (1976), *The Story of a Castle* (1986), *Little Red Riding Hood* (1988).

Recognized as one of the most skillful creators of wordless picture books and pop-up books for primary graders, Goodall is also praised as a storyteller and social historian whose animal fantasies and visual English histories are noted for their excellence of content and design. Compared to English landscape painters such as Constable as well as to such illustrators as Beatrix Potter and Ernest H. Shepard for his watercolor paintings and black and white line drawings, Goodall "has perfected the art of the small picture book without words," according to critic Valerie Alderson. He is also well regarded for his use of the harlequinade or transformation book format in which the flipping of a half page transforms one illustration into another, for his accurate depiction of nostalgic subjects and settings, and for the humor and vitality with which he invests his animal characters. Goodall is perhaps best known as the creator of the Paddy Pork books, ten volumes about a gentlemanly Victorian pig whose escapades—cliffhanging adventures on land and sea and in the air— conclude with the triumphant return of their protagonist. In addition, Goodall is the creator of several books with mice as their main characters, including two stories with period settings about Shrewbettina, an English shrew mouse; two tales about the inquisitive, mischievous Naughty Nancy; and the story of how a mouse couple free themselves from a haunted castle after being locked inside by an evil rat; Goodall has also profiled cats, a dog, a monkey, a toy bear, and a doll in adventures which often include hairbreadth escapes and joyful homecomings.

In addition to his books for younger children, Goodall is respected for introducing middle graders to life in bygone eras with his series of books set in the Edwardian period and series of social histories profiling England from the middle ages through the present. Goodall revolves his Edwardian titles around two upper-class children at the turn of the century, depicting their activities with their family during the English social season, in summer, and at Christmas; also explicit in the books is the distinction between the "upstairs" lives of the aristocrats and the "downstairs" lives of their servants. In his social histories, Goodall blends factual information with humor to show the evolution of a village, a Norman castle, a main pathway, a farm, and a seaside town. His other works include such titles as an autobiography done in pictures that tells Goodall's story from his birth to England's declaration of war in 1939 and wordless retellings of "The Sleeping Beauty" and "Little Red Riding Hood" with mice casts.

As an illustrator, Goodall is celebrated as a superior draftsman whose precise line drawings and watercolor paintings in a representational style, panoramic spreads that reflect both his use of deep, rich hues and more subtle shadings, are well composed and filled with interesting, accurate details. Also a successful landscape and portrait painter whose works have been exhibited internationally, Goodall is the illustrator of works by such authors as Lewis Carroll and E. Nesbit. *The Adventures of Paddy Pork* won the *Boston Globe-Horn Book Award* for illustration in 1969. Named a Freeman of the City of London, Goodall has also received several awards for his paintings.

(See also *Something about the Author,* Vol. 4 and *Contemporary Authors,* Vols. 33-36, rev. ed.)

GENERAL COMMENTARY

Charlotte S. Huck

Through the ingenious use of half pages, John Goodall has managed to add excitement and movement to his many wordless adventure stories. Lovely, detailed watercolors portray **The Midnight Adventures of Kelly, Dot, and Es-**

meralda; a koala bear, a doll, and a tiny mouse, who climb through a picture on the wall and into a charming landscape of a river and boat. Their river outing meets with disaster, as does their trip to a village fair. The three just manage to make it back to the boat, the river, and through the picture, and onto the safety of their own toy shelf. *Shrewbettina's Birthday* and *The Surprise Picnic* are also in full color and use the same imaginative format. *Naughty Nancy* is the tale of an irrepressible mouse who was the flower girl in her sister's wedding. *Creepy Castle* appeals to slightly older children as they "read" the mouse melodrama of the brave knight mouse who rescues his fair damsel mouse in distress. These are long stories with several incidents in each plot, yet the pictures show the action clearly and make them easy and exciting to narrate. (p. 107)

> *Charlotte S. Huck, "Picture Books," in her* Children's Literature in the Elementary School, *third edition, updated, Holt, Rinehart and Winston, 1979, pp. 92-155.*

TITLE COMMENTARY

The Adventures of Paddy Pork (1968)

Turning the pages is half the fun of a tell-it-yourself story, and Paddy's adventures double the pleasure: there are twice as many pages as usual (it seems), half-length between the full-length, and flipping them makes the action occur. You can call it a greeting card gimmick if you want to be stuffy . . . if you can resist laughing when Paddy, towed by his sedate pig mother—turns around for a glimpse of the circus passing through town; or, when she's busy shopping—opens the door and sneaks out; or when he strides along a country lane in pursuit—and comes to a perplexed stop at the crossroads. After a fast getaway from a big bad wolf, a disastrous tryout as a circus performer, Porky, in tears, meets a sympathetic rabbit—who shows him the way to go home. The setting is out of Beatrix Potter, the drawings are crisp and decisive—altogether a delight that's more than a diversion and the children won't be able to keep their hands off it.

> *A review of "The Adventures of Paddy Pork," in* Kirkus Service, *Vol. XXXVI, No. 20, October 15, 1968, p. 1156.*

If this delectable story without words doesn't become one of the hits of the season, your reviewer *deserves* to be sent to the glue factory. Paddy's adventures are pictured against the background of a gentle Beatrix Potter village; his flight to the circus and home again makes a beguiling book that presents only one problem—small children will wear it out looking at it.

> *A review of "The Adventures of Paddy Pork," in* Publishers Weekly, *Vol. 194, No. 18, October 28, 1968, p. 59.*

A charmingly Potteresque bit of mock-Victoriania is John S. Goodall's *The Adventures of Paddy Pork.* There are no words in this page-turner's delight, simply 15 appealing spreads of the English countryside, with ingenious half-page inserts that provide the action and suspense as they

are flipped over. While a few production kinks remain, this tale of a cosseted young piglet and his brief sojourn in the cruel world will delight any child beyond the age of two.

> *Selma G. Lanes, in a review of "The Adventures of Paddy Pork," in* The New York Times Book Review, *November 3, 1968, p. 69.*

Most books without words are gimmicky and so are books which go in for trick effects like half-pages. *Paddy Pork* has both and it is as nice a book as we have met for a long time. Mr. Goodall's exquisite black-and-white drawings tell most eloquently the story of the pig who yearned for the circus and was glad to get home safely. The alternate half-pages impart a sense of urgency and suspense to the wordless tale. The tender humour is as appealing as the picture of an infinitely delightful countryside in which the action is played out . . . . [It] is one of the most pleasing [books of the year].

> *A review of "The Adventures of Paddy Pork," in* The Junior Bookshelf, *Vol. 32, No. 6, December, 1968, p. 352.*

No words; none needed. Between each page there is a half-page insert . . . . In this pattern, a fairly successful physical device, Paddy's adventures can be followed as he escapes the clutches of a fox, tries to attain enough prowess to join a circus family, and finds his way home to mother. The illustrations, black and white, have vivacity and humor; the animal characters have appeal. Slight, but fun. (pp. 93-4)

> *Zena Sutherland, in a review of "The Adventures of Paddy Pork," in* Bulletin of the Center for Children's Books, *Vol. 22, No. 6, February, 1969, pp. 93-4.*

The Ballooning Adventures of Paddy Pork (1969)

Any member of a family will reach for the stocking-size volume, a most dramatic companion to *The Adventures . . .* of the dressed-up pig. Paddy's far-flung journeying by balloon from English shores drops him into the most horrendous near-catastrophes—an encounter with dancing savages from whose stewpot he rescues a weeping, grass-skirted piglet; an encounter with a whale in a stormy sea; and an encounter with bears in a snow-covered forest. Of course, he eventually returns to a triumphant, official welcome. As in the previous book, the cleverly interpolated half-pages accelerate the action. Without text the series of exploits leaves nothing unclear; the ink drawings abound in animated detail, fully characterizing both the endearing pigs and the grosser creatures. There is more real storytelling in this book than in many a picture book with a text.

> *Virginia Haviland, in a review of "The Ballooning Adventures of Paddy Pork," in* The Horn Book Magazine, *Vol. XLV, No. 6, December, 1969, p. 663.*

Like the first book about Paddy, the adventurous pig, this is a story in pictures, each page alternating with a half-page, so that there is partial change of scene with each turn of the half-page. . . . Not very substantial, but there is plenty of action and some humor, and the half-page device very successfully builds suspense.

Zena Sutherland, in a review of "The Ballooning Adventures of Paddy Pork," in Bulletin of the Center for Children's Books, *Vol. 23, No. 7, March, 1970, p. 111.*

An appealing sequel, though not as successful as *The Adventures of Paddy Pork,* this story without words uses the same effective format: half pages inserted between each double spread. When down, the half pages indicate that some unknown action must be occurring; when lifted up, they show what that exciting action is. Thus, readers have the opportunity of coming up with their own imaginative alternatives to each situation, and the adventures, as they are illustrated, are quite satisfyingly sensational for this do-it-yourself approach: Paddy in his balloon rescues a helpless young female pig (in grass skirt) from the stewpot of a group of fierce gorillas; almost blows into a whale during a storm; barely escapes the clutches of menacing polar bears. The highly detailed, Victorian style illustrations will stimulate extra embroidery from the audience, while they clearly delineate the action. This book and its predecessor are two of the best, most inventive examples of textless picture books.

Elinor S. Cullen, in a review of "The Ballooning Adventures of Paddy Pork," in School Library Journal, *Vol. 16, No. 7, March, 1970, p. 128.*

Shrewbettina's Birthday (1970)

In the tradition of excellence set by Beatrix Potter comes an enchanting little book—the story of a day in the life of a shrew mouse. It is her birthday, and we discover Shrewbettina, nightcap firmly in place, fast asleep in a tiny four-poster, under a patchwork quilt. Turn half the page, it's seven in the morning by the cuckoo clock, and Shrewbettina leaps out of bed, washes, has breakfast, and off to the alarms and excitements of the great day itself. Mob-capped lady mice, elegant gentlemen mice in flat caps set neatly between the ears, even a rascally bag-snatching mouse and a policeman mouse—all in beautiful, warm colours, exquisitely detailed. The device of a small half page in between a double-page spread moves the action along—one moment the birthday party is pulling crackers, the next they have paper hats on. The hardest adult heart will be quite melted, and so good is the story-line that only when you have finished the book do you realise that there is no text. Bound to be a classic.

Philippa Toomey, in a review of "Shrewbettina's Birthday," in Children's Book Review, *Vol. I, No. 1, February, 1971, p. 14.*

The format—size, shape, alternate half pages—is that of Paddy Pork but Mr. Goodall has switched to color, scaled up the figures, souped up the action . . . and destroyed most of the charm. Shrewbettina's birthday, which begins with cards and ends with a gala party, is otherwise the oc-

casion for her purse to be snatched and the culprit to be apprehended by an imposing mouse who then becomes her beau—in essence not the homely, comical, interlinked *Adventures of Paddy Pork* and even less so in execution. For the half pages, originally used to surprise and amuse, have here become chiefly a device to advance the action (simply substituting for an additional whole page) or, given the enormity of the figures, a way to startle, to hit the onlooker in the eye. Compared with its predecessors it's a pop-up book—which will not, of course, hurt it with children (though some of them may be bored by the whole courtship business).

A review of "Shrewbettina's Birthday," in Kirkus Reviews, *Vol. XXXIX, No. 7, April 1, 1971, p. 356.*

There are some anthropomorphic animal stories that, because they resemble the work of Beatrix Potter, are almost synonymous with the world of an English nursery. (Their colors are gentle, their characters limited to the smaller creatures of field and forest.) And there dwells in many of us the belief that there is inherent goodness in that world—no wrong can come of anything that hints of Nannies and prams, crumpets and casement windows.

John S. Goodall's *Shrewbettina's Birthday* is such a story. As in his two previous books (about Paddy Pork) the author uses the device of alternating full and half pages for added appeal in a book without words, but this time he works in full color and his tale is touched with homey ease.

Shrewbettina lives in that enchanting world that every child, at one time or another, aches to discover—where shrews and mice and such snuggle under miniature patchwork quilts and travel tiny paths to market for thrifty purchases sturdily wrapped with paper and string. There's more than the usual dose of action here, though—a masked robber sets upon the birthday girl as she starts off to buy the party fixings, there's a timely rescue by a fine gentleman (a suitor, perhaps?) and the weeping culprit is soon in the arms of the law. After much sweeping and baking and donning of finery the festivities finally do get under way. One little mouse hides under the table for the duration, and I didn't notice any other shrews at the party, but no matter, the food is good, the music fine for dancing, and Shrewbettina slips happily into bed in the wee hours of the morning—of such are memorable birthdays (and children's books) made.

Ingeborg Boudreau, in a review of "Shrewbettina's Birthday," in The New York Times Book Review, *April 4, 1971, p. 38.*

Jacko (1971)

[*Jacko* is] likely to meet a varied reception. Although the story is told entirely without words it is hard to suggest an age group for which it is suitable. The small, closely detailed pictures, with their eighteenth-century maritime setting, demand an attentive and perhaps an educated eye to keep track of every twist in the story. It is a beautiful little book, however, cunningly arranged with flaps that turn over to alter the whole point of nearly every picture, and the story, as it unfolds the adventures of an organ-grinder's monkey, carries interesting overtones marking the contrast between human and animal behaviour. Even if the youngest members of the family find the book hard to follow without help, older children and parents may be glad to have it about the house. (p. 1514)

> *"Good Enough to Keep," in* The Times Literary Supplement, *No. 3640, December 3, 1971, pp. 1514-15.*

A charming story told in attractive coloured pictures, about a monkey who escapes from his organ-grinder master, and with a green parrot friend met on the way, gets back to a free life on a tropical island where a welcome awaits him from his wild brothers. The excitement of sailing on a pirate ship which suffers shipwreck, the almost Hogarthian humour of a story which is set in the eighteenth century, and a certain tender feeling for all captive creatures which we somehow know the artist must feel— all these combine to make a book which is sure to appeal to the literate and the illiterate alike, and to all ages. A special congratulation for the use of Goodall's well-known half-pages which are used with such skill to keep up the intriguing game of guessing what comes next. (pp. 24-5)

> *C. Martin, in a review of "Jacko," in* The Junior Bookshelf, *Vol. 36, No. 1, February, 1972, pp. 24-5.*

The creator of Paddy Pork takes to color and his new monkey hero takes to sea in another wordless narrative that moves briskly through a series of alternately full and half-page scenes. Though we could wish for a better color match between the adjacent half and full pages, Goodall's now-familiar device is particularly well suited to the shenanigans of a venturesome monkey whose progress consistently takes place behind the backs or over the heads of the humans involved. Children will enjoy spotting what Jacko's dupes miss as the monkey hustles along from a busy 18th century harbor to a portly ship's captain's house, then off to sea in the captain's chest, later over the plank to a pirate ship whose crew has boarded the first vessel, and finally (sailing under the pirate flag with the captain's parrot for crew) to a tropical island (with fruit piled up as if posing for a still life) that must be home if we can judge from his loving reception by a larger (mother?) monkey. A gimmick perhaps, but once set in motion it never lags.

> *A review of "Jacko," in* Kirkus Reviews, *Vol. XL, No. 21, November 1, 1972, p. 1232.*

Kelly, Dot and Esmeralda (1972; U.S. edition as *The Midnight Adventures of Kelly, Dot, and Esmeralda*)

The series of little picture books which John Goodall has produced, commencing with **The Adventures of Paddy Pork** have provided something unique in the field of picture books for infants. The idea of creating a picture story without words, to stimulate the imagination, is not new and yet few illustrators have exploited it successfully. John Goodall succeeds in three ways—an appealing 'story' idea, excellent illustration reminiscent of Shepard, and the use of a half page illustration which turns over to change the pictures and keep the story on the move. A Panda, a rag doll, and a Mouse are the three characters who come to life on the nursery shelf at midnight. They climb into a picture on the wall and this leads to exciting meetings with many other animal characters culminating in the capture of Esmeralda the Mouse by a feline ringmaster who puts her in a circus act. Her two friends engineer her escape and after a chase they find their way back to the nursery shelf where they all return to the Land of Nod by a quarter past one. A really attractive and charming little book. Highly recommended for three year olds and above.

> *Edward Hudson, in a review of "Kelly, Dot & Esmeralda," in* Children's Book Review, *Vol. III, No. 1, February, 1973, p. 8.*

The twilight-shaded watercolors of John Goodall's tale are so eloquent one forgets there isn't a word in the book. Each picture is worth a few hundred words at least, and think of the fun for the child who discovers them. Here is a story to amuse and interest all. Half-pages inter-leaved with full-size ones allow more mileage per scene and are a delightful gimmick in this absorbing book.

> *Karen Luke, "Bed Table Books: Some Mysteries of the Night," in* The Christian Science Monitor, *May 2, 1973, p. B2.*

Undeniably preschoolers will find a great deal to delight them in the rather drawn-out adventures of the shaggy koala bear Kelly, the rosy-cheeked rag doll Dot, and the tiny mouse-lady Esmeralda with her billowing pink party dress . . . . [Youngsters] will expect to find a villain worthy of a midnight adventure—and a happy ending. They will not be disappointed. Yet adult fans of the illustrator of **The Adventures of Paddy Pork** will find this to be a static piece of work, just another in a series of progressively more expensive, progressively less imaginative books bound to a proven format: a wordless story with a gimmick—full pages coupled with half pages. Soft, detailed miniature watercolors still impress the eye, but there is little to feed the spirit. The reader and the illustrator deserve better.

> *Sheryl B. Andrews, in a review of "The Midnight Adventures of Kelly, Dot, and Esmeralda," in* The Horn Book Magazine, *Vol. XLIX, No. 3, June, 1973, p. 258.*

Paddy's Evening Out (1973)

A very successful story without words in Goodall's familiar small (5" x 7") format with alternating half pages which partially change the previous picture's action. Paddy Pork, hero of Goodall's **The Adventures of Paddy Pork,** begins his adventure by leaning over his theater box to rescue a ladyfriend's fan during a performance. To his embarrassment, he falls into the orchestra pit, lands head-first in a tuba, escapes backstage but repeatedly finds himself back on stage in the midst of the show. The audience sees the humor of the situation even if the leading lady doesn't, and Paddy ends up a celebrity at the stage door after a warm ovation. Taking their cue from the red velvet

From The Adventures of Paddy Pork, *written and illustrated by John S. Goodall.*

theater curtains, the tempera illustrations are in deep, rich colors. Small groups or individual children will be delighted as Paddy's predicament worsens with each turned page.

> *Judith Shor Kronick, in a review of "Paddy's Evening Out," in* School Library Journal, *Vol. 20, No. 6, February, 1974, p. 52.*

While the inserted half-pages that conceal a surprise action are still as entertaining a device as they were in earlier books, this no-words picture book seems more repetitive in structure. The pictures are lively and attractive, but the unfamiliar milieu may make the story a shade less comprehensible than *The Adventures of Paddy Pork.*

> *Zena Sutherland, in a review of "Paddy's Evening Out," in* Bulletin of the Center for Children's Books, *Vol. 27, No. 8, April, 1974, p. 129.*

Paddy Pork makes a return appearance in another comfortably small picture book. The wordless drama unfolds as a show within a show: When Paddy's lady friend drops her fan from her box seat at the theatre, Paddy gallantly tries to catch it and plunges over the rail into the orchestra pit below. Pandemonium follows, as poor Paddy—in the classic low comedy tradition—flounders about onstage and off and finally, as the comic hero, brings down the house. With its all-animal cast and audience, the old-fashioned vaudeville acts, in a setting of red-plush opulence, look like a zoological performance of the famous English Pantomine. But perhaps the now-familiar arrangement of half-pages alternating with full ones (with the discrepancy of color tones as noticeable as ever) will ultimately degenerate into a mere device; it would be interesting to see what other kind of work the author-artist can produce.

> *Ethel L. Heins, in a review of "Paddy's Evening Out," in* The Horn Book Magazine, *Vol. L, No. 2, April, 1974, p. 139.*

Naughty Nancy, the Bad Bridesmaid (1975; U.S. edition as *Naughty Nancy*)

This will probably enchant admirers of *The Midnight Adventures of Kelly, Dot, and Esmeralda,* but for those of us who have found Goodall's recent wordless flap books increasingly cloying it's a new low. The subject is a stylish (old style) wedding, set in soaring church and stately country home, featuring champagne and hanging flower baskets in the reception tent, red carpet and scurrying servants, morning-suited males and ladies in fox stoles and feathers . . . the works. The fact that the participants are all mice presumably adds to the miniature charm of it all, and comic relief is provided in the form of the little pink clad flower girl who is literally into everything—from the wedding cake (before the ceremony) to the bride's trunk as it rides off for the wedding trip in the back of the couple's elegant horseless carriage. There's never a faux pas in Goodall's faithfully detailed, delicately toned paintings, but we'll leave this one for those doting relics of the carriage trade who are given to looking backwards.

> *A review of "Naughty Nancy," in* Kirkus Reviews, *Vol. XLIII, No. 8, April 15, 1975, p. 444.*

Another of John Goodall's delightful picture-books-without-words, in which half-pages conceal the pleasantly shocking scrapes a rabbit-bridesmaid gets into at a Victorian country-house wedding (observed in authentic detail with Beatrix Potter-like colours). The bridesmaid steals the limelight at all the wrong moments, including moving up the aisle on the bride's train and sliding down the marquee roof into a tray of champagne glasses, and finally emerging from the honeymoon trunk as the hapless couple drive off. There is immense verve in the pictures, which should provide a splendid pastime for the very young. (pp. 174-75)

> *M. Hobbs, in a review of "Naughty Nancy the Bad Bridesmaid," in* The Junior Bookshelf, *Vol. 39, No. 3, June, 1975, pp. 174-75.*

John Goodall has perfected the art of the small picture book without words. His latest offering recounts, in this way, the adventures of a mischievous bridesmaid at a mouse wedding. The mice characters are all got up in the style of the Edwardian high society wedding, and through Naughty Nancy, John Goodall is able to poke fun at the pretentiousness of the event . . . . The insertion of half-pages between the full ones allows each single page to live a double life, first on its own and then with the half-page imposed to give a continuous link.

> *Valerie Alderson, in a review of "Naughty Nancy," in* Children's Book Review, *Vol. V, No. 2, Summer, 1975, p. 75.*

Creepy Castle　(1975)

The cloying delicacy of Goodall's wordless half-page miniatures is cut a bit here by the cobwebby gloom of the creepy castle explored one day by an elegant young mouse couple—and by the medieval monster show they run into there after a dastardly, lurking stranger locks them inside. Escape however is almost effortless and the last page finds the pair sipping from tankards before the fire in their cozy "Home Sweet Home"—whose humble style, incidentally, hardly jibes with the lady's high conical hat and pink costume.

> *A review of "Creepy Castle," in* Kirkus Reviews, *Vol. XLIII, No. 19, October 1, 1975, p. 1120.*

Although the artist has made too repetitive a use of the metamorphosis or harlequinade format (a style invented more than two centuries ago), he has chosen a fresh, appealing subject. A young mouse and his lady, adventuring into a medieval castle, are pursued by an evil rat. Locked into a bat- and dragon-infested dungeon, they bravely engineer an escape, and a frog propels them aboard a lily pad from the castle moat. Each panoramic spread carries a bit of the action in soft-hued watercolors. Unfortunately the half-pages interpolated to change the scenes almost always fail to match the adjacent full pages in color tones.

> *Virginia Haviland, in a review of "Creepy Castle," in* The Horn Book Magazine, *Vol. LII, No. 1, February, 1976, p. 42.*

An Edwardian Summer　(1976)

Goodall's watercolors of village streets, country parlors, market places, shops, and parish churches are beautifully painted and packed with details. The button-nosed inhabitants of these nostalgic scenes could have been modeled on Victoria's own collection of penny wooden dolls. Children already hooked on "Upstairs, Downstairs" might appreciate this wordless album but adult Anglophiles will be its primary audience.

> *Merrie Lou Cohen, in a review of "An Edwardian Summer," in* School Library Journal, *Vol. 23, No. 2, October, 1976, p. 106.*

A dream book for looking back at a time of peace and security, this is a miniature exhibit of watercolors depicting two upper-class children running through their summer days in the market, shops, gardens, school, streets, fair, and homes of an idyllic English town at the turn of the century. Aside from Harold Macmillan's brief introduction, which is adult in tone, there are no words to the book, and children familiar with Goodall's other books will not find a story here. They may, however, enjoy the old-fashioned details of the children's world, portrayed with relish in paintings which are worth a good long stare. A collector's item.

> *Betsy Hearne, in a review of "An Edwardian Summer," in* Booklist, *Vol. 73, No. 8, December 15, 1976, p. 606.*

Goodall abandons the use of alternate page and half-page in a wordless picture book that, while nostalgically charming, may direct its appeal to adults more than to children. There are two child characters whose activities through one long, golden summer day are followed in the pictures, but they play a passive role on many of the pages: watching a cricket match, attending a wedding, dropping in on a jumble sale, etc. They go to school in the morning, visit a friend, watch a train go by, and so on. It all affords Goodall a fine opportunity to paint clothing details, the elaborate furniture and ceremony of the era, a pub, a country kitchen and the family kitchen (very "Upstairs, Downstairs") and the splendor of an Edwardian upper-class wedding.

> *Zena Sutherland, in a review of "An Edwardian Summer," in* Bulletin of the Center for Children's Books, *Vol. 30, No. 8, April, 1977, p. 123.*

Paddy Pork's Holiday　(1976)

Like other Goodall books about a lively pig, this has half-pages inserted between each set of full pages, so that turning the half-pages changes the picture. Goodall is one of the more adept creators of such wordless picture books; his story line is always clear, and his tales abound in humor and action. Here Paddy goes off on a hiking trip, is passed up when he tries to thumb a ride with an elegant gentleman but picked up by a friendly family in a caravan. He sets up a tent, goes for a swim, is caught in a storm, climbs a tree and falls into a coal car of a passing train, inadvertently is pushed on a concert stage while wearing a scarecrow's clothes, and eventually reaches home in a fine fettle.

> *Zena Sutherland, in a review of "Paddy Pork's Holiday," in* Bulletin of the Center for Children's Books, *Vol. 30, No. 2, October, 1976, p. 25.*

Paddy Pork is too accident-prone to go for a camping holiday alone. After his eager setting off come disasters, some familiar to all campers, some more dramatic. Having lost all his clothes while bathing, he borrows a scarecrow's dress suit and is mistaken for Herr Grunt the concert pianist. Lesser pigs might have come clean, but Paddy gives his best, to the distress of his audience. All ends well. As always in these delightful books, half-pages hint discreetly at the adventure to come. The drawing is old-fashioned in its care for good draughtsmanship and delicate colour—positively Constable at times in the delectable landscapes.

Paddy Pork needs no words; his simple story comes clearly out of the pictures.

> *M. Crouch, in a review of "Paddy Pork's Holiday," in* The Junior Bookshelf, *Vol. 40, No. 5, October, 1976, p. 262.*

The Surprise Picnic (1977)

With his usual alternate half-pages leading you on, Goodall has a fussily dressed Mama cat and two kittens row off to an island picnic. But the half pages are just a gimmick here, concealing/revealing no unexpected developments, and though there is a surprise when the picnic-table rock becomes a turtle who walks away with the lunch, the rest is a tamer version of *Paddy Pork's Holiday*—with the rowboat drifting off, a storm blowing in, and the cats flying away under umbrella power and landing on a seaside cottage where an outdoor tea party is hastily convened. Pale.

> *A review of "The Surprise Picnic," in* Kirkus Reviews, *Vol. XLV, No. 8, April 15, 1977, p. 422.*

As in the artist's earlier adventures-without-words, the momentum of the plot is heightened by the use of half-page inserts, which provide a quick change of action. While this technique succeeded in his black-and-white work for *The Adventures of Paddy Pork*, it has not always been compatible with the difficulties inherent in color printing. Thus, despite the beguiling sweetness of the feline protagonists, the frequent disparities in color from full- to half-page are obvious as well as disturbing.

> *Mary M. Burns, in a review of "The Surprise Picnic," in* The Horn Book Magazine, *Vol. LIII, No. 3, June, 1977, p. 299.*

The sensibility behind this wordless outing is not so much nostalgia as tasteful antiquarianism. Goodall's Mother and Sister Cat are impeccably turned out in long dresses and sunbonnets; Brother Cat is jaunty in an Eton collar and jacket. Their mini-adventure unfolds via alternating full and half-width pages: Turn one panel and the "rock" on which the cats have spread their picnic lunch is transformed into a giant tortoise. Turn another and a gust of wind takes Mama Cat and her parasol flying. Too often, though, Goodall fails to coordinate the surprises, and the half-page overleaf serves no real purpose. This reduces the format to a gimmick, perhaps, but it's one that very young children respond to.

> *Joyce Milton, in a review of "The Surprise Picnic," in* The New York Times Book Review, *February 26, 1978, p. 27.*

An Edwardian Christmas (1977)

Except for a costume ball extravaganza, Goodall's English *Edwardian Christmas,* like the era it faithfully reproduces, is fussy and overly genteel. The lavish double-page paintings, with minimal continuity from spread to spread, re-semble stage sets of "Upstairs, Downstairs"—beautifully appointed, but there's really nothing going on. (p. 114)

> *Pamela D. Pollack, "Christmas Books '78: A Mixed Bag," in* School Library Journal, *Vol. 25, No. 2, October, 1978, pp. 112-15.*

Goodall's small books, always wordless, are usually embellished by the details of an Edwardian setting; here he's surpassed himself in creating an English Christmas in a nostalgic county/country setting. Family members come to the manor, the children gather holly and mistletoe to help decorate the church, there are Christmas services and family breakfasts, walks in the snow, carolers, a musical evening, and a costume party upstairs that is echoed by the dancing in the servants' hall below. The class structure is clear both in the upstairs-downstairs pictures and in the charitable visit to a cottager. The book may pique children's curiosity, but it should evoke sentimental sighs from the older audience. The paintings, all double-paged, are full without being too busy, nicely composed and detailed, and the restrained use of color contributes to the mellow mood; the night scenes are especially attractive, with Christmas card snow falling lightly on blue shadows.

> *Zena Sutherland, in a review of "An Edwardian Christmas," in* Bulletin of the Center for Children's Books, *Vol. 32, No. 4, December, 1978, p. 61.*

This latest of Goodall's wordless picture books is storyless as well. As in *An Edwardian Summer,* which features the same two children, Goodall contents himself with picturing the innocent joys of family holidays in a spacious house maintained by a large, merrily bustling staff. But the festivities soon pall for onlookers, who might expect to find a suggestion of drama or anecdote but instead meet only one happy scene after another: the ever-smiling, never-wilting participants gather greenery, trim the pulpit at church and the tree at home, dine, play, ride to hounds, ice skate, dance at a masked ball, watch a stage performance (from box seats of course), and more. But even viewers who never got enough of *Upstairs, Downstairs* will feel overstuffed by the end of this unvaryingly joyous vacation.

> *A review of "An Edwardian Christmas," in* Kirkus Reviews, *Vol. XLVI, No. 24, December 15, 1978, p. 1352.*

The Story of an English Village (1978)

It may seem a long step from Paddy Pork to social history, but John Goodall's exquisitely funny picture-stories of his porker are as distinguished for their depiction of a slightly idealised old-world landscape as for their porcine humours. Now the artist, using a larger page but the same technique of wordlessness and alternating half-pages, turns his attention to the growth of a typical English community. We start with a clearing in the forest, making room for a hill-top castle and with the waggon beating a rough road through the lower ground. Then, century by century, the place grows, from a primitive settlement to something a great deal more like town than village, until, foreshadowed by the arrival of the first Edwardian motor-

From Naughty Nancy, *written and illustrated by John S. Goodall.*

car, the full horror of the late twentieth century is revealed. A few constant factors: the castle, the market cross, the church and one house, appear at all stages of the story. Mr. Goodall's pictures are invariably well drawn and careful in detail, a little too clean and tidy, perhaps, especially in the interiors, and they are consistently superficial. But for children too young, or insufficiently equipped in reading ability, for Edward Osmond's 'Valley' here is a useful and fundamentally honest book, and one which will give much pleasure along with the information.

> *M. Crouch, in a review of "The Story of an English Village," in* The Junior Bookshelf, *Vol. 42, No. 6, December, 1978, p. 294.*

As social history, this could be an accompaniment to Trevelyan, but for American youngsters of anything near picture-book age it will all be remote and, in the absence of captions or vivid content, largely meaningless. As Goodall notes in his introductory paragraph, "rural life in England remained remarkably untouched by outside events . . . until the advent of the automobile," so the changes are small and gradual—in six centuries, to the untutored child, a progression from simple to fancy old-fashioned. Suddenly, at the last opening, we're in a mad, mod city which, from the looks of things, Goodall doesn't much like—bringing to a sour close centuries of harmony and order.

> *A review of "The Story of an English Village," in* Kirkus Reviews, *Vol. XLVII, No. 5, March 1, 1979, p. 258.*

An Edwardian Holiday (1978)

The third in Goodall's romantic interpretation of life in Edwardian England follows a family on a seaside holiday. There are no words, though an introduction would expand the understanding for U.S. children, but details of the full-color illustrations enable viewers to share in the pastimes on the pier, fun at the beach, visit to a nearby castle and farm, and trip across the channel to France. Puppets, horses, wading, Punch and Judy shows, picnics, and cro-

quet games amuse the vacationers. The artistry lacks the precision and clarity of *An Edwardian Summer;* colors here tend to be watery and in places muddy, nor does this have the nostalgic charm of *An Edwardian Christmas.* However, the scenes depict a slower, more gentle time of yesteryear, and those who found the others engaging will enjoy this summer outing.

> *Barbara Elleman, in a review of "An Edwardian Holiday," in* Booklist, *Vol. 76, No. 1, September 1, 1979, p. 43.*

In the pattern of *An Edwardian Summer* and *An Edwardian Christmas,* a wordless depiction of tranquil, uneventful days at a British shore resort—so constrained, moreover, as to suggest that the two children of the vacationing family are little models of submissiveness and good deportment. After days of picnicking on the beach and banqueting in the dining room, of meadow walks, croquet, and carriage rides, our little party does embark for a day's excursion to the French coast—which, however, is not going to strike American children in the 1970s as a very different scene. By comparison with Goodall's staid tableaux, Kate Greenaway looks Dickensian.

> *A review of "An Edwardian Holiday," in* Kirkus Reviews, *Vol. XLVII, No. 17, September 1, 1979, p. 997.*

It is in the fidelity and variety of detail that Goodall excels in his wordless books about the Edwardian era; while they tend to show the sunnier side of life and are gentry-oriented, they will probably awaken nostalgia in the oldest and lively curiosity in the youngest. Here a family of four goes to a seaside resort, visits friends and sees their glasshouses; they play croquet, visit the amusement pier, see a Punch and Judy show, and—of course—play decorously on the sands as women emerge from changing rooms clad in the voluminous bathing costumes of the day. Goodall's subtle use of color and a fine eye for perspective and composition add to the appeal of the book.

> *Zena Sutherland, in a review of "An Edwardian Holiday," in* Bulletin of the Center for

Children's Books, *Vol. 33, No. 8, April, 1980, p. 152.*

An Edwardian Season (1979)

A fascinating, mostly "upstairs" view of a London Season, the fourth of Goodall's Edwardian albums. Double-page illustrations record the three months of each year when aristocratic English society enjoyed regattas, receptions, and coming-out dances. Ladies' hats are as large as banquet platters (and piled as high). Children are less a part of this book than the previous ones, as the scenes portrayed are from an adult world. Picture captions are listed only in the front, and scenes are not explained. Only a brief note sets the stage in King Edward's reign; nevertheless, abundant details and lively scenes encourage and reward readers' effort.

Anna Biagioni Hart, in a review of "An Edwardian Season," in School Library Journal, *Vol. 27, No. 3, November, 1980, p. 62.*

The fourth of these Edwardian tintypes and perhaps the one most suited, so far, to the Masterpiece Theater audience rather than to American kids. The "Season" on view is the Social Season starting—as the introductory note explains—"with the Private View at the Royal Academy of Arts"; and continuing, picture-spread by picture-spread, with balls, theatrical performances, regattas, garden parties, horse races, and ceremonious strolls-in-the-park . . . none of which does other than portray a vanished and alien way of life. There's not even an upstairs/downstairs, out-front/behind-the-scenes contrast to give it some reality or drama. Just lots of fancy people in fancy duds disporting themselves (genteely) on one after another occasion.

A review of "An Edwardian Season," in Kirkus Reviews, *Vol. XLIX, No. 1, January 1, 1981, p. 2.*

Paddy's New Hat (1980)

Paddy, an Edwardian pig of considerable charm, has had previous adventures in **Paddy's Evening Out** and **Paddy Pork's Holiday;** Mr. Goodall, justifiably, has had considerable praise for his artistry and mechanical technique (half-page inserts) in those books and others. Here, Paddy's purchase of a straw skimmer, the wind snatching it from his head and the ensuing chase lead him to sign on as a London bobby and on to more trouble before he becomes a hero by rescuing the crown jewels, I suspect, of Pomerania. Although this book has no words, Mr. Goodall's full-color paintings speak eloquently in conveying all the action. (pp. 49,71)

George A. Woods, "These Little Piggies Went to Market," in The New York Times Book Review, *November 9, 1980, pp. 49, 71.*

Alternating full and half pages, Goodall tells a story through the pictures only; each half page changes a scene enough to carry the action forward. The plump Edwardian pig of several earlier stories is the protagonist and, the

title notwithstanding, his adventures have little to do with a new hat. A straw boater, the hat blows off and sails into a police recruiting office; Paddy is signed on, gets into a few scrapes, and catches a burglar. The book ends with Paddy being given a medal by royalty and—last page—strutting down the street with a plume in his hat-band. While the story line is clear, it relies, more than is Goodall's usual wont, fairly heavily on coincidence; however, the action is brisk and often amusing (as when the neophyte bobby makes a total snarl of traffic and runs off) and the pictures are, as always, deftly composed and gracefully painted in soft watercolor.

Zena Sutherland, in a review of "Paddy's New Hat," in Bulletin of the Center for Children's Books, *Vol. 34, No. 4, December, 1980, p. 71.*

Another of the artist's metamorphoses with pages and scenes painted in rich colors. The pictures of Paddy Pork's misadventures need no words to describe what befalls the pig . . . . The mad mix-ups and the contrasting ceremonious honors at court suit the artist's gifts for instilling life and humor into animal characters, both individually, and collectively within the crowd scenes. (pp. 633-34)

Virginia Haviland, in a review of "Paddy's New Hat," in The Horn Book Magazine, *Vol. LVI, No. 6, December, 1980, pp. 633-34.*

Escapade (1980)

John Goodall's new venture into nostalgia enters the world of black-and-white silhouette, with the same wordless narrative and half-page surprises as in his earliest series. In an eighteenth-century setting, a pet Persian and poodle give chase to an escaped canary for their sorrowing mistress. They "ask" its whereabouts of various attractively represented country characters: the outdoor scenes are beautifully and economically designed. After a ducking the pets successfully bring back rather more than what was lost—a pleasant frolic.

M. Hobbs, in a review of "Escapade," in The Junior Bookshelf, *Vol. 44, No. 6, December, 1980, p. 283.*

John S. Goodall's Theatre: The Sleeping Beauty (1980)

[This] book is a lovely fantasy, opening with a picture of a frog, dressed as a busker, advertising the dramatic performance of "Sleeping Beauty." Using the device that has worked so well in his previous little attractions, Goodall alternately conceals and reveals the action with half and full pages. Decorative, very dressy watercolors begin with scenes of a gala crowd arriving at the theater, the curtain going up and the fairy tale enacted (with a huge, menacing rat playing the affronted fairy who casts the spell on the baby mouse princess). The final inspired touch is an overview of the star's fans applauding her as they surround her limousine outside the stage door.

A review of "John S. Goodall's Theatre: The Sleeping Beauty," in Publishers Weekly, *Vol. 217, No. 23, June 13, 1980, p. 74.*

Goodall's technique of using parts of pages to bring a change of scene or character is used to retell the Grimms' "Sleeping Beauty" as a theatrical performance. While other wordless Goodall books have functioned effectively, this does not; the scene shifts, for example, from the infant princess (a mouse, like all the other characters) in her cradle to a room in which a young adult mouse approaches an elderly mouse who is spinning, and there is no visible connection between the infant mouse and the one who comes into the room in the next scene. Nor between that scene and the next, which shows the princess and others in cobwebbed sleep. The illustrations are engaging, but they don't tell the story. (pp. 92-3)

> *Zena Sutherland, in a review of "John S. Goodall's Theatre: The Sleeping Beauty," in* Bulletin of the Center for Children's Books, *Vol. 34, No. 5, January, 1981, pp. 92-3.*

Victorians Abroad   (1980)

Goodall has created another exquisite, wordless book in the same format of his quartet portraying affluent English citizens, **An Edwardian Summer,** etc. Gracefully animated watercolors show Victorian parties leaving home, coping with the hurly-burly of French customs, then tucked into a carriage with stout horses struggling across the Alps to Switzerland. The artist depicts breathtaking scenes of the Grand Tour in the cities of France, Italy, Africa and India. In one view, Victorian gallants (whose ladies are noticeably absent, perhaps shopping at Worth's) are enjoying the exuberant can-can dancers in a Parisian nightclub. The book glows with beauty and exotica, finally revealing the homeward bound on board ship and gazing at the welcoming, really *white* cliffs of Dover.

> *A review of "Victorians Abroad," in* Publishers Weekly, *Vol. 219, No. 2, January 9, 1981, p. 73.*

Sometime during the publication of his Edwardian series, it seems that Goodall put away his pen and began to work without the fine textural definition of his earlier drawings. What he may have gained as a watercolorist, he has lost as an illustrator. His scenes are more crowded with people, the figures stiff and awkward; the exciting composition of his early pictures gave way to static lines of featureless forms dominated by vast backgrounds in which everything looks equally important. In **An Edwardian Season,** the "family" previously engaged in purposeful activities—on a Christmas visit or on a seaside holiday—became obscured by masses of adult figures, all unidentifiable, standing or sitting spiritlessly. In his latest, the unifying family has utterly disappeared, and all that's left is a little album of washy travel sketches that have no style nor rhythm. This excursion into British nostalgia is not of much interest to children and will disappoint even Goodall's adult fans.

> *Wendy Dellett, in a review of "Victorians Abroad," in* School Library Journal, *Vol. 27, No. 8, April, 1981, p. 112.*

Although this has the same format as other Goodall books: same size and no text, it lacks the half-pages that the artist has used in earlier books to show a partial change of scene. Here there is no story; indeed, there is no reason to suppose this will appeal to most children. It portrays a series of scenes of places frequently visited on the Grand Tour for travellers in the Victorian Era. A prefatory page lists the scenes in order, but since no page numbers are provided, it means scanning back and forth. The paintings are charming, with their small-scale details of architecture and period dress, their vigor and pervasive good humor—but to whom does this nostalgic trip appeal?

> *Zena Sutherland, in a review of "Victorians Abroad," in* Bulletin of the Center for Children's Books, *Vol. 35, No. 8, April, 1982, p. 147.*

Before the War, 1908-1939: An Autobiography in Pictures (1981)

Those readers who like looking through old trunks in somebody else's attic will like this picture book. The artist tells his own story in pictures, from his birth in 1908 to England's declaration of war in 1939. Superimposed over many of the watercolor illustrations are paintings of family photographs—servants, relatives and pets who may or may not appear in the larger scenes. Is the bald, bespectacled man showing off an artist's portfolio in the 1920's really the same man who appears bedside on the occasion of Goodall's birth, and is that gentleman also Goodall's father (who is not so bald in a photograph)? It is easy to believe that the illustrations were originally intended as a gift for Goodall's wife and not for publication. The pictures display a variety of styles, individually very pleasing but visually disparate as readers turn from idyllic, almost impressionistic watercolors of the English countryside to the primary colors of a collage, or perhaps to an interior in dark colors with crosshatchings reminiscent of engraving. **Before the War** is a painted photo album by a skillful artist. The very fact that so many of the many details go unexplained would enable imaginative adults and children to use the book as a vehicle for storytelling and to learn about a class of English society in a vanished era—with home birth, nannies, dirigibles, boarding school, tours of the continent. Only a very precocious child would read it alone. (pp. 106-07)

> *Elizabeth Holtze, in a review of "Before the War, 1908-1939: An Autobiography in Pictures," in* School Library Journal, *Vol. 28, No. 1, September, 1981, pp. 106-07.*

Paddy Finds a Job; Shrewbettina Goes to Work   (1981)

[Two pop-ups] **Shrewbettina Goes to Work** and **Paddy Finds a Job,** are much simpler affairs, with no words, suitable for small children. They are pretty, have few moving parts and depict the adventures of a shrew who entraps a thief at a draper's sale, and a pig who has a disastrous career as a waiter. The style of the drawings, with their restrained pastel colourings, is reminiscent of Beatrix Potter; and the absence of a written story will enable the child

From Before the War, 1908-1939: An Autobiography in Pictures, *written and illustrated by John Strickland Goodall.*

to structure his own personal plot, using his own vocabulary and local colour.

> *Ursula Robertshaw, in a review of "Paddy Finds a Job" and "Shrewbettina Goes to Work," in* The Illustrated London News, *Vol. 269, No. 7001, December, 1981, p. 75.*

Paddy Pork makes his return in a pop-up book [**Paddy Finds a Job**] wherein he becomes—very briefly—a waiter in a restaurant. The moving parts in this wordless story add very little to it, and one wonders why John Goodall felt the need to jump on to this particular band wagon. Whereas his alternating full and half-page flap books were truly novel, and encouraged children on to 'story', this one seems dangerously near gimmickry for gimmick's sake. I guess children will play with it, but will they 'read' it? (pp. 25-6)

> *Jill Bennett, in a review of "Paddy Finds a Job," in* The School Librarian, *Vol. 30, No. 1, March, 1982, pp. 25-6.*

We all know Paddy Pork, and to know him is to love him. For all that, Mr. Goodall's new offering [**Paddy Finds a Job**] is something of a disappointment. He has fallen for the allure of the pop-up. His earlier books also played mild bibliographical tricks, with their half-pages, but the pop-up restricts him in the very area in which he excels: the extended joke and joke continuity. For reasons of economics the animated book has to make its points quickly and on the surface. So Paddy's attempt to become a waiter in a high class restaurant, patronized by the best of mouse, duck and cat society comes to its disastrous end almost as soon as it begins. Of course the drawing is as meticulous as ever, and the mechanics are ingenious, even if they do not add much to the impact of the story. There are no words, and indeed none is needed.

> *M. Crouch, in a review of "Paddy Finds a Job," in* The Junior Bookshelf, *Vol. 46, No. 2, April, 1982, p. 61.*

John Goodall takes kindly to the Victorian costumes and settings of his latest pop-up book [**Shrewbettina Goes to Work**], and he varies the gimmicks, with pop-up, lift-up, wheel and slide. Except as novelties—and with such a plethora of these books the novelty is quickly wearing off—these devices do not help his story a great deal. As Shrewbettina pursues and finally catches the sneak-thief in the dress-shop where she has just obtained a post, the excitement mounts only mildly. The drawing is, as always, immaculate.

> *M. Crouch, in a review of "Shrewbettina Goes to Work," in* The Junior Bookshelf, *Vol. 46, No. 3, June, 1982, p. 93.*

Edwardian Entertainments (1982)

Goodall is at his best when his scenes are uncrowded and his figures are large enough to become individuals. Often the many figures—all of equal prominence—tend to confuse the focus. Still, Goodall's *Edwardian Entertainments* is a welcome refreshment after his disappointingly static *Victorians Abroad.* In this newest book the figures are livelier, the colors richer and the details more effective. The close-up portraits of turn-of-the-century stage stars are beautifully rendered, and scenes of street entertainers, a theater dressing room and bicycling in the country are outstanding for their composition, color contrast and breathing space. Nevertheless, the precision and concentration of purpose in his exquisite *Edwardian Christmas* are missing.

> *Wendy Dellett, in a review of "Edwardian Entertainments," in* School Library Journal, *Vol. 29, No. 1, September, 1982, p. 121.*

Paddy Goes Traveling (1982; also published as *Paddy Goes Travelling*)

In his newest adventure, Paddy Pork goes to the Riviera, chases an escaping kite across the beach and gets stuck atop a taxi headed for the mountains. Embarrassed and freezing in his bathing suit, he rushes foolishly into the snowy woods. Rescued by a friendly bear, he is soon properly attired for a sledding race, which he disrupts with typical flair. The illustrations are designed with extra half-pages that can be turned to reveal further developments in the plot. This ingenious idea was elegantly simplified in Goodall's earlier books, carefully drawn, vigorously dramatic picture books with firm lines and brilliant contrasts (especially the first Paddy book, which was in black and white). There was just enough activity in each scene to hold the interest of a young child. But in this latest book, Paddy is lost in the crowds Goodall has allowed to clutter his recent pictures, and the effect is often confusing. Also, Paddy is now an independent grown-up, which puts added distance between him and his audience. Too often the drawings appear to be dashed off, the figures neglected in favor of elaborate backgrounds. Fortunately Goodall still has his delightful sense of humor, so die-hard Paddy Pork fans will enjoy his antics, if they overlook the curious inconsistencies in costumes, which range from Victorian skirts and bonnets, to 1940s beach wear. (pp. 67-8)

> *Wendy Dellett, in a review of "Paddy Goes Travelling," in* School Library Journal, *Vol. 29, No. 3, November, 1982, pp. 67-8.*

John S. Goodall's form is the "harlequinade," or "transformation book," in which a mere flip of a partial page transforms one scene into another. *Paddy Goes Travelling* continues the amusing adventures of the ill-named Paddy Pork, here his being transported from the sunny beaches of the Riviera to the icy slopes of the Alps. Ingenious Goodall can tell through this simple device the most entertaining tale, almost a novel in miniature, all without the use of words.

> *Michael Patrick Hearn, in a review of "Paddy Goes Travelling," in* American Book Collector, *n.s. Vol. 4, No. 2, March-April, 1983, p. 59.*

Lavinia's Cottage (1982)

A reproduction of a book the author made for his four-year-old grand daughter, it has no words and needs none. It is set in the artist's favourite Edwardian period and shows the visit of a lady and her two daughters to a cottager's family.

The fascination of the book for a child is that the pictured doors can be opened to reveal what is behind them, the rocking horse really rocks and the front of the dolls' house opens. At the end of the book a three dimensional model of the cottage 'pops up' as the page is turned.

This kind of toy book may well seem tame to some children after the more startling revelations of haunted houses and the like, but for other children, the presentation has a homely familiarity that has a more gentle appeal and, for adults, a nostalgic charm.

> *E. Colwell, in a review of "Lavinia's Cottage," in* The Junior Bookshelf, *Vol. 47, No. 2, April, 1983, p. 67.*

Enter now a pastoral, proper Edwardian world re-created by John S. Goodall. In this subdued pop-up book a lady with bustle, parasol and two young daughters comes calling at an ivy-entwined thatch-roofed cottage. We assume that Lavinia is the young girl abed with chicken pox, but she's not there for long. She "pops" out of bed and with the two girls climbs a ladder to the attic, where where's a rocking horse, among other delights, then down to the courtyard. And when it's time to leave, we see that one of the young visitors has acquired a kitten.

There's an evocative pleasure to *Lavinia's Cottage,* with its tranquil scenes painted in earth tones and pastels. Mr. Goodall has stocked house and yard with the charming but necessary clutter of the time. A dozen doors—to closets, cabinets, washstands, wardrobes, sheds and gardens—open to reveal further minutiae of daily life. A splendid diorama of the cottage, with Lavinia waving goodbye from a window, unfolds as the visitors depart. We would have loved to stay longer.

> *George A. Woods, in a review of "Lavinia's Cottage," in* The New York Times Book Review, *April 24, 1983, p. 24.*

Above and Below Stairs (1983)

With the mannered charm of his Edwardian books, Goodall promises a look at above and below stairs Britain from the Middle Ages through current times. Wordless pages open to double spreads in this horizontally-held volume, literally showing upstairs, peopled by the upper class, then with the flip of the half page, downstairs, housing support workers. But there are time slippages (some are before-and-after scenes, some parallel) and changes in focus (some show master-servant relationships, some simply varying social classes). And the content of the half page often strains for its artistic relationship to the whole. Did the wine cellar share the vaulted style of the great hall in the time of Henry VIII? Either England through the ages or master-servant relationships would have provided ample field for this confusing book. For all its visual appeal, ***Above and Below Stairs*** is neither period piece nor social commentary, and as such may not be worth the climb.

> *Carolyn Noah, in a review of "Above and Below Stairs," in* School Library Journal, *Vol. 30, No. 2, October, 1983, p. 158.*

Paddy Pork—Odd Jobs (1983)

Wherein, blithely, Paddy Pork hangs wallpaper askew, drops a chimney-pot (on the watching householder's head), flops as a window-washer (occasioning more mayhem), wrecks the village pump (drenching the bystanders) . . . and redeems himself, providentially, by finding a lost baby in a toolshed. (How that baby got in that toolshed . . . .) Zippy—but unlike the jobs, unvaried.

> *A review of "Paddy Pork—Odd Jobs," in* Kirkus Reviews, *Vol. LI, No. 21, November 1, 1983, p. 185.*

The story is commonplace. Paddy, hiring out as a handyman, is engaged to hang wallpaper, replace a chimney pot, wash windows, fix the town pump—and fouls up on every job.

But he reclaims the town's esteem by finding a lost baby. The book's format is inventive. Between its full pages are half pages, which when turned change the full pictures—from an exterior to an interior, a job begun to a job finished, the bottom of a house to the top of a house. I can't imagine any child or adult who wouldn't get a kick out of this ingenious economy. (pp. 45, 51)

> *Charles Simmons, "24 (At Least) Little Pigs," in* The New York Times Book Review, *November 13, 1983, pp. 45, 51.*

Paddy Pork is a rather hapless pig adept at getting himself into difficult situations capped with happy, if undeserved, endings . . . . Even though Paddy runs out after each botched job, leaving the owner with a broken or misshapen mess, this British original is still a charmingly drawn tale with beautiful colors and characters.

> *Anne H. Ross, in a review of "Paddy Pork: Odd Jobs," in* School Library Journal, *Vol. 30, No. 5, January, 1984, p. 64.*

Paddy Under Water (1984)

In the sequel to ***Paddy Pork—Odd Jobs, Paddy Goes Traveling,*** etc., the affable gentleman pig goes snorkeling in the mysterious waters under the sea and gets into more adventures. The famous British watercolor artist has painted resplendent scenes that tell the wordless story. Like Goodall's earlier books, this one springs surprises when the reader lifts half-pages that conceal part of the action going on in the full pages. Paddy's funny, tense exploits put him in the company of exotic fish, lissome mermaids, a sea monster that turns out to be friendly when he realizes that Paddy has saved his tiny child from a marauding octopus. When the hero surfaces, he's toting a treasure chest salvaged from a wrecked ship, a perfect end to the doings and to the charming story. (pp. 82-3)

> *A review of "Paddy Underwater," in* Publishers Weekly, *Vol. 226, No. 6, August 10, 1984, pp. 82-3.*

Paddy Pork to the Rescue (1985; U.S. edition as *Paddy to the Rescue*)

A masked rat-thief, a bag of jewels, a frantic lady pig—a situation perfect for brave Paddy Pork, who pursues the thief down from the roof (an umbrella makes a useful parachute) and out to sea, where a duel with oars between the two boats leaves Paddy to swim ashore; still pursuing, he finally delivers the black villain to the police and modestly receives the thanks of the grateful lady. Flaps increase the sense of action in one more tongue-in-cheek adventure, set in a timeless seaside resort where animals impersonate prosperous townspeople and tourists with gently irresistible humour. Colour, movement, composition, all make words unnecessary in this diverting series.

> *Margery Fisher, in a review of "Paddy Pork to the Rescue," in* Growing Point, *Vol. 24, No. 4, November, 1985, p. 4531.*

The wordless adventure is easy to follow, and Goodall's half-page inserts continue to be a useful gimmick for increasing the suspense in the visual sequences. Rich, warm colors, true lines, and a charming bit of untidiness to the shadings and textures give the artist's illustrations a distinctive character.

> *Denise M. Wilms, in a review of "Paddy to the Rescue," in* Booklist, *Vol. 82, No. 17, May 1, 1986, p. 1310.*

Goodall's cloven-hoofed hero once again romps wordlessly through lovely small-format watercolor double-page spreads, this time pursuing a robber rat who has just stolen a mistress pig's jewels (from around her neck no less!) . . . . The familiar alternating half-pages spur the action on with their near flawless coordination. (An exception is some difference in print color from page to page.) Paddy at last gets his rat, traps him under an empty barrel and hands him over to Constable Hound. As always, Goodall's portrayal of his anthropomorphized animals is accurate but not sugar-coated, and the charming depiction of the English seaside setting is true to life. Another Paddy adventure which will keep young readers turning pages swiftly towards the conclusion but which still offers much to lingerers. A wordless triumph from a master. (pp. 81-2)

> *Patricia Homer, in a review of "Paddy to the Rescue," in* School Library Journal, *Vol. 32, No. 10, August, 1986, pp. 81-2.*

Naughty Nancy Goes to School (1985)

Naughty Nancy is a terror at school, provoking the teacher when her back is turned and entertaining the students. But Nancy also has quick wits; a class visit to the seashore becomes the occasion for her to rescue a stranded swimmer, thereby becoming the hero of the day. All this action plays out in vintage Goodall wordless format. Scenes unfold through right-hand half pages. Richly colored paintings full of action provide lots to look at. The Victorian setting might excuse the somewhat stereotypical portrayal of Nancy's stern, humorless teacher; mischievous Nancy is the opposite extreme. But, while Nancy's independence and wit are admirable, a tired cliché is perpetuated in the teacher's portrayal. Politics aside, this will no doubt entertain children, who will scrutinize the paintings, enjoy turning the flaps, and feel satisfied at Nancy's triumph.

> *Denise M. Wilms, in a review of "Naughty Nancy Goes to School," in* Booklist, *Vol. 82, No. 7, December 1, 1985, p. 571.*

A delightful follow-up destined to be a bigger success than **Naughty Nancy,** this wordless story follows naughty Nancy (and naughty she is) through a day at school. Through the effective format of half pages inserted between a double-page spread, children see the pursuant action by lifting the half page. They'll be able to second guess Nancy's next antic and in most cases won't be disappointed. A great book to share with children of all ages, although equally effective as an independent adventure . . . . Through the detailed yet liquidly colored Victorian-style drawings, warmth and humor spill from page to page as children are charmed by the antics of this playful mouse. This series and the preceding **"Paddy Pork"** series are excellent examples of the power of the wordless text to express action, character and setting.

> *Cathy Woodward, in a review of "Naughty Nancy Goes to School," in* School Library Journal, *Vol. 32, No. 6, February, 1986, p. 74.*

The Story of a Castle (1986)

Goodall's familiar technique of full-page pictures interspersed with half-pages that change the action within the scene works especially well in presenting a drama of historical change. In this book, leaf by leaf, and half-page by half-page, the Norman castle planned and built in the first paintings becomes an Elizabethan garden, a battleground between Cavalier and Roundhead in the Civil War, an 18th-Century estate, a 19th-Century garden party, and a 20th-Century army post. It is fascinating to note that the wedding that is taking place in Victorian times is being held on the site of the medieval stables and to recognize in the World War I hospital the outlines of the original

Great Hall. The book has no text, although the scenes are listed and identified on the frontispiece. Similar in size and plan to Goodall's earlier *The Story of an English Village,* this is a delightful picture book of changing times in English history.

> *Shirley Wilton, in a review of "The Story of a Castle," in* School Library Journal, *Vol. 33, No. 3, November, 1986, p. 88.*

Like Goodall's **The Story of an English Village,** a wordless recapitulation of English social history through a series of richly detailed, beautifully executed illustrations of a single locale . . . . As always, Goodall's research in costume and architecture has been meticulous; the evolution of the arched interior from rough stronghold to panelled and beautifully adorned ballroom is especially interesting, and the chronology of costume will be useful for reference. The cut-page device adds interest and continuity, although in some instances the pictures match imperfectly.

A warm evocation of times past to delight Anglophiles and gather new converts.

> *A review of "The Story of a Castle," in* Kirkus Reviews, *Vol. LIV, No. 24, December 15, 1986, p. 1865.*

The first page of this unusual book is the only one to carry text. Here the history of a typical British Castle is briefly outlined, from about 1170, when the Normans selected a suitable site for a fortress, until 1970, when the owners decided to open the castle to the public.

These events, and others happening in the centuries between, are illustrated on alternate full and half-sized pages. Clever design enables the moment of site choice to be changed to half-way through the building process with minimal effort: similarly, the flip of a half page transforms Cavaliers looking out from the battlements into dead and wounded casualties, overpowered by Roundheads swarming up the castle walls.

John Goodall's ingeniously devised and skillfully executed coloured illustrations establish the continuity of the stout walls of the castle and of human generations, even though the circumstances affecting both may change.

> *R. Baines, in a review of "The Story of a Castle," in* The Junior Bookshelf, *Vol. 51, No. 1, February, 1987, p. 19.*

The Story of a High Street (1987; U.S. edition as *The Story of a Main Street*)

As in **The Story of a Castle** and **The Story of an English Village,** Goodall's eye for historical detail and his talent for making the past relevantly alive combine to act as an animating lens. This time the focus is the Main Street, the pathway, even in Medieval times (when this story begins), where daily business is transacted. People costumed according to period, class, and season go about their mundane tasks, and viewers are street level voyeurs pleasantly and leisurely taking it all in and learning odd bits of information about lifestyles, architecture, modes of transportation, even some relationships between the sexes. The half-

From The Story of a Castle, *written and illustrated by John S. Goodall.*

page flips are used here at times to bring viewers into a shop first depicted from the street and, at others, to move the action forward into time. A stone market cross is the anchor, remaining unmoved and unchanging while all else evolves and revolves around it. Goodall creates scores of people that suggest rather than specify; they are no more important than other items in these engaging tableaux. Watercolors and a deft pencil are all that he uses to create a superbly crowded Edwardian shop at Christmas or to enliven an Elizabethan autumn street scene. Surely a very special slice through time without the dirt, hunger, or death, yet this version of history is not at all sentimentalized, maybe only a bit sanitized. Lots of fine looking here for all.

> *Kenneth Marantz, in a review of "The Story of a Main Street," in* School Library Journal, *Vol. 34, No. 1, September, 1987, p. 174.*

Mr. Goodall is now totally addicted to the use of half-pages, and certainly they have their place in this very attractive 'educational' book. He traces the evolution of a typical town high street in a sequence of full- and half-pages, moving rather hastily from mediaeval to Elizabethan but settling into a rather more leisurely rhythm from the beginning of the eighteenth century. Care has been taken with the details of architecture and costume, but not at the expense of pictorial qualities. Each opening reveals new felicities, and the half-page pictures keep us guessing most pleasurably. And how tellingly the artist presents cultural collapse in the late twentieth century. (pp. 215-16)

> *M. Crouch, in a review of "The Story of a High Street," in* The Junior Bookshelf, *Vol. 51, No. 5, October, 1987, pp. 215-16.*

The drab angularity of the street in the modern period provides a sharp, discordant contrast to the beauty, harmony, and grace that Goodall found in the other ages. Modern times aside, this offering will delight the artist's fans. Goodall's soft colors and intriguing details make this series of full-color illustrations a pleasant tour of the past. Puzzle-oriented children will enjoy pointing out what has

changed or remained the same from one era to another. Teachers may wish to use this in conjunction with Virginia Lee Burton's *The Little House,* Jorg Muller's *Changing Town* portfolio, or Renata Von Tscharner's *New Providence* to show the passage of time dramatically. (pp. 632-33)

> *Carolyn Phelan, in a review of "The Story of a Main Street," in* Booklist, *Vol. 84, No. 7, December 1, 1987, pp. 632-33.*

Little Red Riding Hood   (1988)

In a wordless picture book in Goodall's familiar style—alternating full pages with half pages that flip to modify the scene—mice play roles in Red Riding Hood's family; but, unfortunately, this book is larger than the diminutive format that would have rendered them just life-size—here, they are a clumsy (for a mouse) five inches. The huntsman bear is only slightly larger. Goodall's shadow-dappled forest is lovely, the lurking wolf sufficiently ominous. The beasts that add interest along the way seem to have wandered in from Beatrix Potter's tales: Jemima Puddle-Duck, Jeremy Fisher, Squirrel Nutkin. The business with the wolf is depicted in an unusually grisly fashion: his two attacks are nightmarishly real, including a scene with Grandmother's feet protruding from his jaws; the huntsman's axe is red with gore. Although a wordless version of a familiar story may have value for the prereader and for language development, this one is not well enough thought through to be altogether successful.

> *A review of "Little Red Riding Hood," in* Kirkus Reviews, *Vol. LVI, No. 15, August 1, 1988, p. 1149.*

There's considerable drama in this wordless version that advances the plot through Goodall's often-used format of half pages alternating with full ones. Goodall's lush paintings, casting Red Riding Hood and her Granny as mice, flesh out the plot by having Red Riding Hood encounter several friendly neighbors (a duck, a frog, a squirrel and others) in the course of her trek to Grandma's. The woodcutter is a solicitous bear whom she meets as one of the well-wishers, and the wolf is truly nasty; the scene of him attacking Granny in her bed is one of the most powerful in the book. Thus, the violence of this old tale is evident in the artwork, which shows the woodcutter's bloody ax and the wolf's prostrate body. But all ends happily, with a shaken Granny remerging from beneath the dead wolf. A successful piece of visual folklore not only for its technically strong pictures but also for its ability to evoke the intensity of the story's emotions.

> *Denise M. Wilms, in a review of "Little Red Riding Hood," in Booklist, Vol. 85, No. 2, September 15, 1988, p. 159.*

Goodall's traditional half-page format achieves a pleasing sense of balance and perspective as the main action takes place in the center of the book, with smaller incidents and details flowing out from this focal point. A judicious use of color heightens the drama (the delicate watercolor background of a pastoral countryside is set against the rich and vivid colors used in illustrating the main action). In most spreads, the half-page illustrations are matched, but on several there is a distinct color inconsistency that is aesthetically jarring, and the size proportions are off—the bear woodsman is the same height as the mother mouse. This *Little Red Riding Hood* sets out at a leisurely pace, encountering various animals (an elegant frog gallantly escorts her across a stream), but young viewers familiar with the plot will soon spot the wolf lurking in the background. The tempo speeds up when the wolf arrives at Grandma's and ghoulishly gobbles her up and then Little Red Riding Hood, too. Unlike James Marshall's sheepish wolf (*Little Red Riding Hood* [Dial, 1987]), this one is rotten to the core, with no misgivings. In true folkloric fashion the violence here is graphic and the fear real, but the relief at the rescue is deeply felt.

> *Caroline Ward, in a review of "Little Red Riding Hood," in School Library Journal, Vol. 35, No. 3, November, 1988, p. 102.*

The Story of a Farm (1989)

No wordless books are more eloquent than John S. Goodall's. This one spans seven hundred years, from swine-herds to cream teas, as each spread meticulously plots the progress of a particular dwelling—interleaved with half-spreads to assist the melding of one age into another. Progress? More an endless adjustment of detail, you feel. Whether milkmaids or landgirls, hunting to hounds or an agricultural show, the changes are fixed exactly by the artist's crayon and wash. There could be no better time-line for Juniors with a relish for social history—or for creating that relish.

> *Chris Powling, in a review of "The Story of a Farm," in Books for Keeps, No. 56, May, 1989, p. 30.*

As in his earlier wordless visual histories, such as *The Story of an English Village* and *The Story of a Main Street,* Goodall effectively encapsulates centuries of social change into a series of panoramic views, as absorbing as

they are elegant. His meticulously executed watercolors and choice of subject place him in the grand tradition of English landscape painters. But his interpretations are more than compositions, for they emphasize content along with design so that each spread, with its half-page insert to change the scene, becomes another chapter in the historical chronicle. The central focus is a farmhouse, its humble beginnings depicted in the building of a wattle hut during the early Middle Ages. As the centuries pass, it changes in response to the challenges of the times—from the Tudor inspired structure of the Elizabethan era to an updated twentieth-century version of its Georgian restoration, with a sign advertising accommodations and cream teas. The illustrations capture not only structural modifications but also the changes in the countryside and the economy: the forests of the medieval period give way to well-groomed fields and gardens; the cavalier huntsmen of the Regency are replaced by courteous hikers. The table of contents serves as an effective outline, giving each illustration a title reflecting its intent. Each of the pictures becomes an experience in looking, for, like an absorbing narrative, the book is one to pore over again and again, reveling in beauty while exploring subtle nuances of a society in transition.

> *Mary M. Burns, in a review of "The Story of a Farm," in The Horn Book Magazine, Vol. LXV, No. 3, May-June, 1989, p. 356.*

John Goodall's wordless picture stories are justly celebrated and make superb pre-readers because of the way they draw a child through the book by means of their half-page continuity. Now he is applying the technique to information books, and though the quality of his painting and the richness of his detail are as fine as ever, I have some reservations about this journey through rural history. A child old enough to understand the passage of time could be affronted by the absence of words except on the introductory page. The printing process seems defective, in that the colour values change as one turns the half-flap, so that the essential fit is spoiled. Finally, the movement out from the farm to the countryside means that sometimes one bit of landscape confusingly changes into another. Nevertheless, a teacher could do much with this as a resource for talking with a class about change over time, or by using individual pictures; and imaginative children will lose themselves in the scenes.

> *Audrey Laski, in a review of "The Story of a Farm," in The School Librarian, Vol. 37, No. 3, August, 1989, p. 107.*

The Story of the Seaside (1990; U.S. edition as The Story of the Seashore)

Once again Goodall *(The Story of a Farm)* exposes a rich slice of British society by examining a single scene in its various incarnations during several eras. Here, the seaside town of Weymouth plays host to activities both exotic and familiar. The curtain rises on a royal visit to the resort in the early 1800s; in subsequent spreads, we see adult pastimes such as shopping and tea dances, while children enjoy Punch and Judy shows, boating excursions and digging in the sand. With the advent of WW II, this holiday setting becomes a foreboding coastal defense area; and, on the book's final pages, backpackers, tall buildings and windsurfers testify to the inexorable march of progress. As in all of Goodall's similar works of social history, the central concept of the book is marvelously clean and simple, and is executed with meticulous attention to detail. Readers will be drawn again and again to favorite scenes, and repaid with fresh discoveries each time.

> *A review of "The Story of the Seashore," in* Publishers Weekly, *Vol. 237, No. 2, January 12, 1990, p. 59.*

Using his now familiar device of alternating full and half pages, Goodall provides a table of contents for a wordless book in which watercolors portray scenes at various English seacoast towns that have become popular resorts. From the early 1800s when a royal visit was the catalyst for such popularity, the changes in such resorts as Brighton and Blackpool are pictured; the book ends, with chronological progression and geographical expansion, showing seacoast resorts abroad. Architectural and costume details provide a visual record of change, but the setting and the lack of story may limit audience appeal in the United States despite the lively action on some of the pages.

> *Zena Sutherland, in a review of "The Story of the Seashore," in* Bulletin of the Center for Children's Books, *Vol. 43, No. 7, March, 1990, p. 160.*

Perhaps, one day, there will be a children's picture book which shows life in the countryside as it really is and life in the past as it really was. Almost everyone has a sentimental notion about the country and most of us tend to romanticize the past. The truth is that there is nothing wonderful about rural life and the past was grimmer than we can ever imagine.

Few illustrators of children's books have chosen to see through the romantic cliché and John S. Goodall, the mas-

ter of the flap book, and Thomas Locker, an American artist, comparatively new to the British scene, are no exception. Both idealize the past and show only its charming surface appearance. The thatched cottage may look pretty, but what was it like to live in?

The latest title in Goodall's series of almost wordless history books is ***The Story of the Seaside.*** The passing of time is shown by the ingenious use of the flap pages, but sadly, for this type of factual book, the style of his watercolours is sketchy and vague. The reader longs for greater clarity, more detail and more information.

There is a great concentration on the appearance of people and buildings, but little attempt to convey their social context. Not everyone in the 12th century lived in a castle and few children in the 19th century ran around in Kate Greenaway costumes.

Except for a convincing and quite bloody glimpse of the Civil War, there is nothing grim in Goodall's history. There are no beggars, no open sewers, no disease-ridden slums, no stocks, no gibbets, no public executions, no plague. It is all too like a church summer fête with a Heritage pageant of Merrie Englande. Children brought up on history like this may feel they were born too late. In fact, they should feel thankful to live in a time of unprecedented luxury, health and freedom.

The most realistic part of the books is when they arrive at the present day. Goodall obviously does not think much of it. For him, it is a hideous mess of traffic, crowds, Bingo halls and snack bars, where housing estates swarm up Castle Hill like a besieging army. If the same realism had been applied to earlier centuries, the books would have been more convincing.

> *Raymond Briggs, "The Good Old Days," in* The Times Educational Supplement, *No. 3848, March 30, 1990, p. B11.*

Nette Hilton

1946-

Australian author of picture books.

Major works include *The Long Red Scarf* (1987), *Dirty Dave, the Bushranger* (1987; U. S. edition as *Dirty Dave*), *A Proper Little Lady* (1990).

Acknowledged for her creation of witty, rollicking tales which treat nonsexist themes in a sympathetic and stylish manner, Hilton features child and adult protagonists in stories both realistic and fantastic which are characterized by their inventive use of language and wry tongue-in-cheek humor. Praised for her observant delineation of characters who perform capably while remaining true to themselves, Hilton is also often noted for her literary style: she presents preschoolers and early readers with succinct texts which incorporate onomatopoeia, sound effects, rhythm, and repetition, elements thought to make her books enjoyable both for personal reading and for reading aloud. Hilton's first book, *The Long Red Scarf,* initiates her signature themes of self-reliance and nonsterotypical behavior as it describes how Grandpa learns to knit, producing both a scarf for himself and one for the family baby; *Dirty Dave, the Bushranger* also features an adult male with a nontraditional talent: the father of a family of highway robbers, Dan provides them with a new—and legal—career when his talent for sewing is discovered. Several of Hilton's books highlight boys and girls who possess self-confidence and ingenuity; perhaps the most popular is *A Proper Little Lady,* which describes how tomboy Annabelle, who attempts to become refined by dressing in formal attire, learns that she can still be "a proper little lady" in jeans and sneakers. In *A Monstrous Story* (1990), Hilton departs from her characteristic prose style by using rhyming couplets to explain how a small girl defeats the monster who is threatening her town. *The Long Red Scarf* was highly commended for the Australian Picture Book of the Year Award in 1988 while *A Proper Little Lady* was shortlisted for the same award in 1990.

TITLE COMMENTARY

The Long Red Scarf (1987)

Take heart all you men who enjoy fishing on crisp cool winter mornings. If you do not already have a big long woolly brightly-coloured scarf to wrap round and round your neck and tuck down onto your chest you can knit one for yourself! Grandpa did! When no help was forthcoming from Great Aunt Maude or Cousin Isobel he took a leaf from his friend Jake's book and knitted himself a long red scarf and one for Baby Susan too! This beautifully written, very non-sexist book is full of, warmth and colour. . . . Every home and library should have a long red scarf for family reading times and fishing excursions!

Judith Hall, in a review of "The Long Red

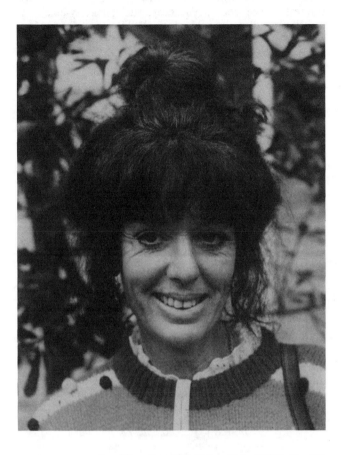

Scarf," in Reading Time, *Vol. XXXI, No. IV, 1987, p. 36.*

There is a great deal of warmth and sympathy in this family story about Grandpa's love of fishing, and his quest to acquire "the biggest, longest, fuzziest scarf in the reddest red in the whole wide world" to keep him warm on cold fishing trips. When Grandpa finds that others can't or won't do it for him, he learns to knit, just as his friend Jake had done, and is then able to knit his own red scarf, together with things for the new baby.

Margaret Power's illustrations are very realistic, and her use of soft pastels to depict minute domestic detail enhances the text. Grandpa and Jake are shown coping with domestic chores like washing and making scones, which underlines the book's themes of old age, loneliness and self sufficiency.

Janeen Webb, in a review of "The Long Red Scarf," in Magpies, *Vol. 3, No. 2, May, 1988, p. 27.*

A fresh story that vibrates with positive energy and that has a sweet, satisfying resolution. . . . The story is quietly told with a rhythm that's calm and calming. There's repetition and a refrain to welcome and snare young readers. Better still is the fact that all of the characters are active, capable, and beyond limitations traditionally accorded to gender and age. Hilton's refusal to acknowledge stereotypes accounts for some of the book's vivacity; [Margaret] Power's lively colored-pencil drawings are responsible for the rest. Those who haven't heard the "clicketty-clack" of knitting needles since Margaret Wild's *Mr. Nick's Knitting* (HBJ, 1989) will receive this book with especially hearty enthusiasm and enjoyment.

> *Liza Bliss, in a review of "The Long Red Scarf," in* School Library Journal, *Vol. 37, No. 3, March, 1991, p. 173.*

Dirty Dave, the Bushranger (1987; U.S. edition as *Dirty Dave*)

A pithy text and watercolors accented with scrawled lines [by Roland Harvey] combine into a picture book that's pure fun. Dirty Dave is an outlaw—he's tough; Sue is his sister—she's rough. But while the duo and their mother rob stagecoaches, their father Dan stays home sewing. Shirts, dresses, curtains, Dan makes them all. One day, in the midst of a robbery, the victims halt in delight. "Who is your tailor?" they demand. Well, the outlaws are abashed, but confess it's Dan. Suddenly, the trio sees a new way to make a fortune, with Dave and Sue as models, and Dan providing the clothes. The last spread shows the family living in luxury, while Dan continues to sew. In a couple of spreads, some of the action is lost in the gutter; but the sprawling artwork is filled with loads of amusing detail and should captivate young eyes. The succinct text may also work for new readers. (pp. 1164-65)

> *Ilene Cooper, in a review of "Dirty Dave," in* Booklist, *Vol. 86, No. 12, February 15, 1990, pp. 1164-65.*

Dirty Dave, the terror of the Australian outback, has a scandalous secret: his father, Dan, likes to sew.. . . . Realizing that there's money to be made here, the gang forsakes highway robbery for high fashion, and soon people are flocking from near and far to purchase Dan's creative couture. Hilton's spare text is deliciously tongue-in-cheek, and the quirky, intricately detailed illustrations—at times reminiscent of Quentin Blake—are full of sly humor.

> *A review of "Dirty Dave," in* Publishers Weekly, *Vol. 237, No. 13, March 30, 1990, p. 60.*

The jacket copy chronicles Australian author Hilton's wish to "give the gentler men their place in history". . . . Hilton's tale is tersely and rhythmically told, with a restrained sense of humor that sets just the right tone for the riotous cartoons of watercolor washes over ink. In a scribbled, energetic style reminiscent of cartoonist Rowland Emmett's, Harvey litters his landscapes with cattle, kangaroos, and an occasional surprise certain to set readers poring over the pages in search of more buried gems. This rollicking tale is thoroughly entertaining, with a clear message to "follow your bliss."

> *Marcia Hupp, in a review of "Dirty Dave," in*

School Library Journal, *Vol. 36, No. 4, April, 1990, p. 91.*

Prince Lachlan (1989)

Prince Lachlan's parents allow their son a free rein as they observe his antics from the sideline with an air of submissive acceptance. But what were they to think when the young lad decided to investigate the aspirations of the greedy Great One living with all his stolen treasures on the other side of Kingdom of Hill?

Nette Hilton has a flair for writing so that stories and reading are fun. No more, no less, but enough that children will enjoy her latest romp and some, especially the spoilt and highly indulged ones, will no doubt relate very well with their young hero. Repetition is well maintained throughout with new "sound" words for the beginning reader to savour. Ann James' jaunty pen and water colour illustrations perfectly match the mood of the text with wacky wit and entertaining characters to attract the 4-6 year olds. (pp. 14-15)

> *Millicent Jones, in a review of "Prince Lachlan," in* Reading Times, *Vol. XXXIII, No. IV, 1989, pp. 14-15.*

This rambunctious royal redhead of the Kingdom of Hill resembles a kilt-wearing human tornado. Prince Lachlan's boisterous good spirits frequently shatter the castle's peace (and possessions), and sorely try his parents' patience. When the royal family learns, however, that the ogreish Great One has designs on the throne, it's Lachlan who saves the day. The frequent sound effects highlighting this caper are sure to delight: "*Shatter* went the window. *Tinkle* went the glass." Chalk up another delectable romp for Australian author Hilton (***Dirty Dave***), whose tongue-in-cheek text is set off splendidly by James's puckish illustrations, chock-full of colorful, unexpected details.

> *A review of "Prince Lachlan," in* Publishers Weekly, *Vol. 237, No. 32, August 10, 1990, p. 442.*

A Monstrous Story (1990)

A rampaging monster is hell bent on devouring the inhabitants of an unnamed village. The story, described by the publisher as a "lovingly, grotesque poem", is written in rhyming couplets which are, on the whole, as oozy as the slimy beast itself.

This humorous tale gathers momentum and with it a clutch of delightfully tricky rhymes. (How many words can you unearth that rhyme with "tourists"?) Can you conceive of what it takes to stop a rampaging monster dead in it's tracks? Can you imagine what the connections between a girl, her cat, her baby brother, a pooey nappy, and a plate of vegetables might be (I suspect not—and if I told you now I'd spoil the story!) Discerning readers will, I'm sure, appreciate the handy hints for simultaneously disposing of unwanted monsters and siblings.

Donni Carter's illustrations are as sprawling and as silly

as the text. They play with perspective in a way that distorts reality and stretches credibility—a perfect match for the text! When all is said and done, the children in bed and monsters vanquished, I am certain that young readers will identify with the message at the heart of this tale . . . EVEN MONSTERS WON'T EAT THEIR VEGIES!!

> *Peter Bansel, in a review of "A Monstrous Story," in* Magpies, *Vol. 5, No. 2, May, 1990, p. 28.*

A Proper Little Lady   (1990)

Cathy Wilcox's art work for **A Proper Little Lady** will undoubtedly be compared with [Bob] Graham's style. True, they both catch character with the stroke of a pencil and convey movement with comic vitality, and both are rich in humour and human observation, but thereafter, they diverge markedly. Wilcox's character, the irrepressible Annabella, stands boldly centre stage, with very little backgrounding and minimal pictorial detail. She is larger than life and ready to take life on, her refined name and proper intentions standing in ironic contrast to her rough and tumble day. The partnership with Nette Hilton is highly successful, the illustrations echoing the text, and the changing sounds of Annabella's deteriorating outfit cleverly bringing an element of surprise to the deliberately repetitive refrain. A captivating, lighthearted book **A Proper Little Lady** has immediate charm and we enjoy it more with each reading. (pp. 22-3)

> *Jenni Connor, in a review of "A Proper Little Lady," in* Magpies, *Vol. 5, No. 2, May, 1990, pp. 22-3.*

A wry look at ladylike deportment with delightfully frenetic illustrations that belie the "propriety" of the lead character's behavior. One day, while peering in the mirror at her flyaway red hair and freckle-covered nose, Annabella Jones decides to be a proper little lady. So she dresses herself in appropriate attire—a dress with a bow, frilly petticoat, shiny black shoes, a long gold chain. Properly bedecked and bejeweled, Annabella swishes and taps her way through her neighborhood, stopping only to rescue a treed cat, instruct two small children in go-cart racing, and join her friends for a quick game of football. She returns home in a bedraggled state, and her mother wisely suggests that it would be easier for Annabella to be a proper little lady in blue jeans and a T-shirt, advice she happily follows. First-time illustrator Wilcox' style is similar to Bob Graham's, although she does lack his technical maturity and economy of line at this point in her career. Her humorous, exaggerated pen-and-ink illustrations brightly washed in watercolor on a plain white background offer visual clues as the story unfolds. A good choice for storytimes, the book has a brief text offering satisfying sound effects and repetition that will enable listeners to anticipate Annabella's next steps.

> *Dorothy Houlihan, in a review of "A Proper Little Lady," in* School Library Journal, *Vol. 36, No. 5, May, 1990, p. 86.*

An amusing, contemporary story that girls particularly will love. Every child has dressed up at some time or another and Annabella Jones does so, page by page with picture on each until she is fully dressed including hat and gloves, and her movements go "swish, swish, swish" (pale blue dress), "tap, tap, tap" (shiny black shoes), "chink, chink, chink" (long gold chain). These words are part of the illustrations in pastel colour wash and lend a vitality to her movements as she parades before the mirror, then goes walking down the street.. . . . A bouncy Australian story for pre-school and lower primary-age children, its spare text, onomatopoeic repetitions (swish, swish, tap, tap, etc) and energetic illustrations will make it a useful addition to any picture storybook collection. (pp. 25-6)

> *Cynthia Anthony, in a review of "A Proper Little Lady," in* Magpies, *Vol. 5, No. 3, July, 1990, pp. 25-6.*

Mollie Hunter

1922-

(Born Maureen McVeigh) Scottish author of fiction and nonfiction.

Major works include *The Kelpie's Pearls* (1964), *The Ghosts of Glencoe* (1966), *A Sound of Chariots* (1972), *The Stronghold* (1974), *A Stranger Came Ashore* (1975).

Often considered Scotland's most distinguished writer for children and young adults, Hunter is celebrated as the author of powerful, memorable novels and stories which profile Scotland in both historical and contemporary times and provide portraits of young people and adults caught up in conflict. Credited with expanding the scope of the historical novel and the fantasy in challenging works considered both universally appealing and essentially Scottish, she is often praised for her skill as a literary stylist and a storyteller, for her ability to evoke place and atmosphere, and for her intimate knowledge of Scottish history, legend, and culture. Hunter is the creator of historical fiction with Scottish backgrounds, fantasy based in Scottish folklore, and realistic fiction with contemporary Scottish settings, works often acknowledged for the brilliance of their writing as well as for the believability of their characterizations. In all of her books, Hunter profiles male and female protagonists who become involved in the struggle between good and evil. Often wreckless in their behavior, her passionate, quick-witted characters prove themselves through courageous acts in both in the natural and supernatural worlds while dealing with difficult, often ambiguous political issues and philosophical questions. Although her works include suffering and death, Hunter stresses such values as loyalty, creativity, truth, and, above all, the redemptive power of love. She writes her books in a brisk, lyrical voice often laced with humor and invests them with a deep affection for her native land as well as with sympathy for the poor and downtrodden.

A self-made scholar, Hunter was forced to leave school in her early teens; her experiences form the basis for two of her most popular books, the autobiographical novel *A Sound of Chariots* and its sequel *The Dragonfly Years* (1983; U. S. edition as *Hold on to Love*). Many of Hunter's works are inspired by her exploration of Scottish folklore and history; in addition to her work as a researcher, Hunter is also an adult novelist, author of nonfiction, and playwright, and has been a producer for and actor in an amateur theater group. Hunter began her career as a writer for children with *Patrick Kentigern Keenan* (1963; U. S. edition as *The Smartest Man in Ireland*), an original folktale that reflects her half-Irish heritage and describes how a mortal cleverly outwits a group of malicious fairies; in her subsequent fantasies, Hunter continues to explore the relationship between humanity and the supernatural world. Characteristically setting these works in such areas as the Orkney and Shetland islands, Hunter integrates such elements as magic, witchcraft, and superstition into descrip-

tions of everyday life and brings her human protagonists into contact with such creatures from Celtic legend as the warlock, the ferlie, and the selkie. She retains her Scottish settings for her historical novels, placing them most frequently in the sixteenth and seventeenth centuries and often referring to the tension between Scotland and England that existed in those times. Hunter uses the form of the romance for such books as *Hi Johnny* (1963), *The Spanish Letters* (1964), and *The Lothian Run* (1970), which share exciting plots often centering on intrigue, and a darker, more serious approach for novels such as *The Ghosts of Glencoe* and *A Pistol in Greenyards* (1965) in which she addresses the tragic Glencoe Massacre of 1692 and the Highland Clearances of 1854; several of her works are also contributions to the mystery and thriller genres. With *The Stronghold,* Hunter recreates the Iron Age society of early Celts on the Orkney Island to describe how Coll, the lame foster son of the island's Druid priest, transcends his handicap and the opposition of the island leaders to successfully design a stone tower to protect his people from Roman slave traders. Hunter is also the author of several novels with twentieth-century settings, most notably *A Sound of Chariots.* In this book, which is set shortly after World War I, Hunter introduces Bridie, a bright, outspoken nine-year-old with a talent for writing who is forced to come to terms with the harsh realities of life when her beloved father dies, leaving her and her family in poverty. *A Sound of Chariots* documents Bridie's growth from the ages of nine to thirteen, a journey which leads her to accept her father's death and her own mortality as well as to better understand her mother. Lauded for its honest portrayal of grief and loss, the novel is also acknowledged as a particularly insightful depiction of the making of a writer. In *The Dragonfly Years,* Hunter portrays Bridie's growing independence and political and social awareness as well as her relationship with a fellow student in the period before the Second World War. In addition to her books for older readers, Hunter is the author of two fantasies for early graders which gently parody the medieval adventure and the courtly romance. Hunter was awarded the Child Study Association Award for *A Sound of Chariots* in 1972 and the Carnegie Medal for *The Stronghold* in 1974. She also received the Scottish Arts Council Literary Award in 1972 and 1977.

(See also *Contemporary Literary Criticism,* Vol. 21; *Something about the Author,* Vols. 2, 54; *Something about the Author Autobiography Series,* Vol. 7; and *Contemporary Authors,* Vols. 29-32, rev. ed.)

AUTHOR'S COMMENTARY

[The following excerpt is from an interview with M. K. in Top of the News.*]*

MK: Your body of work reflects a number of different genres—historical fiction, realistic fiction, and fantasy. Is there one genre which particularly appeals to you?

MH: There's no overriding appeal in any of the various genres I've used. I get a different sort of satisfaction from each—partly because each calls for a technique that's specific to itself and partly because each indulges some aspect of my own nature. In the fantasies, for instance, I'm indulging the dreamy, mystical side of my nature, the side that has always relied on intuition rather than on any reasoning process and that has, consequently, always been attracted to the supernatural; and the technique required to tell a story in these terms relies on a use of language which is simple in itself but is also highly expressive.

I also have a very practical side to my nature, and this comes out in the plot structuring required for my historical novels. These are stories of action where there has to be close integration of incident with the motivation of the various characters, and there has to be a very practical approach to the achievement of this. Welded to this, however, there has to be a very strong sense of theatre, so that—as on the stage—one can build up a scene, highlight it, and then either cut abruptly at a moment of tension or fade down in a way that will tantalise the reader to go on to the next scene. This is something I very much enjoy doing. I used to work a lot in theatre, and I still mentally project in theatre terms for the scenes of my historical novels. But overall in these, of course, the technique called for is still the one that creates the traditional literary form.

That's true also of the books I've so far written in the "re-alistic" vein—although my enjoyment there, I should say, is the very common or garden-variety one of having been able to use personal experience and observations that have lain fallow in my mind over a long period until the opportunity has come to weave them into some story I've had to tell.

MK: Your most recent work, **Hold On to Love,** is a sequel to **A Sound of Chariots.** Why did you decide to continue Bridie's story?

MH: I'd wanted to do so for many years previous to committing myself to the fact. I was aware also that there were many readers who wanted to know more about Bridie; but for me, another book about her wasn't simply a matter of writing a sequel. To write **A Sound of Chariots** had meant going back and reliving all the emotions I had experienced when my father died. I was nine years old then. The event had been traumatic; but by writing **A Sound of Chariots** I had exorcized my ghost and could live at last with my mind at peace. To write further about Bridie, however, taking her on from the age of fourteen where I had left her in the first book, meant going back to a situation where I would again be as vulnerable as I was at that time. And I was afraid of that.

Something else that held me back was that the writing scene for young adults had changed considerably since 1972—the year in which **A Sound of Chariots** was published—and there were many aspects of that scene for which I had no sympathy at all. There's the single-line romance story, which is just like treacle being dripped off the end of a spoon. There's the sex manual, thinly disguised by some stereotyped succession of incidents; and although one must take sexual development into account in any story which takes a character through the adolescent years into adulthood, I felt I owed my readers something a bit better than that.

I've seen them so often, these so-called young adults. They're not, as publishers seem to imagine them to be, around fifteen or sixteen years of age. They're usually not more than twelve or thirteen; but they're girls with the bodies of women, uncomfortably aware of the fact, and yet with a certain small dignity which I find rather touching. That dignity, it seems to me, is an indication that they're aware of themselves as people, aware of the development of their minds as well as the burgeoning of their bodies. They're very conscious of being on the verge of the next significant phase of their lives; and it was my perception of this, I think, that gave me the key to my approach to writing **Hold On to Love** as well as adding an impetus to my desire to tackle that book.

For them, as well as for myself, I knew I had to make it the story of Bridie developing in all the aspects of her nature, the emotional and intellectual as well as the physical; and it was because of the way I had been touched by them, I think, that I finally found the fear of further emotional distress being much outweighed by the strength of my instincts as a writer. (pp. 141-42)

MK: Is there a common theme, or idea, which runs through your books?

MH: All of my books are about conflict. It doesn't matter whether they're fantasies, or historical novels, or realistic novels. At the center of them, there is always a sense of conflict. Throughout them all, there runs a conflict of ideas, with the destructiveness on one side and the creativeness on the other. In effect, it's always the old story of good and evil, and the war between good and evil exists within the human psyche. It's projected through the personalities of the characters.

In my books, this comes out in different ways that relate to the theme of the story. In the fantasies, there is always a confrontation scene, where the human characters are faced with the supernatural characters, who are inimicable to the lives and happiness of the human characters. There is always one enduring aspect of that situation, the one weapon that the humans have against the supernaturals—the capacity to love. The supernaturals by definition are soulless creatures. They cannot understand what it is to love, and they cannot bring their supernatural magical forces to bear on it. If one has that power to love, to sacrifice, to give one's life for another human being—this is something the supernaturals cannot understand.

When it comes to the historical novels, there is always some conflict of ideas in terms of the action of the story, but again it's always a question of people having to make up their minds on which side they're going to stand. In *You Never Knew Her As I Did,* which is simply the true story of the escape of Mary Queen of Scots from her island prison, the sixteen-year-old page who finally organizes the escape has got to come to terms with his own nature. He is selfish, he is careless, he is conceited, and he doesn't care about anybody except himself. Then he is faced with the result of his own behavior and made to realize exactly what he has done, what has happened as a result of his carelessness, his conceitedness, and his selfishness. He's got to live with himself, and the only way he can live with himself is to amend some of the harm that he has done. The conflict of ideas, the war between good and evil in the human psyche—this is the thread that runs all through my books. (p. 144)

MK: What are you trying to achieve in your writing?

MH: I'm just trying to express myself in the way that seems best suited to me. I don't think there should be any other reason for writing. Markets, or the current fad, certainly shouldn't enter into it, nor should ambition. I certainly think that every writer should be striving to produce the classics of his or her particular day. It's the only way to fully realise whatever talent one has. But just think of the millions of books that are written! One would have to be superbly good—or very lucky—to have even one work survive as a classic of its kind.

There's a driving force for me in all this, of course, and that is my native impulse to tell a story. But again of course, one cannot do that in print without having learned the disciplines of a writer; and as soon as one becomes locked into these disciplines, when they become one's life, in effect, there is an inevitable interweaving of one's personal philosophy with what is written. This is what gives a story depth. It's what enables one to create rounded characters with complications of personality that lead to the essential meshing of characterization and incident. Because that's not something one could do in a vacuum of personal experience, or lacking a philosophy bred from that experience. At its lowest, then, what I'm trying to achieve with my writing is just to entertain. At its highest, my writing is an attempt to create form and beauty and maybe a grain or so of truth out of my personal chaos. Usually I fall between two stools and succeed only in producing a readable story. That's not much to achieve, it's true; but if it gives some lasting pleasure to any reader, anywhere, I'll not quarrel with it. (p. 146)

> *Mollie Hunter and M. K., in an interview in* Top of the News, *Vol. 41, No. 2, Winter, 1985, pp. 141-46.*

GENERAL COMMENTARY

Sam Leaton Sebesta and William J. Iverson

Quite different [than the fantasies of Joan Aiken] is the light fantasy of Mollie Hunter. Her *Thomas and the Warlock* has a funny cast of adults ridding their land of witchcraft. In *The Haunted Mountain* a foolish man is enslaved by the fairy "Good People" and then rescued by his son and dog. But Hunter attempts the rich, rhythmical style of the Scottish storyteller and a thematic depth not quite consistent with her playful plots. In *The Walking Stones* a modern boy summons his own double, a mysterious Co-Walker, to foil three modern industrialists who would destroy ancient monuments. The past must give way, the new generation must supplant the old one, the unknown must be confronted—these are heavy themes caught in a light structure. (p. 212)

> *Sam Leaton Sebesta and William J. Iverson, "Fanciful Fiction," in their* Literature for Thursday's Child, *Science Research Associates, Inc., 1975, pp. 177-214.*

Paul Heins

In *A Sound of Chariots,* Mollie Hunter tells how Bridie McShane, overwhelmed by grief at the death of her father, became suddenly, instantly aware of her physical surroundings, "because through all her senses she was filtering into their component parts the whole vast complex of smells and sounds, shapes, colors and textures through which she moved." And she realized that she too must one day die, and her fear of death became intensified "by the fear of the passage of Time along the way."

From the various allusions to Mollie's own childhood experiences in **"Talent Is Not Enough,"** it becomes obvious that *A Sound of Chariots* is autobiographical. But more significant is Mollie Hunter's observation that "the range of a child's emotion has the same extent as that of an adult, and all the child lacks, by comparison, is the vocabulary to match his range." Bridie's emotions and experiences were obviously Mollie's own emotions and experiences, recollected—not necessarily in tranquillity, but certainly with intensity and with a hard-won power to convey that intensity in words. . . . (pp. ix-x)

Although Mollie Hunter's stories are rooted in Scottish soil and history, the range of her fiction is wide-reaching in its sweep and universality. . . . It is worth recalling what some of [her] accomplishments are. *The Lothian Run* and *A Pistol in Greenyards* suggest the novels of Sir Walter Scott for the richness of their historical and narrative textures, and in many ways they are more immediate in their present-day appeal than the works of her great predecessor. *The Kelpie's Pearls, Thomas and the Warlock,* and *A Stranger Came Ashore* are extended narratives developed from the fantasy often implicit in folklore. *A Sound of Chariots* is realistic, intense, immediate. (p. xii)

> *Paul Heins, in an introduction to* Talent Is Not Enough: Mollie Hunter on Writing for Children, *Harper & Row, Publisher, 1976, pp. ix-xiii.*

Peter Hollindale

Mollie Hunter is by general consent Scotland's most distinguished modern children's writer. Scotland is the setting for almost all her stories, and they are rooted almost exclusively in Scots folklore and history. . . . Yet she now enjoys an international reputation, and is read with pleasure not only in her own country or by the offspring of expatriate Scots, but by legions of young children whose prior knowledge of Celtic legend is nonexistent, and by older readers whose acquaintance with Scots history is at best rudimentary.

Whether or not one actually finds this puzzling, it raises a delicate matter which any appraisal of Mollie Hunter's work must start by facing. The fact is that one cannot talk about Mollie Hunter without talking about Scotland. If one finds her work parochial, one finds Scotland parochial. If one is surprised by the international interest shown in her work (given, of course, that it has the major intrinsic qualities that I for one believe it has) one is surprised that Scotland itself should be so interesting. The general idea that a confined setting means a confined range of interest was obviously laid to rest long ago. . . . But somehow the notion persists for some readers that Mollie Hunter's subjects should by all the rules be indigenous, provincial, and abstruse, yet have somewhat eccentrically turned out not to be.

The opposite is true. On the one hand, she has at the disposal of her considerable scholarship the folklore, history, and culture of a nation: she is not a regional—but is a national—writer, and it is in her work that children can find the fullest recent expression of the legend and history which make Scots culture distinctive. On the other hand, she has achieved this without being at all eccentric, difficult, or insular. The chosen geographical bounds of her fiction are narrow, yet they reach to distant horizons. Her 'Scottishness' (even allowing that by birth she is half Irish and that one of her best books is the very Irish *Patrick Kentigern Keenan*) is uncompromising, but it is not limiting: it is also open, hospitable and generous towards readers who are not Scottish, combining an imagination which is charged by the historic energy of a precise locale with a humane moral intelligence that seeks always to be accessible and understood.

The combination is admirable. It is also—if the impertinent generalisation can be pardoned—typically Scots. . . . Here the whole strength of Scots literary tradition is on her side, and without inferring direct 'influences,' it is not hard to see how it has aided her. First, the historical novel is one of its established forms and glories, not as in England a kind of subliterature which has never fully severed the umbilical cord which binds it to 'escapist' romance. This does not mean that it is free of technical problems: each writer must confront and resolve these anew. Mollie Hunter acknowledges her awareness of this in her revealing essay **'The Last Lord of Redhouse Castle,'** where she discusses the problems of writing historical novels for children: 'the first being the one peculiar to Scottish writers in this field—how to set the scene in a country whose history is unknown to non-Scottish children.' But it does enable her to use the form with all the confidence and flexibility of a writer who knows that her national tradition fosters and respects it.

Second, and this is important for a writer who, like Mollie Hunter, is repeatedly concerned with witchcraft and the supernatural, Scots writing has a long history of concern with such phenomena. Indeed, it is a matter of history that witchcraft, as the object of fearful superstition and punitive law, remained a serious issue in Scotland much longer than it did in Britain as a whole. Stories of the supernatural are not, as they tend to be in England and America, a kind of deviant occasional writing for major authors (like *The Turn of the Screw*), and the special preoccupation of minor eccentrics like M. R. James; instead they are serious and central events in a writer's work, like Stevenson's *Dr Jekyll and Mr Hyde* or his story 'Thrawn Janet.' More particularly, the supernatural is not something which intrudes upon the human world only in response to evil or reckless invocation: it is omnipresent and close at hand, hidden from human awareness only by the lightest of shadows. Perilous and rash transactions between the human and the supernatural have never, perhaps, been so brilliantly depicted as they are in that neglected masterpiece, Hogg's *Private Memoirs and Confessions of a Justified Sinner,* a work which is deeply concerned with self-destructive bigotry. A strong available tradition of this kind is clearly helpful to a modern writer like Mollie Hunter, whose historical novel **The Thirteenth Member** is also powerfully concerned with witchcraft and with bigotry, and whose 'fantasies' for younger readers touch constantly on the nearness and unsummoned energies of the supernatural.

Both technically and thematically, then, Mollie Hunter's work is assisted by a long and distinguished national tradition. She is helped, too, by its profound respect for the craft of storytelling. It is not uncommon for the storyteller to appear in some form, often very subtly, as a participant in his own stories; writers as diverse in period and kind as Henryson and Hogg do this. At less-complicated levels of narrative procedure, the Scots novel is full of experiments in first-person storytelling and in identification of author and hero. For Mollie Hunter these have been particularly conscious problems—in achieving the special narrative 'voice' of the fantasies, and in judging the control of first-person narrative, or the correct 'distance' between author and protagonist, in the historical novels. *A Pistol in Greenyards,* for instance, uses a 'double' first person narrative, through which the boy hero tells the story himself telling his story. The seeming oversubtlety of this method is justified both by the greater depth of insight we gain into the boy himself, and by the enhanced attention to some appalling events which is produced by our prior knowledge of their final outcome. This is the careful craftsmanship of a professional writer, but it is also the product of a tradition which regards stories highly as a means of transmitting simultaneous diversion and wisdom. That Mollie Hunter herself regards stories in this way is made clear through such characters, amongs others, as *The Bodach* in the story of that title, and Old Da' in *A Stranger Came Ashore.*

Linked closely to such respect for the storyteller's craft is the absence, in Scots literature, of a clearcut division between 'adult' and 'children's' literature such as exists elsewhere. Mollie Hunter has described, again in 'The Last Lord of Redhouse Castle,' how she came belatedly to discover herself as a children's writer, and her reasons for continuing to address her historical novels to children. But she does not speak of it as some kind of comedown, a half-regretted second best, or something which needs to be *defended* rather than explained. There is a professional certainty about her work which comes, I can only suppose, of writing in a secure tradition which respects children's literature, which acknowledges the adult reader's continuing need for tales, and which has produced a remarkable number of stories which belong to both children and adults alike and appeal exclusively to neither.

What, then, have her gifts and good fortune so far achieved? Her work falls broadly into three sections: the historical novels, the fantasies, and (so far unique in her work) the autobiographical novel *A Sound of Chariots.* It may be helpful to look at each 'group' in turn, since my own view of their relative success does not, I suspect, accord entirely with the general one.

The historical novels are diverse, both in subject and narrative tone. Admittedly, certain preoccupations tend to recur in them. For example, several refer to the tension, not always hostile but always uneasy and ambivalent, in relations between Scotland and England. Again, they show a passionate concern for the poor, the neglected, the dispossessed, the underdogs. Both of these concerns are also present in *A Sound of Chariots,* and insofar as a coherent political mood is discernible in her writing, it perhaps has more to do with the fierce humanitarian socialism so ardently celebrated in that novel, rather than with anything specifically national.

In general, however, it is the diversity that needs to be stressed. The historical novels themselves fall into three groups. Three of them—*Hi Johnny, The Spanish Letters,* and *The Lothian Run*—I would term romances. They have serious themes, certainly, and they do not romanticise history, but the basic emphasis is on the vigorous development of stirring blood-and-thunder plots. Three others have a sharper historical focus and a more-searching investigation of human behaviour in crisis: they each involve, in Mollie Hunter's own words, 'a much deeper ex-

ploration into the themes of courage and conscience.' *The Thirteenth Member* is not affixed to any one notorious historical event, but in its depiction of innocent children trapped between the opposing cruelties of diabolism and superstitious repression—between the witch and witch-finder—it has much in common with *The Ghosts of Glencoe* and *A Pistol in Greenyards.* Here too, in the recreated tragedies of the Glencoe Massacre and the Highland Clearances, young people are snared by forces more powerful than themselves, and must try against the odds to obey the dictates of conscience and keep their bravery alight.

Finally and most recently there is *The Stronghold.* In some respects this book has themes in common with the more 'serious' historical novels mentioned above: it deals with conflicting loyalties; it explores questions of belief and heresy; it presents the realities of power and the plight of the weak; it too isolates the young and tests their wits and courage to the utmost. In this way it develops basic preoccupations in Mollie Hunter's work. But this novel has a new historical dimension and a new, important theme. Its setting, a primitive Orcadian community in Roman times, living a tribal existence under the religious domination of the Druids, is far more remote in time and place, far less documented, than anything Mollie Hunter has previously attempted, and places a different kind of demand on her historical imagination. And in its hypothesis concerning the origins of the 'brochs'—those extraordinary stone structures which are the 'strongholds' of the novel's title—the story explores the marvellous excitement of inaugural acts of imagination: those moments when history is altered by a single original mind. This is the novel's particular achievement—its utterly plausible and moving account of slow, meticulous, and brilliant innovation, a massive act of intellect and will. The historical depth of the novel is enormously enhanced by its reverence for this long-ago event. Coll, creator of the brochs, himself sees them as dispatches to the unknown future, transmitting their message even when their practical usefulness is outlived: 'even then they would still stand for a wonder and a sign of those who had lived long ago. The dream would last.' Through Coll's vision past and present are united. Through the novel we reach out to make contact with our unnamed ancestors. In this way the book is a very impressive achievement.

In other respects, however, the book is perhaps rather less successful. It clearly prompts comparison with the work of Rosemary Sutcliff, not least because its hero, like so many of hers, is a cripple who wins his place in the sun under dreadful handicap. As a total atmospheric recreation of distant times it is less convincing than Rosemary Sutcliff's work usually is. It seems, too, incompletely imagined and structurally flawed, for reasons I should like to reapproach by way of the earlier historical novels.

To return, then, to the 'romances.' . . . Each boy [In *The Spanish Letters* and *The Lothian Run*] is rewarded for loyalty and for that combination of virtues which Mollie Hunter so often links admiringly: 'courage and cunning.' Courage alone is never enough for her; without quick-wittedness and subtlety it is next to worthless. This delight in mental agility as well as physical daring is characteristic of all Mollie Hunter's work. It is refreshing and realistic, but it also raises problems.

In *The Spanish Letters* the problems are negligible. Any moral scruples for Jamie, as a Scottish boy, in serving an English master are resolved by the convenient fact that his own King James VI will shortly be king of both countries. But *The Lothian Run* is a more-complicated issue, and demands a more-complicated plot—a double plot, involving both Jacobite intrigue and smuggling. Here the rights and wrongs are less clearcut, and one cannot help feeling that the smuggling plot is adroitly used to divert attention from Jacobite and Hanoverian politics. The English master whom Sandy serves is, after all, a Customs Officer, and only by chance a political agent. (Attention is further diverted from the straight dynastic conflict by the fact that the chief Jacobite agent is not a committed Stuart loyalist but a cruel, unprincipled mercenary.) In this way contentious political matters, which Mollie Hunter is understandably reluctant to simplify, are instead evaded, and the unambiguous rights and wrongs of smuggling placed in their stead.

The trouble is that these rights and wrongs are *not* unambiguous except in law. Part of Sandy Maxwell's duties on 'secondment' to the Customs Service is to mingle with the fisherfolk of Prestonpans, helping them to repair their boats.

In this way he can eavesdrop on their talk, and draw them into indiscretions. His first target is the fisherman Rob Grierson. This is all very well in the impersonal world of law enforcement. But Sandy's world is not impersonal. Admittedly, he can expect little mercy if his activities are discovered. Nevertheless, these are men whom Sandy has known from childhood, men to whom his mother owes her cherished dish of untaxed tea, men who, so far as their wariness allows, are his friends. When Rob suggests that Sandy's apprentice work may have made him too proud to help with the boat-repairing, he replies: 'Ach, lawyer's work is a dull thing compared to this ploy, Rob! . . . Forbye, you can see I have not lost the skill you taught me in the school holidays!' Later on, Sandy is directly responsible for Rob's capture and imprisonment.

We know that the exploitation of friendships is a time-honoured ruse of efficient law-enforcement. All the same, it is difficult not to feel distaste for Sandy's behaviour here, while also feeling that one is expected to admire its skill and daring. (pp. 109-14) . . .

[Much of Mollie Hunter's dialogue in the historical novels] is intensely dramatic—contentious, suspicious, watchful. Even so, the subtleties of Sandy Maxwell remain questionable, and with them there remains the possibility that Mollie Hunter, in celebrating certain intellectual and moral qualities with such impressive vigour and conviction, tends to overlook other aspects of behaviour, and hence to condone the unpardonable.

The same kind of tension between simple values and complex behaviour is also apparent in Mollie Hunter's love of double meanings. She is clearly fascinated by equivocation and ambiguity. This is another aspect of 'courage and cunning,' and it is the resource of good characters as well as bad. (p. 114)

To return to *The Stronghold,* here we have more double meanings. In the first part of the novel a power struggle takes place between the tribal chief, Nectan, and the Chief Druid, Domnall, and the reader's sympathies are clearly aligned with Nectan. In the aftermath of Domnall's uneasy victory comes his terrible counterstroke, the choice of Nectan's daughter Fand to be the virgin sacrifice at the sunrise festival of Beltane. Coll, whose brilliant mind conceived the brochs, is Fand's foster-brother and lover, and he conceives the further idea of saving her. To do this he need only disrupt the festival enough to delay Fand's death beyond the sacred moment of sunrise, and, having contrived disturbance of the ceremony by fostering doubts of Fand's virginity, he finally achieves his purpose with the superb ambiguous confession: 'I have spoiled the sacrifice.' This is cleverly and bravely done, for love.

However, a consequence of the Beltane festival (in itself an impressive and moving set-piece action) is the transformation of Domnall from enemy to ally. Aversion is abruptly converted to sympathy; religious tyrant becomes aged hero and sage. In itself the change is too sudden and extreme. But it also leaves unresolved the question of Domnall's choice of Fand as the Beltane sacrifice. Was this indeed a choice made by the gods themselves, and mediated through Domnall as their priest? Or was it Domnall's own vindictive revenge on Nectan and his tribe? Or was it a skilful manoeuvre to gain political power? All these are possibilities. When Coll asks him, this is his reply: 'I live close with the gods, but even I cannot always know their will. My duty is therefore a difficult one, but I must still try to do it for the good of all, and thus I have always tried.' And, as Coll realises, there is 'no answer to that . . . no answer except argument, for Domnall's words could be taken to mean anything anyone wanted them to mean.' At this it is left to rest. But it means that the whole distribution of sympathies in the novel, fundamental questions of faith and doubt which it has raised, the whole movement of the plot at the Beltane festival, are left unresolved in a cloud of devious ambiguity. For all its power, the novel thus lacks imaginative wholeness, and its fragile unity rests instead on mere verbal equivocation.

This points, I think, to a self-damaging conjunction of skills in Mollie Hunter's historical novels. They rest, in the end, on a few very simple, very profound values: courage, loyalty, initiative, truth, creative intelligence, and above all on love. Yet their superstructure depends on quite different terms of reference: on the realities of political intrigue and struggles for power, on expediency, on ruthless service to a cause, on ambition and opportunism, on equivocation and duplicity. I do not suggest that Mollie Hunter *approves* of all these things, only that she recognizes their prevalence. The result is a certain imaginative discordancy and moral inconsistency. Two sets of values coexist in unreconciled confusion. Only *The Spanish Letters* and *The Thirteenth Member* (for differing reasons) are entirely cohesive. Of the other novels, *A Pistol in Greenyards* and *The Stronghold* in particular are very impressive works in many ways, and all the stories have their merits. But Mollie Hunter has yet to write a historical novel which is fully commensurate with her gifts.

The fantasies are a different matter entirely.

In this group of stories, which take as their theme the relationship between humankind and the many supernatural beings of Celtic myth, we find a narrative form under immaculate, almost flawless control. The books have much in common. In all of them a child or an adolescent has a crucial role to play—'children see with the eyes of truth'—and even when the child is the hapless victim of adult folly, like Kieron in *Patrick Kentigern Keenan,* he has moments of wisdom beyond the reach of his parents. Usually, however, the child has insights which are closed to adults, and with his understanding comes the need for a resolute courage in facing dangers which he alone knows to exist, or which he alone must undergo. In these stories it is a great happiness to be young, but it is also a solemn and momentous responsibility.

A conspiracy of vision commonly exists between the young and the old, for the old too have insight into the dangers of supernatural magic, but lack the strength to avert them. Sometimes the power of the old is itself magical, sometimes it is simply the ripeness of human wisdom. Whichever it is, it can mean the end of human life. Death is not excluded from the compassionate humanism of these magical stories: Morag MacLeod, in *The Kelpie's Pearls* chooses the end of a life which has no more peace to offer her; *The Bodach* (the old man) sacrifices his life for young Donald, the youthful inheritor of his magical gifts; Old Da', in *A Stranger Came Ashore,* dies and bequeaths both knowledge and responsibility to his child-likeness, his young grandson Robbie. Natural rhythms of youthful strength and aged weakness, of growth and decay, co-exist in the stories with the unearthly everlastingness of the nonhuman world.

Between young and old are the grown men and women, often deprived of the wisdom which belongs to elders and children. The parents, like Peter and Janet in *A Stranger Came Ashore,* or the Campbells in *The Bodach,* are often good-natured and well-meaning, but unsuspicious of strangeness or danger. They are frequently more childlike than their children. This is especially true of those three reckless heroes of stories which resemble each other closely in theme, structure and feeling: Patrick in *Patrick Kentigern Keenan,* Thomas the blacksmith in *Thomas and the Warlock,* and MacAllister in *The Haunted Mountain.* All three are rash enough to challenge the malignant powers of magic; all three owe their final happiness to the reciprocal love between father and son; all three depend above all on their love of their wives, and the faithful, patient, and forgiving love they receive in return. Each of the three stories moves with relentless inevitability towards a climactic battle with the imprisoning forces of magic: these are titanic scenes, and in each of them the human victory is won by love, the redemptive emotion of mortals, which the timeless supernatural can neither feel nor understand.

The value of love is most-explicitly asserted in another, quieter triumph of mortal over fairyland, that of Hob Ha-

zeldene in *The Ferlie,* as he rejects the seductive promise of immortality in the ferlie world. . . . (pp. 115-17)

The otherworld magic is usually malign, though often it is also weirdly beautiful. Magic power invested in human beings can be benevolent, as it is in the Bodach, or malignant, as it is in Goody Cunningham in *The Ferlie,* or dangerously enigmatic, as with the Skeelie Woman in *The Haunted Mountain,* or Yarl Corbie in *A Stranger Came Ashore.* The supernatural is very close to the human world and may choose to meddle with it. For human beings to seek it out is dangerous folly, because the potential cost is their humanness itself—a humanness characterised especially by courage, and uniquely by love.

The matter of these stories accords completely with the manner of their telling. The narrative comes essentially from a *speaking* voice of distinctive quality. It is matter-of-fact and brisk, daring the reader (or listener) to find anything implausible in its strange tales; it is confidential and intimate; but it is also spare and economical, almost bardic in its adroit and dignified simplicity; and it is full of humour and full of music, not least the music of Gaelic idiom and sentence-forms. These diverse qualities merge, with remarkable consistency and control, to express a wide span of moods and emotions within a taut narrative structure. This style is an extraordinary achievement: one example of the effects it allows is the characteristic undulation of mood which occurs near the end of several of the stories. That is a smooth and delicate transition from sorrow and wistfulness to acceptance and joy. *The Kelpie's Pearls* has it to perfection; so do *The Haunted Mountain* and *The Bodach.*

At the end, too, there is often a quiet distancing of the action, a mood not unlike that at the close of 'The Eve of St. Agnes':

> 'ages long ago / These lovers fled away into the storm.'

Wider perspectives of time are allowed to absorb the events we have witnessed, enclosing them in the span of a lifetime, as in *A Stranger Came Ashore,* or a large and hopeful future, as in *The Bodach,* or the passage of lost generations, as in *The Haunted Mountain.* Time, like love, is the human element, an essential condition of our nature and worth.

Mollie Hunter's fantasies, and above all *The Haunted Mountain,* are in my judgement one of the outstanding and most-original achievements of contemporary children's fiction.

Last, and unique in her work, is *A Sound of Chariots.* It is an extraordinary novel, avowedly autobiographical, and of all her works the one least-sensibly labelled a 'children's book.' It is for children, certainly, if they are mature enough to cope with its relentless emotional honesty and the dark valley of childhood tragedy through which it passes. It is for adults equally: a far better, more accomplished, more demanding book than most novels of childhood published with an adult readership in view.

The patterning of the novel is an act of mature imagination. It opens with the central, cataclysmic event: the death in her mid-childhood of Bridie McShane's beloved father. The first half of the novel then reapproaches that moment of shattering bereavement; the second explores its aftermath. This structure invests many moments and episodes with searing irony, or haunting sadness, or almost unbearable pain. Through the shaping process of retrospect Mollie Hunter can also trace the pattern of Bridie's growth: her developing love and command of language, her fierce independence and stubbornness, the rebellious passion for justice that she inherits from her father. She can also highlight the crucial incidents which decide the wider pattern. It is this act of retrospective imagination which transforms the fiction of memory from mere reminiscence to art. And through it we can see the origins of those central themes and energies which inform her other work. As Edwin Muir put it, 'Our first intuition of the world expands into vaster and vaster images, creating a myth which we act almost without knowing it.'

It would be wrong to present *A Sound of Chariots* as a uniformly painful book. It is often very funny, and Bridie's turbulent, youthful spirit provides a counterpoint against the weight of loss and grief. All the same, its central subject is mortality, its central emotion Bridie's obsessive consciousness, having lost her father, with the passage of time and her own inevitable death. Within the mature patterning of the novel—and because of it—we are made vividly intimate with the youthful Bridie, and share with her the appalling clarity of initial experience. The awareness of death the hunter, time the executioner, she finds at last articulated for her in Marvell's lines:

> 'But at my back I always hear / Time's wingèd chariot hurrying near.'

She goes forward from childhood, aware of so much life to be lived, so many words to be written, pursued by a sound of chariots. The novel which emerges from it is powerful, deeply felt, beautifully written, and starkly memorable.

To borrow another phrase from that same poem by Marvell, Scotland has given Mollie Hunter 'world enough, and time.' It is a sufficient canvas for her very distinguished work, and its historical and mythical depths have provided her with that deep time-perspective by which she has remained obsessed. There is an undertone of fateful sadness running through her novels, sadness with which the vibrant energies of youth and the spirit of human love must always find the courage to contend. Perhaps another Scots writer, Neil M. Gunn, supplies in his novel *Butcher's Broom* an appropriate closing image for her work: 'In the centre of this gloom was the fire, and sitting round it, their knees drawn together, their heads stooped, were the old woman, like fate, the young woman, like love, and the small boy with the swallow of life in his hand.' (pp. 117-19)

> Peter Hollindale, "World Enough and Time: The Work of Mollie Hunter," in Children's Literature in education, *Vol. 8, No. 3, Autumn, 1977, pp. 109-19.*

Stanley Cook

[Mollie Hunter] is a most compelling storyteller, yet some-

times one senses she is having a butterfly's troubles with its chrysalis in her use of the formulas of children's fiction. *A Sound of Chariots* is an emotional autobiography apparently and an apologia—and beyond middle school readers. In it her heroine, Bridie, a poet and a rebel, becomes a shop assistant. That is the intriguing thing about the work of Mollie Hunter: how her powerful imagination 'strikes its being into bounds' and relates itself to literary conventions. I won't say that there are not two or three of her books where correlation seems to me inadequate, but often you suspect that the porter carrying your bags is an Olympic weightlifter: no wonder he does an ordinary job so well yet evidently needs extending.

The movement of Mollie Hunter's work is from the historical to the supernatural, to an Old Testament position where natural and supernatural rub shoulders in daily life. In *A Stranger Came Ashore* the king of the undersea Selkie folk comes ashore—and helps with the farming; in *The Stronghold* druid and chief struggle for political power—and the druid cripples a man's arm by his curse. The position is given in terms of the 'old religion' that Christianity superseded, but its exponents have the intensity of John Bunyan; the young men dream dreams and the old men see visions and the latter are in effect the Law and the Prophets. The penetration of ordinary life by the supernatural in earlier days requires, one can argue, this kind of presentation in order to provide an authentic picture. It is necessary even if we do not think it is literally true. As Connal Ross says to Dr Andrew Hamilton in *A Pistol in Greenyards:*

> 'Oh, so it is culture you call it, then!' Mocking him I was, by this time. 'We have simpler names than that for telling stories and making poems.'

There, no doubt, speaks Mollie Hunter. In practice, she writes too well not to achieve 'willing suspension of disbelief'.

It would not be artistically tactful, though sometimes historically possible, for her to introduce Christianity largely or positively. The Devil, as St Paul tells us, believes and fears and he is the most prominent Christian (in a sense) that she allows to appear. But how much does he really appear? Real powers of evil for witches and warlocks can be granted only on Christian terms: therefore with continued tact Mollie Hunter presents witchcraft mainly as fraud and delusion that are only too human. Compare her *The Thirteenth Member* and Shakespeare's *Macbeth,* which both use the account of the exposure of witchcraft in the sixteenth-century *Newes from Scotland,* to see how she explains as politics what Shakespeare suggests is supernatural. To her, witchcraft is to the old religion as pornography is to love stories; and as with pornography people are in it for gain. Thus witchcraft in Mollie Hunter's work is part of her *historical* fiction: her folk tales deal with the imaginative appeal of the supernatural; her stories of witchcraft with the social significance of a superstition.

To look, therefore, at her historical starting point: this is where she both writes to a formula and transcends it. It is the formula, often found in historical fiction for children, of complication to the climax of capture followed by

Hunter (seated far left) at age nine with her brothers and sisters.

escape and resolution in pursuit. It is most obvious in the early *Hi Johnny,* where the kings of Scotland and the gypsies serve for Richard I home from the Crusades and Robin Hood respectively. It tends to write the story, though an exciting one, in *The Lothian Run,* for the hero's psychology is neglected so that he slips into becoming something of a secret police cadet who denounces the smuggler who delivers his mother's tea. *The Spanish Letters* seems to me a much happier version of *The Lothian Run:* its opening is reminiscent of Scott's method where once a stranger has arrived in town action proceeds nonstop. It has a lighter touch than Scott's in using convincing antiquarianism to set the scene. There were the genes of James Bond in Edinburgh in the sixteenth century!

It is unusual for a children's novel to put superstitions so much in historical perspective as does *The Thirteenth Member,* . . . a gripping book but rather grim and definitely, I should say, for thirteen plus. Here and in *The Ghosts of Glencoe* there is, outside any formula, historical fact which has aroused Mollie Hunter's imagination. The choice of historical fact makes *The Ghosts of Glencoe* inevitably parallel to *Kidnapped,* a position it can sustain, for it is a moving story, better in my opinion than *The Stronghold,* which received a Carnegie Medal, and a near-classic. Again I should locate its likely reader at thirteen plus.

[*The Stronghold*] proceeds with the dignity of a medal-winner, i.e. perhaps a shade too educationally when chiefs are not making political capital out of fighting wild boars on foot and single-handed. (It centres, educationally

enough, on the invention of the broch, 'an idea springing from a single brilliant mind'.) Perhaps it is contemporary troubles that make me feel friction over nineteenth-century enclosures in *A Pistol in Greenyards* is rather journalistic. In both these books Mollie Hunter remains the born storyteller and they are successful realisations of interesting periods of history, but I think she does not make quite the clean lift of the story that one comes to expect from her.

Noteworthy achievement though her historical novels are, the form in which Mollie Hunter's Celtic powers move most sweetly and with an inevitability is the folk tale, about the old religion, the little people and, usually, the remoter parts of Scotland. She is the kind of traditional storyteller to whom she herself keeps referring. Above all she *sounds* like one.

I particularly admire *Patrick Kentigern Keenan* and *The Bodach.* For youngest middle school children her stories, linked to come to a climax through varied moods, of Patrick Kentigern Keenan, 'the smartest man in all Ireland', seem to me faultless. Patrick is a comic version of that tangling with the little people of which Yeats's Red Hanrahan is a tragic version. He is, to use the characteristic Irish fairy tale ending, 'living to this very day'. *The Haunted Mountain* is another version of such a battle of wits, where the man who tangles with the little people is not quite so effervescent a character as Patrick and the interest shifts to the hazards of nights on the bare mountain, as is appropriate, for the mountain is more than the scene of a story: 'It was footsteps he could hear, he realised; the kind of long, slow, heavy steps that could be made only by one creature—An Ferla Mor.' Wordsworth was in a boat when a mountain came after him with just the same stride. In *The Kelpie's Pearls* the forceful man who tangles with supernature transfers from the role of hero to that of downright villain. The shift is plausible; there is a moving ending; it is another fine story.

The Bodach is a folk tale set against a hydro-electric scheme: a success and therefore something of a *tour de force*. To combine successfully two such apparently dissimilar elements as modern technology and Highland legend especially requires the charming *sound* I have referred to. 'He lived in a green glen deep among the mountains of the Scottish Highlands, and he was very old' could not bear to have the comma altered. 'I see three men coming to this house, and these three men have but one name between them' has an 'And-the-stars-in-her-hair-were-seven' sound about it. *The Bodach* is delivered direct to the reader. From a practical point of view—and I will make no invidious comparisons—Mollie Hunter's use of her poetic ear to dispense with description must make a great difference when these stories are read to a class.

In Mollie Hunter's most recent book, *The Wicked One,* the hero's temper comes easily to the boil: the reader—or especially the classroom listener—will be pleased with the way in which he keeps coming forward against that four-armed superheavyweight, the Grollican. In fact, I have my doubts about the need to add the sub-plot of his affair with a fairy woman. *The Wicked One* does extend the Mollie Hunter reader's knowledge of the old religion to include the Robin-Goodfellowish type of being 'Who in one night hath threshed the corn / That ten day-labourers could not end', but I felt that, while the story maintained a grip, it was not with as powerful magic as the folk tales I have criticised in my previous two paragraphs. I felt the same about *Thomas and the Warlock.* It ends with witchcraft, something I think Mollie Hunter does not believe in, and she does not make me believe in it either. On the other hand, while I was reading *A Stranger Came Ashore* I felt that its legend was history. This book resembles, but with a different balance, *The Stronghold:* in the latter the supernatural is part of daily life, but in *A Stranger Came Ashore* daily life is part of the supernatural.

The folk tales probably work up through the whole middle school range, in the order: *Patrick Kentigern Keenan; Thomas and the Warlock, The Haunted Mountain, The Kelpie's Pearls* and *The Wicked One; The Bodach;* and *A Stranger Came Ashore.*

Altogether I feel that while some of Mollie Hunter's books are especially memorable—*Patrick Kentigern Keenan, The Bodach* and *The Ghosts of Glencoe* for me—it is the mind behind them that is most compelling. The idea of her chosen landscape alive with people and itself alive is gospel to her. (pp. 108-11)

> *Stanley Cook, "Mollie Hunter," in* The School Librarian, *Vol. 26, No. 2, June, 1978, pp. 108-11.*

Patricia Dooley

"I just like the sensation of wandering back into the past. It's like a country that I have come to know. I like walking back through the past and coming back into my own time with a good story to tell." Mollie Hunter's self-confessed love of history and folklore, and her delight in story, are the two salient (and complementary) features of her work, work which marks her as perhaps the foremost writer for children in Scotland today. She has produced almost twenty books since 1963, all but two of them characterized by either a period setting or a traditional form. But both types share the basic components of "past" and "story"—the historical novels employ traditional patterns of narrative, while the tales summon up a persistent and powerful past—only the proportion, or the emphasis, differs.

Even the two exceptions noted above participate in this pattern, though in a unique way. *A Sound of Chariots* is semiautobiographical: a "story" about Mollie Hunter's own "past." *Talent Is Not Enough: Mollie Hunter on Writing for Children* is a collection of essays, several of which deal explicitly with the process of "storying" and the uses of the past in fiction. Outside the main body of her work, these two books nevertheless make a very good introduction to Mollie Hunter and her work.

A Sound of Chariots is in many ways addressed to the adult trying to remember and understand childhood experience; and it affords a rare glimpse into the making and motivation of a writer. It is also about the perception of life-and-death as part of one whole, and how the revelation of their inevitable interdependence affects a child growing up. Accepting death's proximity enhances, rather than diminishes, the vitality of that child-character, and in many of the other books there are encounters with death, or an awareness of its presence in the wings, giving an added savor to life. Central too is that curiously painful as well as pleasurable sensitivity to both physical and emotional stimuli, an alert response to things and to people; mediated here, as elsewhere, by language. "I think that one is born with an appreciation of language, in the same way that you're born with a good ear for music."

Mollie Hunter's inborn "ear" is attested to by the harmony of her style, enriched by the odd Gaelic word (sidhe, urisk, broch, Bean nighe), strange and delectable to the ear; by resonant place-names, a vivid but homely turn of expression, fluent and lively dialogue. The love of words, their sounds, senses, and power, is a theme reiterated in *Talent Is Not Enough,* where Mollie Hunter gives careful attention to their function as part of a narrative and their potential—and limits—in evoking the past. (p. 3)

Mollie Hunter is . . . concerned with the moral responsibility of the writer to keep the special limitations and needs of a child reader in mind without doing violence to historical truth. The best of Hunter's historical fiction—*The Thirteenth Member, The Spanish Letters, The Stronghold*—deals with strong material without sensationalizing it. Questions of loyalty—political, familial, personal, social—lie at the heart of these and the other historical novels, and Mollie Hunter's refusal to oversimplify the conflicts and ambiguities of such a highly-charged theme has left some of her work vulnerable to charges of irresponsibility in blurring the lines between right and wrong. These lines are *not* always clear (even to the eye of historical retrospect), and Mollie Hunter's sensitivity to language includes a realization of its rhetorical capacity to deceive and obscure. But a young adult reader today should be sophisticated enough to grasp the complex issues here.

A more serious criticism is that these books do not have, somehow, a completely convincing historical "flavor". This is not, I think, accidental, but is in part a consequence of a reasoned philosophy and policy. Mollie Hunter believes that the people who lived in the past "actually were no different from ourselves." In *Talent* she has said that the writer, knowing the thought-process of his historical character, must allow it "to *appear* to dominate, when what takes place in reality is a channelling of this through the thought-patterns of the writer's own time." At the same time she rightly rejects theatrically romantic touches based on popular misconceptions about the past, and renounces, too, archaic language, in favor of "a clear, plain English which in itself is timeless." The absence of "fancy-dress" details, the presence—even veiled—of a modern sensibility, and the medium of a modern English, means that the historical atmosphere tends to be rather thin.

While the timelessness of her style perhaps deprives the historical novels of a legitimate dimension, it is a perfect attribute of these books based on or involving traditional Celtic folk material. The past in such books as *The Ferlie, The Haunted Mountain, A Stranger Came Ashore,* or the recent *A Furl of Fairy Wind* is that generic past covering both "the olden days"—i.e. any and all time before a child's memory—and the static time of country life, which alters very little over the years. Even in such a story as *The Bodach* (published in the U.S. as *The Walking Stones*), where electricity plays a major role, it is assimilated to the flow of history and put in perspective by being introduced as "lightning" in the Gaelic language of the Bodach's vision. *The Kelpie's Pearls* also shares the deft depiction of the strange, uncanny, or magical as credible phenomena in the present. The Scottish setting—specifically, the Highlands—is a key to this successful marriage of the factual and the fantastic. The setting is realistic: scenery, weather, houses, people, are recognizably Scots. But this base of the contemporary is permeated through and through with a sense of the embedded past, and with the writer's deep emotional engagement, and it is realized imaginatively. Thus it is present-day Scotland but something more as well: a place where fairies still have stature and command respect, where the forces of nature, formidable and alien, may still be personified as supernatural beings. To Mollie Hunter the place itself is clearly both real and "magical".

Moreover, she has the folktale's traditional blending of the quotidian and domestic with the amazing and inexplicable to aid her. All these stories take the marvellous seriously: not indeed in the vein of "high seriousness" belonging to some fantasy, but with the un-selfconscious acceptance of powers beyond humble human compass native to the tale. Here again language plays a crucial role: the speech-

rhythms and diction, the heightened pitch but matter-of-fact tone, belong to that colloquial art-form, storytelling. It is a type of artistic expression for which Mollie Hunter's Scots-Irish heritage may peculiarly fit her. Eleanor Cameron has remarked the "Celtic lyricism and beauty" of Mollie Hunter's style; but forthrightness and simplicity are also its characteristics. Even the "poetic" descriptions of nature remain spare, subordinated to the demands of story.

Writing, Mollie Hunter asserts, is the act of a *person* reaching out to another *person,* and narrative is her way of communication. "If you're trying to convey a message, as such," she has said, "then you can't tell a good story." But if the tale is effective, then the personality and ideas of the writer will penetrate in their own way to make contact with the reader. Mollie Hunter's concern with certain aspects of existence—with human capacity for love, for example, or with the exercise of honesty, courage and compassion—is transmitted clearly in her work. At the same time, narrative demands are satisfied. Her fictional forms require action, and her characters are plagued—but also redeemed—by their tendency to rashness and recklessness. Their headstrong embrace of life is perhaps a reflection of the warmth and vitality which invariably impress anyone fortunate enough to meet Mollie Hunter herself. Imagination, dreaming, music, magic may be ways of perceiving the hidden wholeness of the world: but she also understands well the loneliness of the soul marked out by such perception. The importance of caring for another, of finding love, is paramount in her work. Foolhardy and tough, or imaginative and sensitive, the active, pivotal characters in Mollie Hunter's books are most often male: women are cautious, conservative, stay-at-home. This situation, and indeed the rather flat characterization in the tales, are to some extent a legacy of the traditional form. Less traditional and more revelatory of the personality of the writer, is the theme of vocation, or self-fulfilment, the discovery of a sense of purpose in one's life, experienced by many of her characters (and a central theme in *A Sound of Chariots*). (pp. 4-5)

It is clear that Mollie Hunter herself feels such a sense of vocation as a writer: "although I realized it was only the beam of my own imagination reflecting back at me. I still had the feeling of being on a road where *someone* had placed the lights ahead for me." In her books it is the high-road of story, carrying the reader back and forth between past and present, that is illumined by Mollie Hunter's imagination. (p. 6)

> *Patricia Dooley, "Mollie Hunter," in* The Children's Literature Association Newsletter, *Vol. 111, No. 3, Autumn, 1978, pp. 3-6.*

Janet Hickman

[It] is hard to imagine how one could bring more of self to writing than [Mollie Hunter] does. Cultural heritage, life circumstances, love of language, passionate convictions—all the influences on the storyteller are in the stories. (p. 302)

If you cannot visit Scotland for yourself, Mollie Hunter's books are an agreeable substitute. There you will find the "green glen deep among the mountains" of *The Walking Stones,* forbidding Ben MacDui in *The Haunted Mountain,* and the rough shores of the Orkney Islands, site of *The Stronghold.* All of her writing demonstrates her deep feeling for the land where she was born, and where she lives and works.

The settings of her books are not just faithfully represented, they are evoked. In *A Stranger Came Ashore,* the Shetlands village which is central to the story is introduced as "not so much a place, really, as a scatter of houses on hilly ground overlooking the sea." When Robbie takes the boat out to visit the seal pups, the water around him is "the color of melted emeralds." And when the sky is lit by the Northern Lights, " . . . it was like long searchlights of green shooting brilliantly out from a huge and starless black dome."

It is not only the author's ability to call up the sights of her country that makes Scotland so memorable in her books. She has long been interested in its history and folklore, and has expert knowledge in both fields. Born and bred in East Lothian, she recalls that she "absorbed the folklore of the Lowlands as naturally as I ate and drank." . . . She has taken on the Highland lore firsthand also, from long residence near Inverness, "observing, watching, listening, learning."

All her books of fantasy are rooted in this intimate knowledge of folk culture. . . . (p. 303)

Another significant part of Mollie Hunter's writing is historical fiction, a reflection of her interest in Scotland's past. . . . [She] carries "a fairly full and accurate picture of my own country's history in my mind." (pp. 303, 305)

The detailed backgrounds of such books [as *The Spanish Letters, The Ghosts of Glencoe,* and *A Pistol in Greenyards*] require meticulous research as well as general knowledge, and Mollie Hunter is tireless. She does extensive reading and traveling, which sometimes lead to exciting scholarly discoveries. In search of information for *The 13th Member,* a story of the witchcraft plots against James I, she found herself "eventually working with a bundle of documents in Register House, which is where all the archives of Scotland are kept. These were affidavits, sworn testimony, taken down by a clerk of the court from people implicated in these plots, arrested on a charge of witchcraft against His Majesty, questioned by the King himself. . . . and one of these had never before, to my certain knowledge, been quoted in any work on the subject." (p. 305)

[Mollie Hunter's] natural inclination to tell stories is as much a part of her work as is her passion for history or her knowledge of folklore. She grew up in what she calls "a reading family," with a Scottish mother and an Irish father. In these early years she developed a threatrical imagination (she has written, produced, and played for an amateur theater group), and a keen ear for language. She cares intensely about the right word. There is a memorable scene in the largely autobiographical book, *A Sound of Chariots,* in which young Bridie McShane insists on her own turn of phrase—"green broken glass," despite her

teacher's preference for the more ordinary "broken green glass."

Bridie's story also reveals some of the author's feelings about being forced by "economic circumstances" to give up her schooling while still in her early teens. Mollie Hunter is a self-made scholar whose lack of formal education has not kept her from learning, or from achieving. Her characters, too, are frequently unschooled; but they have native intelligence, a wisdom that cannot be taught, and an admirable eagerness to learn. One thinks of the brilliance of Coll's imagination in *The Stronghold,* of Torquil with his gift of King Solomon's Ring in *The Kelpie's Pearls,* and of Adam in *The 13th Member,* whom the alchemist calls "this most teachable of boys."

Again like Bridie, Mollie Hunter's characters are most often intense, strong-willed, passionate, outspoken. . . . Whatever claims her attention claims it fully. It is her habit to be involved, not just in her work, but in community affairs as well. Not long ago she had a part in the restoration of a local mill as a memorial to a much-admired teacher; more recently she has tried to marshal public opinion to defeat a building project that would change the character of her village. A similar conflict between past and present has found its way into her writing in *The Walking Stones,* wherein a Highland glen is to be flooded by the electric company, covering an ancient Stone Circle. Even the old Bodach's magic, his gift of second sight, cannot prevent the flooding; but the magic itself survives, given to a boy who will continue to pass on the Story of the Stones.

Passing on stories is the endeavor to which Mollie Hunter is most deeply committed. The strength of that commitment and her sense of responsibility to children are evident in her book of essays, *Talent Is Not Enough.* The title essay, delivered as the May Hill Arbuthnot Honor Lecture in 1975, paraphrases Emerson: "There must be a person behind the book." Mollie Hunter is the person behind all her books—a complex, caring, vividly alive person. She and her books are well worth knowing. (pp. 305-06)

> *Janet Hickman, "The Person behind the Book—Mollie Hunter," in* Language Arts, *Vol. 56, No. 3, March, 1979, pp. 302-06.*

Roni Natov

In an attempt to offer hope and optimism, earlier generations of writers for children tended to mitigate the painful truths about life, or even worse, to lie about them altogether. In doing this, they ran the risk of losing what of value might have been embedded in that pain. Authors of recent stories for children seem aware that we cannot clean up reality, or separate neatly what was unpleasant or even disastrous from the delights of a moment, an event, or a life. In each of these stories, as in each life, there is pain, and out of that pain, something important is salvaged. These stories reflect the postwar attempt in the best children's books toward honesty, to tell the truth about what was tragic in the hopes of revealing the truth about what it means to be heroic for ordinary people, about what is enduring, inspiring, and creative in each of us that helps us to survive in the face of potential despair.

A Sound of Chariots, Mollie Hunter's autobiographical novel about her childhood in Scotland, chronicles the struggle of Bridie McShane, her nine-year-old heroine, against despair after her father dies, leaving her mother and five children to survive the loss and the ensuing poverty. In each of our lives key moments or events occur after which all else seems utterly changed. For Bridie, her father's death is the event around which all else clusters and through which everything is screened in her consciousness. This highly descriptive novel traces in vivid detail her healing process. (p. 114)

What is heroic in Bridie and what ensures her recovery is her faith in her perceptions, which are given concrete expression in her writings. Despite the bleakness of her family life after her father's death, the poverty and the burden of her mother's suffering, Bridie believes in the value of her writing and in her own vitality. She learns to detach herself from her mother's suffering, ultimately to choose her needs over her mother's in the face of overwhelming guilt. And though Bridie is often told to hide her perceptions, that it is unnatural to see and know as much as she does at her age, along with the conflicting message of being told never to lie, she learns that to survive, "she had to learn to think in two different ways at the same time. . . . In fact, it was almost like being two separate people. On the surface she was a wilder version of the Bridie everyone still expected her to be. . . . Underneath this there was the other part of her mind, like another person watching all her antics and observing the effect they had". (p. 115)

In the sequel, *Hold Onto Love,* Bridie continues to struggle with her vision as a writer and for her independence throughout her teenage years in conservative Scotland of the thirties. In this novel, we see the tension in Bridie between her need to assert her difference from this religious and reactionary society and her need to connect with others. She knows she must avoid the bleak fate of most women, to be dominated by men and saddled with children at a young age. But she has also fallen in love and, aware of her new vulnerability, she avows that "*She* would keep *her* life in *her* hands." While Bridie is careful to distinguish her beliefs from the conservative working class values of her family and neighbors, her hatred of snobbery and social injustice allows her to empathize with others. Her empathetic power ultimately provides a rich source for her writing. (pp. 115-16)

Her insights into the poignant moments in ordinary lives and the courageous qualities of ordinary people and her writer's eye for significant detail allow her to penetrate the surface of reality. She develops her gift for storytelling as she discovers the dignity and heroic strength in the women she meets in the hospital where she has had an appendectomy. She is inspired by the vitality imbedded in their working class pragmatism. (p. 116)

[In] a poor, filthy, tinker woman who fiercely resists being locked up in the hospital, Bridie sees youth and beauty, noticing the luster in her hair and the sensitivity in her eyes. Though tinkers are considered rogues and outcasts, Bridie identifies with her proud, rebellious spirit. At the end of the novel there is a sense of hope and resolution as Bridie and another young tinker woman wait at the train station together for their young men. Bridie has found in her admiration and sympathy for the bravery and fineness of ordinary people a new feeling of community, and, as the title suggests, she has deciced to "hold onto love." She no longer needs to be separate and lonely to maintain her independence. (pp. 116-17)

Roni Natov, "The Truth of Ordinary Lives: Autobiographical Fiction for Children," in Children's literature in education, *Vol. 17, No. 2, Summer, 1986, pp. 112-25.*

TITLE COMMENTARY

Patrick Kentigern Keenan (1963; U. S. edition as *The Smartest Man in Ireland*)

Patrick Kentigern Keenan (the title, in spite of its point, is the only thing I don't like about this book) is about the cleverest man in Ireland—or so he boasts, until the fairies set out to prove him wrong. Among the adventures in which Patrick finds and uses the golden spoon and necklace and the silver bridle, the most dramatic concerns his rescue of little Kieron from the world underground, and the most significant moment comes when he stabs his iron knife into the fairy door to hold back the malicious Little People. Here is a note that establishes the story with ancient lore and not merely with fancy. The language of these tales is easy and in its idiom agreeably Celtic, and a touch of irony saves it from seeming whimsical. The black and white illustrations [by Charles Keeping], also, show that Patrick, though we are allowed to laugh at his bragging, is in the line of Irish mythical heroes.

Margery Fisher, in a review of "Patrick Kentigern Keenan," in Growing Point, *Vol. 2, No. 1, May, 1963, p. 167.*

Everyone in Connemara knows that Irish fairies are master tricksters. How could a mortal hope to outwit them? Yet Patrick Kentigern Keenan boasts that he would do just this. The fairies get the best of him most of the time. . . . When his little son is kidnapped by the beautiful and terrible fairy queen, Patrick proves his innermost courage and ingenuity. Ah, but does he learn from his experiences? Well—maybe.

An exhilarating adventure-fantasy with real Irish flavor in the phrasing; and imagination, humor, gaiety and no doubts about the existence of the "Good People." Everyone who reads the book will know what to do when he encounters these not-so-admirable Celtic fairies.

Ethna Sheehan, in a review of "The Smartest Man in Ireland," in The New York Times Book Review, *November 28, 1965, p. 46.*

Hi Johnny (1963)

The fortunes of humble folk and those of the rich and exalted are mingled in a story of unusual merit, set in and around Edinburgh in 1540. Hi Johnny is a pedlar who comes into conflict with the lawless laird of Hepburn when he tries to rescue from him the Lady Margaret Setoun, kidnapped for her estates. The waif Tom, whose birth is so unexpected, the impressive figure of the gypsy king, and the gaberlunzie whose identity finally links private with national affairs—these characters are well drawn against a background, vividly described, of hovels and wayside inns, towering castle and distant hills.

> *Margery Fisher, in a review of "Hi Johnny," in* Growing Point, *Vol. 2, No. 8, March, 1964, p. 284.*

The Kelpie's Pearls   (1964)

As may be expected from the author of **Patrick Kentigern Keenan** this story of a Kelpie is blended from the folk lore of the countryside, the commonsense of Morag—the old woman whose hill cottage at Abriachan forms a perfect setting for the story—and the loyalty of young Torquil, who had a great gift with animals, and who alone stood by Morag when the whole community would have hunted her as a witch.

The author's previous story was centred in Ireland, but **The Kelpie's Pearls** shows that she writes with the same easy confidence in a Scottish setting. Her simple, economic dialogue forms a direct contrast to the fine prose of the descriptive passages which is embellished by a fitting use of imagery.

> *A review of "The Kelpie's Pearls," in* The Junior Bookshelf, *Vol. 28, No. 5, November, 1964, p. 296.*

Mollie Hunter's **The Kelpie's Pearls** is something of a triumph, for fantasy and magic are made to appear natural and inevitable in a modern context of reporters, buses and policemen. Its range is considerable, from humour to suspense and from pathos to something like primitive fear. Characters and landscape are realized with complete solidity, and what begins as a simple Highland story ends as a touching plea for the recognition of natural magic in the midst of mundane things. Charles Keeping's vigorous drawings exactly catch the spirit of this memorable book.

> *"Breaking the Rules: Engagement and Extravaganza in Never-Never-Land," in* The Times Literary Supplement, *No. 3274, November 26, 1964, p. 1081.*

Supernatural stories like this don't usually happen nowadays (the kelpie even treats Morag to a glimpse of the Loch Ness monster), but this one is so enchantingly told in the gentle dialect of the Highlands that it is a spellbinder from first to last. Read it aloud—in school, home, or library—and you will see!

> *Mary Silva Cosgrave, in a review of "The Kelpie's Pearls," in* The Horn Book Magazine, *Vol. XLII, No. 6, December, 1966, p. 710.*

The Spanish Letters   (1964)

The 'Caddies', that strange band of beggars and guides that formed a distinctive feature of sixteenth-century Edinburgh, provide an exciting human flavouring to the vividly realized, physical setting of Mollie Hunter's story of murder, intrigue, treachery and political conspiracy. Jamie's apprenticeship among this odd brotherhood suddenly acquires a seriousness undreamed of when he is hired to guide Roger Macey, the English agent, sent from Elizabeth's court to attempt to stop the activities of the Spanish plotters, which are designed to overthrow both Scotland and England.

As in her earlier novel, **Hi Johnny,** Mollie Hunter has portrayed an entirely credible society in which not all enemies are without honour. This story will appeal to a wider age group than the previous book and will be seldom found on the library shelf.

> *Gordon Parsons, in a review of "The Spanish Letters," in* The School Librarian, *Vol. 13, No. 1, March, 1965, p. 95.*

[**The Spanish Letters**] combines history with romance, but in the form of a cloak-and-dagger tale with a background of tense Anglo-Scottish relations in 1589. . . . [Jamie] emerges an acceptable hero, despite all the fortuitous circumstances that support his quick thinking and his new mastery of the sword. His reciprocated delight in the fencing master's daughter, a competent lass who creates her own role in the intrigue, adds a significant dimension to the plot. The author, a native Scot, develops a clear sense of time and place, and excels especially in establishing a close sequence of action in the skirmishes, eavesdropping, captures, and escapes. A graphic use of history here.

> *Virginia Haviland, "Tales of Early Britain," in* Book Week—The Washington Post, *May 7, 1967, p. 30.*

As a story of derring-do, romance, intrigue, swash and buckle **The Spanish Letters** has everything; it is saved from being just another dramatic adventure story by the smooth integration of historical details and by Mollie Hunter's deft writing.

> *Zena Sutherland, in a review of "The Spanish Letters," in* Saturday Review, *Vol. 50, No. 19, May 13, 1967, p. 57.*

Jamie Morton, an alert lad of fifteen, is one of the scores of boys organized by the old man known as the Cleek into the loose fellowship of the Edinburgh Caddies. Like the rest of them, Jamie guides strangers, and runs messages but longs to play a more direct part in the affairs that trouble the city in the year after the defeat of the Armada.

His chance comes when Roger Macey accepts him as a guide to the house of the fencing-master John Forbes. . . . There is grave danger for the boy, and moments of pure terror, as well as moments of pride; it is one of his most deadly enemies who remarks 'You are strong and bold and quick in the workings of your mind. And I know also that you are lucky. You have all the attributes of an adventurer but that last is the most important of them all—luck!' And an adventurer Jamie is clearly destined to become, for, as the Cleek realizes, he is older and wiser for his involvement in great affairs. Mollie Hunter has used her fictional character to particularize historical fact and to localize it in the city.

Hunter with her Carnegie Medal, 1975.

Margery Fisher, "Who's Who in Children's Books: The Spanish Letters," in her Who's Who in Children's Books: A Treasury of the Familiar Characters of Childhood, *Holt, Rinehart and Winston, 1975, p. 149.*

A Pistol in Greenyards (1965)

A Pistol in Greenyards confirms the view that, though Mollie Hunter falls short of the magic by which a Sutcliff or a Bryher turns the raw stuff of history into imaginative gold, she is a fine story-teller, able to shape a plot without loss of historical integrity. She has chosen a bitter theme in this latest book—the brutal dispossession of the Highland crofters, little more than one hundred years ago—and softens none of its tragedy: but in the story of the short, doomed resistance of one township, and of a boy's fight against a vicious legal system that has his mother in its grip and is reaching out for his own life, the author has given the theme a spring and elation, a narrative excitement, that make this a book to recommend to two kinds of reader. It will thrill the young historian: and history will rub off from it on the reader who believes he is concerned only with being thrilled.

"Making the Most of Their Time," in The

Times Literary Supplement, No. 3328, December 9, 1965, p. 1147.

This is a most vivid account of the tragedy of the Highland Clearances as seen by Connal Ross, the young son of a crofter. Connal's father is away fighting for England in one of the Highland regiments when through the double dealing of the tacksman, the Sherriff Officer comes to evict the crofters.

This is a most gripping story, the dignity and bravery of the Highlanders in their doomed fight to save their homes makes one of the best historical tales I have read for some time—and it is a reminder that our national heritage has not always been a subject for pride.

A review of "A Pistol in Greenyards," in The Junior Bookshelf, *Vol. 30, No. 1, February, 1966, p. 58.*

The brutal eviction of the tenant farmers of Greenyards, a valley in the Scottish Highlands, provides the core of this entirely absorbing novel. . . .

The valley community is warmly evoked and the acts of simple heroism and affection are as effectively conveyed as the dreadful attack on the women and children which the Sheriff's men carry out. In all respects this is an outstanding book and must be strongly recommended for children of good reading ability, of any age over ten or so.

David Churchill, in a review of "A Pistol in Greenyards," in The School Librarian, *Vol. 23, No. 2, June, 1975, p. 147.*

The action is fast, and the narrative makes compelling reading. It reveals, without hysteria or overdramatisation, the full horror of such evictions, common during this period, and the lack of understanding elsewhere of what was taking place.

To [its] exciting plot is added a range of strongly-drawn characters, especially Connal's sister Katrine, the lawyer who undertakes their mother's defence and Connal himself. The story is presented as written down by him during his voyage to America, and thus the reader sees clearly as Connal changes from cheerful, courageous boy to bitter, hunted young man, the true cost of such ruthless extinction of people's homes and rights. By relating the Greenyards incident in terms of Connal's own struggle with McCaig, Mollie Hunter gives the book an intensity of focus which adds greatly to its strength. She also conveys through Connal's words an unsentimental awareness of the beauty of the Highlands and the depth of the people's love for their own country and way of life.

The book finally is a dignified 'salute to the memory of the people of Greenyards'. (pp. 67-8)

Judith Aldridge, in a review of "A Pistol in Greenyards," in Children's Book Review, *Vol. V, No. 2, Summer, 1975, pp. 67-8.*

The Ghosts of Glencoe (1966)

For Mollie Hunter, place is as important as people and causes. In **The Ghosts of Glencoe** she draws an almost unbearably vivid setting for the massacre of 1692—a brutal tale told in a forthright way. The Campbell's attack on the Macdonalds was for revenge, wrap it up in what political arguments they would; this is her interpretation of the facts, and she has gone back to contemporary documents, army papers among them, for support. She uses too an old tradition about Ensign Robert Stewart and his help for those he was commanded to slay. Stewart is one of the heroes of the book and the very pivot of the plot: the old chief of the Glencoe Macdonalds dominates by his personality: but it is not fanciful, nor need it diminish the power of this excellent writer, to say that the spirit of old Scotland presides. (pp. 834-35)

> *Margery Fisher, in a review of "The Ghosts of Glencoe," in* Growing Point, *Vol. 5, No. 7, January, 1967, pp. 834-35.*

Despite its inept title, this is an excellent book, one of the best accounts of the famous massacre. Perhaps being a Scot without being a Campbell or a Macdonald gives the authoress insight without bias. Certainly she manages to convey the character of both Highlander and the Highlands very vividly. She also succeeds in the difficult exercise of presenting a piece of history as a novel that is convincing as a novel without distorting the facts. The story is put into the mouth of an ensign serving with the Campbell regiment though not himself a Campbell. He warms to the Macdonalds of Glencoe but is not blind to their faults, and though his sympathies are inevitably with them he does not venomously condemn all Campbells out of hand. The reader's understanding is improved by a couple of good maps, photographs of Glencoe and contemporary portraits.

> *A review of "The Ghosts of Glencoe," in* The Junior Bookshelf, *Vol. 31, No. 2, April, 1967, p. 123.*

Mollie Hunter, in **The Ghosts of Glencoe,** gives fictional treatment to an historical event, and one of which every detail has already been closely studied. It would be exceedingly difficult to write an imaginative novel about Glencoe, and Miss Hunter has been content to let the tragedy speak for itself. She has chosen the device of an eyewitness who is not too strong a character to get in the way of the action, although in her concern to rescue him from the effects of his involvement with the Macdonalds she perhaps diverts too much attention from the central tragedy. This is no story for dispassionate treatment, and Miss Hunter rightly declares herself for the Macdonalds without reservation. Her portraits of the principals on both sides are brilliantly done. She is especially successful with the enigmatic Glenlyon who, by a combination of choice and fate, bears direct responsibility for the massacre. In a finely conceived epilogue the spokesman of the story meets Glenlyon behind the lines in Flanders and finds him seeking escape from the ghosts of his victims in the winedregs. This fine story deserves more readers than its austere format is likely to attract.

> *"Casualties of Change," in* The Times Literary Supplement, *No. 3404, May 25, 1967, p. 447.*

Thomas and the Warlock (1967)

Thomas and the Warlock is a very open, active and lively tale; its magic is brisk rather than mysterious. Thomas Thomson, a blacksmith in a Lowland Scottish village, is also a notorious poacher. One day, having temporarily exhausted the laird's coverts, he ventures near the Goblin Ha', which is haunted by the ghost of wicked Hugh Gifford. Then the trouble begins—with supernatural versions of blackmail, kidnapping and assault. But Thomas has allies, in a witch slighted by Hugo and in his bright young son Alexander, and with cold iron and unleashed winds the blacksmith wins the contest in a satisfying, hilarious and exciting way.

> *Margery Fisher, in a review of "Thomas and the Warlock," in* Growing Point, *Vol. 6, No. 1, May, 1967, p. 920.*

The perils of scoffing at the fairy world are . . . brought home hard to Thomas the blacksmith, gay poaching fellow that he is, in **Thomas and the Warlock**. . . . A story in the true Gaelic manner, this book is more impressive in some startling individual vignettes—there is a wonderful description of Thomas, with the aid of all the village boys and their watering-cans, fixing a hot iron rim to the smouldering wooden wheel of the warlock's carriage—than in its sum. For will children really believe—and does the author want them to—that through Thomas's power over iron and his true love for his wife not only was the sinister warlock Henry Gifford overwhelmed, but also all the witches and wizards in the whole of Scotland?

> *"Over the Dream Wall," in* The Times Literary Supplement, *No. 3404, May 25, 1967, p. 451.*

This spell-binding tale will fire the romantic imaginations of ten- to thirteen-year-olds. Set in the Lowlands of Scotland long ago in the days of superstition and witches, it concerns one Thomas—the village blacksmith who falls foul of the terrible warlock, Hugo Gifford. Although Thomas is a poacher, he is well liked in the village, and the local laird, sheriff, minister and neighbours rally to his aid. But the real key to the situation is Thomas's small son, Alexander, who alone knows how the Four Winds could be harnessed to his father's side. In a midnight showdown in the wilds of the countryside, Thomas faces the warlock with terrifying results. . . .

[This] spooky tale is original and exciting and the characters are strongly drawn.

> *Roger Ferneyhough, in a review of "Thomas and the Warlock," in* The School Librarian and School Library Review, *Vol. 16, No. 1, March, 1968, p. 94.*

The Ferlie (1968)

The border country of Scotland is rich in folklore and Scottish author Mollie Hunter mines it well. In her engrossing new fantasy she relates the amazing adventures of small, dark Hob Hazeldene, an orphan, brought up by old witch Goody Cunningham.

Hob is herd boy to fiery-tempered Big Archie Armstrong and is obsessed by a curious, sweet music he hears in his dreams; he is overjoyed when he makes a whistle on which he can play it, little knowing it to be the music of a ferlie, or fairy. After Big Archie, led on by old Goody, steals the ferlie's cattle, sees them magicked away and almost is killed for their theft, Hob is ordered to lure them back with his music.

How he meets the ferlie and resists his efforts to trap him into leaving the real, if cruel world for the ferlie world of beauty and eternal youth puts a dramatic climax on a well-told tale touched with magic.

> *Polly Goodwin, in a review of "The Ferlie," in* Book World—The Washington Post, *November 3, 1968, p. 16.*

The Ferlie is a brilliant, clear-cut, robust story of the mysterious frontier which humans cross at their peril unless they invoke the power of cold iron and the names of saints. . . . Mollie Hunter has a supreme tact in dealing with legendary material. She never over-writes but her clear prose creates picture after picture to carry the story forward. Another frontier has been crossed here, between belief and unbelief; writing of enchantment, Mollie Hunter is in the best sense an enchanter.

> *Margery Fisher, in a review of "The Ferlie," in* Growing Point, *Vol. 7, No. 6, December, 1968, p. 1239.*

Mollie Hunter writes in a narrative style which immediately makes one think of storytelling around the fire. I particularly like her descriptions of everyday things and their linking with magical ones, such as the description of Hob making an elder-wood whistle: music which can charm the fairy cattle into following him. Big Archie, Goody Cunningham, Hob and the Ferlie are clearly defined characters. . . . Any ten-year-old who has enjoyed Mollie Hunter's earlier books should find this new one equally absorbing.

> *Lucinda Fox, in a review of "The Ferlie," in* The School Librarian and School Library Review, *Vol. 17, No. 1, March, 1969, p. 113.*

The Lothian Run (1970)

Edinburgh and its environs in 1736 are the setting for a romantic adventure story with an element of mystery and some meaty historical background. Few writers today are more skilled in this genre than is Mollie Hunter. Sandy Maxwell is a bright lad, clerk to shrewd old lawyer Wishart, who offers Sandy's services to dapper Deryck Gilmour of His Majesty's Customs Service. Gilmour, hunting a smuggler, finds that he has embroiled himself and Sandy in a political plot, and thereafter the story moves suspensefully through a series of intricate and dangerous adventures and counterploys. Gilmour is a glamorous Pimpernel, Sandy a diamond in the rough, and the villains are absolutely heinous. Small print, alas, but a rousing tale. (pp. 69-70)

> *Zena Sutherland, in a review of "The Lothian Run," in* Saturday Review, *Vol. 53, No. 19, May 9, 1970, pp. 69-70.*

The historical novel has various forms. There are those noteworthy for the abundance and accuracy of details about clothes, customs and conditions such as Cynthia Harnett's books. There are the rare few, by Rosemary Sutcliff and Henry Treece for example, which express vividly and without false glamour the spirit of past ages. And there are those in the tradition of *Kidnapped* which use an historical setting to add colour and romance to an adventure story.

Into this category comes **The Lothian Run.** Smuggling and Jacobite scheming combine to provide an exciting plot but the reader's understanding of the attitudes and tensions of life in Scotland in the 1730's is not enriched. The hero is any high-spirited boy who would be equally at home in a contemporary story. But this is a lively, tautly-constructed well-told story which holds the reader's interest. The scenes in Edinburgh and the surrounding countryside are described with authority and are easily visualised.

> *Judith Aldridge, in a review of "The Lothian Run," in* Children's Book Review, *Vol. I, No. 2, April, 1971, p. 55.*

It is only the high standard that Mollie Hunter's earlier novels has established that makes one express an edge of disappointment over her latest. The author's native Scotland provides a setting for a fast-moving story of smuggling and Jacobite plotting which, from many other pens, would be accepted with enthusiasm. The relatively thin characterization and mechanical manipulation of plot, however, both ring strangely from this writer. (p. 260)

> *Gordon Parsons, in a review of "The Lothian Run," in* The School Librarian, *Vol. 19, No. 3, September, 1971, pp. 260-61.*

The Bodach (1970; U. S. edition as The Walking Stones)

A very light fantastic, deftly tripped, as the story seems to tell itself, unfold with no more of a prod than the turn of a page and the surest of elements. There's the old man by the Gaelic name of the Bodach who foresees the bringing of forest, lightning, and death to the glen by three men of the same name; his vision translates into hydroelectric power first damming, then controlled flooding, then reforestation—overseen by Rory Rudh, Rory Dubh, and Rory Ban. There are the Tigers who build the dam under the eye of Callum Mor and every boy in the village especially Donald Campbell, the Bodach's young friend and protege, awed by the old man's promise to forestall the flooding . . . and wondering why. But the how is a marvel: a wild now-you-see-him-now-you-don't dodge and chase with the Bodach positioning himself at the floodgates eluding capture, preventing the flip of the switch, impossibly yet unequivocally. And gradually Donald partakes of the secret of the Bodach's Co-Walker: "It is known of old that this Copy, or Echo, or Living Picture, is under the command of the man of the Second Sight"; and then Donald discovers in Bocca, his private companion, his own Co-Walker. . . . The ceremonious transmigration later of the dying Bodach's power into Donald's self rivals the vigorous this-wordly talk of dam-construction earlier for sheer entrancing boggling, but there's more . . . as Donald paces Bocca through the Bodach's race, now his, holding the waters back just long enough to let the stones that walk once every hundred years complete their rites. Then can the flood rush in, then can the Bodach "go to his herd"; and there will be other glens and stone-circles for Donald. . . . As graceful an unhurried talespin as ever you please or a silver-tongued Bodach could match.

> *A review of "The Walking Stones," in* Kirkus Reviews, *Vol. XXXVIII, No. 15, August 1, 1970, p. 800.*

It takes a remarkable writer to push Mollie Hunter into second place. Here is that rarest of beings, the born storyteller. . . . . **The Bodach** is a tale of the Highlands and could not belong anywhere else. Mollie Hunter paints a loving picture of her ancient hero, a "type" painting rather than a portrait, for the Bodach is a repository of traditional wisdom rather than a person. When the Hydro-Electric Board turn their attention to his valley he holds them off—not for ever—by a mixture of magic and cunning. The author sees no incongruity in the mingling of modern technology and ancient sorceries; nor does the reader, captive as he is to the power of her narrative. It is a charming and approachable story. . . .

> *"Modern Magic and Ancient Sorcery," in* The Times Literary Supplement, *No. 3583, October 30, 1970, p. 1251.*

Subtitled "a novel of suspense," **The Walking Stones** is not really a mystery tale. Rather, in a deeper sense, this story of the flooding of a Highland glen by the electric company is *about* a mystery—the deep mystery of Celtic magic. For the flooding is being held up by the Bodach, a stubborn old man skilled in the ancient Druidic rites, and his young pupil-friend, Donald. They wish to let the towering circle of stones—not unlike Stonehenge—make a final once-a-century pilgrimage to the river on Beltane morning before the flood waters close over the glen forever. And so there is a confrontation—between the magic of ancient Scotland and twentieth-century science.

Unreal? Not in Mollie Hunter's crisply told tale. Readers, fantasy and fact lovers alike, will be caught up in the reality of unreality. As the Bodach says, "Magic is . . . something that happens when everything is right for it to happen." And in **The Walking Stones** the time, the prose, and the story are just right.

> *Jane Yolen, in a review of "The Walking Stones," in* Book World—The Washington Post, *November 8, 1970, p. 8.*

The Thirteenth Member: A Story of Suspense (1971)

Combining in her latest book the feeling for history found

in **The Lothian Run** with the proven ability—as in **The Kelpie's Pearls**—to create an atmosphere of the supernatural, the author has realized a new dimension in her storytelling. Witchcraft and a plot to destroy James the Sixth (later, James the First of England) mingle with the dawning romantic awareness of two young people to form a tale of intrigue and passion set in the late sixteenth century on the superstition-ridden east coast of Scotland. " 'Charity brat' " Adam Lawrie, awakened from sleep in Master Seton's stable outhouse by hunger pangs, spots the timid young kitchenmaid Gilly Duncan, heading out across the moorlands on the 31st of July, Lammas Eve, to meet with the Devil—a clawed figure riding a fiery blue horse. In spite of a desire to remain aloof from the troubles of others, Adam finds himself attracted to the gentle young girl with the gift of healing in her hands. As a result, he is subsequently drawn into the desperate attempt of Gideon Grahame, an alchemist, to prove to the witch covens bent on hexing the King's life that " 'The Devil is the father of lies.' " Gilly—the youngest, the thirteenth member of a coven controlled by the alchemist's twin brother and the Earl of Bothwell—is herself an unwilling witch, dedicated by her mother to the powers of evil from early childhood. Doomed to the "justice-fire" if the plot to kill James succeeds and warned by the witches' executioner, the "Maiden," of death by strangulation if it fails, Gilly joins forces with Master Grahame to defeat the scheme and through this choice unknowingly commits herself to "examination" and torture. The writing is vivid—almost too realistic in certain of the "examination" scenes—while the personalities and motivations of the characters, both fictional and historical, ring true. The relationship between James and Bothwell is particularly well drawn: "The King's fear of Bothwell was rooted in trust betrayed; his hatred was love turned sour." A controlled piece of writing—intense but not sensational—the book is a literary promise kept and a continuing artistic evolution implied. (pp. 489-90)

> *Sheryl B. Andrews, in a review of "The 13th Member: A Story of Suspense," in* The Horn Book Magazine, *Vol. XLVII, No. 5, October, 1971, pp. 489-90.*

The consummate ease with which the background of this unusual and powerful historical novel is set masks the author's careful research into Scotland in the 1590s and the matter and manner of witchcraft. The characters are compelling. . . .

Suspense is maintained on a double level, for while Adam is following Gillie and the witches, not realizing fully the dangers of his meddling, the head stableboy is on the trail of the pair to inform on them.

They are arrested for witchcraft and Gillie confesses under torture. The pace, always fast, increases further when the scene moves to the palace at Edinburgh, the witch trials and the final chase. The study of James VI, shortly to become king of England, the unexpected shrewdness and authority behind the slovenly exterior, and his relationship with his treacherous cousin Francis Bothwell, is masterly. James's curiosity in witches is well shown, and the contrast between Court schemers, simple fools and the three really dedicated witches: Agnes Sampson, dignified even when broken by torture, John Fian the schoolmaster, believing in the "Devil" though aware of his human identity, and the Grand Master himself, who turns king's evidence for spite. . . .

There is a matter-of-fact acceptance of the evil of witchcraft and horrors of torture which neither minimizes reality nor dwells unwholesomely on detail, but creates unforgettably the harsh, credulous atmosphere of the period.

> *"The Matter of Witchcraft," in* The Times Literary Supplement, *No. 3640, December 3, 1971, p. 1509.*

Our attention is caught from the first by the title, the jacket and the opening paragraph. Nor are we disappointed, for the story keeps us engrossed to the end. Readers will gain a clear impression of how some people must have joined covens of witches against their will and been powerless to escape, like the kitchen-maid Gilly. The evil mastermind never does get a chance to explain his behaviour, but we understand from the reluctant confession of his twin brother what could have enticed a man of his intelligence into black magic. It would be interesting for children to read this alongside Peter Dickinson's *Heartsease,* where it is the witch-hunters who are the maleficent group. But don't be misled; Mollie Hunter is writing a swift-moving story—not a sociological treatise!

There is plenty of action, including a convincing fight between our hero Adam and an enemy, and also a night ride to Edinburgh to see King James VI. That puzzling monarch is drawn in a complex and frightening way such that we feel that we are meeting the man behind the puzzle.

Details of life in sixteenth-century Scotland are enough for the needs of the story; perhaps the most piteous appears on the first page, where Adam the stable boy is kept from sleep by gnawing hunger pains. This is the tantalising sort of book which doesn't answer all the questions we expect it to—all the better if it makes the reader think more about it.

> *Maureen F. Crago, in a review of "The Thirteenth Member," in* Children's Book Review, *Vol. II, No. 1, February, 1972, p. 14.*

The Haunted Mountain (1972)

Shakespeare slandered the Little People by giving them pixie names and pretending that they were amusing. Earlier, mostly oral, traditions in the British Isles tell quite a different story.

In Wales, you have the Tylwyth Teg, a strange and beautiful supernatural race, unfortunately much given to the stealing of children. In Scotland, a similar reputation attaches to what they call the Sidhe (pronounced "shee"). . . . [It] is important to bear in mind the older idea of fairies as lordly and terrible creatures, inhabitants of the hollow hills, worshippers of dark gods with ancient magic at their command.

Mollie Hunter's **The Haunted Mountain** takes the Sidhe very seriously, as you would expect of an author who

makes her home in a remote Highland cottage. The story is a powerful synthesis of legend and actuality. MacAllister, a young farmer living in the shadow of Ben MacDui (a haunted mountain) disobeys the taboo that leaves a field of every farm be unworked in case the Sidhe want it. He is stubborn and ambitious, driven partly by his love for his Peigi-Ann and partly by a deep feeling that it is up to him to make a stand for the land which is his life. He ploughs and sows the forbidden patch and reaps a whirlwind of trouble.

At first, the Sidhe are kept away by elemental countermagic—the planting of rowan and elder, the nailing of coins in the troughs to "silver" the water. In the end, their power will not be denied. MacAllister is captured and set to work for seven years as their slave, to be offered later as a sacrifice to their gods. It takes the concerted efforts of his son Fergus and his faithful hound Colm to rescue him, and then only through the intervening blessing of Peigi-Ann's love.

This is an uncommonly well-written tale of suspense with an unforced moral basis. Miss Hunter, while admirably matter-of-fact in the way she treats of wonders and perils, is more concerned at root to find significance in the *human* necessity of her hero's struggle to outwit dark forces. She achieves this by contrasting a sense of the vast and mysterious with a strict attention to what is small and close. (pp. 5, 24)

"There are rules to magic as there are rules to everything." Mollie Hunter keeps to them, and the result is an authentic spell-binder of a book, an allegory of modified good overcoming a sometimes pitiable evil. It is worth mentioning also that *The Haunted Mountain* is very much a told tale, full of the accent of burn and brae, its prose sweet with the speech-rhythms of the Scottish Highlands, elusive as the sting of peat-smoke on the wind. (p. 24)

> *Robert Nye, in a review of "The Haunted Mountain," in* The New York Times Book Review, *May 7, 1972, p. 5, 24.*

The Haunted Mountain does not simply retell an old story, but reworks within the framework of a novel the story of Tam Lane, the man stolen by the fairies and released after seven years' bondage by the enduring power of human love. In constructing her framework Mollie Hunter uses many other familiar incidents and motifs from the fairy world. Set against this world of shadows and illusions is the real world of a Scottish Highland farming community any time in the last century. . . . The deft handling of plot, and the speed and fluency of the narrative, make this an easy read, but in its own fairly slight way it says some important things. About courage and suffering and something too about the dignity and responsibility of being only human?

> *"Celtic Revivals," in* The Times Literary Supplement, *No. 3687, November 3, 1972, p. 1323.*

A writer of historical novels who turns to pure folk-legend may have a chance to use a lot of material that cannot be incorporated into straight historical fiction. Mollie Hunter gives us here a powerful and absorbing tale based on the legends of Ben MacDui, the haunted mountain of the

Cairngorms. Her storyteller's beginning captures the reader and the simple factual style with its strong feeling of inevitability echoes the best folk-tales. The hero, MacAllister, is all a hero should be but his fatal flaw is *hubris,* high arrogance, and he does not seem able to shake this off. His refusal to accept the fairy folk's demands leads him into terrible struggles with them. The eventual resolution shows how he gains his independence but also how he acquires humility. MacAllister's struggle against the fates is a familiar part of the human condition.

Ten-year-olds would probably enjoy this story but it has qualities which could recommend it to older readers.

> *Bill Messer, in a review of "The Haunted Mountain," in* The School Librarian, *Vol. 21, No. 1, March, 1973, p. 83.*

A Sound of Chariots (1972)

Young Bridie McShane, stubborn, blazingly outspoken, is her father's special daughter, "as good as a boy," he had been known to say. Yet even when William is born . . . it is still Bridie her father takes for rambles, talks to about Christ, the revolution, and the wickedness of grinding poverty in the midst of plenty. But Bridie and her family, living on the outskirts of Edinburgh after the First World War on the tiny disability pension of wounded Patrick McShane and the pittance he earns from patrol duty, still know nothing of desperate poverty until after his death, when Bridie is 9.

Patrick is adored by his family. For his wife, his loss bring happiness to an end forever.

As for Bridie, "she was howling through the rush of wind, howling like an animal in the unbearable pain and desolation of understanding at last that her father was dead." But Bridie is indeed her father's daughter. Even before he dies she has the first of a series of insights that continue throughout the book. Eventually they help her to gain steadiness and purpose.

After Patrick is gone, it is the death of a rabbit (whose exact state she is coldly trying to impress upon four-year-old William) that brings home a further knowledge; *that it can happen to her,* this terrible not-being. In her headlong physical flight from that knowledge, her hand is torn by a briar. As the blood wells forth, she is acutely conscious of her own life potent in each drop, sees every detail of the scene around her, hears every sound as never before, and shouts in her mind, "I am alive! I am alive!" But then becomes aware, because of the richness and vitality trembling in those drops of blood, of Time as "a visible specter" fighting on equal terms with her own exaltation. . . .

[Later], as a fledgling writer, she is striving to identify with what lies beyond normal consciousness, to make whatever she wants to express wholly her own before putting it in words. Then, and only then, she seems on the point of escaping "the closed circle of life and death" in which she knows she is caught. Actually, of course, Time is hurrying her on—and the fight between Time and her love of the world in all its myriad aspects is unfailingly expressed in her writing.

Finally, it is the man who feels the poet Andrew Marvell's words ("But at my back I always hear / Time's winged chariot hurrying near") haunting her work who can tell her that she must cease her preoccupation with death, that she must absorb each shattering experience and work outwards, that only a self-destructive spirit burrows in. She must cease to mourn her father's death, as she has unconsciously been doing, and live again, vigorously and creatively, in him.

Mollie Hunter's two best books, to my way of thinking, are her second fantasy, ***The Kelpie's Pearls,*** and this, her first novel of realism, ***A Sound of Chariots.*** What these two have in common is style, a fine fierce ability to share emotion. In ***Chariots,*** I find an increase in Miss Hunter's ability to go directly to the heart of a scene, to wring from it the final drop of meaning. I find an even more skillful interweaving of sights, sounds and feelings as these would be experienced by a child during a moment that will change that child's life forever.

There is a power at work in ***Chariots*** that I haven't met in Mollie Hunter's fantasies. And I cannot help but ask myself if this clarity of vision, that penetrates the smallest detail, may not have been the result of reliving a childhood of loss and turmoil. Whether it is a reliving or not, this is the most memorable of Miss Hunter's books, the distinguished account of a child's traumatic experiences and her struggle to gain the realization of selfhood.

> *Eleanor Cameron, "At Her Back She Always Heard," in* The New York Times Book Review, *November 5, 1972, p. 6.*

Only a poet dares try to convey to the more earthbound of us the emotion he experiences when he sees a rainbow in the sky. A scientist, by reference to refraction, can explain all; but with the explanation the great mystery of artistic experience evaporates like a coastal haze.

Mollie Hunter is a poet, with a strong streak of the scientist in her, a streak which she handles with granite firmness while she uses it to explore the very nature of poetic imagination in her new novel, *A Sound of Chariots.*

A Sound of Chariots is a tough yet tender, humorous yet tragic, sometimes horrific yet always gentle and compassionate autobiographical (surely?) novel. . . .

Though its theme is the growth and development of the poetic imagination, though its heroine is threatened and haunted through a tortured early adolescence, there is no time for self-pity here, no patience with mawkish concern over the psyche, no necessity for those esoteric intellectual fantasies so common in much of today's writing for the introspective young. This is real life, looked at through a sharply focused microscope and given artistic form.

Mollie Hunter, as admirers of her vivid folk stories and full-blooded historical novels would expect, has given us a brilliantly carpentered, no-nonsense novel of the old-fashioned kind: it has shape, plot, theme and heart. Any seasoned reader with a strong stomach, a social conscience, a sense of humour and an interest in the maturing craftsmanship of a writer will read *A Sound of Chariots* with delight—and remember it forever.

> *"The Gift of the Gab," in* The Times Literary Supplement, *No. 3734, September 28, 1973, p. 1113.*

[*A Sound of Chariots*] is a bona fide children's book which shares the best qualities of autobiographical works for any audience. (p. 92)

A certain simplicity of explanation, an occasional withholding of details—what the heroine's father died of, for instance—identify it as a work for children. And Mollie Hunter is, of course, an accomplished writer of children's books. She writes novels of folklore, suspense, and history, books that are heavily plotted and detailed, with a clear, unobtrusive style and a sure sense of storytelling. But *A Sound of Chariots* is a remarkable departure. It seems clearly to be her own story, and while she sustains the narrative at a level comprehensible to children, the writing is dense with lush language and startling, impressionistic passages of discovery and meditation. What's more, for the purposes of this paper, she writes a story that traces the gradual evolution of its heroine, Bridie McShane, from early childhood to young womanhood. And without ignoring the problems and the sense of alienation of adolescence, she places them in a framework of a life, of generations. Hunter offers her reader a sense that there are underlying structures to a life, and that adulthood can be something other than a descent into comtemptible compromise, that it can bring with it a sense of competence, grace, and power.

Fortunately, even though the heroine plans to be a writer, the novel is not written in the first person. In the world of *A Sound of Chariots,* children would not make their voices heard that way. Moreover, Hunter is much too attached to the elegant and rhythmic use of language to limit herself by assuming a voice with less range and maturity than her own. For the progress of the novel is marked by intense, meditative moments of revelation, recorded in baroque swells of prose that describe Bridie's insights and her sometimes frightening epiphanies. When she gains a sudden awareness of the nature of death, for example, she feels the blood coursing through her with the passing of each second, and she understands how each second brings her closer to her own end. . . . (pp. 92-3)

This awareness grows from the central event in the novel, which is the death of Bridie's father, Patrick McShane. His death divides the book into its two parts. The first part opens with his funeral, flashes back to Bridie's life with him, and then closes again with the same scene—the limousine pulling up in front of the house and Bridie's mother getting out of the car. It is an effective structural device, because in the interim between the first scene and its repetition, the reader comes to know the father and to share Bridie's pain at her loss. The second part of the book records Bridie's response and adaptation over the next four years. It involves her obsession with death, once she comprehends the reality of it, her sense of separateness and alienation from her sisters, her hostility to her mother, and their eventual reconciliation. It also involves her growth

from childhood to young womanhood—the condition of adolescence as we commonly regard it today hardly applies. (pp. 93-4)

[At] the end of the novel, [Bridie and her mother] have healed enough to help each other. At that point Bridie begins to sympathize and identify with her mother.

The final chapter opens on a train platform where Bridie is waiting, with her mother and younger brother, for the train which will take her to Edinburgh. Like her older sisters, she has had to leave school, and she is going to work and live in Edinburgh with her grandmother. Although she is only fourteen, she is now dressed as a woman. Feeling awkward and discomforted by the corset "her mother had said she must wear to 'keep her figure in' ", she looks enviously at her brother William "who still got to fidget." But then she exchanges a look of understanding with her mother and suddenly takes pleasure in her new role. "Suddenly she was no longer a school girl uneasily masquerading as a woman. She *was* a woman, a young woman sharing a secret grown-up understanding with an older woman". The transition is convincing, and although Bridie's new position is dictated by her poverty, we feel it will be fruitful. She has a sense of her obligations, and more important, of her own promise. She made her peace with the passing of time and she knows she will write. . . . (p. 95)

The uniqueness and authenticity of *A Sound of Chariots* may stem from the fact that it is autobiographical. Absolutely uncontrived, it captures the mind of a young adolescent the way few adolescent novels do. (p. 96)

> *Geraldine DeLuca, in a review of "A Sound of Chariots," in* The Lion and the Unicorn, *Vol. 2, No. 2, Fall, 1978, pp. 92-6.*

A recurring theme used to express . . . traumatic rites of passage is death. It is, of course, not the death of the protagonists themselves, for then the story would end too soon; but it is very likely a death which causes them severe emotional damage, which comes very near to destroying their psyches.

In earlier books it was often the death of a child protagonist that stirred the emotions—Beth in *Little Women,* Nell in *The Old Curiosity Shop,* or Little Eva in *Uncle Tom's Cabin.* Death now appears as the alien who hurts the children through an attack on their loved ones. Jill Paton Walsh in *Unleaving* expresses something of the view of many modern writers who explore this theme:

> And Peter beside her is saying, "Gran! Gran!" trying to bring her attention back to his question. "Gran, will you mind dying?" "I shouldn't think so, dear," she says. "It isn't our own death that troubles us. We have enough to do surviving other people's."

So, too, in such books as Mollie Hunter's *A Sound of Chariots* and Katherine Paterson's *Bridge to Terabithia,* both gentle, philosophical stories, is death seen as the symbolic end of childhood.

In *A Sound of Chariots,* Bridie McShane is only nine when her father's death sets off her period of struggle. So Bri-

Hunter establishing rapport with young American readers, 1977.

die's journey is one from childhood into adolescence rather than the more unusual passage from adolescence to adulthood. It is also an immensely complex treatment of the intellectual and emotional development of a child sensitive and perceptive beyond her years.

Bridie, as the title suggests, is haunted by the sound of Time's "winged chariot" and has to learn to conquer her fear of death. (p. 42)

Bridie's fear of her own personal death becomes a heartbeat pounding furiously throughout the book; and Mollie Hunter skillfully makes this emotion serve as centerpiece and symbol for all those fears that can dominate a sensitive child's life. Bridie has indeed much to fear—her isolation from her mother and her sisters, the prejudices rampant in her own village, even her own "specialness" as a gifted, articulate person.

Bridie is thus the classic "outsider" and it is this fact that gives the characterization its double dimension of generality and individuality.. . . . (pp. 42-3)

It is important to note that the poetic and philosophic overtones of *A Sound of Chariots* are not allowed to overwhelm the "everyday" flavor of its realism. The story is set in what is obviously beloved and intimately familiar

territory, a small Scottish village on the Firth of Forth in the years following World War I. Not in the slightest degree sentimentalized, it is a landscape that is filled with the awesome reality of the war. As Bridie observes the people from her own street and those who live in the War Veterans' houses, she finds there the firm realities upon and against which to build her inner life.

A Sound of Chariots covers seven years of Bridie's life, a long time-span in which Bridie (and vicariously the book's readers) can absorb her pain and consequent emotional growth and make them more truly their own. (p. 43)

> *Sheila A. Egoff, "Realistic Fiction," in her* Thursday's Child: Trends and Patterns in Contemporary Children's Literature, *American Library Association, 1981, pp. 31-65.*

Two contemporary novels which confront the horrors of modern life yet still proffer hope are Mollie Hunter's *A Sound of Chariots* and Katherine Paterson's *Rebels of the Heavenly Kingdom.* . . . [These] books evoke in my reading self (as far as possible to be distinguished from my critical self), joy, hope, and a sense of transcendence. . . . (pp. 98-9)

A Sound of Chariots looks frankly, almost brutally, at

human vulnerability and fear, particularly the fear of one's own mortality. Bridie McShane's story, like that of Mary Lennox [in Frances Hodgson Burnett's *The Secret Garden*], is one of regeneration; but here rebirth occurs through reenactment, not of the archetype of creation, but of the archetype of sacrifice. Bridie's sacrifice incorporates the death of her father and the paradoxical separation from her mother through a grief which ought to have brought them together.

Bridie is nine years old when she loses her father, the father who had taught her by word and deed that Christ was a revolutionary and with whom she had been one in spirit from the day she was born. When Bridie comes to understand what physical death is—"eyes blind, ears stopped up, senses all swallowed up in coldness and blackness, everything ending in cold black nothing"—and the fact that she too will die, the glory of heaven, which her mother had taught her is but one short death-step away from life, grows impossibly remote to her imagination. What does become clear to her is that she is *now* alive. . . .

Like any of us, Bridie cannot hold on to her moment of exaltation: "Time, like a visible specter, loomed up over her then and fought on equal terms with her exaltation so that she felt her brain would burst with the pressure of the battle going on inside it". Bridie becomes again an ordinary, scared little girl; she rushes home to the comforting arms of her mother but finds grief has closed them against her. "Finding her last refuge had failed her, Bridie broke down and wept too". What the child has realized, what she can never unlearn, is that death sets a limit to finite life and that, [in the words of John MacQuarrie] "like music, life derives its meaning and beauty by working out its material in a finite, temporal pattern". Bridie's new awareness comprehends hope for a rewarding temporal life but has no apparent reference to a life after death; and, despite the presence of Christian allusions and motifs in her story, Bridie's own hope seems areligious and natural.

Continuously aware of "a great and terrible *something* surrounding them all", Bridie is furious, not only at her father's death but at her mother's grief that "lurked in the center of all the dark and interlocking mazes that trapped her". One spring day when Bridie goes to gather some early-blooming violets as a special surprise for her mother's birthday, she jumps the fence onto the flowering bank, as she has before. This time she lands in a viscous mass of lambs' tails, trimmed that morning by the shepherd. In an ensuing symbolic ritual, the child is washed in the blood of the lamb. . . . (pp. 99-100)

Several psychological, pastoral, and religious motifs come together in this scene. The time is April, the season of new beginnings; through the horror, Bridie asserts life, even cruelly, by refusing any longer to be pulled down into the destructiveness of her mother's grief. The violets (whose name derives from the same Greek word as *iodine,* a tincture used for healing wounds) are never picked, and Bridie gives her mother nothing for her birthday. To consummate Bridie's bloody redemption from her mother's darkness and from her own horrific nightmares of the maimed and dying, she partakes of a symbolic eucharist: the shepherd's wife cleans her up and gives her "a bit scone" and

elderberry wine, which "tasted hot and sweet with an after-bitterness" and spread a "warm glow in her chest".

Never able to contemplate nor hope for eternity as Mary Lennox does, Bridie does recover times of self-transcendence in the daily world, for example, in the early morning, as she delivers newspapers. . . .

Before the end of the novel, Bridie has closed her palm gently around a luscious, sun-warmed peach and held in her hand—summer, the time of joy, ripeness, the pride of life.

The end of *A Sound of Chariots* is much less conclusive than that of *The Secret Garden*. Fourteen-year-old Bridie leaves school and home for Grannie's and her first job in Edinburgh. Dr. McIntyre, her English teacher, has helped her to understand that all people "are afraid of the passage of Time carrying them to Death," but that she, Bridie, is one of the very few in each generation who have both the "awareness of each passing moment as a fragment of the totality of Life itself" and "the talent to express their awareness in some creative form". That awareness of kairos within chronos, granted to Bridie at the time of her father's death, is not an end for her; rather it is "a beginning, and in time . . . [she] will learn, [she] *must* learn, to build consciously, creatively outward from it!" For only in such creation can Bridie hope to find "the compensation for [her] loneliness of understanding".

The reader last sees Bridie alone on an Edinburgh tram, traveling hopefully into her future: "No one in the street, no one in the world but Bridie McShane gripping the golden rail that steadied her at the helm of her galleon plunging through perilous seas. And in her head a poem was moving, a poem that held the sudden ghosts of roses in the grape-bloom darkness of an empty room". If the prose seems a bit purple here, it is not because Hunter cannot rise above clichés but because fourteen-year-old Bridie is only just on her way toward becoming a poet and her complete, mature self. The author has taken us further than Burnett into the specific means by which Bridie will continually recover kairos in the world of chronos. All she needs: "A little light. A little time"—the words with which the novel closes. And thus, as Andrew Marvell says in the poem which inspires the title of the book, "though [she] cannot make our sun / Stand still, yet [she] will make him run." (pp. 100-02)

M. Sarah Smedman, *"Springs of Hope: Recovery of Primordial Time in 'Mythic' Novels for Young Readers,"* in Children's Literature: Annual of the Modern Language Association Seminar on Children's Literature and The Children's Literature Association, *Vol. 16, 1988, pp. 91-107.*

The Stronghold   (1974)

The Stronghold takes an enormous leap back in time, to the origins of the brochs—mysterious circular Bronze Age fortresses found only in the Highlands and islands of Scotland.

Choosing the Orkney Islands as their birthplace, she invents the absorbing story of a young genius named Coll, who creates their singular hollow-walled design to defend his people against slave-hunting Romans attacking from the sea.

The force of Druidical magic, and the mercilessness of tribal ritual, are effectively shown without sadistic over-emphasis on detail. And the story of Coll's generation coming of age entwines neatly with the building of the first broch, and the rejection of an ambitious traitor. This . . . is a good book: well-written, original and convincing.

Susan Cooper, "Strains of Mark Twain," in The Christian Science Monitor, May 1, 1974, p. F5.

[Mollie Hunter] has won a deserved reputation in this country for such memorable folkloric fantasies as *The Kelpie's Pearls* and *The Haunted Mountain,* among others, as well as *A Sound of Chariots,* a realistic novel taking place immediately after World War I. In *The Stronghold* she now takes us back to a turning point in the lives of those Iron Age peoples who once inhabited the Orkney Islands off the northern tip of Scotland. (p. 8)

Mollie Hunter has given us a tumultuous yet clearly conceived and tautly constructed novel, narrated in one evoking scene after another in which there are always the swift, telling touches of detail regarding a movement, an expression, a change of mood, the precise shading of colors, the precise timbres of sounds. Too often in historical novels any lasting impression of individual characters is lost in the welter of events. But Coll, the girl Fand (whom Coll loves and who is to be sacrificed to the gods), the fanatic Domnall, the traitor Taran, old Nectan and his wife Anu (the ruthless and compassionate tribal mother), all are given tremendous vitality through the artistry of Mrs. Hunter's telling. An outstanding historical re-creation. (p. 10)

Eleanor Cameron, in a review of "The Stronghold," in The New York Times Book Review, July 21, 1974, pp. 8, 10.

The Pictish broch, in spite of its likeness to the great Mycenean beehive tombs, is unique in its extraordinarily simple and effective defence-plan, and local enough to justify Mollie Hunter's attribution in *The Stronghold.* Setting her robust, exciting story on an Orkney island, she describes a tribe living by the sea, constantly threatened by inland neighbors and by the inroads of Roman ships seeking slaves during the first century B.C., before the first true invasion of Britain. . . . In a long, entirely circumstantial novel, the author justifies her belief that the stone-built defensive tower "must . . . have been an idea before it was a fact; an idea springing from one single brilliant mind'; and in showing how Coll plans his tower, collects materials, stands firm against the opposition of the conservative Druids, she shows us also, most plausibly, what tensions and relationships must have existed in a world where superstition constituted as great a danger as the attacks of raiders or the jealousy of individuals. A close, detailed reconstruction of the past in practical terms—in descriptions of place, weather, buildings—helps to establish a brilliantly imagined picture of an ancient society which we can only know now through conjecture.

Margery Fisher, in a review of "The Stronghold," in Growing Point, Vol. 13, No. 3, September, 1974, p. 2455.

This book is set in a period before recorded history when the inhabitants of the Orkneys were dominated by their Druid priests and terrorised by Roman slave-traders. The story arose from the writer's imagining how the 'brochs', unique circular defence-towers, came to be built. The creation of these towers is set in the context of a clash of opinions and wills between Domnall, the leading Druid-priest, and Nectan, warrior-chief of the major tribe on the islands.

From this has grown a vigorous and engrossing tale which gives an effective picture of the society of the time, bringing its attitudes, beliefs and feelings alive for a modern child. The quiet yet intense relationship between Coll and his Druid-trained brother contrasts effectively with the violence and intrigue initiated around them by their chiefs and ambitious, evil individuals. It is Coll, whose physical handicap has encouraged him to develop his inventive powers, who conceives the idea of the 'broch'. Amidst mounting tension, the threat of Nectan's overthrow, and only after a terrible sacrifice has been made to appease the gods he persuades his tribe to construct a trial broch. It proves successful against Roman attacks and also saves the relationship between Domnall and Nectan.

The writing is taut and strong; the scenes of Druid ritual in particular full of colour and atmosphere; the characterisation is consistent and lively. The whole makes an absorbing tale for lovers of action and for those interested in the past. (pp. 110-11)

Judith Aldridge, in a review of "The Stronghold," in Children's Book Review, Vol. IV, No. 3, Autumn, 1974, pp. 110-11.

A magnificent novel in theme, in plot, in the characters portrayed and in the manner it unfolds its vivid and dramatic story. . . . The glory of this book is the painful playing out of ancient ritual, the patient planning, the victory of loyalty and goodness over greed for power. (pp. 67-8)

Elaine Moss, "Fiction 3: Novels for 11-14 Year Olds," in her Children's Books of the Year: 1974, Hamish Hamilton, 1975, pp. 59-74.

A Stranger Came Ashore (1975)

Mollie Hunter's success with her last book, *The Stronghold,* which recently won the Carnegie Medal, can have had no effect on her new book, which was obviously written long before she heard the news. *A Stranger Came Ashore* is altogether a slighter, less original book than *The Stronghold* but still well worth reading. Its central concern is the fate of young Elspeth Henderson. Will her bridegroom be her old love Nicol Anderson or the new mysterious Finn Learson who comes out of the sea one wild stormy night? Everything is seen through the eyes of twelve-year-old Robbie, Elspeth's brother, so that it is a much younger book than Rosemary Harris's strange story *The Seal-Singing,* which draws on some of the same elements. The hints about Finn Learson are rather heavy-handed, Yarl Corbie should have appeared—or at least have been mentioned—a little earlier in the story, and it seems only for the sake of the plot that Robbie could not swim. But there is plenty here to attract and hold a young reader, and Mollie Hunter's love of the Shetlands and their selkie-legends is pervasive.

> Ann Thwaite, "Fey, Fi, Fo, Fum," in The Times Literary Supplement, *No. 3836, September 19, 1975, p. 1053.*

Mollie Hunter has already written successful junior novels set in the Orkneys and Shetlands. This latest one is a product of her study of the Shetland lore and legend concerning the Selkie Folk, who are the seals that live in the waters round the islands. . . .

The author adapts her style in a remarkably effective way to convey the tension of the story and the impact of its climax. The language is direct, commanding and evocative, and she has a quite outstanding gift for conveying atmosphere. The book will certainly be voted a winner.

> Robert Bell, in a review of "A Stranger Came Ashore," in The School Librarian, *Vol. 24, No. 1, March, 1976, p. 50.*

This is not quite the work expected of a Carnegie winner, but it would make a lesser reputation. The hero is not young Robbie Henderson, who does some brave deeds, but Shetland. The scenery and the culture of the land, and the music of the surrounding sea, pervade the story, bringing an originality of colour to a rather conventional theme. This is in fact the old story of the man upon land who becomes a selkie in the sea. The writer sets the drama of the narrative effectively against the homeliness and simplicity of the island and its inhabitants, drawing the readers by degrees into a feeling of involvement in the beautifully primitive society. As an example of controlled development it could scarcely be bettered.

> M. Crouch, in a review of "A Stranger Came Ashore," in The Junior Bookshelf, *Vol. 40, No. 2, April, 1976, p. 105.*

The Wicked One (1977)

Here is a story that appears at first to be a genuine Gaelic folktale, retold and somewhat expanded. But no, it's a brand-new Gaelic folktale (we need a term for such creations, like "instant antique" but without the pejorative note) devised and related for the first time by the British writer Mollie Hunter. The proper rhythms are here:

"There was this man, it seems, who was troubled by one of these Otherworld creatures that can be seen or not seen, just as they choose." And here are all the ingredients, including a Scottish glen, fairies, changelings (the bovine variety), and charms against evil. Here, too, is the requisite youngest son of three who is both less than and more than his brothers. But Hunter has not been content to tell a sim-

ple folktale, old or new. Instead she has everywhere expanded and developed it, and whether the result is an improvement on the genre or a violation of it is entirely a matter of taste.

The story is about a forester named Colin Grant who lives in the Scottish highlands. It is also about his wife Anna and his three sons. But mainly it is Colin's story, telling of his bedevilment by a creature called a Grollican, and his many attempts to be rid of it. . . .

"Grollican" comes perilously near to being a perfect anagram for "Colin Grant," and indeed it appears that the Grollican is in fact an incarnation of Colin's fiery temper. Anna says, "One of you is as much to blame as the other for the trouble you've had." To escape the creature, Colin finally packs up his family and moves to America but, Hunter implies, one cannot run away from one's bad habits: The Grollican follows and there is a wild, unlikely scene with it on a New York City pier. Only by learning at last to control his temper does Colin learn to control the Grollican.

It's a wonderfully written story and a very entertaining one. However, if you prefer your folktales old, timeless and cosmic rather than new, temporal and utilitarian, then this story may strike you as unnecessary. If you don't give a hoot for the old ways and require only a rollicking story, then you'll have a very good time.

> Natalie Babbitt, in a review of "The Wicked One," in The New York Times Book Review, *June 26, 1977, p. 23.*

Somewhat reminiscent of the author's earlier work **The Kelpie's Pearls,** the book exudes a fine Highland flavor and is an excellent example of the author's ability to interplay strong, solid characters with creatures from the Otherworld in tales of excitement and humor.

> Ann A. Flowers, in a review of "The Wicked One," in The Horn Book Magazine, *Vol. LIII, No. 4, August, 1977, p. 442.*

This time Mollie Hunter is writing in the style of folk tale for ten-year-olds (as in **A Stranger Came Ashore** and **The Haunted Mountain**), not a historical novel for rather older readers (as in **The Stronghold** and **The Lothian Run,** for instance). . . . Action is fast, events are credible and consistent given the magical premises, and a dry humour unobtrusively pervades the whole. . . . Tone and style I found most attractive: apparently casual but always economical; simple but neither patronising nor banal; sympathetic but never sentimental: a good story.

> Norman Culpan, in a review of "The Wicked One," in The School Librarian, *Vol. 26, No. 2, June, 1978, p. 137.*

The Third Eye (1979)

The usually reliable author's latest can best be compared to haggis, a uniquely Scottish dish made primarily from sheep organs; it may be appreciated in its native land, but is unlikely to appeal to the appetites of young readers on this side of the ocean. What plot there is revolves around young Jinty Morrison, the youngest of three daughters in a poor but proud Scottish family during the Depression. Her *Third Eye* (psychic sensitivity) makes her especially aware of the troubles of people around her, primarily those of a gruff old Earl who, by sacrificing himself, seeks to break an age old curse on his family. The tale is told as a series of flashbacks by Jinty, but precious little of interest occurs to her throughout and the various plot threads are neither well integrated nor especially riveting, although a number of the characters, especially Meg's oldest sister and the Earl, are portrayed with sympathy and insight.

> *Chuck Schacht, in a review of "Third Eye," in* School Library Journal, *Vol. 25, No. 8, April, 1979, p. 57.*

What a fine writer Mollie Hunter is! One might think that, with her preoccupation with the Scottish scene, her stories might slip into monotony, but not a bit; she is most resourceful in finding new themes, springing naturally from the conflicts generated between people and their environment.

The Third Eye is largely about a place, Ballinford in West Lothian. In a sense the village is dominated by the colossal figure of the Earl, who is a big man in every sense, but there are others: Archie Meikle, who holds directly contrary opinions on most subjects but loves the Earl like a brother (he is the village blacksmith), his big son Tom who marries the schoolmistress, Mr. Elphinston who rules the kirk and knows all about Hell, Herr Winkel, genius in charge of the Earl's kitchen . . . the list could be extended. Then there are the Morrisons. The action is seen through the eyes of Jinty Morrison, youngest of three girls, not the brightest but the most sensitive. Jinty is fey. Her love for her mother is mixed liberally with fear, and Mistress Morrison is certainly a difficult woman, and one with a past. I guessed the secret which made her so horrible to live with quite early in the story—and most readers will do so too—but this does not spoil the pleasure at all. This is not a mystery story but a complex study in character and a study of a community and a family.

Miss Hunter has adopted rather a difficult device for telling her story, mostly in extended flashbacks. Children are familiar with this, especially from their television viewing, and there should be no real problem. I find it impossible to believe that they will not pay the writer the compliment of total surrender to the powerful narrative and the quiet and persistent appeal of the young heroine. It is a strong drama, but there is plenty of fun to accompany the tragedy and to complete the picture of a whole community. How splendidly Miss Hunter rises to her big scenes, the anvil-wedding and the ice-party. A book to savour, to read slowly and then to read again noting how beautifully every episode is dovetailed into the main structure.

> *M. Crouch, in a review of "The Third Eye," in* The Junior Bookshelf, *Vol. 43, No. 4, August, 1979, p. 221.*

[*The Third Eye* is] an extraordinarily vivid and impressive study of a family and a community in a Scottish town in the 1930's. Attention is held from [the] first sentence right up to the end of the book. . . . Mollie Hunter works out her plot so expertly and directs her narrative so firmly that we are drawn completely into the book, getting to know the characters in the slow, partial manner of real life. This is a book for an active and experienced reader. Using flashback, the author takes us from the Procurator's office back several years, and while Jinty thinks about her first meeting with the old Earl, ponders over the items of local gossip which have troubled her, reflects on the way the community works outwards from the Great House, she is also thinking about her own position in her family. As the youngest of three sisters, and as a child of sudden, startling intuitions, she is shaken by Linda's cool selfishness in forcing independence, and by the apparently brutal way her mother denies Meg, the eldest girl, the home and affection due to her, because she disapproves of her marriage. Though this is not a first-person story, the revelations of a family secret and of the secret motives for the Earl's death are described as they might naturally have been received by a girl of fourteen for whom they bring a heavy responsibility. Unerring in its documentation, lucid and rhythmical in style, this is one of those rare novels which seems to have grown rather than to have been constructed, so that it satisfies as a unique piece of writing.

> *Margery Fisher, in a review of "The Third Eye," in* Growing Point, *Vol. 18, No. 4, November, 1979, p. 3595.*

You Never Knew Her as I Did! (1981)

Had Jane Austen known this latest account of her "bewitching princess" Mary Queen of Scots, she would have exclaimed that the unhappy Queen's friends were now only Mr Whitaker, Mrs Knight, herself *and* Mollie Hunter. With her usual narrative instinct, Miss Hunter singles out a single significant episode, Mary Stuart's imprisonment by her own countrymen on the Island of Lochleven. The story is told by the erstwhile page at the castle, bastard son of the previous laird, a central figure in her successful bid for freedom and her devoted spymaster during her imprisonment in England. The news of her execution has been brought by one of Will's messengers, much the age he had been at Lochleven when he first fell under her spell, and he recalls the past. The first-person narration means that we rely more on dialogue than deliberate evocation of atmosphere. This makes the first chapters, when so much previous history has to be conveyed, a trifle heavy despite the skilful varying of speakers. Thereafter, however, the excitement and suspense of the plot carries all before it. Mary's queenliness in the face of the fanatical Protestant Lindsay and her effect on the entire Douglas household, from the matriarch torn between her bastard son the Earl of Moray, who may be Regent, and the legitimate Geordie who wins Mary's love, to the five Porches, the tall plain Douglas daughters. The men of course succumb to her charm, and the reader too is prepared to accept Miss Hunter's explanations of the Darnley murder and the Bothwell marriage uncritically. The family's complex relationships are well drawn, as is Will's moving confirmation of the identify of his own mother.

> *M. Hobbs, in a review of "You Never Knew*

Her as I Did," in The Junior Bookshelf, *Vol. 45, No. 5, October, 1981, p. 212.*

This is historical fiction about Mary, Queen of Scots, set in Scotland in the mid-16th Century just after the birth of Mary's son James; in one of her escape attempts from her Scots captors, who wish to force her abdication, she is aided by one of the local lord's bastard children, Will Douglas, a 14-year-old boy on the fringe of the castle court, with no real place either as a servant or as one of the lord's family. The Queen's personal attractiveness and her kindness to the boy, as well as the righteousness of her cause, lead the boy to pledge his fidelity to her, and he becomes her trusted servant and lifelong follower. The book investigates an unusual part of the Queen's life, and the first-person narration, from the boy's point of view, lends an immediacy to events. The boy is an obvious partisan of the Queen, but the case for her is not propagandistic, though Hunter and her characters are obviously sympathetic. The book is full of exciting and interesting detail, and the language evokes the times and the dialect of the Scots without being difficult or obscure. The high adventures and chivalry are well sustained and the characters well drawn and well motivated. Both the boy and his queen, though long dead, come alive. (pp. 142-43)

Ruth K. MacDonald, in a review of "You Never Knew Her as I Did!" in School Library Journal, *Vol. 28, No. 2, October, 1981, pp. 142-43.*

The author clearly defines the ambivalent relationships among the characters—relationships complicated by ambitions and power politics clashing with family loyalties. Writing with her natural fluency, never overburdened with historical paraphernalia, she makes the background of intrigue, suspicion, plotting, and counterplotting an organic part of an absorbing story, narrated twenty years later as a memoir by Will Douglas, sorrowing for his beheaded queen.

Ethel L. Heins, in a review of "You Never Knew Her as I Did!" in The Horn Book Magazine, *Vol. LVII, No. 6, December, 1981, p. 669.*

The Dragonfly Years (1983; U. S. edition as *Hold on to Love*)

Bridie McShane did a lot of growing up at an early age. It began, in *A Sound of Chariots,* with the death of her father, whose favourite child she was, and the realization of her own mortality. After wrestling with her own grief and sternly refusing to be paralysed by her mother's, Bridie won her independence and set off for a working life in Edinburgh. **The Dragonfly Years** discovers her there, shortly after Mollie Hunter left her ten years ago, a florist's apprentice and an earnest evening class student, in the period just before World War II. . . .

Her political awareness, already fed by her father's socialist ideals, develops alongside her friendship with Peter McKinley, another evening class student. Their relationship, based on shared enthusiasms, nearly founders when

Peter forbids her to spend an evening with another man. Bridie, who is determined to be a writer, knows that it is more important not to be owned by Peter than to lose him. Peter, equally stubborn, joins the Navy just before war is declared.

This central relationship is somewhat idealized—the other man, for instance, has to be a "bounder" and only after one thing—but what this second novel does chart is the bringing of Bridie's emotional maturity up to the level of her intellect and conscience. "I have given hostages to fortune", quoted Patrick McShane to his daughter in *A Sound of Chariots.* That Bridie does so too, in admitting her love for Peter is, fortunately, not shown as a teenage girl's biological destiny but as a conscious adult choice to adjust her concept of freedom.

Despite the mushy ending, the book makes a powerful point: it is only with the victory of independence that you recognize your necessary involvement with the rest of humankind. Bridie knew, precociously, when her father died, that the bell tolled for her, but it is only in the sequel that she accepts that she is no longer an island.

Mary Hoffman, "No Longer an Island," in The Times Educational Supplement, *June 17, 1983, p. 28.*

The book has interest as a piece of social history, but its success depends mainly on one's reaction to the heroine. Many readers, I know, have deep personal feelings for Bridie, and the small details of her progress towards maturity matter greatly to them. I must confess that I have not surrendered unconditionally to her charms. She is a girl of enterprise, courage and spirit, but somehow she seems to command feelings of respect rather than affection. For me she comes most convincingly to life not in her sympathy with the old Jewish jeweller or in her resistance to Peter's too chauvinistic love, but, more cerebrally, in her passion for Edinburgh and its past. Here, I suspect, speaks both the true Bridie and the true Mollie Hunter.

The book concludes with a clear indication that a sequel must follow, and a full assessment of this achievement of a major writer ought to await the conclusion of the story. (p. 214)

M. Crouch, in a review of "The Dragonfly Years," in The Junior Bookshelf, *Vol. 47, No. 5, October, 1983, pp. 213-14.*

This is a strangely unsatisfying book. *Most* of the characters are realistically portrayed; *most* of the dialogue rings true; *most* of the story line unfolds naturallly; individual scenes stand out clear and sharp. And yet, the whole is not greater than the sum of its parts. Hunter seems an observer rather than creator of her characters and events. She is telling a story, adding in details as they become necessary, rather than constructing a literary whole. Of the three thematic strands, the love interest is most successful. While the historic setting is unusual and interesting, it remains a backdrop rather than an integral factor in the book. Nor is there enough development in Bridie's writing or growth in her personality to involve readers in her life. Ultimately, it is only the love story that captures our attention. Even here, it is difficult to tell whether we care because Hunter

Hunter in the National Portrait Gallery of Scotland responding to congratulations upon the unveiling of the Mollie Hunter portrait in the series "Eminent Scots of the Twentieth Century."

has brought Bridie and Peter fully to life, or because we are aware of the threat of wartime that hung over all, young and old, during that period. As a historical novel or semi-autobiographical character study this is only average; as a teen romance, it is well above the usual run.

> *Barbara Hutcheson, in a review of "Hold on to Love," in* School Library Journal, *Vol. 30, No. 9, May, 1984, p. 90.*

The Knight of the Golden Plain (1983)

Mollie Hunter, a Scottish storyteller praised on both sides of the Atlantic for her folkloric re-creations, here uses the device of one boy's imagining to toy with a host of chivalric clichés. Incidentally, though successfully, she also tells a story.

Banishing witches takes about 30 minutes, and dragon slaying takes even more time, but not long enough to fill Sir Dauntless's day, so he finds himself a maiden in distress. The predictably blonde, blue-eyed maiden is literally dumb; the evil wizard Arriman has turned her voice into a songbird that constantly hails its own reflection in a mir-

rored cage. Death by exhausted narcissism thus awaits "our Dorabella."

One Rapid River and one Dark Forest later, the hero confronts Arriman, who howls "one single and terrible word of magic. Abracadabra. Jets of flame spurted from [his] blood-red talons." The "power of true love" in Dorabella's handkerchief avails the knight naught: " 'I am about to die!' thought Sir Dauntless. And could see no way to avoid this fact. As every knight should do . . . he knelt to say his prayers."

The strength of the deceptively casual prose offsets an occasional lapse into preciousness, as when Sir Dauntless remembers, "On Saturdays there was always chocolate cherry cake for tea. . . . The thought of Dorabella began to fade." But the text is ill served by the illustrations of the Caldecott medalist Marc Simont, whose muddy palette and exaggerated cartoonery play up the author's excesses rather than her lightheartedness.

> *Janice Prindle, in a review of "The Knight of the Golden Plain," in* The New York Times Book Review, *November 6, 1983, p. 43.*

A wish-fulfilment fantasy, written for three grandsons. . . . A small gem of a story, mixing with relish the trappings of high romance and such interests of childhood as ensuring fair shares of chocolate cake. (p. 28)

> *Peggy Heeks, "Traditional Tales," in* The Signal Review of Children Books, 2, *1983, pp. 24-8.*

Set within the framework of a daydream, the story recounts the exploits of a young boy transformed by his imagination into the fearless Sir Dauntless, Knight of the Golden Plain, who rides forth "to do good deeds and to seek great adventures." A gallimaufry of evildoers awaits his presence—from witches and dragons to the demon magician Arriman, who holds in thrall a small golden bird, once the lilting voice of the lovely Dorabella. But the bird is dying, for it is imprisoned in a mirrored cage and compelled to sing each time it sees its reflection. After pledging his vows to the distressed Dorabella, Sir Dauntless proceeds on his quest—into the heart of the Dark Forest. There he finds and releases the singing bird before encountering the dread Arriman, whom he conquers with knightly courage and the power of prayer. Then Sir Dauntless rides home for tea. Unfortunately, the following chapter seems to be an unnecessary epilogue, although it does afford Sir Veritas an opportunity to explain that "the Golden Plain is not a place; it is a *time* . . . the carefree days when you can spin yourself a daydream of any kind of adventure you wish to have." This bit of philosophical musing is both jarring and contradictory, for in the context of the chapter the characters seem to assume a life independent of the boy's imagination. But the flaw is a minor one, for the author's style is rhythmically compelling, her cadenced prose exerting its own kind of magic. And the story itself is a guileless spoof of the heroic tradition and courtly conventions in the spirit of Kenneth Grahame's *The Reluctant Dragon.*

> *Mary M. Burns, in a review of "The Knight of the Golden Plain," in* The Horn Book Magazine, *Vol. LX, No. 1, February, 1984, p. 54.*

The Three-Day Enchantment   (1985)

In this sequel to **The Knight of the Golden Plain** Sir Dauntless does battle with the Giant Hogweed, a blustery, hollow character who boasts, "I shall crush you to mush!" Dauntless mows him down, only to discover that he was the creature of a much more dangerous foe, the sorceress Alkemilla, who has stolen lovely Dorabella. Dauntless must find the witch's lair and break her spell by sundown, or Dorabella is lost forever. For the boy's daydream it purports to be, this tale is remarkably coherent and sophisticated. Never mind. As the raw material for daydreams to come, it's rich and nourishing. Both Hunter's prose and [Marc] Simont's illustrations are notable for verve and fluidity of line; and if the author winks knowingly at her adult audience from time to time, still, the humor is affectionate. Give this to parents who want something longer than usual for reading aloud.

> *Gale Eaton, in a review of "The Three-Day*

Enchantment," in School Library Journal, *Vol. 32, No. 5, January, 1986, p. 58.*

The timeless enchantment of fairy tales is, today, partially credited to features of considerate text—notably, story structure and imagery. Mollie Hunter's **The Three-Day Enchantment** is a good example. . . . [The] story does not depart from the time-honored formula; Mollie Hunter knows how solid it is. She energizes it with vivid language, for words are indeed her servants. Then, too, Marc Simont's paintings reinforce the imagery without revealing too much about the outcome. A book like this leads naturally to renewed acquaintance with older fairy tales. . . . (p. 589)

> *Sam Leaton Sebesta and Peggy C. Moberly, "Critically Speaking: Literature for Children," in* The Reading Teacher, *Vol. 39, No. 6, February, 1986, pp. 588-94.*

Like children's imaginative play, the tone of this story admits it's pretending and then goes on to have a wonderful time. The author's forthright language depends on strong verbs and just the right word rather than too many. Familiar motifs of high fantasy and tales of chivalry are etched in such sharp relief that children who meet them here will recognize them later in more complex stories. The illustrations are simple and dramatically colored, leaving room to imagine backgrounds and detail—a perfect complement to the text. (p. 304)

> *Janet Hickman, in a review of "The Three-Day Enchantment," in* Language Arts, *Vol. 63, No. 3, March, 1986, pp. 303-04.*

I'll Go My Own Way   (1985; U. S. edition as Cat, Herself)

As the only child of a traveller (tinker) family, Catriona McPhie finds herself learning the skills of trapping and pearl fishing from her father along with the traditional 'women's' skills. As a result, she comes into conflict with other traveller families, especially that of her boyfriend, Charlie Drummond. This, coupled with her inheritance of the gift of 'second sight', makes life very difficult for Cat and the problems are resolved only after several very dramatic episodes involving violence and arson.

The novel is as finely crafted as we have come to expect from Mollie Hunter. Her descriptions of wild life and the scenery of Sutherland are especially well drawn, and I certainly learned a great deal about the problems and present-day life-style of traveller families. However, is not Cat McPhie perhaps too refined for someone who has lived her life in relatively primitive conditions? There seems little difference between her and Bridie McShane of **The dragonfly years** and, as with that book, it is very difficult to categorise the work into a readership age level. There are certain episodes (for example, a vivid description of the birth of a child, and a practical one of how petrol bombs are made) which would need mature readers to handle them. Yet the format, the basic style of writing, and the story-line give the impression that the book is intended for the younger end of a secondary school. Given these reservations, I can recommend it as a good story about growing up in general and about present-day traveller family problems; though I would have appreciated the opinion of someone more closely involved before writing this review.

> *Christine Walker, in a review of "I'll Go My Own Way,"* in The School Librarian, *Vol. 34, No. 1, March, 1986, p. 73.*

This story of an extraordinary way of life and a young girl's rebellion against the same traditions that have given her strength and character is peopled with stereotypes who don't come alive: the travellers who are misunderstood children of nature; the townspeople who are suspicious; the obligatory town intellectual whose love of these remarkable people leads him to become their protector and interpreter to the world. Everyone philosophizes too often, and the jargon that sprinkles the pages is often eccentric without being picturesque. Most of the action is bunched into the last half of the book, and although there are flashes of beauty, passion and wisdom, they are few and far between, and few of them ignite into enough dramatic fire to make the characters come alive.

> *Marjorie Lewis, in a review of "Cat, Herself,"* in School Library Journal, *Vol. 32, No. 9, May, 1986, p. 104.*

Travelling life with its wealth of customs, traditions and family feeling is vividly brought to life in this spirited story of Cat, a traveller's daughter who holds a son's place. The family skills are passed from father to son but Cat learns them all and is proud of it. Mollie Hunter writes affectionately of contemporary travellers who face prejudice and hostility from settled communities, but her picture of their life with its strong sex sterotyping and undervaluing of women does not always leave the reader sympathetic. (p. 51)

> *Julia Eccleshare, "Fiction for Older Readers,"* in her Children's Books of the Year, *National Book League, 1986, pp. 45-59.*

The Mermaid Summer   (1988)

Another story set (like *A Stranger Came Ashore* and *The Selkie's Pearls*) in a timeless Scotland that might be now—but where fairy creatures enrich and complicate the lives of ordinary folk. Here, young Anna outwits the cruel, beautiful, but ultimately childish mermaid queen who has revenged herself on Anna's nonbelieving grandfather by exiling him from his family and fishing village.

Giving it her own inimitable flavor, Hunter stirs up a fine broth of hearty Scots ingredients: deftly characterized working people of several generations (the plucky, grieving grandmother is a particularly memorable character); a satisfying series of tricks and countertricks that not only lead to justice for all concerned but echo Anna's physical and moral growth; the magic, which seems altogether possible; and pungent, lilting language, dancing with humor. A feast for fans to savor.

> *A review of "The Mermaid Summer,"* in Kirkus Reviews, *Vol. LVI, No. 11, June 1, 1988, p. 828.*

Mollie Hunter is such an accomplished storyteller that her fishing community in the North of Scotland, whose catch is threatened during *The Mermaid Summer,* becomes real from her first evoking the fearless Eric Anderson (who undergoes a terrible punishment for not believing in mermaids), his family, who suffers more than he does, and in particular the pair at the centre, his grandchildren Anna and Jon, their bravery, together with Anna's faith in his return, bring about the happy ending. The two elders of the village who see further than ordinary are also well drawn, Jimsie Jamieson, the oldest fisherman, and the old witchwoman they called the Howdy. Yet it is hard to become deeply involved in the children's struggle to stave off the threat of the fleet's destruction: the spiteful, greedy mermaid has her moments of creating terror—chiefly by the suddenness of her appearance—but her pettiness militates against the arousing of real emotion, and it becomes at times somewhat of a storm in a teacup, with the narrator working audibly to keep us excited. After all, why *didn't* Anna give up the emerald green comb, her grandfather's gift which is coveted by the mermaid, when she was happy to sacrifice his silk with the colours of the sea, which she wore as the Herring Queen? As Jimsie points out, she was right not to create a precedent for blackmail, but one misses a convincing reason for her first refusal. Let us hope that is an adult's comment, since as soon as one abandons oneself to the style, its rhythm and lilt as always charm away criticism! (pp. 193-94)

> *M. Hobbs, in a review of "The Mermaid Summer,"* in The Junior Bookshelf, *Vol. 52, No. 4, August, 1988, pp. 193-94.*

Belinda Hurmence

1921-

American author of fiction and editor.

Major works include *Tough Tiffany* (1980), *A Girl Called Boy* (1982), *Tancy* (1984), *My Folks Don't Want Me to Talk about Slavery: Twenty-One Oral Histories of Former North Carolina Slaves* (1984).

The author of works for middle graders and young adults that often profile American blacks and use slavery as their basis, Hurmence is recognized for providing young readers both with accurate information on the slave experience and with moving literary experiences. Usually set in North Carolina, the state where she currently resides, her books are noted for their evocative sense of place; their effective use of dialogue, often in dialect; and their strong characterizations. Hurmence writes from the perspective of her young female protagonists in both historical and recent times; in her first book, *Tough Tiffany,* Hurmence describes a frank yet sensitive contemporary eleven-year-old who attempts to provide emotional support for the members of her large family as well as to keep them ahead of the bill collector. Tiffany is fascinated by her grandmother's stories about their slave ancestors; in Hurmence's next book, *A Girl Called Boy,* she introduces Blanche Overtha Yancey, called Boy, who is tired of hearing similar stories from her father. In this fantasy for middle graders, Boy is transported from the present day to a small village in 1853 as a slave and learns to understand slavery through her adventures. *A Girl Called Boy* is acknowledged as an especially distinctive work for expanding on the familiar time travel mode through its slavery background and inclusion of black characters. With her young adult novel *Tancy,* Hurmence premieres her first full example of historical fiction: born into slavery, sixteen-year-old Tancy struggles with her new freedom after the declaration of Emancipation and ultimately discovers the true meaning of independence. Hurmence is also the author of a *The Nightwalker* (1988), a mystery for middle graders which treats both environmental issues and the unconscious life of its twelve-year-old narrator, and is the editor of two collections of interviews taken from the Federal Writers Project slave narratives in which former slaves from North and South Carolina discuss their lives; Hurmence has noted that these narratives provided the background for several of her stories for young people. *A Girl Called Boy* received the Parents' Choice Award in 1982 and *Tancy* won the Golden Kite Award for fiction in 1984.

TITLE COMMENTARY

Tough Tiffany (1980)

This pleasantly poignant slice of life centers around 11-year-old Tiffany Cox, youngest member of a large, poor, Black family in the rural south. Sensitive, curious, and refreshingly frank, Tiffany is sympathetic to the plight of her family, particularly in regard to her pregnant, unmarried 15-year-old sister. Tiffany's perspective is apparent and constant, and her naive, candid point of view brings to light sharply defined characters. The plot consists of a variety of situations that are held together by a continuity of tensions: the sister's pregnancy, Tiffany's fear of furniture repossession. The episodic nature of the narrative occasionally causes it to appear unstructured, even aimless, but this is a minor flaw, as there's a spontaneity in the dialogue and a natural warmth that shines through. (pp. 56-7)

Marilyn Kaye, in a review of "Tough Tiffany," in School Library Journal, *Vol. 26, No. 6, February, 1980, pp. 56-7.*

Tiffany is eleven, a sensitive, curious child who likes to think she's tough; she is tough in the sense of having courage and stamina, but she's also charitable and loving. . . . Hurmence uses enough dialect to flavor the dialogue without burdening it; her characterizations are sharply drawn, and she has—in a fine first novel—used every situation in the book to develop and extend her characters, particularly the redoubtable Tiffany.

Zena Sutherland, in a review of "Tough Tiffany," in Bulletin of the Center for Children's Books, *Vol. 33, No. 7, March, 1980, p. 135.*

No one would guess that this is Hurmence's first novel. She has given readers of all ages a story so full of warmth, liveliness and pure charm that it outclasses the works of many seasoned professionals. Tiffany, youngest in a big family of Southern blacks, is always at the center of the action. . . . But Hurmence's other characters, including the children's Granny—who's as tough as Tiffany—are equally appealing in their various ways because the author has made them all irresistibly human.

A review of "Tough Tiffany," in Publishers Weekly, *Vol. 217, No. 10, March 14, 1980, p. 74.*

A Girl Called Boy   (1982)

A vivid, compelling tale of time travel by a young black girl from the present into the time of slavery. Blanche Overtha Yancey, who prefers to be called Boy, goes on a family picnic and hears her father telling a friend about the "freedom birs," a soapstone carving from Africa that has been in the family for a long time. Boy takes the carving and goes exploring. Soon she is in a small village, it is 1853, and she is a slave. Boy experiences cold, hunger fear, and an odd sense of security at not having to worry about what she should do next. When Boy returns to the present, she doesn't forget what happened. This is a most unusual book. The characterizations are excellent, the historical aspects accurate, and it is a non-preachy revelation for all readers. I cannot recall any other material dealing with a young person's reaction to slavery.

Leila Davenport Pettyjohn, in a review of "A Girl Called Boy," in Children's Book Review Service, *Vol. 10, No. 12, Spring, 1982, p. 117.*

Hurmence can be applauded for breaking new ground here, for she's taken the well-used time-travel fantasy mode and freshened it with black characters and a vivid historical context. . . . Boy gets a taste of what slavery really involved and struggles to survive both mentally and physically in a way she's never had to before. There are many predictable aspects—including plot—but good characterizations and a strong sense of the time are real pluses. The tale's entertainment value is high and so are its discussion possibilities. There is a lot of story here for the money.

Denise M. Wilms, in a review of "A Girl Called Boy," in Booklist, *Vol. 78, No. 21, July, 1982, p. 1445.*

Eleven-year-old Boy is really Blanche Overtha Yancey, black and bright and petulant, and just a little embarrassed when her father talks about his slave ancestors. This is the narrow frame, completed at the end of a time-shift story, in which Boy is transported to plantation life in North Carolina in the decade before the Civil War. . . . The contemporary framework adds little to the story, being simply a launching pad for a story of slavery, save for the facts that Boy had foreknowledge and that she

poses as a boy. This has adequate structure, a writing style with considerable vitality, and adequate characterization, but the effort (not unsuccessful) to depict the lives of slaves seems at times so purposive as to outbalance the narrative.

Zena Sutherland, in a review of "A Girl Called Boy," in Bulletin of the Center for Children's Books, *Vol. 36, No. 1, September, 1982, p. 12.*

Tancy   (1984)

Following the story of Tancy, a house girl for "Miss Puddin" Gaither, mistress of Gaither's Mill, Hurmence conjures up an illuminating and absorbing picture of Civil War-era slavery and the changes freedom brought to southern blacks. Luckier than most slaves because she is literate and because Mrs. Gaither has always favored her, Tancy is one of the last to leave Gaither's when news of the Emancipation Proclamation finally reaches North Carolina. But curiosity about her birth mother, a slave sold off long ago, finally wins out over Tancy's fear of what lies outside the only home she's ever known and her loyalty to Miss Puddin (her mistress is actually a crafty old widow who does little not to her own advantage). Tancy does, in fact, find her mother, a woman not at all like the loving, maternal individual Tancy envisioned, but her search and its outcome are less successful dramatically than they are as vehicles for examining the nature of slavery (including its brutality—Tancy is almost raped twice by Miss Puddin's son); postwar chaos and governmental exploitation of blacks; the insidious dependency that sometimes sprang up between master and slave; and the lot of the freed man and woman. Told from Tancy's innocent perspective with details, dialogue, and earthiness that contribute to a realistic background, this is an effective and vivid novel that will undoubtedly make an impact on its readers for the history it brings to light.

Stephanie Zvirin, in a review of "Tancy," in Booklist, *Vol. 80, No. 18, May 15, 1984, p. 1339.*

Tancy's final integration of all the parts of her life is slightly contrived, but her striving for personal emancipation is movingly depicted against the turmoil of the period; her interaction with a wide range of interesting characters (black and white) dramatizes the suffering of slavery and the hopes and broken promises of freedom.

Zena Sutherland, in a review of "Tancy," in Bulletin of the Center for Children's Books, *Vol. 37, No. 10, June, 1984, p. 187.*

Tancy is a rich, evocative, detailed novel of the brutality of slavery, the era of Reconstruction, and the bewilderment of the slaves forced to choose between the security of slavery and the difficulties of freedom. The story has excellent characterization, humor, realism, and was evidently a labor of love for the author.

Leila Davenport Pettyjohn, in a review of "Tancy," in Children's Book Review Service, *Vol. 12, No. 13, July, 1984, p. 141.*

Certainly this story of a country in turmoil should be more

gripping. Tancy does not seem to have difficult times. She has been favored as a child, and even when she leaves the security of home to see the world on her own, she seems to ride too easy a course. For the adolescent ever so concerned with physical changes, there is little hint of the profound effect this must have had on a young woman given freedom. Her transition from child to adult is too smooth, as her change from slave to free is too simple. A few attempted seduction scenes by a white half brother are handled well, however, and are probably more accurate reflections of the truth.

Despite these failings, the pictures painted of life as a slave and of the South after the war are well drawn; slaves in a basically decent environment afraid to leave, families deliberately broken up, as mothers are sold leaving behind sons and daughters, shantytowns, home to freed slaves faced with no money and no provider; this look at a world most readers would never have imagined is graphic and most informative. The problems faced by formerly wealthy land owners, stripped of their property and slaves are also chronicled, and show that the war affected both sides of society.

Perhaps we may forgive the author for making Tancy's life too easy, her passage too simple. She does such a good job of portraying life in the South, from both slave and plantation owner's point of view before and after war, that I can heartily recommend this book and feel that it is unobjectionable for all readers who fall in the 11 year and older group. (pp. 232-33)

> *Jeannette Pergam, in a review of "Tancy," in* Best Sellers, *Vol. 44, No. 6, September, 1984, pp. 232-33.*

The characterization of Tancy, and the use of dialect in particular, is excellent, as is the incorporation of even the most minute details of slave life. Hurmence examines the confusion of the post-War days through the eyes of a bewildered teenager. Fans of historical fiction will enjoy the protagonist's unique perspective on historical events; Tancy's search for her identity should have even broader appeal. (p. 129)

> *Elizabeth Reardon, in a review of "Tancy," in* School Library Journal, *Vol. 31, No. 1, September, 1984, pp. 128-29.*

My Folks Don't Want Me to Talk about Slavery: Twenty-One Oral Histories of Former North Carolina Slaves (1984)

AUTHOR'S COMMENTARY

Sarah Debro, once a slave in Orange County, North Carolina, put it bluntly: "My folks don't want me to talk about slavery. They's shame niggers ever was slaves."

Sarah's folks are not alone in their embarrassment. Many Americans, white and black, prefer to overlook Sarah's role in that period of United States history. After all, "we" aren't the ones to blame for her enslavement. Why bring it up now? Why talk about slavery?

The answer is *Sarah.* To ignore her life under slavery is to ignore black pioneering in the United States—and, in effect, to deny Sarah's humanity, as it was denied in slavery time. That is why Sarah must be allowed to speak for herself. That is why it is important to talk about slavery.

From the time the new republic came into being, Americans wrestled with the problem of Sarah. Her very existence mocked the validity of a government that guaranteed liberty and justice for the nation's people. One argument maintained that Sarah was property, not a person. The Bible was cited as proof of her inferiority. The argument prevailed, for economic reasons, and a system of government grew up around Sarah that provided for her liability under the law without providing her with protection under that same law. She could not vote; she could not marry; any children she bore became the property of her master.

The system worked well enough that millions of slaves remained in bondage for 246 years in America. It worked poorly enough that increasingly restrictive Slave Codes had to be written to keep the human property under control. . . . Yet the slaves persisted in behaving like human beings. They experienced the same passions as their masters: joy and sorrow, love and hatred, generosity and greed. They had dreams and hopes, and they were aware of their dreams and hopes in the way that all people are aware. (pp. ix-x)

When freedom came to blacks in 1865, hard times came too. Some former slaves complained that their sufferings had not ended with the War Between the States. At least in the old days there had been certainty of food, clothing, shelter. Now there was no certainty, and nobody would listen to their problems.

It was true that nobody wanted to listen. The defeated, smarting South had troubles of its own, and a stunned North, the victor, suddenly had four million needy new citizens clamoring for jobs, education, some land of their own. North and South, so lately enemies, united in bewilderment. The slaves had been set free; why weren't they more grateful? Their unseemly grievances tarnished America's image. If they wouldn't put their past behind them, they ought at least, for history's sake, to keep quiet about it.

And in fact, it took little to silence them. Their children, like Sarah Debro's folks, had stopped listening to slavery stories. Besides, the ex-slaves were accustomed to going unheard, just as though they did not exist. Before long they actually would not exist, for they were growing old. Soon everybody who had experienced slavery would be dead, forever silenced.

Then, unexpectedly, in the midst of the Great Depression of the 1930s, a government agency urged them to speak up, to tell what they remembered of life under slavery. The Federal Writers' Project, created to provide work for jobless writers and researchers, initiated a program in which field workers interviewed ex-slaves wherever they might be found. More than two thousand former slaves participated in the program. Of these, 176 were North Carolinians, among them Sarah Debro.

The ex-slaves talked; the field workers wrote down what they said. Ten thousand typewritten pages of oral histories, assembled under the heading *Slave Narratives,* were deposited in the Library of Congress. (pp. x-xi)

Several years ago, I set out to read *Slave Narratives.* Captivated by a world the history books had never told me about, I marveled at the treasure that lay in our country's library-storehouse. The people came alive in the *Narratives,* and their unique memoir gave me a fresh look at pioneering in the United States and at frontier life in my own state of North Carolina. Slaves could not legally own land as a white homesteader could, but in the sense of the self-sufficiency for which Americans admire their forebears—working the land, building houses, growing and preparing food—slaves were genuine homesteaders. They not only did the work; they endured through bondage to freedom. The idea for *My Folks Don't Want Me to Talk about Slavery* grew out of my admiration of those very real pioneers, and the book is . . . presented in acknowledgment of the black contribution to the nation's development, and to the development of North Carolina in particular.

Some readers may find it puzzling that the people of *My Folks* can speak of their former masters with affection, can even declare, as the ex-slave Mary Anderson does, "I think slavery was a mighty good thing for Mother, Father, me, and the other members of the family. . . . " Such a statement is almost incomprehensible to students educated after the civil rights advances of the 1960s.

The reader needs to keep in mind that these oral histories were collected half a century ago, in a time of depression and deep poverty for many whites and most blacks. The entire nation looked backward with nostalgia during the 1930s. To an aging, destitute black person, bondage may well have seemed less onerous in retrospect, particularly if coupled with memories of an easygoing master, a full stomach, the energy of childhood.

Also, some of the accounts may have been skewed, as all oral histories are likely to be to some extent, by the subjects' telling what they believed their questioners wanted to hear. And the fact that many of the interviewers were white may have constrained some of those interviewed to represent slavery as more benign than it actually was.

Nevertheless, taken as a whole, the oral histories of America's former slaves ring true. The very artlessness of the ex-slaves bestows authenticity upon their words. The same can almost be said of the interviewers, for few of that small army of field workers were skilled in the task given them. They were supplied with a list of questions to ask, told to write down the answers as nearly verbatim as possible, and by and large that is what they did. The result is a remarkably eloquent prose. (pp. xii-xiii)

I am responsible for editing the *Narratives* [presented in *My Folks Don't Want Me to Talk about Slavery*], but all the words of those narratives are the ex-slaves' own. . . . North Carolina's Sarah Debro and her fellow black pioneers talk about slavery, and they speak for themselves. (p. xiv)

Belinda Hurmence, in an introduction to My

Folks Don't Want Me to Talk About Slavery: Twenty-One Oral Histories of Former North Carolina Slaves, *edited by Belinda Hurmence, John F. Blair, Publisher, 1984, pp. ix-xiv.*

The source for this collection is the Federal Writer's Project Slave Narratives. Between 1936 and 1938, interviewers gathered information from some 2,000 former slaves. Eugene Genovese's *Roll, Jordan, Roll* was the first major study of slavery in which the narratives were used to express views of slavery by those who had been slaves. *My Folks Don't Want Me to Talk About Slavery* is a selection of 17 of these narratives from North Carolina. They are somewhat edited versions of the original typescripts. Although this selection covers a limited number of narratives, a substantial amount of information is revealed. This includes conditions of slave life such as food, work, housing, religion, relations with the masters and other whites; experiences during and after the Civil War, among them contact with the Union Army, first knowledge of freedom, patterns of life between 1864 and 1937. The narratives also relate experiences with the Ku Klux Klan, ex-slaves' feelings about their present condition, and attitudes toward the younger generations of blacks. Hurmence is the author of several novels for black children. These narratives are intended for young people and the general reader so they may see that slaves were also black pioneers and homesteaders who contributed to the development of North Carolina and the nation as a whole.

A. A. Sio, in a review of "My Folks Don't Want Me to Talk about Slavery," in Choice, *Vol. 22, No. 7, March, 1985, p. 1064.*

The voices of former slaves interviewed in the 1930s as part of the Federal Writers' Project ring instructively through this fine little book. Despite their brevity, the 21 first-person oral histories comprising this edited collection constitute a worthwhile compilation. The book makes available at modest cost a sampling of a resource that can be used advantageously by either scholars or laypersons. A short but helpful bibliography concludes the volume; at the beginning, the editor's introduction is pointed and pertinent. While the original interviews hewed to a narrow set of questions—and these bounds restrict the remembrances put on paper—the documented answers still give a unique glimpse of slavery viewed from the less well-recorded side, the side of the subjugated. The editor wisely limits herself to the files of those ex-slaves who were 10 years old or older when they were freed. This policy minimizes hearsay and maximizes direct experience reports. Sorrowful or otherwise, the narrated events and observations of the elderly respondents yield a pungent view of the fact that slavery is part of this nation's social past. The book is a useful instrument to better comprehend and learn from history.

Robert C. Bealer, in a review of "My Folks Don't Want Me to Talk about Slavery," in Science Books & Films, *Vol. 21, No. 4, March-April, 1986, p. 206.*

The Nightwalker (1988)

Good atmospheric writing and realistic portrayals of island life on the Outer Banks of North Carolina are the highlights of this mystery, which attempts—and nearly succeeds—to merge larger environmental issues with the inner life of a child. Fires have been burning the local fishing shacks nightly, perhaps as part of a protest of the government's attempts to destroy a local way of life, or perhaps set by the spirit of the "nightwalker," subject of an old Indian legend. Savannah, 12, tries not to believe in such things, but she can't help thinking that her sleepwalking little brother Poco is involved in setting the fires when he goes out at night. Family tensions are sharply drawn as Savannah becomes friends with one of the summer people, the same people who are leading the crusade to turn the Outer Banks into a recreational area. When danger strikes, Savannah discovers that she—and not Poco—is the sleepwalker. An intriguing, sometimes exciting story is occasionally marred by the confusion of Savannah's narration of her sleepwalking episodes (even while she is unaware of them). And without a resolution of the larger issue of fishing vs. recreational rights, the story loses its impact.

> *A review of "The Nightwalker," in* Publishers Weekly, *Vol. 234, No. 16, October 14, 1988, p. 77.*

Hurmence's characters are distinct and engaging, right down to their folklore and their Elizabethan dialect. The setting is intriguing and so sharply defined that even readers will resent the changes that progress is likely to bring. Unfortunately, the plot is less successful. The pacing is jumpy and difficult to follow, and the Nightwalker is too shadowy and indistinct to pull it all together. Readers will find this less a ghost story than it promises to be, and, for that and its lack of focus, somewhat disappointing. But those looking for a reasonably diverting mystery and a finely drawn regional portrait will find **The Nightwalker** all they could want.

> *Marcia Hupp, in a review of "The Nightwalker," in* School Library Journal, *Vol. 35, No. 3, November, 1988, p. 112.*

Suspicious fires, a ghostly nightwalker, and Savannah's own fantasizing spin the twelve-year-old girl into a web of uncertainty, fear, and awakening in the suspenseful tale. The setting is Breach Island, North Carolina, just inland of the Outer Banks. Breach was originally settled by Coree Indians and is now populated by a combination of Coree descendants and the so-called "ditdots," or outsiders who have moved there for the peace of the shore. . . . [Savannah's] growing friendship with ditdot Mary Jean is discouraged by Savannah's father but tolerated because her mother supports Savannah's desire to know about the world beyond Breach. Underlying tension, expressed through descriptions of the locale and effective dialogue—a wonderfully subtle combination of dialect and ditdot English—builds to the climactic fire in Mary Jean's home. While the emphasis is on plot and setting, the characters are realistically drawn and act believably. Savannah comes to know that others besides Poco are nightwalkers and have a shadow side, a subconscious part of themselves that may act without conscious knowledge. The book can be read easily for just a rousing good story, but for the more thoughtful reader the suggestion of the complexity of human thought and action provides substance. (pp. 70-1)

> *Elizabeth S. Watson, in a review of "The Nightwalker," in* The Horn Book Magazine, *Vol. LXV, No. 1, January-February, 1989, pp. 70-1.*

Before Freedom, When I Just Can Remember: Twenty-Seven Oral Histories of Former South Carolina Slaves (1989)

AUTHOR'S COMMENTARY

America's infamous period of slavery casts a long shadow on our national past, a shadow in which those human beings who were most affected are still but dimly perceived. History may readily assess the economics and politics that condemned an entire race to bondage for nearly 250 years, but it continues to conceal from us the *slave* trapped in slavery. After all, history as we know it, is the written record of a people, and the black slaves of America were, by law, illiterate. The writings of Frederick Douglass, Booker T. Washington, and a few others are scarcely representative of the four million slaves who attained Freedom only after a bitter and bloody civil war.

How, then, 125 years after the fact, can Americans learn about the lives of those four million before and after Freedom?

During the Great Depression of the 1930s, various government agencies initiated work programs across the country to provide jobs for the unemployed. . . . One of the projects it undertook culminated in *Slave Narratives,* a collection of black folk histories.

The Federal Writers' Project sent field workers to interview blacks who had lived under slavery and recalled their experiences of it. Most of the ex-slaves were found in the South, although a sizeable number reported from states not generally regarded as southern. The project yielded oral histories on a scale unprecedented at the time. (pp. ix-x)

Ten thousand pages of typed manuscript, representing some two thousand voices, were placed in storage in the Library of Congress. (p. x)

The concept of bondage has always fascinated free Americans. With slavery more than a century behind us, and beyond the recollection of any living person, the fascination still persists. Perhaps the invisible, traumatic ties that bind us evoke a dread empathy with the physically enslaved. Scholars, researchers, and writers have always felt the tug of emotions adherent to the *Slave Narratives.*

They have also felt bewildered by the material. For one thing, there is so much of it. For another, it is so uneven, sometimes joyous, sometimes bitter in tone. Some of the ex-slaves were more articulate than others. The expertise of the field workers in committing personalities to paper varied greatly.

The collection remained virtually untouched for years. In time, the Library of Congress microfilmed the entire ten thousand pages to make it more accessible to scholars. In more time, facsimile pages came to be published in multi-volume editions.

Twelve years ago, in gathering background material for a novel I was then writing, I discovered the *Slave Narratives.* Although I found the testimonies uneven, and the very bulk of them daunting, I saw at once the treasure that lay in the oral histories. The *Narratives* resounded with an authenticity I had not encountered before in any prose dealing with slavery. I set aside my novel and read on. It took me two years to read through the collection, and I ended up with a file of notes thick enough to fill a dozen novels. I subsequently wrote two, based on my notes.

The emotional content of the *Narratives* convinced me that they should be accessible to casual readers as well as to scholars and historians. Thus, I came to edit a selection, first from the North Carolina *Narratives,* and now, as a companion volume, from the South Carolina voices. (pp. x-xii)

> *Belinda Hurmence, in an introduction to* Before Freedom, When I Just Can Remember: Twenty-Seven Oral Histories of Former South Carolina Slaves, *edited by Belinda Hurmence, John F. Blair, Publisher, 1989, pp. ix-xvi.*

From 284 Federal Writers' Project interviews gathered during the 1930s, Hurmence has edited 27 pieces in which ex-slaves from South Carolina discuss their homes, chores, masters, families, and celebrations during slave times. As she notes in her introduction, the former slaves' seeming nostalgia for old times may have resulted from their ages (all were over 80 at the time of the interviews) and Depression-linked poverty, the reality that freedom often meant sharecropping and violence from the KKK, and the fact that their interviewers were white. Nonetheless, the collection offers students a chance to use readable primary sources to research details of the everyday lives of Southern slaves.

> *Alice Conlon, in a review of "Before Freedom, When I Just Can Remember," in* School Library Journal, *Vol. 35, No. 13, September, 1989, p. 287.*

Gordon Korman

1963-

Canadian author of fiction.

Major works include *This Can't Be Happening at Macdonald Hall!* (1978), *Who Is Bugs Potter?* (1980), *No Coins, Please* (1984), *Don't Care High* (1985).

A popular and prolific writer of humorous realistic fiction for middle graders and young adults, Korman is well regarded as the creator of hilarious novels and stories that reflect his understanding of young people and of what appeals to them. Called "the most precociously successful writer in Canada" by critic Eileen Whitfield, Korman, who published his first book at the age of fourteen, is recognized for developing a distinctive formula that includes outrageous plots, fast-paced action, individualistic characters who triumph over adults, and irreverent, occasionally sardonic wit in works noted as refreshing changes from the problem novels usually directed to his audience. The books are also characterized by their lampooning of authority as well as by their consistent respect for the rights and abilities of the young. Throughout his works, Korman's youthful male protagonists encounter parents, teachers, and other adults who are less than competent and often eccentric; by ingeniously manipulating the system through methods that often include wild but unmalicious pranks, the boys achieve victories in the adult world that allow them to retain their personal freedom and quality of life. Praised for his ability to weave intricate plots filled with slapstick or satiric humor around concerns important to children, Korman writes his books in a conversational style that uses wordplay, comic repetition, and dramatization in farces considered zany but still anchored in reality.

Korman's first book, *This Can't Be Happening at Macdonald Hall!*, was written at the age of twelve as an assignment for his English class; set in a private boarding school in Southern Ontario, the story introduces the popular team of Bruno Walter and Boots O'Neal, characters who are also the subjects of four additional novels. In *Macdonald Hall,* mischievous idea man Bruno and his sidekick Boots are roommates in grade ten; separated by Headmaster Sturgeon because of their involvement in practical jokes, they enlist the help of their friends at Miss Scrimmage's Finishing School for Young Ladies and cause so much trouble that they prove themselves unsuitable for any other roommate. In the subsequent novels about the duo, Bruno and Boots raise twenty-five thousand dollars for their school, investigate strange happenings at a local dump, marry off an obnoxious computer expert who is attempting to modernize Macdonald Hall, and try to pass off a star female football player as a boy. Korman is also the author of two books about Bugs Potter, a talented young rock drummer who is also adept at turning around situations to suit himself and to further his artistic expres-

sion. Korman sets his books both in Canada and the United States, notably in his current residence of New York. In *No Coins, Please,* Korman describes a tour from New York City to Los Angeles by a group of six Montreal campers and their two counselors; during the course of the trip, junior con artist Artie Geller invents illegal schemes that net him $150,000 before he is discovered by the U. S. government. Korman's first book for teenagers, *Don't Care High,* depicts how tenth-grader Paul Abrams, recently relocated from Canada to an apathetic New York City high school, plots with his classmate Sheldon Pryor to raise the enthusiasm of the student body. Acknowledged as a writer who has become more sophisticated with each book, Korman has recently moved thematically into larger spheres that encompass social issues, such as in the novels *Son of Interflux* (1986) and *A Semester in the Life of a Garbage Bag* (1987) where the protagonists take over the large companies that are threatening their schools. Korman received the Air Canada Award for the Most Promising Writer under Thirty-Five from the Canadian Authors Association in 1981 for his first five novels; in addition, he received the Ontario Youth Medal from the Ontario Government in 1985, a prize given for his contribution to children's literature.

(See also *Something about the Author,* Vols. 41, 49 and *Contemporary Authors,* Vol. 112.)

AUTHOR'S COMMENTARY

[*The following excerpt is from an interview by Chris Ferns.*]

FERNS: You wrote your first novel [*This can't be happening at Macdonald Hall!*] at the age of 12. How did it all begin?

KORMAN: It was basically an accident. When I was in 7th grade we had this English assignment which I got kind of carried away on, and I accidentally wrote the first book. You know, the characters sort of became real people to me, and they more or less wrote the book for me. The class had to read all the assignments at the end of the whole business, and a lot of people were coming to me and saying how they really liked it. I suppose anyone who writes 120 pages for class is going to attract a certain amount of attention anyway—and I just got the idea of seeing if I could get the book published. It seemed to me like a distant goal, but then again, there seemed to me no reason why it shouldn't get published, as I was pretty sure it was as good as the stuff I'd been reading. (p. 54)

FERNS: Since then you've written—or rather published—eight more books. How do you think your writing has developed since that first novel?

KORMAN: In a number of ways. First of all, I got older—and my characters got a little older. I tend to write about stages which I've just been through, meaning that when I was in high school I wrote about 13 year-olds, and now that I'm in University, the last couple of books are about high school students. My writing's changed in a number of ways: when I was writing the first couple of books I sincerely believed that my strength was not so much as a writer, but more as an idea person: I came up with ideas, and I communicated them the best way I knew how—meaning that a pencil and paper were a lot more accessible to me than two million dollars worth of film production equipment, or video, or something. So I did what I could. I considered myself a guy who had the ideas, and somehow or other managed to find the words to string them all together and express them. But somewhere around the sixth book I began to get the impression that there was something more to writing: that I actually was a writer, rather than someone who just managed to express himself through prose because that was the only way, and I think that now I'm very much a prose writer. I'm studying screenwriting and playwriting at University, and I'm very conscious of my prose background now—to the point where I think it almost holds me back when I try to do stuff.

FERNS: You're becoming more conscious of the actual technique of writing?

KORMAN: Yes. I can play with it more, and if I can say so myself, in the last little while I've gotten good at it. I've just done so much of it that I've eventually picked up the hang of it. (p. 55)

FERNS: *This can't be happening at Macdonald Hall* was highly popular. How did the publishers feel about your branching out from the initial Bruno and Boots saga?

KORMAN: They were very receptive to anything I did, and they've been seeing me move in a number of different directions. Scholastic has always welcomed my experimentation. My work with their editorial department has always been very good, and they've come up with a lot of great stuff. Of course, I've gone in certain areas they didn't like so much.

FERNS: Such as what?

KORMAN: Such as when I was writing *Our man Weston* and *Bugs Potter live at Nickaninny.* What I was dealing with at the time was a lot of contrivance of events. So-and-so does this, and it just happens that at the same time this happens, and it happens at exactly the right moment. Those books tended to have an incredible number of contrived circumstances they also had a large number of adult characters, many of whom were crazy and wild. But those works certainly do just as well as the others, and Scholastic certainly had the vision to see that these books were going to do well, even though this wasn't necessarily what they expected from me.

FERNS: It's funny you should mention those two books in particular. I think those are probably the ones I enjoyed most, partly because there was that sensation of juggling more and more balls in the air and keeping them all going at the same time.

KORMAN: It's very much a question of individual taste. There are going to be people who say: "I liked all your books except *Our man Weston*", and then there are going to be kids who write and say that *Our man Weston* is the greatest thing since sliced bread. But that was a stage. Now my stage, I guess, is writing what they call Young Adult. I think I've already been hitting a good percentage of the Young Adult market, but I've yet to have a book that is technically a YA title. Now I'm writing my favourite stuff—but then I always like whatever's the most recent! My last couple of books have both dealt with high schools. I think they have the most realistic character relationships I've done, and the humour has been a little less slapstick. I'm not going to abandon slapstick, but I'm going to use it differently. I'm going to depend more on my character relations, my sarcasm, and when I use slapstick I'll use it sparingly. But I'll still use it—maybe have a whole page where there's nothing but insanity. It's a development: you can see a little bit of it in *No coins, please.* There are shades of where I'm going.

FERNS: I thought you could see that as early as *I want to go home,* where the actual pacing of the action begins to get more sophisticated. I liked the recurring scenes where everything is seen from the beaver's point of view, where he's trying to get on with his own life, and only sees the actions of the crazy human beings so far as they affect him. I thought that was a very good comic touch.

KORMAN: Yes. That goes back to *Our man Weston,* too,

where no-one really knows what's going on. One person starts something, and then someone else finishes it for him. Another thing I used to do, from *I want to go home* right up to *Our man Weston* and *Bugs Potter live at Nickaninny,* which was working well, but was also really holding me back in some ways, was that I was describing everything. *I want to go home* took place in fourteen days, and it was practically a chapter a day. *Our man Weston* was virtually the same. But in *The war with Mr. Wizzle,* which a lot of people thought was a bit of a regression, I more or less got over my attachment to that one chapter, one day thing. And that was a big thing for me: *Mr. Wizzle* was just a story—it wasn't complicated or anything—but it helped me to do that. To finish off the series, if you like, and move on.

FERNS: Yes. Often realizing that you can get from A to Z without including all the other letters of the alphabet on the way is something it's difficult to learn. Though that's probably something the readers aren't so aware of.

KORMAN: Well, the readers are really going to pick up on two things. Is it funny? And, are the people real? Those are the two most important things. Lately, I've been thinking that "are the people real?" is even more important than "is it funny?" It has to be a little bit funny, but with real people, and genuine character relationships. That's what the readers are going to pick up: they don't care about structure. They won't necessarily see any structural difference between *Live at Nickaninny* and *No coins, please.* If the kids say something, it's more like "I like Bruno and Boots because they're so real". Whereas an adult reviewer might say, "Yes, the book is good, but it does lack a little in believability". The kids don't get that at all—they think that Bruno and Boots are real. Very rarely will there be an event where a kid will say, "I don't buy that." I've never seen it.

FERNS: Perhaps you could say a bit more about the reactions you've been getting from your readers. What kind of feedback have you been getting from the children you've talked to?

KORMAN: Really good. I've been to a lot of schools. I've done a lot of trips across Canada and the U.S.—and the books are getting there. The kids are reading them, and they're liking them. The reactions I'm getting can be very very different, but as a rule nobody hates the books! I don't think I've excluded any kid: maybe a handful here and there. You get a number of different reactions: you get kids who just get so into the books that they take it further. You get a couple of kids who get T-shirts where one says "Bruno" and the other says "Boots", and they go around as self-proclaimed Bruno and Boots. . . . Another reaction is that the kids who are lousy readers get into the books. Many times I've had letters from teachers saying, "This is my fourth grade remedial reading class, and your books have sort of turned them on." The other thing that seems to happen is that the kids get not only into the books, but into me personally—which is good, for the simple reason that it shows I have a distinctive enough style to inject my own personality into the book. So when I get to see a group of kids I'm not just this nothing coming out of a vacuum who just so happens to have his name on the

books—they expect to find a certain amount of my personality in my writing. And when I talk to them I want to show them that, basically, they're right.

FERNS: Do a lot of kids see your writing as semi-autobiographical, then?

KORMAN: Yes. Except that when kids ask questions they tend to over simplify: "Did it happen?" So I explain, well, some of it did—but it's more the feelings. I may describe something totally crazy, but it instills in the mind of the characters and therefore the readers the feeling of something that at some point or other did happen to me. The problem with personal experiences, eight times out of ten, if you use them exactly, is—you've got to be there. You can tell someone something that happened to you, and you may have been dying then, but he just sort of misses it. A lot of times that happens with personal experiences. But it's possible to take a manufactured experience, and use it to create the same feeling between two characters, or humour of the same atmosphere as had happened in real life.

FERNS: Part of the appeal of your main characters is that most of them have a healthy disrespect for authority. Bruno, Boots, Rudy Miller, Bugs Potter—they're all pretty anarchic. But there seems to be a line they themselves draw. In the end Bruno and Boots accept the school's authority. Rudy does stay at the camp. Do you ever feel inclined to let them go still further, and end up in total anarchy?

KORMAN: I was writing at the time of *Animal house,* and things like that. I think one of the things which makes the books fairly strong, so that they defy being compared to things like that, is that they don't cross that line. Considering how crazy the books are, I keep a firm foot in reality. . . . [In] a book—in a movie it may be different, depending on the visual image you're portraying—in a book, if something is going to be crazy, it has to happen in the context of something fairly sane, or else you can't really appreciate how crazy it is. The reason it's great when Bruno and Boots break rules is that in the long run you know that, while they don't necessarily accept the rules themselves, they accept the basic fact that there *are* rules. They accept the fact that they are kids, and that the administration is the administration, and that that's it. And the fact that they do this makes it all the more interesting when they do decide what they can and can't do.

FERNS: You don't see yourself doing something in the vein of Lindsay Anderson's *If,* where breaking the rules finally leads to total rebellion?

KORMAN: I'm trying to think. Rudy Miller is definitely a rebel, but he finds his own energy level. I wouldn't say he respected the rules.

FERNS: No. Scarcely.

KORMAN: But when he leaves, and he drags a counsellor into the water, he goes back to see if the guy is alright. And when he's caught, he's caught. He may try again tomorrow, but once caught, that's it. With Bugs Potter, I think it's a little different. He tries to follow the rules—only there are other priorities so strong that he has to live with them first, and follow the rules whenever it fits in. He's not really actively misbehaving.

FERNS: He's never really aware that he *is* breaking the rules—or if he is, he feels that surely people will understand why he's doing what he's doing.

KORMAN: Yes, because how else could one act? And Sidney Weston has a calling: so what if I break the rules, because I'm saving such and such . . . With *No coins, please* it starts to become a little more ambiguous, because the sympathetic characters set up are the counsellors, almost, and the guy who's crazy is more someone to bounce off them and the other kids in the group. So Artie's motivation . . . I've been getting this real enjoyment, lately, from witholding information—I really think that if Artie had ever said why he wanted all that money it would in some way have robbed the book.

FERNS: Yes. I think it was good to leave that unspecified. Although in the end I think it's pretty clear that it was just the fact of doing it, and that there was nothing he really wanted to spend it on. He just wanted to show himself he could do it. Which is perhaps another of the things which appeals to kids. You show that children can have power, that they can act in an adult world and achieve things.

KORMAN: And that's totally important. I think it's *No coins, please*'s strongest point. How many books have you read—and good books—about a kid who makes money: oh boy, isn't he cute, he raised sixty bucks, a hundred bucks, something like that? I mean, why can't an eleven-year-old make $150,000? If Bugs Potter is a good drummer, why can't he be the best drummer in the world? Whatever an adult can do, somewhere in the world there's one sixteen-year-old who can do it as well. You read about it in the paper—it just keeps coming up. And that's important, because a kid around twelve is just starting to find out that he can do certain things as well as his parents or his teachers. By the time he's fifteen he probably does some things better. You hear a lot of teachers talk about behaviour problems at the grade 7 or 8 levels—perhaps that's because in public school the teachers can do everything better than the students just by virtue of being adults, ninety-nine times out of a hundred. Whereas in high school, teachers have usually accepted that these people are almost adults and can do certain things better than them. It's not out of the ordinary to see that happen. The problem is with the age level where kids are starting to be able to do things, but it still seems unnatural. And I think that's one of the reasons why the books do well in that age bracket, which they're not really supposed to because of their presentation—because they address that situation of kids being able to triumph over the adults, and in many cases with the adults coming to terms with it.

FERNS: One of the things about the way you present, say, Bugs Potter becoming a star drummer, or Artie Geller making a fortune, is that it isn't shown as simple wish-fulfilment. There's a certain lunatic plausibility about the way it happens.

KORMAN: Yes—and I think one of the most important things about *No coins, please* is that while Artie may violate the letter of the law, he never really violates its spirit.

He doesn't really rip anybody off. He extracts a small amount of money from everybody: his fortune comes from the fact that he does it to a lot of people.

FERNS: It comes as quite a shock at the end of the book, when you discover just how many laws he *has* broken. Because he hasn't really done any damage at all. Everyone has enjoyed betting on his toy car races, and buying his attack jelly, and so forth.

KORMAN: I think the books are very respectful of people. In some cases it may be oversimplified, but basically if someone isn't liked, it's because he deserves it. One of the things I couldn't stand about school was that it could very easily happen—it happens in the adult world, too, but in school it's most obvious—that someone could look at your face, and not like it, and want to exclude you from the group, or make your life miserable. In the Bruno and Boots books—in all the books, really—people aren't really disliked or acted against unless they've done something to deserve it. It may be a tad unrealistic—but I think it's better unrealistic. . . . [While] realism is very important, something extraordinary should happen to keep your interest in the book. And that's what I like to do now. I've got a book coming out called **Don't Care High,** about a kid who comes from a small town to a big city, goes to a big city school, and is very shocked by the fact that the city is not what he's used to. Everything seems to work against him: he lives on the thirty-third floor; ninety-nine million things are seemingly going on in the building across the street. In his school there's no school spirit: no-one seems to care—they're all zombies. Every time he tries to eat in a restaurant it somehow destroys his stomach. There's even a local DJ who's yelling at him 24 hours a day: every time he turns on the radio, the guy's there. That's fairly realistic. But then I threw in a very strange and distinctive plot line, which is that he and a friend take the dullest guy in the school and make him student body president, and build an empire around him, and convert Don't Care High into zealots. Which is distinctly non-realistic. It's a question of taking the very very normal, and adding this touch to it.

FERNS: One reviewer talks of your work having "a distinctly Canadian stamp to it". Do you see yourself as a specifically Canadian writer?

KORMAN: In ways, yes, in ways, no. It comes out in parts, but I think there's more to it. In terms of my Canadian identity there may be something to the fact that many Americans think I'm British, and many British think I'm American. I think I'm a Canadian writer because I write books and I live in Canada, and my cultural exposure has been to this place. I wouldn't necessarily call myself a Canadian writer, though: I might just as well call myself a suburban Toronto writer. I don't think it's really important whether or not a Canadian identity comes out in my books, because they don't really mention anyone's identity. There are a certain number of characters who may or may not be representative of a certain percentage of youth. I have a lot of trouble with what the Canadian identity is. Reading all the trade publications, I sometimes believe that in order to achieve the Canadian identity, tragedies have to befall everybody. Or you have to write about native peoples, or something like that. I don't.

FERNS: I thought *Live at Nickaninny* played on that to some extent. It was almost as though everyone wanted there to be someone or something up there in the frozen North.

KORMAN: And the guy's from Manhattan!

FERNS: Absolutely. Also, in *No coins, please,* you show how the group of kids from Montreal who go down to the States find their identity through their shared resentment of everyone more or less saying, Canada, where's that?

KORMAN: And *No coins, please* is probably the book that got the best acceptance from American people. It was written after my first year of school. It comes from the fact that Americans tend to think that Canadians must be exactly like them—only somewhere at the back of their mind there's this vague uneasiness that there may be something different somewhere in there, although they can't imagine in a million years where it comes from. (pp. 56-62)

I want to say that I've got nothing against the notion that I'm a Canadian author, but I definitely don't think that where you're an author from is based on a heart affiliation. Does it make me a New York author, because I live in New York? I don't really think there's a decision at the beginning of a book, of equal importance to the book itself, where you say "Whose identity is this book?" I think it's my identity, and I don't think that national boundaries, or state boundaries really come into that. (p. 62)

FERNS: You're studying Dramatic Writing at NYU, and that involves screen writing too. There's also been a lot of talk about possible films of your stories, possible television series, and so on. Is that something you'd like to get involved in personally?

KORMAN: I'd like to, just for my own "in" in the market, and also to make sure no-one screws it up. That makes me a little bit nervous. I've had various film options on my stuff, and I used to think, "who cares about the books—you've got all these film options?" . . .

I used to put all my hope in those options, and I don't any more, for this reason—I think that one of the reasons the books succeed is that they are *books.* In *I want to go home,* there's a scene where Rudy is pulling Chip along, who's holding on to the mooring line of his boat when he takes off, so that Chip is basically water-skiing on his face. Now that, using very very straight prose to describe something weird, only doing it totally deadpan, comes out very funny. Whereas if you actually saw that happening on a movie screen, while it might be funny, it would be fighting against an entire history of B movies, every single one of which had Don Knotts hanging from a flagpole suspended 500 feet above the street, and all the *Animal house* things. You know: "Sure, O.K., someone's water-skiing on his face—but in this movie someone's *naked!*" I don't think some of the events would cut it as easily on film.

FERNS: Yet there's a very strong visual sense in your writing—perhaps increasingly as it goes along. Also, I think you do something which is very difficult, which is

to *write* slapstick, although the pace of reading is much slower than the frenetic pace you can get in a film. Even so, I'd have thought that something like the concluding scenes of *Our man Weston,* with all the mayhem at the hotel barbecue, or the scene in the Las Vegas hotel in *No coins, please* would work very well in a film context. Scenes like that almost seem as though they were conceived in cinematic terms.

KORMAN: That scene in *Our man Weston* definitely has a lot of visual depth. I'm pretty sure I constructed that scene visually, and layered it very consciously. Although *No coins, please* might be the best book to film. I'm just thinking about it now.

FERNS: Yes. I'd like to see, for example, the model racing track which Artie builds outside the Capitol. Although that's probably something which works better in prose: I'm not sure you could build one as good as the way it's described.

KORMAN: That might be. But something like Attack Jelly would work very well, because you could go for a lot more sales pitch in a movie than you could in prose. The disco might work better, and I think you could do a lot of great stuff with the casino—you know, time-elapse photography of stacks of chips, and so on. There are scenes that I do visually: certain parts of the hotel scene, like the final riot, that's a thing that you layer, right? But for the most part, as with the scene of Artie going to the individual casinos, the intention was to give the impression that he'd gone to a great many of them, but without taking up too much paper. I'm very conscious of not wanting to interfere with the pace.

FERNS: Yes. I think the pacing gets steadily better as the books go on.

KORMAN: And the pacing isn't really visually oriented.

FERNS: You've got nine books behind you, and two more on the stocks—and you're still only twenty. Where do you see yourself going from here? What are your future plans? (pp. 63-4)

[KORMAN:] I'd like to write, not necessarily the great Novel that's going to reshape the world, but a book that makes the sort of splash that *Catch-22* made. I think that's something to aim for, eventually, anyway. But I don't see myself writing an adult book in the immediate future. What I see happening is that one day I'll set out to write about a seventeen-year-old character, and it'll just turn out that this guy isn't seventeen—he's twenty-three or so, and he's an adult. That's how I think the transition will come.

FERNS: Do you see yourself sticking primarily to comedy?

KORMAN: I know that the books I enjoy most are serious books that just happen to be hilarious—so I think that's what I'm naturally going to find myself working towards. As I get older they're going to get that way. In the later books the humour hasn't been so much in the plot: quite serious things can happen, and it's in the discussion of them, or the description of them that funny things come out. (p. 64)

FERNS: One last question. If you were interviewing Gordon Korman, what would you most like to hear him talk about, that he hasn't discussed so far?

KORMAN: I don't know. Off-topic is my middle name. I think I've snuck in more or less everything. (p. 65)

> *Gordon Korman, in an interview with Chris Ferns, in* Canadian Children's Literature, *No. 38, 1985, pp. 54-65.*

GENERAL COMMENTARY

S. J. Freisen

Macdonald Hall, "the best boarding school for boys in Canada", rings with the adventures of a pair of boys who can do anything from shinnying up a drainspout noiselessly in the dead of night, every night, to amassing twenty-five thousand dollars to build a pool. They share their joys and troubles with the fearless peerless denizens across the highway in Miss Scrimmage's Finishing School for Young Ladies. Authority figures take something of a beating at Macdonald Hall, where the Headmaster gets lines like, "I don't care about the budget, my boys must have their evening snack." Parents are shadowy figures beyond the brilliant landscape of the school in which these boys test their strength. The surrounding world consists of standard public figures, like police, and public structures, like banks, which come into play only insofar as they serve the glittering personalities of Bruno, Boots and friends.

Clearly [*Go Jump in the Pool!* and *Beware the Fish!*] will appeal to young readers. They can be quite hilarious and require no more suspension of disbelief than many classics or most bestsellers intended for adults. A. S. Neill, the founder of the renowned Summerhill School, mused in his diary that few young people "have a sense of humour; theirs is a sense of fun. Make a noise like a duck and they will scream, but tell them your best joke and they will be bored to tears." Even after they can appreciate your best joke, the sense of fun remains, witness the antics in college dormitories.

When reading is still hard work, books that are full of fun and adventure may encourage the needed practice. Eric Wilson, a teacher of reluctant readers in British Columbia, states that to become a mature reader a student must read a wide variety of books, a situation he considers possible only when reading is regarded as a recreation. Wilson's own books (*Terror in Winnipeg, Murder on THE CANADIAN,* and *Vancouver Nightmare*) are similar to Korman's in that they employ rapid action and dialogue, as do those of Douglas Hill (*Galactic Warlord*). The concerns are different: Wilson's protagonists worry about cleaning up the environment; Hill's are out to save the earth from destruction and avenge his planet; and Korman's try to save the school or its honour. All would please A. S. Neill; all begin "with 'Hands up, or I fire!' or a kindred sentence."

Whereas Wilson, a teacher, is accustomed to the problem of rolecasting and seems to avoid it by involving girls only peripherally in the world of his male characters, Korman jubilantly peoples his world with females, some of whom are as brave, quick-witted and daring as his males. The girls are, to boot, all-knowing and all-attentive. When the boys must repair a trampled flower garden, the girls feed them a fabulous meal out of doors and do all the gardening themselves, within minutes. They then dirty the boys up and send them back to their Headmaster, whose wife arraigns him for persecuting the angelic darlings. This is rolecasting only insofar as it fits the script.

In these books all the characters are stereotypes. They, like the plot, are merely a frame on which to hang a series of funny incidents and running gags. Unlike Kevin Majors' *Hold Fast* in which everything the protagonist did was in character because Majors was trying to capture on paper a particular Maritimes' approach to life, Korman's characters and events are bent to the purpose of his books—making people laugh. (pp. 39-40)

A more viable criticism of Korman's work would be to question his sentence structure and his lack of feeling for words. Nonetheless, his writing has the qualities which will get it picked up and read, and therein lies the beginning of literacy. A rudimentary definition of literacy could posit that it is the ability not merely to read whether clumsily or quickly, but to know that part of the world is inhabited by people who read and use books. A. S. Neill says, "I couldn't tell you the capital of New Zealand . . . ; all I know is that I could find it out if I wanted to," and "So why learn up stuff that you can get in a dictionary every day?" But you must be able to use that dictionary and know when to turn to it. (p. 40)

Certainly the business of our daily lives is centered on language. As the television documentary "A Requiem for Literacy" pointed out, even the flashing delights of the electronic media have their beginnings in the written word. Yet literacy is more than an ability to find information. It is an enrichment of the whole of one's life, expressed in a greater understanding of oneself and others. Joseph Gold in *A Word to the Wise* says, "But is it adequate that after decades of schooling, our citizens should be no better equipped to lead a richer life of the mind than they are, no freer to find out who they are, what they can do, and how they might order and enjoy their world and their perception of it?" Elsewhere in the same book he says, "the heart of this learning and self-realizing process is language."

These are great things to be asked of books which will appeal to readers around Grades 4 to 6, especially considering that Gordon Korman is just sixteen years old. I have deliberately left mentioning the author's age to the last and have appraised his books in relation to others by mature writers because that is how they will be read. Once a book is printed, bound and sent forth the author's physical age is no longer apparent. Korman is a prolific writer with three books published and two more in manuscript form. He is developing quickly, perhaps almost unconsciously, and will probably find a strong voice of his own soon if he is able to keep his feet through the wave of attention he is receiving. (pp. 40-1)

Meanwhile, his books serve the purposes I have stated, but let it not end there, with a profound purpose laid upon books written out of a sense of fun. Sometimes it is important to take a breather, to get away from whatever you are doing. Not even television, with its constant breaks for commercials, changes of mood, treatment and topic every half hour, can give the refreshment possible from reading. Only a book can give a couple hours of light nothing, a sustained mood, wiping away for the moment all thought, all responsibilities, penances or problems other than those of the other world opened to us by its author. (p. 41)

S. J. Freisen, "Literacy: The Case for Light Reading," in Canadian Children's Literature, *No. 20, 1980, pp. 39-41.*

Eileen Whitfield

In 1976, a manuscript titled *This Can't Be Happening at Macdonald Hall!* made its way to the desk of Fran Buncombe, an editor at Scholatic-TAB in Richmond Hill, Ontario. By the time Buncombe had finished the story (in which the two boys, Boots and Bruno, reduce their boarding school to a shambles), she had decided to publish it. She also knew, by the covering letter, that its author was twelve years old.

Gordon Korman, now twenty-two, is lounging on the sofa in his parents' living room in Thornhill, Ontario. The word "mellow," which he uses often, might have been invented for him. He is pleasant, laid-back, and unpretentious. He is neatly dressed, but somehow looks rumpled. Unlike his fictional heroes, Korman at twelve had never staged a panty raid, liberated an ant farm, or unleashed a skunk on an unsuspecting roommate.

How normal was he? "A *dork*," he laughs. "If my teacher

Korman surrounded by inspiration.

made a mistake, I'd be the person to remind him for the rest of his life. In the sixth or seventh grade you reach a rather unusual point. You realize that teachers are people too." That's how it happens in Korman's stories. In book after book, children are one step ahead of such lovable idiots as parents and teachers. These young characters will do *anything* to protect "the quality of life they're entitled to," says Korman. "What the kids are fighting for is important. You can't talk down to them."

In *This Can't Be Happening at Macdonald Hall!*, Boots and Bruno fight for the right to be roommates by proving too obnoxious for anyone else to live with. In *The War With Mr. Wizzle* they fight to remove a loathsome school administrator from his job. Rudy Miller, in *I Want to Go Home!*, fights to get out of summer camp and takes his revenge on the counsellor he calls "His Cloneship." Most of all, Korman's kids hate boredom, which they combat with the urgency of convicts in a jailbreak.

"When a kid is bored, he's *bored*," says Korman. "It's not a question of how long he's bored or how soon it's going to get better; to the kid it's something really terrible. To an adult, boredom may be deadly dull, but he gets through it by thinking of when it will be over. Kids don't think that far ahead. They live only in the present and can hardly stand it."

No wonder the youngsters in Korman's novels take matters into their own hands, rushing single-mindedly through plots that keep the reader turning pages. (p. 34)

Korman's humour has developed from novel to novel. The earlier books lean toward slapstick. "But as I got older," he explains, "I had fewer inspirations for gags." The humour in his later books grows through a wealth of satiric detail.

This approach is beautifully realized in *Don't Care High,* his latest novel. Don't Care High is really Don Carey High School, named after the designer of the town's sewer system. Students wander through the halls, pursued "by that relentless monster called 'lack of interest.'" Their eyes are "focussed on infinity. . . . If eyes were the windows of the soul, these people had their blinds drawn." The book is also something of a departure. It is set in Manhattan, where Korman lived while majoring in film and dramatic writing at New York University, and where he still keeps an apartment. (His next book, *Son of Interflux,* is set on Long Island.) And after nine books in the "juvenile" category (ages eight to twelve), *Don't Care High* is aimed at teens.

Korman may eventually write screenplays and novels for adults, but writing for children is still a priority; he loves to create highly motivated characters "who always have a reason to get up in the morning. When you're writing," he says, suddenly leaning forward, "you have to *feel* it." Waving his arms, he seems for a moment like an overgrown kid. That may be what has made Gordon Korman the most precociously successful writer in Canada—his ability to feel and re-create the restless energy of children. (pp. 34-5)

Eileen Whitfield, "Novel Approach," in Saturday Night, *Vol. 101, No. 5, May, 1986, pp. 34-5.*

TITLE COMMENTARY

This Can't Be Happening at Macdonald Hall! (1978)

Gordon Korman's first novel shows considerable promise in the difficult field of humour for pre-teens. It is unselfconsciously and comfortably set at Macdonald Hall, a Southern Ontario boarding school of the traditional style, where Bruno Walton and Boots O'Neal are roommates in their grade 10 year. In a drastic effort to curtail their embarrassingly public practical joking, which has culminated in the cat-napping of the York Academy hockey team's mascot, Headmaster Sturgeon banishes Bruno and Boots to separate dormitories in the hope that new roommates will have a settling influence on them. Aided and abetted by the refined young ladies from Miss Crimmage's Finishing School across the road, they plunge the school into merry disruption as they try to make their roommates beg the headmaster to move them out.

Korman uses a conversational style which will appeal to grade five and up. He begins the action immediately, using dialogue and dramatization as the chief carriers of his story. The colloquial element is quite strong, but except for a few recurring catch phrases, I found the tone natural and lively. Characters range from the immediately believable heroes and headmaster to the near cartoons of the exemplary new roommates and the overexcitable Miss Scrimmage, whose exaggerated personalities are integral to the plot's complication. Korman has constructed this novel soundly using a fair variety of techniques for humour and he has a good sense for comic repetition and snowballing details.

I recommend this as a thoroughly funny story for young people. . . .

> *Judy Penteker, in a review of "This Can't Be Happening at Macdonald Hall!" in* In Review: Canadian Books for Children, *Vol. 12, No. 4, Autumn, 1978, p. 67.*

This Can't Be Happening at Macdonald Hall! is a hilarious account of the antics of two boys, Bruno and Boots, at an Ontario boarding school for boys. (p. 57)

This story is a frenzy of hilarious activity from the first page to the last. One imagines the author, a 13-year-old public school boy himself, is recording his fantasies of what a private boarding school might be like and of some of the characters and situations one might enjoy there. While the content of the novel makes no claim to reality—it is purely entertaining, funny and fast-moving—it has nevertheless a distinctly Canadian stamp to it; you know that you are not in an American or British boarding school. The merit of this novel lies less in the characterization than in the sheer imagination Korman possesses in inventing capers for the two boys to perform. It is sure to appeal to any child who goes to school. (pp. 57-8)

> *Susan Kilby, in a review of "This Can't Be*

Happening at Macdonald Hall!" in Canadian Children's Literature, *No. 14, 1979, pp. 57-8.*

Go Jump in the Pool! (1979)

Bruno and Boots return once again to terrorize Headmaster Sturgeon in this sequel to *This can't be happening at Macdonald Hall.* This time, their objective has become refined. No longer are they intent on sheer hellery, but rather, they are attempting to raise $25,000 for a pool. In their efforts, they disrupt the campus with a funny photo contest, set up a toll booth, and play the stock exchange. The ending is inevitable; they surpass their goal, unite the student body, and gain the undying affection of Mr. Sturgeon.

So many authors are intent on writing of adolescent gloom and doom, that Gordon Korman is a pleasant change. While many of his heroes' exploits may be sophomoric, the heroes themselves are good, albeit mischievous boys. Their romps are hilariously funny to young people, and the jokes—real "groaners"—make them laugh. The author, too, is a good model for young people. For teachers who must encourage their students to write, he provides an example of a successful teenage author and because he is Canadian, he is an even rarer species.

> *Maureen Kaukinen, in a review of "Go Jump in the Pool," in* In Review: Canadian Books for Young People, *Vol. 14, No. 3, June, 1980, p. 46.*

Beware the Fish! (1980)

Mysterious messages begin to interrupt regular TV broadcasting in the neighbourhood of Macdonald Hall, a private boys' school near Toronto. They announce the mounting of Operations Pop Can and Flying Fish and end with an ominous warning to "Beware the Fish!" the OPP and the RCMP investigate and encounter UFOs and strange goings-on in the local dump.

The gang from Macdonald Hall—ringleader Bruno Walton and his best friend Boots O'Neal, Elmer Drimsdale, the school genius, Sidney "Butterfingers" Rampulsky, and all the rest—is back, ably supported by the students of Miss Scrimmage's Finishing School for Young Ladies.

This is teenager Gordon Korman's third novel. He's an acute observer of his own teen culture. His characters and conversations are believable and amusing. The events are more than a little improbable, but the story is high-spirited and lots of fun. Each Macdonald Hall book is measurably better than the last. Watch for Gordon Korman and buy lots of copies of *Beware the Fish.* Teenage readers will love it.

> *Adele Ashby, in a review of "Beware the Fish," in* Quill and Quire, *Vol. 46, No. 8, August, 1980, p. 29.*

Who Is Bugs Potter? (1980)

Who is Bugs Potter? is a clever, fast-paced narrative that celebrates teenagers' ability to thrive on music and intellectual challenge; for all its stereotypical plot, it puts the lie to the violence that most adult writers seem to assume is everyone's norm.

> *W. H. New and Moshie Dahms, in a review of "Who Is Bugs Potter?" in* Journal of Commonwealth Literature, *Vol. XVI, No. 2, February, 1982, p. 60.*

I Want to Go Home! (1981)

I Want to Go Home asks the question, "Having fun is what camp is all about, isn't it?" But there is fun and fun, and not everyone can tell the difference. Rudy Miller is sick of camp. Camp Algonquin Island, a.k.a. Alcatraz, is run by The Warden and his gang of clones, a.k.a. counsellors. Rudy has no team spirit and prefers chess and a little sabotage to hearty bouts of baseball, soccer or swimming. He's also a smart-ass who dreams up a scavenger hunt that calls for icebergs, eucalyptus bark, a brontosaurus rib, nuclear waste, a man-eating dandelion, a pterodactyl nest and a Neanderthal man. He escapes from Alcatraz nine times. Six times the clones find him and bring him back, and three times he comes back of his own accord to score himself a point and try again.

I Want to Go Home, the fifth novel by Gordon Korman (of **Macdonald Hall** fame), is his funniest yet. If you are given to laughing out loud, don't read this book in a public place. I was nearly thrown off a streetcar! This book is perfect for everyone, any age, who ever hated camp. We might even let the rest of you read it.

> *Adele Ashby, in a review of "I Want to Go Home," in* Quill and Quire, *Vol. 47, No. 6, June, 1981, p. 34.*

This is 17 year old Gordon Korman's fifth successful book. His many fans love the mocking tone of his stories.

Rudy Miller, the main character in this latest novel, is the perfect anti-hero—a summer camp brat who is determined to upset all order. Unwilling to participate in any organized activities and determined to go home, he creates a big problem for the camp directors. Rudy has no real cause for being anti-camp, he just is, and that is part of the attraction of the story. Korman's heroes do what all kids dream of doing at some time or other—disobeying authority for the sheer fun of it. Rudy "gets away with it" because he is exceedingly talented (baseball, swimming, soccer, etc. expert) and witty.

The story moves with good pace, one adventure following another. The point of view is clear and consistent. Even the "beaver builds a dam" subplot works although it is one of the few obvious contrivances in the tale. While dialogue and action are the main attractions in this book, Korman shows that he is also capable of good description.

It is to be hoped that Canada's "teenage writing sensation" will keep up the good work. Recommended for all nine to twelve year olds—especially boys who think they don't like to read.

> *Frances Baskerville, in a review of "I Want to*

Go Home!" in In Review: Canadian Books for Young People, *Vol. 15, No. 4, August, 1981, p. 46.*

Korman's dedication proclaims, "There's fun and there's fun. This book is dedicated to those who know the difference." Readers of this book will likely discover instead that there's humour and there's humour.

Protagonist, Rudy Miller, who is an ace at every conceivable sport, wants nothing more than to escape from the rigours of Camp Algonkian Island. The plot centres on his many attempts to achieve this objective. The dialogue is stilted, frequently appearing self-conscious and awkward as if the author were unable to place himself inside the characters. Characterization, in general, is shallow; the camp counsellors, for example, are consistently depicted as sports-crazy mental midgets and the camp director as an autocratic totally humourless redneck.

Rudy's single-minded attempts to escape are amusing at first but begin to pall by the end of the book. One successfully funny sequence occurs when Rudy wins a bet and is appointed counsellor for a day. For the most part, however, the one-liners fall flat and the technique of emphasizing a humorous situation by having the characters greatly overreact is not a recommended literary stylistic device.

On the positive side the basic plot is well conceived, the action is fast-paced and the subject is definitely of interest to most boys. In summary, a useful bit of recreational fluff to encourage reluctant readers.

> *Fran Ashdown, in a review of "I Want to Go Home!" in* In Review: Canadian Books for Young People, *Vol. 16, No. 1, February, 1982, p. 41.*

Our Man Weston (1982)

Sidney West, [is] a teenager who is convinced that he and he alone is responsible for the safety of the western world. No one takes him seriously, of course, certainly not his twin brother Tom or the officials of the OPP, the RCMP, the PMO, the DND, NATO or NORAD. Sidney suspects a plot to steal a new advanced plane, the Osiris HE2, from the Trilliam Air Base, which just happens to be next door to the Pine Grove Resort Hotel, where he and Tom are working for the summer. Events prove Sidney right (although he did have some of the minor details wrong, such as who was the spy), and with the aid of a deluxe homing system and a small army of kids four to 10 whom he has personally trained in strategic espionage immobilization techniques, he saves the plane and simultaneously sorts out a few other minor mysteries at the hotel, such as whatever happened to the two missing retrievers.

[**Our Man Weston**] will appeal to . . . [readers] who like fast-paced adventures, populated with dumb adults and kid-heroes who triumph over all. From an adult perspective, it's all wildly improbable, but there is no question there is an audience for the formula. Every library should have several copies.

> *Adele Ashby, in a review of "Our Man Wes-*

ton," in Quill and Quire, *Vol. 48, No. 7, July, 1982, p. 67.*

The War with Mr. Wizzle (1982)

Gordon Korman continues to please his many young readers, but all others beware. It's a pity to watch a promising young writer slide downhill into formula and repetition at age 18, but that's what Korman's last few titles have been, and this one is no exception. **The War With Mr. Wizzle** features wise-guy students Bruno and Boots, the heroes of his earlier books. This time they're on a campaign to rid their prep school, Macdonald Hall, of a martinet computer expert. It's an amalgam of frantic, foolish activity, bald stereotypes and unbearable reiteration of demerits, detentions and line-writing, all climaxed by the appearance of the grotesquely caricatured assistant headmistress of neighbouring Miss Scrimmage's Finishing School for Young Ladies. She seems to have wandered into the plot straight from television's Private Benjamin without even pausing to remove her make-up. Anyone who stays with this tired material to the end will agree that marrying off the two terrible tutors probably serves both of them right. But what to do with the rest of the cast? Keep on serving them up time after time, I fear.

> *Joan McGrath, in a review of "The War with Mr. Wizzle," in* Quill and Quire, *Vol. 49, No. 1, January, 1983, p. 34.*

The boys at Toronto's Macdonald Hall are outraged when Walter C. Wizzle and his Magnetronic 515 computer come to modernize and reform their high school. Bruno Walton and his roommate form a committee to help oust Wizzle and, with the aid of the girls at Miss Scrimmage's Finishing School (who are having comparable problems with former drill sergeant Peabody), they take action in the hope of forcing his resignation. In the end, creative thinking, self-expression and teamwork conquer the mindless computer. The story is consistently packed with fast-paced humor, rapid scene changes and some genuinely funny slapstick episodes guaranteed to elicit chuckles. Unfortunately, the cast of characters is stereotypical ("the brain," "the klutz," "the headmaster's wife") and somewhat immature but the sharp dialogue keeps them afloat. Korman's latest Macdonald Hall adventure makes fun high-interest leisure reading.

> *Patricia Jana, in a review of "The War with Mr. Wizzle," in* School Library Journal, *Vol. 30, No. 1, September, 1983, p. 136.*

Bugs Potter Live at Nickaninny (1983)

The exception that lightens the moral burden of young adult fiction is Gordon Korman. His slapstick rock-music-crazed character, Bugs Potter, is now appearing in his second book, **Bugs Potter Live at Nickaninny**. Bugs not only does exactly what his parents do not want him to do but he does it so well that he escapes being punished for his sins: every adolescent's dream. The whole adult world seems a little silly to Bugs, who only wants to listen to heavy-metal music and get on with playing his drums.

The adult world is in fact Korman's main target for satire. He is not trying to provide laudable role models for his readers, but simply to entertain them. He is undoubtedly successful, because at 19, with eight children's books already to his credit, Korman writes not as a grown-up to a child, but as one young adult to another.

> *Anne Collins, "Driving Home the Moral of the Story," in* Maclean's Magazine, *Vol. 96, No. 27, July 4, 1983, pp. 50, 52.*

Devotees of Gordon Korman will remember Bugs Potter. This time Bugs faces a new test—spending two weeks with his family in the remote northern wilderness without his drums, his radio or access to rock concerts. In the tradition of Korman's most popular characters, Bugs blithely rearranges the north woods to suit his tastes and in the process inadvertently uncovers a long lost tribe of Indians who are the objects of a search being conducted by a fleet of avid anthropologists.

It's all hilarious proof that Korman has not lost his touch. His latest book has a barrel of laughs to punctuate each twist and turn of an intricate and absurd plot.

> *A review of "Bugs Potter Live at Nickaninny," in* Children's Book News, *Toronto, Vol. 6, No. 2, September, 1983.*

Editorial pencils don't have to be sharpened for the latest Gordon Korman title, **Bugs Potter Live at Nickaninny.** Stranded on a camping holiday with his family, the hyperactive Bugs wastes no time in converting the wilderness into a stage for his incredible musical talent and, in the process, manages to make a startling anthropological discovery. For Korman addicts, **Bugs Potter Live** is further evidence that few writers are as adept at creating fast-paced and hilarious plots.

> *Peter Carver, "From the Gripping Yarn to the Gaping Yawn," in* Quill and Quire, *Vol. 49, No. 11, November, 1983, p. 24.*

No Coins, Please (1984)

An afternoon of light-hearted slapstick awaits readers of **No Coins Please. . . .**

Juniortours counsellors, easy-going Dennis and conscientious Rob, are a comedy routine in themselves. But throw in six campers, one of whom is Artie Geller, put them in a white van nicknamed the "Ambulance" and you have a rollicking group careening from New York to Los Angeles.

Artie plays a straight man. His one eccentricity is that he is a master con artist. Little Artie slips away to don tuxedo and conduct truly inventive business schemes. In farm country Nebraska, for example, city tourists are treated to a No Frills Milkstore where Artie offers them the opportunity to milk cows at a dollar a minute; in Nevada, he pulls together a one-night extravanganza called The Pretzel, a disco with a twist.

Sounds too fantastic? No so, since Korman bridges the gap between the possibly imaginable and the absolutely impossible with ingenuity, style, tightly paced action, and the comic eye of a seasoned professional. Korman's sizeable young audience of 8-11 year olds will not be disappointed.

Joan Yolleck, in a review of "No Coins, Please," in Quill and Quire, *Vol. 50, No. 11, November, 1984, p. 13.*

Two counselors and six boys are in one of the vans that are part of the summer camp-and-tour programs of "Juniortours." The two counselors are Dennis, who is stupid and extravagant, and Rob, who has common sense but no power. It's Rob who worries every time eleven-year-old Artie disappears when the group is in a city. They can't stop his vanishing, and they can't find out where he's been. The readers know: Artie is pulling off one lucrative scam after another; eventually the counselors and the other campers find out what Artie's up to and they share in his schemes; in the end, federal agents take over the $150,000.00 Artie has amassed. This is broad farce, with no believable characters, few believable plot developments, and a mediocre writing style. What it has, as appeals to readers, are plenty of action and some humor. (pp. 50-1)

A review of "No Coins, Please," in Bulletin of the Center for Children's Books, *Vol. 39, No. 3, November, 1985, pp. 50-1.*

According to the fly-leaf on this '84 publication, Gordon Korman is twenty years old, no longer the soul mate of Boots and Bruno of Macdonald Hall. Perhaps this accounts for the identification crisis that exists in *No coins, please.* The disarming Canadian hero of this rambunctious Juniortours America trip is hustler Artie Geller, a resourceful eleven-year-old in the mold of Bruno Walton. The familiar conscience-bound foil, however, is eighteen-year-old tour counselor Rob Nevin. Is the responsibility of impending adulthood affecting Korman's vision?

Since his earliest days Korman has been deft at comic invention, and Artie's scams provide some of his best mischievous fantasy. The model car race betting escapade, with its elaborate set, has just enough added complication to be hilarious. Some may be disturbed by the hero's seriously illegal tactics, but the fantasy is so wild it would be difficult to take such an objection seriously. Nevertheless, the author uncharacteristically does take his hero into a situation where he cannot win; even though the chastised Artie seems set to mobilize his fellow tourers at the end, we feel it will not work without his personal style.

Is the maturing Korman seeing a larger world where even in the glitz of Las Vegas fantasies cannot come true? This disenchanted view seems further evidenced in giving the conscience to a young adult rather than to the hero's peer. For all his emphasis on light fun, Korman's paired juvenile heroes always projected the truth of two strong parts of the child's makeup: the part that dares to be individual and the part that holds society's starchy values. Identification and sympathy were at once engaged as one dragged the other into adventure. It is difficult to feel the same interest and sympathy for the older Rob; after all, his motives are tainted by necessity for summer employment and

the desire to attract girls. Neither are Artie's touring peers interesting enough to provide the emotional tension which gives spice to the adventures of Boots and Bruno or Rudy Miller and Mike Webster in *I want to go home.*

No coins, please delivers much of the old fun but destroys the dream of childhood invincibility. It is not comfortable and certainly not fun to look at the world through Rob Nevin's anxious eyes. Has the author outgrown the magic of innocent egotism to be mired in the stifling mundane? A new Korman book should be on the stands now. Will it tell us what has really happened to Gordon Korman? (pp. 55-6)

Paula Hart, "This Can't Be Happening to Gordon Korman!" in Canadian Children's Literature, *No. 43, 1986, pp. 55-6.*

Don't Care High   (1985)

This slapstick fiction from a popular young Canadian writer is based on a new student's galvanizing his blasé New York high school into action by organizing support for a bizarre student president who doesn't even know, much less care, that he's been elected. The humor is forced through repetitive jokes and exaggerated descriptions: the protagonist's mother is forever off to help her sister through various silly household crises; school officials and situations are ludicrously overdrawn. Still, readers suffering the slings and arrows of outrageous education will enjoy seeing it farced.

A review of "Don't Care High," in Bulletin of the Center for Children's Books, *Vol. 39, No. 4, December, 1985, p. 71.*

[Patti Stren's *I Was a 15-Year-Old Blimp* and Gordon Korman's *Don't Care High* are] fast-moving, wisecracking novels about life in the Big Apple that should appeal to teenagers going through the *angst* of adolescence. The characters in each story are high-school kids who are worried about all those issues teenagers are supposed to care most about: dates, dances, zits, sports, school spirit, clothes, and being part of the in-crowd. Not for these kids concerns about war and peace, life and death, drugs, morality, or economic hardship.

For Stren and Korman, adults are figures of fun— distracted scientists working on meaningless experiments, fathers who are never home or who collect airline boarding passes as a hobby, aunts who spend their lives plotting to get a dishwasher, or teachers who operate at various levels of ineptness. Kids are left to work out their own lives, finding their way through the social jungle by themselves.

Stren and Korman each write for the market in a calculated way, not fired by any urge to expand or challenge young minds but, rather, intent on providing diverting entertainment that is relaxing and unthreatening to young readers. They know their audience and the kinds of things so-called young adults are *really* concerned with in their awkward and self-conscious in-between years. . . .

Korman's novels are great romps through barely credible plots somehow held together by the sheer pell-mell desire of his characters for yet one more caper. While the humour lacks the poignancy of Stren's whimsy, there is no denying Korman's uncanny knack for winding up the intricacies of entangled plots that are the envy of more mature writers. . . .

Perhaps because he is closer to the scene he writes about, the 22-year-old Korman is harder-edged in his humour than Stren. There's a satiric bite to ***Don't Care High;*** for example, Paul gapes at domestic scenes from his apartment window and sees a football fanatic who carpets his living room with Astroturf, a man who dons a bunny suit and eats bushels of carrots, a lady who washes her 33rd-floor windows from outside without a safety belt.

Korman's sardonic glimpses of Big Apple bizarreness suggest the writer he may yet become. In this, his 10th novel, the young man who became Canada's one bona fide teen-aged literary idol reveals his debt to the writers he most admires—Kurt Vonnegut and the Joseph Heller of *Catch 22.*

> *Peter Carver, "Wise-Cracking Novels on Growing Up Absurd," in* Quill and Quire, *Vol. 51, No. 12, December, 1985, p. 27.*

In this would-be satire, there are some clever bits: the feudal "Locker Baron" who extorts junk-food payments for combinations in prime locations, the student who is a slave to a terrible addiction—licorice. Other titles of this genre—Stanley Kiesel's affectionately mad *The War Between the Pitiful Teachers and the Splendid Kids* (Dutton, 1980) and Daniel Pinkwater's satisfying tour-de-force *Young Adult Novel* (Crowell, 1982), succeed. Here readers are not persuaded to suspend disbelief. Having missed its mark, the book becomes merely outrageous and offensive. In the characterizations, stereotypes and stick figures abound. The hero instigators are flat personalities for all their rushing about. What makes the pathetic Mike Otis tick is never explained. All of the adults—parents, teachers, etc.—are well-intentioned incompetents or utter fools. Most seriously, in the interest of motivating, the story applauds stealing of confidential records, vandalism and physical violence.

> *Libby K. White, in a review of "Don't Care High," in* School Library Journal, *Vol. 32, No. 4, December, 1985, p. 102.*

Son of Interflux (1986)

Simon Irving, the son of loving parents, has adjusted to the peripatetic life led by the family because Dad is an officer in Interflux, the world's biggest corporation and a manufacturer of what is portrayed as trivial parts: little things that hold other things together (the whip and the handle of a buggy whip, for example). Just beginning to enjoy his classes and his new friends at Nassau County High School for the Visual, Literary, and Performing Arts, Simon is perturbed when he learns that Interflux is going to build on vacant land adjacent to the school. He secretly buys the land with student council money, and "Antiflux" mounts a campaign against his father's company. The details of this campaign are wholly unconvincing

but often amusing. Simon's romance and his art studies give some contrast and are a bit more credible, although every adult is pictured as bizarre, stupid, or both. At times comic, this is overwritten and superficial.

> *Zena Sutherland, in a review of "Son of Interflux," in* Bulletin of the Center for Children's Books, *Vol. 40, No. 3, November, 1986, p. 53.*

This zany, but rather pointless, romp pits Simon Irving against his father, vice-president of Interflux corporation, to save a piece of open land next to his high school. While masquerading as contemporary high-school angst, this novel is pure fantasy bordering on the ridiculous at points. Although there are some funny moments at school and passable character development of Simon and his two best friends, girls and women are reduced to cardboard stupidity or, worse yet, clinging boyfriend fiends. Simon's mother is a culinary fool who follows every whimsical new "health" diet that the newspaper prints. She is the continual target of the longest standing joke in the book. The ending, true to form, depends on the absurd antics of another adult, this time Simon's father's boss, to resolve the dilemma of students fighting the insensitive corporation. Thus, the story ends even more pointlessly than it began. It's easy to pass this one by.

> *Steve Matthews, in a review of "Son of Interflux," in* School Library Journal, *Vol. 33, No. 3, November, 1986, p. 104.*

Waving contrivances like flags of honor, this upbeat spoof lies somewhere between Daniel Pinkwater and M. E. Kerr. Characters, especially Simon and his father, are nicely fleshed out, the plot moves swiftly, and the style is sure-handed and consistent. Though the ending seems a bit deflated, especially in comparison to the rest of the story's pace, and the New York references may be lost to non-New York YAs, this is nonetheless a fast and funny romp, full of oddball characters and off-the-wall situations, sure to appeal to more sophisticated young adult readers who like their humor with a twist. (p. 220)

> *Christy Tyson, in a review of "Son of Interflux," in* Voice of Youth Advocates, *Vol. 9, No. 5, December, 1986, pp. 219-20.*

A Semester in the Life of a Garbage Bag (1987)

"There was something wrong with a world where no one would listen to twenty-two hundred students whose education and well-being were in danger, while an eighty-eight-year-old poet with a yo-yo had the ear of the entire nation." So observes Sean Delancey the pseudo hero in another lunatic view of adolescence by the author of ***Don't Care High.*** The author juggles the determination of Sean to retain his all-important popularity with the bizarreness of his copartner in an English assignment, Raymond Jardine, who will stop at nothing to win a school-sponsored summer trip to a Greek island. Jardine rockets through life fending off Murphy's Law with ingenious and hilarious counteractions yet is quite at home among the other splendidly eccentric citizens at DeWitt High. One student surfs down tipped-up cafeteria tables on a lunch tray; another devotes himself to endless games of poker played for toothpicks; while the principal harbors an obsession for the school's disastrously ineffective Solar/Air Current Generating System. The plot does not so much develop as carom from episode to episode; yet it preserves a zany logic, which includes passing off Sean's perky grandfather as an obscure Canadian poet. Although the jokes may be stretched a bit too thin, the author maintains a refreshingly good-natured view of adolescence in a school that although unbesmirched by sex, drugs, or unseemly language is as lively and antic as a zoo taken over by monkeys. Not for those looking for teenage anguish or anxieties, the book offers entertainment in its nimble-witted conversational exchanges, absurd predicaments, and wholehearted delight in the scrapes and energy of its youthful characters.

> *Ethel R. Twichell, in a review of "A Semester in the Life of a Garbage Bag," in* The Horn Book Magazine, *Vol. LXIII, No. 6, November-December, 1987, p. 744.*

The garbage bag of the title is one Raymond Jardine, a spectacularly unlucky eleventh grader, whose sole obsession in life is gaining one of the coveted six spots on a high school trip to the Greek island of Theamelpos. (The alternative is spending the summer working in his uncle's fishgutting plant in New Jersey.) For reasons far too involved to explain, success in a poetry project for his English class becomes the key to getting there, and Jardine's partner, the hitherto perfectly normal Sean Delancey, gradually finds his life being taken over by the other's obsession—which results (among other things) in Sean's eighty-eight year old grandfather impersonating the obscure (and deceased) Canadian poet on whom they have decided to work. Other characters include Ashley Bach, the stunningly beautiful health food fanatic for whom Sean hopelessly yearns; Steve "Cementhead" Semenski, the moronic muscleman who is the object of Ashley's affections; and a younger sister whom Sean refers to as "Genghis Khan in training". The real villain of the piece, however, is SAGGEN: DeWitt High School's experimental powerplant—thirty-three million dollars' worth of state-of-the-art technology, whose only minor drawback is that is doesn't work.

With his last three titles, Korman has moved from being a writer of children's books into Young Adult territory, and while his lunatic comic inventiveness remains much in evidence, it is accompanied by a perceptive eye for the quirks of adolescent behaviour. Paradoxically, however, the very accuracy of this portrayal of teenage jealousies, antagonisms, image-consciousness creates certain problems. Korman's earlier books depend for much of their effect on his use of a closed environment—school, in the Macdonald Hall books, summer camp in *I want to go home*—which serves to isolate the characters from a larger social context, while allowing Korman's distinctive brand of comedy to develop its own logic and momentum. Here, however, while the main focus is on the life of DeWitt High School, the social context is broader, embracing family life and events beyond the institution. There is a greater realism, too, in some of the characterization: Sean's pangs of jealousy are convincingly rendered, as are some of the

antagonisms between characters—to the extent that it sometimes makes Korman's comic invention seem *too* contrived. In the less realistic world of his earlier fiction, of course, this was never a problem; here, however, the comedy and the observation almost seem to be pulling in different directions. The pacing, too, is affected: more complex than his earlier novels, with more characters, and more aspects of experience to interweave, it moves as a result more slowly, and never quite succeeds in creating the momentum required for the suspension of disbelief which Korman's farcical invention demands. While the climactic self-destruction of SAGGEN is well done, the final resolution, which sends Jardine and Sean to Theamelpos after all, is a little too artificial. And it is surely a miscalculation to make the obsessional Jardine in love with Ashley too, detracting as it does from the fanatical single-mindedness which makes his partnership with the far more normal Sean so comical.

Nevertheless, if the parts do not add up to as satisfying a whole as is the case in some of Korman's other books, this is perhaps an inevitable consequence of what is clearly a process of the author extending his range. It will be interesting to see where he goes from here—and in the meantime, there is much in *A semester in the life of a garbage bag* to enjoy. There is, as always, some splendid slapstick; the poetry of Gavin Gunhold (the obscure Canadian bard) is consistently ludicrous, as is his impersonation by the grandfather, who turns out to be an accomplished yo-yo virtuoso; and there is also the character of Leland Fenster . . . (Leland Fenster is so supercool that he communicates only in a personal dialect so hip as to be totally incomprehensible—except possibly to a Martian: "Affirm, baby, that vub zipped my thinkometer!") Gordon Korman's comic imagination remains as fertile as ever. (pp. 63-4)

> *Chris Ferns, "Escape from New Jersey," in* Canadian Children's Literature, *No. 52, 1988, pp. 63-4.*

[Kids] who like intelligent, hilarious revolt will enjoy the story. Witty, frenetic resistance to school authority, i.e., wild pranks—Korman has been writing in this vein successfully since he was 12 years old. If there is such a thing as a YA novel that is a "screwball comedy," this is it. Although the school and the students are basically believable, the situations are wackier, and the students are more inventive, than would actually occur in real life: Korman goes for laughs. Those who have read his *Son of Interflux* will find much that is similar here—the large high school on Long Island; a big investment at stake that involves the school; kids who like nothing better than manipulating the system and taking control. Korman has almost created a genre of his own, and he certainly will have a following among YA readers.

> *Bette D. Ammon, in a review of "A Semester in the Life of a Garbage Bag," in* Kliatt Young Adult Paperback Book Guide, *Vol. XXIII, No. 3, April, 1989, p. 12.*

The Zucchini Warriors (1988)

Another zany adventure featuring Bruno Walton, "Boots" O'Neal, and the gang from Macdonald Hall.

As in Korman's other books, the plot quickly grows spaghettilike. Macdonald Hall has a new football stadium but a pathetic team—until nearby Miss Scrimmage's Finishing School for Young Ladies furnishes a brilliant quarterback in the person of Cathy Burton. To conceal this illegal player from coaches and the school administration, Bruno and Boots pass her off as Elmer Drimsdale, Macdonald Hall's reclusive science whiz; meanwhile, Elmer's giant Manchurian Bush hamsters escape and discover a perfect nesting spot—under the bleachers, where tons of delicious (to them) fried zucchini sticks have been dumped. Then Kevin Klapper, a Curriculum Inspector and former football addict who is preparing a devastating report on the Hall's new football mania, succumbs and appoints himself coach. He is brilliant; the team claws and stumbles its way into the play-offs. The subplots here are too numerous to mention; suffice it to say that the climactic victory ends in a grand melée of players, spectators, police, hamsters, school officials, and other interested parties.

An expert, if predictable, farce, with familiar character types and plenty of action.

> *A review of "The Zucchini Warriors," in* Kirkus Reviews, *Vol. LVI, No. 15, August 1, 1988, p. 1152.*

Except for the fact that the characters, supposedly Canadian junior high-schoolers, sound older than they are supposed to be, this book lives up to Korman's reputation. It is a silly, funny romp through one football season at a private Canadian junior high school, a school that has never had a football team but puts one together in the hopes that a successful season will translate into a new recreation hall. Elements that add to the laughs, as well as the problems—and successes—of the football team include: a secret female quarterback; nearly extinct but secretly breeding Manchurian bush hamsters; the "blabbermouth" who tells literally everything about everybody from bad breath to ingrown toenails; the "Beast" who spends the season on the bench but wins the big game with his grit and courage; and anti-football fanatic who comes to evaluate the school and winds up coaching the team; and, of course, thousands of "delicious" zucchini sticks!! Even at over 200 pages, this entertaining story should hold appeal for many middle to junior high school students. The football scenes will add interest for sports buffs and the overall zaniness should be fun for all readers. (pp. 182-83)

> *Rosie Peasley, in a review of "The Zucchini Warriors," in* Voice of Youth Advocates, *Vol. 11, No. 4, October, 1988, pp. 182-83.*

After a short digression into the teen-age novel, with ***The Zucchini Warriors*** Gordon Korman has returned to Macdonald Hall and those irrepressible pranksters Bruno and Boots. It's hard to believe this is the 10th anniversary of the publication of the first Macdonald Hall book. Though Korman is no longer the teen-age author who burst on the Canadian publishing scene in the '70s, young readers will

be happy to see that Bruno and Boots are just the same. . . .

Though it does have a smattering of football talk, this isn't a novel for the serious sports fan. The far-fetched plot, breezy pace, and word-play are what readers look for in a Macdonald Hall novel. And Korman hasn't lost his enthusiasm for the Macdonald Hall gang. The same irreverent spoofing that characterized the earlier books is at its best here.

> *Callie Israel, "Bruno, Boots & Margaret Worth Another Look," in* Books for Young People, *Vol. 2, No. 6, December, 1988, p. 10.*

Radio Fifth Grade (1989)

As Korman proves in his funniest book to date, the trials and tribulations of producing a radio show can be sidesplitting.

"Kidsview" airs live on a local FM station every Saturday, and it's up to fifth-graders Benjy, Mark, and Ellen-Louise to pull it together—even if the pet-shop sponsor's Mascot of the Week is flapping vigorously around the studio; the new teacher has to be kept from finding out that her homework assignments are being used for a wildly successful phone-in trivia contest; or the editorial's hysterical warnings about the dangers of ultrasonic sound have 12 second-grade choral readers ready to stampede. To add to the mayhem, sixth-grader Brad Jaworski—the huge, leather-clad "Venice Menace"—has begun commandeering the mike each week to read a series of stories about homicidal kittens. Can Benjy—even with the example of his radio idol Eldridge Kestenbaum to sustain him—stay cool, summon the courage to cut Brad off, avoid the cardinal sin of dead air space, and keep the show on the air? Don't touch that dial!

> *A review of "Radio Fifth Grade," in* Kirkus Reviews, *Vol. LVII, No. 15, August 15, 1989, p. 1247.*

The many elements of the novel's complicated and episodic plot involve a teacher who wins the state lottery, a talking parrot who says all the wrong things, a hair dryer that jams radios and traffic lights, and a school bully who writes stories about two kittens named Fuzzy and Puffy. Although the plot is thin and the characters one-dimensional, this story works well on the level of sheer farce. Korman is good at creating chaotic, if not always believable, situations. And although not all of the jokes work and the perspective is somewhat adult, this book has a fast pace and an amusing, goofy tone that many kids will enjoy.

> *Todd Morning, in a review of "Radio Fifth Grade," in* School Library Journal, *Vol. 35, No. 13, September, 1989, p. 252.*

Although Korman breaks no new ground with this book, he knows his audience and writes for it with assurance and skill. His characters are flat and undeveloped, and description is kept to the minimum necessary to keep the story rolling, but Korman is going for laughs, and he knows how to get them. This light-hearted book will quickly become a favourite.

Fred Boer, in a review of "Radio Fifth Grade," in Quill and Quire, *Vol. 55, No. 10, October, 1989, p. 14.*

Losing Joe's Place (1990)

Confident that they won't jeopardize his brother Joe's apartment lease, 16-year-old Jason Cardone and his two best friends (who don't get along) embark on an adultless summer in Joe's bachelor pad, certain they will have the time of their lives. Unfortunately, Joe never prepared them for his irritating landlord, Mr. Plotnick, who eavesdrops on their conversations and gouges them for every penny he can. Nor is the trio prepared for pretty Jessica Lincoln or Rootbeer Racinette, a seven-foot retired alligator wrestler who barges through their bathroom window, eats 18 cans of soup in one sitting, and announces plans to stay and take up a hobby to ease his tension. Then, too, nobody is expecting Mr. Plotnick to hurt his back and have Jason turn the landlord's greasy-spoon, ground-floor deli into the trendiest restaurant in town. Those are just the highlights of Korman's latest novel, a frenetic string of funny scenes (eventually dovetailing into a plot), supported by a handful of sturdy, basically weird characters and a generous dose of pure slapstick. Rootbeer's bizarre antics and the boys' rivalry over Jessica are simple-hearted in comedic appeal, but part of the humor is derived from negative stereotyping. Consequently, while some readers will laugh out loud, others may not appreciate the mockery. (pp. 1276-77)

Stephanie Zvirin, in a review of "Losing Joe's Place," in Booklist, *Vol. 86, No. 13, March 1, 1990, pp. 1276-77.*

As in all Korman novels, this one calls for a certain suspension of disbelief. But Korman knows just what fantasies 16-year-olds would like to realize. The outrageous situations, fast pace, and appealing characters are on-target for this age group. It's a tried-and-true formula that Korman understands perfectly and manipulates with finesse.

Korman's writing becomes more polished with each book. His style is colloquial but not condescending and his dialogue rings true. This is solid, entertaining fare for young teens.

Callie Israel, in a review of "Losing Joe's Place," in Quill and Quire, *Vol. 56, No. 4, April, 1990, p. 15.*

Surprisingly, it's not the quick twists and turns of the farcical plot that keep this very funny story moving. It's Jason's spirited narrative, his self-effacing sense of humor, and his finely tuned ear for the ridiculous that make these unbelievable antics work and create characters from these caricatures. Young readers will either put this down early with a groan—or, more likely, they'll speed through, slowed down only by uncontrollable laughing fits.

Jack Forman, in a review of "Losing Joe's Place," in School Library Journal, *Vol. 36, No. 5, May, 1990, p. 124.*

Munro Leaf

1905-1976

(Also wrote as Mun and John Calvert) American author and illustrator of picture books, fiction, and nonfiction; journalist; and editor.

Major works include *The Story of Ferdinand* (1936), *Wee Gillis* (1938), *Noodle* (1937), *Listen, Little Girl, Before You Come to New York* (1938), the "Can Be Fun" series.

One of the most popular and beloved creators of American children's literature, Leaf blended humor and instruction in works for primary and middle graders which both address the importance of self-respect and appropriate social behavior and demystify a group of often difficult subjects which children encounter in school. Praised for his clarity and infectious wit as well as for the soundness of his principles, the sincerity of his approach, and his respect for children, Leaf is often acknowledged for possessing a masterful ability to present morals to young people in a painless manner. Leaf is best known as the creator of *The Story of Ferdinand,* a picture book with black and white etchings by Robert Lawson which critic Michael Patrick Hearn calls "a perfect marriage of story and art, perhaps the best modern picture book next to Wanda Gág's *Millions of Cats.*" The story describes a Spanish bull with a gentle, introspective nature who prefers to sit by himself, smelling the flowers under his favorite cork tree rather than engaging in the rough-and-tumble antics of his fellow bulls. When he is stung by a bee, Ferdinand's reaction is mistaken for bravado, and he is taken to Madrid to participate in the bullfights; in the ring, he chooses to sit and smell the flowers in the hair of the senoritas rather than to fight. At the end of the tale, Ferdinand is taken safely back to his cork tree. *The Story of Ferdinand* is considered a classic of children's literature as well as one of the most charming of animal fables. In addition, *Ferdinand* is noted as the first picture book to have been called subversive: the book was burned by Hitler as propaganda, and its message of peace and the importance of individuality has been interpreted as communistic, fascistic, and pacifistic. Ferdinand himself has been the subject of psychoanalysis, and is diagnosed as manic depressive and schizoid as well as having latent homosexual tendencies. Leaf, who was prompted to write the story as a vehicle for his friend Robert Lawson, dismissed these interpretations, calling the story innocent fun and Ferdinand "a philosopher [with] good taste and strength of character." After World War II, Ferdinand became recognized as an international symbol of peace, and the names of Leaf and Lawson are often suggested as possible recipients of the Nobel Peace Prize. Ferdinand was also the subject of an award-winning Walt Disney short as well as a marketing industry that included toys and other items bearing his likeness.

A high school teacher and coach who later served as the director of a publishing company, Leaf was inspired to create his first book for children, *Grammar Can Be Fun*

(1934), when he overheard a mother in the subway struggling to explain to her child why he should not say the word "ain't." Concluding that the boy would have remembered the lesson if it had been accompanied by funny drawings, Leaf composed childlike pictures in red, white, and black line to illustrate frequent grammatical errors, which he depicts through such characters as Gonna, Wanna, and Gimme. *Grammar Can Be Fun* was the first of a series of ten titles in a similar format which introduce children to the principles of appropriate behavior both toward each other and the environment and provide overviews designed to increase his audience's understanding and enjoyment of these topics. In the "Can Be Fun" books, Leaf addresses such subjects as etiquette, health, and safety as well as arithmetic, history, geography, science, and other classroom fare. He is also the author of the "Watchbird" series, four books which teach the rules of kindness and helpfulness by showing their reverse characteristics; based on Leaf's "Watchwords" column, which ran for over twenty years in *Ladies Home Journal,* the entries were edited and collected in the omnibus volume *Flock of Watchbirds* (1946). Several of Leaf's works, both fiction and nonfiction, underscore the value of knowledge and of appreciating quality literature; he also is the author and illustrator of a group of nonfiction titles on ethics, government, and the theory of democracy. His sole work for young adults, *Listen, Little Girl, Before You Come to New York,* is an informational book directed to young women which is noted for its honest evaluation of both job hunting and city life. In Leaf's fiction, he uses fantasy, realism, and a blend of both to address themes centering on individuality and respect for others in books which feature both human and animal protagonists. Leaf is noted as a writer whose informal texts speak to children in understandable language and as an illustrator whose characteristic matchstick figures have special appeal to the young. In addition to their collaboration on *The Story of Ferdinand,* Leaf and Lawson combined their talents on *Wee Gillis,* a popular picture book about a small orphaned Scottish boy faced with the dilemma of whether he should live with his mother's Lowland relatives or his father's relatives in the Highlands; Gillis, who develops his lung power by calling cattle in the Lowlands and learns to hold his breath indefinitely while hunting in the Highlands, finds his solution when he successfully plays the largest bagpipes in Scotland. *Wee Gillis* was named a Caldecott Medal honor book for its illustrations in 1939. Leaf also collaborated with illustrator Ludwig Bemelmans on *Noodle,* the tale of a dachshund who learns to appreciate himself after his wish to become a different shape is granted by a magic poodle. Leaf also edited an edition of *Aesop's Fables,* coauthored an adult book on psychiatry with W. C. Menniger, and produced pamphlets for the United States government, including a field manual on malaria illustrated by Dr. Seuss. In 1960, the American government named Leaf a specialist under the Department of State, a position which took him to over twenty countries as a speaker to children.

(See also *Something about the Author,* Vol. 20 and *Contemporary Authors,* Vols. 69-72 and Vols. 73-76.)

AUTHOR'S COMMENTARY

I can't draw and I never said I could. I think I am an equal to a five-year-old, if he did not go to a progressive school, in giving a rough idea of what I am trying to draw and that is all I cared about in *Grammar Can Be Fun, Robert Francis Weatherbee* and *Manners Can Be Fun. Ferdinand* was written so that Robert Lawson and I could have a good time together and anybody who thinks we didn't have one won't like the book. They won't see why we ever did it and if they can't see that, I won't argue with them—they may be right. (p. 707)

> *Munro Leaf, "Just for Fun," in* Publishers Weekly, *Vol. 130, No. 9, August 29, 1936, pp. 705-07.*

GENERAL COMMENTARY

Hardy R. Finch

Evidence of the continued popularity of the Munro Leaf books is everywhere. Most of his books have reached their fourteenth or fifteenth printings. Library records show that they are read and reread by young people. Bookstores stock and sell many of the titles today.

Why do the Leaf books have such lasting popularity? It is indeed difficult to analyze. However, here are several factors that may be contributing ones:

1. *Sincerity:* Munro Leaf writes from his heart. He is sincere and conveys this feeling to his reading audience of children and adults.

2. *Humor:* His drawings and his writings have the kind of infectious humor that is long remembered.

3. *Style:* He writes with clarity. Although some of his sentences are longer than the usual ones found in young children's books, they are easily understood by the young reader. These long sentences have an added advantage: Parents find them refreshing after an overdose of simple sentences intended for young readers.

4. *Pictures:* Leaf makes full use of his drawings to convey and add to the meaning of the text on the page.

5. *Ideas:* Most of Leaf's books have ideas as well as entertainment for the reader. Possibly that is why parents, teachers, and librarians guide youngsters to them. Many a bewildered parent has, for example, bought *Manners Can Be Fun* for his child because he felt that his youngster might learn some manners from it.

6. *Range of Interest Level:* The interest level in most of the Leaf books ranges from the child who may still need to have the story read to him to the adult who would not ordinarily read a children's book at all. (pp. 410-411)

> *Hardy R. Finch, "Munro Leaf, Writer for All Children of All Ages," in* Elementary English, *Vol. 30, No. 7, November, 1953, pp. 405-11.*

Kathleen Molz

Some thirty years ago, a young publisher overheard a frantic mother explaining to her completely unconvinced five-year-old the reasons why he shouldn't say "ain't". The child obviously did not have the slightest comprehension of what his mother was trying to say, and about all the observer could do was put the whole incident into a pocket of his brain to puzzle over. Surely there was some simpler way of conveying to children their parents' concepts of manners and speech. He began writing a book, titling it *Grammar Can Be Fun,* and, as a guide to the artist, inked in a few drawings depicting for children how their mistakes might look to others. Because the professional illustrators who worked from the sketches made it all seem too complex, the author decided to let his own drawings stand, launching himself, almost by accident, into a career that has made the name of Munro Leaf familiar to two generations of American children.

Now, with forty books behind him, Munro Leaf believes that, from their very inception, those ingenuous line drawings created a bond of equality between himself and children. "Anybody of any age," he says, "hates condescension," and children feel an immediate rapport with a grown-up who peoples his world with stick figures, not unlike those which pop up in their own notebooks. "It is really fortunate," admits Mr. Leaf, "that I draw so badly".

Aware that a "child's thinking vocabulary is way ahead of his writing and reading vocabulary", Munro Leaf has made it "fun" for children to tackle the big imponderables of history, geography, math, and democracy. The words he uses to deal with such topics are simple. He calls them his "nickle" words, for they are the ones that children themselves can traffic in.

Mr. Leaf's own "traffic with the word" began early. An avid reader and a good talker, he was made the neighborhood emissary, singled out for the ticklish job of placating an irate housewife when a ball sailed over her fence. Graduate study at Harvard, a career as a publisher, and several years' experience as a preparatory-school teacher, furthered his appreciation for both good books and interesting talk, and deepened his commitment to children and to the books created for them. Nothing delights him more than seeing a worn-out copy of one of his books in a public library, for that means that the "kid-grapevine" has done its work and put its sanction on a title. With a slow nod of his head, Mr. Leaf denies that he is any Pied Piper, but he impishly concludes that he might be called an "Everyman for small-fry". (p. 45)

> *Kathleen Molz, "Nickle Words for a Golden Mission," in* Wilson Library Bulletin, *Vol. 39, No. 1, September, 1964, pp. 45-7.*

Bettina Hürlimann

[Post-war] America had a number of likeable emissaries . . . . There was, for instance, the children's book which appeared in Germany very shortly after the war . . . whose text, by Munro Leaf, surely held as much significance as Robert Lawson's illustrations. This was *Ferdinand*, the story of the bull who will not fight, a book which set peaceful attitudes and the enjoyment of life above conventional heroism. Munro Leaf himself later took to drawing and he has written and illustrated a number of semi-didactic but always enjoyable picture-stories which have brought ideals of international unity to children all over the world. They have been as quickly understood by the village children of India as by those of the American prairie. (p. 18)

> *Bettina Hürlimann, "Picture Books in America," in her* Picture-Book World, *edited and translated by Brian W. Alderson, Oxford University Press, London, 1968, pp. 18-21.*

TITLE COMMENTARY

Grammar Can Be Fun (1934)

"Ain't" lying prone on the cover is depicted as a cross between a potato and The Yaller Kid. "Yeah," fat and squat and unpleasant; "Gimme" with bee-like body, spiderish arms, and a red tam o'shanter. Frequent mistakes in grammar are illustrated with further curious personifications. Right use of language is similarly treated. At the end of

From Manners Can Be Fun, *written and illustrated by Munro Leaf.*

the book are several blank pages headed "These Next Pages Have Mistakes I Make and the Pictures Are Drawn by Me." What will psychologists say to this provision for impressing mistakes upon their makers? Some grown-ups and some boys and girls will like this book and liking it will find it useful. Others more realistic will prefer to take their grammar dull but straight.

> *Clara Savage Littledale, in a review of "Grammar Can Be Fun," in* The Saturday Review of Literature, *Vol. 11, No. 18, November 17, 1934, p. 295.*

There used, a long time ago, to be a book called *Reading Without Tears*. A similar kindness has now been done to a subject even more under a curse for childhood. Grammar really is fun in this prankish picture-book.

It opens with creatures who should have no place in young society, such as the Wobbly-Necks, Uh-huh and Un-un, who "shake their heads and nod their heads and still no one knows what they want to say," whereas "Yes and No are always happy because everybody knows what *they* mean." These gentry and the egregious Ain't appear as absurd red and black goblins, with the deplorable Gonna, Wanna and Gimme, the messy Got, a weed that grows in sentences like "I have a ball," and No and Not who do not get along well in the same sentences. There is not a word about parts of speech, but a small child cheerfully finds out something about verbs and adverbs at work. . . .

> *May Lamberton Becker, in a review of "Grammar Can Be Fun," in* New York Herald Tribune Books, *December 23, 1934, p. 5.*

Robert Francis Weatherbee (1935)

Robert Francis Weatherbee wouldn't go to school. Then he began to discover drawbacks to not having an education. . . . [Be] sure and introduce Robert Francis Weatherbee to some five-year-old boy and see how he chuckles.

> *A review of "Robert Francis Weatherbee," in* The Horn Book Magazine, *Vol. XI, No. 5, September-October, 1935, p. 285.*

Manners Can Be Fun (1936)

Mr Leaf has proved, in **Grammar Can Be Fun,** that he has the trick of producing what one might call the modern counterpart of cautionary literature: that is, the sort of book that laughs one into doing the right thing rather than shames one out of doing the wrong one. He now goes after bad manners in the nursery and by strong arm methods shooes them away from the society of the young. I like his book: it will be accepted in good part by little children; it does not nag.

Yet we must admit that something must take the place of nagging and do the work of that bad habit, if children are to grow up with the consideration for the comfort of others that is the basis of all good manners. As Mr. Leaf puts it at the very outset: "Having good manners is really just living with other people pleasantly. If you lived all by yourself out on a desert island, others would not care whether you had good manners or not. It wouldn't bother them. But if some one else lived there with you, you would both have to learn to get along together pleasantly. If you did not, you would probably quarrel and fight all the time, or stay apart and be lonesome because you could not have a good time together." Lest this should sound didactic, thus quoted, I hasten to say that there have been already for this amount of text three drawings in red and black of a quite uproarious *grotesquerie,* showing the island and the way ill-behaved people behave on it. The book then proceeds, with a profusion of such pictures and brief sentences in large type, to set for the basic principles of behavior, rightly envisaged as taking in states of mind as well as acts. The Noiseys, the Whineys, the Me-Firsts, the Toucheys, thus come up for judgment.

People who feel the need of an addition to *Goops,* or who want a book for younger children than Mr. Burgess's audience, had better give this one a glance; it is likely to recommend itself even on brief attention.

> *May Lamberton Becker, in a review of "Manners Can Be Fun," in* New York Herald Tribune Books, *September 27, 1936, p. 9.*

[*A revised edition of* Manners Can Be Fun *appeared in 1958.*]

First published in 1936, this is a revised edition. A few pages of new material have been added which include television manners. . . . Describing correct conduct with friends and in school, at home or at play, the author makes it clear that good manners help make one a person pleasant to be with or to live with. The reorganization of some pages and the change to illustrations that are black and white only are minor differences in a book as amusing and effective as ever.

> *Zena Sutherland, in a review of "Manners Can Be Fun," in* Bulletin of the Children's Book Center, *Vol. XI, No. 11, July-August, 1958, p. 121.*

The Story of Ferdinand (1936)

There are two factors in the phenomenon Ferdinand which may interest the psychoanalyst. 1. What the artist expressed by the creation of a bull who refused to fight; 2. why this creation struck a response in the unconscious of so large a portion of the public, hitting apparently upon deep emotional needs; the answer to these two questions may reveal a contribution to the psychoanalysis of the comic and the humor.

The story of Ferdinand is the story of a little innocent calf, born in a paradisiac landscape of green pastures and beautiful trees, flowers and butterflies. Ferdinand gets older and stronger but he refuses to grow up. He remains an eternal child, knowing neither the obligations and conflicts, nor the challenge which is connected with the fate of being a bull. He does not regress; he simply remains locked in his happy innocence, nursing himself with the abundance of infantile pleasure. He gives up even his mother who acknowledged the perfect solution of his narcissism. The only friends, whom Ferdinand accepts, are the flowers around him and the cork tree behind him. There is a suspicious absence of any father figure.

The cork tree belongs to Ferdinand just as a shell belongs to a snail, they are inseparable. The tree appears in all pictures except that at the bull fight episode. Ferdinand's tree is unlike little Washington's cherry tree and also unlike Adam and Eve's tree with the sinful apples of knowledge. It is a cork tree and of a special kind, because the corks grow on it like fruits. They are drawn with special care, so plastic in detail that the onlooker gets the bodily feeling of touching them. This feeling is unique for cork feels like nothing else—if not, somebody may compare it with a thumb without a bone or with a limp penis. The feeling of uniqueness for the *substance* cork is connected with a comical quality of cork as an *idea.* Nobody can take it seriously, it is not heavy enough for that. It is wood and it is not wood; it falls down but it does not seem to have any weight; it floats on water which drowns everything else after a short or long time. In the illustrations of Ferdinand, the cork-stoppers, hundreds of them, hang down from the cork tree. Aimless but distinct, they look as if they were ready to be used as stoppers for bottles—suggesting in this way their symbolic meaning once more.

The physical qualities and the useful function of cork force the reader of Ferdinand to recognize its symbolic meaning as phallus. But it is a special phallus, a limp, a light, a useless and impotent one. This impotence is put into a comical contrast by the large and impressive number of corks and their union with an old, majestic, very protecting and erect, powerful tree which gives Ferdinand the background of serenity and power. It is as if Ferdinand possesses the silly (cork) but still impressive penis (tree) of his father.

Ferdinand, however, prefers not to use it. After having depreciated it by calling it a cork, he could not use it very well anyhow, but its possession makes it possible for him to resign in happy pacifism.

The tree is not only related to Ferdinand and his father. It is an old tree with large, deep, and dark holes, with its roots in mother earth, with its loving and shade-spending branches protecting little Ferdinand—it is, in other words, father and mother together protecting their only child in a very one sided—and that means pre-ambivalent way—a way in which only mothers love their sons. This tree is altruistic in its love for Ferdinand, giving but not taking, spending but not demanding, expecting no return which would be hard for Ferdinand to deliver. In a happy union with his family tree and with the landscape he lives in, Ferdinand grows strong. He is busy smelling flowers, indulging in this without guilty feelings, without fear, which is essentially unknown to him even in the situation of the bull fight. With all the pleasure of the suckling he drinks the smell of the flowers, his nostrils get wide, his eyes closed or even worse, half-closed, like the eyes of a woman in ecstacy. He is not bothered by this appearance because he does not know the difference between men and women. He only knows that this tree is *his* tree and his parents are unchangeably on his side. If someone should doubt that it is just the union of father and mother which makes the cork tree so important and gives Ferdinand his inner harmony and security, he may turn back once more to the first picture in the book *Ferdinand* and look at the castle, so very high, so very erect, so powerful with its high roof and towers, so continued into the sky by a high pile of clouds and so deeply cut by a dark canyon. Here we have again the symbolic expression of father's powerful phallus with mother's gigantic womb, forming the background of this picture. From here the onlooker's eye is drawn into the foreground, into the center of the picture to the repetition of the same motif: little Ferdinand under the cork tree.

Ferdinand would not be a comical person but only an idyllic one if his happiness, innocence, and resignation would be achieved and kept without any conflict. The bumble bee stings him, of course, without malice, but in self defence because Ferdinand tried to sit on her. The sensible and tender-nerved Ferdinand reacts as if in danger of death (or mortal danger) with a terrific anxiety attack. To put it mildly, he over-reacts.

The fear of insects, especially stinging insects, is wide spread among many persons. After getting stung, the affected place gets painful swollen, red and hot. We know from dreams how terribly frightening insects may become

and that the unconscious sees in the sting of a bee something like a poisonous dagger. Ferdinand jumps into the air like a girl who sees a mouse, and the artist does not forget to show that he even destroys flowers and a little branch off the cork tree. For a moment Ferdinand loses the symbols of his security.

The experts from Madrid take the shocked Ferdinand as a man in fighting mood and off he goes to the sacred ordeal of the bull fight. Mistaken for that which he wanted to avoid, he is to be killed in ritual forms. He gets all the fame and reputation of a primitive totem animal when he is thought to be ferocious and wild, dangerous and heroic, ready to fight and die like a guilty Oedipus.

"But not Ferdinand." He refuses to be made the dying king Oedipus, ready to die for his dreadful desires and deeds. The smell of the flowers in the ladies' hair is enough for him. He is not out for forceful defloration. He quiets down and does not confess intentions which he never had. He refuses to die and is taken home in disgrace. No one can be allowed to kill the totem who apparently refuses to be one. Back home, "he is happy" again.

The book *Ferdinand* may or may not have been written for children but its interest is surely not limited to them. As a matter of fact it is one of these books which the *adult* accepts because it is not directed to him but to children. Children like Ferdinand as an animal and as a bull but not as Ferdinand. They like it best just in all these situations in which Ferdinand is not behaving like Ferdinand but in which Ferdinand behaves like El Toro Ferocio. Ferdinand may be bought for 50¢ as a toy. In utter neglect of his true character, children play with him in the way in which Ferdinand does not behave and perform. They let him fight with everything. Because Ferdinand is made of iron–rubber he can stand it and belongs to the few indestructible children's toys.

Adults like to read this book to children telling them in this way that Ferdinand enjoys everlasting love, peace and happiness so long as he behaves like a nice little calf who does not grow up. In this case the book is used as a clear cut castration threat, like most famous books for children (Struwwelpeter, Alice in Wonderland).

Ferdinand found his way into the unconscious of the masses, the book became a perennial best-seller, he volunteered successfully as a movie star. He enriched the English language with a new word with the meaning "conscientious objector" and fell short of being a national hero. He is not heroic in the common sense of the word because he is not the super-man but a victim, he is not great but small, he has not the features of the sublime but of the tragi-comic and of the humorous. He cannot be called a hero nor can he be called a totem animal; in the usual sense of the word he is not a sacred symbol of the father and he has not the sacred fate and the ceremonial death of a totem animal but he had some of these features in disguised form, maybe in a form which is typical for our present time. Ferdinand is not only the son who successfully avoids the fate of Oedipus; he is also the depreciated father about whom the son laughs before he identifies himself with him. After all, little Ferdinand is not as harmless as he succeeds in making us believe. Helene Deutsch pointed out similar features in the figure of Don Quixote, and Jaeckels is of the opinion that depreciation of the father and giving him the features of a son is the main motive in the creation of every comedy.

The heroic and beautiful beast of the bull fight is a totem animal symbolizing masculine power, fighting spirit, and preparedness even to die. These features of the father totem are destroyed by Ferdinand who simply smiles at everything that father might have done in a similar situation. After depreciation of the powerful father and after laughing at him and his defeat, we can like and love him again. After the death of the totem animal we may incorporate him, identify yourselves with him and we are then ready to accept him as some form of an ideal. In the case of Ferdinand, it is the ideal of the sociable citizen. "You must be like Ferdinand in order to live in these days of bull fights."

Ferdinand is not a pitiful figure. Our super ego would not permit us to laugh if he was. According to Freud, laughter is aroused where energy is saved. In the form of wit, aggression is freed, in a form of the comic: thought; in a form of humor; emotion. We save the emotion of pity because Ferdinand is not unhappy. We laugh it off with tears in our eyes, so typical of true humor. After all, Ferdinand is the victor-like Charlie Chaplin, who also wins out through his innocence and naivete. He simply refuses to accept defeat by reality. Ferdinand and Chaplin, they do not believe in castration, always asking in moments of danger, "So what?" with disarming results. This is an overcoming of reality by the denial of its existence.

This denial must be made possible by certain reality conditions, otherwise the reader of the book or the spectator at the movie could not follow. The denial must be accepted as credible, it must be described convincingly. The special condition which enables Ferdinand to live as he lives and the reader to identify himself with him, is the inner security and harmony which he gains from the knowledge of possessing father and mother.

The collective unconscious accepts Ferdinand not only because of this but even more because of the unconscious recognition of a little Ferdinand in every one of us. We have all considered for a period of time, more or less seriously, with more or less successful and lasting results, avoiding the curse of being an Oedipus. During the psychoanalytic treatment a similar feeling may often be observed. When the patient is freed from his most disturbing symptoms he often is puzzled: freed to do what? On the couch with the psychoanalyst behind him, he feels like Ferdinand backed by the cork tree, quite satisfied and most certainly not going to move.

Ferdinand is by no means altogether castrated even though he does not enjoy manifest genital activity. He enjoys the sense of smelling with all the signs of real excitement. The childish paradise of Ferdinand is beautified by childish pleasures. Freud knew the importance of the suppression of the sense of smell in humans and he even states that man's turning away from the earth and his repression of the smell pleasures are "largely responsible for his pre-

disposition for nervous diseases." Ferdinand does not make this repression, he enjoys smell and he does not even need to fight for it—partially because he does not take away anything from anybody by smelling and partly because his understanding mother does not mind it.

Sigmund Freud recognized humor as a regressive phenomenon: as a triumph of the narcissism, a denial of reality, a victory of the pleasure principles. In humoristic attitude, the super ego acts toward the ego like an adult toward a child. The super ego speaks a kind word of comfort to the desperately depressed and bewildered ego. The contrast to such benevolent attitude is the "Spartan attitude" (Franz Alexander) with which the sadistic ego demands sternly the fulfillment of unpleasant duties. Because of this relation between ego and super ego the humoristic attitude is possible within one and the same person, no listening third is needed (Kris). In the case of Ferdinand, the super ego demands are satisfied without much conflict; the kindliness of the super ego is partially pictured in the tolerating mother who does not mind Ferdinand's strange behaviour and his smell perversion, and partially in the matador who does not kill Ferdinand when he refuses to fight back.

From the economic point of view the humoristic phenomenon is a saving of energy, a saving of emotion—again following Freud. Wit has a close relation to sadism, as Dooley pointed out, and humor has a close relation to masochism. Humor may be found where the Oedipus complex is going down under the weight of disappointment, fear, and

From The Story of Ferdinand, *written by Munro Leaf. Illustrated by Robert Lawson.*

guilt. The typical Oedipus complex, the tragic guilt about the Oedipus desires, are denied and displaced by Ferdinand; and this may give some more information about how the ego manages to be treated in such an unusually kind way by the super ego, as Freud suggested. The super ego is so kind because it is put aside by the desperate and aggressive ego. The ego relapses into primary narcissism. In the case of Ferdinand, it regresses into narcissistic resignation. Ferdinand behaves as if the world were not real but, as he wishes it to be: peaceful. In this way, as Bergler describes it, the ego assumes the child's behaviour of inner freedom about logic, thought, and emotion: a repetition of life before logic and before the Oedipus complex, a life in happiness and in pleasurable mastery of word and thought. The opposite of laughter is not weeping. In the instance of humor, the laughter occurs with tears. As a matter of fact we seldom laugh about Ferdinand. Usually, we only smile, using in this way a sublimated form of laughter. (pp. 34-40)

The disguise of what really is meant in the story of Ferdinand seems to be successful. In the disguise of the little Ferdinand, a totem animal and a father figure is depreciated, humiliated, is killed and revived in a form which is now acceptable even for a very strict Super Ego. This acceptance is not based upon special kindness of the Super Ego but is based on a desperate effort by the ego by means of regression, denial, negative hallucinations, and masochistic resignation. The aggression stimulated by all associations contained in the idea of being a bull is suppressed and the emotional pity for the castrated father is saved by the happiness of Ferdinand who succeeds in gaining a happy reunion between father and son, not even losing the mother's love. Smilingly we enjoy the mastery of the infantile past by infantile means. Then again after the reassurance of such an experience it is easier for us to subdue ourselves under the government of logic, rational behaviour, reality principle, and the super ego. (pp. 40-1)

> *Martin Grotjahn, "Ferdinand the Bull: Psychoanalytical Remarks About a Modern Totem Animal," in* American Imago, *Vol. 1, No. 3, June, 1940, pp. 33-41.*

The book **Ferdinand the Bull** may have been written for children, but its appeal is not limited to them. It is one of those books which adults accept because it is directed not to them but to children. Children love Ferdinand as an animal and as a bull, but hardly as Ferdinand. They like him best in those situations in which Ferdinand behaves not like Ferdinand but like El Toro Ferocio. He used to be sold as a toy, and children playing with him would make him fight with everything, in utter neglect of his true character.

Adults like to read the book to children, telling them in this way that Ferdinand enjoys everlasting love, peace, and happiness so long as he behaves like a nice little calf who does not grow up. The book is used as a disguised, contemporary castration threat, like so many famous books for children. It is as if the grown-up reader says to the unconscious of the listening children: And five bad men came—like five fingers of a hand with bad intentions—and they wanted Ferdinand to be bad, and Ferdi-

nand got mad and excited and wild, but then he controlled himself and was saved.

Ferdinand found his way into the collective unconscious. He became a perennial best-seller and successful movie star. He was a national hero until times changed, the Second World War broke out, and the nation could no longer afford dreams of peace and passivity.

Ferdinand cannot be called a hero nor can he be called a totem animal, representing the incarnation of the sacred father who has to be killed and eaten at periodic intervals, but he has some of these features in disguised form. Ferdinand is not only the son who successfully avoids the fate of Oedipus; he is also the depreciated impotent father about whom the son laughs. In a passive and peaceful way, the ideals for which the father is ready to kill and to die are quietly and efficiently depreciated. Little Ferdinand is not quite so harmless as he wants us to believe. Little Ferdinand has done to the father what the father intended to do to his son; he has effectively and neatly castrated him. He has done so by defiance and a passive sit-down strike. The father's ideals have been treated with contempt, and the poor father is left stranded, bewildered, and helplessly looking at his victorious son, seeming to ask: What now?

The heroic and beautiful beast of the bullfight is a totem animal symbolizing masculine power, fighting spirit, and preparedness to die. These features of the father totem are destroyed by Ferdinand, who quietly smiles at everything that Father might have done in a similar situation. After depreciating the powerful father and laughing at him and his defeat, we may incorporate him, identify ourselves with him, and accept him as a form of ideal. In the case of Ferdinand, it is the ideal of the well-adjusted, resigned citizen: You must be like Ferdinand in order to live in these days of bullfights.

Ferdinand is not a pitiful figure. We would not allow ourselves to laugh if he were. We save the emotion of pity because Ferdinand is happy. He has many reasons to be happy: he has defeated his father; has, as the analyst would say, castrated him. Then, after the depreciation, he became like him; he behaves like a castrated father himself. Oedipus behaved differently; after he slew his father, he himself became king and husband to his Queen Mother. Not so Ferdinand. The depreciated totem animal of our time pays a high price in order to remain alive.

To the end, Ferdinand is the victor, like Charlie Chaplin, who wins out through his innocence and naïveté. Each steadfastly refuses to accept defeat by reality. The meek will inherit the earth. Ferdinand and Chaplin do not believe in castration; they always seem to ask disarmingly in moments of danger: So what? Reality is overcome by the denial of its existence. Ferdinand symbolizes victorious defiance in a humorous setting. By being castrated, he castrates.

A different defiance in aggressive and witty form is contained in the following story:

A woman in New York tells her neighbor how worried she is about the behavior of her son; she has taken him to a psychiatrist, and the doctor has diagnosed the poor boy as suffering from "an Oedipus." With great cheerfulness the neighbor reassures her: "Oedipus, schmoedipus! Don't worry, so long as he loves his mother." That is Ferdinand's solution. He loves his mother and is loved by her like a baby, which renders the father helpless. Let the father puff and snort—so long as the son peacefully sleeps on the breast of the mother. This is the ultimate defeat of the father by the infant son. It symbolizes the goal and final victory. It leads us in the end to the last embrace, which is Death. (pp. 216-20)

> *Martin Grotjahn, "The Importance and Meaning of Ferdinand the Bull and Mickey Mouse," in his* Beyond Laughter, *McGraw-Hill Book Company, Inc., 1957, pp. 205-234.*

No adult ever forgets his first surprised examination of the small pink book bearing the picture of a mild-looking bull and the title **The Story of Ferdinand.** Munro Leaf's brief, succinct text, together with some of Robert Lawson's finest drawings, achieves a droll perfection that is hard to account for.

Ferdinand, the peaceful bull, accidentally sits down on a bee, is stung into wild action, and is mistaken for the "fightingest" bull of the whole countryside. He is carted off to the city for a bullfight, but once in the arena he merely returns to his favorite occupation, smelling flowers, and so is ignominiously sent back to his meadow.

Why does this small tale include such prolonged chuckles? First, it has a genuinely funny situation: peaceful Ferdinand cast in the role of a frightful monster! Ferdinand's plight suggests amusing human parallels. Probably every adult has at one time or another found himself in the thick of some battle for which he was never intended; some awful committee he should never have been put on; some exalted public task he is supposed to work at brilliantly when all he really wants is a little spare time to go his own way and sniff peacefully at such fine flowers of leisure as life affords. So adults, identifying themselves with the absurdly miscast Ferdinand, are much amused with his tribulations. But children like this story, too. The youngest take it literally. They say gravely, "Did the bee hurt Ferdinand?" Older children are entranced by the drawings and catch the fine humor of the text. (p. 400)

> *May Hill Arbuthnot, "Animal Stories," in her* Children and Books, *third edition, Scott, Foresman and Company, 1964, pp. 398-425.*

It seems probable that [**Ferdinand**] earned the approval of adults in the 1930s because it could be seen as upholding ideals which were markedly popular at that time. One of these was kindness to animals. In 1932 Hemingway had published his *Death in the Afternoon,* which tended to glamourize bullfighting but predictably aroused protest against the sport as cruel. Political overtones may also have seemed timely here: the Spanish Civil War did not begin until 1936, too late to have affected the composition of **Ferdinand,** which was published that year, but there were many signs of trouble long before 1936. Mussolini invaded Ethiopia in 1935, for example. Many who sensed war coming elsewhere were actively trying to maintain peace: this was the era of Peace in Our Time and America

First. Peacemakers may have seen a satisfactory moral in Ferdinand's dislike of fighting, and his final state makes a splendid emblem of the joys of peace. Those who knew their Bible might be reminded of the description of the Day of the Lord in *Micah* 4: 3-4:

> And he shall judge among many people, and rebuke strong nations afar off; and they shall beat their swords into ploughshares, and their spears into pruning hooks: nation shall not lift up a sword against nation, neither shall they learn war any more. But they shall sit every man under his vine and under his fig tree. . .

In Ferdinand's case the fig tree is replaced by a cork tree, but a cork tree with corks on it, which brings the whole scene close to the nonsense world—as does the bull who sits down to smell flowers. This nonsense is absolutely necessary to the book. It is, of course, amusing to children of the age for which this picture book was intended, which is not an age likely to be receptive to undisguised propaganda about whatever worthy causes or global issues may concern their seniors. Even more important for this audience, however, is the function of nonsense in controlling the reader's reaction to cruelty: nonsense is the picture-book illustrator's prime device for "distancing" events which might otherwise seem uncomfortably close-to-home. Carried to an extreme (as it usually is with Lear's limericks) nonsense removes the scene from any possible comment on reality; but a mixed style of the sort represented by the illustrations of **Ferdinand** need not undermine serious implications: it simply mitigates unpleasant aspects of the world depicted.

Unfortunately, though, adults rarely seem to understand nonsense and its functions. Among possible adult mistakes in this respect is the confusion of serious nonsense with mere buffoonery, the mistake the Disney people evidently made in their interpretation of Ferdinand. Of course, pacificism was not such a fashionable attitude by the time the film was made, and imminent war may have been a factor in turning the tale into a didactic story inculcating the norms of male behaviour by poking fun at the sissy who played with girls ("the heifers all called him *amigo*") and had not mastered the manly arts of self-defense ("he never learned to fight").

If all this now seems offensive to feminists (and others) as well as thoroughly tasteless, it may be consoling to consider the extreme unlikelihood of any such message reaching the children who read or listened to the book itself then, or those who are still enjoying it. The work of the illustrator, Robert Lawson, makes it perfectly clear that this is a book about the cruelty and stupidity of the adult world. While the bull has his comic aspects (as do other heroes and heroines of the best modern fantasy for children), it is obviously the people who are truly ridiculous—especially the "bull experts." Their evident stupidity is almost sinister, needing only a change of headgear and an eyepatch or two to qualify them for the crew of the *Hispaniola*. It is hard to see how anyone could fail to identify with the bull, who looks so tiny in the great arena. To poke fun at Ferdinand is as bad as it would be to make Alice a figure of fun, setting up the standards of the Duchess or the Red Queen for us to admire, for, like *Alice in Wonder-*

land, Leaf's book is the type of fantasy, bordering on satire, which exploits a bemused innocent's view of an irrational (or inhumane) world. (pp. 8-9)

> Constance B. Hieatt, *"Analyzing Enchantment: Fantasy after Bettelheim,"* in Canadian Children's Literature, *Nos. 15 & 16, 1980, pp. 6-14.*

[*The following excerpt is from an essay by Margaret Leaf, the wife of Munro Leaf.*]

Few bulls, if any, have birthday parties, and certainly not to celebrate 50 years of life. But Ferdinand, the bull who liked to smell the flowers, has been having not just one but several birthday parties in various parts of the country. The peaceable bull and his little book—all 800 words of it, written by Munro Leaf in about 40 minutes one Sunday afternoon—are still going strong and show no signs of aging.

In 1935, Munro and I were living in one room on 60th Street in New York City, working our way out of the Depression. Munro was an editor and a director of F. A. Stokes Co., and I was the manager of the children's department at Brentano's. Munro had written and Stokes had published **Grammar Can Be Fun** in 1934 and **Robert Francis Weatherbee** in 1935. **Manners Can Be Fun** was scheduled for 1936. (**Manners** is also celebrating its 50th anniversary this year and has never been out of print.) We had become friends of Robert and Marie Lawson; she had designed some book jackets for Stokes and he was spending his time etching. Munro promised him that he would write a book for him to illustrate.

One day I was trying to read a manuscript, and Munro persisted in talking to me. Finally, I told him to go away and amuse himself. Less than 40 minutes later, he handed me six pages of yellow legal-pad paper. It was **The Story of Ferdinand.** Munro wanted to write about an animal and decided that stories about bulls weren't common. Since the story was set in Spain, Munro named the bull after King Ferdinand—it was the only Spanish name he could think of.

We went at once to the Lawsons' and they read it. We all knew we had something out of the ordinary, and I insisted that we give it to Viking, because they had the best manufacturing man—Milton Glick. Munro had a contract for his next book with Stokes, but Mr. Stokes graciously gave him permission to publish Ferdinand elsewhere. Bob made up a dummy, and we brought it to May Massee, who accepted it at once. She wouldn't even let Munro take it home.

The book, published in the fall of 1936, soon after the start of the Spanish Civil War, met with immediate controversy. This innocent bull was branded a communist and an anarchist. There was a special burning in Germany where the book was labeled "degenerate democratic propaganda." Articles about the bull appeared in the *New Yorker, Life* and *Look.* Munro was attacked in the *Cleveland Plain Dealer* for subverting the children of America. His reply was as follows: "I have been accused of defending or attacking practically every 'ism' that has popped up in the last few years. As far as I am concerned, there is one story there—the words are simple and quite short. They try to make sense and if there is a message in them, as many people seem to want, it is Ferdinand's message, not mine—get it from him according to your need."

Harold Ginsberg, president of the Viking Press, had suggested postponing publication until "the world settles down." Fortunately, May and Munro decided to go ahead. The first printing was small—only 5200 copies—and all the fall advertising money had been allocated for a book now long forgotten. What happened with **Ferdinand** is still a mystery. After Christmas, sales increased every week, and within 13 months eight editions had been published. Ferdinand appeared as a giant balloon in the Macy's Thanksgiving Day Parade; Eleanor Roosevelt wrote about him; a Ferdinand song made the hit parade; and in December of 1938, **The Story of Ferdinand** nudged *Gone with the Wind* off the top of the bestseller lists.

Within several years, there were over 60 translations, an Oscar-winning Disney short, jewelry, dress material, games and toys; then the book settled down to steady sales year after year. Worldwide, over 2.4 million copies have been sold to date.

Now in 1986, the book seems right for the times. It is being bought for children by grandparents who say they were raised on it. There are new editions in England, Germany and Poland (where Ferdinand was the only noncommunist children's book allowed during the Stalin period). A puppet show has been touring the U.S for years, and there is also a puppet show in Japan. The story has been reprinted in Spain, where it was not published until 1978. A reviewer in Madrid said that Ferdinand should have won a Nobel Prize. The Academia de la Lingua Asturiana in Orviedo is publishing it in the Asturian language. (Asturian is spoken by a small population in the northwest corner of the Iberian Peninsula, and translation is reserved for a handful of classics of world literature.) A number of other translations are also in progress. Ferdinand has made his television debut as well: Trebitsch Productions International of Hamburg recently filmed a reading of the book by Peter Ustinov, with the Hamburg Philharmonic Orchestra playing in the background while Lawson's illustrations are shown. . . .

Recently, I spoke to a group of 60 children at a birthday party for Ferdinand held in a library. One small boy raised his hand and asked why Ferdinand sat and smelled the flowers when everyone wanted him to fight. I told him what I believe is the message of the book: that Ferdinand has the courage to refuse to do what he knows is wrong for him. Munro always maintained that he meant no message, that he meant only to entertain. But I have a photo of him as a small boy lying down in front of a family group, and he is smelling a flower.

> Margaret Leaf, *"Happy Birthday, Ferdinand!"* in Publishers Weekly, *Vol. 230, No. 18, October 31, 1986, p. 33.*

The Story of Ferdinand is a perfect marriage of story and art, perhaps the best modern picture book next to Wanda

Fire-bug Nit-Wit. *From* Safety Can Be Fun, *written and illustrated by Munro Leaf.*

Gag's *Millions of Cats.* In Lawson, Leaf found his Tenniel, his Ernest Shepard. Lawson was not only a deft draftsman but also a master of characterization and picture-book pacing. Each figure is individualized, each spread a new surprise as Lawson expanded the understated humor of Leaf's tale through the beautiful and hilarious pictures. These contain countless small, witty details (such as Ferdinand's growth chart, the patches on the other bulls and those on the vain Matador's stockings, Ferdinand's whimsical cork tree) which fascinate young readers. It is no wonder that Walt Disney for once did not wander far from Lawson's original drawings when he adapted the book for animation in 1939.

Leaf's little lesson is as true today as it was during the Spanish Civil War. Like the Cowardly Lion in *The Wizard of Oz,* Ferdinand the Bull is not what others expect him to be. He is a social misfit who refuses to go against his nature. Like Melville's Bartleby the Scrivener, Leaf's Ferdinand just prefers not to. Every child knows what it is like to be forced to do something that he or she just does not want to do. Another writer would have clumsily transformed timid Ferdinand into a hero of the bullring. But Leaf knew that true courage is being true to one's self, no matter what anyone else might say. And it is within himself that Ferdinand finds true happiness. Happy Birthday, Ferdinand. (p. 22)

> *Michael Patrick Hearn, "Ferdinand the Bull's 50th Anniversary," in* Book World—The

Washington Post, *November 9, 1986, pp. 13, 22.*

Noodle (1937)

If young Mr. Leaf keeps on at this rate, he may get it through the heads of people who have not read a child's book since they were in elementary school that it is now possible for them to read one, even in public, without losing face. His *Ferdinand* made history. As for *Noodle,* I have for several days, as an experiment in human nature, carried a copy with me on the subway and turned the pages each time for two perfect strangers, one on each shoulder.

This is the more noteworthy for *Ferdinand*'s type of humor is distinctly adult, while that of *Noodle* is the sort that appeals particularly to the young. No doubt much of this appeal is due to the pictures, since Mr. Leaf has been once more twice-blessed in his illustrator. Noodle is a dachshund, and Ludwig Bemelmans knows and appreciates a dachs from the brain cell out. One can almost see him charging a brush with brown paint, making a couple of expert dashes at the paper and holding off the result to look at it—one may say without irreverence—with the same sort of delighted satisfaction with which the Creator must have leaned back and regarded the first dachs. . . .

In this moral tale, Noodle is digging for a bone and wishing himself some other shape because digging might be easier, when his nose touches a buried wishbone. When he emerges, there is the dog-fairy—naturally in the shape of a white poodle—to grant his wish. Noodle, having profound commonsense and the rest of the morning to spare, promises to make his choice after dinner, and goes to the zoo to look over the animals. Each one naturally advises his own shape. Noodle feels that he cannot agree with the hippo, the zebra or giraffe in this matter, or consent to become anything so silly as the ostrich. So he wishes to be "just exactly the size and shape I am right now"; the dog-fairy says "that is a very wise wish" and the tall-piece shows Noodle meekly asleep and looking much like a pretzel.

A good, happy little book, it will get itself happily remembered by any child who gets it. I sincerely hope that a great many will.

> *May Lamberton Becker, in a review of "Noodle," in* New York Herald Tribune Books, *September 12, 1937, p. 7.*

Those who look for another *Ferdinand* will not find it here. They will find here a merry little tale, its humor less sophisticated, told with a crisp economy of words, which has its own quality of absurdity combined with sound common sense, and a tinge of the wistfulness which practically every dog story, fanciful or otherwise, manages to contain. Its success depends equally on the manner of its telling, and upon Ludwig Bemelmans's drawings, grotesque, ridiculous and wholly expressive of the story's flavor.

> *Ellen Lewis Buell, "Dachshund's Choice," in*

The New York Times Book Review, *September 19, 1937, p. 12.*

Listen, Little Girl, Before You Come to New York (1938)

Listen, little girl—but you needn't be afraid that all you are going to hear is "Don't." Munro Leaf, studying the field of employment for young women in New York City, is much more helpful than that, even if he is not over optimistic. This is a book of positive information. Here are the facts about that work you think you'd like, your chances of getting a job and keeping it, how much you would probably be paid, and how well you could expect to live on your earnings. It is a book of the clearest and most concrete detail. And its valuable information sinks in no less deeply for being presented with liveliness and humor.

As possible workers in New York, Mr. Leaf addresses his readers in three groups: the Beautiful, the Brainy and the Nice. The Beautiful learn what it is, and what it pays, to be a model; what chances the stage offers, and how; what one can do, and earn, in a night club. The Brainy are introduced to the requirements and rewards of advertising, editorial work, executive positions in department stores. The Nice—girls whose character is a more important asset than appearances or intellect—learn the demands and the hopes that center in teaching, social work and secretarial responsibilities. And under each general heading there are groupings of smaller, less important or less remunerative activities as well.

The material is concentrated and practical. It is also curiously interesting. Mr. Leaf has covered his subject with zest as well as care and comprehensiveness. His book should help his ambitious young reader not only to look for a job in the Big City but to make good, without disillusionment, if she gets it.

"Jobs in New York," in The New York Times Book Review, *May 1, 1938, p. 12.*

Anybody who has ever had much to do with wistful young girls from the hinterlands who come to New York in search of a career ought to feel a devout gratitude to Munro Leaf, who has just written this book with all the answers. He is the same Mr. Leaf who wrote about the charming young bull called Ferdinand, who loved flowers, and he realizes that these young ladies love flowers too, and everything else connected with glamour, and think there are more to be found in New York than anywhere else. There are, but the book makes it plain that you have to be good to get them, and even then there aren't always enough to go around.

The book isn't unfairly discouraging. It gives plain facts gaily and entertainingly, in spite of the grimness in some of them, and if the facts relating to each field are as accurate as they are in connection with those I happen to know intimately, the author has done a very thorough job. . . . The book ought to clear up a lot of vagueness in the minds of ninety-nine and nine-tenths per cent of the young women planning to come to the big city to be "advertising women" or do "fashion work" or "write" or what have you. It tells about the various branches in all these fields and a good many more, and what talents are needed for them, and it should be very illuminating to the innumerable young ladies who haven't yet realized that there *are* different branches.

But it's the last chapter in the book that should be given out as a tract in high schools and Sunday schools and by fond mamas and hopeful suitors. The one about the boarding-houses where the landlord's family have to pass through your room to get to the front door; and the rooming houses with the gas rings and the smell of stale cabbage and cheap cold cream; and the girls' clubs with golden oak bureaus and female callers only; and the terrible food at a good many places. A lot of girls who could stand the work described, couldn't stand the hours when they wouldn't be working.

If a girl can read about all that, on top of all the rest, and still believe that she can come to New York and make herself a career, she'd better come. As the book points out, thousands do every year—and hundreds actually get the careers.

Marjorie Hillis, "Jobs and the Big City," in The Saturday Review of Literature, *Vol. 18, No. 2, May 7, 1938, p. 16.*

Munro Leaf is a highly talented young man. Several seasons ago he wrote a book for children about a bull named Ferdinand, and the book at once became a classic among grown-ups. Now he has written a book with no bull in it, and it is safe to prophesy that it will become a handbook for the ambitious young thing who wants to achieve maturity in the city known for its Great White Way.

To start with, Mr. Leaf warms that part of this reviewer's heart, ordinarily called cockles, by not advising the adventurous post-adolescent to keep away from the big, brutal city. Being young himself, he knows that to the vital creature who seeks her destiny in New York, obstacles do nothing but add flame to her desire. She will starve, she will be friendless, she will know desperate loneliness. All right. She'll see restaurants and night clubs which some day she thinks she can crash; she'll be part of the crowds in subways and streets, she will meet other human beings as lonely as herself. At any rate, it's worth a try.

Mr. Leaf, then, takes it for granted that the girl is here and that she has come equipped with some talents to enable her to take part in the exciting world that is New York. What are her opportunities for survival, how does she go about making contacts, what are the pitfalls, what the entrance wedges? These are questions Mr. Leaf answers with knowledge whose research and seriousness are hidden by a delightfully humorous and colloquial style. Make no mistake about it: this book is instructive, but the instruction is given in a way that doesn't hurt.

Not only will the girl from the sticks profit from this book but the tens of thousands who are more or less native here, confused by their desires and the seeming richness of choice of occupation, if not of opportunity. . . . A swell city, New York, and a swell book, Mr. Leaf.

Rose C. Feld, "Advice to Young Things," in

New York Herald Tribune Books, *May 8, 1938, p. 9.*

Safety Can Be Fun (1938)

The "nit-wits" in this book describe people whose foolishness is always bringing them into grave danger, resulting in fatal accidents. The cartoons in black and red lines are highly humorous but drive home a lesson. The text and illustrations cover a great variety of the foolish practices followed by children (only nit-wits of course) such as the Stick-in-the-mouth Nit-wit who runs with a lolly pop in his mouth; the Dumb-walking Nit-wit who walks on the wrong side of the roads where coming cars cannot be seen. Youngest children will see the point.

> *Mary Katharine Reely, in a review of "Safety Can Be Fun," in* Wisconsin Library Bulletin, *Vol. 34, No. 10, December, 1938, p. 204.*

[*A revised edition of* Safety Can Be Fun *was published in 1961.*]

A new edition of the 1938 publication, in which the original text is not changed; the revision consists in the addition of eight new pages of illustrated stupidities in the child's world. The violators of safety rules new to the book are the tool-foolish nit-wit, the new-building nitwit, the never wait nitwit, etc. The line drawings, the breezy language, and the striking red-black-white of the original have been used for the new pages, and the book will undoubtedly prove as durably popular as the original edition.

> *Zena Sutherland, in a review of "Safety Can Be Fun," in* Bulletin of the Center for Children's Books, *Vol. 15, No. 2, October, 1961, p. 31.*

Wee Gillis (1938)

However much you may have heard of the book beforehand, there is a genuine surprise at the climax of **Wee Gillis,** the new Leaf-and-Lawson offering about a small boy whose ancestors on the one side were Lowland Scots and on the other Highland, so he, like George Gray Barnard's famous statute, felt two natures warring within him.

Wee Gillis—so called because his full name was too long and too Gaelic for mortal mouth—went to visit his uncles on both sides of the family, being an orphan who would one day have to make up his mind on which side he would settle. In the misty Lowlands he learned to call cattle until his lungs and the noise he could get out of them resembled a foghorn and its results, only far more so. Then he went to stay in the Highlands where his relatives spent their time hunting stags and when he let out his breath louder than a mental sigh they all jumped on him. So there he learned to hold his breath practically indefinitely. But he did not forget the other accomplishment. How he reconciled the two, and by what perfect means he found a way to use both his talents and settle his personal problem, must be left to some of Mr. Lawson's most temperamental

pictures to reveal. They run like those in **Ferdinand,** one to every sentence or so, on a large page; the book has a handsome tartan cover and jacket, and if a large proportion of Scotty pups named during the next two years are not named Wee Gillis I miss my guess.

> *May Lamberton Becker, in a review of "Wee Gillis," in* New York Herald Tribune Books, *October 9, 1938, p. 8.*

Munro Leaf and Robert Lawson have done it again. Though **Wee Gillis** may possibly have a less sensational success than Ferdinand, it has already won the hearts of children and adults. The pictures of the Lowland farms and the craggy Highlands of Scotland have sufficient beauty to make any one who comes from that lovely country homesick for its hills and heather.

Boys and girls from 7 on are deeply interested in the small Scottish lad who called the cows in the Lowlands and stalked the deer in the Highlands, while his lungs meantime grew stronger and stronger until at least he was able to play the largest bagpipes in Scotland. . . . With its gay plaid cover, beautifully reproduced illustrations and fine design, this is a distinguished volume.

> *Anne T. Eaton, "In Scotland," in* The New York Times Book Review, *November 13, 1938, p. 39.*

[Wee Gillis's] is not quite so subtle a fable as Ferdinand's, but perhaps an even better story to read aloud. Of course you should have a bagpipe record to go with it. Mr. Lawson brings us the Highlands and the Lowlands just as vividly as he did the atmosphere of pre-war Spain. His Scotchmen's faces are superb. Welcome, Wee Gillis! May many a Christmas puppy be named for you. You have solved the unhappy border-land problem in a year when the grown-ups made a mess of it.

> *Louise Seaman Bechtel, in a review of "Wee Gillis," in* The Saturday Review of Literature, *Vol. 19, No. 4, November 19, 1938, p. 18.*

Lawson, in a style much like James Daugherty, demonstrates his skill as an artist in his renderings of Scottish geography and native dress. His illustrations offer a humorous and gentle interpretation of a boy faced with a dilemma. But the format of the book, a page of text faced with an illustration, does little to enhance or enliven the story; if the audience takes the time to look beyond the superficial monotony of the illustrations, they will quickly realize the skill of the artist, even though Lawson chooses to use only black and white. If anything is amiss, it is the text that comes across as the weakness of this Honor Book, and it seems the merits of the illustrator alone have been the influencing criteria in the book's inclusion as an Honor Book in [1939] (pp. 239-40)

> *Linda Kauffman Peterson "The Caldecott Medal and Honor Books, 1938-1981," in* Newbery and Caldecott Medal and Honor Books: An Annotated Bibliography, *by Linda Kauffman Peterson and Marilyn Leathers Solt, G. K. Hall & Co., 1982, pp. 235-378.*

The Watchbirds   (1939)

Here is a further development of one of the most easily administered books of advice for the nursery, **Manners Can Be Fun.** As in that welcome work Mr. Leaf develops basic principles of baby—or little child—behavior; here he does it by absurd case-histories with arresting names and portraits both ludicrous and true to spirit. When he draws a Sulky, a Floor-piler, a six-handed Grabber or a Bedbawler in action, the most heedless youngster knows precisely what he means. This book laughs the littlest child into some of the reasons for manners. Nobody else does it in this way—or quite so well in any other way.

> *A review of "The Watchbirds," in* New York Herald Tribune Books, *May 7, 1939, p. 8.*

Fair Play   (1939)

Best of Mr. Leaf's juvenile guides to the good life, it uses the same methods as **Manners Can Be Fun:** type large, spacing wide, pictures crude and vigorous, funny but never too funny. Nobody could doubt for a second what one of these extraordinary people was doing or even thinking. With directness, wasting not a line or syllable, he

From Wee Gillis, *written by Munro Leaf. Illustrated by Robert Lawson.*

drives home a better idea of what democracy is and how it works than I have found in a dozen adult academic articles. Starting from the fact that if you were the only person in the United States there would be none of a number of pleasant things you take for granted—"in fact there would be only you and a lot of wild animals and I don't think you would have much fun"—he shows by practical and lively instances, drawn at first from playground and drinking fountain, how the traffic laws of human conduct are based on fair play, and how an individual known as Justme can make everything unpleasant for everybody, including himself. This leads to a simple survey of our government, showing how it works on the principle of fair play, and revealing law to a child as his friend and protector. It may even reveal to him the essential nature of law.

Mr. Leaf has deserved well of his own country and of the embattled democracies, for a book that could have been perfectly awful—as some others have been—if it had not been just right. But, you see, it *is* just right.

> *May Lamberton Becker, in a review of "Fair Play," in* New York Herald Tribune Books, *October 1, 1939, p. 7.*

This is full of sound ideas on self-government and national government too. This would be a good gift for a school or a class rather than an individual child, for it has a touch of the text-book in spite of its lively cartoons, and is meant to instruct and improve and inspire patriotism in the youthful breast.

> *Rosemary Carr Benét, in a review of, "Fair Play," in* The Saturday Review of Literature, *Vol. 21, No. 4, November 18, 1939, p. 22.*

Mr. Leaf is a convinced moralist. Sometimes he dresses the moral up in story form, as in the incomparable **Ferdinand** and **Robert Francis Weatherbee,** sometimes he is content to let the moral stand up for itself. He has the gifts of clarity and humour which make his message at once pointed and acceptable. His subject this time is citizenship, and he tackles it with the same zest and fun which made such an unpromising subject as personal behaviour so irresistible in **The Watchbirds.** His text is a model of simple statement, with just the right amount of repetition, and with a happy choice of references from general to particular. In explaining the basis of good government to the very youngest children he is helped by his own illustrations. The simplicity of these is most deceptive, as anyone will find who tries to imitate their style. And how very charming they are. "I love this artist", said one six-year-old to whom I read the book. Mr. Leaf indeed inspires affection and respect, both of which feelings I take to be highly desirable.

This book, subtle, wise, witty and simple, deserves the warmest welcome from parents, teachers and librarians. (pp. 58-9)

> *M. Crouch, in a review of "Fair Play," in* The Junior Bookshelf, *Vol. 14, No. 2, March, 1950, pp. 58-9.*

John Henry Davis (1940)

Munro Leaf may go down to history as the man who made morals attractive to the American child. One after another our boys and girls take these funny books, chuckle over the advice because the pictures that go with it are so absurd, and find themselves agreeing with what he says because it strikes them as sensible. A perceptible improvement in home conduct always follows his ***Manners Can Be Fun***: ***Fair Play*** started many of our small fry on the road toward democracy, and now the experiences of a kid known as J. H. D. with a tough guy of his own age, slide into a young intelligence the strange but salutary conviction that being tough is only another way of being awfully dumb.

Though in most ways he is just like any other small boy with a red head and average grades, J. H. D. has one trait not so common. Every now and then He Thinks. You can see him doing it, in Rodin's own pose, absently patting his dog the while. Then comes a boy who has clamped his face into a tough mug, and cannot talk out of the middle of his mouth. Why, he demands, is this dog being petted? Are not animals to be tormented? Why doesn't J. H. D. slap his little sister, and not be a sissy? "Why should I?" he reasonably replies. "I like her and what's wrong with that?" And as the young thug seems open to reason, J. H. D. takes him to see the powerful elephant letting children ride him; to the firehouse, where the glorious driver is painting a picture; and so on through experiences with he-men too brave to be tough, till they meet J. H. D.'s friend the State Trooper, at whose very sight the tough guy takes to his heels. Yes, says the boy to the Sergeant, being tough cheats yourself out of a lot of fun.

This is not slipping over a moral on a boy; it is showing one in action. It is also showing thought at work, and that's not a bad idea.

> *May Lamberton Becker, in a review of "John Henry Davis," in* New York Herald Tribune Books, *September 15, 1940, p. 7.*

The author's spontaneous clever manner of teaching the young is almost missing but children from four to seven years of age will probably enjoy and profit by the book. The drawings in black and red are amusingly suited to the text. . . .

> *Sonja Wennerblad, in a review of "John Henry Davis," in* Library Journal, *Vol. 65, No. 17, October 1, 1940, p. 813.*

A War-Time Handbook for Young Americans (1942)

This is so much the best book to tell boys and girls under twelve what they can do "to help win this war and bring it to an end just as soon as we can," that the best advice I can offer parents of young children is to see that they own it as soon as possible, and to later writers along these lines that they use it as a model.

It is so good because its principles are so sound and its spirit so convincing. A child under twelve not only belongs to a family unit: he gets his own sense of personal value and social security from belonging to a family, and whatever he does will be best done within the family. Munro Leaf's standing with children as an adviser is good; he talks a language they understand; his rude drawings are in their own technique. All this is now brought to bear upon rousing and using a child's sense of responsibility within the family. Any parent knows, and no child resents being told, that whatever the grown-up may be doing to win the war, "it takes only one noisy, quarrelsome, grouchy brat to spoil a home." I submit that this is the spirit in which to develop the self-discipline we will need quite as much after the war is won.

It is sound democratic advice to "have a meeting of the family and divide the work so that each one has special duties that are his and his alone." It is the right idea to follow this with such duties as children can undertake, so presented that a child pants to undertake them. For through an aroused sense of personal responsibility the child has reached that sense of personal value on which the right working of all democracy depends. He has not only been given outlets of action, but the assurance that this action counts. Sometimes it is relatively long-term, sometimes immediate; it is always described clearly and so as to tighten the strings of courage and determination that tune up the spirit to active patriotism.

Many a book for children's wartime work will be "made to order" before this war is won, and some will be pretty awful. But this one was evidently made to the personal order of one American father who knows just what he means when he says "American," and because he is clearly aware of what we are fighting for, and what we are fighting against, can speak, not only for the fathers of America, but for the Founding Fathers.

> *May Lamberton Becker, in a review of "A War-Time Handbook for Young Americans," in* New York Herald Tribune Books, *August 16, 1942, p. 7.*

Participation in the war effort is the surest cure for the jitters and war nerves which parents fear for their children in these days of anxiety and tension. Just how to achieve participation and how to use the energy and the earnest desire to help which is so natural and so lovable a quality of nice children is a problem which has perplexed many a parent and teacher of late and one to which Munro Leaf has given here some valuable answers.

His handbook is for children of 7 and up, for any child in fact who is old enough to carry messages or gather salvage, although its style and format will probably find its major public under 12. The suggestions addressed directly to the young in informal, easy style are succinct and wholly practicable, and many of them will continue to be helpful to a harmonious family life in peacetime too. Thus harassed parents will appreciate Mr. Leaf's plea for cheerfulness, his stress on the duty of a young patriot to get plenty of the right food, exercise and sleep (and all this without "whining and howling") and his plan for a division of household chores. There are specific suggestions for actual service with direct bearing on the emergency, such as learning the rudiments of first aid, gardening, running errands, collecting salvage, and there is good sound advice on learning about one's community and how to be a good neighbor, which is after all the prime requisite of a good citizen at any time. The whole mounts up to an appeal to a child's sense of responsibility, which is a surefire method, as a wise parent knows, of enlisting his interest and help. The advice, both as to practical matters and to attitude, pointed up by drawings in the author's drolly grotesque style, should do a lot toward building a generation of cooperative democrats.

> *Ellen Lewis Buell, in a review of "A War-Time Handbook for Young Americans," in* The New York Times Book Review, *August 16, 1942, p. 9.*

Health Can Be Fun (1943)

Some parents ask themselves, wistfully watching the effect on their children of Mr. Leaf's guides to the good life, what he's got that they haven't got. They offer tactful advice on table manners and Johnny's elbows stay on the table. He says something on the subject with about as much tact as a poke in the ribs, and Johnny, grinning broadly, removes his elbows from the board. The same straightforward method works in the latest of the series.

"If there is one creature that makes everybody tired," says he, looking choosy children in the eye, "it's a food grumbler that won't eat what is good for it, and mumbles and grumbles about eating anything except just what it thinks it likes. It won't eat this and it won't eat that until people get so tired of it they almost don't care what happens to it at all." He then puts in a picture of a food grumbler—these skeleton Leaf effects are getting so much better if he doesn't look out the first thing he knows he'll find he can draw—and the incident, so far as intelligent human beings go, is closed. Such an appeal to reason, offered in the spirit in which children offer it to each other, seldom fails.

In this book it succeeds in the case of exercise, posture, going to bed ("without fussing about it like a two-year-old"), open windows, keeping clean and changing clothes without having to be nagged into it. . . . It tells an audience from four to seven about looking out for colds and co-operating with the doctor. It winds up with the conviction that "staying healthy is a game we play all the time." Your very good health, Mr. Leaf; your book deserves it.

> *May Lamberton Becker, in a review of "Health Can Be Fun," in* New York Herald Tribune Weekly Book Review, *September 12, 1943, p. 6.*

In this day when everyone is so health conscious **Health Can Be Fun** by Munro Leaf should be read by the entire family. As usual, Munro Leaf is humorous, both in text and pictures, but there is a seriousness too that even youngsters will feel.

> *Evelyn Sarnes Littlefield, in a review of "Health Can Be Fun," in* Library Journal, *Vol. 68, October 15, 1943, p. 821.*

3 and 30 Watchbirds (1944)

The Watchbirds have been delighting *Ladies' Home Journal* readers for six years now, and here is another collection in book form. They might be defined as today's "good books", for they serve the same purpose in teaching principles of good behavior to small fry, rules of kindness and helpfulness, by making reverse characteristics thoroughly unprepossessing.

> *A review of "3 and 30 Watchbirds," in* Virginia Kirkus' Bookshop Service, *Vol. 12, No. 4, February 15, 1944, p. 95.*

Thirty-three new Watchbirds are introduced here in the same format as his previous book, **The Watchbirds.** They are ready to watch Braggers, Never-minders, Bike-busters and all the others; and to help them become just the opposite. And too, there are some wartime Shoe-scufflers, Food-wasters and Gabblers who need special watching today. The interest and timely value to younger children is superb.

> *Vera Winifred Schott, in a review of "3 and 30 Watchbirds," in* Library Journal, *Vol. 69, March 15, 1944, p. 264.*

Watchbirds will not be found in cages; they perch invisible in homes where children don't behave and, in effect, stare them out of countenance. "This is a Never-Help," one says. "Do you think it's going to help set the table? Not unless somebody makes it do so, and then it will probably squawk." A pause. Then, with the help of red ink, the Watchbird says searchingly., "Were YOU a Never-Help today?" In like manner it serves up, roasted, Stubborn, Never-Mind, Bathroom-Wrecker, Wrong-Time Reader, Droopy-Hand, "about as nice to shake as an old wet dish rag;" Dirty-Plate, Snitcher, Lump, Shoe-Scuffer, Sprawler, Waster, Meany, Blamer and so on. It will be seen that some of these names could be used later in life; I myself, chuckling as usual straight through the book, found self-analysis strongly setting in.

As usual, Mr. Leaf's remarks on bad behavior pull no punches: the "Pokers" who run up to people and yell Bang "ought to be painted red like a load of dynamite." Children rightly approve of this downrightness; they don't want you to be tactful in such matters if you mean to get results in short order. Mr. Leaf's books get them, as many mothers know.

I gather from hints in this book that a nest of Watchbirds is hatching whose gaze will be fixed on grownups. Our manners are due for a lift.

> *May Lamberton Becker, in a review of "3 and 30 Watchbirds," in* New York Herald Tribune Weekly Book Review, *June 11, 1944, p. 5.*

Gordon the Goat (1944)

Gordon was a goat who lived in a Texas ranch with lot of other goats. "He didn't work very hard. All he did was just go on being Gordon day after day and every once in a while he would get his hair cut," because he was a mohair goat. When Gordon went to walk, he followed a lead goat and went where that did. . . .

[After the lead goat took the goats into a tornado, Gordon] has kept on for himself ever since. "Never again would he just tag along from one place to another just because every one else did." Without laboring the point, Mr. Leaf then bows himself out and leaves children from four to eighty-four in possession of a Good Idea.

The pictures are in color, funnier than ever. They are also better drawn. I hope this goes no further, but if Munro Leaf really learns to draw, he may stop making those peerless figures by which he educates our infants in good behavior.

> *A review of "Gordon the Goat," in* New York Herald Tribune Weekly Book Review, *November 12, 1944, p. 39.*

Gordon always followed the lead goat, without thinking, along with the other goats. One day he followed the lead goat straight into a Texas tornado. When he got back to Texas, Gordon decided to think for himself. This delightful story will be readily comprehensible to American children. Perhaps Mr. Leaf would be willing to draw a mustache on the pictures of the lead goat for the benefit of small German children, who might well begin their re-education with this wise and gay little story.

> *Marjorie Fischer, in a review of "Gordon the Goat," in* The New York Times Book Review, *November 12, 1944, p. 6.*

Not one of Munro Leaf's major items, but on his name it will have a wide market. . . .Munro Leaf has that rare ability to preach a sermon without making it obvious, and his little moral tales are really funny.

> *A review of "Gordon the Goat," in* Virginia Kirkus' Bookshop Service, *Vol. XII, No. 19, November 15, 1944, p. 519.*

Let's Do Better   (1945)

Some people can talk to children so they listen; some can even talk in such a way that children remember what they say. It gets into the marrow of their minds, because the right thing was said with the straight face that carries both fun and conviction much better than a smile does. After this manner Munro Leaf has been addressing our children, to their advantage and amusement, ever since he proved that grammar could be fun. He has also been putting his ideas into pictures, using the technique of one who, despairing of being able to explain how something works, grabs a pencil and cries "Here! I'll show you. . . . " and somehow does. He still uses this method; the pictures have gradually taken on a style as distinctive in its own way as Thurber's are in his. In this latest book both pictures and text reveal an intense earnestness back of the fun. Let's do better, he says—and you feel the other, unspoken half of the sentence . . . "it's about time."

So he shows our ancestors living in dark, dank caves, scared of their lives, looking so funny even a small child at once takes an interest. That was when strong and clever

people either beat up the others or tricked them into being dead or out of the way. "Then some wise people had the very simple idea that if some of them got together and worked together there might be food and shelter enough to go round, and they did so as tribes, gangs, groups, or anything you want to call a lot of people who live together." Civilization gets under way. War comes in. "The sensible way of living just wouldn't work—unless everybody felt the same way about it." I never saw an "Outline" that put so much history into so few facts. There isn't a proper name or a date, or a portrait save these absurd caricatures of Everyman in his various phases, or even a program tied up like a packet of tea. All it gives is a hint, direct as an elbow in the ribs. "What we do and how we think when we are young is as important as it ever is when we are older," and we see once more the picture of the dark, dank caves to which our ancestors retreated to save their lives. "It could happen to any of us." While this book was going through the press, it was happening. "Let's be Thinkers all over the world, strong kind and unselfish Thinkers, and Let's Do Better!"

If children are ever in their lives going to think, they start early. Sometimes a laugh sets them thinking, if it has earnestness—and truth—behind it.

> *May Lamberton Becker, in a review of "Let's Do Better," in* New York Herald Tribune Weekly Book Review, *September 23, 1945, p. 6.*

Only Munro Leaf could get away with this kind of moralizing on the course of the history of War and Peace, and he manages to get his ideas across to the children, without sugarcoating the pill. Amusing, lively cartoons, in his particular style, make this a good companion piece—with a broader significance—for *Manners Are Fun,* etc. Black and white with a splash of red. Humor and a barb of not always palatable truth.

> *A review of "Let's Do Better," in* Virginia Kirkus' Bookshop Service, *Vol. XIII, No. 19, October 1, 1945, p. 435.*

It is a long way from the nineteenth-century "book with a moral" to this one where high ideals and principles are presented in humorous drawings by Munro Leaf. Here in a few pages he tells the story of man's ascent from the cave dweller to modern times under the various forms of government.. . . . Children will enjoy the pictures and, although it takes a mature mind to understand theories of government and war and peace, the very young reader will, thanks to Munro Leaf's simple and humorous interpretation, get at least a first glimpse of these difficult subjects.

> *Blanche Weber Shaffer, "The Way of Democracy," in* The Saturday Review of Literature, *Vol. 28, No. 42, October 20, 1945, p. 44.*

Flock of Watchbirds   (1946)

The Watchbirds need no introduction—this is an omnibus volume, containing a good selection of the favorites,—the thumb sucker, the nail biter, etc. For the watchbirds are guardians of morals and manners, done in such humorous mood that children get fun out of them, while parents reap benefit.

A review of "Flock of Watchbirds," in Virginia Kirkus' Bookshop Service, *Vol. 14, No. 12, June 15, 1946, p. 274.*

Somehow Munro Leaf can point out faults in children's behavior in the most uncompromising manner and yet retain not only respect but affection of the far-from-faultless. His Watchbirds, flying through three volumes, can look a Bed-Bawler straight in the eye and tell it "how it yowls and howls and moans and groans when it is time to go to bed," and the Bawler will stop to laugh at the absurd picture of itself, and like Mr. Leaf the more.

May Lamberton Becker, in a review of "Flock of Watchbirds," in New York Herald Tribune Weekly Book Review, *July 7, 1946, p. 7.*

How to Behave and Why   (1946)

How to Behave and Why, by Munro Leaf, is another of his honest but rather forced attempts at teaching basic rules of conduct. It is not mere captious criticism to wish Mr. Leaf would use simple, correct punctuation.

A review of "How to Behave and Why," in The Catholic World, *Vol. CLXIV, No. 982, January, 1947, p. 382.*

Honesty, fairness, strength and wisdom are the foundations of good behavior according to the author, who has liberally illustrated the text with his typical figures. Children will find the pictures more appealing than the message.

Marguerite M. Smith, in a review of "How to Behave and Why," in Library Journal, *Vol. 72, No. 1, January 1, 1947, p. 83.*

Munro Leaf's good-humored hints on etiquette, previously offered in his special fashion to very small children, have made a special place for themselves because they are not concerned with conduct alone but with the mainsprings of conduct. The second part of the title of this book indicates this spirit. It brings etiquette for children down—or up—to its essential, the reason for good behavior.

This is a book for the very young about how to have the most fun in living. It begins: "The two biggest questions to ask ourselves in life, at any age, are: Are most of the people I know glad that I am here? Am I glad I am here myself? Any one who can honestly answer 'Yes' to those two questions most of the time has learned to behave in this world and to live a happy life." If that sounds didactic, the illustrations that go with it at once remove this curse. They are typical Munro Leaf pictographs of a widely humorous nature. A child old enough to read the book—whose vocabulary is very simple—or listen to it, laughs at the absurd drawings while attending to the words, which boil down to four things we have to be: honest, fair, strong and wise. And the direct, forceful manner

in which these ideas are introduced into the young mind is such that the chances are they stay there.

May Lamberton Becker, in a review of "How to Behave and Why," in New York Herald Tribune Weekly Book Review, *January 5, 1947, p. 8.*

Sam and the Superdroop   (1948)

Here's a book parents and children will enjoy—together and separately. It's a burlesque on comic books that manages to be hilarious even with the library-card advice ending. Sam, it seems was a regular fellow but he came down with comic bookitis—a common disease. The monster, Superdroop, appeared and he and Sam went on some fiercely boring adventures—Rhett Race who righted all wrong, villainous Punkinhead, Mouse-Mouth Macaroni, stooges, black limousines, bombs, guns and phoney ammunition galore: there is a priceless adventure with a super cowboy in High Wind Canyon country which undoes Tom Mix types forever, and a malicious chase through the "funny" comics with a few mean and nasty practical joker characters. In fact, any peeve you have ever had you will find here and everyone will be relieved to end up safely in the public library. Public libraries will naturally love it, parents will love it and squirm a bit at the criticism they'll meet, and young people will never find comic books quite as good again. Good fun plus Munro Leaf's drawings—and morals.

A review of "Sam and the Superdroop," in Virginia Kirkus' Bookshop Service, *Vol. XVI, No. 15, August 1, 1948, p. 364.*

Up to now comics have been like the weather: everybody complains about it but nobody does anything. Now it has been done. In his funniest story Munro Leaf has enlisted the one force that can really deal with the comics—the sturdy common sense lurking somewhere in the make-up of every small boy. . . .

[On] successive excursions, Sam meets Rhett Racey, the best R-man on the force, and Side-saddle Samson of Wyoming, who talks Western lingo quite unlike that of Sam's uncle who lives in Cheyenne. He meets lovely Torso the Jungle Queen and Plutanium, Secret Scout of the Interstellar Patrol. He even visits what for some reason are called the funnies, just clean fun like getting the woiks. Try reading any one of these out loud, especially the one about Torso. Try it on anybody, young or old. It just can't be beat.

What to do about the comics? Believe it or not, the last chapter tells just what. Sam and his parents come to a conclusion that works. Congratulations, Mr. Leaf.

May Lamberton Becker, "From Elizabethan Times to Today's Comics," in New York Herald Tribune Weekly Book Review, *November 14, 1948, p. 8.*

Any boy or girl who may be taking the comics a little seriously will certainly take them less so after reading this,

By watching them and copying the way they do things and listening to what they tell us, we learn to

walk

dress ourselves

comb our hair

talk to people

brush our teeth

wash ourselves

feed our- selves

help others

be kind to animals

From Reading Can Be Fun, *written and illustrated by Munro Leaf.*

even if the should miss some of the delightful satire. Both story and pictures are grand fun for the whole family.

> *Frances Smith, in a review of "Sam and the Superdroop," in* The New York Times Book Review, *November 14, 1948, p. 4.*

Boo, Who Used to Be Scared of the Dark   (1948; British edition as *Boo, the Boy Who Didn't Like the Dark*)

The "buck up, it's all nonsense, old man" attitude of Mr. Leaf has proven reassuring to the parents of children, and here, in lavish illustrations by Frances Tipton Hunter, and a healthy and sensible text, the long campaign continues for a healthy mind in a healthy body. Boo was a little boy who was afraid of lots of things, also the dark. But he had a cat who spoke to him, man to man, and who taught him that it was silly to be frightened. He even took away Boo's fear of the dark. Eye-catching, and merchandise-worthy in the big, bright illustrations of a darling boy and a cat, and with pleasant, alternating black and whites.

> *A review of "Boo," in* Virginia Kirkus' Book- shop Service, *Vol. XVI, No. 21, November 1, 1948, p. 570.*

Both the story and the pictures will amuse small children as well as contribute to the relief of their anxiety. Parents, too, will have reason to be grateful to Mr. Leaf for meeting this universal problem on a child's own terms.

> *Helen Adams Masten, in a review of "Boo, Who Used to Be Scared of the Dark," in* New York Herald Tribune Weekly Book Review, *November 28, 1948, p. 6.*

What a pity! No one today points a moral more dexterous- ly than Munro Leaf, and he has written a little story which deals sympathetically, and simply, with one of childhood's greatest terrors. Alas, instead of his own inspired scrib- bles, we are given some devastatingly sweet and sentimen- tal pictures by Frances Tipton Hunter. I am still shudder- ing.

> *A review of "Boo, the Boy Who Didn't Like the Dark," in* The Junior Bookshelf, *Vol. 18, No. 4, October, 1954, p. 190.*

Arithmetic Can Be Fun   (1949)

Mr. Leaf has proved that a lot of horrid old bugaboos can

be "fun" when he leads the way into thinking about them. He has taken up health, manners, safety and grammar all so merrily that his name is beloved in homes, libraries, schools and book-shops. They will all bless him for taking up arithmetic.

First he introduces the numbers; goes on to addition, subtraction, simple fractions, simple measures, the calendar, telling time. To tell the truth, we have all seen arithmetic practice books that look a lot like his pages. But as you read, it is his words, his lively approach, the nonsensical little stories, the irresistibly funny pictures, like those of a clever child, that make this the most painless arithmetic ever invented. One can only hope that every child who is starting this horrible subject can have a copy. Romping through one at home is a sure way to put your little one at the head of the class.

> *A review of "Arithmetic Can Be Fun," in* New York Herald Tribune Book Review, *November 13, 1949, p. 8.*

"One of the big reasons that arithmetic isn't much fun to so many people is that they never learn about it so that it makes sense," says the author-illustrator. Mr. Leaf then proceeds to give meaning to numbers in his most recent effort to humanize knowledge.

Parents and teachers will appreciate the educationally sound technique used here. Six-to-9-year-olds enjoy the imaginative line sketches and the simple, entertaining style in which Mr. Leaf tells them about counting, measuring, adding and subtracting, and about money and telling time.

Most children will want to meet the challenge on the last page: "If you know everything that is in this book, you already know more than all the grown-up men and women in the world knew for thousands and thousands of years."

> *Alyce L. Seekamp, " 'Fatso' Zero & Co.," in* The New York Times Book Review, *January 8, 1950, p. 18.*

This is a book for the parent, not for the child. It is amusingly written and illustrated and designed on exactly the same lines as modern arithmetic textbooks for the young, but with much more letterpress.

Learning to read and learning to count are elementary processes usually undertaken together and no child at this stage in arithmetic would be able to read or even to understand the text. Those who could read and understand would find the arithmetic much beneath their dignity. The parent, on the other hand, could help a child in the earlier stages of learning with instruction based on the methods used here.

> *A review of "Arithmetic Can Be Fun," in* The Junior Bookshelf, *Vol. 15, No. 5, November, 1951, p. 216.*

History Can Be Fun (1950)

From ancient Egypt to the United Nations in a skip and a jump (with side hops in English and United States histo-

ry). Mr. Leaf's whimsical style and stick-figure illustrations are justly popular, so expect a large market for this one. Beginning with the declaration that "the story of history is really the story of YOU", and a fanciful excursion in a genealogical rash of "great-great-greats etc." Mr. Leaf tells the story of long ago people—the Egyptians, Phoenicians, Greeks, Romans, Medieval Europeans, Crusaders, Moslems, with their contributions to civilization. Then there is a brief history of the English people, the settling of America, the Revolution, Civil War and America and the world today. Just enough detail for a young child to take—with gay little scribblings to make history really fun.

> *A review of "History Can Be Fun," in* Virginia Kirkus' Bookshop Service, *Vol. XVIII, No. 18, September 15, 1950, p. 557.*

"Grammar and arithmetic can be fun," said Mr. Leaf, and the children who moaned at the very words dipped into his clever pages and came up smiling. So they will do with his new book, for to most children under twelve the great path of the past is a disconnected blur.

Mr. Leaf announces some very fine, serious purposes, actually the same which already have animated such writers as Hendrik van Loon, Katherine Shippen, Genevieve Foster, Gertrude Hartman. But this introduction to world history is not a history, nor is it long enough to fulfill such hopes; it is a most stimulating little essay on how to think about history. It is plenty serious in text; the familiar allure of the clever, funny Leaf pictures is all that ties it to the previous titles. It puts great eras, and some great ideas, into dynamic brief pages which should interest any child under twelve.

This reviewer has long struggled with the difficulties of younger children who approach stories as well as learning with no historical pegs on which to hang their ideas. She uses a "help" which some children think is "fun," a "Ladder of Time."

After seven years of testing, this "ladder" still seems to me marvelous, and I wish Mr. Leaf would make a "funny one" for the endless reprints his new book will have. His thoughts are fine, his pictures are fun, but "time" is the strange element still left mysterious, in fact not talked about very much in his pages.

> *A review of "History Can Be Fun," in* New York Herald Tribune Book Review, *November 12, 1950, p. 14.*

After proving that health, safety, grammar, manners, arithmetic can be fun, Munro Leaf has focused his talents upon history. Whoever doubts that man's story, from the caves to the United Nations, can be made intelligible to young children within one thin book, must read this remarkable condensation. Its selection of details and its appealing style make the reader feel like a spectator of the great parade. While the centuries roll by, and powers rise and fall, the human quest for a better life emerges as the dominant pattern. A child too young to have begun the study of history in school will easily comprehend that he has an important role in the pattern's future shaping.

The author's characteristic humorous drawings help convey these vital ideas. Here is a needed introduction to the long march of history, especially valuable in the present crisis.

> Irene Smith, "The Great Parade," in The New York Times, December 17, 1950, p. 17.

Geography Can Be Fun (1951)

Again the Watchbird man seems to have as much fun as the reader, as he uses the familiar tipsy little scribbled figures to point out a great deal of information. Although for steady all-year-'round consumption we prefer a less whimsical and more solid approach . . . , Mr. Munro Leaf's excursions into the mysteries of "difficult" studies serve as excellent introductions to subjects about which the child may be somewhat wary. This story of geography covers—literally—a vast amount of territory; around the world and back again, up in the sky and down to the ground; but most important, it simplifies the aims of the study of geography, which many teachers are apt to ignore in the pursuit of map-drawing and principal industries—that is, what the earth is like and "how and why people live there or don't live there". The sun, moon, water, animals, vegetables and minerals, solids and liquids, lands and oceans and divisions of same receive a lively and illuminating once-over lightly.

> A review of "Geography Can Be Fun," in Virginia Kirkus' Bookshop Service, Vol. XIX, No. 19, September 15, 1951, p. 529.

The last of the famous Leaf "can be fun" books, those merry supplements to dull teaching, was about history. It was good, but not funny; it offered few pegs on which to hang your beginning struggles with dates and eras. The geography is quite different, being Leaf at his best, in talkative text and lots of informal, amusing pictures.

At first he introduces you to George, who lives where North and South meet at Gettysburg. George's father gets him straightened out about the very beginnings of geography, and you see George's picture lists of animal life, vegetable life and minerals. There is a nice halt where the author takes a page to speak of the value of reading, and seeing far places through books. Then we go on to investigate our country, with George, and the sense he gets out of it is pretty elegant. The rest of the world is covered very briefly, and the last page holds a good final thought for young minds to hold fast to.

Yes, parents, when your young ones announce that they are starting geography and don't like it, you can rush for the new Leaf, and be fairly sure it will help them out, at ages eight to ten.

> Louise S. Bechtel, in a review of "Geography Can Be Fun," in New York Herald Tribune Book Review, September 16, 1951, p. 8.

Curiosity concerning natural phenomena, places and people seems deeply rooted in all children. Munro Leaf's approach to such serious questions is light but accurate. . . .

While some readers may regret that there are no maps on which to locate their state, home city, or other area, most children will enjoy this unusual book and learn from it. Parents will be amazed at the simple clarity with which Mr. Leaf presents facts that puzzled them in their school days. The drawings are delightful, amusing and to the point.

> Marian Rayburn Brown, "Places and People," in The New York Times Book Review, September 23, 1951, p. 36.

Reading Can Be Fun (1953)

Inimitably, Leaf conveys the wonder of the world of books in a way you fervently hope will captivate just one, or ten, a thousand, a million children. In simple story and his own sketchy pictures he tells how very different it is to be able to talk instead of just saying "Whaaa!" like a baby—what a vast improvement the alphabet was over picture writing—how reading, as necessary to your mind as food to your body, presents you with a vast and exciting new set of friends and ideas. All told in direct relationship to its young audience—from pre-readers who will get the idea from listening to it, to kids in the throes of rejecting their books for funnies and TV—a perfect and humorous antidote to the many modern factors that undermine a true literacy.

> A review of "Reading Can Be Fun," in Virginia Kirkus' Bookshop Service, Vol. 21, No. 18, September 15, 1953, p. 632.

Munro Leaf's spontaneous new book, **Reading Can Be Fun,** springs from the sincere, child-like quality of his own thinking. Who but someone that understands could say: "Knowing how to read is almost like having a private telephone all your own"—and then illustrate that statement with a picture of two telephones on a curlycue wire with a child on one end and—of all people—Columbus, on the other, speaking into his phone and saying, "This is Columbus, 1492."

"When you know how to read," writes the author, "you can have for your own friends the wisest and the best and the greatest people who have ever lived in the world."

A quite young person, who stands on the very threshold of discovery will find this last one of the Can Be Fun series a big help. With informal illustrations and large type, the young reader is carried into a marvelously populated world of print.

> Olive Dean Hormel, in a review of "Reading Can Be Fun," in The Christian Science Monitor, November 12, 1953, p. 11.

[The] author presents in breezy, rather tongue-in-cheek text and stick-figure drawings something of the history of written language, practical uses of reading, and the pleasures that come from books of all types. The extreme superficiality of the treatment creates some misconceptions, as when the act of reading is said to depend on simply knowing the 26 letters and the 44 sounds that make up English. Most of the text is written at about a fourth grade reading level, but the book is such a conglomeration of the babyish and the adult that it will have little meaning for children of any age.

A review of "Reading Can Be Fun," in Bulletin of the Children's Book Center, *Vol. 7, No. 6, February, 1954, p. 47.*

Lucky You (1955)

It is a popular belief that "Munro Leaf can do no wrong." Certainly he does nothing to disprove the theory in his newest book, which will be wasted if it's read only by the young. Mr. Leaf has a way of distilling facts, so that only the pure truths come thru. In **Lucky You** he points out with devastating clarity just how many things children of today have to be thankful for, and what would have been their lot had they been born Ugh, a boy of cave dwelling days. With his disarmingly simple sketches, he gets his message across and makes it all good fun.

Maurine M. Remenih, in a review of "Lucky You," in Chicago Tribune, *Part 4, November 13, 1955, p. 10.*

The author uses the device of contrasting the everyday lives of two boys, Ugh of caveman days and Younow of the present, to point out what SCIENCE has done for us. Illustrations, format, and type style all give the impression that the book is intended for the comparatively young reader, but the concepts and sentence structures are too difficult for beginning readers. No help is given the reader in attempting to comprehend the passing of time, except for a very brief section at the beginning. The airy treatment leaves the reader with an unfortunate feeling of smugness rather than any awareness of the magnitude of the changes that have occurred over the centuries—this in spite of a precipitous section at the close on the science of human relations, which is a subject for a book in itself.

A review of "Lucky You," in Bulletin of the Children's Book Center, *Vol. 10, No. 5, January, 1957, p. 68.*

Three Promises to You (1957)

The basic premises of the United Nations, a body whose tasks are to prevent wars, see that all people get fair treatment and to find ways for people to live better—are given pat and plain treatment. The Leaf drawings, along with a text pared to the simplest of elements, give some solid facts about people and nations, why they fight, why they shouldn't fight and what to do about it. Fine for that first course in civics.

A review of "Three Promises to You," in Virginia Kirkus' Service, *Vol. XXV, No. 4, February 15, 1957, p. 138.*

As a message of good will the UN has asked Munro Leaf to tell the children of the world very simply what the organization is trying to do. In a masterly fashion he contents himself with a very few basic truths. The eldest and wisest of us can ponder them with the children. First he shows

photographs of the United Nations buildings. Then with the jolly, familiar figures with which he has delighted and enlightened children in writing on arithmetic, safety, manners and many other subjects, he talks about "You." "You are an important human being—a person." Like all persons, "you like to have good things to eat, a pleasant place to live. You want to enjoy a happy, healthy life." "You hate to be scared," to have some one come and "smash, wreck and destroy things that make your life good." That happens in war. Nations (groups of persons) quarrel. Some wars start because nations are afraid of what will happen if they do not fight. So, after a big war the leaders of many nations planned the United Nations to try never to have war again. The United Nations wants them to know that it is "working day and night to keep its three promises: 1. No war. 2. Fair treatment for all human beings. 3. Better living for everybody by sharing what we know. Three promises to you." This is "Fair Play" on a world scale. A book for primary children that does not simplify foolishly or make vast generalizations about an immediate Utopia. It makes them see what is earnestly being attempted, and why it is terribly important to them and to every other person on earth.

Margaret Sherwood Libby, in a review of "Three Promises to You," in New York Herald Tribune Book Review, *May 5, 1957, p. 10.*

Here is a new book for children! Munro Leaf's pictorial story of the aims of the United Nations provides instruction on the benefits of world government for the six to ten-year-old group. In pursuit of internationalism, Mr. Leaf emphasizes three major promises made by the United Nations to the children of the United States and the world: 1.) No War, 2.) Fair Treatment for all human beings, and 3.) Better living for everybody by sharing what we know. The fact that this is a book for children, was, we assume, Mr. Leaf's reason for failing to mention that we have been sharing a good deal more than just our knowledge.

The drawing of a table around which all nations sit and discuss their problems is Mr. Leaf's answer to the utilitarian's dream—but is the greatest good for the greatest number, unquestionably, the greatest good? He believes that once fear and inequality are eliminated, universal happiness and peace will automatically follow. The chance that teaching children to believe that all forms of fear, competition and success are wrong might easily develop a nation of mediocrity—from the world governed nursery to the international old age home—has somehow eluded Mr. Leaf's subtle pen.

There are two specific sentences in the book that deserve special notice; one implies that people will hate you if you eat better food than they eat. Thus at the tender age of six is sown the seed of fear that our good fortune can only bring dislike and the pattern is set for squandering our national assets via continual foreign aid loans. A second sentence states that the United Nations belongs to "You" the children. This should be of interest to parents who, discovering that no one is allowed to wander above the first floor of the United Nations Building without an official guide, have taken the trouble to escort their progeny on one of the "every-ten-minute tours" that show "You" *your* building at a cost of $1.00 for adults and .50 for children. If "You" haven't the money "You" can't see *your* U.N. It's rather like owning a doll and not being able to play with it, but then with such thought-provoking subjects in children's books as world peace, perhaps the six-to-ten-year-olds don't play with dolls anymore. (pp. 152-53)

> *G. S. H., in a review of "Three Promises to You," in* American Mercury, *Vol. LXXXIV, No. 401, June, 1957, pp. 152-53.*

Science Can Be Fun   (1958)

It was inevitable that science would join arithmetic, manners and the rest, and prove to be fun when presented by the prolific and inspired Munro Leaf. In lively text, accompanied by the familiar quasi-cartoon illustrations, this enthusiastic narrative explains some of the fundamentals of the scientific principle and indicates practical methods of testing each statement empirically. A lively curiosity, plus a rubber ball, an orange and a clothesline provide the essentials he demands of his young scientist. Add to that an appetite for Leaf's bold and entertaining approach and you have it,—a real help, both in presentation and in the encouragement of further reading.

> *A review of "Science Can Be Fun," in* Virginia Kirkus' Service, *Vol. XXVI, No. 17, September 1, 1958, p. 659.*

This author-artist has that particular genius for imparting

From Metric Can Be Fun!, *written and illustrated by Munro Leaf.*

knowledge to the young, whether it be manners, arithmetic, or anything one could mention. It was inevitable that he should attack science, and here it is: a book that explains scientific fundamentals with simple experiments any child can perform. A challenging book with step-by-step drawings.

> *Charlotte Jackson, in a review of "Science Can Be Fun," in* The Atlantic Monthly, *Vol. 202, No. 6, December, 1958, p. 97.*

The Wishing Pool   (1960)

Three children make wishes. One wishes to be a knight, one a cowboy, and the third, a pilot. And in these zany episodes which casually mix possibility with fancy, their wishes come true. And since Munro Leaf, author of the *Can Be Fun* series, is the necromancer, the adventures unfold in a rhythmic prose which is simple and pleasurable to read. Illustrations by the author punctuate the atmosphere of good natured adventurousness that underlies this book.

> *A review of "The Wishing Pool," in* Virginia Kirkus' Service, *Vol. XXVIII, No. 14, July 15, 1960, p. 554.*

In a new series for beginning readers, this "easy to read" book tells about the dreams of three of the children who play at the wishing pool. While the knight-rescuing-his-lady theme may seem a bit sophisticated, the jet flight to the North Pole should certainly have appeal. No *Cat in the Hat* or *Little Bear* but entertaining and useful, nevertheless.

> *Miriam S. Mathes, in a review of "The Wishing Pool," in* Junior Libraries, *September 15, 1960, p. 57.*

Turnabout   (1967)

No one who recalls Ferdinand, the effete bull, can recall author-illustrator Munro Leaf with anything but good will. But Mr. Leaf is also a moralist, and in *Turnabout* that strain is at its strongest. The book has to do with a lad who ties a can to a dog's tail and is subsequently brought to trial before all the world's animals, and you can imagine the heavy-handed preachment *that* situation engenders.

> *Clifford A. Ridley, in a review of "Turnabout," in* The National Observer, *November 27, 1967, p. 21.*

A switch on man bites dog. Two small boys tie a tin can to a dog's tail, and in a dream they both must answer to the whole animal kingdom. The moral, cruelty begets cruelty, is timely, the illustrations, vintage Munro Leaf. But the punch of the book is lost in too many words.

> *A review of "Turnabout," in* The New York Times Book Review, *January 21, 1968, p. 28.*

There is too much text here and it nags away at a point that is too obviously made from the start. The child-style illustrations, which are supposed to be comic, aren't; they are poorly composed, badly drawn, and the color is unevenly scrawled on. The story starts with Jack and Tommy tying a can to a dog's tail. When Tommy falls asleep, he dreams of being put on trial by all the world's animals. This dream sequence is set in Malaysia and Jack is replaced by a Malaysian boy named Ali. This setting and the character substitution are purposeless. The animals that gather are a windy bunch who indict Tommy and mankind for cruel practices and bloody sports. Finally, Tommy is warned that boys who are cruel to animals become men who are cruel to each other. Then Tommy wakes up. Children might stay awake for this with the author telling it while dashing off illustrations, as he recently did in Malaysia according to the jacket copy, but in book form it's a sleep-inducing sermonette.

> *Lillian N. Gerhardt, in a review of "Turnabout," in* School Library Journal, *Vol. 14, No. 6, February 15, 1968, p. 80.*

I Hate You, I Hate You   (1968)

It takes a grandfather, Munro Leaf of Ferdinand fame, to poke fun in a grand way at all the hating going on in the world today. Two children fighting over a red truck, the Pakistanis mistrusting the Indians, the Chinese chasing the Malays and, conversely, the Indonesians chasing the Chinese—all this, according to author-illustrator Munro Leaf, is "nonsense." This, he says, "is a book of foolish ridiculous stupid nonsense."

In delightful simple prose and Munro Leafish illustrations this popular children's author makes fun of all the hating being expressed between races, religions, nationalities, grandchildren. *I hate you, I hate you,* a slim paperbound volume, may find a comfortable place in college book stores next to *A Friend Is Someone Who Likes You.*

It will also be just right for little children as a picture book. Yes, it is a message, but in this age of McLuhanism the medium is part of the message—or massage, for those who like chewing on their picture books.

The title is bold: "I Hate You, I Hate You." But the anecdotes are subtle. The pictures are subtler. And the final question, "Hasn't this gone on long enough?" confronts the reader with the force of atomic energy.

> *C. P., "Not-So-Flower Children," in* The Christian Science Monitor, *November 7, 1968, p. B9.*

Who Cares? I Do   (1971)

Two stick figures state the case, "You Know What? Our country is getting to be a mess," then point to photos of trash and litter and drawings of the SPOILERS (divided into DROPPERS and WRECKERS) who are doing the damage. Their accompanying second-person exhortation advises that "boys and girls your age can really change the thinking and the ways of a lot of people. . . . Not by preaching at them or nagging. . . . NO/ All you have to do is act like a decent human being yourself." There's no

positive reinforcement in the pictures or the lecture, only a tired watchbird admonishing litterbugs. (pp. 935-36)

> *A review of "Who Cares? I Do," in* Kirkus Reviews, *Vol. XXXIX, No. 17, September 1, 1971, pp. 935-36.*

Man's seemingly inborn tendency to be a litterbug and defiler of beauty is clearly illustrated in **Who Cares? I Do.** As the reader proceeds through this book, he is presented with full-page photographs of horrendous acts of vandalism or littering. On the page facing this environmental obscenity are a few lines of text and a simple sketch of two bewildered observers. While the ecological concept of the book is simple—"don't mess things up"—it is also appropriate. The complexity is suitable for early elementary children. In fact, the young reader is portrayed as an active leader in the cause. By his good example, he can educate sisters, brothers, and friends and even, heaven forbid, parents and other grownups. Munro Leaf's book is especially commendable because its message is not presented in terms of good or bad morality. Rather, the author identifies the problem and appeals directly to the child's own rationality for a solution.

> *Thomas A. Butler, in a review of "Who Cares? I Do," in* Appraisal: Science Books for Young People, *Vol. 5, No. 3, Fall, 1972, p. 24.*

Metric Can Be Fun!   (1976)

Though Leaf's stick figures might help demystify the subject, they don't (despite his title) make it look as much like fun as Lustig's cartoons did in Branley's similarly simple but stronger *Measure with Metric* last year. Advising readers to "forget that you have ever heard of inches, feet, . . . pecks and bushels," Leaf gives them a decimeter-long guide to making a meter stick—from which a liter box can follow—and a number of suggestions as to what to measure. As for units of weight, if you haven't a metric scale, "check labels in stores for a general idea." For those who can't quite forget the old way, equivalents are appended. Usable, but it can't measure up to the Branley.

> *A review of "Metric Can Be Fun!" in* Kirkus Reviews, *Vol. XLIV, No. 9, May 1, 1976, p. 539.*

Munro Leaf's book goes right to the heart of the matter, with a quotation from Alexander Graham Bell: "All the difficulties in the metric system are in translating from one system to the other, but the moment you use the metric system alone there is no difficulty." It's rather like learning a language—comes a moment when you stop translating into English and start thinking in, say, French. After that it's easy.

But a problem defined is only the beginning of a problem solved. How do we create a *tabula rasa* where measurement is concerned so that we can begin thinking in the metric system? What Leaf has done is provide a skillful mix of assumed prior knowledge and new information. Although distances, quantities, weights and temperature are approached in elemental fashion, some familiarity with the entire concept of measurement would be of help. Initially, the reader is provided graphically with a line ten centimeters long and instructed that "you will need a straight stick or a piece of cardboard ten times longer than this line" in order to carry out the suggested measuring activities that follow. Throughout, metric measurement is related to the familiar—"your father may weigh about 80 kilograms," or "on a January evening you may hear that it is . . . 2 degrees centigrade in Princeton, New Jersey."

By doing just what he states as the best approach at the outset—using the metric system alone—the author does a commendable job with what could have been an exercise in equivalents and boredom. Leaf invites reader participation and suggests activities. The pen-and-ink illustrations resemble humorous decorations in a science notebook.

> *Ingeborg Boudreau, in a review of "Metric Can Be Fun!" in* The New York Times Book Review, *May 30, 1976, p. 11.*

This book covers most aspects of the metric system in relatively simple language with plenty of interesting drawings. While this is an introductory book, teachers will need to provide background on measurement of area, perimeter, quantity and weight. The relationship between meters, li-ters and grams is described well in simple, clear language. In addition, while the author mentions the full range of units (kilo, hecto, deca, deci, centi and milli) his main emphasis is on the more commonly used prefixes, kilo, centi, and milli. Leaf also lists good projects and examples to relate the metric system with everyday items—how tall are you, what is the area of your bed, how heavy is your father? The discussion of temperature measurement is good. Finally, for those who have mastered the metric system, there are two pages of conversion tables from English measuring units to metric.

Editor's note: [from *Science Books and Films*] This book was also evaluated—strictly for metric accuracy—by the National Bureau of Standards. The NBS reader noted the following: 1. Degrees Celsius should be used instead of degrees centigrade (p. 49). 2. "Stere" is obsolete (p. 28). 3. Commas should not be used to separate groups of three digits (p. 42). 4. Throughout the text deka is incorrectly spelled "deca."

> *Alison Taunton-Rigby, in a review of "Metric Can Be Fun!" in* Science Books & Films, *Vol. XII, No. 4, March, 1977, p. 209.*

William Mayne

1928-

(Also writes as Martin Cobalt, Charles Molin, and, with R. D. Caesar, as Dynely James) English author of fiction and picture books and editor.

Major works include *A Swarm in May* (1955), *A Grass Rope* (1957), *Earthfasts* (1966), *Ravensgill* (1970), *A Game of Dark* (1971), *The Jersey Shore* (1973).

The following entry emphasizes general criticism of Mayne's career. It also includes a selection of reviews to supplement the general criticism.

Often regarded as the most important British author of books for children and young people from the primary grades through high school, Mayne holds a distinctive place in the field of juvenile literature. Praised as a phenomenon, a virtuosic genius who possesses a totally original vision and voice, a thorough understanding of children and adults, and a remarkable ability to evoke the power of landscape, he is also characterized as the creator of eccentric, idiosyncratic books which have little or no appeal to young readers due to their difficulty, denseness, subtlety, lack of emotion, and absence of strong narrative flow. Mayne is sometimes perceived as an adult author masquerading as a creator of children's literature due to the sophistication of his prose and the darkness of his subjects and themes; however, he is often celebrated for broadening the limits of juvenile literature, for contributing to its artistry, and for preparing his audience for the style, content, and complexity of adult fiction. The author of approximately one hundred books in most genres which are published at the rate of one to five times per year, Mayne addresses the adventure story, the time travel fantasy, the picture book, the school story, the ghost story, and the adolescent novel as well as the folk tale and the allegory in works often lauded as outstanding contributions to their respective genres. Writing in an oblique, elliptical style which stresses dialogue and utilizes such techniques as inversion, wordplay, and grammatical shifts, Mayne presents his audience with a fresh world view in which he describes the interplay of the present, the past, people, and place in a poetic manner that stresses cosmic awareness both through locale and the perceptions of his young male and female protagonists; "All I am doing," he has said, "is looking at things now and showing them to myself when I was young." Mayne often steeps his books in English history, tradition, and legend, a characteristic credited for giving many of his works a mythic quality; despite the often serious nature of his stories, Mayne invests them with a playful, whimsical humor which he reflects most frequently in his consistent use of puns.

Born in Yorkshire, the setting for many of his books as well as his current residence, Mayne attended the Choir School at Canterbury from the ages of nine to thirteen; he uses this background for his popular quartet of Cathedral Choir school stories *A Swarm in May, Choristers' Cake*

(1956), *Cathedral Wednesday* (1960), and *Words and Music* (1963). A self-taught writer, Mayne began his career with family stories which involve mysteries and treasure hunts, books in which he first explored the nuances in relationships among members of all generations. *A Grass Rope,* the story of how two children attempt to discover the source of an old legend, is often considered the precursor of many of his later works, which continue to investigate the intricacies of time and space. Several of Mayne's books are considered classics; among the most highly regarded is *Earthfasts,* his first venture into pure fantasy. Based on an eighteenth-century Yorkshire legend about an drummer boy who went into a hole in the rock of Richmond Castle in search of King Arthur's treasure and was never seen again, *Earthfasts* describes the events, both natural and supernatural, that occur when two modern boys, David and Keith, encounter the drummer boy Nellie Jack John after he emerges from the castle. Mayne is also especially acclaimed as the author of *Ravensgill,* the story of how teenage cousins Bob and Judith reconcile a family quarrel which has existed for nearly fifty years and includes the possibility of murder, and *The Jersey Shore,* a novel set in the United States in the early 1930s in which Arthur, a young Englishman, learns about his family's past from his grandfather; the U. S. edition of this book eliminates the fact that Arthur's grandfather is black. Perhaps Mayne's most controversial work is *A Game of Dark*, a fantasy-cum-psychological novel which describes how fourteen-year-old Donald comes to terms with his dying father and aloof mother as well as with the memories of his dead sister by entering into an alternate life; as a squire in a vaguely medieval time, Donald kills the vile worm that is terrorizing a feudal village and thus is able to accept himself and his home life. Criticized for its spare, cool quality and for the questionability of its Oedipal theme for teenage readers, the novel is also considered a powerful reading experience which is perhaps Mayne's most ambitious work. In addition to his books for readers in the middle grades through high school, Mayne is the creator of several picture books and stories for younger children; especially well-received are *No More School* (1965), a humorous tale which describes how a group of Yorkshire schoolchildren teach themselves when their regular teacher becomes ill, and the Hob stories, four volumes of short stories about an English household spirit. Mayne is also the editor of several anthologies about legendary and supernatural figures as well as the composer of the incidental music for *Holly from the Bongs* by Alan Garner, a writer to whom he is often compared. Mayne received the Carnegie Medal for *A Grass Rope* in 1957; he was commended for this award for *A Swarm in May* in 1955, for *The Member for the Marsh* and for *Choristers' Cake*, both in 1956, and for *The Blue Boat* in 1957, while *Ravensgill* was named a Carnegie honor book in 1970. *Earthfasts* received the Lewis Carroll Shelf Award in 1968, while *The Mouldy* was a Kurt Maschler Award runnerup in 1983. Mayne is also the recipient of two prizes from the International Board on Books for Young People (IBBY), the writing award for Great Britain for *All the King's Men* in 1984 and an honor listing for *A Year and a Day* in 1978.

(See also *Contemporary Literary Criticism*, Vol. 12; *Something about the Author*, Vol. 6; *Something about the Author Autobiography Series*, Vol. 11; and *Contemporary Authors*, Vols. 9-12, rev. ed.)

AUTHOR'S COMMENTARY

[*The following excerpt is from an interview with Mayne in 1969 by a group of children's literature professionals.*]

It has been said that a writer of top quality ought not to be so productive.

I should have died at thirty-six, like Mozart, then it wouldn't have mattered. (p. 48)

Why do you write for children?

I don't. I write for myself, but myself of long ago. Perhaps I think of some dismal Tuesday afternoon when it was raining in 1941. I knew I hadn't anything to do and I was bored. I wished I'd had a book to read, so I think, well, I'll write it now. But it doesn't help because I never read them. Awful, to try to read one's own books. I think that's all, you know. It's purely selfish.

Do you know why you write for yourself of long ago and not for yourself now?

I don't think I've got anything to say to myself now. I'm just trying to give myself a good background. (pp. 48-9)

Why are you preoccupied with the pastness of the present?

I'm not. The present's alright. It's just different. I'm just an observer in the present. If I want to project it into the past, why not? I think I can see things more clearly now than I could when I was young. One's so busy when young and there's no time to do things. You are always slaving away at arithmetic and all that sort of stuff at school. It doesn't give you any time to develop or become educated. All I am doing is looking at things now and showing them to myself when I was young. If anyone else wants to look over my shoulder, that's alright. If they don't, that doesn't matter either. All I really want from a book is just a nice copy. I know it's got a coloured jacket on but I can always take it off. Yet it seems so impolite to take it off when the artist has gone to all that trouble. I put it on the shelf and that's the satisfaction. They send money as well and that's another satisfaction. Nineteen pounds ten a year!

To what extent are you working something out as you write? Do you find that by writing, your vision of a particular thing or of life generally becomes more sharply focused, or do you find that the nature of your vision is altering?

If I write something it's because I can't see it before I begin. If I am having difficulty with a landscape or a situation of some sort not necessarily quite my own, I think a way of coming to some agreement with that particular thing is perhaps to write a book about it. Not that you the reader would know that I was writing about that at all. It might appear quite differently. So I am therapizing myself no doubt.

Would you care to say to what extent your ideas about writing or life generally have changed as you have moved from one book to another, to what extent they have come more sharply in focus, or do you take each book as it comes along without any necessary reference to what has gone before?

I'm an existentialist I think, and each one just happens. I have no doubt that they do influence each other and I am always hoping to get better or even to find out how to do it. I always forget between books how it's done. I don't know at all. I don't even know how it's done when I do it. It's not a question of general philosophy.

Do you really prefer observing and then you've enjoyed it so much that you've got to put in down?

Observation is all. What is one's purpose in life? I don't know whether it is just to come down here on earth and look at things. Perhaps we are reporting back to Mars. But we must look at things. This is all that scientists do—they look at things.

But you do delight in it, don't you, and then you feel you've got to put it down?

Yes, I think so. I put it down because I like it or sometimes because I don't like it. I still have to put it down if I don't like it because I haven't understood it. I analyze it and it's always nicer when it is analyzed.

You are very keen, it seems to me, on a truthful kind of dialogue, sometimes in a Pinteresque kind of way. Are you conscious of overhearing children speak?

Well, they do talk don't they? But if you use their words, the publisher will say 'This is a funny bit, it's not quite natural, a bit stilted, this bit, isn't it?' and—difficulties you know. One has to be crafty, if not artful.

But your dialogue is very distinctive, isn't it?

Is it? I don't know. I only think it's any good if it says exactly the opposite of what I meant, because I think that might be more natural. If it's lifelike that's luck, isn't it?

Are there any aspects of human nature that you haven't explored that you would like to explore? Would this lead you away from writing for children?

Well, they are all human even if they are children. It's not been proved but I can assume they're human, so they've got the same nature all the way through as people. There's no great difference except they are not so expanded in some directions.

Are there any aspects you would like to explore further or are there any fresh aspects you would like to explore?

I don't know. If I come across them, I'll write about them. That's all I can say because I haven't any classifications of these things in mind at the moment or perhaps at any moment. I'm not too good on human nature. (pp. 49-51)

Do you believe in your work seriously? Could you get to the end of a book if you didn't believe in it?

I don't know whether it's worth doing or not at any point. I know I've got the idea in mind and I know the shape of the thing and I've got to finish it. I know when I get two-thirds of the way through, it just becomes a bit of a labour and a bore and I think 'Oh heck, I've never given up yet' and I struggle on to the end.

But have you got to finish it? You haven't. What makes you?

Tidiness. Can't have this thing lying about unfinished.

*I wonder if you could say a little about how **Earthfasts** came to you?*

I just happened to be mowing a hayfield with a farmer and he said 'By gum, there's a lot of earthfasts this year.' I thought what a good word. It had been a dryish, wettish, dryish, wettish season and all the rock had come up through the grass and the blades kept catching. It was just the right sort of day apparently. There was this word and these stones were growing. Then I had this other idea, not an idea, but a local story—which of course is perfectly true—about the drummer boy going into the ground and beating his drum. Then it stopped. They were following him up above. I wondered what had happened to him. I'd often wanted to use it as a motif or something. Then I thought, well, perhaps if he came out . . . then you'd have to start meddling with time and things. I used that, reluctantly I would say, but I didn't dislike it. It's just too diffi-

cult to deal with. You can't go beyond a superficial thing because of science fiction or something. Mess about with dimensions and you don't know where you are.

Were you not then satisfied with the book when you finished the story?

Oh, when it had had a few coats of paint it was alright. Any building's got a few bits that have been patched over. I have to admit that. I was going to say 'It's only fiction . . .' but there are loose ends that can't be tied down in a book. Sometimes you use them boldly and say 'Lo and behold, here are loose ends lying about. They are part of the flavour.' There are loose ends in **Earthfasts.** That's alright. There have to be. I haven't disguised them, I hope.

Are you satisfied with the ending when somebody essentially of the past becomes somebody of the present—the drummer boy settling down?

I was going to kill him off but people said 'No, don't.' I felt quite free to do what I liked there, so as they'd expressed a preference for having him alive still, I thought it made a nice *tierce de Picardie.*

*Would you say that in your last two books, **Over the Hills and Far Away** and **Earthfasts,** there is a change of direction?*

It's the exigencies of the plot, I think. The plots didn't work without a bit of disruption of normality. That was all. I couldn't have done either story without. To me fantasy is just a tool of the trade. If I want to use it I will but I am not particularly interested in fantasy. Yet it's all right. It's a difficult thing because you get so tangled up. If you move one physical element or one physical law you upset the whole lot. The world only just holds together anyway.

The assumption has been made that if you plonk a child down in a room full of books, he's going to become an avid reader. Our experience tells us that this is not so, it doesn't happen with a lot of children. You may be mainly concerned with the child who comes to books naturally but we are concerned with the child who doesn't.

I'm sorry. I'm only concerned with the one who is an avid reader already because what I've done is written some things down. That's up to him, or somebody, to read it. I can't do anything more about that. I've just produced these particular bricks. If you can't build with them, I can't do anything about that.

Perhaps this is our job, to bring these children to you. Have you any observations to make about our place in this, as partners rather than as antagonists?

I don't know. This is a different sort of expertise. On the whole I don't want to feed that information into my computer. I don't think my computer has any way of processing that material. This is a different machine.

*Children who start off reading those simple books like **The Big Egg** can be led on to the others. You are not throwing down a whole lot of finished difficult books, you are leading children into your work.*

I can programme the computer to a certain extent, yes. A publisher has a series. The books are such and such a length or for such and such an age. I can feed that information in. It's not information I work on at the moment of sitting at the typewriter, but months before. There's a lot of stuff floating about and I can put down a net with the right weave and pull up the things that I want. I hope to anyway. That's all I can do. (pp. 52-3)

Do you look back on the children in your novels as perhaps rather unsuccessful cardboard figures in certain books and in others successful and pleasing to yourself?

I think that they have all got the status I intended them to have. Some are bound to be made out of cardboard. People are at different distances from the camera—some are in focus and some aren't. Different sorts of focus. It depends upon their function in the story. This is a purely technical thing, not of any interest to anybody but me, I think. I don't know—I haven't read the books you see—whether they are right or not.

Postscript by William Mayne

I've read this through and don't like it very well. I think I was driven to teasing the audience a little and I believe they thought I was tiresome and flippant. At one point in the session a publisher leapt up in my defence and told them to stop bullying me. I am certainly aware of not having been able to respond quite as I had hoped to the gathering and I could not bring myself to do what one delegate wanted: 'open the door wider so that they could see more than the hall wallpaper'. My own defence is that I am not a public speaker about myself. I'm quite good on subjects like housing and drainage and the iniquities of the Northallerton and Dales Water Board, but not on me. My public expression is what I write, and I don't see that 'I' am relevant. I am an observer who makes small temporary classifications, not an interpreter of anything. I apologize to the reader for the formlessness of the article—sometimes in the sort of session reported the proceedings achieve form, or at least momentum. (pp. 53-4)

> *William Mayne, "A Discussion with William Mayne," in* Children's literature in education, *No. 2, July, 1970, pp. 48-55.*

The Junior Bookshelf

Children will greatly enjoy this story [*Follow the Footprints*] of a hunt for hidden treasure. It moves swiftly and is really mysterious and exciting. Mr. Mayne has a delightful touch of wit and his children, Andrew and Caroline, are thoroughly tolerable. Our only complaint is that the writing lacks style and clarity here and there. Nevertheless we look forward to an improvement in the author's next book.

> *A review of "Follow the Footprints," in* The Junior Bookshelf, *Vol. 17, No. 3, July, 1953, p. 121.*

The Junior Bookshelf

Some might quibble at the whimsical humour and allusive conversations in [*The World Upside Down*], but read in the right mood it is delightfully refreshing, with its nice civilized children making quotable (and quotation-filled) remarks, and finding pleasure in being alive as well as a proper treasure of golden crowns and coins. The treasure is kept in proportion by the accompanying need to retrieve family honour, to say nothing of a charming grandfather, by the Oxford student who helps Jack and Lucy in their search. There is style in the writing, warmth and wit in the family relationships, and reality behind each character, even the poacher who sounds almost too much a character to be true. The kind of light reading which will stand up to many re-readings, and pave the way to the best kind of adult light fiction.

> *A review of "The World Upside Down," in* The Junior Bookshelf, *Vol. 18, No. 5, November, 1954, p. 247.*

Betty Brazier

The main plot of William Mayne's [*The World Upside Down*], the search for hidden Cavalier treasure, is ordinary enough, but he has happily interwoven other more original themes and raised the book well above the level of an ordinary "quest" story. There is Jessop, the old poacher whom the bailiffs are after, the large fish taken in private waters twenty years back and fed by old Kinross, the appearance of his unknown grandson, trout tickling, and a picture of farming a small-holding in a Yorkshire Dale. Too frequently in children's books the unwanted adults are conveniently non-existent, but William Mayne has not only made the grown-ups friends of the two children, Jack and Lucy, but has created a particularly happy relationship between them. The author understands children and he has drawn parents with hearts as young as their offspring's. There are some banal descriptions of the children's doings, but the beauty of the woods and becks and dales of Yorkshire is rendered in simple clear-cut pictures.

> *Betty Brazier, in a review of "The World Upside Down," in* The School Librarian and School Library Review, *Vol. 7, No. 5, July, 1955, p. 361.*

G. Taylor

[*A Swarm in May* is] a delicious recounting of the traditional Beekeeping ceremony in a choir school. The story of how the youngest Singing Boy fulfilled his major role on this occasion, discovering meanwhile the haunts of the earliest Beekeeper to the cathedral, is richly told. Boys and masters come alive, the cathedral and its precincts are all around, but only the maturer reader who can give himself up to the spell of the writer can walk with him into this world which he knows so well.

> *G. Taylor, in a review of "A Swarm in May," in* The School Librarian and School Library Review, *Vol. 8, No. 1, March, 1956, p. 69.*

The Times Literary Supplement

Without going outside the familiar convention of seek-and-find adventure in an English country setting, William Mayne has quickly established himself as the most original good writer for children in our immediate time. At this stage ([*The Member for The Marsh*] is his fourth) it is possible to see something of the pattern on which his imagination works. He writes on the edge of the past rather than on the edge of the future; he dismisses the age-barrier between friends; he makes his own traditions (among schoolboys, for instance), but they seem to lighten life, not burden it. He also expects his readers to think speedily. If it is a scramble to follow his quick wit at times, the book can always be read again; and the second reading often gives more pleasure than the first.

> *"The Edge of the Past," in* The Times Literary Supplement, *No. 2828, May 11, 1956, p. vii.*

The Junior Bookshelf

William Mayne is certainly the most excitingly original writer for children to emerge in the last five years. This is not to say that he is, even potentially, the most popular. *The Member for the marsh* confirms the impressions of his three earlier novels that he has an insatiable passion for oddities. When many writers are haunted by the shadow of the backward reader, he writes joyously and unashamedly for the top flight of the grammar school, for those who may be expected to enjoy fine style, original and provocative ideas and rich characters. He writes, one suspects, to please himself, as most of the best books are written.

Mr. Mayne is a master of the use of setting. This time his scene is the fascinating flat country of western Somerset. He knows the country well and communicates his appreciation of its not-very-obvious charms. Into this setting he puts—but no, they live there already—four very odd boys, the Harmonious Mud Stickers, who relieve the tedium of a daily bus ride to school with song and elevating conversation. Never were there less typical schoolboys, but each is drawn consistently and convincingly. Their activities, in which schoolboyish fun charmingly breaks through the solemnity, are too good to give away. Mr. Mayne tells a good story, with certainty and without haste. Not a book for children, but definitely a book for the child who can deserve it.

> *A review of "The Member for the Marsh," in* The Junior Bookshelf, *Vol. 20, No. 3, July, 1956, p. 144.*

The Times Literary Supplement

To come to *Choristers' Cake* is to enter a new world, from the flat drabness of monochrome engraving to the colour and movement and depth of real life. The scene is that of *A Swarm in May,* but the viewpoint is changed. The Choir School is seen through the eyes, and interpreted by the rather muddled brain, of an older boy, one who does not easily find a place in the cooperative society of school. This is a most skillful study, and there is nothing contrived about Sandy's gradual achievement of self-recognition.

Psychological insight is not the whole of Mr. Mayne's armoury. He is a master—*the* master in contemporary English writing for children—of setting, and the hero of *Choristers' Cake* is not Sandy but the Cathedral. The Cathedral is ever-present. Its traditions provide the story with its main theme. Its services mark the passage of time. The precincts are the boys' home and their playground. The many, and delightful, minor characters are the Cathedral's servants: the gentle-hearted organist, the aggressive and psalm-quoting verger, the unforgettable Pargales who take care of the fabric.

Choristers' Cake may be a by-way of children's literature. Its virtuosity and verbal richness, as well as the undoubted oddness of many of its characters, put it beyond the range of the average reader. But for the child who can meet its demands it will be a deep and memorable experience. In insight, in gaiety, in exuberance of idea and language, it is in a class apart. Mr. Mayne is certainly the most interesting, as the most unpredictable, figure in children's books today. He has all the talents, and he has devoted them to the creation of a little world, self-contained and absorbed, in spite of quarrels and rivalries, in its work of praising God.

> *"Willingly to School," in* The Times Literary Supplement, *No. 2856, November 23, 1956, p. vii.*

The Junior Bookshelf

Mr. Mayne, in the second of his novels about a choir school [*Chorister's Cake*], evokes most beautifully the spirit of the cathedral and its people.

Mr. Mayne is not an easy writer, as we know. His love of words, his range of ideas and his interest in psychology, which are the very essence of his art, all act as stumbling-blocks to the young reader. One suspects that Mr. Mayne is not unduly distressed by this. He writes, as he must, to please himself. Will he at the same time please others? Yes, he will delight those who deserve writing of this quality, the children, a minority but not an insignificant one, who can recognise the truth of his observation of boys' behaviour and who can relish the convincing oddity of his adults.

This book is not a sequel to *A Swarm in May.* That inimitable book said the last word on its subject. In *Choristers' Cake* we look at the same school from a different viewpoint. The central character is an older boy than John Owen, who in this story is a very small and unimportant singing boy. Sandwell is one of those boys who fight a solitary war against school tradition and discipline. He is intensely real. Every school has such a one. The main theme of the story is that of Sandy's progress towards self-harmony. There is a background theme of the rivalry between the two halves of the choir. There is a splendid climax on Guy Fawkes' Day, when three guys of a quite horrifying and malignant grotesqueness meet a merited end. (p. 341)

> *A review of "Choristers' Cake," in* The Junior

Bookshelf, *Vol. 20, No. 6, December, 1956, pp. 341-42.*

The Junior Bookshelf

Mr. Mayne continues to pursue his own course, unaffected by fashions and undeterred by criticism. [**The Blue Boat**] is as delightful, and as difficult, as **The Member for the Marsh,** and the characters are more odd than ever before. Hugh and Christopher, two small boys, spend their holidays with Mrs. Wrigley while their parents are in Africa. Sent out every day to play nicely on the beach, they in fact spend their time exploring a mysterious mere, with an island inhabited by giant, goblin, bear and other strange things. With the aid of the goblin, his friend the alchemist, and their animal supporters, the boys challenge the giant to battle. In a somewhat contrived ending, they return to Mrs. Wrigley's to find that their parents have come home.

Of the many shots in Mr. Mayne's locker, perhaps the most effective is style. His writing always has great beauty, subtlety and evocative power. He has a remarkable gift for bringing a scene vividly to life. He loves landscape and knows how to use it as an essential actor in his story. His humour is of the sort which creeps up on the reader unawares; instead of laughter it brings a warm glow of satisfaction. He has the most profound and intimate knowledge of boys and their ways. His two principals are delightfully contrasted; Hugh, who lives in a world of the imagination, Christopher, who clings to reality as a protection from the terrors of his fancies; and he shows how the boys influence one another. He is a master of revealing dialogue.

I have no doubt at all that this is a very fine book, infused with wisdom, gaiety and deep understanding. It is not so clearly a book for children, many of whom will be baffled by its strangeness and by its blending of realism and imagination. It should, nevertheless, be put within children's reach, for to the right child it will come as the opening up of a new world. (pp. 143-44)

A review of "The Blue Boat," in The Junior Bookshelf, *Vol. 21, No. 3, July, 1957, pp. 143-44.*

Jennie D. Lindquist

[*A Swarm in May*] has a most unusual plot. It is based on an old tradition: the youngest Singing Boy is always the Beekeeper; he must "come before the Bishop one Sunday in May, to sing a short solo and recite the ritual assuring the Bishop that the organist will supply good beeswax candles for the Cathedral throughout the coming year." . . . The Cathedral background, the music, the beekeeping and the very real boys combine to make a story that will be loved by those children who are always looking for English books and by others who are lucky enough to have adults share it with them. (pp. 307-08)

Jennie D. Lindquist, in a review of "A Swarm in May," in The Horn Book Magazine, *Vol. 33, No. 4, August, 1957, pp. 307-08.*

The Times Literary Supplement

Mr. Mayne makes no concessions to the young reader [in *A Grass Rope*]: his children, his adolescents, his adults are all unerringly themselves. To whom are *Songs of Childhood* and *Peacock Pie* addressed—to child or grown-up? *A Grass Rope* could and will be read by the young; but it is the parent who will recognize the accuracy of Mr. Mayne's characterization and the artistry of his narrative. His portrayal of Mary the younger girl and his evocation of the mystery and wonderment of her private universe thrusts us back into that dewy *pays sans nom* which is the child's Eden for a span of no more than two or three years in the very morning of life but which, long before he reaches puberty, has faded and left not a rack behind. Mr. Mayne reminds us, as Alain-Fournier, Forrest Reid and de la Mare remind us, that the dream may be the reality and our vaunted maturity the dream.

"Domesticated Adventure," in The Times Literary Supplement, *No. 2907, November 15, 1957, p. iv.*

The Junior Bookshelf

Mary [of *A Grass Rope*] believed in fairies. Adam didn't, but after all he *was* Head Boy of the Grammar School; but he did believe in the fundamental truth of the old legend about the Unicorn and the hounds. Between them, and with help from Nan, Peter and others, including Hewlin that "sackless gummock" of a dog, they tracked the legend to its source deep under ground. A treasure-hunt, in fact, but a treasure-hunt with the difference that Mr. Mayne imparts to everything he touches. No one could be more traditional in his material; no one could touch the dead material of the adventure story into vivid life with such sure, individual and wonderful magic.

Mr. Mayne has infinite resources. First, style. He has the gift of describing everyday things as if he were seeing them for the first time, and he shares this freshness of vision with his readers. "Daddy's hole grew slowly. The stones came out moist one by one: each had time to dry to grey speckled with golden powder before the next stone fell beside it." He has, too, a fine sense of landscape and of atmosphere. The harsh Pennine country of this story is an essential actor in the drama; one sees it all the time, as one feels the hill mists, and hears the distant rush of water and the barking of foxes. He has a deep understanding of children. No one ever acts or speaks out of character. He is, moreover, a fine story-teller, who knows how to set his narrative in motion so that it gains in momentum as it goes. And everything is coloured with his characteristic sober humour.

Is *A Grass Rope* a book for children? It isn't the answer to the C-stream's prayer. It is difficult to read, with the twin obstacles of dialect and uninhibited vocabulary. It depends on subtleties of writing and observation. It is, nevertheless, completely in tune with childhood. It is written from the child's point of view, not from that of an adult thinking about children. Experience of other novels by Mr. Mayne has shown that their appeal is unpredictable. The most unexpected children take them to their hearts. They are unlikely to be enormously popular, but here and there, and in larger numbers than most adults would expect, there are children whose eyes are opened to the beauty and the mystery and the fun of life by seeing these treasures first through the eyes of William Mayne. *A Grass Rope* is an original and enchanting book. No one else could have written it. (pp. 318-19)

> *A review of "A Grass Rope," in* The Junior Bookshelf, *Vol. 21, No. 6, December, 1957, pp. 318-19.*

The Times Literary Supplement

To say that *Underground Alley* is not William Mayne's best book does not mean that it is not still one of the outstanding books of the year. Real life springs from every page he writes; in his hands even the most conventional seeds of plot blossom wonderfully. . . . More than anyone else now writing Mr. Mayne is able to get down to twelve-year-old height. Looking upwards with the unblinking stare of a child he sees all he sees as something new.

> *"Extraordinary-Ordinary Worlds," in* The Times Literary Supplement, *No. 2960, November 21, 1958, p. viii.*

The Junior Bookshelf

No doubt we shall have sober people explaining how in this passage Mr. Mayne has succeeded, in that failed, here written within the child's range, there soared far beyond his grasp. Labour in vain! William Mayne is one of those rare writers—there are seldom more than one or two in each generation—whom one takes on his own terms or not at all. *The Thumbstick* is a very good Mayne; that is, a very good book for intelligent readers of all ages and all environments. Whether it is a children's book depends on one's definition; it recalls C. S. Lewis's dictum: "A children's book which is enjoyed only by children is a bad children's book." It will certainly lift the right child on tiptoe; it is one of those tales in Lamb's words "which make the child a man, while all the time he suspected himself to be no bigger than a child."

The Thumbstick is one of Mayne's Yorkshire stories. Like all his books it is a tale of living traditions. It is also about a treasure-hunt. Like every one of Mayne's books, too, it is astonishingly unlike every other one. For all that, it has his characteristic qualities; a style which is a miracle of flexibility and range, a superb sense of atmosphere, brilliant characterisation and subtle observation, above all a poet's interest in the commonplaces of every-day life and an awareness of their cosmic significance. (p. 152)

> *A review of "The Thumbstick," in* The Junior Bookshelf, *Vol. 23, No. 3, July, 1959, pp. 152-53.*

Hamish Fotheringham

[Mayne's] first published story was *Follow the Footprints,* the story of a "treasure hunt," a motif which William Mayne has developed with freshness and originality in the majority of his books. Caroline and Andrew Blake come with their parents to live in an old Tollhouse in Cumberland. From local legends the children learn of treasure hidden in the former abbey of Saint Elda and set out to

find it. . . . The children are portrayed as being staunchly independent, clever, but never too clever, thank goodness, and neither precocious nor prigs. They are aware that independent action free from adult control can bring with it occasional discomfort and much hard work. (pp. 185-86)

This framework of well described country setting, local legends, excellently drawn pen portraits, sparkling dialogues and a plot rich in incidents is used by the author in his other "treasure hunt" stories. Framework is hardly the correct term. Variations on a theme would perhaps be a better description, for William Mayne has a poet's ear for the music of language—the sound as well as the sense. (p. 186)

The plot [of *The World Upside Down*] is a little complex but utterly logical. The description of the inverted reflection on the wall which provides the main clue—and the title of the story—needs more than one reading to fix the detail, but it fits together perfectly. All the characters have the breath of life. The old poacher Jessop, a likeable old rogue, is particularly well done, although the broad Yorkshire dialect of his speech may offer occasional difficulties.

William Mayne has produced a rich portrait gallery of shrewdly but affectionately observed, well-rounded characters. One thinks of young Mary, the Yorkshire farmer's daughter, in *A Grass Rope* with her unshakeable belief in fairies. Or the brothers in *The Blue Boat,* Hugh, highly imaginative opening up a world of phantasy to the more serious minded Christopher who, thanks to boarding school, feels it is easier to avoid trouble by conforming to the rules imposed by grown ups.

How much of the material in the two books about Canterbury Cathedral Choir School is autobiographical, one wonders? (pp. 186-87)

In *Choristers' Cake* the main figure is Peter Sandwell who tries to shirk being up-graded to the rank of chorister and is, in consequence, sent to Coventry by his school-fellows. His gradual awareness that his behaviour is anti-social is presented with a skill and insight which will be appreciated more by parents than by young readers. The atmosphere of the centuries old cathedral is beautifully fixed. Thanks to Mr. Mayne's art—aided perhaps by having actively shared the milieu—there is nothing "pye" about the choristers. They remain boys throughout, with whom the reader can identify himself, not surpliced and ruffed little angels.

Perhaps William Mayne's chief asset lies in not confining his characters to one particular age group. He always shows complete harmony existing between children of different ages and of both sexes and this same harmony marks the child's relationship with the adult world. Each child possesses a distinct personality with the right—one can almost say the DUTY—of expressing an opinion. They all take an active part in discussing plans and carrying them out. In the "treasure hunt" stories it is quite clear that they are successful in their search only because THEY ARE A GROUP with each child of whatever age making an important contribution to the common aim. (p. 188)

William Mayne is not an easy author. He never writes down and concentration is needed to keep up with his lively imagination. But is this, after all, such a bad thing? There are children prepared to make the effort of meeting an author on his own terms, and to them Mayne's stories are exciting and wholly satisfying. (p. 189)

> *Hamish Fotheringham, "The Art of William Mayne," in* The Junior Bookshelf, *Vol. 23, October, 1959, pp. 185-89.*

Margaret Sherwood Libby

The simplicity and potency of William Mayne's writing is extraordinary. Ever since we read of the choir school in *A Swarm in May* and *Chorister's Cake,* the boys and their teachers, especially Dr. Sunderland, the organist, have been as surely a part of our life as the girls of Orchard House or Thumb, Thimble and Nod, but we have yet to receive a glowing report of these books from a child under thirteen. Again [in *The Blue Boat*] the author has created characters and an environment that you simply do not forget when you close the book. . . . In the course of [Christopher and Hugh's] explorations they discover a real world that seems compounded of enchantment, pure enchantment for Hugh, imaginary enchantment for Christopher. As Hugh said afterwards, they "had a jolly good time even when they were frightened," for frightened they were by the very small man they called goblin who lived in the woods with a bear and some talking ravens, the "giant" who had a huge house with gigantic yew-tree figures in his garden, and the alchemist. Truly a rare book which we hope will find young readers patient enough to follow the boys until the moment, half through the book, when they come upon the blue boat which makes it possible for them to meet these men, who enjoy providing the suspense and magic that is expected. If a few do, that is sufficient; they and the older people who will be fascinated with the glimpses of these children's minds, the interplay of their imagination, their swift changes of mood, will have a satisfying reading experience.

> *Margaret Sherwood Libby, in a review of "The Blue Boat," in* New York Herald Tribune Book Review, *April 3, 1960, p. 9.*

The Times Literary Supplement

Schoolboy society is in William Mayne's *Cathedral Wednesday*—cathedral choir school society once more. For those—now or years ago—distinguishing with difficulty between "collect" and "collection" on an Anglican service-sheet, or for those with little musical language, this is a specialized world. (Nowadays Mr. Mayne kindly explains such words as "antiphonally".) But the issue is straightforward: an epidemic removes most of the boys from the school, disorganizes the routine (so that most days have to become "Cathedral Wednesday"), and promotes the hero to temporary head-prefectship and to delicate problems of insubordination.

As always, Mr. Mayne's writing is brilliant—so brilliant that there is a perpetual, restless surface-shimmer that can become tiresomely dazzling. But children learning to appreciate play of language and image will enjoy the wit, even the atrociously ingenious puns. Above all, Mr.

Mayne's writing has exactness ("four steamed puddings *robed* in jam") and individuality.

> *"Family and Friends," in* The Times Literary Supplement, *No. 3065, November 25, 1960, p. xii.*

The Junior Bookshelf

Cathedral Wednesday is, like *A Swarm in May,* a story about responsibility. Owen, in the earlier book, tries to evade the responsibility of his job as Beekeeper; Young, in this, finds it difficult to accept the problems of maintaining discipline when Trevithic goes sick and he find himself Acting Head Boy. The difference between the two books is that *A Swarm in May* works out its social and moral problems through a most original and profoundly interesting treasure-hunt; Andrew Young's dilemma is almost the whole of *Cathedral Wednesday.*

This is not to say that Mr. Mayne's new book is lacking in interest. It shares with the other "Choir School" stories the fascination of the Cathedral setting and of the complex and traditional life of the school; it has too its delightful clutch of odd characters and, because Young is a day boy, glimpses of a typical Mayne domestic interior in which the clarinet is played in the bath and mutton broth is laced with China tea. The writing is as exquisite as ever. Mr. Mayne's dialogue is a miraculous blend of naturalism, wit and individuality. His narrative prose glows. His insight into human behaviour, adult and child, is uncanny. I have no doubt at all that *Cathedral Wednesday* is a very lovely book, with much to delight and amuse and develop the child reader. Many of them however will miss the point and be left wondering if there is a point at all.

> *A review of "Cathedral Wednesday," in* The Junior Bookshelf, *Vol. 24, No. 6, December, 1960, p. 370.*

Margery Fisher

Unique among writers for children is William Mayne, who gives to his wildest treasure-hunts a background of balanced and complete family life. . . . I know no recent children's stories more *actual* than William Mayne's, whether he is writing about a school or a village or a small town; and perhaps he is a little difficult for children to appreciate just for this reason, because he utterly ignores any compromise, any of the formulas which endear more popular writers to children. But the child who plunges into his stories, forgetting fashion, listening to the dry, crisp dialogue, and seeing in his mind's eye the scenes so minutely and economically visualized, has found a companion for life, no less. (pp. 280-81)

> *Margery Fisher, "Little Birds in Their Nests Agree: Family Stories," in her* Intent Upon Reading: A Critical Appraisal of Modern Fiction for Children, *Brockhampton Press, 1961, pp. 270-96.*

Marcus Crouch

William Mayne's debut in 1953 with *Follow the Footprints* passed almost unnoticed. Although this story contained in embryo all the elements of his later books, and although the plot was most characteristic, it lacked a vital spark. The same was true of his second book [*The World Upside Down*]. With *A Swarm in May* it became apparent that a major novelist had arrived. *A Swarm in May* was, of all outmoded things, a boarding-school story, but there had never been a school-story quite like this. The setting was a cathedral choir-school, with its long history and ancient traditions. The hero was a very small boy but the story concerned the whole school, including the staff. It was a picture of a complex and fascinating society. The story was one of hidden treasure—another outworn theme—and the working-out entirely original and unexpected. Mayne's book, like all his subsequent books, was whole and indivisible; plot, setting, characters, writing, all contributed to the final effect; but the writing was the catalyst. Mayne's prose was a delicate, sensitive instrument, exactly suited to its purpose. The dialogue was exquisitely right, the description (which was never extraneous but always dedicated to forwarding the narrative) was spare and beautiful. Mayne's prose never slipped into poetry, but his eye was that of the poet; he saw the commonplaces of the world around him with the poet's (or the child's) clarity and freshness. Critics who begrudge a child the best in anything have claimed that Mayne is an adult novelist *manqué*. Certainly any of his books is worth the attention of the most exacting adult reader, but in the fine simplicity of his vision as much as in his profound understanding of the minds and instinct of children, he is essentially a children's writer.

Mayne is a prolific writer, and books followed at intervals of less than a year. Although the theme of a search for treasure was recurrent, each story was strikingly original. The scene ranged wide, from Canterbury Cathedral to Sedgemoor, from the Pennies to the Wiltshire downs. Places are important to Mayne. His stories grow inevitable out of their settings and their characters. He has a fine ear for dialect, and skill in reproducing it in acceptable form. He has become increasingly successful in portraying human relationships, whether simple—in the family atmosphere of *The Member for the Marsh*—or complex—in the situation between Patty and her stepmother in *Underground Alley*. In spite of his love of ancient traditions, he is essentially a contemporary writer. He belongs to the post-war world and understands the social phenomena which have developed since 1945. Understanding and a deep unsentimental affection for young people enrich his wise, subtle stories. (pp. 121-22)

> *Marcus Crouch, "Widening Horizons," in his* Treasure Seekers and Borrowers: Children's Books in Britain 1900-1960, *The Library Association, 1962, pp. 112-38.*

The Junior Bookshelf

Puffin books, with their high standard of selection, couldn't have found a better author than William Mayne for their newest venture—"Original Puffins"—for he is surely the most original and stimulating writer for children of our day. Here [in *A Parcel of Trees*] is the usual bounty of freshly observed scenes, emotions, conversations and characters, each indicated with the minimum of words and contrivance, the maximum of humour and

sympathy. The story is one of his most approachable and the problem is less elaborately worked out than some he has evolved. Susan at fourteen wants a place of privacy and finds that the old orchard just beyond the railway line might be hers if twelve years usage can be proved. There are three stories within the story, the tales of an oldest inhabitant, a betting man, and the boys who launched a series of rockets from the site. And always there is the background of Susan's family and the bakery they operate— her younger sister and the father who doesn't understand about people like her, and her mother, so quick with her answers—it is a sure thing Mr. Mayne will never have to kill parents off or send them on a cruise. Everyone else in the book is equally worth writing about and treated as an individual, not just a type, even when he appears for only a sentence or two; each is made instantly and completely *there*. As in real life some of the allusions and explanations are obscure at first but there is plenty to intrigue and please and it is all even better the second time round—and the third and fourth, for the Mayne books make some of the best re-reading ever written and always the wonder grows—how does he do it, all so deftly and astonishingly right without ever forcing the pace or being merely clever?

> *A review of "A Parcel of Trees," in* The Junior Bookshelf, *Vol. 27, No. 3, July, 1963, p. 156.*

John Ashlin

[*Words and Music*] is a sequel to the remarkable trilogy *A Swarm in May, Choristers' Cake,* and *Cathedral Wednesday. . . .* Has the magic been achieved yet again? No one is more conscious than William Mayne of the difficulty of maintaining the level of interest over a number of volumes and in *Cathedral Wednesday* he adopted the unusual and successful device of looking at the school through the eyes of a day-boy. Now we are back again as boarders and with the fabric of the cathedral playing a part in the story as it did in *A Swarm in May.* Readers must judge for themselves but I felt that he has once more met the challenge successfully, but one or two characters such as Trevithick are becoming more remote and vague—time they moved on to their public schools perhaps. The style is just as lucid, clear and clever, and a delight as usual; most of the characters drawn by the author show that he understands the workings of a prep schoolboy's mind as perhaps no one else does. (pp. 206-07)

> *John Ashlin, in a review of "Words and Music," in* The School Librarian and School Library Review, *Vol. 12, No. 2, July, 1964, pp. 206-07.*

Margery Fisher

Reviewers can very easily fall into a kind of literary accidia—'I've heard all this before'; but once in a while a book is published that makes you feel language and thought have been new-born. Such a book is *Earthfasts.* Here is much that is familiar in Mayne's books. Two boys, Grammar School in their conversational wit and in the tenderness of heart and thought never far below the surface. A superbly visualised Yorkshire dale with a few households (of a farmer, a doctor, a solicitor) skilfully depicted. An antiquarian mystery chosen for associations

(Arthurian, this time) which will be sensitively alive in very many readers. An evanescent humour, prosaic, used as Shakespeare uses it to lower tension but also to heighten awareness.

What is different in this book? First, most obviously, Mayne has moved into what, for the sake of categorising, I may call fantasy, deepening and enlarging the hints of other-worlds in *A Grass Rope*. David and Keith are involved with a natural phenomenon (a boggart accepted quite naturally by the farmer and his wife), and also with supernatural happenings. In 1742 a drummer boy had gone underground from the Castle to look for King Arthur and his knights in their legendary sleep. He emerges in 1942 bearing a candle from the Round Table and so breaking the age-old sleep and releasing into the world of David and Keith ancient warriors, giants (long changed to standing stones) and invisible beings. There is terror, danger, almost death, before the reconcilement when the candle (and time) are restored to the proper dimension.

William Mayne is a very literal writer. *Earthfasts* . . . opens with a description of earth opening as precise and matter of fact as if it were a description of a tree falling—neither more nor less probable and real. For everything outside reason there is a factual counterpart. The candle with its cold flame is tested by David with a boy's scrupulous earthly experiments. The links of mail worn by Arthur make the kind of sound you would expect chain mail to make, and, to Keith, 'they shone in places and were dull in others, as if the only cleaning they had had was the cleaning of use and no metal polish or duster had touched them.' The invisible boggart climbs on to David's knee and Mrs. Watson gives the boy a saucer of milk:

> David took the saucer and held it at knee level.
> There was movement, but no weight, at his knee,
> and the saucer emptied. Then, when every drop
> had gone, the saucer left his hand and cracked
> against Keith's head, and fell to the ground.
> Then David's lap was empty, and the farm cat
> was hurrying round the table looking over its
> shoulder.

All this has a steadying effect on the story and at the same time helps the imagination to accept its deeper events. These events are not, as in most fantasy, tied to a contest of good and evil. What is involved is Time—the dimension of time interfered with, the speed of time altered. It is perhaps to stress this that the author plans his story in widely spaced episodes, each one striking and terrible and each divided from the next by a recovery period when human clocks, as it were, take over.

Stylistically, the book is magnificent. The prose has at times an almost painful richness and at others Mayne uses a flat, abrupt tone of statement that seems new to him, to clinch something unbelievable that we have to believe in. 'The dead boar was taken to the police station, and a zoologist called, because boars have not been wild in this country for two centuries.' Again, when describing the candle, for instance, he uses words with Biblical intonations; and even the plain bridging paragraphs have a glow and rhythm more striking than anything he has written before. I have read *Earthfasts* twice already and it left me just as

startled and tingling the second time. If I had to make any guess at why it is so much grander and stronger than anything Mayne has done before, I would say that he seems more deeply committed than he has ever been before. The touch of Olympian detachment in his stories has disappeared: book and writer are entirely one. To suggest that he is wiser because older or that he is more prepared to let his characters disturb him emotionally is probably impertinence beyond a critic's licence. But I can think of no other way to emphasise the quality of this book. For many people it will be a landmark in the progress of children's literature. (pp. 769-70)

> *Margery Fisher, in a review of "Earthfasts," in* Growing Point, *Vol. 4, No. 2, July, 1965, pp. 769-70.*

Margery Fisher

Ruth and Shirley [in *No More School*] are at the top of the village school: Susan and Bill don't go yet; Fletcher, the farmer's son, seizes any excuse to stay away. Altogether, there are fourteen children who are at a loose end when Miss Oldroyd falls ill and the school is shut. After two or three days inaction drives most of the children to mischief, till Ruth decides, with the magnificent confidence of her temperament, to open the school again. Perhaps the curriculum is a little unorthodox, and the school dinners vary from a tolerable stew to a trifle made of grass and apple leaves, but the children learn what they can do, and Mayne teaches us once more to look at both sides of a word and hear its echoes as he places it unerringly in a sentence. The construction, detail and piercing rightness of his stories make most others seem halting by comparison.

> *Margery Fisher, in a review of "No More School," in* Growing Point, *Vol. 5, No. 4, October, 1966, pp. 546-47.*

Geoffrey Trease

You either surrender to Mayne's spell or impatiently don't. Myself, I admire so many of his talents singly—his poet's eye and ear, his word-magic, his evocation of atmosphere—but I cannot make the surrender, and feel sure that at no age could I have done so.

> *Geoffrey Trease, "Golden Age," in* New Statesman, *Vol. 72, No. 1861, November 11, 1966, p. 708.*

The Times Literary Supplement

Three new books this autumn bring the total of William Mayne's stories to twenty-eight in less than half that number of years. This journal was only mildly enthusiastic about the first two novels, *Follow the Footprints* and *The World Upside Down*, but the reviewer of *A Swarm in May* declared Mayne an "eccentric genius", and John Rowe Townsend, ten years later, wrote: "Quality and quantity have not often gone so formidably together."

After reading straight through a substantial selection of Mayne's output, the present reviewer would agree with these comments, yet cannot forget the exasperated words: DOWN WITH MAYNE, reported to have been seen on the blackboard of a particularly well-read class of eleven-year-olds. Their uncompromising frankness points the paradox. Mayne is a superb writer, probably the most original of children's authors writing today. Yet many children, and by no means insensitive or unbookish ones, do not like his writing. They find it difficult or boring. Are their views to be dismissed because grown-up critics find Mayne so enjoyable?

The question is apt, for his recent novel, *Earthfasts,* is claimed to be a new departure and at once one asks: in what direction? Will it take Mayne nearer his readers or farther from them? After two readings, one is obliged to say: the barriers are up. This is one of Mayne's most difficult books. It is his very virtues that make him hard reading. His refusal to use stock situations and stereotyped characters is part of his excellence. He can be intricate and, indeed, downright obscure, but he is incapable of being commonplace. To use Hugh's word, in *The Blue Boat,* Mayne is "disordinary". On the other hand, his intoxicated use of words, of puns and dialect, allusions and private jokes, can reach a point where they become a deterrent and thus some children will be debarred from the rewarding experience of reading Mayne, rewarding because the themes which obsess him have an enduring validity which will not disappear with childhood.

Earthfasts is a vehicle for two motifs which Mayne has explored with tenacity in most of his novels: the strength and depth of human relationships, and our awareness of the thin wall dividing what we are accustomed to call reality from the supernatural. Many of his plots, *Earthfasts* included, have been built around some kind of treasure-hunt, or unexpected discovery, and this may give a clue to Mayne's way of thought. At the beginning of the early novel, *The World Upside Down,* the author sets a short poem, presumably by himself, the last line of which reads:

> Are we on either side staring at what
> > we seek?

The novel is not one of his best, but the sentence is revealing. As Mayne knows, children have readier access to these worlds at which we stare, often uncomprehendingly. Rilke says something of this in one of the Duino Elegies:

> a child
> sometimes gets quietly lost there, to be
> > always
> jogged back again.

Mayne often shows this supernatural world suspended between the disbelief of the older characters and the acceptance of the younger.

> Nan did not know where the grass rope had been: down into Fairyland by one door and out again through another secretly: nobody knew but Mary.

Thus William Mayne in *A Grass Rope.* But in *Earthfasts* there is no younger child to catch the fabulous unicorn and persuade us to accept the magic. All are involved equally and men as sceptical as magistrates and constables and doctors are compelled to record what they cannot explain and acknowledge that "there are supernatural phenomena we don't know about".

While Mayne's attitude to "magic" has altered considerably, his treatment of human relationships has only changed in that it has become steadily more profound and convincing, reaching perfection, for this reviewer, in *Sand.* In spite of the fairly obvious middle-class milieu of *A Swarm in May* and its sequels, Mayne is a very classless author, and one is always made aware of his characters as people, whether it is a boy who cannot read, like John Much in *Pig in the Middle,* or Profound, the coloured bus-conductor in *The Twelve Dancers,* or the village boys of Bourne Bridge in *The Rolling Season.* His lack of emphasis on class mirrors the world of the young with far more truth than the self-conscious excursions into working-class life which now form quite a corner in children's books. Sharply characterized as individuals, Mayne's diverse characters achieve their unity through easy communication. Seldom has an author depicted so well, with such unerring sympathy, the friendships of young people, and the inter-relationships of grown-ups with children. Unsentimental, usually based on common interests, and enlivened with humour, they provide, after reading Mayne in depth, an extraordinarily hopeful picture of the way people can live together, and how much this state of affairs depends upon respect, tolerance and affection.

Mayne's characters are in tune with each other. Their remarks are like balls tossed from one to the other. This can be seen in very simple form in one of his best stories for younger children, *The Man from the North Pole:*

> "It'll be lessons at home", said Mother. "Come and do some arithmetic on the dinner. Divide by five."
>
> "And no remainder", said John.
>
> "I'll deal with the remainder", said Mother. "It's the washing up."

There is often a kind of mad inconsequence about the conversation, but this has become less noticeable in Mayne's later books, and has virtually disappeared in *Earthfasts.* It is in any case a less important hallmark of his style than his cunning technique of maintaining the thread of thought behind the words of the different speakers. In real life, this does exist between people who know each other well. Unfortunately it often makes conversation puzzling and esoteric to an outsider. Once absorbed by a Mayne story, a reader will come to relish his language and be eager for more, but there are some who will be put off at the start. There may be something to be said for reading the novels or at least parts of them aloud. The reading aloud of a story bridges the gap between the almost extinct art of story-telling and reading to oneself.

Mayne's respect for people is matched by his respect for words. He can put into direct and vivid, sometimes startling, imagery the whole gamut of the sensations. This is something that children do not find it easy to express, though, released through the medium of their own poetry, they often use words with unselfconscious daring. Mayne is economical, and often achieves his effect through a single word. Though not invariably—which might make it a mannerism—he often uses a metaphor of a particular kind, one which relates physical phenomena with human feelings, and this is such a feature of his style that it deserves a few examples.

In *A Swarm in May,* "Owen walked round the Cathedral on the gravel, passing the round east end and walking on the grass, because his feet made too insolent a noise on the path". Who but Mayne would have thought of that word "insolent"? In *Sand,* Ainsley's shirt, after a cold night, "was made of cold cloth and frozen buttons. . . . It had been starched with ice", and later, Alice sees, in the sand-swept garden, "a red polyanthus with sand in its throat". This is not a use of the pathetic fallacy, but something rather different, springing perhaps from Mayne's strong sense of the unity of the whole natural world of which man is a part.

It is odd that a writer who uses words with such precision can sometimes lapse into obscurity. This reviewer has on many occasions had to turn back and reread passages, puzzled at some lacuna or contradiction in time or place. There is often a disparity between Mayne's eye for detail, his capturing of feel, smell and sound, so uncanny in its accuracy that you exclaim: Of course, that's what it is like! and his muddled and inept treatment of practical things: the making of the raft, for instance, in *The Member for the Marsh.* No one wants Mayne to spell it all out syllable by syllable, but there is a point at which too much can be loaded upon a child reader, and he will simply give up because he cannot understand.

Earthfasts is marred by much obscure writing and a daunting array of dialect words, most of them unexplained. There is even a touch of arrogance, one feels, in the very title of it, for the "earthfasts" are only referred to briefly in the book as soil that moves in ploughed land. A search in reference books produces the information that "earthfasts" are in fact stones fixed in the earth. This is only one of the rare words in which the book abounds, few of them clear even in their context. They are fascinating and one is grateful for them in this age of verbal poverty, but their profusion and lack of explanation makes the reading an obstacle race that many will not survive.

This interesting and disturbing novel raises some hard questions in the mind of one reviewing it as a children's book. The supernatural events are very different from the mild magic of earlier novels. Now we are confronted with happenings which are unbelievable, yet true because they totally disrupt the lives of the characters. The treatment of friendship also is on a deeper level. Here we have no longer the friendly bickering of the group, with its in-talk and badinage, but a solid friendship between two mature boys, nearing the end of their schooldays.

Earthfasts, like several of its predecessors, is based on a local legend and is set in the familiar Dales district. A drummer boy, Nellie Jack John, emerges from the soil before the eyes of David and Keith. He has been on a treasure-hunt which has brought him abruptly into an age two hundred years beyond his own. And by his coming, and through the cold-flamed candle that he carries, the world is changed for the two boys. They have moved on from

childhood, when they stared at what they sought on either side, to find themselves facing "the threatening edge of the world, a wall that should not be looked at". It is David who insists on utilizing the cold flame to show him mysteries. He is a boyish Faust, playing with more dangerous elements than he knows, and he pays dearly for his aspiring mind, though to say more than this would spoil the dramatic climax.

Throughout, David attempts to reduce what is happening to a rational explanation. He cannot do it. All he can do in the end is to record the extraordinary events released from the past. Just as earth heaves up its earthfasts, so, it seems, does time, casting up something from the present into the future, from the past into the present. Such speculations have often been indulged in by children's writers but few have admitted fully the fear that such events would give rise to, and this is a very frightening book. It is also, on the human level, a moving one. The boys are two of the most likable characters Mayne has created. The tragic event which separates them inspires the author to this metaphysical statement:

> He [Keith] understood, now that his face was put against it, what David had known by instinct, that the lost places are in this world and belong to the people in it and are all that they have to call home.

This far from simple statement, which occurs two-thirds of the way through, is not threaded into the rest of the book or made explicit. Indeed, from this point on, the novel falls to pieces. The supernatural element becomes a congested tangle of events in which King Arthur's part is far from clear or even relevant. The tragic situation which dominated the climax is resolved by merely bringing back the status quo, a most unconvincing and unsatisfactory conclusion. If this is the new direction, it is not an altogether happy one, and one may begin to question whether Mayne is writing for children at all. If he is, it is not unreasonable to ask that he should be intelligible, verbally.

> *"William Mayne: Writer Disordinary," in* The Times Literary Supplement, *No. 3378, November 24, 1966, p. 1080.*

The Junior Bookshelf

[*Earthfasts*] is a book in a thousand; William Mayne at his very considerable best, and quite impossible to put down from start to finish.

David and Keith are drawn into an old legend about King Arthur, his Knights and his buried treasure when they witness Nellie Jack John, the drummer boy of the legend, emerging from a crack in the ground. They follow Nellie Jack John to try and save him from the worst shocks of a world 200 years later than his own. They are drawn closer into the legend, strange inexplicable happenings surround them and David is enthralled by the clear white light of an ever burning candle which the drummer boy carries until he himself is absorbed into the subterranean world of the legend where time is measured differently from the world above ground. The merging of reality and legend is a triumph of imaginative writing, no cheating wakings from dreams, but instead a frightening fight to regain the world as we know it.

A review of "Earthfasts," in The Junior Bookshelf, *Vol. 30, No. 6, December, 1966, p. 386.*

Margaret Meek

The pace of the plot of William Mayne's latest *tour de force* [**The Battlefield**] is slow and measured, country style. Spurred on by weird legends, Debby and Lesley, daughters of the innkeeper at the Battlefield spend their winter freedom exploring the rock, the lookout tower and the moor near their home. With the help of Thomas and his tractor they pull out a stone, which distresses Billy Calvert, who is building a new cross on the village green, and next a cannon, which upsets the shepherd who knows the legends. The climax is conceivable only because by the time it comes the girls have woven themselves into the readers' consciousness by the quaint acuteness of their speech, their 'cleverness' in the northern sense. The author exploits the way they experiment with language before reality encroaches on metaphor. The result is an exploration in depth of sense experience, almost Keatsian in its richness, laced with good humour and memorable characters. I smell that shepherd yet.

Margaret Meek, in a review of "The Battlefield," in The School Librarian and School Library Review, *Vol. 16, No. 1, March, 1968, p. 111.*

Ruth Hill Viguers

Mr. Mayne's settings are most often Yorkshire villages, his characters ordinary middle-class people—except that they are never really ordinary. To browse through a number of his books at the same time is to realize how many people he has brought to life in print and how complete an individual each one is. The children disagree, sometimes quarrel and weep, but the atmosphere that one remembers in his many stories is good humor. The relationships are affectionate and amusing, the dialogue full of quips and jokes and amiable insults. **Sand** is an especially good example of the individuality of characters, **The Battlefield** of the quick wit and the lively give and take in the conversations. The Yorkshire dialect sprinkled through the stories is less confusing to American children, I believe, than Mr. Mayne's tendency to make three words do the work of twenty. He has been called a "verbal magician" and his genius in finding the right word and his ability to tell a story almost entirely through dialogue are continually astonishing. The abundance of details packed into a few lines demands the most careful attention or the thread of meaning is lost. There is no racing through Mr. Mayne's books, and herein may lie the reason for the reluctance of some children to read them. (pp. 571-72)

Ruth Hill Viguers, "Experiences to Share," in A Critical History of Children's Literature by Cornelia *Meigs and others, edited by Cornelia Meigs, revised edition, Macmillan Publishing Company, 1969, pp. 567-600.*

Eleanor Cameron

William Mayne's **Earthfasts** . . . puts him triumphantly among that small group who have shown such an audacious and original grasp of the possibilities of time fantasy [and lures us into] another kind of magic. It is one which, rather miraculously for a fantasy, manages to absorb into itself and to interlace throughout the book, not only legend and folklore, but the kind of dry, witnessing, factual exchanges one would expect to hear at an ESP conference, as well as observations of the author's, through his own words and through the words and thoughts of his boy protagonists, very often phrased in the language of science. At times, indeed, one is almost inclined to say to oneself that this is not fantasy at all but the story of a psychic phenomenon in which the whole countryside has been caught up. And yet, in the end, when Keith enters the cave and beholds, as he replaces the Candle of Time in its stone socket on the Round Table, King Arthur and his knights change back to stalagmites, what is felt then, purely and simply, is a power brought into play by the supernatural.

Earthfasts is a wild, glimmering, shadowed, elusive kind of book which, like all of William Mayne's best, demands more than one reading. The past, the evocation of legend and folklore, haunt every page and from this evocation wells the magic that grips it. Earthfasts, to begin with, are humps or rises in plowed land, and out of one of these at "half past eight dusk of a day at the end of summer," a "higging" (confusing? cavilling?) time of day, two boys hear a throbbing in the earth which they think may be badgers, or possibly underground water, but which proves to be the drumming of a drummer boy of the time of Napoleon who had gone into a cave under Garebridge Castle to search for King Arthur's treasure. And when he emerges, beating his drum with one hand and in the other holding a candle that burns with a cold, spinning, indestructible flame, he sets loose all the ancient, sleeping forces of this corner of Old England: a boggart that had lain quiescent until this moment, giants that had stood in the form of the huge Jingle Stones up on Hare Trod but which now, at first imperceptibly, then more swiftly, begin to move and to leave dragging trails at their feet in the thick turf, some invisible, madly whirling force that causes havoc in the marketplace, and stone shapes that had remained frozen in underground darkness since the year of Arthur's death. (pp. 123-24)

The candle [which William Mayne's drummer boy carries with him out of the past into David Wix's and Keith Heseltine's present] is not only a concentrate of time-magic but is as well the moving force of the book, for it compels both boys to action and Keith to a comprehension which brings the story to its climax. Furthermore, its nature serves to reveal, through their reactions to it, the differing characters of the two boys: the essentially reasoning, inquiring, experimental nature of the brilliant David and the usually more subjectively biased, intuitive nature of Keith. (p. 126)

Yet William Mayne is far too much of an artist to see David as purely and simply "the scientific type," devoted only to facts and to logic, for it is David who says that "Science doesn't know everything" and rebukes Keith for thinking it will be interesting to see what the drummer boy will do when he beholds strange and unfamiliar things, saying that it would be cruel to experiment with him. David combines in himself clarity of intellect with compassion; he is, in many ways, more adult than Keith, more spiritually courageous; in the beginning he has qualities which Keith has yet to realize, and it is the candle which brings Keith to a more mature stage of himself.

Keith's reaction to the candle, upon first discovering that it gives out a cold flame which the wind does not affect, that it casts no light and that its two inches have been not in the least consumed while it lay steadily burning overnight in the drenched grass, is to fling it down in disgust "as if it had been a maggot that suddenly wriggled between his fingers." But David, observing that not only does the candle cast no light but that (like Time) nothing affects it, nothing can change it, and that it is perfectly self-contained and enduring, takes it home and says nothing more about it. But there he studies it, tests it, and persists in looking into the heart of its unearthly fire, until what he sees brings him to extinction as far as the world of the present is concerned. Meanwhile, the revelations gained from his "seeing" have presented him with precisely that view of Time (though possibly he does not realize this) which formerly he had rejected when Keith expressed it. . . .

Time is a globe now for David instead of the line going straight into a wall.

He comes to understand as well, because of the candle, something beyond logic about Time and the Jingle Stones. The fearful dragging trails which the moving stones left in the turf have vanished into the vastness of the moors, and Keith and David one night see the shapes of giants walking far off on the black skyline against the lingering light of evening and know at last, because the candle has been brought from King Arthur's table, what the Jingle Stones have become.

> "I'm thinking," [David] said, "I'm thinking what I would have done if I was a Jingle Stone. It's not logic in the ordinary way. . . . I can see with the eyes of a stone, and think with its thoughts, and feel with its layers and strata, and I just stand whilst the world rushes by like a wind. I think the wind is time. And then time stops and I can get out of where I'm standing, and I'm a person again. . . . It's an understanding I've got," he said. "I understand it from looking into the flame. I know what it is. I know."

And after David vanishes, and Keith takes the candle and begins learning from the flame, he too sees the Jingle Stones and what they have become as expressing something about Time that he needs to know, which leads him to what he must do. (pp. 127-29)

A mingling of poetic and scientific insights is continual throughout *Earthfasts.* Again and again they are set in juxtaposition, each intensifying the other, setting off the other, as David and Keith by their differences, which are never pure differences, reveal and enhance, bring out aspects of one another. The mood of shadowed, portentous magic, of fatefulness, of inexplicable movements in half darkness (reminding one, in a way, of Ingmar Bergman's film of medieval life, *The Seventh Seal*) is constantly striated by objective observations having to do with cause and effect, while words relating to experiments in physics or chemistry are found in paragraphs of feeling, of intimation, of seventh sense.

Keith, having begun to look into the heart of the candle flame, is aware of "shadows with him during the day, as if there were strange atomic assemblies behind doors and blackboards, things just hidden behind settees and busses, more people present than the room really held." He explains these shadows to himself as "phantoms from his own eyes. . . . They were all tinged with green, and that must be the reflexes of the candle flame, like the colour that stains a white wall after looking at a coloured object, the complementary of what has been seen." The candle flame itself he thinks of as "a spindly molecule."

Having gained a certain knowledge from the flame which brings him into the presence of what had snatched David from his own time, he is aware that "something moved away very rapidly. It was not so much a going away as a re-ordering of the darkness. There was nothing to see, it was more like an invisible and inaudible precipitation or crystallization in some compound. The resistance went from the night, and he could move, but there was the feeling that there had been a chemical change in the darkness." (pp. 129-30)

The extraordinary uniqueness of William Mayne's conception of simultaneous existences in two different times is nowhere more evident than in his description, through Keith's thoughts, of King Arthur's army waiting outside the boy's window. Keith and that army have not yet arrived at the point where they will stand together in one time, and though the men and their horses seem quite real, he sees them as "set, somehow, against the grain of the world, so that Keith himself felt slightly as if he were leaning." It is as though those men in chain mail were obeying the laws of a different field of force; it is what you feel in those incomprehensible fun houses built over magnetic centers where you struggle over a flat floor as up the steepest mountain, or where "a marble runs up the sloping floor and then up the wall and out of the window." He saw the army "as if they were held, like iron filings, and prickly like them too, against a different force from the one that held Keith to the house and to the floor of the world." A moment later, though there is no opening to another time that Keith is aware of—"only the brightening sky and the frosty earth and yonder hill fringed with giants," and "Excalibur with the dull green back and the sharp bronze edge that held light from everywhere, from star and morning and candle"—Keith and the King are no longer obeying the laws of different force fields, existing at different angles, but are standing on the same plane; they have come to their meeting place. "And the King had his sword."

It is the visualization of an idea which the mind and the imagination can play over with the greatest pleasure because of its strangeness and potency; they can go back to it in wonder as they do to Nellie Jack John, the drummer boy, straining toward Keith and David with his hair streaming out behind him and his clothes pressed against his body, but moving at a snail's pace because he is running against the grain of Time instead of with it. (pp. 130-31)

> *Eleanor Cameron, "Fantasy," in her* The Green and Burning Tree: On the Writing and Enjoyment of Children's Books, *Atlantic-Little, Brown, 1969, pp. 3-136.*

The Times Literary Supplement

The special features of Mr. William Mayne's enthralling talent sometimes distract attention from those features of it which link him with the most famous and gifted children's authors of the past. There is, for example, the way in which the outline structure of his plots—triumphantly disguised with a daunting ingenuity—is fundamentally uncomplicated and traditional at heart. There is the repeated use of the convention of tireless daring and resourcefulness in children, often used to outwit (though gently) the intentions of their undiscerning elders; the originality of the means and the deep understanding of relationships between generations serve to mask it. And least noticeable of all, perhaps, is a pervading moral emphasis—worked out through detail and by means of implication rather than proffered by generalization and stark obviousness.

This last feature appears in *Ravensgill* in its usual painstakingly subtle form. Mr. Mayne's greatest gift is his ability to inhabit the moment-to-moment consciousness of the young, remember and understand their confusions, register in an elegantly precise prose narrative and dialogue their partial and yet illuminating sense of the world of objects and people, and enter into their games of perception. It follows, but almost imperceptibly, that the most sensitive are the most virtuous and that the reward of virtue—almost invariably allied, inseparably, with moral strengths like courage and persistence—is triumph. But one notable mark of his originality is that the process of winning is frequently a process also of achieving understanding. The two main child characters in his new novel work away at the mystery which grips and bewilders them, until they solve it in a way which yields a moving comprehension of adult values, rituals and obsessions.

Bob and Judith are young adolescents living on two Yorkshire moor farms, separated by some miles of intractable terrain and by an inexplicable family hostility which has kept their very cousinhood secret all their lives. Forty-six years before, a man in one family died, in circumstances suggesting murder. Someone in the other family was responsible, but what was the motive? And what were the dark personal facts which rendered it necessary to hush it up for half a century? Bob is resourceful and Judith thoughtfully persistent in teasing out the problem. Bob's Grandma, lovably (not *too* lovably) slatternly and flamboyant, will not let on; she burns the mysterious letter from Judith's Gran which brings the news that the pestering constable who suspected her for years of harbouring the murderer has at last died. The lad unintentionally hits upon a secret tunnel (the bare bones of the outline structure show through here), confronts Judith with his suspicions, researches through old newspapers and struggles through to some fragments of the truth. Judith's and his separate efforts combine, with just a little contrived coinci-

dence, to effect a reconciliation of the two families and the clearing of a dead man's name. The book ends with a risky but moving and credible, "burial of Grandma's innocent husband when a prepared memorial stone is ritually set above the place where his bones were found. Underneath, but far underneath, the surface, the elements are traditional and familiar. But the skill with which they are re-shuffled and re-interpreted makes *Ravensgill* a solidly original achievement, even if it does not represent Mr. Mayne at his arresting and alarming best.

As always, his sense of setting and his perception of the interrelation of people and places are remarkable. The action of *Ravensgill* happens against the background of a rural community that is essentially modern but which functions at a leisured pace, in time with the seasons and the subtlest movements of the weather. From the farms the children go down to a mixed comprehensive school from which changing habits and fashions of thinking will spread up the dales—the values of old and young are set beautifully and discerningly at odds. No one senses and portrays these shifts and changes more accurately than Mr. Mayne. No one now writes with more knowledge of, and compassion for, people in all their roles. And no one contributes more through sheer sensitivity and virtuosity of style and treatment to our increasing realization of children's fiction as an art in its own right.

> *"Yorkshire Family Quarrel," in* The Times Literary Supplement, *No. 3566, July 2, 1970, p. 713.*

Leon Garfield

William Mayne's *Ravensgill* has already been praised highly elsewhere; but that is no reason for not praising it again. It is, I feel, his most considerable book for some time. In addition to the usual brilliance of his writing, there is a chilling depth that lends the story a rare excitement. Little by little a long-forgotten crime is brought to the surface—both literally and metaphorically—and the weird grandmother who stands at the plot's centre becomes a shifting, fascinating character exhibited in the dimension of time. There are many memorable passages in the book, but one in particular stands out. Apparently unrelated to the movement of the plot, yet providing a necessary emotional balance, there is an episode describing a game of French cricket that is pure magic. (p. 608)

> *Leon Garfield, "Labels and Categories," in* New Statesman, *Vol. 80, No. 2068, November 6, 1970, pp. 608, 610.*

Pat Smyth

With this new story [*Royal Harry*], the adult reader finds his attention gripped with the same intensity as that of any child. This is an ideal situation for a genuine sharing of its experience.

What are the qualities of the book that contribute to its peculiarly universal character? The magical appeal of the core of the tale demonstrates ancient fealties and gives us hints of treasure to be discovered and a throne to be regained. The reader is refreshed by his journey deeper into the past and closer into the wild countryside untouched by urban and industrial development; but he is not allowed to make his 'escape'. All the happenings of the story are firmly embedded in the reality of human existence, the same then as now, and the same in childhood as when we are grown up. Harriet, the heroine, values her strange and exciting encounters mostly for the opportunities they afford her for being secret and private. When her world is invaded or things become too public she is at best embarrassed and at worst rather cross. Her desire for secrecy is the separateness that each of us needs in order to emerge as a person. And as we are only persons in our relationships with others so Harriet is seen as a member of her fascinating family. Dad, lovable and loving, has 'never settled'. He finds in his daughter's inheritance of the Archdale house a timely opportunity to avoid paying another week's rent on their old home. He is more than tolerated by Harriet's mother, good-hearted and businesslike who, in the midst of all the mysteries, settles down to scrubbing and dusting. Even the shadowy French intruders have some very work-a-day mishaps, and the extraordinary Old Mole and Missus who live inside the mountain conduct their lives in terms of real hardship.

Much has been said in praise of William Mayne's dialogue. The conversations in this book have many of the characteristics of the give and take of the best kind of improvised drama. They distil the quality of the relationships, and delight us by their dryness and wit. Much too could be said of the incidental details that enrich the fabric of the story's reality.

'Have you read *Royal Harry?* '. The question from teacher to pupil will indeed be the same question he will ask his friends. They will relish it together. (pp. 262, 265)

> *Pat Smyth, in a review of "Royal Harry," in* The School Librarian, *Vol. 19, No. 3, September, 1971, pp. 262, 265.*

Natalie Babbitt

William Mayne's prose style has a club foot. For the first few pages of [*A Game of Dark*], the phraseology seems awkward, ill-assorted and confusing: "Donald resisted slightly, and Nessing let him walk straight ahead, and Donald let him lead now." And then very subtly Mayne's unique rhythms begin to assert themselves. The reader finds he has fallen into step with them and is no longer parsing sentences to get at their meaning. The gracelessness has become a kind of power instead, a power well suited to such a strange tale as this.

Donald Jackson is a 14-year-old boy who lives, in his English town, a life that is utterly bleak. His mother is humorless and withdrawn, his father an engrossed paralytic, and both, when they speak at all, are given to sermonizing. . . . Donald realizes that he neither loves nor pities his father, and because of this and his own rejection of his family's religious (Methodist) views, he is lost in guilt, shame and confusion. The escape he takes is backward in time into the feudal period and here he acts out a role so laden with symbolism that it must be examined very gently.

In the first place, it seems clear that this is no "Connecti-

cut Yankee" fantasy adventure but rather a variety of schizophrenia. Donald slips effortlessly in and out of his imagined world, and embodies there the emotional chaos of his real life in physical forms which he can touch, cope with and understand. He becomes page, then squire, then knight to a feudal lord in a town menaced by a gigantic and voracious worm which eats whatever it can find, including people. In fighting the worm by the rules of honorable combat, the lord is killed and Donald, called only Jackson in this shadow life, becomes lord in his stead. He tries to fight the worm by the rules himself, sees that this means defeat and death, and runs away, returning later to slay it in the only possible way—through guile. By violating the code, he knows he has made himself an outcast, but still his method has been successful and he is still alive. Returning to reality, he discovers that he can now love his father, but his father dies immediately of a fever and Donald "lay and listened to the quiet, and went to sleep, consolate."

What is to be made of this? The worm is unmistakably and grossly phallic, and its killing insistently reminiscent of Zeus's castration of his father, Cronus. On the other hand, the lord whom Jackson serves may be a symbolic Lord of Heaven sacrificed senselessly to the blindness of Christian ethics so that Jackson, in killing the worm dishonorably, is severing his own ties with his parents' loveless piety, thereby setting himself free to love purely outside any prescribed code.

Probably Mayne intends both of these interpretations, though the Zeus-Cronus side is the stronger. I can think of no other reason why Donald, freed, should be "consolate" at his father's death unless the author intends us to understand that the father, castrated, is no longer a threat and can be loved without fear and lost without remorse.

Mayne is relentlessly, gloriously graphic in his descriptions of the horrors of the worm and pitiless in his exposure of the people in Donald's real life. There is no shred of warmth in a single word of the novel—only alienation and the all-pervasive bleakness—but it holds the attention completely nevertheless. However, it will take an extremely unusual young person to pluck from this story anything but the genuine color and suspense of the worm episodes and the surface tensions of Donald's relationship with his father. Like much of modern poetry, the rest is so personal, fragile and involuted that more patience is required to understand it than perhaps it merits.

> *Natalie Babbitt, in a review of "A Game of Dark," in* The New York Times Book Review, *October 10, 1971, p. 8.*

John Rowe Townsend

Next to that of Enid Blyton, the name of William Mayne is probably the one most likely to start an argument about children's books. It is much the same argument, though approached from opposite ends. Enid Blyton's books are popular with great numbers of children, but deeply disliked by adults who care about books. William Mayne appeals strongly to adults with an interest in children's books, but frequently fails to arouse a response in children, even highly intelligent ones! 'A marvellous children's writer for grown-ups,' I have heard it said of him, 'but is he such a marvellous children's writer for children?'

I do not myself see how it can be held against a writer that his work is a minority taste. It may affect his pocket, or his publisher's pocket, or the number of copies of his books that a library needs to order, but it does not diminish the merit of the books themselves. This is one of the points at which our frequent confusion of standards can be seen. And even if I make the deliberate switch from 'what the book is' to 'what the book can do for the child', I can find no method of weighing a superficial pleasure given to many thousands against a deep personal experience which may come only to a few. My own conviction is that if a book opens windows in the imagination of only one child, it has justified its existence.

William Mayne has never made any concessions to the lazy or inattentive reader; he has never written the fully-automated book. In any case, we cannot all like the same things, and even among books of comparable merit there must always be some that strike a more popular note than others. Nevertheless, the impression of Mayne as a writer of somewhat rarefied excellence—one who operates at a high literary altitude where the air is thin—still persists, and may have some justification. Re-reading many of his novels in a short time—after having previously read and admired them individually at the time of publication—I am inclined to feel that Mayne as a writer has a characteristic which deprives his work of a substantial and vital element.

This, I think, is a tendency to shy away from the passions. Children feel strong emotion and can be deeply conscious of strong emotion in others, even when it is not understood. Life without it is less than the whole of life. Mayne is aware of the passions, most notably so in *Ravensgill*, but even there he appears to define deep feeling by drawing round its edges rather than plunging in. One senses in *Ravensgill* that the air is full of old guilt and fear, grievance and feud and loss; but one is never there in the middle, experiencing these things. Pity and terror are rare in Mayne's books; the expression of love, in any of its many forms, is to the best of my recollection absent. To say this is not to make an adverse criticism of any book. *Ravensgill* seems to me exceptionally fine, and I do not suggest that the author could or should have written it differently. But there is a limitation here. I suspect that it is a lack of robustness and of red corpuscle in Mayne's work which often causes it to make a less satisfying impact than that of writers who are more crude in their perceptions and far less gifted artistically.

There is no lack of evidence on which Mayne's progress can be judged. For a 'quality' writer he is remarkably prolific. Between 1953 and 1970 he published some forty books: an average of more than two a year. He started young and shows every sign of reaching his century. His first book, *Follow the Footprints,* published when he was only twenty-five, is in many ways characteristic, and could not be mistaken for the work of anyone else. It is an elaborate treasure-hunt in which a mystery from the past is solved and reputedly supernatural phenomena turn out to have a rational, though highly complicated, explanation.

This is not yet vintage Mayne—he has done the same thing in several later books and done it better. But it is full of typical Mayne dialogue: oblique, elliptical, or going off at curious tangents. (pp. 130-32)

I did not read *Follow the Footprints* when it first came out, so I cannot say how it seemed when Mayne was new and when the number of good current children's books was much smaller. I do, however, recall the first appearance of *A Swarm in May,* which seemed then, and seems now, an outstanding piece of work. In this novel, set in a cathedral choir school based on the one he had attended as a boy, Mayne created or re-created a closed, complete and satisfying world, in which a large cast of characters was clearly distinguished, and in which a story was clearly told and a mystery satisfyingly solved. And behind these individuals, behind the daily life of school and the puzzle from the past, emerging out of the mist to dwarf them all, was the cathedral itself. Indeed, the cathedral seemed in the end to become the frame of the story: a frame filled with cathedral space, a space filled with cathedral music, with the choir's singing and Dr Sunderland's organ-playing. It is hard to fault *A Swarm in May.* Within its limits—and in this case I believe the limits were a source of strength—it is as near to perfection as any children's book of its decade. Even *Tom's Midnight Garden* is of no greater formal excellence, although it has a depth which *A Swarm in May* lacks. But then, the latter was a young man's book; indeed, it gives the impression that it might have been written by a marvellously talented schoolboy, a literary Mozart.

In the books which followed, Mayne seemed to be elegantly treading water. Individually his books were of obvious distinction and were duly acclaimed, but, collectively, they began to add up to a disappointment. Three more choir-school books—*Choristers' Cake, Cathedral Wednesday* and *Words and Music*—followed *A Swarm in May* and added very little to the original achievement. There were more treasure-hunts, too. *A Grass Rope* won the Carnegie Medal which to my mind should have gone to *A Swarm in May.* I do not think it is Mayne at his very best, though there is excellence in its evocation of that Yorkshire dalescape which is Mayne's own and in which several later books have been set. With *The Thumbstick, The Rolling Season* and *The Twelve Dancers* the treasure-hunting element became ever more convoluted, and the last of these books is more an ingenious puzzle than a story.

In 1964 and 1965 a change of direction came with *Sand* and *Pig in the Middle.* These were about the everyday lives of boys and young adolescents, doing quite ordinary things with no elaborate mysteries to be solved. The setting of *Sand*—a Yorkshire coast town that is being slowly suffocated by sand-dunes—is splendidly drawn; sand can almost be felt on the reader's eyeballs; and there is a memorable relationship between the hero and the elder sister who refers to him with distaste in the third person:' "Look at him laying the jam on," said Alice. "Doesn't it disgust you, Mother?"' Here too—a new departure for Mayne— we have a group of boys who are desperately keen to get to know some girls, though they don't quite know how to set about it. *Sand* comes close to being a very good story, but is marred to my mind by a seemingly-endless account of an attempt by the boys to excavate the tracks of an old narrow-gauge railway. Their persistence in this pointless task is entirely convincing, but the description of it comes to share its own pointlessness; and although the excavation leads to the pleasing climax in which the boys dump a huge, supposedly-prehistoric skeleton in the girls' school yard by way of getting acquainted, it takes a long and weary time to reach this point. I have heard praise of *Pig in the Middle,* a story about boys in an inner-city district who try to rehabilitate an old barge; but it seems to me that Mayne is not at home in this setting, and its greyness has communicated itself to the book.

At this stage, with the new writers of the 1960s becoming prominent, it seemed that Mayne was almost becoming a back number. But in 1966 he published *Earthfasts:* an extraordinarily fine book in which at last he surpassed his early work. I believe that in *Earthfasts* there is an element of response to the novels of Alan Garner. At last Mayne makes use of the supernatural, which previously he seemed to have avoided, and he uses it superbly. In Garner's manner he brings the fantasy-world into the here-and-now; and to make it more credible he has as his main characters two modern, scientifically-minded schoolboys who look for rational explanations of everything. When *they* are convinced that the impossible has happened, we are all convinced.

On a Yorkshire hillside one evening, David and Keith see a stirring in the turf and hear a drumming; there's movement as if someone was getting out of bed, there's light, 'increasing light, pure and mild and bleak,' and out of the hillside marches a drummer-boy, who'd marched into it in 1742 and hadn't been heard of since. He carries a candle that burns with a cold, white, unchanging flame, and he has been searching for the supposed burial-place of King Arthur and his knights. The drummer is a matter-of-fact Yorkshire lad, and he marches off to look for the cottage where he used to live—which is still there—and the girl he left behind him—who is not. When the boys convince him of his situation he doesn't make too much fuss but marches back into the hillside.

The drummer-boy's appearance resulted from something like a geological fault in time. Over the next few weeks there are strange phenomena: huge footprints appear, a wild boar roams the streets, prehistoric stones move from their places—but are they stones or giants? Strangest yet, David, by looking into that cold candlelight, acquires some kind of second sight, more a danger than a gift; and one day he vanishes from the earth—struck, people think, by lightning. From here the story, like some swift, intricate dance, swirls eye-defeatingly faster and faster until the moment when Keith, replacing the cold-flamed candle in the centre of a round table in an underground cavern, stops everything, turns moving figures into stalactite and stalagmite, and seals up the fault in time.

The sheer sweep of *Earthfasts,* swift and wide and totally under control, has never been matched by Mayne. It has its flaws at the level of simple surface probability—surely

two boys finding themselves in possession of an ever-burning cold candle would have taken it straight to be analysed—but it marks a breakthrough, and it remains, in 1970, its author's best book. It also seems to have begun a new lease of artistic life. In 1968 Mayne took up another time theme, but played it the other way round, with his present-day characters journeying into the past. This was *Over the Hills and Far Away,* in which Dolly and Andrew and Sara, pony-trekking on a visit to their Gran, find themselves switched into post-Roman Britain, into a tale of old unhappy far-off things that they can't understand or even really believe in. And Sara, who has flaming red hair, is looked on by the tribesmen among whom she finds herself as a witch, a saviour, a sacrifice. *Over the Hills and Far Away* is notable for an outstandingly clear, almost transparent, style of writing, and for the effective contrast between the fluid, dreamlike nature of the action and the enduring solidity of the Yorkshire landscape through which it moves. *Ravensgill* is set, yet again, in the Yorkshire dales, and at first sight has a resemblance to Mayne's work of the *Grass Rope* period, a dozen years earlier. Here are families on two farms, estranged by an unsolved crime of half a century ago. Here is an elaborate and ingenious solution to the mystery. But there is a sombre note in *Ravensgill* which is new to Mayne; and the dominant character, Grandma, the impetuous girl who lost her man long years ago and has grown into a foolish, pathetic, but spirited old woman is one that I would once have thought outside his range.

William Mayne is a writer with striking strengths and weaknesses. He has a genuinely distinguished, if sometimes unduly whimsical, mind. He writes superbly. He can evoke a landscape, a time of day or year, a kind of weather, the feeling of the way things are, as in *Sand:*

> The shirt was made of cold cloth and frozen buttons. It lay on Ainsley's bed like a drift of snow. The cold spring wind blew the curtains and moaned under the door. Ainsley stroked the shirt. It had been starched with ice.

He has an unfailing gift for the precise and vivid simile:

> Her heart banged in her like a wildcat in a sack.

> The flame perched on the wick like a bright bird.

These examples are both from *Over the Hills and Far Away.* Occasionally he can lapse into archness, however, as in *Ravensgill:*

> It was Sunday sunshine, that seems to be as hot as any other, but is not doing any work with its heat, because of the day.

He has a fine imagination, and a gift for story construction and narration when he cares to use it, which is not always. If he feels so disposed he will turn aside from his story to chase images like butterflies, snatching significant and insignificant detail alike from the air. He will allow the action of a story to mount towards climax and then, casually and disappointingly, let it down. His plot structure may sag in the middle, as in *Sand;* and he seems unworried by disconcerting shifts of viewpoint, as in *Over the Hills,* which has a complete change of cast after the first fifty pages.

He is a notable writer of dialogue, and, like many who excel in this field, appears to have a gift of mimicry. In *The Twelve Dancers* almost all the characters are Welsh, and although not a word of Welsh is spoken, their English is Welsh English. His ear is unfailing and one hardly needs to be told that he is a musical man. He knows how things are done, and can tell you; he seems to have an instinctive understanding of all trades, their gear and tackle and trim. But his books are not notable for their characters. Between Dr Sunderland, the rumbling-voiced choirmaster of *A Swarm in May,* and Grandma in *Ravensgill* fifteen years later, I find that few Mayne characters spring unbidden to mind. On looking through the books, one finds many who are well drawn, and hardly one who fails to ring true, but few who come vigorously off the page with a life of their own.

Mayne has written that 'the best part of a book is the plot . . . I don't bother with the characters until I have begun'. To my mind this is a weakness. There are only a few basic plots, and they have all been used again and again. Character is infinite, and, for my money, characters make novels. But, on the whole, Mayne children mostly resemble other Mayne children. Of the numerous mothers and fathers, the only one who stays firmly in my memory is Marlene's sharp, narrow, down-to-earth mother in *The Twelve Dancers,* who sends three-year-old small brother Porky to school to get him out of the way, but grouses at having to pay dinner-money: 'He can't eat a shilling a day if he tried.'

The reluctance, noted earlier, to become involved with any depth of feeling may have something to do with Mayne's relative failure in the area of characterization. Often one feels that the emotional life of his characters is weak or is simply left blank, and they are correspondingly enfeebled.

Interestingly, William Mayne's books for younger children about everyday life are among the best in that rather barren genre. A pleasure in fantasy can be shared by writer, parent and quite small child; but most authors seem to find that the restricted range of a child's experience makes it difficult to tell a worthwhile story for the younger age-groups about actual life. *No More School,* which tells how Ruth and Shirley keep the village school unofficially open while the teacher Miss Oldroyd is ill, is a small gem of a story, for all that there is nothing in it beyond the understanding of a child of eight or nine. *The Fishing Party,* in which a class of children is taken to catch crayfish and cook them on the spot, is simple, unaffected, and totally absorbing, whatever the reader's age. *The Toffee Join* is a story about three sets of cousins and the contributions they take to the sweetmaking of their joint Granny. It is perfectly on the level of a very small child, and it is perfectly and properly serious.

Mayne's special quality as a writer for young children is that he never sees things with the used adult eye, or fails to see them because of the preoccupied adult mind. Everything is experienced afresh. He notes exactly the things that children do but adults have forgotten. . . . (pp. 132-38)

There is never any condescension, and nothing is dull or commonplace about the small details of daily life as seen by William Mayne.

His principal work, nevertheless, consists of his numerous novels for older children. They are for the most part individual, original, enjoyable, admirable. Their flavour is unlike that of anything else. Some of the recent books have shown the author reaching out towards new achievement: *Earthfasts, Over the Hills and Far Away* and *Ravensgill,* especially, show signs of a maturity as a writer which had been long delayed after early brilliance. In spite of having written forty books, Mayne still has plenty of time on his side, and there is every reason to suppose he will go on filling out as a writer. In 1955 one felt of the author of *A Swarm in May* that he might do anything. In 1970 one feels much the same about the author of *Ravensgill.* (p. 138)

> *John Rowe Townsend, "William Mayne," in his* A Sense of Story: Essays on Contemporary Writers for Children, *J. B. Lippincott Company, 1971, pp. 130-42.*

Robert Bell

It is almost becoming a *cliché* with reviewers to say that William Mayne's latest book is 'his most powerful to date,' but really one cannot avoid saying it of this one [*A Game of Dark*]. How he is able to go on giving us books which evoke ever higher and higher praise is nothing short of astounding. Donald Jackson, the central character in this story, can remember when his father had been a normal, attentive and amusing parent, but a railway accident has left him crippled emotionally as well as physically, and he has become a petulant and intolerant stranger. Donald's mother teaches in order to keep the home going, and this leaves her little time to give the boy the attention and understanding he needs, and inevitably stresses build up. He finds an escape by retreating into a fantasy world of medieval adventure and knight-errantry, where the town in which he lives is terrorized by a monstrous and loathsome 'worm,' which has killed every knight who has challenged it. Donald himself manages to despatch it, but only by hiding in its lair and giving it no chance to fight. This is regarded as a breach of knightly conduct and he is banished from the town. The way the action slips from one world to the other and back again, and the subtle interaction between fantasy and reality, make the story totally absorbing. The dream world, although an escape, is no cosy, fairy-tale, place, where everything comes right, but from the grimness and horror, and even his own 'honour rooted in dishonour', Donald derives a strange strength and consolation when his father dies. This is a most profound and moving book which stays long in the mind. (pp. 63-4)

> *Robert Bell, in a review of "A Game of Dark," in* The School Librarian, *Vol. 20, No. 1, March, 1972, pp. 63-4.*

Margaret Meek

The day you start work is the initiation ritual. For Mason

Ross [in *The Incline*] it means more than 'going to business' at the bank; it includes passing to the men's side and seeing the world of the quarry, where until now his father seemed unchallenged, as a microcosm of human insecurity and his father no stronger than others. Then there is Moira, the quarry owner's daughter, and Lizzy in the bakery, who scatter his feelings, unpredictably. The network of adult concern is focused on the Incline, where the quarry waggons pass up and down.

Although we now know how to become enmeshed in Mayne's characters despite the external simplicity of the situation, we can never capture in a short account enough of the complexity of feeling he portrays. This book is more direct than *A Game of Dark,* as if the author were offering us a tale of rural Yorkshire in the early days of this century, but its linear plot is no less subtle than those of the other recent books, and draws the reader into as many contrapuntal moves as any adult novel. Mason's reactions are finely gauged, perhaps more so than the girls who are the source of them. Whereas the mothers are credibly drawn with a few deft strokes, the girls are observed more from the outside. The dialogue is sheerly poetic, yet as tense as steel, a thing of great beauty and wonder.

This is a book to make adolescents pause, if only because it brings boys' matters close to the reader in a way that no adult novel can do so directly any more. For this reason alone Mayne is in a class by himself. (pp. 259-60)

> *Margaret Meek, in a review of "The Incline," in* The School Librarian, *Vol. 20, No. 3, September, 1972, pp. 259-60.*

Joan Aiken

When writing for children it is important to be absolutely sure of your own meanings and intentions and to take the utmost pains to convey these to the reader. For a child, reading something he has not read before can be very nearly equivalent to having the experience itself for the first time; it should be presented with integrity; it should not be cursory or makeshift. William Mayne is marvellous at this; his characters speak in the voices of real people. If he describes sand blowing along a street, you feel that he has just come in from going out to look at it before he chose his words. (p. 18)

> *Joan Aiken, "Dialect and Colloquial Language in Children's Books," in* Children's literature in education, *No. 9, November, 1972, pp. 7-23.*

Helen Stubbs

William Mayne was given the Carnegie Award for *A Grass Rope* in 1957. Over the previous five years he had made increasingly, indelibly his distinct and unique contribution to children's literature. How did he do this?

In *The Unreluctant years,* Lillian H. Smith says "that a new book's claim to stand beside a well-loved favourite rests in the degree to which it possesses the magic of a Lewis Carroll or a Stevenson or a Mark Twain."

With what infinite certainty do we realize in Mayne's books that children do things 'with blitheness,' are end-lessly searching for lasting truth, and in the process, reveal to us the heart of the matter. "The eager, reaching, elusive spirit of childhood is here. It has its own far horizons and a friendly and familiar acquaintance with miracle." It is because of this quality, which is innate in the books of William Mayne, that we cannot fail to recognize his universality, his disarming truth, his power to re-create for us the essence of the heart of a child, by the strength of his expression and insight into the ways they think and act. This power makes us all renew within ourselves, if for a short time only, the inexpressible things of that rare and fleeting receptive time that was our own childhood.

In his studies of children, he is able to express for us their essential thought-workings, projected as they are, from imaginative conception into real adventure. The children think things out before us and act in accordance with intensity and feeling. Everything is real to them and has meaning. Because we can read about ideas as they are being crystalized into action for us through the eagerness of vision that only a child can have, we too are able to draw on inner capacities and can give ourselves, the readers, a rare treat. We are able to feel safe again in a world which is true, where there are no conventions, and no delusions. They rediscover for us a kind of symbol of the eternal, and the intensity of our pleasure in being able to recapture it is real indeed.

If we wonder with C. S. Lewis whether the 'excitement' in a story may not be an element actually hostile to the deeper imagination, we shall wonder again with William Mayne, when we find ourselves accepting with shivers and delight, the range of ideas which are embodied in his tales. We find the secret to our pleasures lies largely in his style and especially in the style of the dialogue and the undertones and overtones of his settings. It takes the whole story to build up for us the atmosphere that his imagination re-creates for us, and it is achieved almost entirely by talking. His appeal is to the whole 'idea' of the things he mentions. If it is 'unicorns,' he makes everything which goes into the conception of a unicorn, count. He is able to capture for us the essential truth of the basic idea. With Mary, whose faith can move mountains, and who can unerringly follow her own imaginative direction to the end, we find ourselves following with our own grass rope.

He makes for us, as a story-teller, the kind of 'Secondary World' that Tolkien talks about in his essay on Fairy-Stories, which our minds can enter. Inside it, what he relates is true; it accords with the laws of that world. We enter it through the clear, true heart of a child because he makes us aware, with a child's intense feeling, of the immensity and luminous quality of what is for them absolute and eternal. The boundaries of life are for them uncharted, free, innocent, and defy the measurements of time and place. He re-creates for us that joyous state of being which was once our own proud, unconscious possession. Whether as a child or as an adult, this intrigues us. We emerge from the experience with our senses quickened.

I think Mayne in all his books is also acutely aware of the fresh, unsullied, direct approach to the world of nature and life in general, that is in the heart of childhood itself. He suggests it to us at every turn of phrase.

"What is the use of a book without conversations," says Alice. That being so, William Mayne excels here too. Because it is by means of conversations, direct, by implication, at times elliptical and often dialectal, that the motivation and charm of his books unfold. Through his use of conversation we are able to feel the whole process of thought growing in the characters. It is a procession of ideas really, one thing suggesting another. At times it is as stimulating to read in one sense, as the conversations in *Tea with Walter de la Mare*. One's appetite is continually being whetted, as the relationship of thought, idea, character, and action, is projected before our eyes.

It is entirely true to the child mind. Based on everyday living, sharpened and attuned to legend and tradition, and illuminated by imagination, the 'adventure' of the book is the complete realization of all three. We thus step within that real world of childhood again when we read the books of this engaging and skillful writer. Children have no such thoughts when they read his stories. They don't have to. They *sense* reality—the reality which is basic in things mortal and immortal.

Tradition or legend to him is unequivocally English, and just as alive today as it was in the Middle Ages. The quality and influence of that tradition penetrates the present and is the motivation behind the writing in his cathedral choir school stories. It absorbs us, the centuries are rolled away and we make our way in and about and around the living cathedral of today.

He shows us the comfortable, easy relationship that can be between boys and masters. His values are sound. His ideas move into other dimensions, particularly the world of the spirit. His motivation—a combination magically mixed—of the real and imaginative stimulation at work in the minds and hearts of the young. Because it is the core of his writings—all adults are swept along with it and move within the radiance of this reality too. We are shown by this creative mind of Mayne that the world of fantasy is really not blurred by the real world, but rather set in motion by it.

Whether it is an English cathedral; whether it is an eerie marsh in Somerset full of untold fears and possible mud monsters that snarl and snap amid close dead stalks; whether it is a mere, an island and a borrowed **Blue Boat;** or Mary wandering in the misty dales of Yorkshire, searching for her unicorn—he gives us a world of heightened reality. The atmosphere he creates lives for us. He has infinite capacity to suggest, rather than describe, and to integrate character, story and a sense of place, with evocative power.

The adults in the books are completely understanding and play their part with an unusual degree of spontaneous lightness of heart, appreciating to the full that the world of a child is very real, both inside and out, and so very rich in a number of inexpressible, unexplainable things.

In all his style is deceptively simple. His acute perception of boys—their different habits, ways of thinking, their manner of influencing one another and the entirely lovable Mary of *A Grass Rope*—unforgettable. His rich character studies of adults remain extraordinarily vivid in our minds—personalities in the flesh.

Mayne gives us in his description of everyday things, thoughts and feelings by implication as if experienced for the first time. Thus, with subtlety of writing and observation, by being completely in tune with childhood, with provocative ideas, rich characterization, a sense of tradition and landscape, he offers us a unique realization of the power of communication, by which the everyday world in which we live can be transcended. By a subtle blending of all these things and others, yet more intangible, into a whole state of being, and illumined by his imagination, he shows us the mirrors of a mind. The experience to us is an enriching one. It is an art that conceals art.

Since winning the Carnegie Award in 1957 William Mayne has continued to travel in his own particular and stimulating country of the mind, offering to the world some 20 more books for children and young people. The same qualities which arrested us in his earlier writings still appear, to a greater or less extent depending on the degree of creativity which concerns his mind and the purpose to which, at the time, he directs his thoughts. (pp. 5-7)

Mayne's books, with all their tonal variations remain true to the arpeggios of life as he knows them. No false note is ever struck. His style is literary, distinctly original and individualistic in its expression. It can breathe atmosphere in a single phrase, is often incisive in its physical perception, and charms with startling and often unexpected insight into the workings of the mind and heart of all his characters, especially children. He writes with a controlled and polished style and is often elliptical, with flashes of humour that tease and delight the imagination with their genuine quality of surprise. Though never of universal popularity in their appeal, his books, in the experience they afford to individuals, cannot be adequately assessed in any general terms. A master craftsman in his particular art, he brings together myth, legend, tradition and human nature, and etches in for us their interplay especially in the elusive and thinking minds of children. Because he clothes it all in the cloak of an adventure in imagination he catches for us, with classic art, that particular spark of vitality which feeds its own flame. In a little more than 20 years he has given to the world of children's literature a contribution that vibrates with intimations of immortality. (pp. 13-14)

> *Helen Stubbs, "William Mayne's Country of the Mind," in* In Review: Canadian Books for Children, *Vol. 6, No. 1, Winter, 1972, pp. 5-14.*

Myles McDowell

In *A Parcel of Trees* Susan wins from the Railways the right of possession of the orchard because on the whole she deserves to. She has proved herself worthy of the heritage. It isn't merely a conventionally happy ending; no other ending for the child reader would have made sense. (pp. 54-5)

In *A Parcel of Trees* Mayne evokes a languid, summery world of long and lazy days and slow quest. He unfolds his story unhurriedly, drowsing and droning, so it seems.

But the impression is deceptive—a retrospective impression. In fact, the story seldom stands still, and then only for the shortest passages.

> Susan felt melancholy rise in her like joy. Here she was alone, but there was a way back. Here she was not in the year that surrounded the rest of the world, but in the first year and the last year of time. This vision was perfect. It began in the mist, like a dream, and then the sky began to be blue overhead, and the mist sank, until the treetops were out of it and the sun shone on the apples. Then it was warm on her face and warm on the wall, and then was slanting across the grass and mottling it with the indistinct profiles of the branches above. The sunshine showed in the still heavy air, and the shadows were hollow, so that the air was veined. The day began to be hot. Susan thought she must have been out all morning, and went back in again, hoping not to be late for dinner.

Back to action again! Though the sun has been active and changing throughout this relatively still passage, Mayne's art is to give the impression of languidness without lulling the reader to sleep. He does this, among other means, by the obliquity of his dialogue.

> Mr Ferriman looked into the shop on his way home at midday.
>
> 'Burwen rock,' he said, and went at once.
>
> 'Caerphilly Castle,' said Rosemary.
>
> 'Don't stock it,' said Mum, shaking her head. 'I don't believe it's made. Weston-Super-Mare is what he's thinking of.'
>
> 'Tom Royal,' said Susan. 'That's the name of something. He doesn't mean seaside rock.'
>
> 'Are you sure?' said Mum. 'We'll go and look at Burwen Hill and be certain.'
>
> She went outside. Susan went with her. Burwen Hill, with its rocky top, stood out clear against the paler edge of the sky. 'That's it,' said Mum. 'It looks no different, so he must mean what you think.'
>
> 'He does,' said Susan.

There is with Mayne a sense of a slow, deep, steady current of understanding underlying the lighter surface show. The surface carries the reader buoyantly; the undercurrent it is which is remembered. And this, of course, is Mayne's strength, this hiding of the introspective, reflective quality in dialogue and incident.

> 'It must be water,' said David. 'It's water rocking a stone about, or a boulder or something, and then it's going to break out here and be another spring. At least, it won't be another spring, because there isn't one in this field, even though it's called High Keld. This must be the High Keld itself, and it dried up and went. Now it's coming back.'
>
> 'Oh well,' said Keith. 'I'd rather have badgers.'
>
> 'Of course,' said David. 'Of course.'

What a wealth of private understanding, of a history of reflection, of a scale of values, of a way of life shared is conveyed in those short strokes, 'Of course . . . Of course.' (pp. 55-7)

> *Myles McDowell, "Fiction for Children and Adults: Some Essential Differences," in* Children's literature in education, *No. 10, March, 1973, pp. 50-63.*

Penelope Farmer

[*The following excerpt is from a collection of essays written by a group of authors, critics, and other professionals who were invited by* Children's literature in education *to discuss "the best children's book I read during the last year."*]

I have to choose **A Game of Dark.** William Mayne is one of the most considerable, and certainly in some respects the most interesting writer for children now and this is undoubtedly his best book. Less rich and localized in its fantasy than **Earthfasts;** less rich in human terms than **Ravensgill;** not as affectionately funny as **A Swarm in May,** it is still all those things in a highly concentrated and synthesized form, besides demonstrating Mayne's recurring obsession with mysterious family pasts and relationships. And it goes far deeper than any of the others.

Mayne's sheer brilliance has always been one of his drawbacks as a writer. Some of his books could almost be described as cons—marvellous writing concealing the fact that they are uncontrolled, perverse, peripheral, even one dimensional in human terms (all those patient, understanding mothers. . . .). But here he goes straight to the centre, shirking nothing. There are not tricks, no verbal fireworks. It is pared down, precise, plain, using images sparingly, highly economical in form, yet possessing an extraordinary translucence and clarity. It has however drawn upon itself the most surprising and unprecedented abuse culminating in the accusation that Mayne is working out his hangups on adolescents—as if most hangups weren't conceived in childhood and first encountered in adolescence anyway. His, in all events, are beside the point and to say the least it would be impertinent to speculate.

The hangups in the book relate to Donald's family: his cool, priggish, teacher mother who forgets and calls him Jackson at home; his dying minister father and his own ambivalent feelings towards both of them—his horror at his father's illness, his guilt at his lack of felt love. The problems here are intensified maybe, but they seem to me central to adolescence; what we feel—or don't feel—about our families, once we cease to take them for granted, the guilt aroused by our ambivalence. We are a guilt ridden, depressive society, and perhaps, underlying the declared concern for the young in the cries of hate against this book, is a reluctance by many to look at such aspects of themselves.

Otherwise the adjectives used seem inexplicable, 'confusing' for instance: 'disgusting'—well the stench and habits of white worm Donald faces and slays in his otherdimension world are disgusting, but so is the guilt which it symbolizes. The descriptions are not merely there to shock, but are integral. (And ultimately Donald wins.)

Cold—yes, but there is also Donald's search for warmth and sometimes his finding it in the family of the Anglican parson, Berry (homosexual overtones?—if so, marginal, and they don't invalidate the warmth) . And despite all Donald's depression and withdrawal, warmth keeps creeping in—in his other-dimension relationships with Carrica and the lord; in Nessing, the schoolboy, enemy of authority, yet who '. . . at the funeral of the . . . very old Mrs Lesley . . . had been seen in tears'; in the humour, always warm and affectionate—describing, for instance, Berry's wife's muddled housekeeping.

It is still not an easy or comfortable book. I would not expect it to reach many adolescents (but that does not mean it should not be offered them; to a few it may say a lot). Nor do I think it is flawless. The railcrash is slightly melodramatic. The whole ending is not quite right—you grasp momentarily what it says and feels, and then lose both. But on any reckoning it is important and considerable. The fact that it was ignored by last year's selection committees for awards and 'best books', indicts only their members, not Mayne himself. (pp. 37-8)

> *Penelope Farmer, in a review of "A Game of Dark," in* Children's literature in education, *No. 11, May, 1973, pp. 37-8.*

The Times Literary Supplement

The act of writing appears so easy to William Mayne that one should not be surprised at the increasing virtuosity of his technique, or at his increasing range of experiment with ideas. Yet surprised one is, every time, and here is **The Jersey Shore,** as subtle and skilful a piece as anything he has done.

Arthur, an American boy, comes with his mother to a lonely coastal village in New Jersey. "Nobody told me geography this far east", says the mother. It is Arthur's first visit to his grandfather and his Aunt Deborah; in typical Mayne fashion these two relatives live incompatibly apart. The boy on most days goes to the old man's wooden house in the sand, and hears the tale of his unknown family in the far-off East Anglian fens. It is the tale of a labouring boy who learnt that he could not change his lot, of a passage of bygone time that often has all the grief of a ballad: of children lost in the marsh; of loves and partings and disappearances; of the poverty of the poor when the great house is displeased. The boy learns too of a stranger out of the sea, a shining dark man hung with chains, the only survivor of a wreck. He had settled in the village and married a village girl, and there his descendants remained. One of these was the grandfather's unattainable love through life.

Arthur never sees the old man again—but he sees the village by chance, some ten years later, when he is in the US Air Force and is posted to East Anglia. "Nobody told me geography this far east", says the tail gunner. But the place is there, church and marsh, just as it was in his mind. And he goes to find what the old man lost, to mend what was broken, to break the chain hanging on the wall, the fetter of the slave. Something read and forgotten, maybe, gives this story an oddly insistent likeness to that of Clare: the lost unattainable village love, the name of Martha the

wife, the descriptions of the children who came and went, the long walk back to home, the haunting prose throughout. . . . But Mr Mayne is also writing fiction, and the final design is his own. Even if this were his only book it would mark him out as a very considerable talent. Technically, it ranks with the best that he has done. By giving most of the narrative to the old man he avoids all but a dash of the whimsical chit-chat that is the most dispensable part of his writing.

Much of the prose can be reread as often as poetry. The end has a stunning impact, almost as much for its art as for what it tells. Looking back, one can see how cunningly the clues have been laid down in the text. But it is also the theme itself which gives this seemingly quiet story its range and depth. A whole village world unfolds, its people open to the bitterness both of the winds and the social powers. And one thing more, which must be Mr Mayne's surprise.

The old question can still be asked: what young will read this book? Child readers Mayne certainly has; they are those who do not want to travel the motor road of fiction—the whole thing stretched out flat and straight in front. The theme itself is not at all out of youthful reach or grasp. It needs to be read more than once, of course— but a book that does not invite a second reading, even if primarily through pique or perplexity, is only a middling sort of book, and generally very much less. Middling is not an adjective that could be applied to **The Jersey Shore.**

> *"Old Man's Tale," in* The Times Literary Supplement, *No. 3719, June 15, 1973, p. 674.*

Brian Alderson

It seems to me that **Over the Hills and Far Away** and **A Game of Dark** are as important for their exploration of time and place as ever they are for the stories that they have to tell. In both books we stand like Magra and Korva 'surrounded by a misty edge where one time ran into another' and it is the uncanny skill with which Mayne summons up . . . an utterly convincing past and mingles it with the present in a particular place that gives these two books their peculiarly haunting quality. The effect is fairly obvious in **Over the Hills and Far Away,** but has not been so widely noticed in **A Game of Dark.** Reviewers, with a whiff of Freud in their nostrils, have gone chasing phallic symbols and Zeus/Cronus patterns and have neglected what is emotionally and technically one of the book's triumphs: Donald's ambivalent relationship with his Other World and the absolute reality of that place as a paradigm of his home world.

The skill that has gone into this book and its predecessor can be seen emerging gradually through Mayne's whole writing life—like Nelly Jack John from under Richmond Castle—and the success with which it is carried out can perhaps be measured by comparing Mayne's work with that of Alan Garner in the recently published *Red Shift.* For all the force of Garner's historical imagination he does not achieve that fugal intensity with which William Mayne plays off past against present simultaneously so that the reader too feels the chill of 'being in a place before the map knew about it'.

It is through their intricate play with time that *Over the Hills and Far Away* and *A Game of Dark* can be seen as closely related to William Mayne's latest novel *The Jersey Shore.* With considerable daring he has elected to set the scene for what he has to say in the United States in the early 1930's and the small happenings of this part of the story concern a boy, Arthur, and his mother who are spending a longish holiday on 'the Jersey shore' with an oddish aunt. It is quite possible that American readers will find fault with some of Mr. Mayne's characterisations in these scenes and it is for the more knowledgeable to say whether Arthur—who is one quarter escaped Negro slave—speaks, or at least thinks, in a manner altogether too akin to one of Mr. Ardent's young gentlemen.

This part of the book, with the exception of a superb, somewhat enigmatic Negro Preacher, is fairly conventional Mayne family-portrait stuff (however unconventional such may be by most writers' standards of perception). What gives the book its energy are the communings between Arthur and his English grandfather who, incompatible with the aunt, his daughter, lives farther down towards the shore. In a series of meetings the old man conveys to the boy not just recollections of his own feckless past as a labourer in the Norfolk fen-country, but something which is the essence of that distant locale, its people and the generations of family life. And to say 'conveys' is to be as exact as possible—for communication between the two of them is only partially in words—the brilliantly caught accents of one man from one place—much of it is in transferred images. The old man's narrative may be direct recollection:—

> 'Osney, where I was a lad; the parson there. See him, a wild man, devout to hawk and hound, him. Great, tall, broad, lord of the manor, the roaringest man that ever backed horse . . .

Or it may be reflection:—

> 'We're small things . . . There's no greatness to us, because there isn't anything but ourselves to see what we've done; there isn't a bigger animal, you might say, to tell us how good . . .

Or it may be as Arthur recognises that:—

> 'There were things waiting to be told between them that would need more than speech, that would need long times of sitting on the stoop against the wall, and waiting for the thoughts to join his mind.'

So where your conventional children's writer would have had Arthur down on the beach with his bucket and spade, terrorised by his aunt and awaiting tales of buried treasure from his grandfather, Mr. Mayne provides passivity and apprehensions, tiny novels in themselves, beyond any immediate event: a black galley-slave washed ashore a century before, the marauding Fleetmen an age before that. '"So see us, see us"' says the old man and Arthur sees with heart-breaking clarity the deaths of children at the hands of the sea.

It is quite impossible to more than simply sketch thus William Mayne's highly idiosyncratic method of once again bringing his readers up against the almost physical interlocking of past and present (and the abrupt denouement of the book reinforces this in a fashion which seems to have surprised even the author, who drops for a moment his elaborate guard of irony and allows us a sixpenny cliché). But along with its masterly presentation of the past life of Osney Cold Fen, it also sets before the critic a further instalment of those arguments that are to be found rambling through so many discussions of William Mayne's writing: can this really be called a children's book?

Now while most reviewers, critical or not, were prepared to admit that *Over the Hills and Far Away* was just such a thing—even though 'for the thoughtful who wonder about time' (*Times Literary Supplement*)—it was a regularly occuring objection to *A Game of Dark* that it was unsuitable for and incomprehensible to young readers. ('Amusing for amateur psychoanalysts, but not really for children' said *The Teacher,* predictably enough); while the only reason that Mr. [Aidan] Chambers had to welcome it was so that he could use it, with some regularity, as a stick to beat reviewers who get too 'awed about obliquities and stylistic perfections'.

As always though, such charges are levelled without the accuser offering a firm view on what distinguishes 'children's books' from any others, and without him facing up to the question of whether criticism in this field is to be replaced by the simpler judging process of counting heads. Will it not take a lot of the pretentiousness out of criticising children's books if we opt for the obliquities and stylistic perfections of Capt. W. E. Johns and let 'the thoughtful who wonder about time' go watch Captain Kirk on the star-ship Enterprise? For William Mayne has never shown himself particularly willing to tailor his writing to the requirements of educationists and social philosophers and the truth of the matter is that if we regard 'creative fiction' as 'opening the door of emotional understanding of oneself, other people and the world about one' (A. Chambers: *The Reluctant Reader* p. 40) then a novel like *A Game of Dark* would seem to figure.

During the last year or two however rather more precise attempts have been made to distinguish the characteristic features of 'creative fiction' in children's literature—among the most perceptive being Myles McDowell's essay 'Fiction for Children and Adults' in *Children's Literature in Education No. 10* (March, 1973) and Jill Paton Walsh's recent statement to the Exeter Conference (which presumably will eventually be printed in that magazine). At the heart of these two statements was a view of the good children's book as one which 'makes complex experience available to its readers', while the good adult book 'draws attention to the inescapable complexity of experience' (McDowell), or that the book may 'stretch' its readers without relinquishing the necessary, traditional 'strand of story' (Walsh).

By either of these definitions, backed up with their more mechanical provisos on such matters as length and content, *A Game of Dark* remains a book as much for older children as for anyone else (though 'hard' admitted Mrs. Walsh). The momentum of its plot, the brilliance of its historical episodes (the more so for their lowered key) and its direct relationship to the archetypal stories of dragon slaying all link it to the traditions of the genre, but it is a book which leads beyond those traditions and towards the territory of the modern adult. It stands on the littoral between the innocent and the experienced reader.

With **The Jersey Shore,** however, it seems to me that William Mayne has crossed 'the misty edge' and written a book where the complexity of experience requires more than childish resources for its appreciation. The fulcrum of the story is not Arthur, down there on a visit, but Benj Thatcher and his profound but unco-ordinated recollections. The angle of the obliqueness has shifted decisively against the child, for whom the disparate elements of past and present, place and family will surely not fuse into the compelling unity that they do for an adult. Like so much of William Mayne's writing the tones of the book's voices echo in the mind long after it has been finished, the pictures that it summons up live in the memory, but the truth of its emotion speaks from maturity to maturity. (pp. 134-35)

> *Brian Alderson, "On the Littoral: William Mayne's 'The Jersey Shore',"* in Children's Book Review, *Vol. III, No. 5, October, 1973, pp. 133-35.*

Russell Hoban

William Mayne, in **A Game of Dark,** has taken on not only the Oedipal conflict but the basic existential one of staying or going, holding on or splitting. Fourteen-year-old Donald Jackson lives with his crippled father and a mother who teaches at the school he attends and calls him by his surname as frequently as his Christian one. His dead sister is a constant shadowy presence. The atmosphere is piously oppressive and physically corrupt.

Appropriately the story opens with a feeling of sickness and a pervasive stench. The bad smell of Donald's life has carried over into a second life in which he must ultimately fight a stinking worm who leaves a slimy track behind him as he preys on a feudal village. Needing to be a man, Donald drifts into a world where he is needed as a man. He rescues a girl who is reminiscent of his dead sister, and he is pressed into the service of the local lord. He can live in either of his two lives. . . . (p. 73)

Mayne is technically unlimited—he can do anything with words—and he handles his psychical shifts suavely. For a time Donald chooses the second life in the feudal village. Eventually he kills the worm, not in the proper knightly fashion but with the ingenuity and tenacity of desperate courage. At the end of the book people assume workable places:

> Carrica was not his. She was his mother or his sister, and of those two he knew which was which, and he knew that the man in the other room was his father, whom he knew now how to love. Carrica was a phantom if he wanted her to be, and the house in Hales Hill was another, and he had the choice of which to remain with.

Donald finally chooses the world of everyday reality, and his father conveniently dies.

Mayne has taken on themes that require considerable force and depth of the writer; how well he has done with them is less important to me than that he regards them as being within his province. (pp. 73-4)

> *Russell Hoban "Thoughts on Being and Writing,"* in The Thorny Paradise: Writers on Writing for Children, *edited by Edward Blishen, Kestrel Books, 1975, pp. 65-76.*

Charles Sarland

William Mayne is the great "problem" amongst modern children's writers. Everyone seems agreed that he is a writer of great subtlety and complexity, that he has an uncanny knack of seeing the world through the eyes of children, and that he is the most assured stylist of all modern children's authors. Yet he remains obstinately unread by children, and short of saying that he is a very sophisticated writer, which he is, no one has satisfactorily explained why. I do not intend, in this article, to question his critical standing, though I will declare a personal bias towards **Choristers' Cake** and **Words and Music** and some of the shorter books he has written about younger children like **The Big Wheel and the Little Wheel** and **The Last Bus** as opposed to **Ravensgill, Earthfasts** or **A Game of Dark.** Whatever their relative merits, however, I intend to confine myself to the four Cathedral Choir School books for they contain elements that are common to everything that he has written, from **Follow the Footsteps** to **A Game of Dark.** I want in particular to look in some detail at the writing style, for it seems to me that valuable clues are to be found in it that go a long way to explaining precisely why many children find it difficult to come to terms with a writer who, on the face of it, would seem to have so much to offer.

On first reading the earliest of the Chorister books, **A Swarm in May,** one is struck by three things: the meticulously detailed descriptions of the physical environment; the uncanny insight into a small boy's concerns; and the wordplay, the witty allusions and puns that inform the book. These three aspects of Mayne's work turn out to be characteristic of his whole output, and all three things relate to his style. First and foremost then, he is concerned to show exactly what it feels like to be a small boy in a choir school. He does this by detailing the physical environment from precisely the point of view of such a small boy, re-creating for the adult reader that forgotten time when the immediate physical environment was a continual source of interest and even wonder. Consider for instance the climax of the book, the passage where Owen collects the bees with the aid of a strange-smelling globe attached to a large key by a chain that they have found. (pp. 107-08)

It is the tiny detail that is telling; for instance, "he smelt the strange smell of it *through the burnt gas*", "where the chain hung through his fingers", or the description of the swarm. Furthermore it is immediately clear that the insight into Owen's concerns is achieved precisely by this concentration on detail. But something else also emerges from a consideration of this passage, and that is Mayne's handling of pace. The book is here nearing its climax, and the reader's concern is that Owen shall successfully negotiate the ordeal of the service. Yet the detail slows the pace deliberately: instead of warming the globe in his hand as he approaches and letting the bees gather until he has a fair-sized arm, he must forget to warm it, take the globe back to the house, and even then he doesn't run, and then further detail is presented, the bubbling water, the weight of the swarm, the feel of the swarm, and so on. The reader must forget the action and concentrate instead on the sensations of the moment.

If one examines the wordplay of the same book one gets some idea of the idea of the mental processes that Mayne expects his readers to apply. For instance, one of the teachers, Mr. Sutton, has a nickname, Brass Button. At one point Owen puns on his name " 'No fear,' said Owen, 'Brass Button's come quite unsown with me' " and later in the book he develops the metaphor in answer to Dr. Sunderland, " 'He won't for me, sir,' said Owen. 'I weaken his threads too much.' " And here is Trevithic, the head chorister, with two musical puns in the same breath, the one obscure and the other more obvious, " 'You are burbling out the dullest passages I ever heard,' said Trevithic. 'I think you must have gone slightly decomposed in the afternoon.' " In order to appreciate such jokes—indeed in order to understand them, for their metaphorical applications have specific meaning within the narrative and emotional context of the book—the reader must stand back and make the connecting links that Mayne deliberately leaves out. In other words the wordplay alienates the reader from the drama of the narrative and draws his attention instead to the formal linguistic elements that serve to unite Mayne's delineation of character. In the above example on the two occasions that Owen puns on Mr. Sutton's name the reader is reminded of Owen's apprehension of Mr. Sutton but remains objective in his consideration of that apprehension.

Once again the technique is devoted to dissipating the immediate dramatic impact and replacing it with a contemplative consideration of the situation. The Brechtian term "alienation"would seem to fit the bill very precisely here, for Brecht's alienation devices were conceived with exactly the same purposes in mind. I am not suggesting that Mayne is a Brechtian writer, merely that he has adopted and adapted the technique for his own use. In passages of dialogue the same result is achieved by somewhat different means. Take for a example a crucial interchange in *Cathedral Wednesday.* A dayboy, Andrew Young, finds himself acting head chorister because of illness. He has a lot of trouble with the two boys next below him in seniority. Finally he puts them on the prefect's "list", a grave step. There follows this conversation when he meets one of them:

> "Is it . . . ?" said Silverman and stopped.
> "Hmn," he said, and shook his head.
>
> "Better line up, " said Andrew quietly.
>
> "Yes," said Silverman. He looked fully round at Andrew. "Is it Book Boys?" he said.

"What do you think?" said Andrew.

"But honestly," said Silverman, "we . . ."

"Line up," said Andrew. "Attention, left turn, quick march, left, left, left."

This is, potentially, a highly dramatic exchange in which Andrew, for the first time in the book, asserts his authority. Yet the conversation is interrupted by passages of description, "He looked fully round at Andrew" and "said Silverman and stopped. . . . he said, and shook his head", so that the passage takes far longer to read than it would have done to say. And even if it is objected that these would have been legitimate details under any circumstances, one still has to explain why there are so many "he saids" in the latter half. The passage might well have gone:

> "Is it Book Boys?"
> "What do you think?"
> "But honestly, we . . ."
> "Line up," said Andrew.

and immediately there is an increase in pace and drama. So clearly Mayne wishes to prevent his readers from becoming emotionally involved either in Silverman's desperation or in Andrew's triumph and they are encouraged instead to take a more objective view.

On other occasions he will deliberately create a situation in which he is forced to break off the narrative in order to explain what is going on. Here is Mr. Lewis, late for breakfast in *Words and Music:* " ' . . . go and make the toast for me. It's my breakfast.' He didn't mean that the toast was for him, but that he should have been downstairs seeing that everyone else got it in time." Instead of a clear exposition of the total situation within which the drama can unfold, Mayne gives the reader little snippets of exposition in order to clear up the puzzlement that he himself has created.

If the opening section of *Choristers' Cake* is examined in detail it will be seen to exemplify all these points. It is the description of one of those games where a ball is rolled down between the legs of teams of boys standing in long lines. If the ball gets outside the legs it has to be fetched back to the same place. The game is never described directly, however; instead a number of sense impressions are presented which, as it were, move inside the structure of the game rather like a planet moves inside an orbit, and the reader has to posit the structure from internal evidence, rather as man posits a possible orbit from observation of related phenomena. . . . (pp. 108-10)

What is in fact being described here is a competitive game, but none of the excitement of such a game gets into the words. Instead we have the visual description of the ball and its attendant shadows, and when Sandwell commits his crime by sending the ball outside the line of legs it is not explained that it is a crime, though such can be deduced from the conversation which follows.

> "Perfect fool," said Trevithic, loudly, from the head of the team.
>
> "Don't tell him," said Lowell, who had come up

from the back of the other team and was now leading it.

"He's an augmented fool," said Madington, brushing his hair more on to the top of his head in case Trevithic barged into him bonily again.

"Sandwell," said Trevithic, "fetch it."

"Run, Sandy," said Meedman, removing his weight from Sandwell's shoulders.

"Me?" said Sandy, sitting down on the Latin verse and exchanging his view of the sometime Dean for one of the bright coats of arms in the cloister vaulting.

The whole team lifted their heads and turned their bodies without moving their feet, and urged him to hurry. Sandy thought they looked like a row of startled looper caterpillars. The ball lay quietly against the door to the Bishop's garden. Sandy fetched it and ran forward to the head of the team with it. They bent themselves down as he ran past them. "Like the backbone skeleton of an animal," the thought; and fed the ball to Trevithic.

The point of course is that, with in the context, it would not need to be explained to Sandwell that he had boobed so Mayne does not explain it; rather, he gives us the next aural impression that Sandwell would have had, Trevithic's comment.

The conversation itself bears close examination. It is the dramatic core of the scene yet the drama is held at arm's length. In the first place there is the musical pun of perfect augmented fool. Secondly, there is the apparent meaninglessness of Lowell's remark until the reader works out for himself that it is because Lowell is in the opposing team that he does not want Sandwell told. Thirdly, there is the puzzlement about Madington brushing his hair to the top of his head, for nowhere in the passage previously has it mentioned that Trevithic has barged into him. Of course Mayne's "again" carries all the implication that he wants. Fourthly, there is the whole little episode of Meedman removing his weight from Sandwell's shoulders, an episode which has to be considered in the light of the second paragraph to be fully understood. In fact here, as with Madington's hair, there is a concealed causal relationship. What in fact happens is that Meedman has virtually been sitting on Sandwell, and Sandwell has been pressing upwards in compensation. Thus when Meedman removes his weight Sandwell overbalances and sits on the floor. Mayne does not make the causal link, the reader has to do it; and even then he has Sandwell sit on the Latin verse, not the floor, and looking not immediately at the ceiling but first at the coats of arms which are then placed in their correct context. In order to appreciate fully what is going on, the reader must carry Mayne's wealth of detail in his head because it is within the matrix of this wealth of detail that the structure of the book will unfold.

There is then this irony: that a more conventional author would give the reader an objective view of the situation, and by doing so, assuming a degree of competence on the writer's part, would engage him in the action, while Mayne, by presenting a subjective viewpoint, forces the reader to a more dispassionate consideration of what is going on.

In *Choristers' Cake* the central character, Sandwell, is unsympathetic. He is conceited, obstinate and foolish. At various points in the story he makes the wrong decisions. Yet he remains the central character, and it is through his eyes that we perceive the action. If it were not for his alienation techniques Mayne would never be able to handle such a delicate situation and retain an objective moral viewpoint. But the book requires a degree of sophistication in the readers that would not normally be found in children of the same age as his characters. It is clear from the way that he uses pace, dialogue, causal relationships, puns and wordplay that the last thing that he wants is that the reader should be carried along on the tide of the narrative. Always the requirement is that out of the sense impressions that he supplies the reader should construct his own pace, his own drama, his own causal and verbal links, and it is a measure of Mayne's mastery that they are there to be constructed. He admits no ambivalence of response, but the reader must work hard to pick up all the cues that are laid down for his guidance.

There are a number of conclusions that present themselves. One is that Mayne will quite simply remain a minority taste. Another is that perhaps the publishers could usefully look at the age range for which they are intending his books. There is a case for saying, for instance, that *Choristers' Cake* is suited to a thirteen- or fourteen-year-old audience rather than a ten-year-old audience. Certainly *Ravensgill* would seem out of place in a list of books for eight- and nine-year-olds. One hopes that the fact of his unpopularity will not discourage publishers from ensuring that the best of his books remain in print. (pp. 111-13)

Charles Sarland, "Chorister Quartet," in Signal, *No. 18, September, 1976, pp. 107-13.*

Mary Cadogan and Patricia Craig

William Mayne has devised a kind of dialogue in which the character speaks principally to himself, to clarify some facet of his personality for his own benefit. His children are surprisingly articulate but leave much unsaid. The possibilities for ambiguity, for private interpretation, are endless here, but the device is used also to project unequivocal feelings and uncertainties. . . . In *Earthfasts* the author's concern with psychological effect is everywhere apparent: he has got inside the characters who are confronted with a variety of phenomena, in order to express more explicitly their efforts to extend conventional definitions to accommodate their experiences of the supernatural. (p. 356)

The author's explanations are entirely convincing; his reordering of "natural" events has in it a matter-of-fact quality and controlled tension which combine authoritatively. Everything is worked into this book; legend, superstition, a "scientific approach", psychological detail, a surface interest, a powerful evocation of scene; and everything *works,* because it is given just the right degree of emphasis. The characters are driven to extremes of feeling and experience (one even "dies") but there is not note of hysteria, no sense even of make-believe. (p. 357)

> *Mary Cadogan and Patricia Craig, " 'Time Present and Time Past. . . ', " in their You're a Brick, Angela! A New Look at Girls' Fiction from 1839-1975, Victor Gollancz Ltd., 1976, pp. 355-72.*

Edward Blishen

[There] is no reliable means of measuring the general effect of a children's writer on his readers; but I must say I suspect that those who argue that William Mayne is an adult's children's writer and not a children's children's writer are expressing nothing better than guesses.

It is not only more generous, but far more sensible and grateful, to say what a good writer he is, and what a welcome effect he is beginning to have on writing for children here. The effect has not taken the form of imitation; he is strictly inimitable, though easy to parody. (I think he is not guiltless of parodying himself.) But what his writing has shown is that stories for children need not drive straight from opening to end; they can shape themselves by a sort of sly oblique process, emerge sideways and even backwards out of dialogue and hints. In fact, all his stories have strong narrative spines; but they are not rigid ones. He has also come so close to the true nature of children's talk and to the way they feel and think that it must be more difficult than it was for a writer of any sensitiveness to reproduce that blunt form of dialogue, always obviously to the purpose, and that falsely consequent rendering of patterns of young thought and feeling, that are conventions of writing for children. In a sense, Mr. Mayne has reminded us of the precise nature of children.

To begin with, children fool with words. It is often a very serious foolery. Most dialogue in most children's books assumes that children use words as adults do. . . . To children, much of the vocabulary and phrasing their elders have come to accept calls for questioning. A mother, in one of Mayne's books, says that a village wants money, and her small son comments: 'I didn't know villages wanted money. I thought people wanted money.' And of course, children spend much of their time in a world of puns; they ransack words for jokes and secondary meanings, they put phrases under the strain (which causes them often hilariously to disintegrate) of literal examination. They have an alertness, too, to the unsaid thing lying behind something said; they have ears inside ears. William Mayne's stories are full of this pure true comedy of talk among children, of talk between children and adults (the adults sometimes exasperated or bemused by it, or without the leisure that enables the child to give it full attention; though the old, as they are often portrayed in William Mayne's stories, are seen to have re-acquired their sense of the intricate meanings of language). And, apart from his purely comic concern with words, William Mayne understands beautifully that language is itself part of the adventure of being alive and that, by misleading or puzzling or illuminating, it can inspire or direct events.

It is perhaps this feeling he has for the role played in life by language—especially in the lives of children, able to be so attentive—that more than anything makes Mayne a highly original and rare children's writer. He can be arch, and over-playful, and is capable of, as it were, doodling in the style of William Mayne; at times (I detected this especially in a recent story, *The Battlefield*) his children had the way they talk reflect the writer's agility with words, his inability to leave them alone, rather than their credible selves. He is an extraordinarily prolific writer—two and sometimes three books a year since he was first published in 1953. I fancy this causes some of the critical hesitation about him; a writer of such quality ought not to be so productive. I find this an odd point of view: there is no reason in the world why sensitiveness should not be combined with stamina. But certainly this large output is responsible for the passages of doodling and of near-self-parody. It is also to be seen as a kind of generosity: he has spread his attention over many audiences, from the youngest to the most sophisticated. And because to each of those audiences, in each of the varied settings of his stories, he addresses himself in the same manner, in the tone of this dancing and devious concern with language (as well as because the structure of his writing is *never* difficult, and he is indeed a master of the short sentence), I cannot believe that those who say he is writing over the heads of children, or only for those with a special taste for words, are analysing the situation correctly. In so far as there is a resistance to his work, it comes sometimes, I believe, from adults who cannot imagine that work of high quality might have a wide appeal; and sometimes from a certain shaping of children's appetites, as readers, that may have occurred by the time they come to Mayne. The point is that most writing for children *is* blunt and uninventive in its use of language; and that children may have come to believe that this is the proper tone of any story whatever.

I have read William Mayne to the most unlikely audiences—apparently cheerfully blunt boys in Islington, for example—and have found that, if the stories are properly presented (and in this case I simply mean if they are read aloud by someone who enjoys them), they cause great delight. This has its roots in that use of language I've already discussed—that grave fooling with language that is an activity of children everywhere. It lies, again, in William Mayne's witty and perceptive treatment of the life of the senses. From the moment you enter one of his stories, all your senses are deeply and very precisely involved. . . . [The] beauty of William Mayne's style is that it is never purple—there is rather this constant deft attentiveness to the sensations of being alive, usually expressed with a wholly unstrained wit. (pp. 99-101)

But what is most important is that all this texture, to which I have found it necessary to pay attention before looking at anything else—this perpetual lively alertness to language and to sensations—is wholly at the service of Mr. Mayne's stories. It can be enjoyed for its own sake, but it does not exist for its own sake. The little group of books he wrote about life in a choir school—beginning with *A Swarm in May*—stand slightly aside from the rest. They form a loving tribute to a special way of young life. The stories embody characteristic themes—the impact on the present of complex mysteries with their roots in the past, the conflict of attitudes to tradition, the relationships of the young and their elders—but, to my mind, exist as an achievement separate from the rest. They include some of William Mayne's best inventions: for example, the family of Pargales, who have tended the fabric of the cathedral for centuries, and whose notion of time, as of the relation of generations among themselves, has become tied to the enormously leisurely pace at which stone crumbles, gargoyles weather and fall and must be replaced. In the other stories, two major preoccupations emerge. One is that of the treasure hunt, of the search for clues to some mystery that carries the characters back into the past. This is a common theme in writing for children, but William Mayne handles it in a most uncommon manner. Not only is there his usual teasing obliqueness of narration, at once crystal-clear and devious; but there is also a constant ambiguity that enables a story to be interpreted in the light both of the most sober common sense and of the most extravagant imagination. Fantasy and realism are beautifully enmeshed. This is the manner of stories such as *The Thumbstick, The Rolling Season, The Battlefield:* and is at its best, in my opinion, in *A Grass Rope,* . . . in which the various possible interpretations of the near-magical events has its convincing advocate among the characters: a child who believes in magic, a clever boy who brings scientific reasoning to the quest, the children's parents who are simply sensible about it all. The conclusion is perfectly poised: the reader may believe any of the explanations, and perhaps that reader is most worthy of the author who manages to believe all of them. This is a very serious achievement of William Mayne's, I think: to preserve such an active and enchanting neutrality as between all the levels of our experience. Beside this achievement, much writing for children—wholly embracing fantasy or opting for thorough realism—falls awfully short. . . . Interestingly, even when Mayne is writing less ambitious stories, as close to plumb realism as he ever comes, the shadow of a proper mystery is allowed to fall upon the commonest things—as surely it does in the lives of all children. An example is a recent story for very young readers, called *The Yellow Aeroplane,* in which a common or garden tower in a wood, in fact a vent for the railway that passes through a tunnel below, is (for the unaccountable smell and sounds it emits) taken to be some supernatural, haunted edifice. A common wood near a common housing estate is touched with that Grimm-like uncertainty and sense of splendid peril which, as much as matter-of-fact realism (which they also love), so often shapes children's response to whatever world is around them.

The second large theme often, but not always, stems from this first one. It is the theme of enormous makings and destructions. The boys in *Sand* find what appear to be the remains of a prehistoric creature under the sand; they set out on an elaborate task of secret rescue, trying to retrieve these mysterious bones. The complications of their labour are vast; and so, too, are its consequences. In *Pig in the Middle,* a group of boys set out to transform an old barge into a seagoing vessel; as in *Sand,* they become intricately involved in the task. One of them, then they have achieved part of it 'suddenly understood the beginnings of the Bible'. It is this business of making things—of planning for a construction, or of actually constructing—that again and again William Mayne celebrates; and again, of course,

there could be few things closer to a child's heart. But so often in these stories the making leads to a vast unmaking, a catastrophe. In *The Battlefield,* the children's interest in the old tower in the marshes, the steps they take to investigate and make use of it, lead to near-fatal consequences, a huge scene of flood and displacement. The children are in fact warned by an old shepherd that, with so many forces at work—those of nature and of history, for example—those exerted by inquiring man may be too much. The attempt to transform the old barge in *Pig in the Middle* leads to immense disaster again—or at any rate is closely associated with it: the complete collapse of the mill buildings in which the barge is housed. It seems to me that this theme of making and breaking, sometimes separate from the magical theme, sometimes part of it, is again a concern that takes William Mayne close to the young reader, much of whose own life is devoted to bold constructions and to curiosity about the consequences of interfering with nature.

It is easy to say that William Mayne is an uneven writer. That must be true of anyone who writes so much. The comment is sometimes made by critics who appear not to distinguish between the more ambitious stories and those that are less serious in intention. It is also easy, and I think quite wrong, to claim that he is a writer for a highly literate minority; as I have said, I believe this view is an invention of those who see only the freshness, sublety and obliquity of the writing, and do not observe that it is always tied to stories of considerable narrative strength or that children everywhere have a delight in verbal ingenuity. These are, in fact, extremely *sensible* stories, and in my experience are recognised as such by a wide range of children. They are sensible because the heroes are never improbably heroic, and pure villains have no more place in the stories than they have in life itself. They are sensible also because Mr. Mayne understands the fluctuating relationships of child with child, the tangle of emotional attitudes which is part of the reality of children's lives, and of which so many children's writers seem inadequately aware. One should add that William Mayne is a brilliant reporter on the nature of family life, on the role of mums and dads. Parents impose a framework, but that is not all that can be said about them; one of the best things about this writer's work is that he understands that, at intervals in their busy round, adults are likely to be as much influenced by their children as their children are by them. The children of the sixties are fortunate to possess a writer who can make such a robust and copious literature out of a balance of so many gifts, all of them uncommon. (pp. 101-03)

Edward Blishen, "Writers for Children, 2: William Mayne," in The Use of English, *Vol. 20, No. 1, Autumn, 1978, pp. 99-103.*

Diana Waggoner

The magical blending of times and spells in [*Earthfasts*] is made more effective by Mayne's matter-of-fact attitude. His tight, intricate plotting, skillful prose, and distinctive, individual characters, especially the drummer boy and gentle, passive Keith, combine with the immense profundity of his invention to make this one of the best of all fantasies, a classic of speculative literature. (p. 240)

Diana Waggoner, "A Bibliographic Guide to Fantasy," in her The Hills of Faraway: A Guide to Fantasy, *Atheneum, 1978, pp. 125-302.*

Peter Hunt

One of the few things which commentators on William Mayne seem to be agreed about, is that his books lack passion; curious, then, the strength of the passions he seems to arouse. For some, he is among the best, if not *the* best, of contemporary writers for children. . . .

The opposition, which seems to react almost as much to Mayne's supporters as to his work, feels that he is full of sound (if not fury), overblown, repetitive, and uneven (if not actually pretentious), with a style that is a negative affectation. . . . (pp. 9-10)

Unusually, and unlike the Cormiers, Farmers, and Southalls, his subject matter is rarely an issue, even when he deals with serious adolescent problems as in *A Game of Dark,* or when his books fall into the no-man's-land between the children's and adults' lists, as with *The Jersey Shore.* Much of the difficulty seems to hinge on his style. . . .

Thus the two camps seem to polarize into those who feel that Mayne is a major literary talent, to be encouraged regardless of his supposed audience; and those who feel that he has little to offer children, and that his lionization is likely to have a deleterious effect not only on them, but on the already ambiguous position of children's books. . . . (p. 10)

[It] might be softly pointed out that there is a third, somewhat Brobdingnagian camp around: that of those literate, well-educated, and well-read people who have never even heard of William Mayne. . . . [This] large majority of outsiders might have something to offer by way of criticism—perhaps corrective to both sides—were they consulted. What if such readers were presented with an author and asked to disregard his classification? This might reveal a good deal about the filters through which those professionally involved with children's books read them.

These filters are of several kinds. The first are those which depend on the use of the books: we may read "on behalf of the child", making our responses in terms of *their* supposed responses. This may have practical value if we have to teach or market a book, but what child are we thinking of ? Whether it is ourselves as children, or an ideal or theoretical child, or a composite drawn from our experience of children, we are in great danger of distorting our responses—and of not having much to communicate to other people.

Secondly, because of the classification of the book, or even simply its cover, we will have expectations (however subconscious) of what the book should be like. This is not just a matter of content; it extends to the vocabulary, sentence structure, and register; narrative devices (notably internal monologues); structural resolution, and, as we shall see, a predominance of narrative itself. Again, we are reading in a special way—a way which *may not* be demanded by the book.

Equally, such an approach may reveal the preconceptions of "value", "quality", or "literary merit" held by other readers. Even the best of children's-book criticism tends either to alter its coinage to suit the audience for the texts . . . , to relate to children's response, or, as has been frequently pointed out of reviewers, to have no standards at all. If Mayne is an important writer, then he must be approached with rigour, even . . . as potential literature, and only secondarily, if at all, as material *for* a particular audience. Whether we like it or not, we are adults, must read as adults, and must, or should, talk to other adults about children's books.

Thus, an experiment in reading and response; rather than taking Mayne in isolation, I have attempted to test reactions to him from uninvolved readers. This seems to me to be a first step in at least identifying the problems which face us. The first problem was to find the readers—a neutral but skilled audience.

The Postgraduate Seminar in the Department of English at the University of Wales (UWIST) in Cardiff, in common with similar groups in most universities, meets regularly to discuss the department's research interests. It seemed that its members were an ideal group for commenting on an author like Mayne who is, at least potentially, capable of appealing to any audience. . . . The only four attributes that they had in common were that they were all adults; they were all skilled readers; they had all either never heard of, or had never read, William Mayne; and they had no professional interest in the conclusions reached.

The ostensible object of the exercise might best be explained by giving an extract from the brief issued to each seminar member.

> One of the aims of my research has been to examine and reassess authors who, because they supposedly write children's books, remain virtually unread by adults. Such criticism as is applied tends to be partial (if not biased), or to concentrate on characteristics not normally considered by critics. If an author could be given a fair hearing, there *may* be no reason why he should not be accepted into the canons of literature—and thereby be more widely read and criticized (among other less dubious benefits).
>
> I propose, therefore, to introduce an author, William Mayne, ignoring as far as possible his classification or status as children's author. Let us try to imagine that he is a contemporary author who, by some curious oversight, has not been looked at . . . We might then discuss whether we feel him to be a writer of literature (as opposed to reading matter), and of what status, and why (or why not).

(pp. 10-12)

The first way of operating this kind of experiment is to use unidentified extracts from books. . . . Seminar members were each asked to read at least one complete novel. The books issued (purely for logistic reasons) were *A Game of Dark, The Jersey Shore, The Incline, Earthfasts, Royal Harry, The Battlefield,* and *No More School.* We also discussed an extract from *The Twelve Dancers.*

Before looking at what happened in the seminar, it might be as well to declare my own bias (at least as it existed before we began), if it is not already obvious. Possibly because I am not primarily concerned with children, but rather with books and literary theory, I feel that Mayne is a major writer, who should be recognized as such. That opinion is based on the *oeuvre,* rather than on any single book. . . . In his style, Mayne is an original, one of the few true stylists of the twentieth century; if the language echoes a somewhat idealistic view of a child's perceptive processes, it is nonetheless at its best with the apparently inconsequential, avoiding patronizing either the characters or the implied readers. It sets up, in short, an honest narrative contract.

Consider, for example, the opening of *The Twelve Dancers.* . . . (pp. 12-13)

I feel that the passage offers precisely what literature should offer; something essentially different; something unique. More prosaically, it is remarkably economical in setting the character and background for the novel, and the irony operates—unlike many other writers'—on both the writer-child and the writer-adult levels. If all that is known is known through the child's eyes, that does not invalidate its acceptance by the adult; and Mayne can extend this technique to virtuoso lengths, as in *Royal Harry.*

It may be true that his characters rarely stand out, being functional parts of enclosed worlds (or, as Mayne himself has said, secondary to the narrative), for some readers rather in the manner of the early Lawrence—and this derives from his total approach. While avoiding direct emotional involvement, his capacity to see over the heads of his characters—as in much of *A Grass Rope*—gives a compensatory dimension, in a tradition running from Fielding to Ford Madox Ford and P. G. Wodehouse.

Not to make this a catalogue, I might cite, as others have done, his use of dialogue, which is Pinter-esque, at least in its obliquity and its implication of social infrastructures, if not in its verbal density. This goes hand in hand with his capacity to draw rounded families from suggestions (as in *The Battlefield*) or complete communities from casual details (as in *A Parcel of Trees*). (pp. 14-15)

Since 1953 Mayne has produced over fifty books, an output not normally associated with quality. With *A Swarm in May* he produced a major contribution to the then moribund school-story genre; he is a master of the "regional", particularly with novels set in Yorkshire, but also those set in Wiltshire (*The Rolling Season*), Somerset (*The Member for the Marsh*), the Welsh Marches (*The Twelve Dancers*), and, among other places, America in *The Jersey Shore.* And he has treated most of the conventional plot areas: the treasure hunt (*Underground Alley*), the detective story (*Ravensgill*), the supernatural (*Earthfasts*), children's games and projects (*Sand*), time travel (*Over the Hills and Far Away*), and half-forgotten aspects of childhood (*The Changeling* and *Summer Visitors*). To all of these he has contributed something highly individual which has often transformed the subgenres. His most impressive recent works have dealt with problems of adolescence, using imaginative psychological extrapolations in

A Game of Dark, social history in *The Incline,* and an almost Jamesian insight in *The Jersey Shore.* He has also, not for the first time, ventured into apparent self-satire with *It.*

Where . . . does Mayne stand, or where might he be placed? (p. 22)

Perhaps the most fruitful attitude to take was that of the last critic quoted: we must judge works *by the basic tenets which they set up for themselves.* You can only judge "good of its kind". In *children's literature* we may be discussing a creature which bears a relationship to, but does not necessarily coincide with, its adult counterpart. This difference has virtually nothing to do with form, hardly anything to do with the supposed predominance of narrative over style (or thought), and it should have little to do with accessibility (is *Finnegans Wake* accessible?). Nonetheless, if an author is tacitly writing over the heads of his audience or possibly writing first for the adult audience which must necessarily *process* the work, then the audience cannot be expected to perceive what is being attempted to be communicated. And if literature is part of a communicative act (however odd, fossilized, or complicated) then the author must necessarily fail. We, whatever our roles, are not part of that act, and we have no way of knowing either what was intended, or what was achieved. (Writers are as unreliable as children in reporting what goes on—and for the same reason: neither can be expected to understand it or articulate it in terms that mean anything to anyone but themselves.) This may well mean, as, for example, with the study of an author like Defoe, that we are imputing qualities which the author neither intended, nor was aware of; and which exist only in us. [If we think that that is a bad thing, we should at least accept that it is inevitable; that no committed group has any more claim to the validity of their own armory than any other. If this experiment has done no more than demonstrate *that,* however laboriously, or has shown the complexity of classification and evaluation in this field, it will have done something.]

The seminar members agreed. The majority were glad to have had the opportunity to encounter Mayne, either for his stylistic interest, or his artistry, or both. If there was a general conclusion, it was that the style/content dichotomy was intriguingly shown in this author; melded successfully, that success could be extremely impressive. Equally, as an exercise rarely possible among those professionally interested in books, it caused many of us to reinspect our literary values in a slightly different light—and to consider, perhaps for the first time, the role and problems of the children's author. (pp. 23-4)

> *Peter Hunt, "The Mayne Game: An Experiment in Response," in* Signal, *No. 28, January, 1979, pp. 9-25.*

Frank Eyre

William Mayne's name must inevitably appear frequently in any discussion of the late twentieth-century children's book. Not only because, despite conflicting views about his work, all critics agree that it is important, but also because he has written so many different kinds of book, for so many different ages. He is the one living writer of real stature who has already established a secure reputation. Whatever else he may write from now on he has written sufficient to demonstrate an instinctive understanding of the real nature of children, an infallibly sure ear for the truth of children's conversation, and a subtly complex way of looking at life, people and things which makes him unique among contemporary writers.

There are still many people who argue about William Mayne's work, who say that children don't like his books; that they sit on the library shelves; above all, that children don't *talk* like that. Anyone who believes this has never listened properly to children talking among themselves. Few children may use the actual words or constructions that Mayne uses, but what he achieves, for those with ears to hear, is the authentic sound and *feel* of children talking.

William Mayne's use of dialogue is, in fact, the distinguishing mark of his work. Children (and adults) who do not enjoy the finely strung tension and wit of the kind of dialogue that he writes (and it *is* a sophisticated taste) are not likely to appreciate his books. Because, to a much greater extent than with any other contemporary writer for children, his stories are introduced, developed and concluded with talk. Not to such an extent that, as with Ivy Compton-Burnett's novels, if you do not concentrate on every single word of the dialogue you are likely to miss an essential part of the plot, but at least to the extent that if you have the kind of visual rather than intellectual imagination that demands constant description to keep you 'on scene' you are likely to miss the essential point of his books—and may even lose your way in them. There are few descriptive passages; he rarely sets a scene—and when he does it is not particularly well done—so that the reader sometimes has to work hard to understand what is being described. Instead the reader is made aware of the effect the scene had on the people who were present and becomes vividly aware of what it felt like to be there. His books are about people and feelings rather than things. A 'thing' is often the superficial centre of the plot (an old barge, a disused railway line, a boat, a 'parcel of trees') but it is the people who matter and what they are like is communicated to the reader not by description but by what they say. If he wants his readers to know that a boy who has just come into the room is big and burly and angry he rarely tells you that he is—instead, he makes him *sound* big and burly and angry.

William Mayne is particularly good at conveying by small details of dialogue the inevitable tensions of close family relationships, and there are many fine examples of this in his books. . . . Mayne never makes the mistake of overdrawing these tensions until they become false tragedies. He knows that family life is not like that. But he has a wonderfully sure touch for the complex love-hate, friendship-dislike, need-for-yet-wanting-to-be-away-from that all close families share, and a family, though it is seldom the centre, always plays an important part in his books. He is almost but not quite as good with the relationships between children at school and at play.

The world of William Mayne is an intimate one, restricted to a few people closely observed, and circumscribed always by the normal ranging abilities of children and their inescapable necessity to report home for meals and bed and to school during term-time. It is, in fact, the true world of children. But it is in some ways a *mental* world, the projection of someone whose own deeply-felt love of childhood has never been lost, and who spins his wonderfully fine web of imaginative truth from the truth he knew rather than the truth he sees. It is a world which has something in common with Kenneth Grahame's. Not because there is any similarity between their books, but because both look backwards at childhood with an adult mind. Both are genuinely thinking hard about children, striving to get their essential nature down on paper, to tell us how they think and feel, what life seems like to them, what they think of us, to make it possible for us to share a child's world. But Kenneth Grahame never succeeded, in those of his books which are about children, in making them truly *for* children, whereas William Mayne does. His world is one which children and their parents inhabit equally and this is the second distinguishing mark of his books—that no part of them is ever included cursorily. Everything that is in them is there for a purpose and each part is handled with the same kind of observation and affection. The world of school, the world of home, the world of play are indivisible to him, they are all part of the world of childhood, and that is the world he writes about. (pp. 139-41)

He is unlikely to write a better book [than *A Swarm in May*]. It has all the Mayne qualities, fine dialogue (the way in which the characters of the different masters are brought out in discussion is remarkable) and a lovingly observed *mise-en-scène* superbly served by one of his best plots. . . . The story [of *Sand*] contains some of Mayne's best dialogue, and the talk and behaviour of the girls and boys is not only finely observed and accurately recorded but is also at times very funny. Many of Mayne's stories are set in [a small coastal town or village], where the past is still a living one, the population is small, everyone knows everyone else and relationships are close between a small group of mostly working-class families, shopkeepers, electricians, railwaymen, painters and other tradesmen. *Pig-in-the-Middle* has much the same kind of plot. . . . But, as with *Sand,* it is not the story that matters, it is the people in it, and Michael's family is one of Mayne's best-sustained portraits. (pp. 141-42)

[*Earthfasts*] is an uncanny book, with an extraordinary power of conviction that impresses one again with Mayne's great gifts. The suspension of disbelief while reading is so complete that the sense of chill that the boys experience comes through vividly. Only at the end, when many readers will reject the idea of the drummer-boy being left alive above the ground, to settle down and become an ordinary human boy again, is the reader brought up suddenly by a question. . . . It is interesting to note that he first thought of killing the boy off and only left him alive because others asked him to do so.

I have no wish to belittle William Mayne's work, because I think him the truest and most creative of those few major authors who are genuinely writing *for* children. But it would be a mistake to think that his books will be widely popular, or that all children will enjoy them. So much so that parents, teachers or librarians who try to force children who do not like them to read them are doing the author a real disservice. Those children who do appreciate and enjoy them will come back to them again and again, but they are always likely to be in a minority. (pp. 142-43)

> *Frank Eyre, "Fiction for Children," in his* British Children's Books in the Twentieth Century, *revised edition, Longman Books, 1979, pp. 76-156.*

Fred Inglis

[William Mayne] is an extraordinarily prolific writer whose writing addresses itself time and again to the point at which past and present, individual biography and historical movement may be caught in intersection. I spoke earlier of the exceptional purity of his prose, and the fidelity of his attention to children's lives. These are the really indispensable attributes of the rare children's writer who is also, at times, a great writer. To adapt a famous formulation, Mayne seems to be making major fiction out of a minor mode—'as if, that is, the genius of a major poet were working in the material of minor poetry' [in the words of F. R. Leavis]. The point about Mayne here is not so much his major or minor status, however, as the strength and breadth of a man whose writing about and for children gives him a subject-matter and diction in which to make a series of structures capable of encompassing some of the main experiences of the present time. His gifts make him an exception to Yvor Winters's stricture on most of the adult novelists now around, and turn our cheerful and our generous optimism about children's novelists into something rather more qualified:

> The most damnable fact about most novelists, I suppose, is their simple lack of intelligence: the fact that they seem to consider themselves professional writers and hence justified in being amateur intellectuals. They do not find it necessary, so far as one can judge, to study the other forms of literature, or even forms of the novel other than those they practice; they do not find it necessary to think like mature men and women or to study the history of thought; they do not find it necessary to master the art of prose. And these remarks are equally true, so far as my experience goes, of those novelists who write primarily for profit, and who boast of being able 'to tell a good story', and of those who are fiddling with outmoded experimental procedures in the interests of originality and who are sometimes praised in the quarterlies. In fact the history of the novel is littered with the remains of genius sacrificed to ignorance and haste
>
> (pp. 228-29)

Mayne's rarity and relevance . . . are that he has found new, simple, and piercingly familiar metaphors with which to render and understand the presence of the past. (p. 229)

> *Fred Inglis, "History Absolves Nobody—Ritual and Romance," in his* The Promise of Happiness: Value and Meaning in Children's Fiction, *Cambridge University Press, 1981, pp. 213-31.*

Judy Reade

When we look back at developments in children's literature, we do so with an air of sophistication, aware of the qualities of a particular work and mindful of its role in the extension of the genre. What we cannot reproduce, however, is the excitement that a body of work generated when it first appeared, making a break with previous examples of literature for children. Such a body of work is the stories of Arthur Ransome, written between 1930 and 1947, and centred around the Walker and Blackett children. Not that Ransome considered himself an innovator at the time, but merely a recorder of the adventures of a group of children, based on his own experiences when he was young, and filled with details of activities at which himself was proficient—boating, camping, swimming and fishing.

In spite of his disclaimer, Ransome's stories did usher in a new component in the spectrum of children's literature—the holiday adventure story. (p. 5)

Arthur Ransome's success as a writer and innovator was marked by the award of the first Carnegie medal for his *Pigeon post* in 1936. A Carnegie medal was won just over twenty years later by a story which shares with the Ransome tales an existence on the dual plane of the imaginative and the practical—*A grass rope . . . A grass rope* has many of the elements [of Arthur Ransome's stories]. It takes place within a short space of time, it involves a group of children of differing ages, and the adventure is provided by a hunt for treasure, in this case for the silver collars of a group of hounds which disappeared underground in the Yorkshire dales at the time of the crusades. Like Ransome, Mayne knows the area he writes about very well, but in this story there is no attempt at transformation—the author lets the countryside be its own eloquent spokesman. . . . (p. 7)

Although the story takes place during school time, the activities of school remain in the background; the focus is on the events which happen after school each day, when the children are back in their home environment. Adult characters, although more in evidence than in the Ransome stories, are again never allowed to intrude. The story is carried along by the activities of the children, with their parents acting as regulators or consolers. The adults only take charge when the crisis occurs at the very end of the story. Like Ransome's adults, however, they are sympathetic to the enterprises of the children and the working-out of the mystery. . . . (p. 8)

In *A grass rope,* the action on this dual imaginative/practical level centres around the youngest child of the group, Mary. In the Ransome stories, all the children enter into the imaginative framework of the adventure. In Mayne's story, on the other hand, although all the children combine to pursue the adventure, only Mary, through the use of her imagination, sees its magical possibilities. It is Mary who believes the hounds have been called underground by the fairies and that a unicorn was among their number. . . . Unicorns can only be captured with a rope of grass woven by a maiden. Mary weaves such a rope in readiness. On a walk across the dales, the children discover an old mineshaft. It looks the place where hounds may have disappeared and Mary decides to act:

> Adam helped Mary down from the wall, and led the way round the pit. Mary stayed behind for a moment, now that she had found a place where fairies lived and could be heard, though they were out of sight and no one at all could get there. She left them something to remember her by, in case they had the unicorn down there and so that they could make it tame and ready for her. She undid her belt, took off the grass rope, coiled it tightly, and threw it over the brink, ribbon and all; and it vanished.

While Mary continues to view the legend as fact, the remaining children (her older sister, a cousin and a friend) persist in viewing it on a more practical basis. It is Mary who precipitates the climax of the story. Exploring the mineshaft at night, she succeeds in locating the collars. A fox cub, which has fallen down the shaft, is mistaken by Mary as one of the hounds of the legend. . . .

The legend, as it happens, has a practical solution, but some of the group prefer not to hear it.

> 'Go on,' said Adam. 'There must be an explanation. What is it?'
> 'Don't tell us,' said Nan. 'I don't want to hear.'
> 'Don't listen,' said Daddy. Nan blocked her ears whilst Daddy explained to Adam.

As in Ransome, Mayne's characters are real children and his stories have a rational setting and give a rational explanation for any mystery. As an adventure story, however, **A grass rope** goes beyond the Ransome books, by introducing the element of fantasy, the 'irrational of all time and the poetic below the events of the ordinary life' [in Margery Fisher's words]. The inclusion of this element gives the work of this author a more literary appeal. His works therefore do not have the immediate attraction of the Ransome books. 'Mayne', says Marcus Crouch, 'is writing to satisfy himself.' But then again, so was Arthur Ransome. (pp. 8-9)

> *Judy Reade, "What Fun, What Fun! Characteristics of the Holiday Adventure Story," in* The School Librarian, *Vol. 32, No. 1, March, 1984, pp. 5-12.*

Jon C. Stott

[Mayne's] best work can be divided into three categories: realistic experiences of children growing up; attempts to solve mysteries from the past; and time travel. (p. 183)

No matter what his subject matter, Mayne in his best books succeeds for three reasons. First he places his characters in fully realized settings, especially in his Yorkshire novels. Second, he presents clearly the difficult and often conflict-ridden interrelationships between young people growing up. Finally, he sees the world as his characters see it, varying his viewpoint according to their ages, circumstances, and temperaments. (p. 184)

> *Jon C. Stott, "William Mayne," in his* Children's Literature from A to Z: A Guide for Parents and Teachers, *McGraw-Hill Book Company, 1984, pp. 183-84.*

Aidan Chambers

William Mayne, always published as a children's author but notoriously little read by children and much read by adults, may, for all I know, intend to be a writer for children. But what the tone of his books actually achieves, . . . is an implied author who is an observer of children and the narrative: a watcher rather than an ally. Even his dramatic technique seems deliberately designed to alienate the reader from the events and from the people described. This attitude to story is so little to be found in children's books that even children who have grown up as frequent and thoughtful readers find Mayne at his densest very difficult to negotiate. He wants his reader to stand back and examine what he, Mayne, offers in the same way that, as nearly as I can understand it, Brecht wanted his audiences to stand back from and contemplate the events enacted on stage. . . . (pp. 43-4)

There is . . . an ambivalence about Mayne's work that disturbs his relationship with his child reader. And this is made more unnerving by a fracture between a narrative point of view that seems to want to ally the book with children and narrative techniques that require the reader to disassociate from the story—to retreat and examine it dispassionately.

What Mayne may be trying to do—I say 'may be' because I am not sure that he *is* trying for it—is not impossible to achieve, though it is very difficult indeed to achieve for children. (p. 44)

> *Aidan Chambers, "The Reader in the Book," in his* Booktalk: Occasional Writing on Literature and Children, *The Bodley Head, 1985, pp. 34-58.*

Margery Fisher

William Mayne cannot be said to have invented the treasure-hunt tale, but he brought to it certain qualities which remain unique to him, in spite of the many writers who have followed his lead. The treasure is always unexpected, even strange (a forgotten ritual dance or a railway track or row of shops, an old family mystery explained, a lost water-course, a hound-whistle) and the finding depends on the intense observation of a particular place; there is a strong sense of community, often stronger because it comes through an outsider; relations between children and adults are respectful on both sides and unusually relaxed, particularly in dialogue, and there is a sharp sense of personality in minor characters; the narrative style is elliptical, enigmatic and selective (the main reason why Mayne has often been considered 'minority reading').

A Parcel of Trees is Mayne at his best, mystifying but not confusing, with a neatly jointed plot carried on concrete detail, every word weighed and important. The quest is a simple one. Susan, elder daughter of the village baker, looking for somewhere to escape a cross-grained, intrusive small sister, sets out to prove that a piece of land at the foot of the garden, beyond a railway, is still family proper-ty. To confirm continuous use of the 'parcel of trees' (a spinney with a ruined hut and other natural and man-made features) she must delve into local history. Through her questioning Mayne lays before us, by implication, sev-eral decades of village life. There is humour here, a mental map easy to visualize and, above all, that sense of popu-lousness, of a world of people and events inside and out-side and around the immediate story, which is perhaps Mayne's most significant gift to fiction for the young. (pp. 47-8)

> *Margery Fisher, in a review of "A Parcel of Trees," in her* Classics for Children & Young People, *Thimble Press, 1986, pp. 47-8.*

Margery Fisher

Because of his extremely terse, subtle, elusive and allusive selection of words, William Mayne will always be a minor-ity writer, in the sense that not all young readers are will-ing to match his uniquely observant, elliptical style with an awareness of their own. Yet his own particular merging of place and procedure have made some of his mystery-adventures experiences in reading beyond any other.

Mystery is the key to the continuity of his books, a puzzle whose solving the reader is invited to follow (but not to anticipate) in sympathy with the characters. Many of the objects sought and found belong to the long tradition of mystery-adventure, with tunnels, buried treasure, lost documents as the common coin. Mayne mints his coin afresh by conditioning each central object, scrupulously and with unique force, in a particular environment and with his camera-eye observing that environment at both close and distant range. This continual change of focus means that the place he has chosen is not only the *cause* of the puzzle but is also a peopled background, a place in which behind the active, foreground figures whose actions make up the story we can glimpse a more distant world going about its business. This invaluable device [is one] of populousness, of thrusting sharply, momentarily, beyond the bounds of the story. . . . (p. 322)

It is in the unity of sense-impressions and character-perception that Mayne has pushed the adventure story to its limits, as Peter Dickinson or Emma Smith have done in other ways. His special selectiveness in detail, operating powerfully in his use of dialogue, affects the settings of his stories towards the creation of secondary worlds—that is, of clusters of places and people assembled from reality (we always know which county we are in, though the actual places may be fictional) and extended and confirmed by imagination. The basic, familiar treasure-hunt plot which is his staple—the search for a well, a document, a lost house or a tunnel, a boat—is defined by its position and its importance in a particular place. In *Ravensgill* a family feud is composed after twenty years through the explora-tion of an underground watercourse; in *The Rolling Sea-son* a Wiltshire village is saved from the effects of drought by the discovery of a well at the foot of a certain hill; his first book, *Follow the Footprints,* depends on a close scru-tiny of minute changes in a path and a rock, due to light and damp. Always the reader is left with an impression, an almost physical recognition of a place, which has a

compelling power far beyond the scope of any form of il-lustration. Mayne's books have been punctuated agreeably by many illustrators but none has even tried to assume the prime duty of words. (p. 326)

> *Margery Fisher, "Techniques of Description," in her* The Bright Face of Danger, *The Horn Book, Inc., 1986, pp. 318-44.*

Zena Sutherland and May Hill Arbuthnot

Many of Mayne's books present stylistic difficulties, espe-cially in his use of dialect and idiom; like other great styl-ists, he will probably never be one of the most popular children's writers—but he is one of the greatest contempo-rary writers. (p. 360)

> *Zena Sutherland and May Hill Arbuthnot, "Modern Fiction," in their* Children and Books, *seventh edition, Scott, Foresman and Company, 1986, pp. 332-402.*

Neil Philip

Gideon Ahoy! shows William Mayne back on form after a series of quirky and disappointing books. In its assured depiction of the unstated intimacies of family life it recalls the strengths of *Ravensgill* and *The Incline.* Like them, it is demanding and not every reader will have the patience to enjoy it. It is an oblique book, in which things are appre-hended by the shadow they cast on their surroundings rather than by direct examination. As in all his best work, Mayne refuses to choose one story from the many poten-tial narratives.

This is not to say the book has no narrative drive. The sense of impending crisis is strong. But the story springs from the characters; they don't serve the story. Although the Gideon of the title is a deaf, brain-damaged teenager, *Gideon Ahoy!* is about as far from the manufactured "problem" novel as it could be.

It is, for a start, full of the pure wit which has always been Mayne's richest quality. It delights in the possibilities of language. Its syntax and phrasing have, in Mayne's phrase for Grandpa's building work, "A right and inevitable ex-actness". It is astonishing that Mayne can be so craftily precise and yet remain, as he does, entirely lucid and straightforward.

Language is one of his themes: the way language allows us to look round blind corners. For example, Gideon can-not speak: ("Gideon using his middle word. 'Baooch', somewhere between 'Rauh' and 'Dthth'.") But in one way he can speak more clearly than anyone, for his sounds, his actions and his emotions are inseparably meshed. Even with his limitations, he can make his inner life available to his family and, through Mayne's careful prose, to the readers. . . .

The reader is made to feel the weight of Gideon's disability because his fifteen-year-old slowness is set off by the mer-curial make-believe life of his young brother and sister, whose existence is a kaleidoscope of willed self-deceptions. Between these two poles is twelve-year-old Eva, whose viewpoint overlaps significantly with that of the book's ob-serving eye. These children, in their home on the barge, together with Mum, Dad and Grandpa, make up that rare thing in children's literature, a family which is a living entity rather than a background for plot development.

William Mayne is one of the best guides we have to the perplexities and intensities of feeling in childhood. In *Gideon Ahoy!* he shows those perplexities and intensities at work in a character who is unable to express them with anything other than varied inflections of "Baooh", "Rauh" and "Dthth". Gideon is not a static character: he develops in response to circumstances; in his own way, he grows up. The story of how he does so is moving, engrossing, and real.

> Neil Philip, "The Language of Light," in The Times Literary Supplement, No. 4385, April 17, 1987, p. 421.

Michele Landsberg

William Mayne is particularly unclassifiable; there is no more assured and skillful writer in the whole field of children's literature, and there are few forms he has not tried, all with astonishing success; fantasy, time travel, adventure, preschool stories, adolescent novels, school stories. . . . [Parents] of talented readers ought to be looking for his books from the time their children are about seven years old. The difficulty lies not in his vocabulary or his plots, but in his elusive, oblique manner of expression. It is extremely condensed and evocative, and perfectly honed to catch the flicker of mood and feeling just below the surface of action. Such accomplished writing provides a complex, distinctly literary pleasure for the advanced reader, but may prove too much of a challenge for the less practiced. (pp. 32-3)

> Michele Landsberg, "Taking the Plunge," in her Reading for the Love of It: Best Books for Young Readers, Prentice Hall Press, 1987, pp. 9-34.

Alison Lurie

Once upon a time children's books were the black sheep of fiction; like detective stories and westerns, they were tended mainly by specialists, critics of popular culture, or nostalgic sentimentalists. In libraries they were—and still are—herded together into a separate room, or quarantined from the rest of literature in the stacks under the letters PZ.

Recently, though, children's literature has begun to be discovered by mainstream theorists and scholars. Learned volumes on its significance crowd the library shelves, and the professional journals are full of articles that consider every classic from *Alice* to *Charlotte's Web* as a "text."

And yet, apart from the few people who write for these journals and the—I suspect—even fewer who read them, many of the most interesting children's books are little known. A case in point is William Mayne, one of the most gifted contemporary British writers. His thirty-five years in the field . . . have produced picture books, family stories, tales of mystery and adventure, and some of the best fantasy and time-travel fiction to come out of England since Tolkien.

Mayne's dialogue has been likened to Pinter's, his "exploration of sense experience" to that of Keats, his "alienation effects" to Brecht's, and his sensitivity to landscape and primitive emotion to Lawrence's. By and large, these comparisons are not all that far off. Mayne also manages to treat extremely sophisticated ideas and subjects—such as the ambiguities of perception and the shifting relations of present and past—in a lucidly simple manner, so that he can be read by children. If most of juvenile literature, however original and brilliant, was not still largely in quarantine, he would also be read by adults.

The first things about Mayne's work that strike most critics are the vividness and economy of his language and his acute, subtle sense of how the world looks and sounds. In *A Game of Dark,* a story of a boy who loses himself and finds himself again in an imagined medieval world, fallen leaves are "circles of faded carpet along the streets, . . . and between these circles with their unsewn edges lay the starlit desert of cloudless pavement." When he describes a train starting, the rhythm of his sentences is onomatopoeic:

> Then there was a sort of small shake in the engine, and from the wheels there came a noise like sugar being trodden on, which was the rust on the rails being powdered. From the engine itself came a puffing roar and there was movement, and then there was going. [*Salt River Times*]

Even the briefest simile can open out:

> There was [a bird] quite near, and he heard its wings flutter against the air like a book being shaken. [*The Yellow Airplane*]

The reader, if he or she chooses—and no doubt some do so choose—can test this comparison by shaking the volume in which it is printed, so that the book becomes the bird. It is the sort of odd reverberation that occurs in Mayne's work.

He is also acute in describing mental phenomena. . . .

A related gift of Mayne's is the ability to enter sympathetically into the minds of a wide range of characters. It is perhaps most brilliantly demonstrated in *Salt River Times,* a series of interlocking sketches set in a working-class Australian suburb. With what seems effortless ease, Mayne reproduces the speech and thoughts of an elderly Chinaman, a squabbling married couple, and a whole gallery of children and adolescents. . . .

Though Mayne's portraits of adults are often skillful, his important characters are usually children or innocents—unsophisticated, half-literate people, separated from the contemporary world in some way: they are gypsies, uneducated servants and laborers, farmers in remote Yorkshire villages, or inhabitants of an earlier period of history.

In Mayne's books such protagonists or narrators see nature and human relations uncontaminated by received ideas, and speak a language that is both simple and original. They also have the child's or the primitive's relation to time: it is not regulated by clock and calendar, but is free to expand and contract according to subjective perception. In the mind of the old serving woman who is the narrator of **Max's Dream,** today and sixty years ago melt into each other.

Several of Mayne's books are marked by an alliance between the very young and the very old, who have clear if idiosyncratic memories of the past, and speak to children as equals. Middle-aged people, such as parents and teachers, are often preoccupied and uncomprehending. Their interaction with the children is practical: they make rules, set tasks, and pack lunches. When children and parents (or teachers) speak to each other, the tone is detached and cool—sometimes, indeed, "Pinteresque." In *A Parcel of Trees,* for instance, Susan (age fourteen) is sitting on her bed reading one hot day, when her mother challenges her:

> "I don't know how you're going to make out at all," said Mum. "Or I wouldn't if we didn't all feel the same. It's the weather."
>
> "It's the dreadful life we lead," said Susan.
>
> "What do you mean?" said Mum. "You're the dreadful life, lying about like an old stump."
>
> "I haven't any branches," said Susan. "Do you think my soul's died first, and I'm going on automatic?"
>
> "To think you used to be a sweet little girl," said Mum. "I enjoyed having you."

Even between children real connection is unusual. What matters is not how they feel about each other but how they feel about themselves and the country or town they live in, or the success of some common enterprise.

Though Mayne often stands back several feet from his characters, his descriptions of Yorkshire are close and loving: he knows its economy of farming and sheep raising, its plants and animals, its weather and seasons. His preference seems to be for late autumn and winter, when the land is bare of leaves and of outsiders. . . .

As with many other British writers, Mayne's sense of place is intertwined with an almost archaeological sense of the past. He rejoices that every field has an ancient name, and that popular legends keep old beliefs and events alive. For him history is literally hidden beneath the landscape, and may appear at any time, as when Patty in *Underground Alley* discovers a five-hundred-year-old street of houses buried under a hill behind her cellar.

Occasionally the reappearance of the past is supernatural. In *Earthfasts* an eighteenth-century drummer boy called Nellie Jack John emerges into the modern world from beneath a ruined castle, carrying a candle that burns with a cold, unextinguishable light. His interpretation of contemporary events transforms them:

> A car started in the market place, went up the steepness in a low gear. . . . "Wild boars," said Nellie Jack John. "They come up by the town of a night."

Mayne's fascination with the past is not unique. Much of the population of Britain today appears to be living in the shadow of history, and sometimes, to judge by films, television, and popular literature, heroism, virtue, relevance, even meaning seem to have ended after World War II. For Mayne, however, this history is sometimes dark. Patty's "Underground Alley" turns out to be a decoy built to entrap and destroy a caravan of horses and men carrying treasure from Wales; the bricks of its pavement are gold, but behind the false fronts of its houses lie bones. What is concealed underground, in the past, is often both death and treasure.

William Mayne has now written more than seventy books; as might be expected, his work is uneven. But at his best he is remarkable. (pp. 11-12)

> *Alison Lurie, "Underground Artist," in* The New York Review of Books, *Vol. XXXV, No. 2, February 18, 1988, pp. 11-13.*

Penelope Farmer

Returning to William Mayne after a long gap has been a revelation. The sometimes whimsical self-indulgence of a writer who could, you felt, catch the uncatchable without trying, has gone almost completely. In this spare, compelling piece of story-telling [*Antar and the Eagles*], the tone is both mythic and throwaway in the manner of the best folk tale, and also of vintage Mayne. . . .

Antar is the son of a roofmaker in a time and country unspecified; when he conquers his fear of heights and climbs to the spire his father is working on, the eagles take him. They want an unvertiginous boy, small and light enough to learn to fly to rescue the stolen egg of their next great eagle. They make no concessions to Antar's youth, his size, his non-eagleness. He is bullied, derided, half starved, pushed off cliffs. Yet he is not to be pitied for this, except in passing, nor the eagles blamed.

Antar himself at the end knows he had received little kindness from them. But only because they did not think kindness important. But they had given him a lot of attention and that was important to him." And it is the attention he is given, the sheer physical reality of eagleness, described with the minimum of anthropomorphism, that makes this book so remarkable.

Any naturalist can list the facts of eagle life. But it is something else to convey with such utter conviction what it feels like, as Antar feels it—from the moment the eagle talons grip his clothes "as if a rope had been wound round his waist and chest three times and pulled tight"— through his attempts to eat the raw meat pushed into his mouth by his eagle sentinel and to keep nest space amid the savage nestlings brooded with him—above all through his struggles to make his wings and fly: "Something came up under him and held him steady, so that he no longer dropped and dropped. He was hanging on air . . . supported by the feathers he had sewn."

It is an equally remarkable and very moving portrait of a child, always a child, yet growing through appalling but unavoidable privations from the helplessness expected of young humans to a mature understanding of his mentors' capabilities and his own. I don't know if children will take to this wise, strange, uncompromising, yet warm, book, but I hope so.

> *Penelope Farmer, "Strange Nestling," in* The

Times Educational Supplement, *No. 3826, October 27, 1989, p. 25.*

Kevin Crossley-Holland

It's a pity that, among the plethora of prizes given to British authors, there is no Nobel-type award for children's writing: not to be given for a single work but for an *oeuvre,* a distinguished succession of books written over a number of decades. Such an award would suit William Mayne. He has long been a master of characterization, dialogue and atmosphere; he is a wonderful storyteller; his prose is dry, tight, unshowy and graceful, like a clean window that offers you a view and doesn't draw attention to itself; and he says things that are really worth listening to.

> *Kevin Crossley-Holland, "Flood Warning," in* The Times Educational Supplement, *No. 3858, June 8, 1990, p. B9.*

Stephen Fraser

A writer of protean gifts, William Mayne consistently lifts the world of children's books to new levels of literary excellence with each new work. He writes in the best storytelling tradition and knows how to keep his listeners' rapt attention with strong images, clean solid language, and momentum built by foreshadowing and cliffhanging chapter endings. He is a master.

> *Stephen Fraser, in a review of "Antar and the Eagles," in* The Five Owls, *Vol. IV, No. 6, July-August, 1990, p. 109.*

Francine Pascal

1938-

American author of fiction and scriptwriter.

Major works include *Hangin' Out with Cici* (1977; also published as *Hangin' Out with Cici; or, My Mother Was Never a Kid*), *My First Love and Other Disasters* (1979), *The Hand-Me-Down Kid* (1980), the "Sweet Valley High", "Sweet Valley Twins", and "Caitlin" series.

One of the most popular and controversial writers for young readers in the middle grades, junior high, and high school, Pascal is best known as the creator of the series of paperback formula novels about the lives of the teenage and preteen characters who reside in the mythical middle-class suburb of Sweet Valley, California; she is also well regarded as the author of contemporary realistic fiction acknowledged for its humorous and sensitive treatment of adolescent and preadolescent concerns. Pascal addresses her works to young women, whose enthusiasm for the Sweet Valley books, together with extensive marketing and promotion, has helped to make publishing history; for example, the "Sweet Valley High" series, which includes more than fifty volumes, has sold over forty million copies internationally, and the Sweet Valley High Super Edition *Perfect Summer* (1985) was the first young adult novel to be represented on the *New York Times* best seller list. Described by Pascal as "romances in the classic sense," the Sweet Valley books are also credited with opening the market for formula fiction for their audience. Most often centering around issues of love and friendship, the stories are often compared to soap operas for their use of continuing characters and cliffhanger endings. The "Sweet Valley" series revolves around the problems of identical twins Elizabeth and Jessica Wakefield, the most popular girls in school, who possess radically different personalities: Elizabeth is friendly, studious, and sincere, while Jessica is snobbish, superficial, and devious. The events in each story, which usually focus on relationships with boys or other personal issues, take place with a minimum of adult intervention. Initially profiling the Wakefield girls as sixteen-year-old high school students, Pascal created prequels with the "Sweet Valley Twins" series which feature them as sixth graders; she later introduced a new character, Caitlin Ryan, one of the richest and most popular students at Carleton Hill University, in a separate series. Currently, Pascal retains artistic control of the "Sweet Valley" and "Caitlin" series but delegates the actual writing to others: she provides the plot outlines and descriptions of character and setting for each new volume, all of which are produced by a stable of writers at the usual rate of one title every three months.

Pascal began her writing career as a magazine journalist, and later collaborated with her late husband John on scripts for a soap opera and an adult nonfiction title on Patty Hearst; Pascal is also the author of an adult mystery novel and is the coauthor of the script for the Broadway

musical *George M!*. Her first book for young people, *Hangin' Out with Cici,* is set in Pascal's old neighborhood in Queens, New York. The story centers on how Victoria Martin, a self-centered and trouble-prone fourteen-year-old who is sent home early from a weekend with her aunt when she is caught smoking marijuana, is transported to 1944 and becomes friends with wild teenager Cici, whom Victoria discovers is actually her mother as a girl. Pascal is also the creator of two sequels about Victoria, *My First Love and Other Disasters* and *Love and Betrayal and Hold the Mayo!* (1985), as well as *The Hand-Me-Down Kid,* which describes how Ari, a overly sensitive eleven-year-old, learns to stand up for herself. Based greatly on Pascal's high school experience and on her fantasies about how high school might have been, the "Sweet Valley High" series and its offshoots have become notorious for delineating an idyllic, almost exclusively white suburb peopled with idealized characters who are usually beautiful and rich. Although her non-Sweet Valley books are often acclaimed for Pascal's wit, facility with dialogue and setting, and understanding of her characters and their situations, the "Sweet Valley" series has received a strongly negative reaction from adult professionals, who fault Pascal for such problems as simplistic plots, unbelievable characterizations, blatant morals, and facile writing, as well as for sexism and racism; some of the titles have also been removed from schools and libraries, as has *Hangin' Out with Cici* for its inclusion of drug use and frankness about teen sex. However, other observers note that the Sweet Valley books could serve to capture the attention of reluctant readers and nonreaders by providing them with high-interest subjects and characters with whom they can readily identify, thereby introducing these young people to the enjoyment of reading. *The Hand-Me-Down Kid* won the Dorothy Canfield Fisher Children's Book Award and was chosen for the *Publishers Weekly* Literary Prize list in 1982. *Hangin' Out with Cici* and *The Hand-Me-Down Kid* were also adapted as ABC Afterschool Specials in 1981 and 1983 respectively.

(See also *Something about the Author,* Vols. 37, 51; *Authors & Artists for Young Adults,* Vol. 1; and *Contemporary Authors,* Vols. 115, 123.)

GENERAL COMMENTARY

Steve Dougherty

When Francine Pascal introduced the identical twin heroines of her teen novel series *Sweet Valley High* five years ago, she modestly announced that they were "the most adorable, dazzling 16-year-old girls imaginable." Right from the start it was as clear as their unblemished complexions that Elizabeth and Jessica Wakefield would not be your garden-variety adolescents. No braces or gangly legs for them, no Clearasil, no anguished moments spent studying themselves in the mirror. True, it turned out that beneath their dazzle the twins were as different as girls who wear matching gold lavalieres can possible be. Elizabeth was "friendly, outgoing and sincere", Jessica was "snobbish and conniving." Around these polar-opposite twins revolved a whole world of familiar teenage problems, and upon them Pascal has built an empire.

In perpetual attendance at mythical Sweet Valley High, the Wakefields are forever the most popular girls in school. In fact, they may be the most popular girls of all time in teen fiction. Unlike such sleuthing predecessors as Nancy Drew and the Hardy Boys, Elizabeth and Jessica help friends solve figure flaws, not crimes, and they're after cute guys, not bad guys. Since making their debut in *Double Love,* in which they fought over "tall, lean" Todd Wilkins, the good and bad twins have appeared in 45 *Sweet Valley High* books (for girls 12 and up) and in 19 more of the *Sweet Valley Twins* series, a spinoff for preteens. . . . With more than 40 million books in print in the U.S. alone (they have also been translated into 15 languages), the *Sweet Valley* series is a publishing phenomenon. It made history in 1985 when *Perfect Summer* (about a romantic bike trip) became the first young-adult novel ever to make the *New York Times* paperback best-seller list. (p. 66)

Besides, she insists, she never works simply by formula. "If I don't choke up at the end of an outline, it's no good, and I go back to the typewriter," she says. "It's really got to get you right there," she adds, indicating her heart. "It"

almost always gets readers, too. Pascal receives up to 1,000 letters a month from young fans, many of whom say that she got them hooked on books. To critics who accused her of grinding out junk food for kids starved for nourishing reading, Pascal argues, "These books have uncovered a whole population of young girls who were never reading. I don't know that they're all going to go on to *War and Peace,* but we have created readers out of nonreaders. If they go on to Harlequin romances, so what? They're going to read."

Pascal is convinced that, potentially anyway, *Sweet Valley* could go on forever. "No matter when you were born or where, puberty is the same," she says. "It's the same for your parents as it is for you—what's happening in your body dictates everything. Sweet Valley is the essence of high school. The world outside is just an adult shadow going by. The parents barely exist. Action takes place in bedrooms, cars and school. It's that moment before reality hits, when you really do believe in the romantic values—sacrifice, love, loyalty, friendship—before you get jaded and slip off into adulthood." (pp. 66-7)

Pascal became a novelist "one day in 1975, when I had a revelation. I said, 'John, what if'—my two favorite words—'a 13-year-old girl who can't get along with her mother goes back in time to her mother's childhood and becomes her best friend?' I just loved the idea so much. So I sat down and wrote it." *Hangin' Out with Cici* (later made into an ABC special) became a hit in the lucrative young-adult market, and Pascal began turning out a new novel each year. (p. 67)

> *Steve Dougherty, "Heroines of 40 Million Books, Francine Pascal's 'Sweet Valley' Twins Are Perfection in Duplicate," in* People Weekly, *Vol. 30, No. 2, July 11, 1988, pp. 66-8.*

Mary M. Huntwork

What do you do when your good reader, that eager consumer of a couple of stacks of library books per week, suddenly changes her habits? The hardcovers with their appealing jackets sit untouched, even the ones marked YA with the more grown-up subject matter. Instead, the drawerful of skimpy-looking paperbacks with the rosy-cheeked blonds on the covers get all the attention. As a librarian-in-the-making, I recognized the signs of the preadolescent paperback fetish, but as a parent I couldn't face the fact that my 11-year-old daughter had fallen prey to formula romances. Fortunately for me, there were papers to be written, research to be done. Why not, I thought, attack the problem head on—find out why these books attract and hold their audience and what, if anything, can be done to broaden the reading habits of formula fans?

The first point my research uncovered was that my daughter and her friends were not alone in their enthusiasm for *Sweet Valley High* and other romances. In every survey I found, girls consistently listed romances when asked to name the kinds of books they preferred. (p. 137)

Obviously, superior marketing answers a large part of my question about why girls read these books. Bantam has followed the historically successful formula in the paperback industry—predictability equals profit. If publishers can identify a category of book and the people who seek that category, then they can predict sales and avoid costly mistakes. Following the adult romance tradition, Bantam targeted an audience, determined what that audience wanted, and made it readily and widely available. (p. 138)

When teenage girls got word of the new books, they did not have to go farther than the book rack at their nearest supermarket, drugstore, discount chain, or mall to find them. And no matter how large or crowded the rack, *Sweet Valley High* books stand out immediately. The pastel covers (at least a dozen different shades), the circle crowned with the series title and encompassing the portrait of the main characters, and the provocative titles all reach the browser from six feet away. Closer up, potential readers get an idea of the plot from the details of the portrait and from the questions beneath: Has Jessica found someone new? Will Elizabeth lose her best friend? Some teen romance publishers use photographs on the covers, but designers at Scholastic and Bantam now consider color portraits with photographic realism more romantic looking.

Features such as the small pennant on the cover bearing the number of the book, the lists and order forms for other titles, and the hook paragraphs at the end of each novel leading into the next story, all emphasize the serial nature of the books. The series approach appeals to the "collect all twelve" mentality most children have grown up with. A phrase Roger Sutton once used in an *SLJ* piece put a new focus on the books for me. Sutton said that reading one of the choose-your-own-ending romances is more "like playing with a Barbie Doll than hoping and suffering along with the heroine." Barbie and *Sweet Valley High*'s Wakefield twins belong to the same fantasy consumer world. Just about the time girls outgrow Barbie at age 10 or 11, the Wakefields step in to take her place.

What I learned about teenage romances as consumer items confirmed my preconceptions of the books as skillfully marketed junk food. I had no trouble finding sources critical of their literary merit or redeeming social value—particularly during the early 1980s, when the series romances began to flourish. Critics of the books commonly named these characteristics: poor character development; weak writing; use of stereotypes; emphasis on superficial and materialistic values (clothes, makeup, cars, popularity, physical appearance); sexism (female characters find value only in relation to boyfriends); and finally, failure to reflect real life (predominance of white, middle-class characters, facile solutions to dilemmas).

Journalist Margo Jefferson wrote one of the most scathing commentaries [in *Nation*, May 1982]. She faulted the books for promoting the "notion that a threatening world can be made begin and orderly through external means (magic and fate) or internal means (conformity and submission) . . . What these books are really marketing is wishful thinking—the state of mind many teenagers are in when they experience intercourse, pregnancy, abortion, or childbirth."

Armed with criticisms like these, I felt a bit smug in my approach to the books. However, as I consulted *Genreflec-*

ting: A Guide to Reading Interests in Genre Fiction (Libraries Unlimited, 1986), a reference book on adult romances, I was brought up short by the following dedication page quote: Rosenberg's First Law of Reading—*Never apologize for your reading tastes.* Thus, Betty Rosenberg, author of the guide and senior lecturer emerita, UCLA Graduate School of Library Science, set the tone for the next phase of my research.

This nonjudgemental attitude also predominated in an eye- and mind-opening book by Janice Radway, *Reading the Romance: Women, Patriarchy, and Popular Literature* (University of North Carolina Press, 1984). Radway asserts that critics cannot explain why women read romances just by examining the books themselves. She rejects the idea that the text of a book is a fixed object. The reader, she says, brings assumptions and strategies to the book that give the text meaning. (pp. 138-39)

On one level, the romances seemed to provide "a utopian vision in which female individuality and a sense of self are shown to be compatible with nurturance and care by another." Vicariously, through the novels, the women see their mates transformed by love from dominate and insensitive to nurturing and caring individuals.

In addition, Radway theorized that a romance functions both as a novel and as mythology. Reading a romance, like oral myth telling, is a "ritual of hope" in which the same events occur again and again in the same pattern. Yet the romances also function as novels with characters and situations that seem new with each story. Even though teen romances differ greatly from their adult counterparts, Radway's reader response approach and her view of romances as mythology offer new ways to look at these young adult formula books.

Mary Anne Moffitt, of the University of Illinois, took a similar approach in her study of 14 high school girls from a white-collar, middle-class community. . . .

The girls read a minimum of two books a month, with most reading six to 20 romances in that time. Most of them read *Harlequins* and other adult romances, but one-third also read *Sweet Valley High* and other teen romances.

Moffitt observed that the girls surveyed felt strong identification with main characters. Some stated that they briefly "became" or pretended to be that character. The romance provided "a portable and intensely absorbing fantasy escape," Moffitt wrote. "The struggle they feel between what family and society expect of them and what they feel capable of accomplishing is managed in one way, through this leisure reading practice."

Interest in the opposite sex motivates romance reading. The girls indicated that they liked the long conversations between the male and female characters and descriptions of what boys were thinking. They also liked fights in which the girl spoke her mind without ending a relationship. Moffitt wrote that the books helped the girls capture a feeling of being in love and being loved. In a way, the girls could try out life (personal relationships, developing a sense of self, breaking with parents) through their reading.

Pascal with twins auditioning for the television version of "Sweet Valley High."

Moffitt made some interesting comments on fantasy and reality. Children accept fantasy-as-truth in their reading, she said, while adolescents read the novels as *understood fantasy.* Perhaps this process accounts for adolescent acceptance of plots and solutions that seem unrealistic to adults. Also, Moffitt's subjects explained how they exerted control over the text, constructing their own images if they were not pleased with story details (such as hair color, for example).

Both Moffitt and Radway emphasized the satisfaction and pleasure romance readers receive from leisure reading. (p. 139)

Many reading specialists who choose to write about romance reading do not condemn it as a worthless activity. Instead, they seem to share a practical attitude. Formula fiction, they might say, will always be with us. Why not use the books to motivate readers and fight aliteracy? As reading educator Lucy Fuchs put it, "Out of these early reading experiences will come the habit of reading. . . . By accepting their reading choices at this sensitive age and by talking to them about what they have read, we can provide them with perspectives on love and life."

Not all librarians in the trenches are threatened by *Sweet Valley High* books, either. In a Jan./Feb. 1988 *Book Report* article titled "You Can't Make Them Read Any-

thing," Sherry York urged librarians to "Respect the individual student and his or her needs. Never mind that you'd like to see Janie read at least one hardcover sometime this year. If Janie is reading paperback romances ad nauseum, at least she has recognized that reading is a pleasurable activity, and she might even expand her vocabulary."

After several months of research on teenage romance fiction, I too no longer view *Sweet Valley High* as a threat. I will not be overly concerned if my daughter lingers there a while longer. Still, doubts remain. I found no study that assessed the reading habits of teen romance readers two, five, or ten years after they have outgrown the books. What accounts for the difference between those young people who moved on to *Harlequins* and those who branch out into many kinds of pleasure reading?

I suspect that reading mentors—teachers, librarians, parents, and friends—make a difference. In Andrea Sledge's description of the ideal mentor, I found a model for the librarian/romance-reader relationship. Sledge describes reading mentors as "close, trusted, experienced counselors and guides in the development and promotion of a wide variety of reading interests."

Part of building trust, of course, is acceptance, not only of the adolescents themselves, but of their reading choices.

Each time a girl selects a *Sweet Valley High* book, she is telling us something. Publishers know this and have listened closely. The strong response to their romance series told them that not all teenagers identify with the characters of the heavier problem novels, that some teenagers want to read about situations closer to their own. Publishers responded not only with more series books, but with changes in their young adult trade books as well. Likewise *Sweet Valley High* readers told publishers that they liked buying books in convenient places. Now we are beginning to see more quality children's and young adult paperbacks in the discount stores.

Taking a cue from the publishers, reading mentors also need to listen carefully to the echoes from *Sweet Valley High.* (p. 140)

> *Mary M. Huntwork, "Why Girls Flock to Sweet Valley High," in* School Library Journal, *Vol. 36, No. 3, March, 1990, pp. 137-40.*

TITLE COMMENTARY

Hangin' Out with Cici (1977; also published as *Hangin' Out with Cici; or, My Mother Was Never a Kid*)

"Kids will be kids" might be the moral here, though bratty, self-centered Victoria, whose only talent seems to be for getting caught, isn't as easy to identity with as Pascal intends her to be. Somehow Victoria, returning home early from a weekend visit after her Aunt discovers her smoking a joint, unconsciously wishes herself back some 30 years to 1944 where she pals around with an even wilder girl named Cici. Minor shoplifting, sneaking cigarettes, and some ruckus in a movie theater soon escalate to full-scale havoc when Cici gets caught trying to buy a purloined science test with money snitched from a USO collection box. Meanwhile Victoria, who first thought she was in a weird, old-fashioned sections of Queens, has realized that Cici is really her mother . . . Victoria urges Cici to confess; wakes up—still on the train—to find that Cici was only a dream; and later realizes that her school principal is the same Ted Davis who tried to sell Cici that science test. Although Mother never catches on to what has happened (neither do we, entirely) she and Victoria end up sharing a kind of girlish solidarity. Actually, they're very different: Cici's pranks are high-spirited whereas Victoria's are unrelievedly sad and self-destructive. And like both girls the author enjoys setting up wiggy situations but can't always handle the consequences.

> *A review of "Hangin' Out with Cici," in* Kirkus Reviews, *Vol. XLV, No. 3, February 1, 1977, p. 99.*

After several hilarious escapades, Victoria realizes that Cici is her own mother, and the discovery gives her a new perspective on her own problems. Although the plot line lacks the precision of Rodgers' popular *Freaky Friday* (Harper, 1972) the effect is just as entertaining and the characters just as believable.

> *Diane Haas, in a review of "Hangin' Out with Cici," in* School Library Journal, *Vol. 24, No. 1, September, 1977, p. 134.*

The story contains some funny episodes and a particularly good appreciation of the changes in New York City from 1944, when it was safe and pleasant, to the hazardous present day. Cici is an appealing girl, quickwitted and lively, and the instant friendship is quite understandable. Even Victoria's rapprochement with her mother and her sincere but not yet perfect change of heart—she still fights with her sister—is believable. An amusing fantasy with realistic adolescent characters.

> *Ann A. Flowers, in a review of "Hangin' Out with Cici," in* The Horn Book Magazine, *Vol. LIII, No. 5, October, 1977, p. 541.*

My First Love and Other Disasters (1979)

Victoria's infatuation with gorgeous looking Jim Freeman prompts her to get a summer job as Cynthia Landry's mother-helper on Fire Island, where her ideal plans to spend his vacation. Though determined to capture Jim's attention, Victoria is ecstatic but surprised when she does—even after a late night petting session that leaves her embarrassed in the morning and in trouble with her employer for staying out too late. Overburdened by the demanding children and taken advantage of by their usually absent mother, Victoria lets the children spend a day with their grandfather, against Cynthia's wishes, with nearly disastrous results when the old man takes the youngsters out on rough seas. Needing help, Victoria turns to Barry, the boy who's been there all along, and is finally able to see through Jim's self-centered egotism. Wittily told in the first person vernacular of a 15-year-old, the story captures the kaleidoscopic complexities of living through a first love. The perceptions reached for but never realized in Pascal's first novel, *Hangin' Out with Cici* come through more surely here, and, despite a tendency to dwell on Victoria's day-to-day chores, the plot reaches successfully into a young girl's head.

> *Barbara Elleman, in a review of "My First Love and Other Disasters," in* Booklist, *Vol. 75, No. 12, February 15, 1979, p. 936.*

The denouement—predictable but satisfying—finds Barry and Victoria cast as hero and heroine in a storm at sea and Jim exposed as the selfish cad he is at heart. The story is a rousing good one and Victoria's colloquial narration fraught with verve and wit. But the real plus here is the delicate balance Pascal strikes between the explicit and the sensational; she writes about teen-age sex with candor and sensitivity. (p. 150)

> *C. Nordhielm Wooldridge, in a review of "My First Love and Other Disasters," in* School Library Journal, *Vol. 25, No. 7, March, 1979, pp. 149-50.*

To hear her tell it, the biggest disaster in Victoria's life so far has been turning 14. Whether this is also a disaster for you, the reader, depends on your visceral reaction to the nonstop patter of this clothes- and boy-crazy heroine. In fairness, Victoria's glib account of her summer as a mother's helper on Fire Island and, especially, her blow-by-blow report on how she fends off the advances of an over-insistent date will no doubt be avidly read by some of her peers.

Francine Pascal has good comic timing and she has created a few truly funny scenes, but she hasn't given us a character who can sustain credibility between laughs. Adults are likely to find Victoria exasperatingly shallow, and I suspect that the beach-blanket set will be bored by her relentless naïveté.

Joyce Milton, "All for Love," in The New York Times Book Review, *April 29, 1979, p. 38.*

The Hand-Me-Down Kid (1980)

"It's awful to be the littlest in the family. By the time you come along everyone is bored stiff with babies and everything's been done already." As this comment indicates, eleven-year-old Ari Jacobs, self-styled "hand-me-down kid," has a decidedly negative view of life. Then she meets Jane Richardson, whose situation is identical—except that she, in contrast to Ari, is a prime candidate for a power-of-positive-thinking award. By happy coincidence the two become friends at precisely the right moment for Ari, who is about to sink into a mire of deception—beginning with her borrowing, without permission, her older sister's new ten-speed bike for the class bully Rhona Finkelstein to ride in a race. The bicycle is stolen before Rhona ever rides it, and Ari desperately begins to fabricate one excuse after another in order to evade her sister's wrath; the penetrating questions of the police; and the ostracism of the outraged, and bikeless, Rhona Finkelstein. Narrated in the slightly skewed grammatical style typical of today's adolescent, the story is an amusing contemporary novel with an urban setting, which maintains a perspective on everything from training bras to older brothers and sisters and offers hand-me-down kinds a believable example of assertiveness training. (pp. 302-03)

Mary M. Burns, in a review of "The Hand-Me-Down Kid," in The Horn Book Magazine, *Vol. LVI, No. 3, June, 1980, pp. 302-03.*

Eleven-year-old Ari Jacobs goes to a private school in Greenwich Village; she has an older sister and brother who tease her constantly, she's always getting their cast-off clothes and skis and skates, and she cries when frustrated, which is often. Altogether—like the narrator of *My First Love & Other Disasters* —she's a bit much. The tears flow like tap water when Ari secretly borrows her sister's new ten-speed Peugeot, only to have it stolen by two young punks. Afraid to tell the truth, Ari fakes a basement break-in that the police try to pin on her sister's Puerto Rican boyfriend; then she ventures into the dangerous wilds of the East Village in search of the thieves and nearly gets clobbered by her parents for staying out too late. But not only does everything work out just fine, Ari even learns to stop crying—thanks to her assertive friend Jane who demonstrates that, for the victimized youngest in the family, the best defense is a good offense (Jane to sister, re brassieres: "You're practically sixteen, and you don't even have half as much [as I do]. Ironing board!"). Trendy

and overdrawn—but anyone in Ari's fix might learn a thing or two from Jane's ripostes. (pp. 714-15)

A review of "The Hand-Me-Down Kid," in Kirkus Reviews, *Vol. XLVIII, No. 11, June 1, 1980, pp. 714-15.*

This first person narrative is related by 11-year-old Ari Jacobs, the youngest of three children, who is bullied by sister Elizabeth, brother Ned, and the school tough girl, Rhona Finkelstein. . . . Though too prone to self-deprecation, Ari is a charming character and this well told, humorous, absorbing tale skillfully depicts her confrontation with sibling rivalry, her coping with peer pressures, and her final triumphant assertion of herself.

Millicent Lenz, in a review of "The Hand-Me-Down Kid," in Voice of Youth Advocates, *Vol. 3, No. 4, October, 1980, p. 27.*

Relationships develop in fiction through dialogue but just as much through silence. The writer has to fill that silence by taking us into the minds of the characters and implying what they feel and what, perhaps, they would like to say. This is where first-person narrative, that most taxing device, can be useful; with one character at least we can feel we have a direct, not a mediated contact. In *Hand-me-down Kid* Francine Pascal has avoided the main pitfalls of I-stories. Ari Jacobs, who is eleven, is telling us how awful life is with a sister of sixteen, Elizabeth, who treats her like a servant and scornfully passes on worn out garments, and a brother whose jeers are truly unpleasant; but self-pity is kept at bay because of the narrative is in the historic present so that events move us briskly through the girl's perplexities and frantic plans. For Ari is in real trouble. A domineering school-fellow has forced her to borrow Elizabeth's new bicycle so that she can enter a contest in Central Park; two boys steal the bike and Ari tries desperately to hide her part in the disaster and to track down the thieves. Excitement and humour are very naturally expressed in her headlong tale, whose conclusion casts back to the deeper issues in the story. Ari finds the bike but she also finds a friend, a dauntless girl, also the youngest in her family, who has worked out an effective way of holding her own against oppressive siblings. Another danger of first-person narratives is that they can easily become rambling and diffuse; in this domestic tale from America the problem of the lost bicycle affords a firm, satisfying structure under which a shrewd picture of changing relationships is built up. (pp. 4311-12)

Margery Fisher, in a review of "The Hand-Me-Down Kid," in Growing Point, *Vol, 23, No. 3, September, 1984, pp. 4311-12.*

Power Play (1983)

[*Power Play* was written by Kate William.]

Power Play is the fourth in a series of novels dealing with the adventures of the Wakefield twins (Jessica and Elizabeth) at Sweet Valley High. This is formula fiction in its darkest hour, folks. The characters are both unbelievable and one dimensional; the plot depends upon a legion of cliches, and it is probably kinder to skip over conflict and theme. Having said all that, I must add that our 13-year-old read and liked it. The pity of books like *Power Play,* which give a number of reassuring, if simplistic messages to young teens (heavy girls can transform themselves into being beauty queens in a few months; poetic justice reigns) is that they offer no insight, no real handle on social rejection or sibling discord. They are ephemeral, the cotton candy of young adult fiction, as opposed to the meat and potatoes of a Mary Stolz.

> *Judy Mitchell, in a review of "Power Play," in* Voice of Youth Advocates, *Vol. 7, No. 3, August, 1984, p. 146.*

Jessica Wakefield thinks only of boys, clothes and status, while Elizabeth, aghast at her twin's shallow behavior, is dedicated to working on the school newspaper. When Jessica does her sneaky best to blackball a chubby, unpopular classmate from her snobbish sorority, Elizabeth schemes to get Robin in and teach her sister a lesson. A subplot concerns a rich friend of Jessica's who shoplifts because her father neglects her. This story, full of perky couples and dialogue like "Omi-god," is contrived, simplistic and over-dramatic. Personalities are explained rather than developed; everyone is described in superlatives. People are the wealthiest, snobbiest, shyest, smartest, etc., at Sweet Valley High. The snobs get their comeuppance, but who cares? The morals jump out, but the methods of resolving the problems are faulty. A book for junior high school students should not appear as if it were written by one.

> *Annette Curtis Klause, in a review of "Power Play," in* School Library Journal, *Vol. 31, No. 1, September, 1984, p. 136.*

Dangerous Love   (1984)

Dangerous Love is the sixth in a series on Sweet Valley High School, the Wakefield twins, Elizabeth and Jessica, and adolescent love. In this volume, the love of Elizabeth and Todd is tested by his new motorcycle which she is forbidden to ride. She does; there is an accident which leaves her in a coma as the book ends. Buy next month's volume to find the outcome of the medical crisis.

Because of this unresolved climax, format, purchasers should buy the series, not an individual volume. The appeal will be to the junior high age. High school students will find it simplistic. The characters are poorly developed. The work fails to address the pressures and problems today's young adults have in their relationships with members of the opposite sex.

> *Sarah Simpson, in a review of "Dangerous Love," in* The ALAN Review, *Vol. 11, No. 3, Spring, 1984, p. 23.*

Love and Betrayal and Hold the Mayo!   (1985)

Although Victoria gets several early hints that her summer with her best friend Steffi as camper/waitress at Camp Mohaph isn't going to be Perfect with a capital P, she has no idea just how bad it's going to get until Steffi's boyfriend Robbie arrives, and she falls head over heels in love with him. Keeping Steffi in the dark and staying clear of Robbie is difficult in itself, but to make matters worse, Victoria's thoroughly nasty bunk mate catches on to what's happening and applies a little blackmail. Even Victoria's waitressing is fraught with disaster. All in all, Torrie would have been better off at home, especially when Robbie makes a play for her, and she finds herself faced with deciding whether a great romance is more important than her loyalty to a friend. Torrie gets caught up in a few too many bizarre, slapstick situations, but her flip, frenetic telling will still have appeal as a humorous portrayal of the impetuous infatuations of teenage life in the extreme. A sequel to Pascal's *My First Love and Other Disasters,* this can be read on its own.

> *Stephanie Zvirin, in a review of "Love and Betrayal & Hold the Mayo!," in* Booklist, *Vol. 81, No. 14, March 15, 1985, p. 1052.*

The resolution is an exceptionally satisfying one, but not surprising. For Torrie and Steffi are both sharp, attractive, intelligent "winner" types, whose integrity makes them eminently likable. Although the two girls aren't flawless, their good judgment and loyalty to principle make them both real and ideal. The dialogue is contemporary without contrivance, the story compelling without melodrama and the characters and situations capably drawn and credibly delivered.

> *Catherine vanSonnenberg, in a review of "Love and Betrayal & Hold the Mayo!" in* School Library Journal, *Vol. 32, No. 1, September, 1985, p. 148.*

Showdown   (1985)

Jessica and Lila are both in love with handsome, sexy, and exciting Jack. But why the big mystery about his background? And so goes another crisis at Sweet Valley High where all the guys and gals are just too beautiful and rich to be true, and where parents and homework are only vaguely in the picture. The book ends with a "cliffhanger" to entice the reader towards the next novel in the series.

> *Myrna Feldman, in a review of "Showdown," in* Voice of Youth Advocates, *Vol. 8, No. 4, October, 1985, p. 264.*

Alone in the Crowd   (1986)

Following in the success and style of other Sweet Valley High novels, this one is no exception. Lynne Henry feels like an outsider until Guy Chesney, the keyboard player of a popular band, enters her life. They soon became friends even though Lynne is secretly in love with him. There is no need to go on. The rest of the story follows in the tradition of other Sweet Valley High novels. If you are a follower of this series, I'm sure you will enjoy this. If you are a newcomer to these novels such as I, this book can also be enjoyable. Speaking from a man's point of view, I found this book to be readable as well as interesting. This book could be enjoyed by men as well as young ladies. ***Alone in the Crowd*** was far from spectacular, but if you enjoy this type of novel, I'm sure it will maintain your interest as well as your loyalty.

Tony Ling, in a review of "Alone in the Crowd," in Voice of Youth Advocates, *Vol. 9, No. 5, December, 1986, p. 231.*

Bitter Rivals (1986)

When Elizabeth Wakefield gets a letter from Amy Sutton, an old childhood friend, to say that she is moving back to Sweet Valley, Elizabeth is thrilled. But when Amy arrives, Elizabeth realizes that she's changed. Instead of being the shy, skinny tom-boy of Sweet Valley Grade School, she's now Sweet Valley High's biggest hit. She's vivacious and beautiful, the newest member of the cheerleading squad, and has become good friends with Jessica, Elizabeth's twin, and Lila Fowler. What is worse, she and Enid Rollins, Liz's current best friend, seem to be heading for a showdown.

This book is a pretty good addition to the Sweet Valley High series of which I have been a dedicated reader until a few books ago. But I have just one thing to ask. Why has Jessica become a secondary character next to Elizabeth in this series? (pp. 231-32)

Susannah Neal, in a review of "Bitter Rivals," in Voice of Youth Advocates, *Vol. 9, No. 5, December, 1986, pp. 231-32.*

Best Friends (1986)

[*Best Friends* was written by Jamie Suzanne.]

Here is a "soap opera" for the younger set complete with a "cliffhanger" to entice the the reader to borrow/purchase the next volume in the series. Identical twins Jessica and Elizabeth Wakefield have always dressed alike, have had similar tastes in friends, and have participated in the same activities. Now that they are sixth-graders at Sweet Valley Middle School, they are having identity crises. Jessica, the older, wishes to join the Unicorns, an exclusive all-girls club. Elizabeth doesn't feel comfortable with these people, and initially doesn't wish to become a member of the group. She prefers to join the school newspaper, Jessica decides to dress differently from her sister. Elizabeth can't understand why they can't continue to look alike. Even thought the characters are wooden and stereotyped, and the plot simplistic and predictable, the book is fast-paced and easy to read. Many pre-teens will probably pick this up and breeze through it.

Civia Tuteur, in a review of "Best Friends," in

Voice of Youth Advocates, *Vol. 9, No. 5, December, 1986, p. 232.*

A New Promise (1987)

This book is about Caitlin Ryan, one of the richest and most popular girls at Carleton Hill University. In this episode of her life, Caitlin is more confused than ever. She just broke up with Jed, her loyal boyfriend from high school and Caitlin's new boyfriend, Julian, is only after revenge. Caitlin must decide which boy she loves the most before her reputation is ruined. With Jed 2000 miles away and Julian right next door Caitlin favors Julian. However, Julian doesn't really love Caitlin. He just wants to hurt her because she is rich and his family is very poor. As the story unfolds and Caitlin discovers more of Julian's plan for her destruction, thoughts of Jed come flooding back to her. Emily, one of Caitlin's closest high school friends, senses Caitlin's confusion and talks to Jed, who is still in love with Caitlin. With much persuasion from Jed, Caitlin goes back with him and Julian is left alone to discover that he had fallen in love with Caitlin. He tries to make her fall in love with him again, but Caitlin's heart lies with Jed.

When I started this book, I dreaded the ending. The characters seemed so cruel that I knew someone would end up hurt. I'm glad it was Julian! His scheme to make Caitlin fall in love with and then to destroy her publicly was vicious. He shouldn't have held it against her that she had more money than he did. My idea of the book changed when Jed came back to win Caitlin's affection. He loved Caitlin more than anything else and deep in her heart Caitlin loved him. Jed was the only one who could see through Julian enough to realize he would hurt Caitlin. I was in suspense about how she would find out Julian was a fraud. It was during this time that I realized that these characters were no more cruel than some people are today. Therefore these characters made the book even more realistic. I was glad the book ended with Caitlin in Jed's arms and Julian was unhappy because in trying to make Caitlin fall in love with him, he fell in love with her. In my opinion some of the details of the book were dragged out, but the ending was too short. Everything was solved so quickly that it became like a fairy tale. I hope the author writes another Caitlin book so that I can find out what happens to Julian and his family and if Jed and Caitlin can stay together.

Jennifer Harvey, in a review of "A New Promise," in Voice of Youth Advocates, *Vol. 10, No. 2, June, 1987, p. 87.*

Amy Schwartz

1954-

American author and illustrator of picture books and editor.

Major works include *Bea and Mr. Jones* (1982), *Mrs. Moskowitz and the Sabbath Candlesticks* (1983), *The Purple Coat* (written by Amy Hest, 1986), *Oma and Bobo* (1987), *Annabelle Swift, Kindergartner* (1988).

Considered one of the most promising American creators of picture books to have emerged in recent years, Schwartz is praised for writing and illustrating warmly humorous stories which reflect both her personal background and her understanding of universal childhood experience. Often setting her books in periods such as the 1940s and 1950s, Schwartz is acclaimed for accurately detailing historical milieus while investing her texts and illustrations with a distinctive contemporary slant. She is also noted for creating resourceful characters who meet challenges and surmount problems by learning to rely on themselves. Her works, which often feature young girls or older women as protagonists and are written in a style noted for its rhythm and wry wit, address such themes as the love between generations, the joy in having a mentor and in realizing one's capabilities, and the anxieties of starting school, of having an assignment due, or of moving to a new home. Celebrated as an illustrator, Schwartz is well known for the pen and ink and watercolor pictures which grace her works. In her illustrations, which are compared to those of Wanda Gág and Lois Lenski, Schwartz characteristically portrays rounded or elongated figures with expressive faces and incorporates patterns and cross-hatching in both background and foreground for color and the effect of three-dimensionality.

Raised in Southern California in a close Jewish family, Schwartz moved to New York to become a children's book illustrator; several of her works are set in either California or New York City. Her first book, *Bea and Mr. Jones,* which describes how kindergartner Bea and her executive father successfully change places after becoming disenchanted with their respective roles, was inspired by her observations of the Manhattan business world as well as by her memories of wondering what her father did at work. Schwartz again addresses the problems of a five-year-old in *Annabelle Swift, Kindergartner,* the popular story of how Annabelle vindicates herself in kindergarten after being embarrassed by the advice of her older sister; Schwartz based this book on a story written by her eldest sister at the age of thirteen. In *Oma and Bobo,* she uses characters based on her grandmother and family dog to tell how disgruntled Oma learns to love the troublesome puppy owned by her young granddaughter. Two of Schwartz's books, *Mrs. Moskowitz and the Sabbath Candlesticks* and *Yossel Zissel and the Wisdom of Chelm* (1986), reflect her Jewish heritage: in the first story, an elderly woman adjusts to her new apartment as she prepares

to celebrate Shabbat, while the latter is a original noodlehead tale based on the traditional stories about the country where simpletons are considered wise. Schwartz is also the adapter of *The Lady Who Put Salt in Her Coffee* (1989), a chapter from Lucretia Hale's humorous classic *The Peterkin Papers.* For this story, which describes how Mrs. Peterkin learns why her coffee tastes so dreadful, Schwartz revised the text to increase its suitability for the picture book format. Recently, Schwartz selected eighteen Mother Goose rhymes with Leonard S. Marcus for *Mother Goose's Little Misfortunes* (1990), a collection which marks a departure for her as an illustrator; in this work, Schwarz places stylized forms against large amounts of white space and surrounds her pictures with thin colored borders. Schwartz is also the illustrator of works by such authors as Eve Bunting, Mary Stolz, her father Henry Schwartz, and Amy Hest, whose *The Purple Coat,* the story of how Gabrielle's grandfather tailors a coat that pleases both Gabrielle and her mother, is especially well received. *Mrs. Moskowitz and the Sabbath Candlesticks* won the National Jewish Book Award for illustrated children's books and the Association of Jewish Libraries Sydney Taylor Book Award for best picture book, both in 1984, while *The Purple Coat* received the Christopher

Award in 1987. Several of Schwartz's other works were named among the best books in their years of publication by both children and children's literature professionals.

(See also *Something about the Author,* Vols. 41, 47; *Contemporary Authors New Revision Series,* Vol. 29; and *Contemporary Authors,* Vol. 110.)

AUTHOR'S COMMENTARY

[*The following excerpt is from an interview by Leonard S. Marcus.*]

Leonard S. Marcus: What are some of your childhood memories of books and reading?

Amy Schwartz: I read a great deal when I was young. I had a very strong fantasy life, and reading offered a way of becoming totally engrossed in another world. . . .

Lentil and *Blueberries for Sal* were favorites, and I loved the Madeline books. When I was a little older, I read *Harriet the Spy* repeatedly, and the Little House books. I was—and still am—fascinated by Garth Williams's illustrations. His characters look so wise to me, with their soft, almond eyes and full lips. There's a real humanity in his work that I felt even as a child. (p.36)

LM: How did you first become interested in writing and illustrating children's books?

AS: A friend of mine remembers my wanting to be a children's book artist when I was in the fourth grade. But as I grew up, the books of my childhood became more remote, and my artwork developed in other directions. It was only in my twenties that I started getting interested in children's books again. I had graduated from art school and was doing my own drawings, which were mainly portraits of friends, as well as some illustration work. A friend from art school was talking about getting into book illustration and this rekindled the idea for me. (pp. 36-7)

LM: How did working on your first children's book, *Bea and Mr. Jones,* feel in relation to what you had been doing up to that point?

AS: It was satisfying to have a story to tell, in contrast with doing single portraits. I found it enjoyable to take a character from scene to scene. And I liked being silly.

LM: In *Bea and Mr. Jones,* which you illustrated in black and white, wild geometric patterns run through the pictures—on the floors, on the teacher's dress, and so on. It reminds me somewhat of op art and M. C. Escher and seems like a way of being colorful without having color.

AS: I enjoy the way patterns look on the page. My drawings are flat—I'm really working on the surface—and I think the patterning gives the drawings unity and depth.

LM: How did *Bea and Mr. Jones* come about?

AS: The story has to do with my reactions to the New York business world after moving East from California and with memories of wondering just what exactly *did* my father do all day when he put on his hat and coat and left home every morning.

I wrote and started illustrating the book in a children's book class at the School of Visual Arts in New York. When I first came to New York, my intention had been to be an illustrator, not a writer, but as I was making the rounds with my portfolio, a number of editors suggested that it might be easier to break into the field if I also wrote. I really started writing so that I would have something to illustrate. Now writing seems like a natural part of me.

LM: When you write a story, do you revise a lot?

AS: I write many, many, many drafts. I usually start out by vastly overwriting, explaining too much. In the early versions of the opening of *Bea and Mr. Jones,* for instance, I went on and on trying to tell everything that was going on in Bea's mind. In the final manuscript I was able to sum it all up in Bea's first bit of dialogue, " 'I've had it with kindergarten!' "

LM: There's a very clear parallel structure to the story in the way it switches back and forth between Bea and her father's activities. Did you have that plan from the start, or did it emerge from all the paring down and editing you were doing?

AS: I think I came up with that quite readily. Having a gamelike structure made the book somewhat easier to write. Once the structure was established, it was mainly a matter of playing out variations on a theme.

LM: Did you know all along how *Bea* would end?

AS: In my first version, I had the characters going back to their original roles at the end of the story because I thought that was what I had to do for it to be a nice, acceptable children's book. My instructor said, "What about having them remain in their new roles?" I said, "You mean I can *do* that?"

LM: Has the question of what might be unacceptable for a picture book come up often in your work?

AS: When I write a book, I want it to be something that will appeal to children as well as satisfy my own idea of what a picture book is. That idea, of course, has been shaped by picture books that I've read and by conversations with teachers and editors. In the case of one of my books, I had to simplify the vocabulary in a way I didn't always think was necessary. But usually my editors have felt as I do—that a child will learn an unfamiliar word.

LM: In *Oma and Bobo,* was it a problem to have the grandmother speak a few words of German?

AS: I was pleased and amazed that it was never an issue. In that book there is also a reference to Rin Tin Tin, which children today might not recognize on their own. But it adds to the period flavor of the book, and I was very happy to be able to include it.

LM: In the past, it would have been unusual for a picture book story to be set among palm trees in what is apparently California. Were you aware of doing something exotic from this standpoint?

AS: I started out thinking that a picture book had to be set in the East. Most of the books I saw as a child were, and even as an artist it was a while before I could question this convention. The first book that I set on the West Coast was *Jane Martin, Dog Detective* by Eve Bunting. I placed it specifically in Southern California because the author and I were both Californians, and so was the publisher. It felt rather daring. (pp. 37-40)

LM: *Mrs. Moskowitz and the Sabbath Candlesticks* is a story about making a home for oneself. It is also your first specifically Jewish book. How do these two focuses of the book come together?

AS: I wanted to talk about the ritual of Shabbat—the candle lighting, baking the challah—and also about the feelings of home, family, and continuity that come with observance of the Sabbath. I drew upon my own experiences and associations with the holiday. When I first moved to New York I often spent Shabbat with neighbors. I remember being struck by the strong feelings of permanence and home that I experienced in their company. I also realized that the ritual objects of Shabbat become inseparable from one's feelings about the holiday, that such objects become more than themselves. That's really what my story is about.

LM: Is there an autobiographical element in *Her Majesty, Aunt Essie?*

AS: *Aunt Essie* is about a little girl, Ruthie, fantasizing that she was meant to lead a very grand life. I certainly had those feelings as a child—I think a lot of kids do. I used to speculate after a presidential election that my father had four years to become president, and then I, too, could live in the White House.

LM: How would you describe the children you've written about and drawn? Do you think of your heroines—Bea and Ruthie, Alice in *Oma and Bobo,* and Annabelle in *Annabelle Swift, Kindergartner*—as having certain qualities in common?

AS: They all want to be respected in their world, and sometimes they have to scramble to get there. They start by casting themselves in a difficult role, which they then have to live up to. So they share an odd combination of insecurity and worry, while also having a very strong sense of self.

LM: What were the origins of *Oma and Bobo?*

AS: It started with a quirky recollection piece I wrote in a children's book workshop in 1982. In my original story, Bobo—our family dog—was contemplating becoming a human. Later I thought of turning it into a story about the relationship between Bobo and my grandmother, Oma, who lived with my family while I was growing up.

Oma and Bobo was published in 1987, so it took me five years to write the story. I reached many impasses along the way. I began with a mother and a father and a grandmother and four children—my family, essentially. One of the first things I did was to get rid of most of these characters, because it made the story too confusing. The climax of the story is Bobo's dog show. In real life, Bobo flunked the event. So, in my story, that was originally how I had it. In a writing class I was told that this was just too depressing, so I changed it to a victory.

From The Purple Coat, *written by Amy Hest. Illustrated by Amy Schwartz.*

The next problem was how to get from the beginning to the end of the story. I had to show how the change in Oma's feelings for Bobo came about. It's the most important thing in the book, and I found it very difficult to do—to have the reasons for this change be clear—without hitting the reader over the head. As I revised the story, first it got too long and overly emotional, then it got too short and flip. Finally, I read over all my revisions—quite a stack by this time—and tried to combine the best elements of each manuscript. That's when the final story really came into being.

I dummied up the text many times while I was working on the manuscript. This was helpful in getting the pacing of the story. Working on *Oma and Bobo* was like focusing and refocusing a camera, wanting to get things sharper and sharper. (pp. 40-3)

LM: When you began to do the art for the book, did you start with the first illustration?

AS: I actually did. Often an opening illustration introduces the characters in a simple and straightforward way. *Oma and Bobo*'s first illustration depicts Alice's birthday party. It shows each of the principals in a characteristic pose—Oma indignant, Alice excited, and Mother calmly neutral. It serves as a kind of prologue to the action to come. When this first illustration was completed, I then also had models to work from for the rest of the book.

LM: Do you think of other pictures, within the format of the picture book, as serving certain functions? Are there way stations running through a picture book?

AS: One goal in designing a picture book is to echo and accentuate the rhythm of the story. A well-written story will have variations in tempo; so might the illustrations. A series of spot illustrations, for instance, might be appropriate when the speed of the action is picking up in the text. Or I might introduce a double-page spread for a scene I think important, to make the reader stop and look.

LM: Even though **Oma and Bobo** was a story about characters you knew very well, was some research required?

AS: I went to look at the house that I lived in until I was four years old, and I looked at pictures of my grandmother. I took photos of two old German china cabinets that sit in my parents' home and that I put in Alice's house. As a child I wove elaborate fantasies about the contents of those cabinets, which my grandmother had brought over with her from Europe. I relied on memory, too—selective memory, I'm sure—in creating interiors that bear a certain resemblance to the two houses I grew up in.

LM: Is it when the artwork is done that you and others start thinking about the choice of type? Or has that already begun?

AS: Usually, the type is chosen after I've done a first illustration, so we can pick one that goes well with my artwork. That way, I also have the type for size; I can see how much room to allow for it on the page.

LM: Is it possible to say what makes for a good type in relation to a certain kind of drawing?

AS: The first thing is simply that it's visually pleasing. Often the designer will pick a type in which some element of the line is mirrored in the artist's line. In **Oma and Bobo** we chose a type that had a graceful capital *O.* For **Bea and Mr. Jones,** I remember my editor telling me that he'd found just the right typeface: it was nice and clunky, just like my illustrations! . . . Different typefaces seem to express different moods, and so a well-chosen type can contribute significantly to the telling of a story. (pp. 43-5)

LM: Do you consider yourself finished with a book when you turn the artwork in, or are you involved in what happens at the printer?

AS: I do like to go on press, because what is created there is all most people will ever see of my artwork. There are many limitations in four-color printing, and it's always difficult to see the exact shade that I worked so hard on just disappear. But one can make a lot of changes at the printer in terms of adjusting and balancing color, and I want to be a part of that process.

LM: What do you want your readers to come away with at the end of one of your books?

AS: Each of my characters starts off in a quandary. Ruthie solves her problem by sheer faith in her vision. Annabelle rejects her sister's overbearing advice and goes back to her own strengths and resources. Despite herself, Mrs. Moskowitz makes a home for herself by her refusal to be self-pitying. So I want my readers to feel that they'll be able to find a way out of their own quandaries, too. And, most of all, I want them to have laughed and to have felt that they've heard a really good story. (p. 45)

Amy Schwartz, in an interview with Leonard S. Marcus, in The Horn Book Magazine, *Vol. LXVI, No. 1, January-February, 1990, pp. 36-45.*

GENERAL COMMENTARY

Maureen J. O'Brien

As with many authors, Schwartz bases her stories on a combination of personal experience and general observation. Of the seven children's books she has written, all of which have been praised for accurately capturing a child's point of view, Schwartz has explored the pressures of working in midtown Manhattan (**Bea and Mr. Jones**), the anxieties of starting an important new project (**Begin at the Beginning**), the joys of having a glamorous role model (**Her Majesty, Aunt Essie**), the loneliness of leaving home (**Mrs. Moskowitz and the Sabbath Candlesticks**), the rewards of being unique (**Yossel Zissel and the Wisdom of Chelm**), the wonders of watching love blossom (**Oma and Bobo**) and the pride of being intelligent (**Annabelle Swift, Kindergartner**).

Characterized by her comically droll illustrations, virtually all of Schwartz's books include one overriding theme: that anything is achievable if you just put your mind to it.

"When I'm trying to come up with a story," Schwartz interjects, "I think I am more inclined to write about internal victories. That's probably why I often pick these tough, ornery types as main characters—both in little girls and grandmotherly figures. I think it's a part of me, a part of the people in my family." (pp. 176-77)

Maureen J. O'Brien, in Publishers Weekly, *Vol. 233, No. 8, February 26, 1988, pp. 176-77.*

TITLE COMMENTARY

Bea and Mr. Jones   (1982)

Schwartz's first picture book exhibits a talent for satire that she may use more constructively in time. The "story" is really a flat recital of foolishness, lacking the credibility that pure nonsense tales need. Bea complains to her father about the babyish activities in her kindergarten class; Mr. Jones moans about his humdrum work as an advertising executive. So Bea and Dad trade jobs. She commutes to Mr. Jones's office in the city, where she excels at inventing slogans and earns a promotion. Mr. Jones shines at kindergarten projects and becomes a favorite of the teacher and the kids. The drawings depict locales and things with admirable accuracy, but Schwartz goes overboard in burlesquing the characters; they are more unprepossessing than funny.

A review of "Bea and Mr. Jones," in Publishers Weekly, *Vol. 221, No. 22, May 28, 1982, p. 71.*

In this fantasy a precocious kindergartener and burned-out advertising executive father swap daily routines. It's visual caricature all the way set against straight narrative: each is readily accepted into the new environment and each joyfully succeeds. Most of the fun comes from the juxtaposition of the efficiently trimmed and noncondescending story with the surreal images of a balding kindergartener spelling "antidisestablishmentarianism" with blocks while his daughter, in his business suit and carrying his attaché case, goes about meetings and business lunches (ice-cream sodas rather than martinis if you please). The softly modeled black-and-white drawings are equally trimmed of all but essential details. Patterns are stressed (clothing stripes and checks, wood grains, lattice fence-work, etc.) and the human figures are rounded rather than angular, more symbolic of kindly peoplehood than naturalistic actors in life's drama. Indeed, the book is a parable about the way we organize our lives, about our uniforms and rules and the possibility of finding happiness in a bureaucratic society.

> *Kenneth Marantz, in a review of "Bea and Mr. Jones," in* School Library Journal, *Vol. 28, No. 10, August, 1982, p. 105.*

Every now and then on *Sesame Street* you'll run into a gag—like the Bruce Springsteen muppet singing "Baby, We Were Born To Add"—that's hilarious to tots, but can be fully appreciated only by their parents; a bonus of sorts. Similarly, kindergartners will enjoy the idea of Bea Jones trading places with her father for the day. But when the day turns into forever—"Mr. Jones and Bea had each found their proper niche in the world"—parents can enjoy, besides the wry little voice telling this story, its possibly unintentional parody of a well-worked (by Mary Rodgers and Walt Disney) theme. Best of all are the pictures. Full of chubby little dumpling people bearing purposive expressions, they form an extended cartoon satire of kindergarten teachers, businessmen, waiters, and good little children who *like* playing stupid games.

> *Janice Prindle, in a review of "Bea and Mr. Jones," in* The Village Voice, *Vol. XXVII, No. 50, December 14, 1982, p. 76.*

Begin at the Beginning (1983)

A lesson; a dull, hackneyed lesson (growing out of a contrived situation besides). Sara has been chosen "to do the class painting for the art show tomorrow." Miss Weinstein expects "something *wonderful*"—but, says Sara to her mother, "I don't have even one idea." This takes Sara through the evening: trying to paint "the earth—and the sky—and the day and the night, and-the-summer-and-the-winter-and-everything"; not knowing how to begin; getting conflicting advice from everyone at dinner; and, finally, being reminded by her mother that "you can only begin at the beginning." She'd originally thought to paint the tree outside her window; now, as they look out the window, that's it. The black-and-white crayon drawings strain for a little satire and a little frenzy; the text tries for some quasi-Ruth-Krauss, patterned speech. It all falls flat.

> *A review of "Begin at the Beginning," in*

Kirkus Reviews, *Vol. LI, No. 3, February 1, 1983, p. 119.*

Sara's frustration, her family's well-meaning but aggravating suggestions and the stalling will all strike a sympathetic chord, as will the lesson to bite off what you *can* chew. The pudgy people in the pencil drawings (sort of a surreal Lois Lenski Family Small for the '80s) convey reality, but in a refreshingly unique style.

> *Nancy Palmer, in a review of "Begin at the Beginning," in* School Library Journal, *Vol. 29, No. 10, August, 1983, p. 58.*

The simply drawn figures, black and white, have a clothespin-doll solidity; the story, albeit brief, touches on an experience with which most children can identify, the structure is adequate and the solution to Amy's problem realistic and moderate.

> *Zena Sutherland, in a review of "Begin at the Beginning," in* Bulletin of the Center for Children's Books, *Vol. 37, No. 3, November, 1983, p. 57.*

Mrs. Moskowitz and the Sabbath Candlesticks (1983)

Elderly Mrs. Moskowitz is sure that her new apartment will never hold the memories that her house did. She is gloomily surveying her surroundings when her son Sam brings in yet another box of her belongings. As she unpacks it, she finds her Sabbath candlesticks wrapped in a soft, white cloth, and she reminds Sam of some of the happy Sabbath times the family shared. Later, the sight of the candlesticks prompts her to polish them, which in turn makes her locate a nice tablecloth, mop her floor, arrange her furniture, and, finally, buy food for the Shabbat dinner. There is just one thing missing, and Mrs. Moskowitz fixes it with a phone call—she invites her children and grandchildren for dinner so they can share the Sabbath peace and begin making new memories. To appreciate fully this warm, loving story, readers will need an understanding of the Jewish Sabbath, which Schwartz provides in a clearly written afterword. Her pencil drawings are full of emotion and humor; even more than the text, they show that when one door is closed, another can be opened.

> *Ilene Cooper, in a review of "Mrs. Moskowitz and the Sabbath Candlesticks," in* Booklist, *Vol. 80, No. 22, August, 1984, p. 1629.*

Her Majesty, Aunt Essie (1984)

When Ruthie's Aunt Essie comes to stay, the girl realizes what no one else seems to—that her aunt is definitely a member of royalty. The girl draws this conclusion from her aunt's mannerisms, mementos, and the statement, "When I was a girl I was a little princess, Ruthie, not like some children I know." On the basis of this evidence Ruthie makes a rash bet with her friend Maisie. She will prove that Aunt Essie is royal, or else Maisie can have Ruthie's dog, Joe. Some clues are dropped throughout the afternoon (isn't that a little gold crown on Aunt Essie's slip?), but there's not enough evidence to convince Maisie.

Bobo trotted over to the potholder, and, triumphantly, he carried it back to Oma in the third row.

"Hurray!" Alice cheered. "We passed. I knew we would. Hurray!"

Oma was on her feet! She was waving an old red potholder above her head.

"*Achtung,* Bobo!" she cried. She tossed the potholder across the room. "Fetch! *Herbringen!*"

Bobo's ears perked up. His tail thumped the floor.

Then he stood up!

From Oma and Bobo, *written and illustrated by Amy Schwartz.*

However, the issue is resolved when Aunt Essie leaves the house for a date in full regalia—stole, long gown, and tiara. She dubs her niece Princess Amy, and after that, even Maisie doesn't argue. Although the oversize format, large pictures, and minimal text would indicate that this book is for preschoolers, its premise is far too sophisticated for them, especially since there is little to indicate why Amy has chosen to go off on this tangent in the first place. There is also the matter of the artwork. Schwartz provides wonderful full-color pictures, reeking of the story's late-forties milieu, but little ones may not realize the story is set in a different era. Slightly older kids may not either, but they will have a better appreciation of the intricate patterning and the amusing fashion nuances. All ages will enjoy Schwartz' roundly shaped people, who manage to pack a good deal of emotion into their small features.

> *Ilene Cooper, in a review of "Her Majesty, Aunt Essie," in* Booklist, *Vol. 81, No. 9, January 1, 1985, p. 643.*

The brightly colored illustrations nicely capture the over-stuffed comfort of Ruthie's brownstone apartment and the formidable contours of Aunt Essie herself. Sharp-eyed readers will enjoy their perception of Aunt Essie as a bossy and overweening visitor and at the same time sympathize with Ruthie's determination to manipulate ordinary events to support her own misguided conviction.

> *Ethel R. Twichell, in a review of "Her Majesty, Aunt Essie," in* The Horn Book Magazine, *Vol. LXI, No. 1, January-February, 1985, p. 48.*

Why is it that American writers seem able to produce humorous work for sixes-to-nines so freshly, whereas too much of our home-grown publishing is *still* either outdated, or patronising, or hackneyed?

Aunt Essie is a wonderfully larger than life creation. The pictures skilfully catch both quirky characters and urban settings. The ending, when the heroine graciously loses a bet with her friend, has irony and pathos that is still too rare in books for the age group. Find this one.

> *Colin Mills, in a review of "Her Majesty Aunt Essie," in* Books for Keeps, *No. 41, November, 1986, p. 15.*

The Purple Coat (1986)

[The Purple Coat *was written by Amy Hest.*]

Together Schwartz and Hest capture a quintessential moment of childhood with which both youngsters and their parents will identify. Young Gabrielle knows that autumn means a new coat. Every fall she and her mother take the long train ride into New York City to Grandpa's tailor shop. And every year Gabrielle knows exactly what she will get—a plain navy blue coat with gold buttons. But this year she has something different in mind, something in purple. When her mother leaves the shop Gabrielle tries to persuade her reluctant grandfather to make a purple coat. It is not until he remembers how much Gabrielle's mother longed for (and got) a tangerine dress that he comes up with his ingenious solution—a reversible coat in royal purple and navy blue. Schwartz' signature shapes—round, chunky, and unnaturally elongated—work beautifully here, especially in the city scenes filled with all types of people. The artwork is full color, and the deep shades and vibrant colors (especially that purple) are arresting. The numerous details and patternings catch the eye and make for pictures that can be looked at over and over; each time the story's satisfying conclusion rings sweetly true.

> *Ilene Cooper, in a review of "The Purple Coat," in* Booklist, *Vol. 83, No. 1, September 1, 1986, p. 62.*

Each fall Gabrielle rides on the train and the subway with her mama to Grampa's tailor shop in New York City to be measured for a new navy blue coat. This year, however, she yearns for something different. Her request for a purple coat, and Grampa's creative solution, provide a delightful story of intergenerational love and understanding. Schwartz' familiar brightly colored illustrations provide warmth and humor as they portray every detail of the text. The story is realistic, the characters believable, and the whole will elicit an affectionate response from children.

> *Susan Scheps, in a review of "The Purple Coat," in* School Library Journal, *Vol. 33, No. 3, November, 1986, p. 78.*

If every child must tailor his imagination to the measurements of reality, survival as an adult often depends on a fanciful solution to a practical problem. One part of growing up is learning what we can't have; another entails finding out how to get what we want. [**The Purple Coat** and Harriet Ziefert's *A New Coat for Anna* are two dissimilar books which] celebrate the triumph of imagination, resourcefulness and hope and still manage to tell wonderfully specific stories of two little girls and the occasion of getting a new winter coat.

Every fall Gabrielle, the heroine of **The Purple Coat** accompanies her mother on the Silver Express from Meadowlawn to Pennsylvania Station, then in the subway to Grampa's tailor shop for a lunch of pastrami and salami sandwiches and a new coat for Gabby. The ritual is always the same and so is the coat—navy blue "with two rows of buttons and a half belt in back." But this year Gabby wants a purple coat. Mama only laughs and goes off to do her shopping. Though Grampa is a consummate tailor, he is a reluctant to fashion a coat of a different color as Gabby is to switch from her usual salami to Grampa's favorite pastrami.

To divulge how Grampa and Gabby reach a compromise between practical accommodation and colorful adventure would be to spoil the suspense, but Amy Hest knows all about the tendency of ragg knee socks to slip down around the ankles, the changes in Grampa's face when he frowns and the way bubbles rise in freshly poured cream soda. And Amy Schwartz's witty, richly detailed pictures create a world, poignantly familiar to many adults, through which a child can wander endlessly. Bolts of fabrics in a rainbow of colors rise from floor to ceiling; button boxes, each with a mounted sample, are stacked against one wall; patterns with half-finished garments hang from racks; the

skyscrapers of Manhattan where Mama disappears for the afternoon loom outside the windows. The image of Gabby and Grampa perched on his cluttered desk with their sandwiches could change every child's eating habits.

[**The Purple Coat**] reverberates with a nostalgic reality. . . .

> *Ellen Feldman, "Growing Up Hopeful," in* The New York Times Book Review, *November 9, 1986, p. 60.*

The comfortable relationships in the family are echoed in the warm, colorful illustrations. The details of Grampa's tailor shop are carefully rendered with the bolts of cloth on their shelves, the boxes of buttons, the spool board near the sewing machine, and the bare windows looking out over the roof tops of the city. Readers will enjoy the book both for its picture of a time when coats for little girls could be made by a grandfather in his small tailor shop as well as for the pleasant and very natural interactions among the members of this loving family. (pp. 46-7)

> *Hanna B. Zeiger, in a review of "The Purple Coat," in* The Horn Book Magazine, *Vol. LXIII, No. 1, January–February, 1987, pp. 46-7.*

The loving family dynamics are clearly reflected in the writing as Grandpa passes on his wisdom to Gabby ("Once in a while it's good to try something new"). The illustrations, however, project the relationship even more strongly, as the two homely figures echo each other's stances, positions, and expressions. Appropriate in a story about fabric, there is much attention to texture and pattern in the art, with clothing a palpable presence in all the figures and a focus of contrast or coordination with the surroundings. A rich observation of childhood experience.

> *Betsy Hearne in a review of "The Purple Coat," in* Bulletin of the Center for Children's Books, *Vol. 40, No. 6, February, 1987, p. 107.*

Yossel Zissel and the Wisdom of Chelm (1986)

A butcher in Chelm receives word that a rich uncle has left him a fortune. He travels to Warsaw to claim it, but finding the bags of gold too heavy to carry, he trades them for animals, then trades the animals for feather beds. Even they prove heavy, so he slits them, imagining that the wind will carry the feathers to Chelm. Since the feathers are blown throughout the world, Yossel Zissel and the other Chelmites now travel everywhere to recover them.

Schwartz's lighthearted text moves the story briskly along. Her black-and-white illustrations are appropriately zany, although some of the reproductions have a muddy quality. Yossel Zissel's ability to be content despite setbacks is refreshing in our age of enticing materialism.

The tales of Chelm, where simpletons are the wise men, are a well-established part of Jewish folklore. Some are available in collections of Isaac Singer and Solomon Simon. This is a good introduction to these foolish but lovable characters for younger children.

A review of "Yossel Zissel and the Wisdom of Chelm," in Kirkus Reviews, *Vol. LIV, No. 22, November 15, 1986, p. 1726.*

This is an amusing inclusion for a story hour of numskull tales, with a hearty Jewish flavor all its own but motifs similar to "Gudbrand on the Hillside" and others. The black-and-white illustrations are spacious and, in the best compositions, have a rhythm of rounded shapes somewhat reminiscent of Wanda Gag's work.

Betsy Hearne, in a review of "Yossel Zissel and the Wisdom of Chelm," in Bulletin of the Center for Children's Books, *Vol. 40, No. 5, January, 1987, p. 98.*

Oma and Bobo (1987)

While Schwartz' backdrop has changed—Spanish-style houses and wide open spaces have replaced her typical New York City brownstones and sidewalks—her elongated yet lumpy figures are as vital as ever. Here they come to full life in a story about a grandmother, her granddaughter, and a dog. When Alice's mother gives Alice a dog for her birthday, Oma's reaction is *"Mein Gott,"* her words accompanied by a wicked scowl. Gradually, though, Oma warms up to Bobo, growing from hostility to peaceful coexistence and finally to friendship. It's hard to tell who the star of this book is—Oma or Bobo, for each is funnier than the other in expression and action. Alice is pretty charming herself, but she has strong competition for the limelight, including the characters at dog obedience school, who look very much like rejects from a Fellini movie. **Oma and Bobo** has all of the elements that a pic-

ture book *should* have: a strong story, memorable characters, and pictures that are self-explanatory. Like Bobo, it deserves a blue ribbon.

Trev Jones, in a review of "Oma and Bobo," in School Library Journal, *Vol. 33, No. 7, March, 1987, p. 150.*

Schwartz provides a rather scarce commodity these days—a picture book whose story has a beginning, a middle, and an end. Vividly written, it is insightful as well as entertaining. As in her other books, Schwartz' pictures are unusual in the best sense of the word—a California ambience complete with palm trees provides the setting and the early fifties is the time. Schwartz peoples her drawings with characters who are overly fat or overly thin, all unique in their oddities. Cross-hatching, patterning, and clever detailing add to the visual interest. There is special appeal here for older children, who will best appreciate the story's subtle tension between Bobo and Oma.

Ilene Cooper, in a review of "Oma and Bobo," in Booklist, *Vol. 83, No. 15, April 1, 1987, p. 1210.*

This is a fresh portrait of an unlikely friendship that allows room for both humor and dignity. Schwartz's eccentric illustrations have a 50's mood colored by an 80's sensibility, and are filled with witty details and patterns (check out Alice's paisley pedal-pushers) exactly suiting the dry tone of the text.

Roger Sutton, in a review of "Oma and Bobo," in Bulletin of the Center for Children's Books, *Vol. 40, No. 10, June, 1987, p. 196.*

"Annabelle Swift?" Mr. Blum called.
Annabelle jumped up. She cleared her throat.
"Annabelle Swift, Kindergartner!"
All the kids on the green rug started laughing. Except the chubby boy.
Annabelle sat down. She wanted to crawl under the rug.

From Annabelle Swift, Kindergartner, *written and illustrated by Amy Schwartz.*

Annabelle Swift, Kindergartner (1988)

Annabelle's third-grade sister, Lucy, makes sure that Annabelle is well prepared for her first day at school, with mixed results.

Officious Lucy teaches Annabelle the "fancy stuff"—on Mom's dressing table, the colors are not just red and blue but Raving Scarlet and Blue Desire. But when, on Lucy's instruction, Annabelle responds to Mr. Blum's roll call with "Annabelle Swift, Kindergartner," she is mortified to have everyone laugh. After Lucy's color names also prove inappropriate, Annabelle learns caution; but the class's esteem is fully restored when she is the only one who can count the milk money—Lucy taught her that, too.

Schwartz's well-designed, cartoonish illustrations are brightly colored and wonderfully expressive of five-year-old emotions and a cozy, well-equipped classroom; you can almost smell the vast, fresh-scrubbed cafeteria where Annabelle goes to fetch the milk. An exceptionally perceptive look at sisterly relations and the ups and downs of beginning school.

> *A review of "Annabelle Swift, Kindergartner," in Kirkus Reviews, Vol. LVI, No. 1, January 1, 1988, p. 59.*

Schwartz knows how to tell a good story, and this one, laced with humor, makes for a delightful read. The unique pictures, many two-page spreads, show both freedom of movement and attention to detail, and the happy colors tie it all together. A satisfying wedding of art and text, perfect for the intended age group.

> *Ilene Cooper, in a review of "Annabelle Swift, Kindergartner," in Booklist, Vol. 84, No. 11, February 1, 1988, p. 936.*

In illustrations that carefully evoke the naive and awkward drawings of children, Schwartz captures the essence of childhood complete with pedal-pushers, pinafores, and 6¢ milk. Line and wash illustrations in crayon-bright colors reveal a classroom that is cheerful, warm, and inviting. The children pictured are universal yet individual, while the adults are solid and supportive. Schwartz is in fine form summoning the fears and feelings that all children experience at one time or another. Preschoolers will readily empathize with Annabelle's plight, while beginning readers will enjoy a giggly head start on such school stories as Cleary's *Ramona the Pest* (Morrow, 1968). Schwartz' humor lightens the gravity of Annabelle's early problems without negating them so that young readers will cheer all the louder at Annabelle's decisive victory. (pp.87-8)

> *Jeanne Marie Clancy, in a review of "Annabelle Swift, Kindergartner," in School Library Journal, Vol. 35, No. 8, May, 1988, pp. 87-8.*

The Lady Who Put Salt in Her Coffee (1989)

When Mrs. Peterkin finds that she has put salt in her coffee instead of sugar, the whole family searches for a remedy . . . but neither the chemist nor the herb woman can restore the taste. Not until the family consults the sensible lady from Philadelphia (who suggests brewing a fresh cup) can Mrs. Peterkin enjoy her morning coffee. In this adaptation of the first—and perhaps funniest—chapter of Hale's *Peterkin Papers* (Sharon, 1981), Schwartz has removed some of the wordiness without changing Hale's style or the droll flavor of the original, better suiting the story to the picture-book format and making this classic more accessible to today's children. Full-page watercolor and pen-and-ink illustrations are filled with the abundant patterns and clutter associated with Victorian decor—fringed lamp shades, ornate furniture, and swarming patterns on wallpaper, carpets, and clothing. Using only tiny lines to denote facial features, Schwartz has endowed her whimsical characters with wonderfully expressive faces. Full pages of text on white background are sometimes embellished with smaller illustrations, adding to the pleasing format. A charming spoof of Victorian family life and an example of nonsense in early American writing revived by a gifted illustrator of today. (pp. 85-6)

> *Susan Scheps, in a review of "The Lady Who Put Salt in Her Coffee," in School Library Journal, Vol. 35, No. 14, October, 1989, pp. 85-6.*

This story, from Lucretia Hale's *The Peterkin Papers*, was published in a magazine in 1867 and as part of a collection of stories in 1880. Still available in libraries, the book is little read by children today. Schwartz rescues this, the best-known episode from those droll tales, and provides a smooth revision respectful of Hale's language. She also presents a new generation with artwork that re-creates the Victorian setting while echoing the humor of the narrative. Fine black lines delineate the elaborate Victorian interiors and outdoor scenes, while soft, rich watercolors provide warmth, patterns, and shading. The exaggerated figures and deadpan faces of the characters express the story's essential wit. A treat to read aloud, particularly to children who have yet to meet the Peterkins.

> *Carolyn Phelan, in a review of "The Lady Who Put Salt in Her Coffee," in Booklist, Vol. 86, No. 5, November 1, 1989, p. 558.*

Adapting a classic is a challenging process. Fortunately, Amy Schwartz has succeeded brilliantly, showing respect for her material and appreciation for the time and place in which it is set. Textual changes are minimal: a few judicious omissions of material that slowed the pace and the rearrangement of paragraphs into sequences better suited to the picture book format. Lucretia Hale's words and wry humor remain as brisk and appealing as always, brightly burnished for a contemporary audience. Always a favorite with storytellers, **"The Lady Who Put Salt in Her Coffee"** is one of the original "noodlehead" tales about the Peterkin family—long on charm but short on commonsense—who are rescued from their self-induced dilemmas by the practical wisdom of the lady from Philadelphia. In this episode, Mrs. Peterkin mistakenly puts salt instead of sugar in her coffee. . . . The solution—to brew a new cup of coffee—will certainly charm today's listeners and readers as much as it did those in 1867, when the story was first published. The animated, finely detailed, colorful illustrations capture both the absurdity of the tale and the wonderfully fussy Victorian atmosphere. Like a Gilbert and Sullivan operetta, the story not only stands the test of time but benefits greatly from a new and thoughtful production.

> *Mary M. Burns, in a review of "The Lady Who Put Salt in Her Coffee," in* The Horn Book Magazine, *Vol. LXVI, No. 1, January-February, 1990, p. 51.*

Mother Goose's Little Misfortunes (with Leonard S. Marcus, 1990)

A charmingly idiosyncratic selection of 18 nursery rhymes that, as Marcus says in his excellent introduction, "remind us all of the supreme virtue of being able to laugh at oneself . . . [and] recast misfortune so that it looms less large." Some of the choices here are pleasantly familiar; more are refreshingly less so. In her best illustrations to date, Schwartz swirls the beleaguered but cheerful characters across the pages, deftly delineating forms with an airy line against the generous white that sets off her judicious, sparing use of bright color. There are some splendid compositions, from Peter White following his nose right off the first page to Anna Elise, seen six times as she bounds rhythmically across a double spread; from the vibrantly stylized cats of Kilkenny, all mouths and about to eat each other up, to the wise men of Gotham, who conclude this delightful book by sliding off the round world in their round bowl. Not to be missed.

> *A review of "Mother Goose's Little Misfortunes," in* Kirkus Reviews, *Vol. LVIII, No. 12, June 15, 1990, p. 879.*

[*The following excerpt is from a review of* Mother Goose's Little Misfortunes *and* The Orchard Book of Nursery Rhymes, *selected by Zena Sutherland.*]

Pray, what's the right age for a Mother Goose fix?
Post-natal, post-teen-age, post-geriatrix.
While teevee numbs duller and dimmer each day,
these rollicking rhymes indelibly stay.
So welcome, wassail, hooray and halloo
to two grand collections with pictures brand-new.
One is traditional, one is quite mod,
each rates a rousing affirmative nod.

Mother Goose's Little Misfortunes: the title is poor,
hardly engaging the reader as lure,
but open the pages and find there instead
a sampling far better read than dread.
Lest one worry a tot might be got insecure,
Leonard Marcus's preface will reassure.
Yet even without the warning disarming
no child would find this book alarming,
so skip the prose intro, jump in with both feet
and clap your hands to the joyous beat.
Amy Schwartz's pictures are buoyant, up in the airy,
goofy, guffaw-y, never too scary.
My favorite fall guy is Dr. Fell,
but most of the others I like full well;
the watercolors are bright, there are white open spaces
to leave laughing room for the fuming faces,
the merry mishaps, the clown-y rages.
One capsule complaint: not enough pages.

> *Eve Merriam, "Clap Your Hands to the Joyous Beat," in* The New York Times Book Review, *November 11, 1990, p. 31.*

Is there a place on the shelf for yet another compilation of Mother Goose rhymes? The answer can only be *yes* when the collection is as fresh, well focused, and intelligently chosen as this. Marcus and Schwartz include some old favorites, but most of the eighteen poems are less familiar. In all, trouble is afoot, whether impossibly silly or scarily possible—'Jerry Hall/He is so small,/A rat could eat him/Hat and all." Marcus's cogent two-page introduction comments upon the universal appeal of these rhymes to encourage us to laugh at ourselves: "Nonsense is only partly what they're about; by a delightful paradox, their nonsense restores our sense of proportion." Schwartz's illustrations are immediately recognizable as her own, yet different from what we have come to expect. Her figures sport pink, oval faces and prominent noses; placed on stark white backgrounds, embellished and decorated with splashes of bright, child-appealing color, they take on an energy which the thin, single-color borders surrounding each page or double-page spread are barely able to contain. Stylized shapes, unusual perspectives, and exaggerated sizes combine to create a graceful and pleasing whole.

> *Ellen Fader, in a review of "Mother Goose's Little Misfortunes," in* The Horn Book Magazine, *Vol. LXVI, No. 6, November-December, 1990, p. 755.*

Alvin Silverstein

1933-

Virginia B(arbara) Silverstein

1937-

Alvin—(Also writes as Dr. A) American author of nonfiction and journalist.

Virginia—American author of nonfiction.

Major works include *Life in the Universe* (1967), *Guinea Pigs: All about Them* (1972), *Alcoholism* (1975), *So You're Getting Braces: A Guide to Orthodontics* (1978), *Aging* (with Glenn Silverstein, 1979), *AIDS: Deadly Threat* (1986), the "Systems of the Body" series, the "Story of Your . . . " series.

Considered among the most outstanding writers of informational books for middle graders and young adults, the prolific husband and wife team of the Silversteins are respected for addressing both complex subjects and topics with special interest to young people in a clear, authoritative, and engaging manner. Covering a variety of subjects in such areas as biology, zoology, chemistry, genetics, bionics, and robotics, the Silversteins are praised for the timeliness and high-interest level of their topics, the thoroughness of their coverage, their successful integration of basic findings with the newest materials in the field, and their balanced, nondidactic approach. The collaborators are also acknowledged for creating works which are often the first, or the best, introductions to their subjects for the grade or high school audience. Operating from the premise that learning should be enjoyable, the Silversteins write in a straightforward, informal style that often incorporates anecdotes and personal experience. Noted as excellent teachers as well as superior writers, the team is often celebrated for their ability to impart the excitement of science to young people through their books.

A college professor of biology who is also the writer of the syndicated juvenile fiction column "Tales from Dr. A," Alvin has collaborated with Virginia, a former analytical chemist and freelance translator of Russian scientific materials, on approximately seventy books for children and young adults; in addition, the Silversteins have collaborated with two of their sons, Robert and Glenn, on their children's books and have written college textbooks and a work of adult nonfiction. The Silversteins base much of their juvenile literature on material from Alvin's biology lectures and on personal experience, such as their raising of hamsters, gerbils, rabbits, guinea pigs, and other creatures as family pets. The Silversteins structure most of their books in a consistent format: they begin with an overview of their subject, including its various attributes and functions, and follow these surveys with descriptions of current scientific opinion. After providing detailed historical backgrounds which highlight the major discoveries in the field, the books conclude with experiments or sections on possible future developments and applications.

The Silversteins are perhaps best known for their series on the systems of the body, which explains such features of human anatomy as the endocrine, skeletal, reproductive, and excretory systems as well as the senses, brain, and heart, and for their "Story of Your . . . " series, which addresses the ear, mouth, hands, and feet. They are also well known for their books on animal life, which cover mammals and insects as well as such topics as symbiosis and elementary life forms, and for their works on such diseases as alcoholism, epilepsy, diabetes, and AIDS; genetics research, engineering, and technology; bionics; fruits and vegetables; and such varied subjects as sleep and dreams, gnotobiology, aging, and speech. Often praised for their lack of condecension, the Silversteins are the creators of several books written especially with the interests of the young in mind, such as braces and orthodontics, acne, glasses and contact lenses, and left-handedness; the team has also written three biographies of prominent scientists and two books in which they utilize a fictional structure to introduce scientific information. Three of the Silverstein's books were named

Outstanding Science Trade Books for Children by the National Science Teachers Association: *Animal Invaders* in 1974, *Itch, Sniffle, and Sneeze* in 1978, and *Nature's Champions* in 1980; many of their works have also appeared on lists of recommended science books for children. Alvin Silverstein was named national chairman of the National Collegiate Association for the Conquest of Cancer from 1968 to 1970 and chairman of the Foundation for Research Against Disease and Death from 1979 through 1982.

(See also *Contemporary Literary Criticism,* Vol. 17; *Something about the Author,* Vol. 8; *Contemporary Authors New Revision Series,* Vol. 2; and *Contemporary Authors,* Vols. 49-52.)

AUTHORS' COMMENTARY

Our seventh-grade daughter Laura came home the other day with a sheepish expression. "You may not like this very much," she began.

"What?" we asked.

"Well, in class the teacher was giving us words like 'state' and 'animal' and we were supposed to write down whatever we thought of. So when she said 'author' I put down 'Alvin and Virginia Silverstein'."

"What's wrong with that?" we asked, smiling. "That doesn't sound like something to be upset about."

Laura looked down. "Well, then the teacher asked who had parents who did interesting things and could come in and talk to the class about them and she said, 'Laura, why aren't you raising your hand?' So I did, and now she wants to know when you can come and talk to us about your books."

Laura was right. It's rather fun telling children about writing books and answering their questions about the mysterious world of publishing, but raising six children, teaching in college, translating scientific Russian, and writing books often seems to be a little more than two people can readily handle and doesn't leave much time for fitting such excursions into our schedule.

We'll go, of course, and although we haven't met this particular group before, we can guess in advance what many of their questions will be.

"How did you get started writing books?" The male half of the team usually answers that one. "I'd been teaching college for years," he says, "and often students would say to me, 'Dr. Silverstein, I'm not sure what kind of a career I want. I'm interested in science, but I really like English, too.' I had advised quite a few of them to try their hand at writing science books, before it finally occurred to my wife and me that we ought to take that advice too. We finally did, about eight years after we were married, and we've been writing together ever since."

That makes a good story, and actually it's true. But the whole truth is a bit more complicated. Before the first children's book, there was a college text. That was under contract and well on the way to completion when one of the book salesmen who normally make the rounds of the colleges stopped in at the office to say that he'd left the book-selling business and had joined a prominent literary agency. Now he was scouting around for some likely talent and had heard about the textbook contract. "How about letting us handle your next textbook?" he suggested. When you are in the midst of writing a 1600-page manuscript, the "next" textbook is the last thing you want to think about. But then the conversation got around to an idea for a children's science book we had, and the next thing we knew we were actually writing it and sending it to our new agent. She placed the book (*Life in the Universe*) on her second try. (pp. 3-4)

"How do you get your ideas?" That's another question children and teachers ask us every time. It is a question with a number of answers.

Our first book, *Life in the Universe,* grew out of a childhood fascination of the male half of the team with astronomy. A number of our books—*A World in a Drop of Water,* for example, and the entire "Systems of the Body" series published by Prentice-Hall—were distillations of material that he teaches to his college classes. They were supplemented, of course, by extensive reading in various references, but we had a good head start in the fact that he believes the learning process should be fun wherever possible and has always interspersed his lectures with a variety of pertinent anecdotes and attention getters.

Some of our books, such as *Germfree Life* and *World of Bionics,* grew out of our lively interest in "science watching"—keeping up with news of the current frontiers of science. (The last time we counted, we were subscribing to some 85 magazines and journals, but more have been added since then.) Our recent book, *The Genetics Explosion,* would have fallen into that category, except that before we had a chance to approach a publisher with the idea, we received a phone call from an editor we'd never worked with before, asking us to do a book on that subject.

Editors have been the source of ideas for some of our books. The first book we wrote in response to a specific editor's request was *Cancer.* The then president of the John Day Company told us his wife thought there was a real need for a readable reference for children on this subject, and that we would be ideal people to write it. We agreed readily about the need but were quite unsure about our ability to interpret such a topic effectively for young readers. By that time, we were customarily signing contracts on the basis of a title and an outline, but on *Cancer* we insisted on writing the entire book first "on spec," before accepting any advance, to see whether we actually could come up with a product that would satisfy both us and our editors. Apparently we did, since the book is already in its second edition. Since then, we've written a number of other books on diseases, so that we've come to be informally known in the trade as "the disease people."

Judging from the fan mail we get, young readers seem to know us even better as "the animal people." Our books on guinea pigs, hamsters, rabbits, gerbils, and cats have been extremely popular. We're pleased at that, because those are the books we've had the most fun writing. We both have had a lifelong love for animals, and for our pet books we have raised each kind of animal and drawn heavily upon our own experiences and observations. There are the books that have the most of "us" in them. They also tend to be family affairs, with photographs of our children, who help in the caring for the animals. Our newest book in this genre, *Mice: All About Them,* was even more of a family project, since many of the photographs were taken by our son Robert.

"How do you write books together?"—that's another frequent question. We've tried some variations, but most of the time we sit there, one of us at the typewriter (changing places at intervals—we speculate on whether our typist can tell who typed which parts of the rough manuscript according to the characteristic types of typographical errors), and throw ideas back and forth. Often one will begin a sentence and the other will finish it. Occasionally we disagree, but the disputes are surprisingly infrequent; usually our ideas and styles mesh smoothly. The writing generally goes rather slowly at the beginning of a book, but then, as we get a "feel" for the material, the pace accelerates, and we often finish on a total-immersion, "crash program" basis, with 14- or 16-hour work days. (We periodically vow to work in a more sensible manner, but with occasional exceptions such as *Nature's Champions,* written at a steady one-chapter-a-day pace, it rarely seems to work out that way.) The actual writing of our books may take from about two days (for some of our very-young-reader books) to several weeks, but it is preceded by a period of researching that is usually far longer than the writing. We don't generally revise very heavily at that stage (having two people writing provides a sort of automatic "quality control" as we go along), but an editor may later call for expansions, reorganizations, or shifts of emphasis. We are glad to accept editorial suggestions that we feel will improve a book, but we stand firm when we believe a suggestion or change is invalid. (pp. 4-6)

> *Alvin Silverstein and Virginia Silverstein, "A Visit with Alvin and Virginia Silverstein," in* Appraisal: Science Books for Young People, *Vol. 14, No. 2, Spring, 1981, pp. 3-6.*

GENERAL COMMENTARY

Harry C. Stubbs

Once upon a time a science course consisted entirely of a body of facts to be memorized—chemical formulas or the descriptions of animals and their habits. Then the trend toward scientific method developed and expanded, and fewer and fewer facts were taught; and with all due respect to the importance of thought as compared to memorization, I sometimes think the trend may have gone too far. When I meet a student who has passed a high-school chemistry course but cannot tell me what happens when sodium is dropped into water, I become sure of it; and at such times I look around for a nice, old-fashioned, descriptive science book nicely loaded with facts. Perhaps you know the sort I mean; it tells you how to distinguish a frog from a toad, or how many pores there are in the human skin, or how long it takes a red blood cell to make

a round trip through the circulatory system. I settle down and try to read the book with my brain shut off except for the recording portion—no effort to calculate the cooling power of the skin or the horsepower of the heart. The trouble is, most books make one think even if they are purely factual; brains are hard to shut off.

Three small volumes by Dr. Alvin Silverstein and his wife Virginia seemed worth trying at one of these moments. They are *The Respiratory System: How Living Creatures Breathe; Circulatory Systems: The Rivers Within* (no, the final s's are not misprints); and *The Digestive System: How Living Creatures Use Food.* As the titles suggest, all three follow a similar plan. Each system is described as it appears in the human body; then scientific and engineering reasons for its structure are clarified by describing the corresponding equipment in similar organisms.

The job is well done, though not wholly without slips. I raised my eyebrows at page 4 of the respiration book, where it is stated that the human body has more than a hundred trillion different *kinds* of cells (a hundred trillion *cells* is more like it). In the book on digestion, page 25 perpetuates a widespread canard about acids. It is true that gastric juice contains hydrochloric acid, to the tune of about half of one percent; but I commonly use HCl about forty times as concentrated in the high-school lab with no trouble. It will damage clothing if left thereon, but there is plenty of time to walk, not run, to the sink for a wash if the stuff is spilled on the hand. Even without the errors, though, I still had to think, for the Silverstein books were stimulating. (pp. 629-30)

> *Harry C. Stubbs, "Views on Science Books," in* The Horn Book Magazine, *Vol. XLVI, No. 6, December, 1970, pp. 629-31.*

Zena Sutherland and May Hill Arbuthnot

Alvin Silverstein is a biology professor and Virginia Silverstein a translator of Russian scientific literature; they have collaborated on over thirty books for young people, from books that deal with a narrow area, such as *Apples: All About Them* to books on such complex topics as *Sleep and Dreams.* Their work is carefully organized and written in a clear, direct style, and is dependably accurate. The more complicated subjects are not always covered in depth, but they are given balanced treatment, and the Silversteins' writing usually shows their attention to current research and always maintains a scientific attitude.

Hamsters is one of a series of books for the middle elementary school grades, all subtitled *All About Them*. . . . Following a brief discussion of the way in which hamsters were introduced into the United States as research animals and became popular as pets, the text gives detailed advice on the care of hamsters, including information on housing and breeding. A concluding chapter describes the importance of the hamster in laboratory studies. Pervading the book is an attitude of respect for the rights and well-being of pets, and there is no trace of fictionalization or anthropomorphism. Another book in the series is *Mice.*

The Silversteins have written many books in a series called "Systems of the Body," with books like *The Skeletal Sys-*

tem and *Heartbeats* that have accurate texts, include facts on recent research, and give lucid explanations of intricate physiological functions. Their emphasis on current research is evident in this book and in *Runaway Sugar: All About Diabetes.* It is stressed particularly in *The Code of Life,* which explores genetic engineering as well as genetic inheritance and how it functions, and in *The Chemicals We Eat and Drink,* which discusses the benefits or dangers of chemicals in foods, with findings based on testing programs and research studies. The book also considers, as do other Silverstein books, effects on the society, and suggests citizen support of pollution control and of supervisory legislation; a concern for the sociological implications of biological problems is paramount in *Aging.* (pp. 501-02)

> *Zena Sutherland and May Hill Arbuthnot, in a review of "Hamsters: All About Them," in their* Children and Books, *seventh edition, Scott, Foresman and Company, 1986, pp. 501-02.*

TITLE COMMENTARY

Life in the Universe (1967)

Presenting an easy introduction of the multiplicity of life forms on the earth, their requirements of oxygen, liquid water, radiation, etc., the authors go on to point out the rarity of these essentials in the rest of the solar system. Then, there is a brief but stimulating chapter on the attempts to discover other intelligent life in the universe. . . . [The] presentation is excellent, but the bits of original verse at the beginning of each chapter are silly; the authors are not poets. Nevertheless, they teach well. The only error is one that could not be helped because it has so recently been discovered that the count of Saturn's known satellites now stands at 10.

> *James S. Pickering, in a review of "Life in the Universe," in* School Library Journal, *Vol. 14, No. 3, November 15, 1967, p. 71.*

In *Life in the Universe,* Alvin and Virginia Silverstein cover a much wider field for still younger readers [than does David C. Knight in his *Comets*]. Any such book must, of course, stir astronomical and biological facts together to give a picture of what life needs and how likely other worlds are to provide it. The Silversteins stress the astronomical material somewhat, but the biology is by no means neglected. They have done an unusually good job of expressing ideas in language which young readers can follow, without saying things which will disturb their readers' physics and biology teachers eight or nine years from now.

> *Harry C. Stubbs, in a review of "Life in the Universe," in* The Horn Book Magazine, *Vol. XLV, No. 2, April, 1969, p. 191.*

Rats and Mice: Friends and Foes of Man (1968)

The difference between a *dirty rat* and a *man who's a mouse* is enormous, the difference between a rat and a mouse in reality simply a matter of size; so there's justification for lumping them together, then separating the marauders who live on man from the denizens of field and forest, as this compendium does. But the organization of the first third is so loose, the statements so generalized, that the reader has difficulty determining just what distinctions are being made. Furthermore, some are unexplained (e.g. why rats are more intelligent, why mice are more timid). The chief drawback of the book as a young juvenile, however, is the paucity of illustration: very few of the types described are drawn [by artist Joseph Cellini], and such aspects of behavior as the lodges of the wood rats, which may reach five or six feet, beg for pictorialization. Information, then, on rats and mice in history, in legends and literature, as found throughout the world, as pets and as laboratory specimens for use where necessary since there's nothing similarly comprehensive. But it's not tempting as bait or satisfying as a study. (pp. 1172-73)

The association of rats and mice with men is older than recorded history, for human habitations have provided a dependable source of food for these small mammals, more dependable than the natural habitats of fields and forests to which some species are still native but others deserted long ago. Although some kinds of rats and mice are destructive of stored human food supplies, are a menace to growing crops, and are also dangerous disease vectors, others have a beneficial aspect as destroyers of insects and as food for other animals. As experimental animals, rats and mice have aided in genetic, physiological, pharmacological, psychological, and other researches that have yielded results highly beneficial to man. Rats and mice have been mentioned in folklore and fiction. All these fascinating life history, ecological, economic, and other aspects of small rodents and their relation to man have been woven into an interesting and instructive narrative. For those interested in small rodents as pets, there are instructions on how to care for them. A classification of rodents is in an appendix, also there are suggestions for further reading, some of which are excellent for older readers but are too difficult for the audience for which the book is intended. Altogether it is a worthwhile book for libraries, classroom collections, and for the young person's own library.

> *A review of "Rat and Mice: Friends and Foes of Man," in* Science Books: A Quarterly Review, *Vol. 4, No. 3, December, 1968, p. 230.*

How dichotomous can we get in our reactions to mice and rats? Pet mice are kept in home and laboratory, rats are invaluable in medical research, both are obnoxious in the field. This dichotomy becomes apparent in this handy review.

Most small rodents are an important link in the foodchain for predators, birds, mammals and reptiles. The prodigious populations that arise crash, through disease and hysteria.

So closely are these rodents connected with man's life that a commensal relationship exists between the unwilling host and his four-legged acquaintances. This closeness has resulted in legend and folk-lore from the Pied Piper, to the three blind mice and Mickey Mouse.

For the early 'teens this is a useful initial reference book which should help to counteract some of the repugnance given even to thinking of rodents by most folk. (A minor correction—the black rat should be included in the list of animals introduced to Great Britain).

> *R. S. G., in a review of "Rats and Mice: Friends and Foes of Man," in* Children's Book Review, *Vol. I, No. 3, June, 1971, p. 102.*

Unusual Partners: Symbiosis in the Living World   (1968)

Unusual associations of animals, or plants and animals, make a very interesting and informative book for young people who are beginning to learn about ecology. Some of the associations discussed, such as helpful relationships between man and domestic animals, pollination of flowers, or the role of intestinal microflora, are familiar to almost everyone. However, the Silversteins discuss some less familiar relationships that are very fascinating, such as the honey guide (a bird) and the honey badger (or ratel) who work together in raiding bees' nets for food, or the plover who cleans the crocodile's teeth, the tickbird who feeds on ticks that burrow into the hide of the rhinoceros, or the ants who milk their "aphid cows." A variety of mutually helpful, parasitic, and harmful relationships are mentioned. . . . The final chapter, which summarizes the book, contains suggestions that will stimulate the young naturalist to undertake some field observations on his own initiative. Needed by all school and public libraries.

> *A review of "Unusual Partners: Symbiosis in the Living World," in* Science Books: A Quarterly Review, *Vol. 4, No. 4, March, 1969, p. 298.*

Although generally accurate factually, this account of plant and animal relationships lacks originality in the material presented. It merely represents a typical survey of the more widely known cases of symbiosis. All of the examples given have been used before by many authors. The terminology sometimes lacks the concise definitive quality sought by the scientist. It is distressing to see so many living things lumped together as creatures. Calling bacteria creatures leaves much to be desired.

> *Douglas B. Sands, in a review of "Unusual Partners" Symbiosis in the Living World," in* Appraisal: Children's Science Books, *Vol. 2, No. 3, Fall, 1969, p. 23.*

The Origin of Life   (1968)

An excellent book describing the latest theories on the formation of life. After a simplified discussion of what is life, the authors give a sound, understandable analysis of DNA, RNA, and the earliest to the latest theories on how life began on earth. Experiments by Redi, Spallanzani and the Russian, Oparin are described simply, yet with detail, and are documented with careful illustrations [by Lee Ames]; the pictures of bacteria, viruses, DNA molecules, etc. are clear and give a fairly good likeness to the real thing as seen through a microscope. The picture book format with its large heavy type is misleading because this is a sophisticated book, on a highly complex subject, that introduces and defines many difficult biological and chemical terms and concepts, and is crammed full of more interesting and useful information than can be grasped on the first reading; except for the first chapter, there is no talking down to the readers. Fifth and sixth graders might use this under the guidance of a teacher. The only thing really lacking is a glossary to help define the terms employed. An important title for school and public libraries.

> *Linda Greenberg, in a review of "The Origin of Life," in* School Library Journal, *Vol. 16, No. 1, July, 1969, p. 161.*

A World in a Drop of Water   (1969)

Spectacular photographs and clear diagrams are unfortunately accompanied here by a copy presentation of oversimplified, erroneous concepts together with superficial presentations of complex material insufficiently explained for this age level. For example, the Silversteins say that algae "drink in the energy of the sunlight and make their own food"; that plant spores " 'sleep' until good weather comes again"; that rotifers "can stay asleep this way for years"; that "most hydras give birth to young by a process called budding." Plants do not drink or sleep; they absorb or are inactive—both concepts within the grasp of students at this age level. "Give birth" implies sexual reproduction, while budding is an asexual process. Later, the authors mention conjugation of *Paramecium and Spirogyra* without developing the genetic reasons for this conjugation; they also state that water is carried out of the flat-

Photograph by Dr. Alvin Silverstein and Virginia B. Silverstein from their Gerbils: All about Them.

worm's body without elaborating on the significance of this process in the vital maintenance of water balance in the organism. The concepts of conjugation and water passage are fairly sophisticated for this age level, and, if introduced at all, require more thorough explanation. The superbly detailed photographs of tiny plants and animals are worth the purchase price of this book, and adults can make discriminating use of the text for a science-oriented read-aloud, but there are too many inaccuracies and misleading statements to suggest this as a reliable purchase for older independent readers.

> *Robert H. Stavn, in a review of "A World in a Drop of Water," in* School Library Journal, *Vol. 15, No. 7, March 15, 1969, p. 156.*

Young scientists and no doubt their teachers will be grateful to the authors for this clear but very wide-ranging account of water and what is to be found in it when its secrets are revealed under the microscope. The text has no element of writing down but boldly presents the facts and names of things which live in water. The black and white illustrations are very good and clear, and work in excellent partnership with the text to make this a valuable introduction and setting-off point for further exploration of the subject. (pp. 44-5)

> *H. Budge, in a review of "A World in a Drop of Water," in* The Junior Bookshelf, *Vol. 35, No. 1, February, 1971, pp. 44-5.*

Microscopic aquatic life is a fascinating subject, and this attractively produced little book . . . seemed set for a warm reception. There is, however, heavy concentration on the formal textbook types such as amoeba and hydra, neither of which is likely to be among the first organisms encountered. One must, I fear, limit response to the lukewarm for failure to do more to *supplement* reference material already and readily available.

Reference to amoeba as a living *glob* (my italics) may have been acceptable to reviewers of the original American edition, but this is surely a four-letter word we can do without.

> *H. M. Thomas, in a review of "A World in a Drop of Water," in* The School Librarian, *Vol. 19, No. 1, March, 1971, p. 92.*

A Star in the Sea (1969)

A boy and a starfish make for a poetic pair, as [illustrator] Symeon Shimin is well aware. One look at his poetic pictures demonstrates his awareness. And the authors have written, in clear, straight fashion, a boy's discovery of the wonder of the starfish's story. Only one complaint: your reviewer wishes they had resisted the temptation to give the starfish a name. Starfish is evocative enough. Stella is superfluous.

> *A review of "A Star in the Sea," in* Publishers Weekly, *Vol. 195, No. 15, April 14, 1969, p. 97.*

Good natural history writing in the form of a beautifully-illustrated adventure story has produced a unique life history story of the common starfish, which fills a gap in zoological literature for young readers. Spawning starfish are discovered in a tidal pool whose many other inhabitants are mentioned also. To carry the story one of the tiny newly-hatched starfish is named "Stella" (but here the device is not objectionable). Morphological development is traced from a larva to a small fully-formed adult. The competitive nature of the tide-pool environment and the many hazards to survival are vividly described. Then a violent storm comes again and the inhabitants of the tide pool are swept out to sea, and the young starfish becomes adapted to an ocean environment. The descriptions of feeding activities, a victory over a predatory gull resulting in the loss of one arm, the regeneration of a new arm, a successful encounter with a large cod, and other adventures are vivid. The final phase of the story is rescue by a boy from the beach on which Stella was stranded. He placed her in a tide pool where she recovered, was joined by another starfish the boy had captured, and after a time the starfish spawned and the life-cycle began again. It is an excellent book to read to very small children, for older ones to read, and for enrichment material in the classroom or on field trips to the seashore.

> *A review of "A Star in the Sea," in* Science Books: A Quarterly Review, *Vol. 5, No. 2, September, 1969, p. 155.*

Conceived in a tidal pool, returned to sea in a storm, then washed upon a beach, Stella (from the Latin word for star, *stellaris,* but still a bit too coy) is returned by a boy to another oceanside pool where the cycle of starfish life begins again. Children, naturally fascinated by this unusual sea denizen, will find answers to most of their questions in this cogent, story-like presentation—the only one available for this age group.

> *Mary Jane Anderson, in a review of "A Star in the Sea," in* School Library Journal, *Vol. 16, No. 1, September, 1969, p. 105.*

Frederick Sanger: The Man Who Mapped Out a Chemical of Life (1969)

This short biography of Frederick Sanger, who was awarded the Nobel Prize in Chemistry in 1958, for children was written with his cooperation. The book follows Sanger from his boyhood in the Cotswold Hills of England, through Downs School, Bryanston, and Cambridge University where he received the Ph.D. degree in 1943. Particularly exciting areas of the book are in the discussions of Sanger's discovery of the DNP reaction, and in the tracing of some of the details surrounding the search for the structure of the protein, insulin. Experimental techniques used by Sanger and his coworkers are described carefully and clearly. Good photographs and excellent sketches illustrate the book. There are illustrated diagrams of models of some chemicals such as amino acids, peptides, water, a generalized structure of insulin, and several others. A brief chronology of significant events in Sanger's life follows the text. There are a glossary to help with the more difficult scientific terms, and a short index. The teacher of elementary science would probably find this book worth reading, and with some help the elementary student should find it very fruitful. This biography would be a worthwhile addition to a young person's own library. In Sanger's quote in the book, "I am always wondering what is around the next corner. And there's always another corner to go around and look at." These words and other similar statements should serve as encouragement to the young readers contemplating a scientific career. (pp. 235-36)

> *A review of "Frederick Sanger: The Man Who Mapped Out a Chemical of Life," in* Science Books: A Quarterly Review, *Vol. 5, No. 3, December, 1969, pp. 235-36.*

If the purpose of this series is to introduce various scientists to very young children, this one fails since the subject of biochemistry, however one might simplify it, is just too complicated for 7 to 10 years old. The authors dedicate most of the book to describe the work of Frederick Sanger in all its intricate and suspenseful odyssey. A fairly good knowledge of chemistry is needed to enjoy and be excited by the painfully slow progress of a research that brought so much honor to Sanger and so much ferment to the scientific world.

> *Laura Musto, in a review of "Frederick Sanger," in* Appraisal: Children's Science Books, *Vol. 3, No. 2, Spring, 1970, p. 20.*

"Studying Science" should mean more than learning the facts, principles, concepts and methods of science. It should also include learning about the "human" side of science: what scientists are like, what kind of problems they work on, how they work together and communicate with each other, how they got interested in science, what their personal lives are like, and so on. Unfortunately, there are too few popular works that show scientists as anything other than sterile, mission-oriented, mechanical laboratory workers who attain instant success in their projects. The Silversteins have made an earnest effort to present a balanced and realistic picture of one of the great biochemists of our time, Frederick Sanger. The book is delightfully written, technically sound, and beautifully illustrated [by Frank Vaughn]. Its only drawback is the level of subject matter. Trying to explain to youngsters age 7-10 the structure of a complex protein and the methods by which that structure is determined is a herculean task. In spite of an admirable attempt, it is doubtful whether the authors have succeeded. I don't think that a young child can follow the technical aspects of the story, even granted its lucid exposition. This should not distract from a fine book, but should suggest a somewhat older audience for it.

> *David E. Newton, in a review of "Frederick Sanger," in* Appraisal: Children's Science Books, *Vol. 3, No. 2, Spring, 1970, p. 20.*

Carl Linnaeus: The Man Who Put the World of Life in Order (1969)

This very simply written book does well what it purports to do. It introduces very young children to a great name

in science and to his life and achievements. The emphasis is on the story of his early struggles and disappointments, and finally his gain of great popularity, fame, and success, but there are limited explanations of his scientific work and the importance of it is not clearly shown. (p. 20)

> *Laura Musto, in a review of "Carl Linnaeus," in* Appraisal: Children's Science Books, *Vol. 3, No. 2, Spring, 1970, pp. 19-20.*

This book presents very little insight into the science of taxonomy or botany, or into Linnaeus as a scientist. It appears to be a biographical sketch of a young man of the 18th Century. There are many missed opportunities for interesting side notes; e.g., Dean Celsius—thermometer scale; Linnaeus' relative, Humerus—name of bone.

> *Irving Leskowitz, in a review of "Carl Linnaeus," in* Appraisal: Children's Science Books, *Vol. 3, No. 2, Spring, 1970, p. 20.*

Cells: Building Blocks of Life (1969)

[*Cells: Building Blocks of Life,* is] acceptable for the exceptional fourth grader and ideal for sixth graders. The thorough, clear text gives complete coverage to the birth of a cell, its work, and how the combination of cells makes us what we are. Pronunciation keys, attractive and detailed illustrations [by George Bakacs], and simple experiments guide readers to scientific understanding. A fine book on a subject not covered as well elsewhere for this grade level. . . .

> *Pat Barnes, in a review of "Cells: Building Blocks of Life," in* School Library Journal, *Vol. 17, No. 3, November, 1970, p. 106.*

Germfree Life: A New Field in Biological Research (1970)

Gnotobiology is the study of the effects of specific microorganisms on germ-free plants and animals living in a sterile environment. Controversy over the benefits of a germ-free existence began a century ago. Early research, halted by World War I, led to the perfection of techniques and equipment. Today gnotobiological experiments are providing useful or potentially useful information that may radically change some aspects of world health. Among the questions considered here are the possibility of immunization against tooth decay, the effects of bacteria on production of some vitamins, and the efficacy of microflora in slowing the process of cancer. The straightforward, brisk writing is lucid, the material neatly organized, the subject one of the most intriguing on the biological frontier.

> *Zena Sutherland, in a review of "Germfree Life: A New Field in Biological Research," in* Saturday Review, *Vol. 53, No. 34, August 22, 1970, p. 53.*

This is an unusually lucid and remarkably up-to-date interpretation of highly technical subject matter, although the text grows a bit pedantic in places. It does seem unfortunate that the reader must get well beyond the halfway point in the text before the historical background information gives way to accounts of present-day problems and applications. I suspect that the lengthy historical preamble might "turn off" some young readers who would otherwise be captivated by the space-age relevance of the topic. The illustrations, nearly all photographic, are of uniformly high quality; but they often convey a sense of bewildering complexity. Some simple schematic diagrams would have been a helpful addition.

> *Ronald J. Kley, in a review of "Germfree Life: A New Field in Biological Research," in* Appraisal: Children's Science Books, *Vol. 4, No. 3, Fall, 1971, p. 23.*

Harold Urey: The Man Who Explored from Earth to Moon   (1970)

Complete with glossary and table of salient biographical events, this is an instructive introduction to scientific method in practice, a book that troubles to explicate (not just enumerate) the concepts behind the discoveries. Dr. Urey, a Nobel laureate for his isolation of deuterium, a hydrogen isotope, has restively applied his special knowledge to physical chemistry, the wartime nuclear energy project (less than complacently), oceanographic studies, the problem of life origins, the geology of the moon. The questions he asked, the experiments he initiated, the conclusions he reached and followed through into new hypotheses for new research evolve here into a coherent pattern uncommon at this level. Nevertheless the text is uneven, inasmuch as the chemistry is more rigorous than the boyhood chronology—though even that relates significantly: Urey was first bent on teaching Latin in country schools and grew only gradually into his lifetime pursuit as exposure and opportunity coincided with readiness. Much is unsaid, but the rudiments are firmly gripped and fastidiously conveyed.

> *A review of "Harold Urey: The Man Who Explored from Earth to Moon," in* Kirkus Reviews, *Vol. 39, No. 1, January 1, 1971, p. 6.*

The primary theme is Harold Urey's scientific career but an adequate amount of personal and family history is included to provide human interest and give a fairly full picture of the man. Urey's discovery of deuterium and his subsequent work on isotope separation, the use of isotopic oxygen ratios to determine paleotemperatures, his experiment with Miller on the atmospheric origin of organic compounds necessary for life, and his work on the origin of the moon and planets is covered. The scientific basis for each of these topics is adequately presented for young readers. It should make interesting reading for its intended audience and it could be an inspiration for a scientific career.

> *A review of "Harold Urey: The Man Who Explored from Earth to Moon," in* Science Books: A Quarterly Review, *Vol. 7, No. 2, September, 1971, p. 110.*

Metamorphosis: The Magic Change   (1971; British edition as The Magic Change: Metamorphosis)

This is not a new book insofar as the information is available in many other children's books: metamorphosis in butterflies is widely treated, as is the metamorphosis of frogs; somewhat less common are the life cycles of honeybees, dragonflies, sea squirts, starfish and eels. It is uncommon, however, to make metamorphosis the central theme of a book dealing with these animals and more, and this the Silversteins do in a readable fashion. They describe each organism and its activities at the various stages, the process of reproduction, and the changes that occur in transition from one stage to another. A major biological generalization is emphasized—that these peculiar life cycles represent evolutions toward better environmental adaptation.

> *A review of "Metamorphosis: The Magic of Change," in* Kirkus Reviews, *Vol. 39, No. 4, February 15, 1971, p. 178.*

An excellent development of the biological theme of metamorphosis in its broadest sense. Butterflies, moths, frogs and dragonflies receive a standard treatment, but the last half of the book, containing discussions on sea squirts, starfish and eels, provides a distinct contribution to existing children's literature. Unlike most authors, who merely describe metamorphosis, the Silversteins include a very interesting discussion of the adaptive survival value of this phenomenon, thus making the book unique and of particular interest to teachers. Fine black-and-white photographs augment the text to spark maximum reader interest. (pp. 110-11)

> *A. C. Haman, in a review of "Metamorphosis: The Magic Change," in* School Library Journal, *Vol. 17, No. 8, April, 1971, pp. 110-11.*

It is useful to have assembled in one book descriptions of the various types of metamorphosis; true, descriptions of bee and frog are plentiful enough in children's books but other subjects such as eels are harder to find. Yet it is a pity that the authors cannot decide for what age they are writing, for a child who needs to be asked "Have you ever noticed how quickly the little puddles . . . dry up when the sun comes out?" is hardly ready for the explanation of survival on page five nor interested in the addition of thyroxin to the water in which axolotls live (if he does get as far as consulting the glossary he will not be much wiser if he does not understand what a thyroid gland or a salamander is). Young children need to do a good deal of practical observation before wanting to read a book like this, and older children may be put off if they think they are at times being treated like six-year-olds. Nor does it help to have animals treated in anthropomorphic terms as "starfish are very greedy", nor to write about frogs without using the words frogspawn or amphibian. The adjective in the subtitle is inappropriate as is the description of the dragonfly emerging with "tissue paper wings". Children take things very literally and this book purports to deal with science, not fairy tales. (pp. 167-68)

> *C. Martin, in a review of "The Magic Change:*

Metamorphosis," in The Junior Bookshelf, *Vol. 36, No. 3, June, 1972, pp. 167-68.*

Mammals of the Sea (1971)

Mammals of the Sea is an interesting, lively, and timely book for children. Its central theme clearly points out the need for conservation and protection of sea mammals. At one time many of the sea mammals were in danger of either extinction or being drastically reduced in numbers, not by natural predators—but by the greed of man. The book has just enough information concerning some of the natural activities of these animals mixed with lively stories about some happenings with these mammals to keep children's interest high. It certainly would be an impetus to some children to read further about some of the interesting phenomena briefly mentioned by the authors; e.g. the ability to withstand great pressures upon diving; the ability to go without breathing for long periods of time; and the amazing intelligence of these mammals with regards to learning and vocalizing.

> *A review of "Mammals of the Sea," in* Science Books: A Quarterly Review, *Vol. 7, No. 1, May, 1971, p. 65.*

A fine book for young readers that does the unique job of discussing in general all the various mammals that live in ocean waters. Since the book is only 90 pages long, it cannot be considered a complete reference work in any respect; however, it does serve to pull together (without bogging readers down in scientific terminology) basic facts about the different kinds of seals, walruses, whales, porpoises, dolphins, dugongs, manatees, and sea otters. Some of the general myths surrounding sea mammals are discussed, and the authors explain how these ideas could have developed.

> *Donald J. Schmidt, in a review of "Mammals of the Sea," in* School Library Journal, *Vol. 17, No. 9, May, 1971, p. 70.*

The Endocrine System: Hormones in the Living World (1971)

A competent treatment of the functions and malfunctions of the pancreas, thyroid, pituitary and other glands, the growth and sex hormones and the glands that secrete them, and some examples of hormones in animal and even plant life. Edith Lucie Weart's *The Story of Your Glands* (1963) covers much the same ground, but the Silversteins add interest with their scattered references to recent findings, reporting not only the information but the experiments by which the information was obtained. Thus we observe hens changed to roosters and vice versa by the application of testosterone or estrogens, and discover the existence of a death-signaling pheromone as a community of ants tries to bury an obviously live-and-kicking comrade that has been sprinkled with the secretion. . . . [The] prose is clear and the research up-to-date and the subject has not yet been done to death.

> *A review of "The Endocrine System: Hor-*

mones in the Living World," in Kirkus Reviews, *Vol. XXIX, No. 14, July 15, 1971, p. 744.*

This is a general discussion of the endocrine system of the human body, the role of hormones, and the special role of sex hormones and the thyroid pituitary glands in the regulation of human processes. Learning human biology as a special case of general biology has many conceptual values for the student. Later chapters discuss the roles of plant and animal hormones. . . . The material in this book is rather difficult and, despite the aids to pronunciation of terms and the assistance of labeled diagrams (some are misleading, however), most students will tend to become lost in the detail. Calcitonin is omitted, and the use of trade names for standard substances, such as "adrenalin" for epinephrine, occurs. The book would serve best in a situation in which a teacher shares it with students, or an informed parent or older person works through it with an individual child.

> *A review of "The Endocrine System: Hormones in the Living World," in* Science Books: A Quarterly Review, *Vol. 7, No. 3, December, 1971, p. 255.*

This is a very ambitious book. Information on the endocrine system is presented in an engaging and precise fashion. Interesting parallels from daily activities are used to explain the function of individual hormones and hormonal systems. Problems related to the overabundance or insufficient supply of hormones are succinctly discussed. All in all, the book presents a thorough discussion of the endocrine system. In certain places, however, too much technical terminology and anatomical detail is included.

> *Harry O. Haakonsen, in a review of "The Endocrine System: Hormones in the Living World," in* Appraisal: Children's Science Books, *Vol. 6, No. 1, Winter, 1973, p. 30.*

The Sense Organs: Our Link with the World (1971)

A good book, not unlike others on the topic, that describes the structure and functioning of the sense organs and makes suggestions for testing some reactions (finding the blind spot in one's eye, differentiating between foods while holding the nose, etc.) and discusses some of the sensory operations of plants and animals. The writing style is stolid, but the material is well-organized and the information given clearly. An index is appended.

> *Zena Sutherland, in a review of "The Sense Organs: Our Link with the World," in* Bulletin of the Center for Children's Books, *Vol. 25, No. 2, October, 1971, p. 33.*

The coverage of the five senses and the inner senses (kinesthetic receptors) in muscles, tendons, and ligaments is at best adequate; and, occasionally, the information provided is too scanty: e.g., the names of the three bones in the middle ear are omitted; in the demonstration of "blind spots," the text does not specify that you must close your right eye in order for the dot to disappear, etc. A fuller presentation, including some of the same experiments, is Zim's *Our*

Senses and How They Work (Morrow, 1956); however, the Silversteins also treat plant sensitivity and modern research to improve the senses, and, unlike Zim, include an index. Best bets, however, are the books on the individual senses by Irving and Ruth Adler—*Your Ears, Your Eyes* (both 1963), and *Taste, Touch, and Smell* (1966, all John Day)—which contain the same material in much greater detail for the age group.

> *Nina M. Walsh, in a review of "The Sense Organs: Our Link with the World," in* School Library Journal, *Vol. 18, No. 2, October, 1971, p. 115.*

This very good presentation is a topic interesting to the intermediate and junior high school student. The two introductory sections make for a smooth transition into the main body of the work where the sense of sight receives its greatest emphasis. Vivid, uncluttered diagrams [by Mel Erikson] enhance the text. However, in the diagram of the human eye, crossed label lines between the upper iris and the cornea are confusing. Similarly, the diagram of the semicircular canal does not convey the orientation alluded to in the text. The concluding sections on plants and sense research, together with a good index, complete an interesting and well-balanced book.

> *John J. Padalino, in a review of "The Sense Organs: Our Link with the World," in* Appraisal: Children's Science Books, *Vol. 5, No. 3, Fall, 1972, p. 33.*

The Reproductive System: How Living Creatures Multiply (1971)

Another serviceable but unexciting system book from the Silversteins, tracing the one in question through various animals from the amoeba on, with special emphasis on humans and a brief chapter on plants. The closing chapter on "frontiers of research" is disappointing here, exploring only the well-settled territory of the birth control pill, IUD, fertility drugs and artificial insemination (with a bare mention of "test tube babies"). And the authors' obeisance to the trend of weaving simple experiments into the text results in some pretty silly suggestions: the reader is directed to put a handful of broken toothpicks in his pocket and throw another handful on the grass to demonstrate that offspring given more care by their parents are more likely to survive. The subject of genetics is not considered, nor are questions of human sexuality—a legitimate limitation of scope that is carried to extremes when intercourse is described as a process that occurs "when a man and woman wish to have a child." Obviously then, this will neither stimulate young scientists nor answer children's personal sex questions, but as a strictly mechanical survey of the mechanics of reproduction, it might have some classroom utility.

> *A review of "The Reproductive System: How Living Creatures Multiply," in* Kirkus Reviews, *Vol. XXIX, No. 22, November 15, 1971, p. 1216.*

This book is a good addition to the considerable number

on the subject of reproduction in animals and plants. . . . The few activities for the reader are simple to carry out and effective for teaching the point presented. The material is generally valid; however, although it is true that the testicles are first formed inside the abdomen, ordinarily they have successfully migrated to the scrotum before birth, not shortly afterward as the text states. The word "sperm" is regularly used for both singular and plural forms—"sperms" is not used for a plural in speech or writing. **The Reproductive System** does not demand any considerable background in biology, but it teaches a good deal. It should be interesting and useful to children from sixth grade level on. At this grade level the phonetic assistance to pronunciation is probably unnecessary and an irritation to the reader; and since some of the vowel sounds are given false values, the cause of good speech may be ill-served.

> *Esther H. Read, in a review of "The Reproductive System: How Living Creatures Multiply," in* Appraisal: Children's Science Books, *Vol. 5, No. 2, Spring, 1972, p. 34.*

An attempt to present the facts of reproduction without placing any value judgements is difficult; however, the Silversteins have done a commendable job. Reproduction in animals and plants, both sexual and asexual, is succinctly presented, and there is a brief discussion of cloning. Minor flaws in the text detract from its quality. For some children, the assistance of an informed adult may be necessary for understanding some of the concepts. (pp. 47-8)

> *A review of "The Reproductive System: How Living Creatures Multiply," in* Science Books: A Quarterly Review, *Vol. 8, No. 1, May, 1972, pp. 47-8.*

Guinea Pigs: All about Them (1972)

Children introduced to these "ideal pets" and deservedly famous lab animals through the Meshover-Feistel-Hoffmann *Guinea Pigs That Went to School* (1968) will be further enlightened by the Silversteins' able report on the origin, family tree, varieties, habits, and uses of the animals scientists call *Cavia porcellus.* The section on guinea pigs as pets is a particularly useful manual on their housing, care, feeding and breeding, written with a Dr. Spockish clarity, instinct for what questions need answering, and attention to emotional needs (a solitary guinea pig needs an extra portion of play and attention). Regarding their advantages as lab animals, the Silversteins point to their convenient breeding habits and their peculiar similarities to humans (both species, for example, unlike horses, dogs, cats, rabbits, rats, mice, and most other mammals, are unable to make their own vitamin C), and illustrate their usefulness in nutrition and genetics studies and the germfree research the authors surveyed in **Germfree Life.** Roger Kerkham's apt photographs of guinea pigs newborn, nursing, nesting, playing, receiving injections, or being held, fed, housed, and groomed by children, are another reason why readers will be eager to set up their own guinea pig laboratories.

> *A review of "Guinea Pigs: All about Them," in*

Kirkus Service, *Vol. XL, No. 4, February 15, 1972, p. 199.*

From origin and characteristics to guinea pigs as pets to their research contribution as laboratory animals, the information provided here is explicit, easy to understand, and indexed. The section on breeding guinea pigs is particularly well done. Black-and-white photographs show various types of housing and capture the guinea pig's appeal. Sections on guinea pigs are included in *Shelf Pets: How To Take Care of Small Wild Animals* by Edward Ricciuti (Harper, 1971) and *Gerbils and Other Small Pets* by Dorothy Shuttlesworth (Dutton, 1970) and detailed instructions for building a hutch are given in Alfred Morgan's *Pet Book for Boys and Girls* (Scribners, 1951). However, the Silversteins' book is the most complete manual with an attractive format on this popular animal.

> *Julie Cummins, in a review of "Guinea Pigs: All about Them," in* School Library Journal, *Vol. 19, No. 1, June, 1972, p. 136.*

Everything you ever wanted to know about guinea pigs: where they came from, what varieties there are, how useful they are as laboratory animals, and—in infinite detail, and with some repetition—how to care for them. The authors discuss the guinea pig's life cycle, diet, sleeping and feeding habits, and behavior; they explain how to breed the animals and how to build hutches for them, how to handle them, play with them, and train them. The writing style is brisk and dry; some of the photographs are useful, others merely of casual interest.

> *Zena Sutherland, in a review of "Guinea Pigs: All about Them," in* Bulletin of the Center for Children's Books, *Vol. 26, No. 7, March, 1973, p. 113.*

The Long Voyage: The Life-Cycle of a Green Turtle (1972)

Readers who aren't put off by the attribution of "a strange restlessness" to the migrating turtles and "a feeling of fullness" in one six-foot-long mother-to-be will follow the pregnant wanderer from the shores of Brazil to her egg depository on Ascension Island, then switch to one of her offspring for the return trip. As in the Silversteins' *A Star in the Sea,* the inevitable sameness of the life cycle formula is relieved by the introduction of some human characters—here biologists from a floating laboratory who electronically tag the newly hatched turtles and track them for months across the sea. This device is carried a bit far with a boy from the ship who becomes personally attached to one of the turtles, rescuing her from various predators along the way and reencountering her on the same Ascension Island twelve years later when the boy is a marine biologist and the turtle is returning to lay her eggs. On the whole, however, mind-reading the turtles is kept to a minimum and the people do add variety and a bit of scientific information to the long voyage.

> *A review of "The Long Voyage: The Life-Cycle of a Green Turtle," in* Kirkus Service, *Vol. XL, No. 6, March 15, 1972, p. 332.*

This life-cycle account of the green turtle also provides information about the study techniques used by marine biologists. The technology surrounding the study of these animals, who travel more than a thousand miles to lay eggs and mate, includes fastening a small radio transmitter to the shell of newly hatched turtles for tracking purposes. . . . Unfortunately, while there is little material on this type of turtle, the text here is directed to older readers than would be attracted by the picture-book format.

> *Linda Lawson Clark, in a review of "The Long Voyage: The Life-Cycle of a Green Turtle," in* School Library Journal, *Vol. 19, No. 2, October, 1972, p. 114.*

This is the story of the trip of a giant (six-foot long) sea turtle from the coast of Brazil to Ascension Island to lay its eggs, and the danger-filled return trip to Brazil of the newly hatched baby turtles. It is also the story of the marine biologists (accompanied by a young son) who observe and track this voyage with the help of radio transmitters attached to the shells of a number of baby turtles. Though the underwater illustrations [by Allan Eitzen] are esthetically pleasing, they do nothing to fill the wide information gaps left by the text. Young readers might be expected to know the whereabouts of Brazil, but the location of Ascension Island remains a mystery—a map should have been included. Also, it is gratifying to learn that the young boy in the story grows up to be a marine biologist and works in a program for protective breeding of the turtles. It would have been of greater interest to know what was learned by tracking the turtles on their fantastic voyage and why they are in danger of "disappearing from the oceans forever." This slight book does succeed in making you care about the survival of this turtle. With more information it could have been a very good science book.

> *Hanna B. Zeiger, in a review of "The Long Voyage: The Life Cycle of a Green Turtle," in* Appraisal: Children's Science Books, *Vol. 6, No. 2, Spring, 1973, p. 34.*

The Muscular System: How Living Creatures Move (1972)

A readable introduction to human and animal muscles: the different kinds of muscle cells and how they contract, a bit about their chemistry, and a look at how different animals get around. Basic concepts are simply explained and nothing is assumed: there are brief digressions on such physical phenomena as buoyancy, hydraulic compression and air resistance when they help to clarify the different process of locomotion. This is an easy subject for direct observation and the Silversteins frequently suggest moving certain muscles, watching a dog walk and run, etc., thus demonstrating points being made in the text. Throughout comparisons and analogies vivify without over-simplifying: an ant can carry 50 times its weight, comparable to a man carrying three automobiles on his back—but if an ant as big as a man could exist he probably wouldn't be much stronger. Functional, and it moves easily along.

A review of "The Muscular System: How Living Creatures Move," in Kirkus Reviews, *Vol. XL, No. 10, June 1, 1972, p. 627.*

Although somewhat misleading in title, since movement of plants, ciliated protozoa and various hydraulic structures are included, this is an interesting . . . and very readable account of movement in various species. The authors explore the ways the human muscular system is similar to that of of other animals—the contractile protein of the paramecium, the specialized muscles of earthworms, the streamlining of water animals—and the ways that the human muscular system is especially suited to human activities. The organization of material is not altogether logical, but the defect is fairly well compensated for by a full index. More careful editing would have caught such errors as attributing involuntary blinking to smooth muscle action and using "stomach" instead of "abdomen." A very good feature is the large number of simple experiments, using the reader's own body or readily available materials, interspersed through the text.

A review of "The Muscular System: How Living Creatures Move," in Science Books: A Quarterly Review, *Vol. 8, No. 4, March, 1973, p. 344.*

The Skeletal System: Frameworks for Life (1972)

Backing up their **Muscular System** . . . , the Silversteins perform a similarly workmanlike job on the cells, structure, development, and workings of the bones. Surveyed also are the production of blood cells in the marrow (with a discussion of the effects of atomic radiation) and the processes of bone breaks and recovery (with recent findings on how electric current helps in healing). Animal skeletons are considered in terms of analogous (birds' wings and insects' wings) and homologous (birds' wings and human arms) structures, and a final chapter examines fossilized bones as "clues to the past." Solidly and smoothly articulated.

A review of "The Skeletal System: Frameworks for Life," in Kirkus Reviews, *Vol. XL, No. 10, June 1, 1972, p. 628.*

Although this resembles Elgin's *The Skeleton* . . . in its accuracy and clarity, the writing here is fuller, digressing to ancillary (but pertinent) material. Both books use phonetic spelling for difficult words. . . . The Silversteins give an added dimension by discussing skeletal systems other than that of the human body, so that the text provides some information about comparative structures, and while not all of the digressions are informative, many give depth and add color to the text. An index is appended. (p. 17)

Zena Sutherland, in a review of "The Skeletal System: Frameworks for Life," in Bulletin of the Center for Children's Books, *Vol. 26, No. 1, September, 1972, pp. 16-17.*

Details of our bone system are presented in a well-organized manner. Make-up, functions of our skeletal system and comparison of our bone system with that of other animals are noted. Research and medical practices in regards to bones are described. While the material is clear, concise, and complete, the overall format is generally dull and uninviting: pages and pages of close text, ordinary diagrams and illustrations, [by Lee J. Ames], matter-of-fact style of writing. This appears to be a book that a student might quickly consult for an answer to a question but certainly not read cover to cover.

M. Letitia Kelley, in a review of "The Skeletal System: Frameworks for Life," in Appraisal: Children's Science Books, *Vol. 6, No. 2, Spring, 1973, p. 34.*

The Excretory System: How Living Creatures Get Rid of Wastes (1972)

As usual, the Silversteins' construct their lecture on bodily systems with stoutly utilitarian examples, demonstrations and drawings (the kidney looks like a kidney bean, the bladder like a balloon filled with water, etc). But there's no false modesty in their explanations of observable phenomena (why urine is darker in the morning) or in their suggested experiments (keep a record of daily urine output and observe changes due to salt intake). The chemical reactions which underlie waste production are briefly but clearly explained and the text is solidly packed with self-pronouncing vocabulary words such as *homeostasis, hemoglobin,* and even *bilirubin.* Medical sidelights—from bedwetting to kidney transplants, final chapters on the waste removal systems of non-human life forms (amoebas, fresh water vs. salt water fish, plants) and even a reference to the waste recycling problems anticipated on long space voyages—complete a factual, variously engrossing introduction which belies its modest appearance.

A review of "The Execretory System: How Living Creatures Get Rid of Wastes," in Kirkus Reviews, *Vol. XL, No. 19, October 1, 1972, p. 1149.*

Although the scientific vocabulary appears difficult—such terms as osmosis, nephric filtrate and urobilin are introduced—the phonetic pronunciation for such words is given and an adequate explanation of each term follows. This reviewer feels that such scientific terminology should be introduced rather than substituting some inadequate phrase to describe the process. Some simple experiments are outlined to help the reader understand renal function and sweating, and adequate precautions are indicated. . . . The excretory processes of man, water and land animals, and plants are compared. The book ends with a discussion of the frontiers of research in excretion and provides insight into the problems of patients on kidney machines as well as the problems of waste elimination during space travel. After finishing this book, the reader should better understand these topics which are frequently mentioned on radio and television.

A review of "The Excretory System: How Living Creatures Get Rid of Wastes," in Science Books: A Quarterly Review, *Vol. IX, No. 1, May, 1973, p. 80.*

The authors have attempted to pack too much information in too small a space, covering the excretory systems of man, animals, and plants in 74 pages. Much of the information presented is interesting, although one questions the necessity of encouraging a child to perform a three-day test on his own urine in order to determine his normal patterns of urination. The function of kidneys, sweat glands and lungs are carefully explained in great detail, but the function of the liver, gall bladder and large intestine in getting rid of solid waste is summarized in two short pages. An extensive glossary of terms together with page references is badly needed even though terminology is explained as the book progresses. A short chapter on excretory research including dialysis and recycling of waste concludes the book. Useful as an additional book on the subject.

> *Selina J. Woods, in a review of "The Excretory System," in* Appraisal: Children's Science Books, *Vol. 6, No. 3, Fall, 1973, p. 34.*

The Skin: Coverings and Linings of Living Things (1972)

Having presumably exhausted all systems the Silversteins now turn to the less interesting subject of skin and related tissue. The basics on skin—its layers, functions, coloring as determined by melanocytes, skin senses—are treated in somewhat less detail than might be expected; then, rather than stretch the subject too thin the authors pad it out with material on hair and nails, linings (of stomach, blood vessels, nose), and (following Silverstein formula) the integuments of different organisms from the amoeba on. The brief section on "frontiers of skin research," almost totally concerned with grafting, is disappointing in comparison with parallel material in the systems books. One feels that the Silversteins might have tried harder with this one; but it is a serviceable once-over that covers the subject. (pp. 1149-50)

> *A review of "The Skin: Coverings and Linings of Living Things," in* Kirkus Reviews, *Vol. XL, No. 19, October 1, 1972, pp. 1149-50.*

As in other volumes in the series, phonetic aids to pronunciation and the use of labelled diagrams are helpful. In this reviewer's opinion, the book suffers from poor organization and from inclusions of extraneous material, thus detracting from the main point. For example, the discussion of fingerprints is so long that the continuity of the description of the anatomy of the skin is lost. The young reader will also tend to be confused by the inclusions of cursory discussions of other epithelial and endothelial surfaces. (p. 81)

> *A review of "The Skin: Coverings and Linings of Living Things," in* Science Books: A Quarterly Review, *Vol. IX, No. 1, May, 1973, pp. 80-1.*

The Skin (coverings and linings of living things) is the study of integuments for different kinds of organisms. The main emphasis is on man. The informative style is a bit pedantic; the efforts toward drama are weak—"your body is constantly in a state of seige; an invading army

Photograph by Dr. Alvin Silverstein and Virginia B. Silverstein from their The Left-Hander's World.

awaits"—although bits of humor refresh the text. "Did you know that an octopus could blush?" On the whole, it is satisfactory for a middle-school child. Let's hope he has a sparkling teacher and some exciting equipment to accompany it.

> *Ann Janes, in a review of "The Skin," in* Appraisal: Children's Science Books, *Vol. 6, No. 3, Fall, 1973, p. 34.*

The Chemicals We Eat and Drink (1973)

The pollutants we eat and drink are well known by now to most of us, but the Silversteins' non-technical report on items of current concern and recent headlines—additives such as cyclamates, nitrites and MSG, accidental contaminants like strontium 90, mercury and DDT, "our daily drugs" alcohol and caffeine, and others less notorious—offers the most informative and systematic coverage at this level. There is also a timely warning against the organic food racket, and although the closing suggestions as to "What should we do" seem ludicrously inadequate, the preceding up to date survey avoids both alarmism and false assurance.

> *A review of "The Chemicals We Eat and Drink," in* Kirkus Reviews, *Vol. XLI, No. 7, April 1, 1973, p. 393.*

Well organized and indexed, this covers both beneficial and harmful chemicals in food, alternative food sources, and guidelines for staying healthy. The carefully researched text cites FDA efforts to keep food pure and case histories on the effects of synthetic food additives, chemical residues, and common drugs. Pertinent information, previously available only in periodicals, is made easy to understand in this simplified but scientifically accurate report.

> *Mary Neale Rees, in a review of "The Chemicals We Eat and Drink," in* School Library Journal, *Vol. 20, No. 7, March, 1974, p. 110.*

A very promising title is **The Chemicals We Eat and**

Drink . . . The title does not deceive; the authors do indeed express concern about the host of compounds which go into practically everything we consume. However, being competent scientists, they warn of the dangers of extremism and point out that all our foods—natural or not—are chemicals. They tell about the additives currently arousing the ire of the food faddists and, admittedly, of others. But the authors also make clear the alternative to using fertilizers, pesticides, and preservatives: the inability to produce enough food for our present population. The Silversteins have written as balanced a book on the subject as I have seen.

> *Harry C. Stubbs, in a review of "The Chemicals We Eat and Drink," in* The Horn Book Magazine, *Vol. L, No. 2, April, 1974, p. 169.*

Exploring the Brain   (1973; revised edition as *World of the Brain*)

Though juvenile material on most of the topics here covered—the nervous system, animal brains, the "primitive" midbrain and the "higher" cerebrum, memory and learning, sleep drugs, ESB, headaches, mental illness and robots—is already widely available, the Silversteins do a superior job of integrating basic information with recent findings, pointing up the wide and various roles of chemicals in brain function, and making the whole interesting and easily understandable. It is unfortunate that the authors choose to pronounce on the controversial issue of sex differences without bothering to document their assertion that although "some people believe that . . . men tend to be more active and aggressive than women simply because they are taught to behave that way . . . studies of the brain indicate that this view is incorrect." Nor do the Silversteins get into the intriguing territory of past and present brain research so ably surveyed by Freedman and Morris in *The Brains of Animals and Man* (1972). However, this is a readable, generally responsible introduction—far more balanced and mature than Zim's *The Brain* (1972). (pp. 604-05)

> *A review of "Exploring the Brain," in* Kirkus Reviews, *Vol. XLI, No. 11, June 1, 1973, pp. 604-05.*

Although similar material on comparative brain anatomy and experimentation with the brains of man and other animals can be found in Friedman and Morris' excellent *The Brains of Animals and Man* (Holiday, 1972), this is a useful complement to their book because of the chapters on human brain disorders and mind altering drugs. A glossary of technical terms is helpful. . . .

> *A. C. Haman, in a review of "Exploring the Brain," in* School Library Journal, *Vol. 20, No. 3, November 15, 1973, p. 68.*

Although the number of topics covered results in short shrift being accorded some, this is a good overview of what is known about the human brain; some aspects of the subject have been accorded full texts (sleep, drugs, morphology of the brain) in books for children and young people, but this gives coverage of these subjects in adequate, if superficial, fashion. The authors describe the functioning of the brain and the nervous system, going into especially fascinating details about areas of the brain that have been studied and mapped. Some of the ancillary aspects, such as how the functioning of the brain is affected by drugs or illness, are made clearer by the citing of laboratory experiments. It is, however, in the compilation of findings of recent research that the text is strongest.

> *Zena Sutherland, in a review of "Exploring the Brain," in* Bulletin of the Center for Children's Books, *Vol. 27, No. 4, December, 1973, p. 71.*

[*The following excerpts are from reviews of* World of the Brain *published in 1986.*]

This is one of the best in the many good books on medical or biological subjects by the authors. It is serious, comprehensive, well-organized, and clearly written. It discusses the new tools that facilitate and expand the medical profession's ability to diagnose and treat illnesses that emanate from brain malfunction or that affect the brain; it describes in fine detail the brain's structure and its myriad functions; and it informs readers of the results of recent research.

> *A review of "World of the Brain," in* Bulletin of the Center for Children's Books, *Vol. 39, No. 10, June, 1986, p. 197.*

This is on the whole a well-organized and informative book, with generally helpful illustrations [by Warren Budd]. Illustrations, mostly drawings, are few and black-and-white; the overall aspect of the book is pages of print. This implies a serious reader, and for my taste the authors approach their subject more gradually than the assumption of a serious reader would require. The pages of print, clear and legible in themselves, might have been aided by subheads or other devices. Picture captions, which unlike the main text are in sans-serif type, intrude a tacky note. Some topics are treated in gingerly fashion—IQ differences between races and sexes (politically hot) and ESPO (scientifically iffy)—but they *are* treated. I would have thought that the recent analysis of slices of Einstein's brain—which revealed an unexpectedly high proportion of glial cells—was in time to be included, but perhaps not. All in all, though visually pedestrian and thus somewhat hard to get excited about, this book seems to do its job very well.

> *E. Bruce Brooks, in a review of "World of the Brain," in* Appraisal: Science Books for Young People, *Vol. 20, No. 1, Winter, 1987, p. 65.*

Rabbits: All about Them   (1973)

Another capable all-round report, copiously illustrated [by Roger Kerkham] in the manner of the authors' *Guinea Pigs.* The Silversteins begin with a catalog of the different kinds of rabbits and how they and their relatives—the hares and pikas (the habits and features of all three are reviewed later on)—differ from the rodents, since blood serum tests have proved them to be less closely connected to rodents than they are to the hoofed mammals. The advice on how to choose, house, feed, and breed this clean, affectionate animal who might be "just the pet for you" includes an informative, to-the-point description of how they mate and reproduce as well as extensive directions for building a hutch—the latter recommended over the authors' own "run of the house" approach in view of rabbits' tendency to chew on everything and anything from important papers to the vacuum cleaner cord. A quick pan over the functions of rabbits in field and laboratory, lore and legend completes the agreeable picture.

> *A review of "Rabbits: All about Them," in* Kirkus Reviews, *Vol. XLI, No. 22, November 15, 1973, p. 1270.*

This well-organized compendium of rabbit fact and fancy gives the reader far more than other standard works on the subject. After an admirable section on care and feeding of rabbits as pets, the remaining chapters examine both the hare and rabbit as laboratory research subjects, then describe their zoological, behavioral, and ecological characteristics, and end with a tasteful survey of rabbit legend and lore. . . . The authors are moderately anecdotal without cheapening their straightforward writing style, which is devoid of condescension toward the young audience. Suggestions for further reading are appended.

> *A review of "Rabbits: All about Them," in* The Booklist, *Vol. 70, No. 11, February 1, 1974, p. 602.*

In an informal narrative, the Silversteins present clear information for young readers on both wild and domestic species. From their own experiences raising rabbits, the authors offer much practical advice on identification and selection of healthy pets; housing arrangements; feeding; breeding; etc. In addition to a section on the importance of rabbits to science (e.g., germfree rabbits are raised and used to study the cause of diseases), final chapters cover problems of rabbit ecology and population and "Rabbits in Legend and Lore." For slightly older children than Zim's *Rabbits* (Morrow, 1948), this is an excellent treatment of the topic.

> *Bonnie Tolman, in a review of "Rabbits: All about Them," in* School Library Journal, *Vol. 20, No. 8, April 15, 1974, p. 61.*

Sleep and Dreams　(1974)

Though it might seem that the topics of EEG sleep research, REM deprivation, the function of dreams and the like have been done to death, the Silversteins have come up with a crisp, intelligent report that puts to shame Deming's droning reiteration in *Sleep Our Unknown Life* (1972). Their descriptions and discreet interpretations of experimentation with animals and people are well integrated with background explanations of inner clocks, brain parts and functions, etc., and animated with relevant and interesting incidentals—about cats who prowl and stalk in their sleep when the brain center that suppresses muscle tone is disconnected, about the night terrors that occur during stage four (thought to be the deepest and

most restful stage of sleep), about thirsty subjects who wake up satisfied if they dream of drinking but still thirsty if they don't . . . The authors note that though "man has speculated on the nature of sleep for millennia . . . the scientific study of sleep did not really get started until the invention of the electroencephalograph"; we suspect that EEG's haven't scratched the subsurface of this mysterious third of life, but the Silversteins make present knowledge and current speculation—on what makes us sleep, what happens when we do, why we need it, and how safely to induce it—both accessible and stimulating.

> *A review of "Sleep and Dreams," in* Kirkus Reviews, *Vol. XLII, No. 7, April 15, 1974, p. 438.*

Sleep, that condition in which we spend approximately one third of our lives, is a no man's land which scientists have begun to penetrate only in recent decades. Today, new discoveries about sleep are being made constantly in laboratories around the world, and with each new finding, new questions arise. This lively book by Alvin and Virginia Silverstein covers the basic knowledge that has accumulated so far and describes some of the ingenious methods research scientists have used in their attempts to pin down the illusive facts about this universal but highly subjective experience. The help of the blind, for example, has been enlisted in studying the nature of dreams (test subjects who had been born blind dreamed only in sensations of smell, taste, touch and sound).

The Silversteins first survey the many subtle and mysterious rhythms that govern all forms of life on this planet, from day lilies and beans to monkeys, oysters and men. Sleep is an integral part of these rhythmic patterns, and succeeding chapters are devoted to the sleep of animals, the various phases of human sleep and the chemical and psychological factors associated with human sleep and sleeplessness. In their chapter on dreams the Silversteins contrast the theories of Freud and Jung with the experimental work currently being conducted in sleep laboratories. For good measure there are chapters on How to Get a Good Night's Sleep, Remedies for Troubled Sleep and The Long Sleep, which is what they call hibernation. The Silversteins have compressed a lot of interesting material in simple, lucid prose that is mercifully devoid of the florid metaphors science writers sometimes feel obliged to impose on the more tolerant adult reader.

> *Paul Showers, in a review of "Sleep and Dreams," in* The New York Times Book Review, *July 28, 1974, p. 10.*

Although the title includes both sleep and dreams, the main focus is on the subject of sleep and the array of new knowledge made available as a consequence of the widespread use of the REM (rapid eye movement), electroencephalographic, all-night monitoring technique. The authors have come up with an informative and well-written summary of these new data, which they have presented clearly and non-technically and yet in sufficient detail to answer questions arising in the minds of readers. A wide net is cast so that the research surveyed covers the range of both animal and human experimentation, the phenomenon of hibernation and estivation, and the significance of this new knowledge to the many unsolved sleep problems, both clinical (insomnia, exacerbation of certain disorders during REM periods) and other (jet travel, space exploration). The authors have done a good job not only in touching on the high points of these findings, but in showing relationships and implications. Photographs and charts are well selected and helpful. This slender volume is excellent as collateral reading and for classroom use as an introduction to the subject. (pp. 138-39)

> *A review of "Sleep and Dreams," in* Science Books: A Quarterly Review, *Vol. X, No. 2, September, 1974, pp. 138-39.*

Epilepsy (1975)

This is less substantial than the Silversteins' book on *Cancer* but also more likely to be of practical use to the intended age group. The authors describe, very briefly, the different kinds of seizures ("electrical storms in the brain") and advise onlookers on what to do about a *grand mal*. Stressing that what epileptics most need now is understanding, they survey their fate through history, the drugs currently used to control the condition, and ongoing research on its causes and treatment. Pointing out that there is no connection between epilepsy and high or low intelligence, they end reassuringly with lists and photos of famous and physically active epileptics.

> *A review of "Epilepsy," in* Kirkus Reviews, *Vol. XLIII, No. 7, April 1, 1975, p. 382.*

This book is very readable and easily comprehended by all ages. It does much to remove the mysteries and misconceptions about this common but at times frightening disease. The authors explain the fears and misunderstandings of epilepsy in the past, what is being done now to help patients, and what can be expected through the use of drugs and surgery. They describe in detail the cause and effect of seizures, what onlookers can do to help, and how important it is to realize that in almost all cases there is no danger or after-effects. This little book is highly recommended and should be available to all in the hope of correcting false ideas about a most misunderstood disease. (pp. 31-2)

> *Sallie Hope Erhard, in a review of "Epilepsy," in* Appraisal: Children's Science Books, *Vol. 8, No. 3, Fall, 1975, pp. 31-2.*

This is a fine book, excellent for any school, college, or general library. It is clear and interesting and should give anyone a good elementary grasp of the total situation. The book is wholesome. It does not suffer from the usual failings of writing for laymen on epilepsy: hostility, defensiveness, and sentimentality.

> *Esther H. Read, in a review of "Epilepsy," in* Appraisal: Children's Science Books, *Vol. 8, No. 3, Fall, 1975, p. 32.*

Beans: All about Them (1975)

It's nice to know that Cicero's family took its name from

the chickpea . . . and about the industrial uses of the soybean . . . and just how the legume family shapes up. . . . But as the Silversteins proceed, paralleling the excesses of *Oranges,* it becomes apparent just how slapdash this compendium really is: certainly a whole chapter on flower parts and pollination is redundant in this context; and the recipe section (mostly stuff like pouring condensed cheese soup over frozen limas) doesn't even mention that many of today's dried beans require little or no soaking. Half-full of b–ns—or more like Peter Limburg gone bananananas. . . .

> *A review of "Beans: All about Them," in* Kirkus Reviews, *Vol. XLIII, No. 21, November 1, 1975, p. 1237.*

History, types, and uses of *Beans* are included in a book with a promising title and attractive dust jacket. However, the promise is not kept; inside it is badly written and put together (the worst feature is the print pattern—inner margins are 4/10 of an inch but outer ones are 2 1/5 inches with the result that print seems to run across pages). Organization inclines to be random, with a lot of material put in willy-nilly, and an erratic system of italicizing further complicates reading. No illustrations [by Shirley Chan] are labeled, though over 65 italicized technical words (plus those not italicized that should be) ought to have suggested the advisability of naming the parts. Despite the need for a children's book on this subject, purchasers should wait until a better one comes along.

> *George Gleason, in a review of "Beans: All about Them," in* School Library Journal, *Vol. 22, No. 5, January, 1976, p. 56.*

Beans sprouting in a glass container never fail to excite and interest students from 5 to 15, and *Beans* is an entertaining source of answers to questions children ask about beans as growing plants. With a bag of dry beans and this small volume, a student can do experiments in germination, photosynthesis, tropisms, make bean soup, chili con carne, or play bean versions of Go, and Fox and Geese. Teachers will find a wealth of information applicable to studies of seeds, plants, genetics, economic botany, history of foods, geography and folk legends. Various bean sayings ("Full of beans," "doesn't amount to a hill of beans," "Jack and the Beanstalk") are discussed, including the jingle "beans, beans, the musical fruit . . . " (one of the few references not given enough explanation, considering the frequency with which children ask about it). Varieties of beans from around the world are discussed in terms of appearance, economic importance, history, preparation and even hints on how to buy. Soybeans, a major cash export crop of the United States, get two chapters, not only because of their diverse uses in foods and industry, but also because of their future potential as a high-protein diet supplement. This book is a well developed, single-topic book. Happily, it does not read like a textbook chapter, as do some of the other volumes in the Silverstein series. Recommended as a highly readable reference for classrooms and elementary and secondary school libraries.

> *Claire K. Goldsmith, in a review of "Beans: All about Them," in* Science Books & Films, *Vol. XII, No. 2, September, 1976, p. 107.*

Alcoholism (1975)

Alcoholism and [Stanley L. Englebardt's] *Kids and Alcohol, the Deadliest Drug,* are straightforward and comprehensive books that set out to give the facts so that young people can make up their own minds. They don't dodge any of the issues, and each is written in a style readable enough for intelligent high school or junior high school students. Both include good, candid discussions of alcohol as it influences our culture and affects our bodies. The chapters on alcoholism may be frightening and disturbing, but only because alcoholism is frightening and disturbing. The authors try hard not to preach.

In the end, and to their credit, they are ambivalent because there can be no simple answers about alcohol for young people, or for adults. "One sure way to avoid becoming an alcoholic is never to drink at all," write Alvin and Virginia Silverstein in *Alcoholism,* "but many people feel that such a decision means missing out on one of the pleasures of life. . . . To drink or not to drink should be a personal decision." . . .

The real challenge of alcohol education—as with sex and drug education—lies in effectively reaching a peer-oriented adolescent audience with little tolerance for outside advice. By conveying the notion that alcohol is a continuing source of trouble among adults as well as young people, and that the old and the young might do well to worry about it together, these books stand a good chance of succeeding.

> *David C. Anderson, in a review of "Alcoholism," in* The New York Times Book Review, *January 18, 1976, p. 14.*

This little book is packed with information and it is an excellent source for anyone (particularly teenagers) seeking basic knowledge about drinking. It is especially noteworthy that the authors avoided preaching and using scare tactics—common pitfalls in this field. Although this is an elementary level book, it will be widely useful, with its greatest value as collateral reading in a junior or senior high school hygiene course. In addition, it is highly recommended for the general reader.

> *W. A. McConnell, in a review of "Alcoholism," in* Science Books & Films, *Vol. XII, No. 2, September, 1976, p. 100.*

This informative, fact filled paperback describes alcoholism as a disease and treats excessive drinking as a personal decision. The book gives technical, historical, and current information, and ends with advice to teenagers who may have alcoholic parents or who may themselves be considering if, and how much, to drink. Strangely enough, there is not a single mention of the staggering amounts the liquor and beer industries spend on advertising to encourage *more* drinking.

The book *does* tell us that Chinese Americans "have traditionally been a very family-centered culture, with ties extending to a broader group of relatives. A strong emphasis is placed on the welfare of the group. . . . Heavy drinking is acceptable. . . . But consequences of drinking that might harm the group are strongly disapproved and penalized. As a result, though drinking is common, problem drinking is rare, among Chinese-Americans."

The authors do not tell us that doctors returning from the People's Republic of China report there is no alcohol problem, and that hard drugs—for many years a major problem—are no longer used there. Venereal disease has also been eliminated. Alcohol is freely available, but there is no profit to be made through its sale. And intensive campaigns of public education, public pressure, public penalties, plus retraining of hard-core abusers have been responsible for this dramatic change.

Is China the only country in which this could be accomplished? Are Chinese physically immune from the "disease" of alcoholism? Or can the USA also cure alcoholism *socially,* instead of trying to cure individual alcoholics while the yearly toll keeps claiming more victims?

Young readers should be respected enough to have that basic question posed to them in any book on the subject of drug abuse. (pp. 245-46)

> *A review of "Alcoholism," in* Human—And Anti-Human—Values in Children's Books: A Content Rating Instrument for Educators and Concerned Parents, *edited by the Council on Interracial Books for Children, Inc., Racism and Sexism Resource Center for Educators, 1976, pp. 245-46.*

Gerbils: All about Them (1976)

Not the first at this level but undoubtedly the best introduction—even outclassing Dobrin's commendable guide—to this gentle, curious, clean, frisky Mongolian rodent first imported as a laboratory animal in 1954. From researcher Dr. Victor Schwentker's five females and four males have issued all of today's proliferating pets, as well as the wild gerbils ecologists are watching for effects on nature's balance. (Importing them is now against California law.) The Silversteins describe the species, its adaptation to desert life, and its relatives; they report on its behavior at home on the Gobi (evidence of territoriality has been observed), in the lab (gerbils flunk maze tests because they're more interested in investigating than in the rewards), and in the family room (an odd, temper-tantrum-like foot stamping has owners stumped); and they offer helpful advice on selecting a healthy specimen, arranging a marriage (or avoiding a population explosion, as you choose), and generally feeding, housing, amusing, training, and breeding these almost perfect pets. Anecdotes from the authors' experience add a personable immediacy. . . .

> *A review of "Gerbils: All about Them," in* Kirkus Reviews, *Vol. XLIV, No. 8, April 15, 1976, p. 479.*

Writing from close observation of gerbils raised in their own home, the Silversteins give a far more thorough and interesting account of gerbil behavior and care than has previously appeared in children's books on the subject. Historical background, a careful description of the Mongolian and related species, detailed information on the care and breeding of pet gerbils, and appropriate experiments and training are covered. An attractive assortment of black-and-white photographs [by Frederick J. Breda] are both helpful and appealing accompaniments to the smoothly written text.

> *Margaret Bush, in a review of "Gerbils: All about Them," in* School Library Journal, *Vol. 23, No. 1, September, 1976, p. 125.*

The narrative of the book is quite clear and simple and includes interesting background information about the subject as well as very practical instructions and suggestions about raising of gerbils. The description of the usefulness of these animals for experimental work in scientific laboratories is particularly well written and instructive. The authors write with humor and clarity, especially on the subject of raising gerbils at home, and this book would be a handy guide for families with new pet gerbils. As such, it is a recommended addition to the adult shelves in public libraries. It is also recommended for classroom use for both students and teachers, and it would be most useful for classes who are raising gerbils as a group experiment.

> *R. S. McCutcheon, in a review of "Gerbils: All about Them," in* Science Books & Films, *Vol. XII, No. 3, December, 1976, p. 161.*

Potatoes: All about Them   (1976)

The ubiquitous potato is examined from innumerable angles: its history, its nutritive value, the ways in which it is processed and served, the way it reproduces, potato diseases, using potatoes in arts and crafts, games that involve potatoes, et cetera. Some recipes are included, and an index is appended. The material is organized well, the writing is straightforward and clear, experiments are suggested, and the whole book has a brisk, competent air.

> *Zena Sutherland, in a review of "Potatoes: All about Them," in* Bulletin of the Center for Children's Books, *Vol. 30, No. 1, September, 1976, p. 18.*

Coverage of the history of potatoes is extensive, informative and even fascinating (e.g., in Shakespeare's time potatoes were considered an aphrodisiac). Well chosen information about raising potatoes, conducting experiments with them and cooking them is clearly and usefully presented. Considering the paucity of reliable material (except for government pamphlets) on the subject, this title in the Silversteins' series on vegetables and fruits is well worth having.

> *George Gleason, in a review of "Potatoes: All about Them," in* School Library Journal, *Vol. 23, No. 1, September, 1976, p. 139.*

[The] subject is treated as thoroughly as the title promises—from historical and botanical aspects through production and marketing, some science experiments and crafts . . . and cooking. . . . Use of subheadings would have been helpful; instead, within each chapter, everything covered merges together. Also, those few illustra-

tions [by Shirley Chan] which are related to the text are not labeled, and the others are only decorative. Thus several good opportunities are missed to illustrate important concepts, such as leaf structure. There is nothing particularly outstanding about [this book].

> *F. E. Hunt, in a review of "Potatoes: All about Them," in* Science Books & Films, *Vol. XII, No. 3, December, 1976, p. 163.*

Heart Disease   (1976; revised edition as *Heart Disease: America's #1 Killer*)

A systematic explanation of the functioning of the heart and the causes and consequences of its dysfunction. Especially worthwhile is the discussion of ways young people can prevent heart disease. The photographs and [Diane L. Nelson's] diagrams are helpful in understanding difficult concepts as are the definitions which follow each of the technical terms, and the index is very thorough. The most extensive juvenile coverage to date, this is especially useful for school libraries serving health education programs.

> *Owen M. Borda, in a review of "Heart Disease," in* School Library Journal, *Vol. 23, No. 7, March, 1977, p. 148.*

A comprehensive survey of cardiovascular disease is soberly written but not dry, gives authoritative information, and is logically organized and amply illustrated. The authors describe the structure and functioning of the heart and the rest of the circulatory system, the various malfunctions or defects that are popularly grouped under the term "heart disease" and the devices and techniques used in heart surgery. Subsequent chapters discuss heart attacks and what to do if one has or sees such an attack, the relationship between heart ailments and exercise, diet, and the pressures of modern living, and research and preventive measures. A most useful book, not alarmist but candid and sensible.

> *Zena Sutherland, in a review of "Heart Disease," in* Bulletin of the Center for Children's Books, *Vol. 30, No. 9, May, 1977, p. 150.*

The Silversteins give a panoramic view of the major problems in heart disease and present methods of treatment. Initially, the anatomy and physiology of the cardiovascular system are briefly reviewed, followed by a rather incomplete section on congenital and acquired heart disease. The signs and symptomatology of a heart attack are documented, and the account of the present feelings about the effects of diet and exercise on heart disease is well written. The final chapters of the book deal with the hazards of our civilization affecting the heart, including smoking, water pollution and noise pollution. A review of some drugs is included. In the chapter on frontiers of heart research, the authors list echocardiography, vectorcardiography and electronic pacemakers, all established techniques which, although they may continue to advance, do not represent the frontiers of heart research. There are several instances in which the reader may become misinformed. For instance, the authors give the impression that the arteries of the body intrinsically contract rhythmically as does the heart and this is entirely false. In the discussion about open heart surgery, the reason for stopping the circulation is to not influence the associated blood trauma. The authors state that overeating sugars for many years can result in the development of diabetes, but there is no clear-cut scientific evidence to support this statement. The impression given that external pressure as circulatory assist is a well-accepted, widely utilized technique is incorrect. The discussion on pacemakers is concise and accurate, but no mention is made of utilization of the transvenous route and in fact only epicardial leads are depicted. Yet despite minor imperfections, this book is of overall good quality, easily readable, and would be of interest to most junior and senior high school students as well as to a good segment of the general population. Its major drawback is that none of the references are cited, which limits the book's classroom use.

> *Herbert W. Wallace, in a review of "Heart Disease," in* Science Books & Films, *Vol. XIII, No. 2, September, 1977, p. 86.*

[*The following excerpts are from reviews of* Heart Disease: America's #1 Killer *published in 1985.*]

This revision of the 1976 edition includes up-to-date information on treatment, prevention and causes of heart disease. New theories about the roles of fat and cholesterol are explained. Diagnostic equipment such as the CAT scan, angiocardiography, echocardiography and the nuclear magnetic resonance scanner is discussed. Drug treatments such as vasodilators, beta blockers, calcium blockers and anticoagulants are covered, along with new surgical remedies, including coronary bypass, balloon angioplasty and heart transplants. The discussion of the artificial heart is current through the Barney Clark case, and the Silversteins raise the moral and ethical questions of who should receive an artificial or transplanted heart and who should foot the bill. The Silversteins pack a lot of information into this clearly written book, which begins with a thorough explanation of how the cardiovascular system works. Students needing easier general information on how the heart works will find useful Brian R. Ward's *The Heart and Blood* (Watts, 1982), which includes numerous color diagrams and information on blood not found in the Silversteins' book. High-school students will find **Heart Disease** a useful springboard into the American Heart Association's *Heart Book* (Dutton, 1980; o.p.) and DeBakey and Grotto's *The Living Heart* (McKay, 1977; o.p.). Both are comprehensive books written for the layman on all aspects of heart disease and treatment.

> *Joyce Adams Burner, in a review of "Heart Disease: America's #1 Killer," in* School Library Journal, *Vol. 32, No. 5, January, 1986, p. 75.*

Since the book is targeted for the young teenager, it is puzzling why the authors chose to use adult examples (blood pressure readings for adults when discussing hypertension, a picture of a middle-age male with protruding abdomen on a scale to indicate overweight as a risk factor, and a middle-aged male suffering a heart attack). It is too bad that the authors, when discussing risk factors, omitted reference to smokeless tobacco and the effect that nicotine has on the heart. Cigarette smoking was appropriately covered. The authors pointed out that "women taking birth control pills have a considerably higher risk of heart attack than women who do not." What should have been pointed out is the fact that women who take birth control pills *and* smoke cigarettes have a *much* higher risk.

The authors state that "overeating sugars for many years can result in the development of diabetes." This is not supported by scientifically-based data. Fortunately, the authors include few statements that are not based upon published studies. Occasionally the young reader might misinterpret comments the authors make ("When young people were given vitamin C pills, their blood cholesterol levels promptly dropped,") and embark upon a regimen of vitamin-pill popping. The inclusion of a picture of a young teen on a stationary bike seems incongruous, especially when lifetime sports skills are mentioned in the text.

This book is for the reader who wishes to delve deeper into the topic of heart disease and for the reader who has a command of scientifically-related language. (pp. 64-5)

> *Evelyn E. Ames, in a review of "Heart Disease: America's #1 Killer," in* Appraisal: Science Books for Young People, *Vol. 20, No. 1, Winter, 1987, pp. 64-5.*

Allergies (1977)

After a brief historical sketch, the Silversteins get down to a cell-level description of how allergy works; this is reasonable, but less satisfying than Arehart-Treichel's explanation in *Immunity* (1976) and less careful than we'd expect: what, for example, are these "special cells called mast cells" and where do they come from? Elsewhere the authors survey the varieties of allergies, and their symptoms, diagnosis, and treatment; they mention briefly the "controversial suggestion" that food allergies can cause behavior problems and declare more firmly that "most physicians today" consider emotional problems mainly an effect, not a cause, of asthma. Throughout, they make clear that this is an area of pesky uncertainty and contradiction—skin tests are unevenly reliable and the results affected by all sorts of extraneous conditions: repeated bee stings might sensitize one person to further stings and give another immunity. But their synopsis-style report lacks the sense of shared inquiry, the stimulating integration of ongoing research, of such Silverstein titles as **Sleep and Dreams** and **Alcoholism.**

> *A review of "Allergies," in* Kirkus Service, *Vol. XLV, No. 22, November 15, 1977, p. 1204.*

As a practicing allergist, I will be recommending this book to many of my patients as it clearly presents the fundamental information that allergic people would like to know. The authors carefully avoid emphasizing one particular philosophy of diagnosis and treatment. The basic presentation of the main immune mechanisms is written in a manner that is understandable to an unsophisticated readership. (I plan to use the book as source material in teaching student nurses.) I am particularly pleased that the Silversteins emphasize the tremendous amount of research and the day-to-day changes that are expanding our knowledge of allergy, indicating the areas in which there is debate and in which research information is most rapidly changing. The book should remain useful for some time even though certain concepts presented are already outdated. My only criticism is the inadequate list of sources of further reading.

> *Austin T. Hyde, Jr., in a review of "Allergies,"* *in* Science Books & Films, *Vol. XIV, No. 3, December, 1978, p. 172.*

The Left-Hander's World   (1977)

Among the aspects of left-handedness that the Silversteins discuss are handedness among wild animals and some plants, well-known people who are or were left-handed, and left-handers in sports. The more pertinent chapters, for most readers, will probably be those that describe the functioning of the left and right spheres of the brain, left-handed writing, and the problems left-handed people have in adjusting to the many objects (scissors, can-openers) that are designed for the right-handed majority. An interesting book, but rather heavily written and padded by the comparative unimportance of such chapters as "Famous Left-handers," this concludes with sources of further information and of some manufacturers who make products especially for the left-handed. An index is appended. (pp. 166-67)

> *Zena Sutherland, in a review of "The Left-Hander's World," in* Bulletin of the Center for Children's Books, *Vol. 31, No. 10, June, 1978, pp. 166-67.*

Three million American children may feel that the book was written especially for them. The one child in ten who is left-handed already knows he faces certain inconveniences, but he should realize that many more exist, as he reads about the difficulties with left-handedness in our own and in other societies. The authors consider many other aspects of handedness: They look at "left-handed" plants and animals, such as vines and certain snail shells; describe the development of left and right hemispheres in the brain; discuss handwriting; and mention famous lefties from Leonardo da Vinci to Babe Ruth. . . . The book is attractive and should be entertaining to righties as well as lefties.

> *Sarah Gagné, in a review of "The Left-Hander's World," in* The Horn Book Magazine, *Vol. LIV, No. 3, June, 1978, p. 308.*

Handedness has always been an intriguing human trait, especially to the 10 percent who favor the left. This little book treats left-handers as another minority group, presenting facts, speculations and personal experiences to provide the left-handed child with a sense of identity and pride about his or her differences. The factual material includes descriptions of asymmetries in the natural world and recent research on dominance in the human brain, as well as sociological, historical, and psychological aspects of left-handedness. The authors carefully separate fact

from pejorative superstition, and inform us that many well-known and successful people are included in the ranks of the left-handed. Practical help for left-handers is limited to a short appendix listing relevant books, articles, products and organizations. There is a chapter on left-handed writing, perhaps the greatest bane of the sinistral, but it is devoid of helpful advice on struggling with this problem. To this (left-handed) reviewer, this is a more significant need than the problem of a negative self-image. Moreover, I know of no evidence supporting the authors' contention that successful lefties got that way through compensation nor that others—such as Jack the Ripper—became antisocial through the bitterness of coping with a right-handed world. I am certain, however, that such conjectures are of no benefit to the young reader. Even so, the book will be of interest to teachers, children and families of both bents.

> *David Gostnell, in a review of "The Left-Hander's World," in* Science Books & Films, *Vol. XIV, No. 2, September, 1978, p. 69.*

So You're Getting Braces: A Guide to Orthodontics (1978)

A must for any youngster faced with braces; their parents, too, might benefit from reading about how teeth and jaw can go awry and how orthodontists set bands, wires, and devices to work in straightening misaligned teeth. The text is clear, straightforward, and supportive; the Silversteins' own children wear braces, and their differing problems and experiences add interest to portions of the text. The hindrances braces pose in enjoying gum, certain candy, and foods are frankly acknowledged, as are the aches and pains they might give. Warnings are posted on getting broken or loosened parts fixed quickly (see a regular dentist if you or your orthodontist is out of town) lest desired movement be set back, and there is insistence that wearers not shirk in cooperation: "you can't fool your teeth . . . the better you cooperate, the sooner the treatment will be finished." A first-rate primer on a common, expensive adolescent pain, with a list of sources for further information. (pp. 1260-61)

> *Denise M. Wilms, in a review of "So You're Getting Braces: A Guide to Orthodontics," in* Booklist, *Vol. 74, No. 15, April 1, 1978, pp. 1260-61.*

Delving into the history of orthodontia and explaining some of the techniques used today to produce pleasing and functional tooth arrangements, this book goes a long way toward helping parents and children understand how this procedure works, what can be reasonably expected of it and the ease and comfort with which it can be done.

Written in clear, lay terms and illustrated with many fine drawings [by Barbara Remington] and numerous photographs (the authors' three teenaged children were willing subjects), the Silversteins have taken the mystery out of orthodontia and provided a very readable book.

Anyone facing the prospect of orthodontic treatment would benefit from reading this book.

Irwin I. Getz, in a review of "So You're Getting Braces: A Guide to Orthodontics," in Kliatt Young Adult Paperback Book Guide, *Vol. XII, No. 6, September, 1978, p. 33.*

This short book is an aid to prospective orthodontic patients and their parents. The authors write from their children's experience, lending a human, compassionate, humorous tone to the account. . . . Some of the historical attempts at solving these problems give perspective about who should or should not have orthodontics. (At this point, the authors might have raised issues such as the cost effectiveness of orthodontics or the comparisons between culturally determined norms of aesthetics of other cultures [e.g., the Chinese binding of feet] with those of our own.) The mechanics of bands, arch wires, torques and forces are discussed; they can be used to alter tissue growth. The Silversteins put the mechanics of orthodontics into perspective—useless without patient cooperation. Recommended for dentists' waiting rooms. (pp. 104-05)

Mike McKay, in a review of "So You're Getting Braces: A Guide to Orthodontics," in Science Books & Films, *Vol. XV, No. 2, September, 1979, pp. 104-05.*

Aging (with Glenn Silverstein, 1979)

Like *Cancer,* another Silverstein title, this might seem a less than compelling subject for a children's book. But whatever its readers' motivation, they will find here another of the Silversteins' exemplary research reports. Every animal or plant species seems to have its own typical life

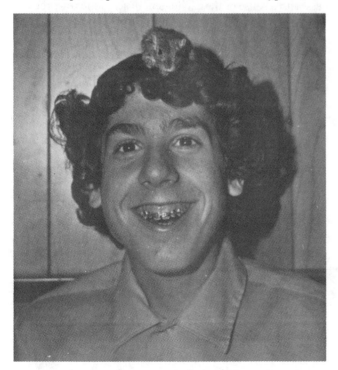

From So You're Getting Braces: A Guide to Orthodontics, *written and illustrated by Dr. Alvin Silverstein and Virginia B. Silverstein.*

span, they note; and though many of the physical and mental concomitants of growing old are not so much inherent, inevitable processes as the results of disuse or accumulated wear and tear, a limit of about a hundred to a hundred-fifteen years seems to be programmed into our genes. The recently celebrated long-lived populations such as the Hunzans and the Soviet Georgians were really just faking their ages, most researchers now believe, and all youth elixirs from the fabled fountain to yogurt and royal jelly have proved illusory—though recent studies with mice and rats, based on investigations of the probably many and varied causes of aging, have found a number of substances that stretch out their lifespans. The Silversteins don't consider how we will handle the population pressures if the dreams these studies encourage ever come true, but they end with a perhaps more realistic look at the plight of forced retirees.

A review of "Aging," in Kirkus Reviews, *Vol. XLVII, No. 19, October 1, 1979, p. 1148.*

This brief book deals with the process of aging, the scientific efforts to understand this basic phenomenon of biology and the changing role of the elderly in our society. The authors relate much information in a very readable way. Although anecdotal in style, this book succeeds in presenting the subject of aging in an exceptionally positive manner and includes a number of photographs of renowned individuals in their late but still productive years. As an easy-to-read, enjoyable and enlightening book, it should be a hit for those in senior high and above.

Knight Steel, in a review of "Aging," in Science Books & Films, *Vol. 16, No. 1, September/October, 1980, p. 6.*

The Silversteins, who have written a number of competent books on human disease and other scientific subjects, give aging a once-over-lightly. (p. 20)

It's all there—the conventional material in a conventional format. The point of view is generally humane and enlightened, although somewhat limited by the arrogance of the medical establishment. Yet the presentation is, on the whole, rather dull. Often there is simply a recital of names, dates and facts without much sense of continuity and direction. This is a frequent flaw in books of this kind for young readers—the effort to be clear and simple results in a colorless style and circumscribed presentation of the data.

On the other hand, the book does give deep and obviously sincere respect to older people and their achievements. It points to their roles and their contributions—not only of the famous people it cites so frequently but also of ordinary men and women. Unfortunately, this aspect of the book is weakened by a serious omission, which becomes especially evident in the photographs of older people scattered throughout. Every single older person mentioned or pictured is white. There is not a darker face among them. It would not be hard to think of any number of Asian, Black, Native American or Latino people whose pictures would have given perspective and inspiration and a truer sense of reality to young readers. Such racist insensitivity is most unfortunate in a book that, despite its faults, performs a useful function. (p. 21)

> *Betty Bacon, in a review of "Aging," in* Interracial Books for Children Bulletin, *Vol. 11, No. 7, 1980, pp. 20-1.*

The World of Bionics   (1979)

Beginning with the explanation that bionics is the study of the systems and structures of nature and the application of these principles for human use, the Silversteins delve into the research being done in prosthetics, radar, bioluminescence, robots, and more. All is presented clearly and concisely, but little is found here that does not duplicate information in Melvin Berger's *Bionics* (Watts, 1978). Libraries with high demand on the subject may want both, but for the rest, either would suffice.

> *Denise L. Moll, in a review of "The World of Bionics," in* School Library Journal, *Vol. 26, No. 6, February, 1980, p. 61.*

From early prosthetic devices and newer bionic limbs with sensors to provide feedback, the Silversteins branch out to a general discussion of how models of animal senses and other "good ideas" from nature are yielding military, TV, aeronautic, and other technological applications. One new-style prosthetic device is the Chanley hip joint, a steel ball and plastic socket planted in 15,000 arthritis sufferers annually; from electronics comes a variety of "seeing" devices, though true bionic eyes are well in the future; and among our attempts to borrow from nature are projects that would simulate biological clocks for navigation systems and bioluminescence for heatless light. Computers are being turned into true "thinking machines" (though the examples given here are unimpressive); and robots—for exploring Mars or scrubbing floors—are definitely on the way. The book itself seems an assemblage of spare parts and it's a bit diffuse for the Silversteins. Still, it's a straightforward and readable summary and, with descriptions of the animal eyes and other natural systems we're hoping to simulate, less gadget-oriented than Skurzynski's *Bionic Parts for People* (1978).

> *A review of "The World of Bionics," in* Kirkus Reviews, *Vol. XLVIII, No. 4, February 15, 1980, p. 220.*

Although this covers much of the same material as do *The Bionic People Are Here,* by Arthur Freese and *Bionic Parts for People,* by Gloria Skurzynski, it has a rather different focus, approaching the subject from the viewpoint of basic research on the animal world, and the application of that research (focused on each of the senses) to supplying the bionic knowledge. It includes, as do the other books, information on the prosthetic devices or machines that help human beings. The material is logically organized. The coverage is broad, the writing competent and authoritative. (pp. 201-02)

> *Zena Sutherland, in a review of "The World of Bionics," in* Bulletin of the Center for Children's Books, *Vol. 33, No. 10, June, 1980, pp. 201-02.*

The Sugar Disease: Diabetes   (1980)

The Silversteins have filled a large gap with this offering on diabetes. Covering symptoms as well as causes, diagnosis, history, current treatment methods, and the implications of recent research, this is intended for both interested lay people and diabetics themselves. While the introduction is pompous, it does not detract seriously from the text itself, which is clearcut and fascinating. Much better than John P. Connelly's patronizing and dated *You're Too Sweet* (Astor-Honor, 1968) this title should make a welcome addition to any collection. Sources for further information and a bibliography are appended. (pp. 147-48)

> *Kathryn Weisman, in a review of "Diabetes: The Sugar Disease," in* School Library Journal, *Vol. 26, No. 1, September, 1979, pp. 147-48.*

As Dr. Charles Nechemias (a diabetes specialist at Mount Sinai) notes in his introduction, this is a "what is" rather than a "how to" book, intended for non-diabetics as well as for patients and their families. The Silversteins do include chapters on testing for and living with diabetes, but they also treat the disease—its causes, effects, and possible treatments—as a subject of inquiry. Their history of diabetes research shows how the insulin breakthrough caused other significant findings to be overlooked and how current practice is leaning back to the pre-insulin emphasis on diet (though the diets are different and insulin still important). The history also supplies some incidental human interest in a story of unfair assignment of credit in the 1923 Nobel Prize. And, like other Silverstein reports, their final chapter on frontiers of diabetes research leaves readers with a sense of the excitement of scientific research and an awareness that there are many leads to follow.

> *A review of "The Sugar Disease: Diabetes," in* Kirkus Reviews, *Vol. XLVIII, No. 11, June 1, 1980, p. 716.*

This is an engaging and well written book which covers the symptoms of diabetes, the history of its investigation, and its causes, diagnosis and treatment. After a lucid review of glucose metabolism, the authors differentiate nicely between the different types of diabetes and discuss current theories about the causes. There is an interesting chapter on the historical aspects of its investigation which makes very entertaining reading. The chapters on diagnosis and treatment are current but not particularly technical. The authors end with a discussion of current research and potential future developments. This book will be of interest to anyone of high school age or older wanting to know more about diabetes. In addition to general audiences, medical personnel, I believe, would benefit from this and enjoy it. The book tends to avoid the cookbook approach so often seen in diabetic manuals and instead educates and entertains the reader. Because of this, I would recommend it highly.

> *Mark Sullivan, in a review of "The Sugar Disease: Diabetes," in* Science Books & Films, *Vol. 16, No. 3, January/February, 1981, p. 147.*

The Genetics Explosion (1980)

Just as Nixon's recent *Real War* should be widely read for realization of our political perils, this book deserves wide acquaintance for an understanding of the new biology frontier on which we are poised. Even the most frivolous need to know the meaning of DNA research and its widely varied implications and possibilities. . . .

This book, probing beneath sensational headlines about cloning and recombinant DNA research and about genetic engineering, provides a thought-provoking analysis of a complex issue. As with nuclear power and cloning (to name but two issues today) there are both good and bad possibilities in the new knowledge but we can hardly stifle the growth of knowledge out of fear of evil potential. If we could cure genetic diseases such as hemophilia, sickle-cell anemia, Down's syndrome, Huntington's chorea and others, or if we could induce the body to grow spare parts to replace a lost arm or leg, even if we might clone an endangered species, we should greatly profit therefrom, to say the least. In any case, we are entering a bold new era about which we must be fully aware. While some may be frightened by this research, others find it very exciting. Perhaps we must risk the unwitting production of some plague of mutant bacteria which might wipe out life on earth before it could be stopped. How can research be controlled, and by whom? Who has found reasonable answers? Teenagers might read this book and try to decide for themselves.

> *William H. Archer, in a review of "The Genetics Explosion," in* Best Sellers, *Vol. 40, No. 6, September, 1980, p. 211.*

One of the fastest growing areas in scientific research today is that of molecular genetics, the study of the chemicals of heredity. The Silversteins have contributed a first-class book full of excitement and suspense as they introduce us to this most fascinating subject. The authors begin with a history of genetics from Gregor Mendel's experiments in crossing green-seeded peas with yellow-seeded peas, Thomas Hunt Morgan's work with the fruit fly, the discovery of DNA and RNA and then the bombshell—the double helix—the model of DNA discovered by James Watson and Francis Crick. The authors have written many fine books on the human body—its functions and diseases. It is not surprising that they have included a most exhaustive chapter on genetic diseases: why do they occur; what can be done for the sufferers; and with the progress in research what does the future hold? Other chapters describe attempts to read the chemicals of life, the making of genes by a special enzyme called reverse transcriptase, and the importance of a technique known as cell fusion. The chapter on recombinant DNA discusses some of the issues and furor which has existed over carrying on certain types of research which could prove harmful. Finally, can man improve on nature? What is the role of cloning? Could replacement organs be grown from a person's own cells thus thwarting the bodies rejection of a transplant? Will we be able to reprogram our genes? This is not easy material to absorb in one reading. It takes study, and the fact that enthusiasm is generated to demand one's attention is what makes this such a great book.

> *Ann F. Pratt, in a review of "The Genetics Explosion," in* Appraisal: Science Books for Young People, *Vol. 14, No. 1, Winter, 1981, p. 57.*

This book is very timely in its subject, basic genetics and genetic engineering, and excellent in both its organization and content. The material included is organized so that a young reader or a nonbiologist can understand the basic genetic concepts, and then the techniques of genetic engineering are presented. The reader will gain an adult understanding of both genetics and the potential for both good and bad in genetic engineering. In today's world a responsible citizen is likely to need such an understanding. The treatment of Mendel's peas would have been clearer had $y+$ and y been used in place of Y and g. The rate of speed of growth of genetic knowledge is somewhat exaggerated, as is the proportion of human births classified as defective. The estimate of the number of genes in higher organisms is speculative. In each case (except that of Mendel's peas) the authors are being consistent with the general opinion within the field. A single misplaced period, a single misspelled word and two instances of failure of agreement between verb and subject in number do not detract significantly from the book. The glossary is very good and the index is complete. Both increase the considerable value of the work.

> *Raymond R. White, in a review of "The Genetics Explosion," in* Science Books & Films, *Vol. 16, No. 3, January/February, 1981, p. 138.*

Nature's Champions: The Biggest, the Fastest, the Best (1980)

From the fastest runner (the cheetah), the largest reptile (salt water crocodile), and largest bird (ostrich) through 25 other record-breakers to the smartest: the human being, that "champion of champions" who can fly higher than the highest flier and faster than the fastest, generates more electricity than an electric eel, and is more deadly than a black widow spider. The Silversteins amass impressive statistics and explain or describe the achievements of the various champions, all in a manner somewhat more adjective- and exclamation-studded than in their previous, more centered and substantial books. The change conforms to the format, which is oversize, cardboard-covered, and illustrated [by Jean Zallinger] with pallid, conventional indifference.

> *A review of "Nature's Champions: The Biggest, the Fastest, the Best," in* Kirkus Reviews, *Vol. XLVIII, No. 23, December 1, 1980, p. 1520.*

A delightful book in many ways, **Nature's Champions** contains unusual facts about a variety of animals and describes particular ways in which they excel. The titles of the chapters would immediately stimulate the curiosity of a child: "The Highest Flier," "Layer of the Most Eggs" and "The Most Shocking," to name a few. The last chapter is on human beings, whose outstanding characteristic is being "The Smartest." . . . I highly recommend this book. A school librarian would find **Nature's Champions** to be one of the most popular books checked out.

Martha K. Piper, in a review of "Nature's Champions: The Biggest, the Fastest, the Best," in Science Books & Films, *Vol. 16, No. 4, March-April, 1981, p. 220.*

Teachers and librarians, harried by questions such as "What animal is the fastest? the biggest? the loudest? the smartest?" will appreciate this book. It includes all sorts of interesting trivia, particularly fascinating to younger students, about twenty-nine of "nature's champions." For example, don't be shocked, but an electric eel can discharge up to 650 volts. That's enough to kill a person!

The difficulty comes in determining the accuracy of the facts presented. No two sources will agree on exactly how far a kangaroo can jump or how long an elephant's tusk can grow, etc. Nonetheless, most of the facts in **Nature's Champions** do not seriously deviate from facts listed in other reliable sources. (Since the book has neither footnotes or a bibliography, the reader cannot judge for himself the accuracy or reliability of the sources used.)

Martha T. Kane, in a review of "Nature's Champions: The Biggest, the Fastest, the Best," in Appraisal: Science Books for Young People, *Vol. 14, No. 2, Spring, 1981, p. 43.*

Runaway Sugar: All about Diabetes (1981)

Addressing a younger audience than the readers of last year's **The Sugar Disease: Diabetes,** with more emphasis on the concerns of patients and their friends and families, and less information on diabetes as a subject of scientific inquiry, the Silversteins do an admirable job of explaining the mechanisms involved in the body's sugar control system and the different ways they might go wrong in diabetes. The symptoms, tests, control, and possible crises of diabetes are also explained simply, in easy sentences, but not superficially; a basic understanding of how and why these tests and treatments work is conveyed along with the how-to-tell and what-to-do guidelines. A good example of how a thorough grounding on the authors' part can result in light and clarity at the easiest level.

A review of "Runaway Sugar: All about Diabetes," in Kirkus Reviews, *Vol. L, No. 1, January 1, 1982, p. 9.*

FutureLife: The Biotechnology Revolution (1982)

The Silversteins' report on biotechnology begins with breathless references to the revolutionary "war" against the unknown being waged "all over the world," and ends with a two-page barrage of questions which suggest some of the difficulties posed by biomedical advances: conflicts between scientific freedom and expertise, on the one hand, and the "average citizens' " right to curb possibly dangerous research, on the other; the ethics of tests on humans; the prospect of "some future dictator" abusing genetic engineering. (There is no attempt, however, to put the medical wonders in perspective vis-à-vis current world priorities.) The bulk of the book, glossier than the Silversteins' **The Genetic Explosion,** with which it overlaps, is a posi-

tive review of sophisticated gadgets such as the CAT, PET, and NMR scanners; spare parts; and the applications of genetic "tinkering." The tone and the viewpoint are bland and sometimes simplistic, whether the topic is the brain patterns of mental patients, the use of growth hormones in livestock, or the possibility of shaping our heredity ("Some people find prospects like that frightening; others find them exciting")—or of living forever ("Some scientists believe that this could happen"). Superficial.

A review of "FutureLife: The Biotechnology Revolution," in Kirkus Reviews, *Vol. L, No. 22, November 15, 1982, p. 1243.*

This slender volume surveys virtually all aspects of technology as it is applied to biological life today. It includes descriptions of new tools used in medicine such as CAT scanners and ultrasonography as well as artificial organs and "body parts." DNA recombination and the whole gamut of genetic products and problems from oil-eating microbes to test-tube babies and cloning are mentioned. A final chapter on "New Questions and Hard Choices" does examine problems associated with biotechnology, but it is too brief. The facts are presented clearly in a very readable style. . . . Although there is an excellent glossary and index, there is no bibliography. Combining all of the aspects of biotechnology does not enable great depth or detail, but as a timely survey of the "state of the art" this book is valuable. Other books such as Eve and Albert Stwertka's *Genetic Engineering* (Watts, 1982) and the Silversteins' own **Genetics Explosion** don't cover the medical tools and artificial organs, but do provide details missing from the genetic section of this book. (pp. 197-98)

Judith Rieke, in a review of "FutureLife: The Biotechnology Revolution," in School Library Journal, *Vol. 29, No. 7, March, 1983, pp. 197-98.*

Heartbeats: Your Body, Your Heart (1983)

Heartbeats seems designed to interest the casual reader, with its spacious format, fairly large print, deemphasis of medical terms, and running text without headings or chapters. Yet the majority of readers are apt to use the book for school projects, in which case, chapter headings would have been extremely useful—the more so for students just learning to organize material. Students would also have been helped, not hindered, by some emphasis on terms. For example, a long description of "congestive heart failure" is offered, but these words are used only once, toward the end of the discussion. Two other terms—*arteriosclerosis* and *hemophilia*—are defined in the glossary but are not mentioned in the text. Helpful diagrams [by Stella Ormai] of heart and lung anatomy are included, and numerous drawings often show children, thus adding interest. Generally the text is clear and interesting—important for such a complex subject.

Sarah Gagné, in a review of "Heartbeats: Your Body, Your Heart," in The Horn Book Magazine, *Vol. LIX, No. 3, June, 1983, p. 333.*

Complete with a list of the technical terms and their definitions, this little book gives the reader a very good picture of how the heart operates. Remarkably thorough in their treatment of the subject, the authors explain how the blood circulates through the arteries, veins, and capillaries, and the parts played by the oxygen and carbon dioxide.

I would like to have seen a little attention paid to the role of the hemoglobin as an oxygen carrier. Heart defects are featured. Although the heart never seems to rest, when the atria are filling, there is a brief opportunity for relaxation by the muscle. (pp. 58-9)

> *Douglas B. Sands, in a review of "Heartbeats: Your Body, Your Heart," in* Appraisal: Science Books for Young People, *Vol. 16, No. 3, Fall, 1983, pp. 58-9.*

There is considerable complexity in the circulatory process and the interaction of the cardiovascular and pulmonary systems, but these authors have successfully rendered much of that complexity comprehensible by any interested eight to ten-year-old. The comfortable, conversational discussion of the structure and function of the heart also manages—at appropriate points—to touch on congenital defects, diagnostic technology, hormonal controls, immune factors and transplantation, and anticoagulant and antihypertensive therapy as well as nutritional, behavioral, and genetic factors that predispose one to heart disease. . . . The inclusion of both a glossary and an index underscores the quality and thoroughness of the Silversteins' effort and adds to the book's effectiveness as a learning tool. In summary, this fine little volume is a surprisingly comprehensive primer on how the heart works, what can go wrong with it, and how modern medicine attempts to set it right again.

> *Barbara S. Bynum, in a review of "Heartbeats: Your Body, Your Heart," in* Science Books & Films, *Vol. 19, No. 3, January-February, 1984, p. 160.*

The Robots Are Here   (1983)

Beginning with an overview of mechanical men and robots in history, in literature and in the movies, the book covers the invention and sophistication of "real" robots (as differentiated from show robots) from the mid-1900s through today's computer-operated "intelligent" models. Many descriptive examples of current industrial and experimental models (with photos) show what tasks the modern robot can accomplish and what can be expected of future creations. The Silversteins have included chapters on the use of robots in industry, medicine, space and the home. They describe several homemade models and a few fun-and-games androids, concluding with some predictions for the future of robotics. A glossary, a bibliography (including periodicals, organizations and suppliers of robot materials) and a thorough index are appended. This obviously well-researched volume is mainly an overview of extant types of robots and their capabilities. A more complete chapter on robotic history and origins and a detailed discussion of the workings and movements of various models can be found in David C. Knight's *Robotics: Past,*

Present and Future (Morrow, 1983). Hilary Henson's *Robots* (Warwick Pr, 1982) has excellent color charts, diagrams and photographs but Barbara Krasnoff's *Robots: Reel to Real* (Arco, 1982) remains the most thorough and best-written book on robotics to date for this age group.

> *Susan Scheps, in a review of "The Robots Are Here," in* School Library Journal, *Vol. 30, No. 7, March, 1984, p. 165.*

Avoiding the production of just another robot book is an increasing difficulty these days, but it can be overcome in two ways, both of which the authors have utilized effectively. One way is to make use of the newest material in a field that is growing explosively; the other is to use imaginatively what material has already been available. In this book the latter method takes the form of portraying in an unusually clear way the difficulties of designing a robot capable of learning a new job. To professional programmers, specifying procedures in all their necessary detail is a standard part of life; to young readers this is seldom the case; but as computer courses at the high school level increase in number and, one hopes, improve in quality, the situation may change. Medical diagnostic robots, robot surgeons, and robot housecleaners as well as robot assemblers in factories all need to react to minor changes in job detail and, ideally, to respond effectively to major ones. As the Silversteins make clear, we are gradually developing machines and programs able to do both these things—although we are far from real robotic thought and intelligence. As is usual with a well-done book of this sort, even a fairly sophisticated follower of modern technology can be surprised at the current state of the art; if you just want to sit back and be amazed, read the book, anyway.

> *Harry C. Stubbs, in a review of "The Robots Are Here," in* The Horn Book Magazine, *Vol. LX, No. 2, April, 1984, p. 227.*

The Story of Your Mouth   (1984)

A clear, organized account of the anatomy and physiology of the mouth, this begins with a general overview of the parts and their functions—in eating, speaking, breathing, and as sense organs—and then discusses in detail the teeth, tongue, and salivary glands. The scientific information is presented simply and objectively, enlivened with vivid examples (the power of the jaw muscles is demonstrated in trapeze artists gripping a bar with their teeth), comparisons with other animals, and facts of recent medical research. Diagrams [by Greg Wenzel] and text are not always well-synchronized; the diagrams are sometimes more technical and they use terms not mentioned in the text. Nevertheless, this should prove a useful and readable source of accurate information. An index is appended.

> *Zena Sutherland, in a review of "The Story of Your Mouth," in* Bulletin of the Center for Children's Books, *Vol. 37, No. 10, June, 1984, p. 192.*

Readers will be able to see this remarkable organ in a new light. In major chapters on the tongue, teeth, digestion, and disease, a wealth of facts is incorporated into the text.

For example, sensitive lips convey the fact that food is too hot, and they can use muscles to form consonant shapes for speech. The jaws can clamp down with a force of two hundred pounds. Three sets of salivary glands make food slippery, and in the saliva there is a germ-killing enzyme that can attack bacterial cell walls. All this information is presented in readable style. . . . While the text is clear, it occasionally leaves one wishing for more information: Are sugar-eating bacteria ever attacked by the "germ-killer" enzyme? How can an electric current stimulate teeth to move to their proper positions? What is known of how ventriloquism works? Brief explanations of these points would have improved the text. Still, readers will get a helpful picture of an organ they seldom think about.

> *Sarah Gagné, in a review of "The Story of Your Mouth," in* The Horn Book Magazine, *Vol. LX, No. 5, September-October, 1984, p. 628.*

The up-to-date information is detailed in a straightforward writing style. Italicized scientific expressions are clearly explained. However, not all of the black-and-white drawings and diagrams are clearly labeled; some are not near textual references. In addition, the format resembles that of a book written for much younger children. *The Story of Your Mouth* contains mainly valuable, occasionally trivial and often entertaining data; it is unfortunate that the level of its presentation does not match that of the text.

> *Sue A. Norkeliunas, in a review of "The Story of Your Mouth," in* School Library Journal, *Vol. 31, No. 3, November, 1984, p. 128.*

[*The Story of Your Mouth*] deserves praise for its integrity—it is a thorough exposition on everything one would want to know about the mouth. With abounding organization and accuracy it illustrates the anatomical and physiological aspects behind tasting, eating, digesting, breathing, and communicating. This detail is augmented with tidbits on the effects of inflation on tooth fairies, sharks' teeth, halitosis, and the sources of common mouth-words and phrases. Current information on the herpes simplex type virus (and its implications), vaccines that fight tooth-decaying bacteria, and new electrical techniques used by orthodontists indicate the care the authors took in researching the subject and their awareness of the concerns of the readership. Difficult anatomical terms are italicized and handily explained within the text. Although this text is best suited as a reference for upper elementary student research, it is sufficiently spicy to stimulate interest in the directed casual reader. (pp. 34-5)

> *Nancy Murphy, in a review of "The Story of Your Mouth," in* Appraisal: Science Books for Young People," *Vol. 18, No. 2, Spring, 1985, pp. 34-5.*

Headaches: All about Them   (1984)

The Silversteins have done their usual outstanding job on a topic that will prove useful both for school reports and teenagers' own personal reading. It is surprising that this seems to be the first book on the topic aimed directly at young readers, even though headaches are common enough ailments among children and young adults. As a basic text, this is a model of clarity and organization, covering the various types of headaches (including but not limited to migraine, cluster, and tension headaches). It offers some history, current medical research and theories, and practical suggestions for headache sufferers: just what people have come to expect of the Silversteins! It would not be surprising to see this cropping up on adult library shelves as well, or wherever a well-organized, easy to understand, and not too lengthy text is appropriate.

> *Susanne S. Sullivan, in a review of "Headaches: All about Them," in* Appraisal: Science Books for Young People, *Vol. 18, No. 1, Winter, 1985, p. 35.*

This comprehensive, practical, and attractively written book should be of particular interest to medical personnel and those suffering from or interested in headaches. . . . The text is comprehensive and up to date in its discussion of the latest diagnostic and therapeutic measures, ranging from the use of propanolol to acupuncture or acupressure, biofeedback, and progressive muscle relaxation. The roles, relative efficacies, and limitations of various strategies are clearly and fairly presented. The historical section fails to mention Aretaeus of Cappadocia's description of migraine half a century before Galen introduced the term "hemicrania," and a description of the peculiar headache that may accompany hyperostosis, frontalis interna, was omitted. However, given the length, scope, and intended audience of the work, such criticisms are insignificant. This book is highly recommended as an easily read but comprehensive, accurate, up-to-date overview of the subject.

> *Paul J. Rosch, in a review of "Headaches: All about Them," in* Science Books & Films, *Vol. 20, No. 3, January/February, 1985, p. 150.*

Don't be misled by the bland title. This is a fascinating, if discouraging, study of this most common malady. After tracing sufferers through history, the Silversteins categorize headaches, with patient profiles, research, drug intervention/drawbacks and coping techniques for each. Though the writing is clear and technical vocabulary is explained in context, the more exposure readers have had to physiology, the better they will understand the text. Mechanisms of headaches and drug names and actions permeate, and the text occasionally reads like a Russian play, with chemicals as the characters. Acupuncture and biofeedback are examined as alternatives to drug treatments. In addition to its obvious use for health assignments, the book will be useful for readers who suffer themselves or who have close relationships with sufferers. The authors are thorough in describing pros and cons of particular drugs and non-drug therapies, as well as the emotional and physical triggers of headaches. (Readers who don't have to cope with recurring headaches will count their blessings after the description of cluster headaches.) There are no illustrations or glossary. Acknowledgments document cases quoted and suggestions for further reading precede the index.

> *Symme J. Benoff, in a review of "Headaches:*

All about Them," in School Library Journal, *Vol. 31, No. 7, March, 1985, p. 182.*

AIDS: Deadly Threat (1986)

Strong, reliable writers of health and science materials for young people, the authors contribute a solid overview of AIDS (acquired immune deficiency syndrome) that avoids most of the problems of Hyde and Forsyth's *AIDS: What Does It Mean to You?* and includes several topics Hyde and Forsyth do not cover. An explanation of how the immune system operates provides background to the well-ordered text, which (despite the unfortunate subtitle) generally steers clear of loaded words and phrases as it summarizes current knowledge about causes, symptoms, spread, and treatment of the disease. Firmly establishing AIDS as a problem of international scope—not a "gay plague" or a drug abuser's due—the Silversteins highlight events surrounding the discovery of the AIDS virus and look at the competition for scientific credit that has ensued. Their consideration of treatment options available to patients embraces discussion of the ethical dilemmas that have arisen concerning the use of experimental drugs on disease victims. AIDS patients are viewed from the humanistic as well as the medical perspective in other areas also, with special attention paid to the controversy over rights of afflicted children to attend school. An informative, straightforward introduction that neither understates nor overemotionalizes its serious subject.

> *Stephanie Zvirin, in a review of "AIDS: Deadly Threat," in* Booklist, *Vol. 83, No. 3, October 1, 1986, p. 215.*

The Silversteins have combined their lively style and careful research (through early 1986) to outline the latest findings about AIDS with thoroughness and accuracy. About 50% of the text deals with medical detail, but they make it vividly readable. Readers will be left with no doubts about how AIDS is transmitted, and clear directions are given for prevention. Toll-free national AIDS hotline numbers are listed. The chapter on child victims covers the school-attendance debate. Worldwide reaction during the 1980s illustrates the need for more accurate, objective information on the spread and cure of AIDS and its related syndromes, including AFRAIDS (Acute Fear Regarding AIDS). This book is non-judgmental, expressing sympathetic reactions to AIDS patients and impatience with the plague mentality. Both [*AIDS: Deadly Threat* and Margaret O. Hyde, and Elizabeth H. Forsyth's *AIDS: What Does It Mean to You?*] will be dated fairly quickly, but now, for the young victim, the student, and the curious general reader, the Silversteins' book is the top choice. (p. 118)

> *Anne Osborn, in a review of "AIDS: Deadly Threat," in* School Library Journal, *Vol. 33, No. 4, December, 1986, pp. 117-18.*

The market has recently been flooded with a variety of books on the subject of AIDS. Issues surrounding this disease are so complex and controversial that one must set very high standards for a "successful" book on this topic. Such a book should be up-to-date, accurate, comprehen-

sive, and emphatic to the needs and feelings of those humans touched by the disease. The Silverstein's book rates highly on all these criteria.

The emphasis in the book tends to be somewhat toward the technical side of the AIDS question, although social, psychological, and political issues are not ignored. The glossary and suggested reading list at the end of the book are helpful. I think it might also have been useful, however, to mention magazines and journals in which information might be found in the future. The very nature of this disease and of the publishing business guarantee that this text will be somewhat out of date as soon as it is published. The additional list of resources would help the reader know where to turn for even more current information.

My only other suggestion would be that a specific list of safe sex techniques might have been very helpful. Although the authors do discuss the concept of "safe sex", I'm not sure that readers will know precisely what it is that is "OK" to do sexually and what is probably or definitely risky.

Highest recommendation, in any case. (pp. 58-9)

> *David E. Newton, in a review of "AIDS: Deadly Threat," in* Appraisal: Science Books for Young People, *Vol. 20, No. 2, Spring, 1987, pp. 58-9.*

The Story of Your Foot (1987)

Although young readers have seldom evinced a burning interest in the subject, the Silversteins' treatment is brisk, authoritative, and informative enough to win that interest. Most of the material is anatomical description, including evolution, form, structure, and function or malfunction. A final chapter, "Foot Fitness," gives advice to any health-conscious reader, and especially to joggers, run-

Photograph by Dr. Alvin Silverstein and Virginia B. Silverstein from their Cats: All about Them.

ners, and boys and girls who participate in any sport. An index is appended.

> *Zena Sutherland, in a review of "The Story of Your Foot," in* Bulletin of the Center for Children's Books, *Vol. 40, No. 11, July, 1987, p. 218.*

[This] covers everything children ever wanted to know about the foot—and then some. The book begins with background information on how the human foot evolved, comparing it to various animal feet, including those of monkeys and apes. "The Outside Story" discusses footprints, foot structure, parts, skin, development, and deformities. "The Inside Story" examines skeletal structure, joints, muscles, and the nervous system in relation to the foot. "Feet in Action" is just that: standing, walking, and exercise of various types. Finally, "Foot Fitness" explains foot problems, disorders, injuries, and footwear. The writing is clear and concise, with technical terms italicized and defined within the text. Short anecdotes are included, usually references to one of the authors or their children. . . . A three-title bibliography is included. This book provides a good, updated alternative to Robert Krishef's *Our Remarkable Feet* (Lerner, 1968), and offers more comprehensive information on the foot itself than does Vicki Cobb's *Sneakers Meet Your Feet* (Little, 1985), which devotes much of its text to footwear. And although the subject matter is more specialized than most students' anatomy studies and reports encompass, it would be useful in almost any library serving the age group. (pp. 135-36)

> *Denise L. Moll, in a review of "The Story of Your Foot," in* School Library Journal, *Vol. 34, No. 2, October, 1987, pp. 135-36.*

The Story of Your Foot is a marvel. This fascinatingly thorough text includes anatomy and physiology; normal growth and development; injury, disease and common treatments; evolutionary differences between man and various animal species; common reflexes; historical and cultural influences as foot binding and wearing high heels; reflexology; foot fitness etc. The black-and-white ink drawings [by Greg Wenzel] are excellent; they rival any college text in clarity and detail. They greatly enhance the book. A detailed index and brief bibliography are included. No glossary is present but highlighted terms are defined within the text. This is an excellent resource for 10-year-olds through general audiences.

> *Renee Blumenkrantz, in a review of "The Story of Your Foot," in* Appraisal: Science Books for Young People, *Vol. 22, Nos. 1 & 2, Winter & Spring, 1989, p. 80.*

The Mystery of Sleep　(1987)

The authors of the more lab-oriented **Sleep and Dreams** here take a good middle path between accessibility and technicality. They build a fact-based overview of the mental and physical phenomena of sleep. Satisfyingly information packed, the book links research findings with readers' experiences while being neither oversimplified nor patronizing. Special attention is given to problems such as snor-

ing, sleepwalking, and nightmares. There is a sensible view of insomnia and a non-hysterical look at sleeping pills. While there are a few questionable calls—hibernation is not distinguished from sleep; the natural human sleep cycle is taken as 24 hours (it's actually a little longer)—they seem to be considered rather than negligent. . . . This is a fine book for readers curious about an aspect of themselves that they can't observe directly.

> *Paul Bogrow, in a review of "The Mystery of Sleep," in* School Library Journal, *Vol. 34, No. 4, December, 1987, p. 98.*

A good, little book packed full of interesting information about sleep. Although some sleep research results are undergoing vigorous "debate" in various scientific circles, the author proceeds to write in a reasonably confident manner, resulting in a readable book which is accessible to the juvenile reader. Due to the tentative nature of some of the sleep research, a reviewer can too easily find fault, yet to do so would be to miss the purpose. As a juvenile book on the topic of sleep, this one serves rather well.

Unfortunately, the text deserves better illustrations. The illustrations [by Nelle Davis] give the impression that they would be more appropriate for a children's picture book on some less technical topic. On page 10, for example, drawings or photographs of EEG machines attached to a subject would add useful information to supplement the text.

Despite the foolish illustrations which bear little relationship to the text, this is still an informative book on sleep, and it can be read by the juvenile reader who might be put off by a book which looks too technical.

> *Clarence C. Truesdell, in a review of "The Mystery of Sleep," in* Appraisal: Science Books for Young People, *Vol. 21, No. 3, Summer, 1988, p. 40.*

Wonders of Speech　(1988)

Clear writing, good organization of material, broad coverage, and the inclusion of recent research all contribute to an exemplary informational book. The authors discuss the ways in which sound is produced in the human being, the functioning of the brain in storing and sorting bits of the intricate communications network, the learning of language, speech disabilities, artificial languages, and other aspects of speech. Books that are entitled "The Wonders of . . . " don't always seem wonderful; here it is moot which is the more wonderful, the ability of people to speak or the extent to which scientists have discovered the complexities of how the brain operates to produce speech and the memory on which it depends. (pp. 167-68)

> *Zena Sutherland, in a review of "Wonders of Speech," in* Bulletin of the Center for Children's Books, *Vol. 41, No. 8, April, 1988, pp. 167-68.*

In a grab bag of topics about the immense subject of language, two veteran science writers cover the physiology of the speech organs and how the brain works in understanding and formulating speech; they go on to discuss research in psycholinguistics, the history of English, effective speaking (in both conversation and speeches), communication of the deaf, the role of body language, computers, and many other subjects. The biology chapters are the best, technically detailed and clear, but some of the other sections are unfocused and superficial. This cursory treatment is exacerbated by the lack of documentation, so that, except for the chapter on speech making, readers will not be able to explore further for themselves: at best researchers' names and institutions are given, but often references are as vague as "studies show." Still, the ideas and facts are fascinating—from babies' first language to the limits of artificial intelligence—and the style, informal without being condescending, will draw readers in much the same way as a good magazine article does.

> *Hazel Rochman, in a review of "Wonders of Speech," in* Booklist, *Vol. 84, No. 20, June 15, 1988, p. 1729.*

This book ambitiously undertakes the large task of introducing middle- and high-school students to the broad topic of speech and its disorders. Individual chapters survey speech production, the psychology of language, how children acquire language, communication disorders, animal communication systems, language change over time, and the art of speaking effectively, with the last topic quite tangential to the book's main thrust. Overall, the general tone is lively and engaging, and information is conveyed in a clear and interesting manner, but this book does have flaws. There are some factual errors, such as the explanation of the functions of Wernicke's area and the explanation of vowel production that attributes vowel articulation to the lips, rather than the tongue. There are not many errors of this kind, but the book also lacks a reference list, suffers a bit of organizationally, and contains some unsupported assertions. Rather than references, a small list of books for "further reading" is provided, comprised almost entirely of texts on speech improvement, animal communication, and sign language. (In any college-level nonfiction work, this lack of references would be considered a grave failing). In terms of lack of organization and unsupported assertions, the chapter on speech disorders is somewhat incoherent and makes the indefensible assertion that the development of stuttering is triggered by emotional stress. At another point, the authors attribute certain adult speech disorders to overlearned patterns of childhood "cuteness," another unsupported opinion. In sum, this book is a clear and interesting but a rather flawed and incomplete introduction to a complex area of study.

> *Nan Bernstein Ratner, in a review of "Wonders of Speech," in* Science Books & Films, *Vol. 24, No. 3, January/February, 1989, p. 147.*

Nature's Living Lights: Fireflies and Other Bioluminescent Creatures (1988)

Striking format and lucid text are combined in an unusually appealing look at bioluminescence in both plants and animals.

Deep-blue pages with white type and illustrations [by Pamela and Walter Carroll], interspersed with blue-on-white pages, provide a vivid background for dramatic facts about living light sources—including the familiar firefly and glowworm as well as the less familiar flashlight fish, angler fish, brittle star, dinoflagellates, and fungi. The Silversteins discuss how the light is produced and its functions for its hosts, including some current research. Also useful to man, bioluminescence is used by the fishing industry to locate schools of fish, by environmentalists to track pollution, and by the navy to track submarines. Medical scientists use it to test for infection and for early warning of bone, muscle, and heart disease. New studies focus on recombinant DNA: transferring light-producing genes to better understand heredity.

Excellent science writing; an outstanding piece of bookmaking. Scientific names and works are italicized; brief glossary.

> *A review of "Nature's Living Lights: Fireflies and Other Bioluminescent Creatures," in* Kirkus Reviews, *Vol. LVI, No. 10, May 15, 1988, p. 767.*

This explanation of the production and use of bioluminescence by bacteria, insects, larvae, sea animals, and plants and fungi provides an adequate although sketchy introduction to an intriguing phenomenon. The Silversteins explain the chemical process involved and the uses that various species make of the light with some emphasis on the well-known firefly. A short discussion of human uses of the chemical agents luciferin and luciferase is tantalizing but frustrating in its brevity. Similarly, explanations of the physiology of some of the light-producing species is superficial when included at all. The unlabelled white figures and print on dark blue pages are more visually interesting than useful; they do not augment the minimal explanations. There is a glossary but no index, and the fairly difficult text in a thin volume narrows the audience. A better choice is Francine Jacobs' *Nature's Light: The Story of Bioluminescence* (Morrow, 1974; o.p.).

> *Margaret Bush, in a review of "Nature's Living Lights: Fireflies and Other Bioluminescent Creatures," in* School Library Journal, *Vol. 35, No. 1, September, 1988, p. 195.*

This seems to be a rather specialized subject matter for this age level. Additionally, students might be able to find material on this subject in pre-existing references. This book does however have some unique qualities.

The illustrations are good and, in places, interesting. What better place to have reverse printing than in a book about night-time creatures? Perhaps a good and a bad point: some of the material borders on the somewhat technical. It may be above some of the children. On the other hand, they may not find these kinds of explanations elsewhere. The danger with "bordering on" the technical is that to give clear explanations, you may need more room than you want to—or are able to—use.

Perhaps in order to be "a desirable purchase" or "a must purchase" this book needs to be a part of a series of oddities in nature called *Nature's: Living Lights* where all of the books are titled *Nature's* . . . No doubt about it, the prolific Silversteins could do it. (pp. 78-9)

> *Dana Richard Freeman, in a review of "Nature's Living Lights," in* Appraisal: Science Books for Young People, *Vol. 22, Nos. 1 & 2, Winter & Spring, 1989, pp. 78-9.*

Glasses and Contact Lenses: Your Guide to Eyes, Eyewear, and Eye Care (1989)

All about eyes and eye care, including the structure of the eye, how vision works, and the development of glasses, contact lenses, and surgery techniques used to correct vision. This outstanding science title is clearly written, carefully researched, and up-to-date. The authors discuss the ten distinct layers of the retina, common vision problems from myopia to hyperopia, and how to read a lens prescription. A history of eyeglasses takes the reader from the first written mention—in 1626—by English scientist Roger Bacon to the 1988 introduction of bifocal contact lenses using holography. Laser surgery, braces for eyes, radial keratotomy, and corneal sculpting are all included.

> *A review of "Glasses and Contact Lenses: Your Guide to Eyes, Eyewear and Eye Care," in* Kirkus Reviews, *Vol. LVII, No. 10, May 15, 1989, p. 771.*

The Silversteins continue their investigation of body parts and related apparatus in this readable, up-to-date report on the state of eyewear. After a brief look at the history of corrective lenses, the book presents a comprehensive overview of the structure and operation of the eye. . . . Clearly written but not oversimplified, with some personal references that seem to be the authors' trademark, this should be useful to many readers, either for reports or to satisfy personal curiosity. It's a first choice for those who have nothing on the subject, and should be considered as a timely update to Alberta Kelley's *Lenses, Spectacles, and Contacts* (Elsevier, 1979; o.p.).

> *Denise L. Moll, in a review of "Glasses and Contact Lenses: Your Guide to Eyes, Eyewear, and Eye Care," in* School Library Journal, *Vol. 35, No. 10, June, 1989, p. 130.*

High-school science students will find this to be a useful source for term papers as well as for information about their own need for vision correction. It will also give them insight into careers in the eyecare field. Adults also will find many of the topics helpful, including the comments on bifocal glasses. A great majority of the many facts are presented accurately. However, in chapter four, statements about vision defects are not completely correct. For example, most young people with hyperopia can see both distant and close-up objects; only those whose hyperopia is of a high degree cannot see close-up objects well, yet the book implies that this is true of all hyperopic persons. A later error that is probably typographical indicates that a donor cornea is ground *up* after being frozen; what is meant is that frozen corneal tissue is reshaped by a procedure analogous to lens grinding. Such misstatements are

few in number in this otherwise well-written, well-organized book. (p. 30)

> *Ronald W. Everson, in a review of "Glasses and Contact Lenses: Your Guide to Eyes, Eyewear, & Eye Care," in* Science Books & Films, *Vol. 25, No. 1, September/October, 1989, pp. 29-30.*

Overcoming Acne: The How and Why of Healthy Skin Care (with Robert Silverstein, 1990)

A familiar writing team discusses one of the banes of teenage existence (90 percent of the young people between the ages of 12 and 17 have it in one form or another), stressing that while acne is not curable, it is treatable. Writing in a straightforward fashion, the Silversteins first present basic background on the structure and functioning of the skin. They go on to explain how lesions form, take a look at theories about external factors involved in acne development, and consider what can and cannot be done to treat the condition. Their information about over-the-counter treatments (brand names are not used) is appropriately cautious, and they provide a realistic sense of what to expect from a dermatologist.

> *Stephanie Zvirin, in a review of "Overcoming Acne: The How and Why of Healthy Skin," in* Booklist, *Vol. 86, No. 16, April 15, 1990, p. 1621.*

From womb to tomb: acne can affect infants prenatally; King Tut, who died as a teen-ager, was put to rest with medications for his skin problems—these plus many other, more useful facts can be found here. Using comfortably informal parlance ("zits"), the authors elucidate the action of the skin as an organ. While helping young people laugh at themselves with expressions like "microbe menagerie," their message is serious: the roles of hormones, sweat glands, cleanliness, and diet, and an up-to-the-minute comparison of over-the-counter medications with dermatologist-prescribed treatments. A section enabling readers to understand what triggers their own eruptions is especially useful. Little, if anything, else is available on this high-interest topic. Glossary; index.

> *A review of "Overcoming Acne: The How and Why of Healthy Skin Care," in* Kirkus Reviews, *Vol. LVIII, No. 11, June 1, 1990, p. 803.*

Lyme Disease: The Great Imitator (with Robert Silverstein, 1990)

The Silversteins, long known for their clear, well-researched books on health topics, are here joined by their son—in a detailed look at a troublesome disease that has recently become more widespread.

A foreword by Leonard H. Sigal, M.D., suggests that the book's purpose is "to allay fear and to educate." The latter goal is met well as the Silversteins survey the history of Lyme disease, describe its course, and present the tick's life cycle. With many specifics, they give a sense of the disease's bewildering array of symptoms and possible treatments, the difficulties in diagnosing it, and the status of research. But aside from the fact that Lyme disease—though it can be exceedingly disagreeable—is rarely life threatening, and that even in high-risk areas the chances of getting it are not overwhelming, there's little comfort here. The choice remains: stay inside; take the chance of venturing out as usual; or go to laborious but not guaranteed lengths to baffle or repel the dread tick.

Dry and occasionally repetitious, although the information is well researched and well organized, serving not only to inform but to exemplify how the medical and research communities address a peculiarly knotty problem. A question-and-answer chapter serves as an excellent summary. Suggested reading; list of organizations; glossary; index.

> *A review of "Lyme Disease: The Great Imitator," in* Kirkus Reviews, *Vol. LVIII, No. 12, June 15, 1990, p. 881.*

CUMULATIVE INDEX TO AUTHORS

This index lists all author entries in *Children's Literature Review* and includes cross-references to them in other Gale sources. References in the index are identified as follows:

AAYA: *Authors & Artists for Young Adults* Volumes 1-6
CA: *Contemporary Authors* (original series), Volumes 1-133
CANR: *Contemporary Authors New Revision Series,* Volumes 1-33
CAP: *Contemporary Authors Permanent Series,* Volumes 1-2
CA-R: *Contemporary Authors* (revised editions), Volumes 1-44
CDALB: *Concise Dictionary of American Literary Biography,* Volumes 1-4
CLC: *Contemporary Literary Criticism,* Volumes 1-66
CLR: *Children's Literature Review,* Volumes 1-25
DLB: *Dictionary of Literary Biography,* Volumes 1-107
DLB-DS: *Dictionary of Literary Biography Documentary Series,* Volumes 1-7
DLB-Y: *Dictionary of Literary Biography Yearbook,* Volumes 1980-1989
LC: *Literature Criticism from 1400 to 1800,* Volumes 1-17
NCLC: *Nineteenth-Century Literature Criticism,* Volumes 1-32
SAAS: *Something about the Author Autobiography Series,* Volumes 1-12
SATA: *Something about the Author,* Volumes 1-65
TCLC: *Twentieth-Century Literary Criticism,* Volumes 1-41
YABC: *Yesterday's Authors of Books for Children,* Volumes 1-2

CUMULATIVE INDEX TO NATIONALITIES

Nationality Index

CUMULATIVE INDEX TO TITLES

Title Index

Title Index

Title Index

Title Index

Title Index